FIST OF THE NORTH STAR

VOLUME

3

STORY BY
Buronson

ART BY
Tetsuo
Hara

FIST OF THE NORTH STAR

VOLUME

3

CONTENTS

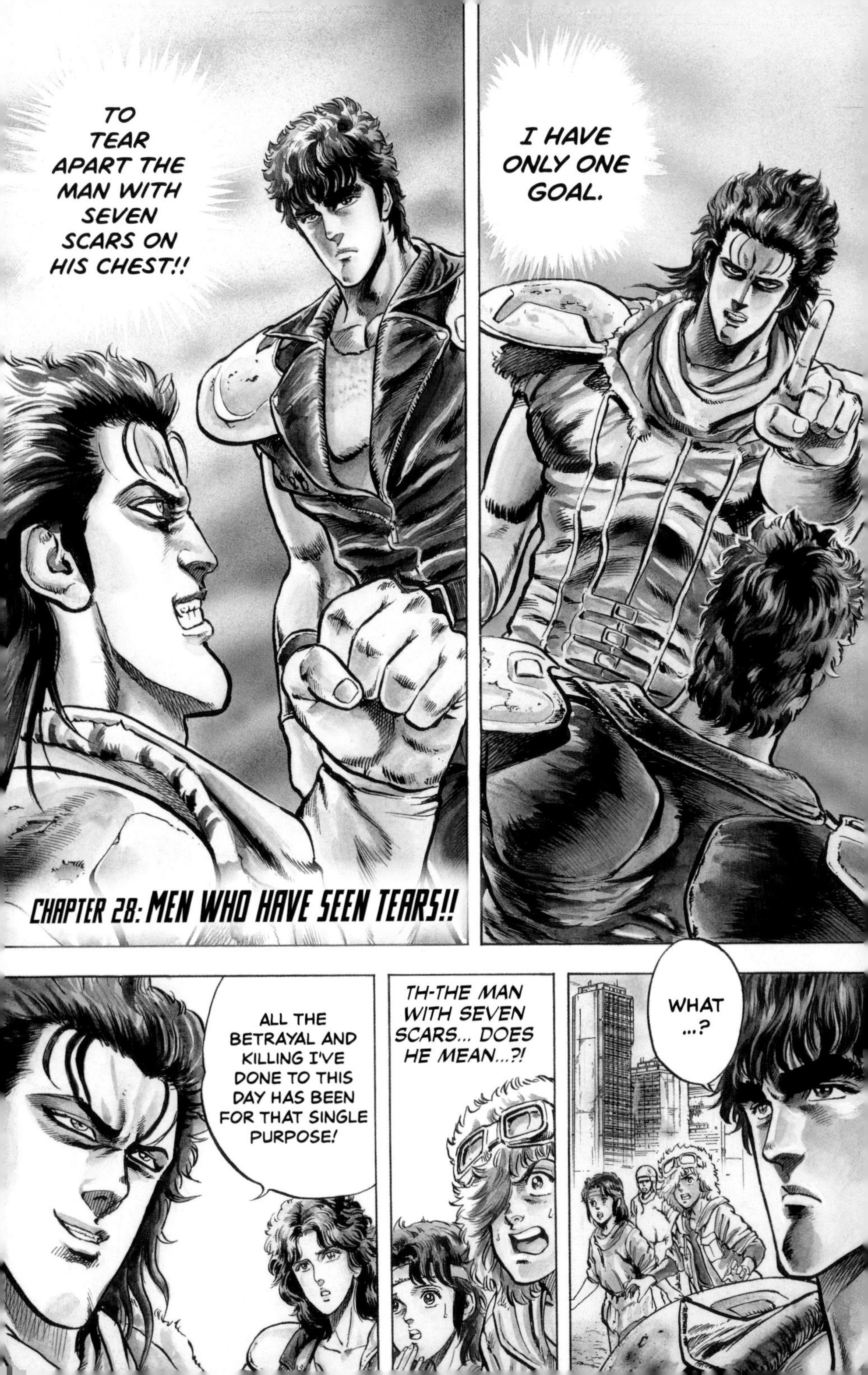
I HAVE ONLY ONE GOAL.
TO TEAR APART THE MAN WITH SEVEN SCARS ON HIS CHEST!!
CHAPTER 28: MEN WHO HAVE SEEN TEARS!!
WHAT ...?
TH-THE MAN WITH SEVEN SCARS... DOES HE MEAN...?!
ALL THE BETRAYAL AND KILLING I'VE DONE TO THIS DAY HAS BEEN FOR THAT SINGLE PURPOSE!

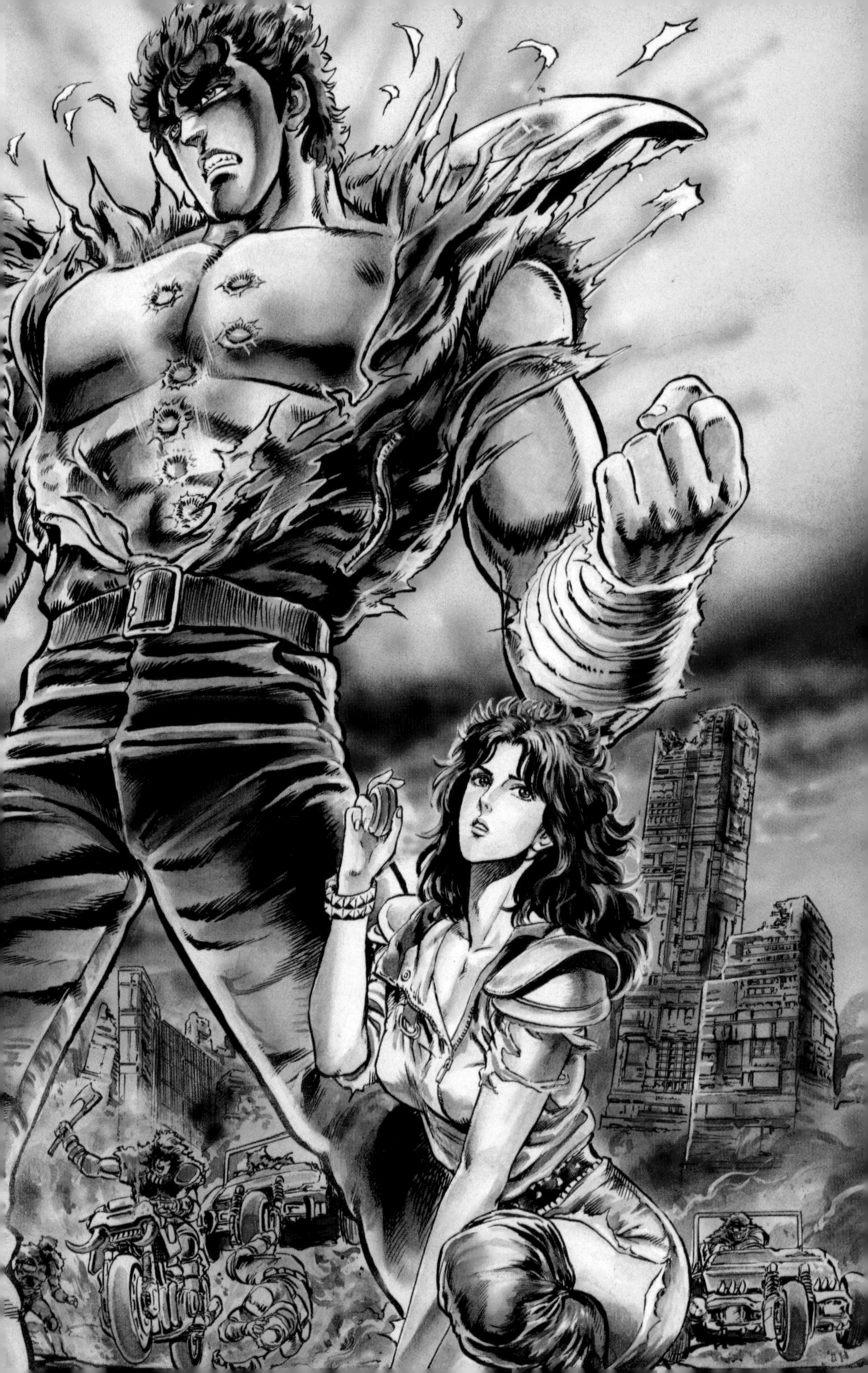

CHAPTER 28: MEN WHO HAVE SEEN TEARS!!

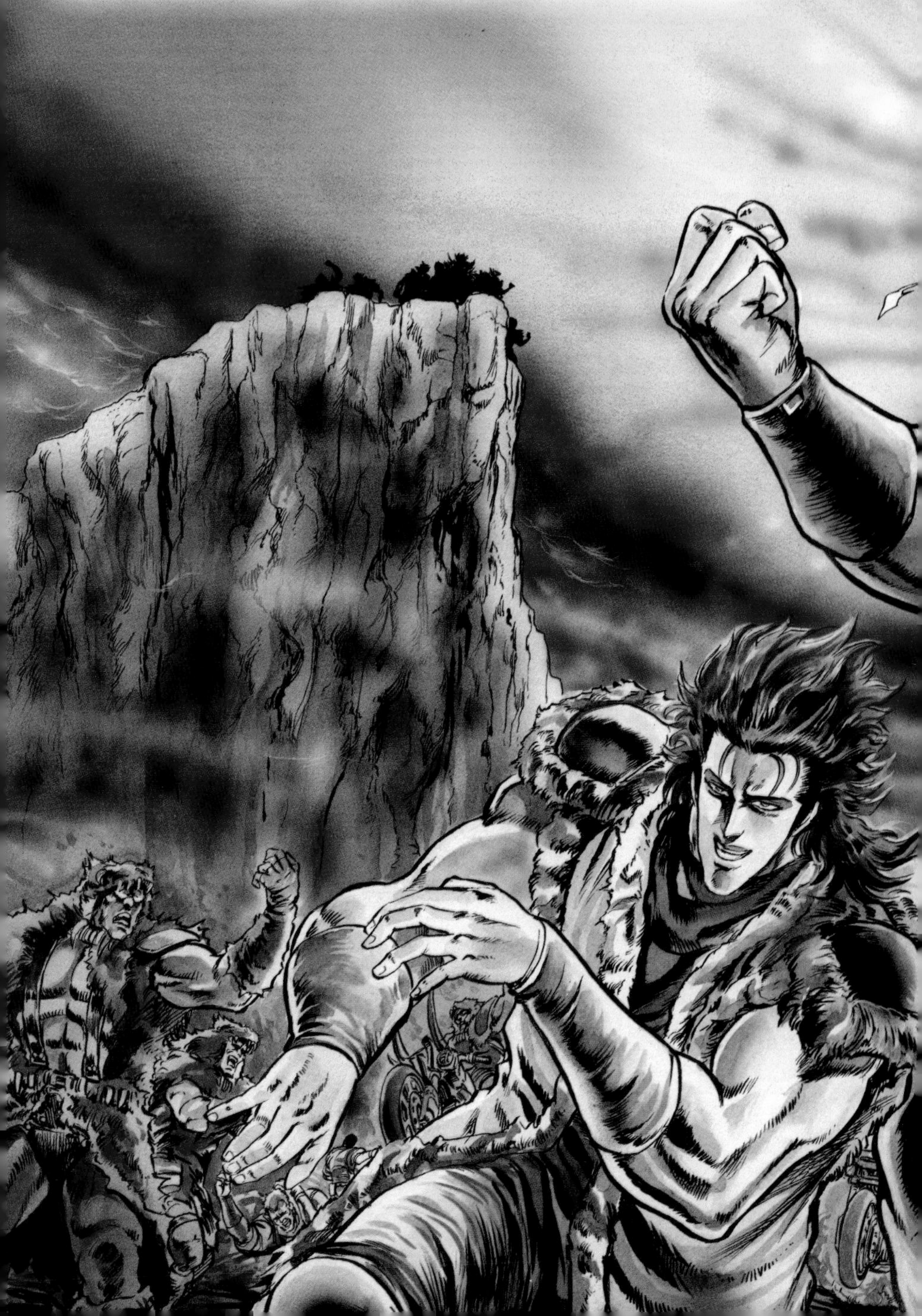

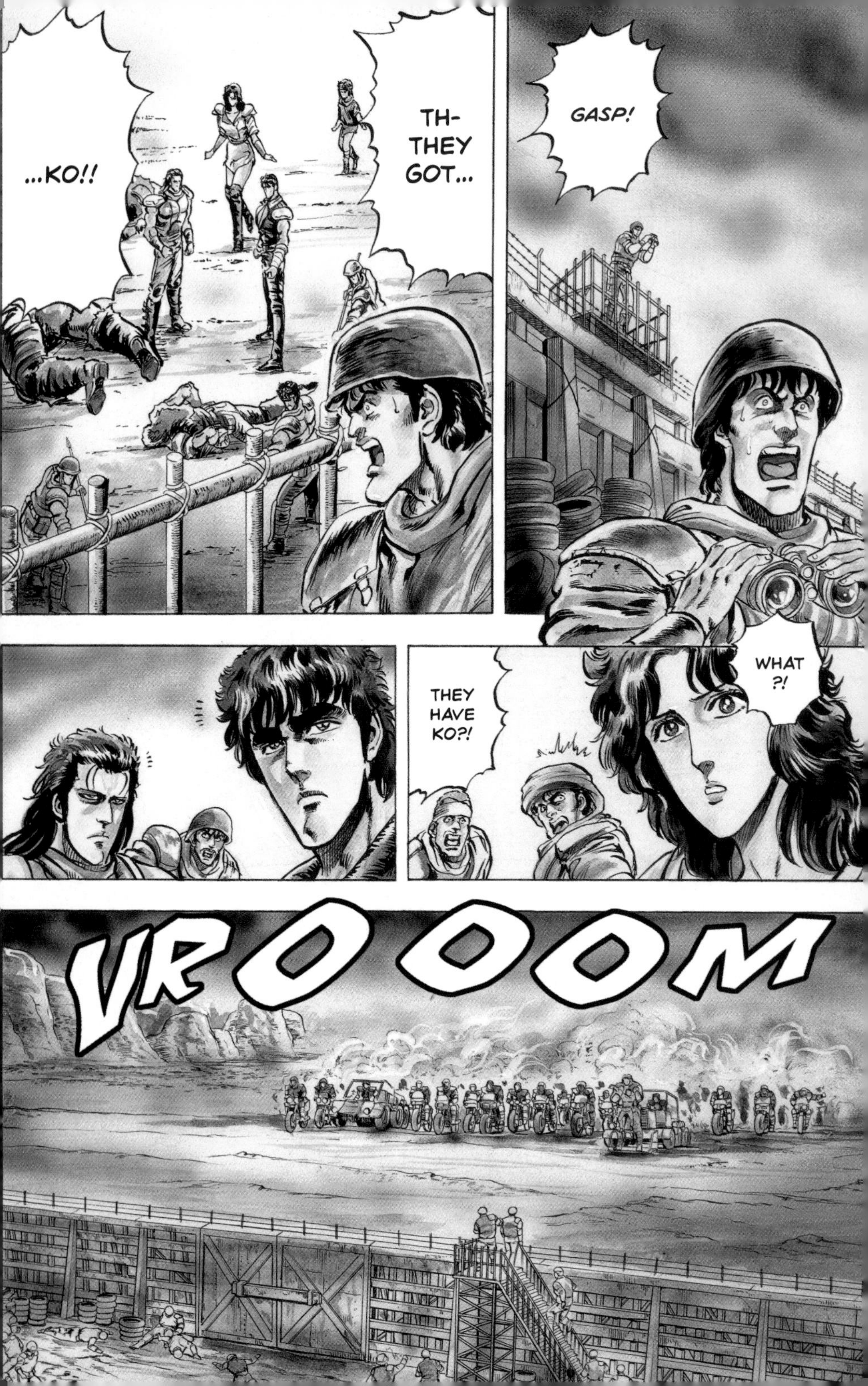
GASP!
TH- THEY GOT...
...KO!!
WHAT ?!
THEY HAVE KO?!
VROOOM

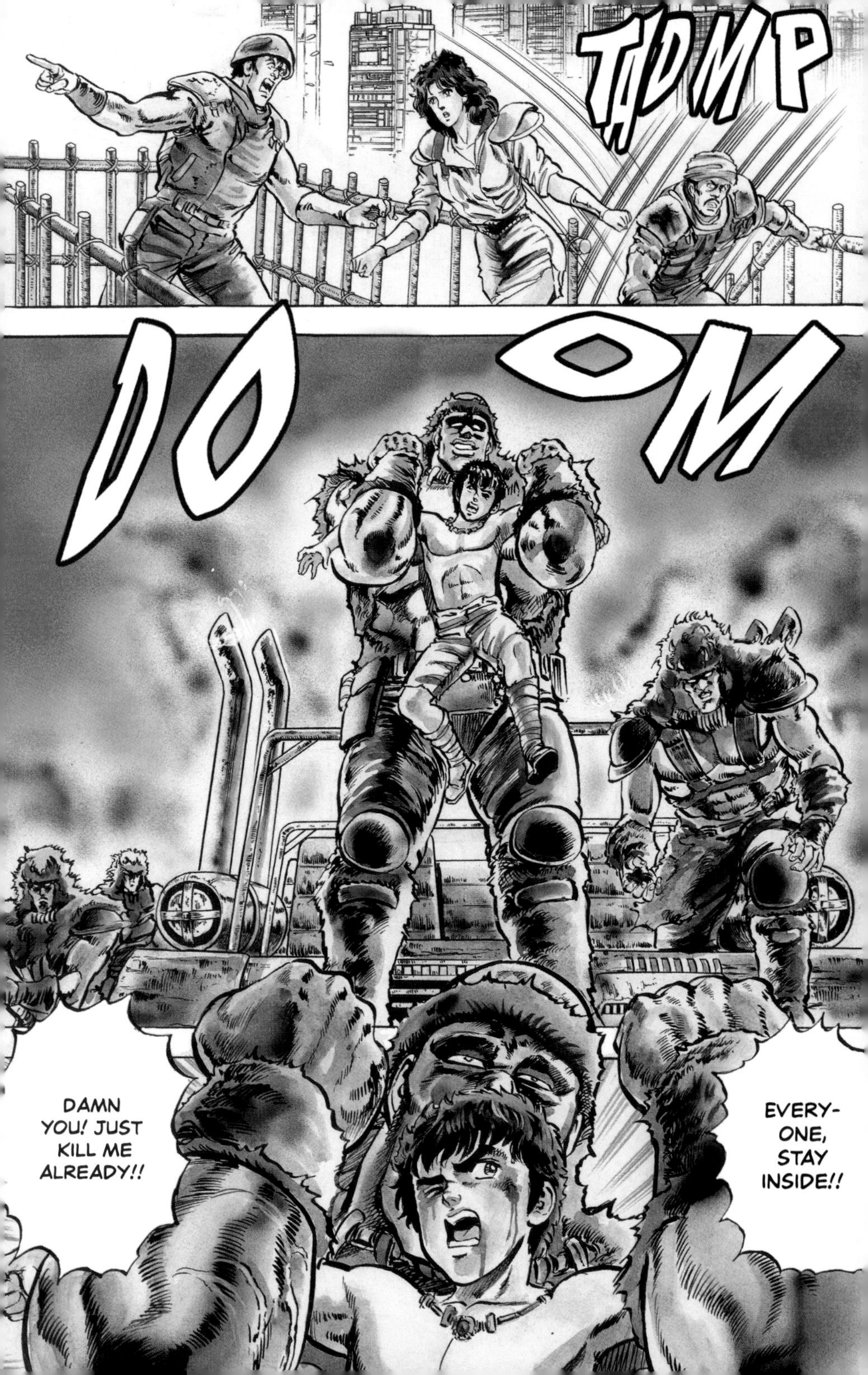
DOOM
EVERY-ONE, STAY INSIDE!!
DAMN YOU! JUST KILL ME ALREADY!!

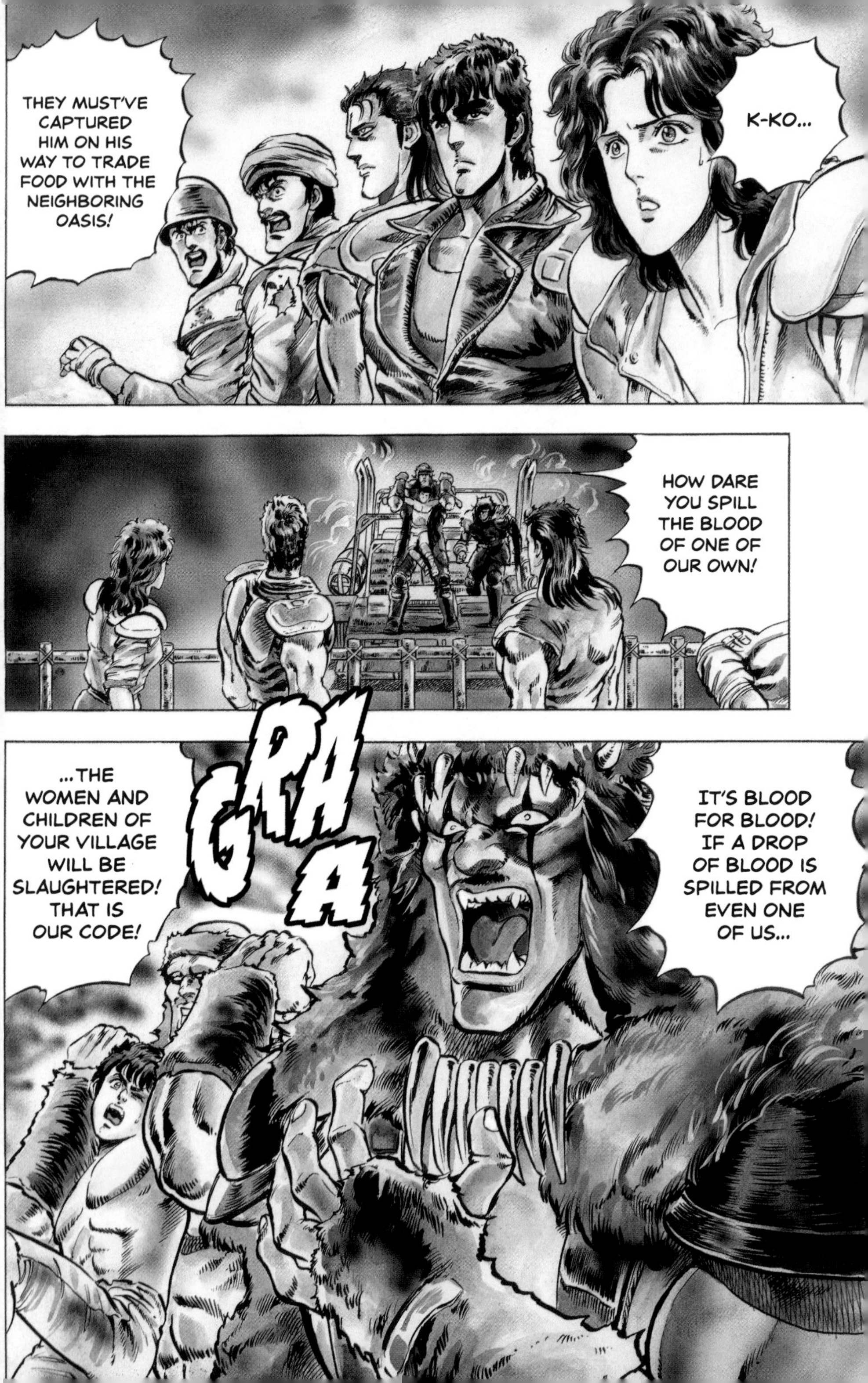
K-KO...
THEY MUST'VE CAPTURED HIM ON HIS WAY TO TRADE FOOD WITH THE NEIGHBORING OASIS!
HOW DARE YOU SPILL THE BLOOD OF ONE OF OUR OWN!
IT'S BLOOD FOR BLOOD! IF A DROP OF BLOOD IS SPILLED FROM EVEN ONE OF US...
GRAA
...THE WOMEN AND CHILDREN OF YOUR VILLAGE WILL BE SLAUGHTERED! THAT IS OUR CODE!

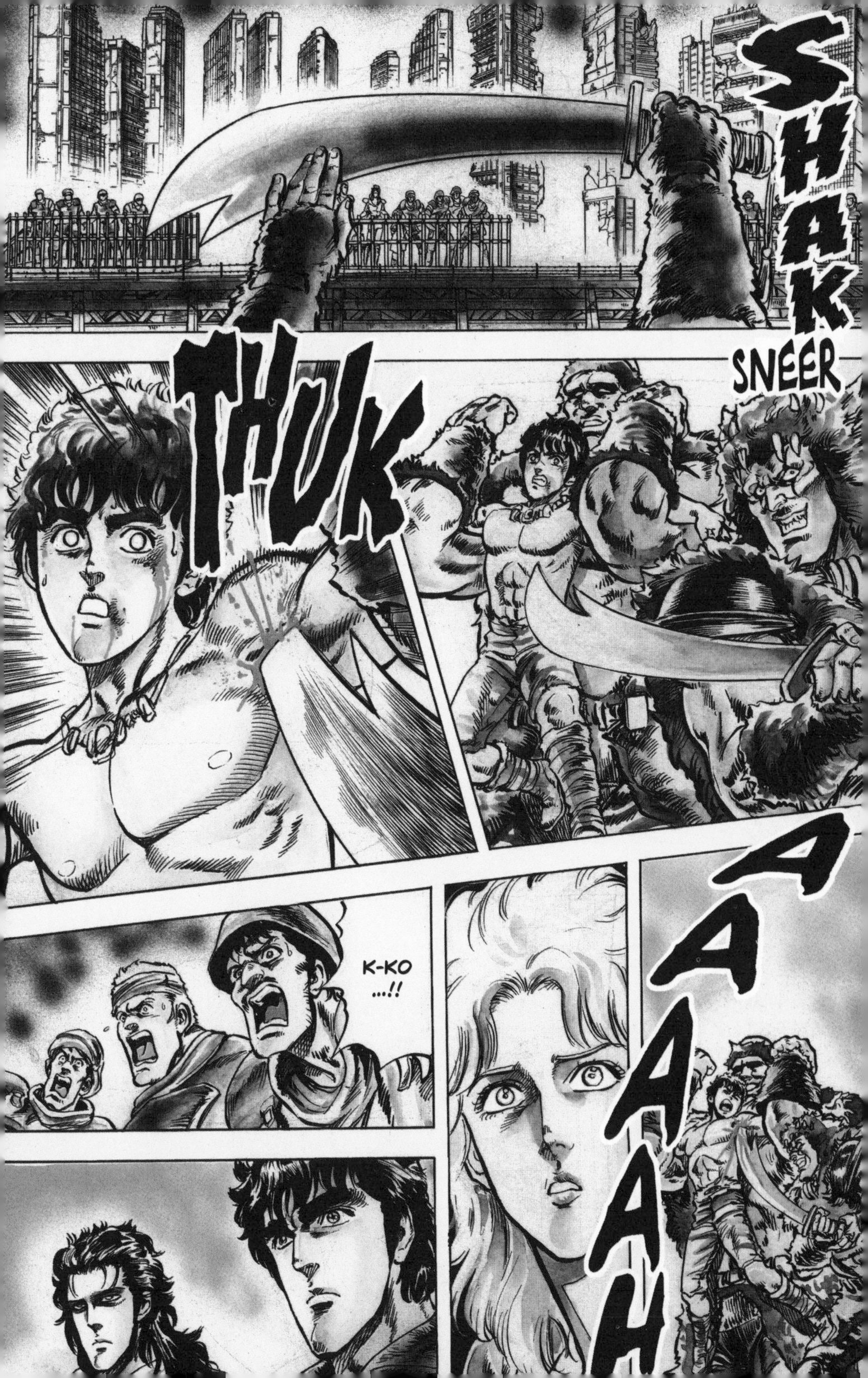
SHAK
SNEER
THUK
K-KO ...!!
AAAAH

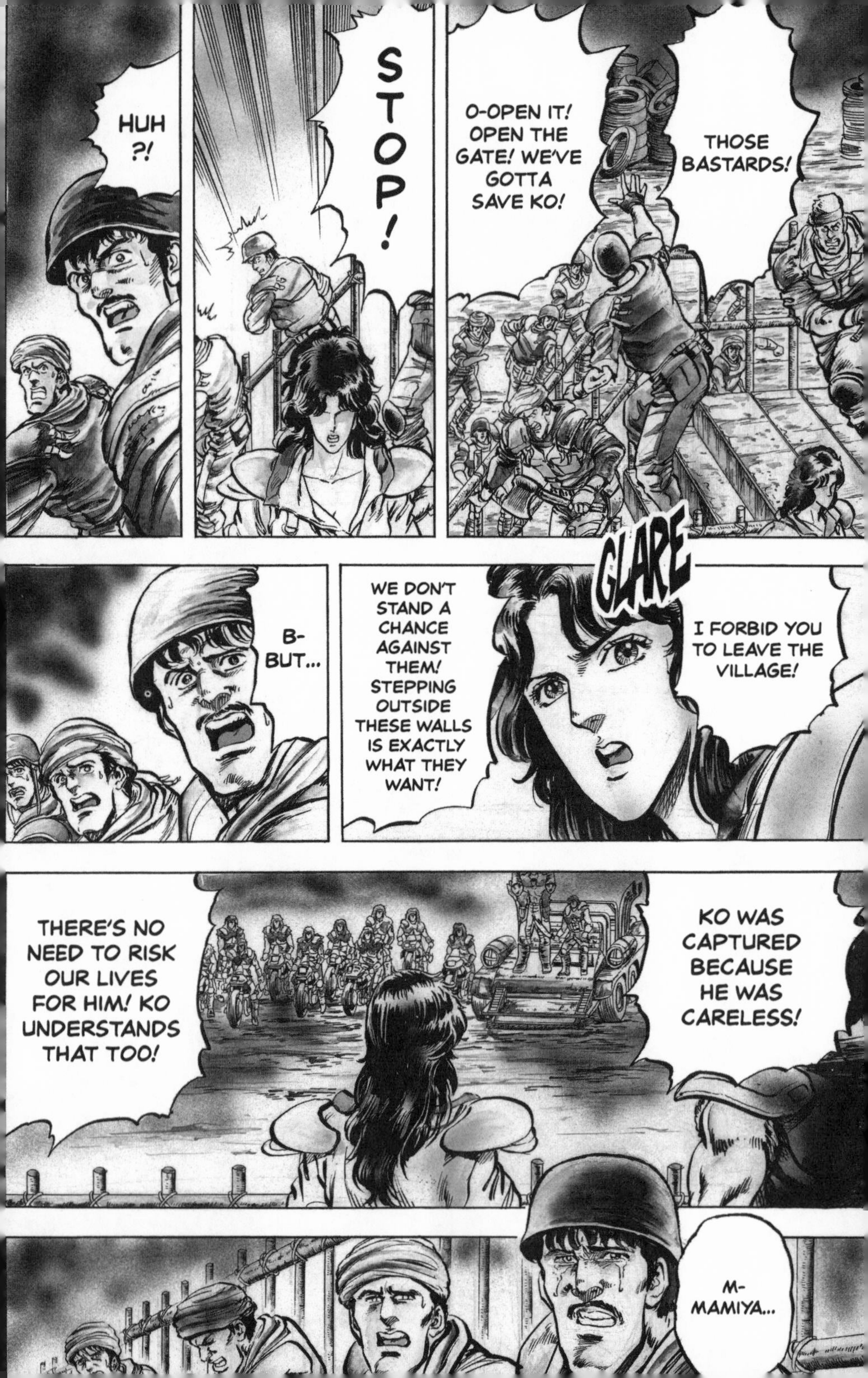
THOSE BASTARDS!
O-OPEN IT! OPEN THE GATE! WE'VE GOTTA SAVE KO!
STOP!
HUH ?!
GLARE
I FORBID YOU TO LEAVE THE VILLAGE!
WE DON'T STAND A CHANCE AGAINST THEM! STEPPING OUTSIDE THESE WALLS IS EXACTLY WHAT THEY WANT!
B-BUT...
KO WAS CAPTURED BECAUSE HE WAS CARELESS!
THERE'S NO NEED TO RISK OUR LIVES FOR HIM! KO UNDERSTANDS THAT TOO!
M-MAMIYA...

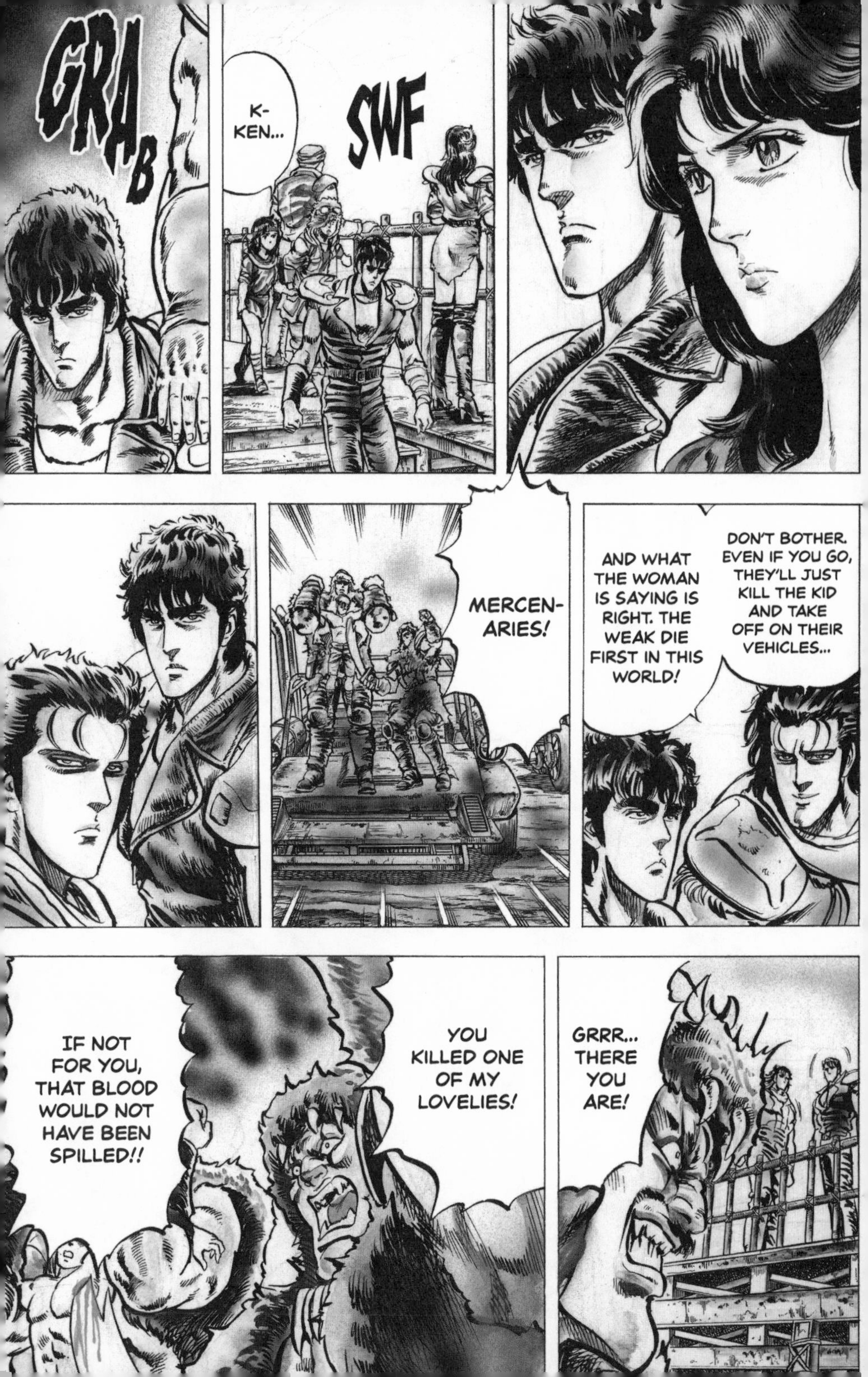
K-KEN...
SWF
GRAB
DON'T BOTHER. EVEN IF YOU GO, THEY'LL JUST KILL THE KID AND TAKE OFF ON THEIR VEHICLES...
AND WHAT THE WOMAN IS SAYING IS RIGHT. THE WEAK DIE FIRST IN THIS WORLD!
MERCEN-ARIES!
GRRR... THERE YOU ARE!
YOU KILLED ONE OF MY LOVELIES!
IF NOT FOR YOU, THAT BLOOD WOULD NOT HAVE BEEN SPILLED!!

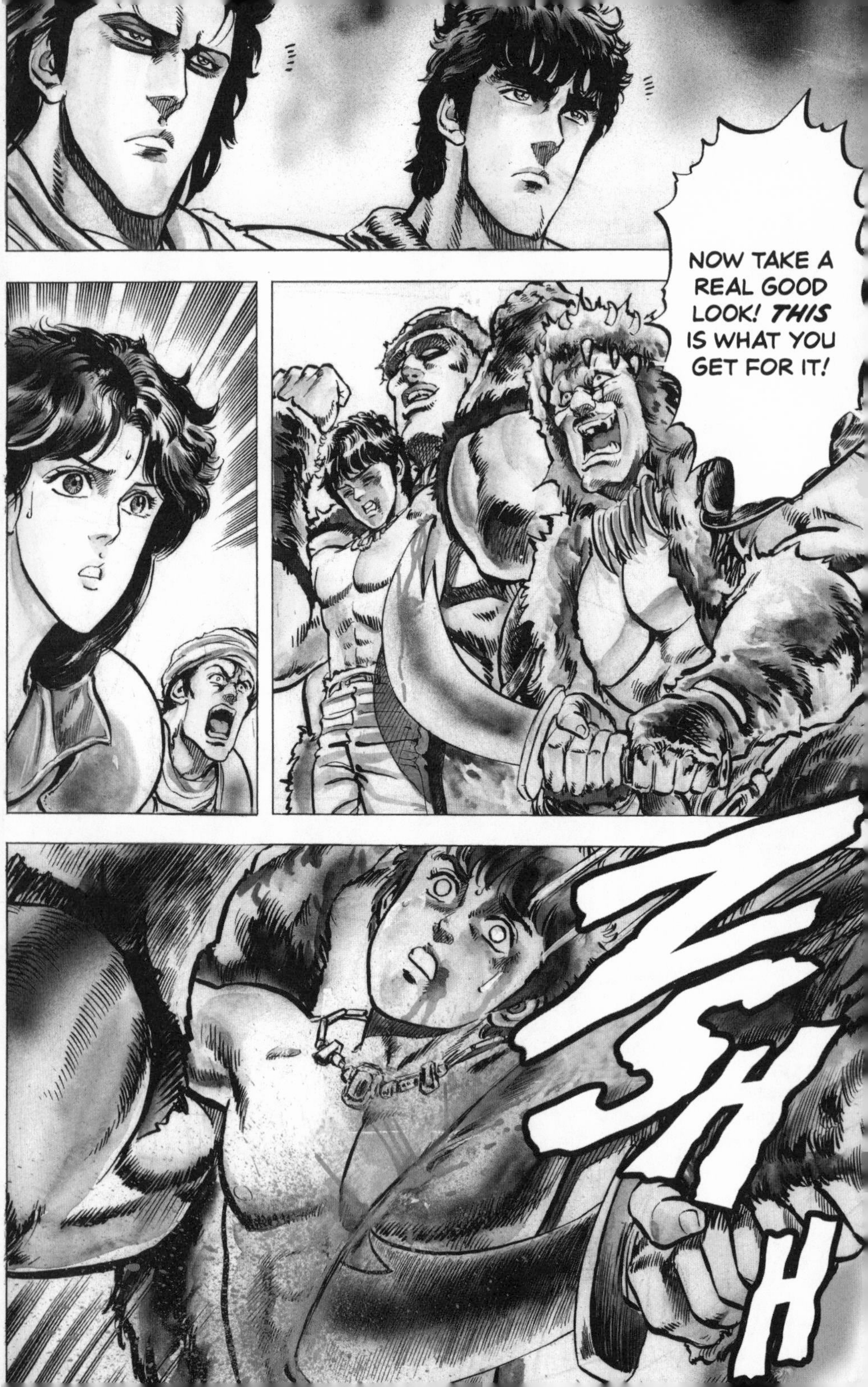
NOW TAKE A REAL GOOD LOOK! *THIS* IS WHAT YOU GET FOR IT!
ZSH

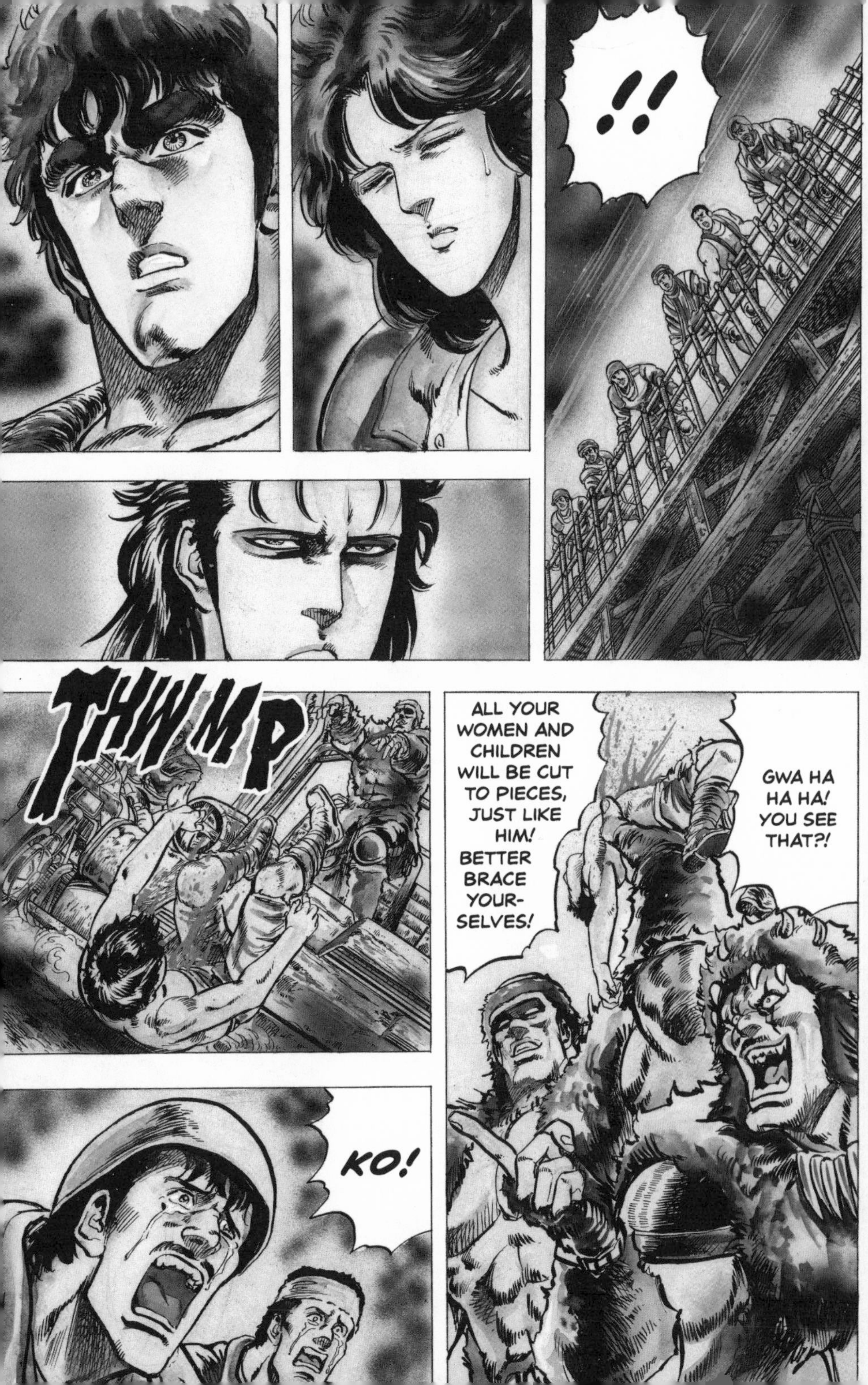
!!
GWA HA HA HA! YOU SEE THAT?!
ALL YOUR WOMEN AND CHILDREN WILL BE CUT TO PIECES, JUST LIKE HIM! BETTER BRACE YOURSELVES!
THWMP
KO!

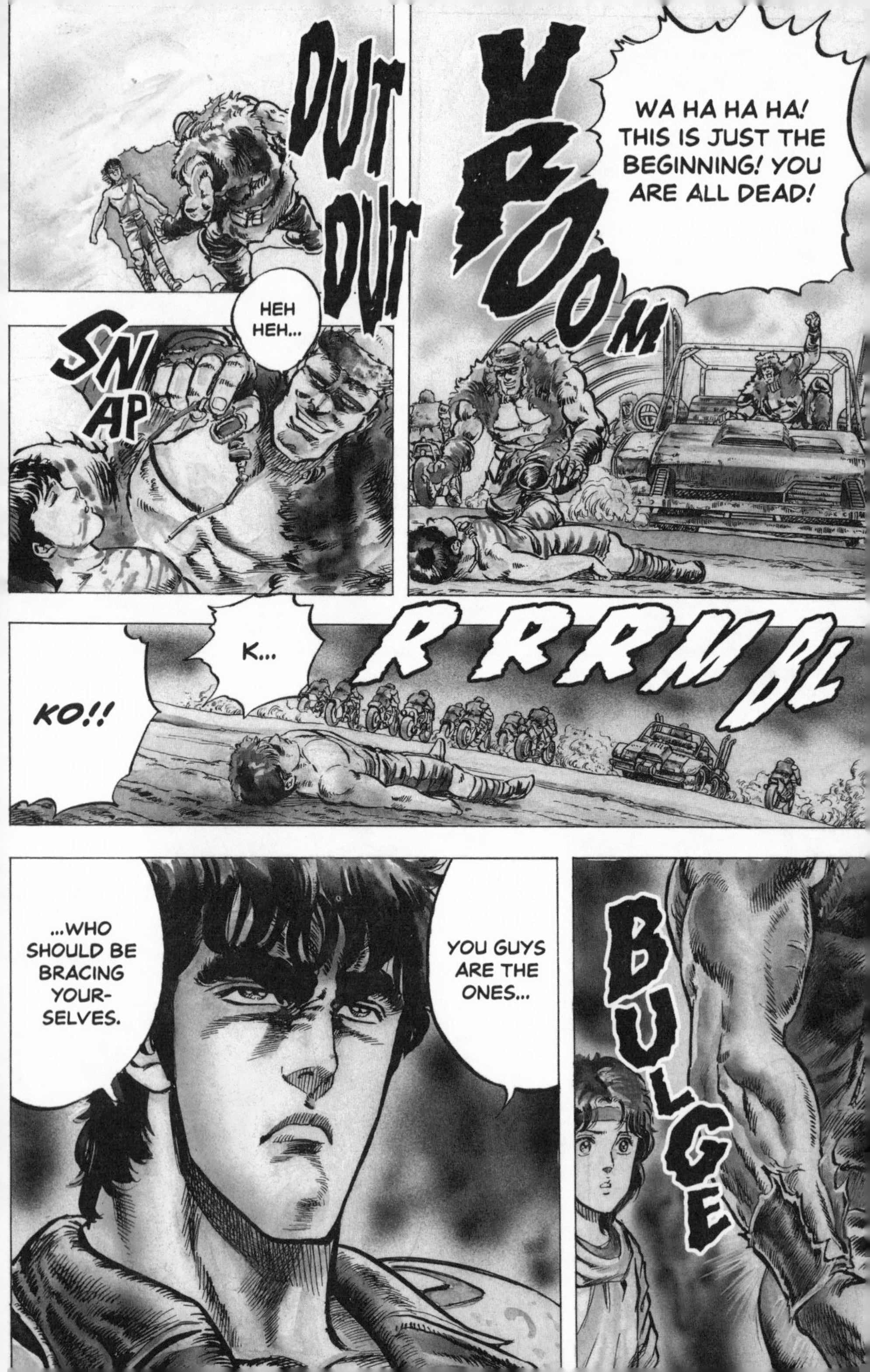
VROOM
WA HA HA HA! THIS IS JUST THE BEGINNING! YOU ARE ALL DEAD!
DUT DUT
HEH HEH...
SNAP
RRRMBL
K...
KO!!
BULGE
YOU GUYS ARE THE ONES...
...WHO SHOULD BE BRACING YOUR-SELVES.

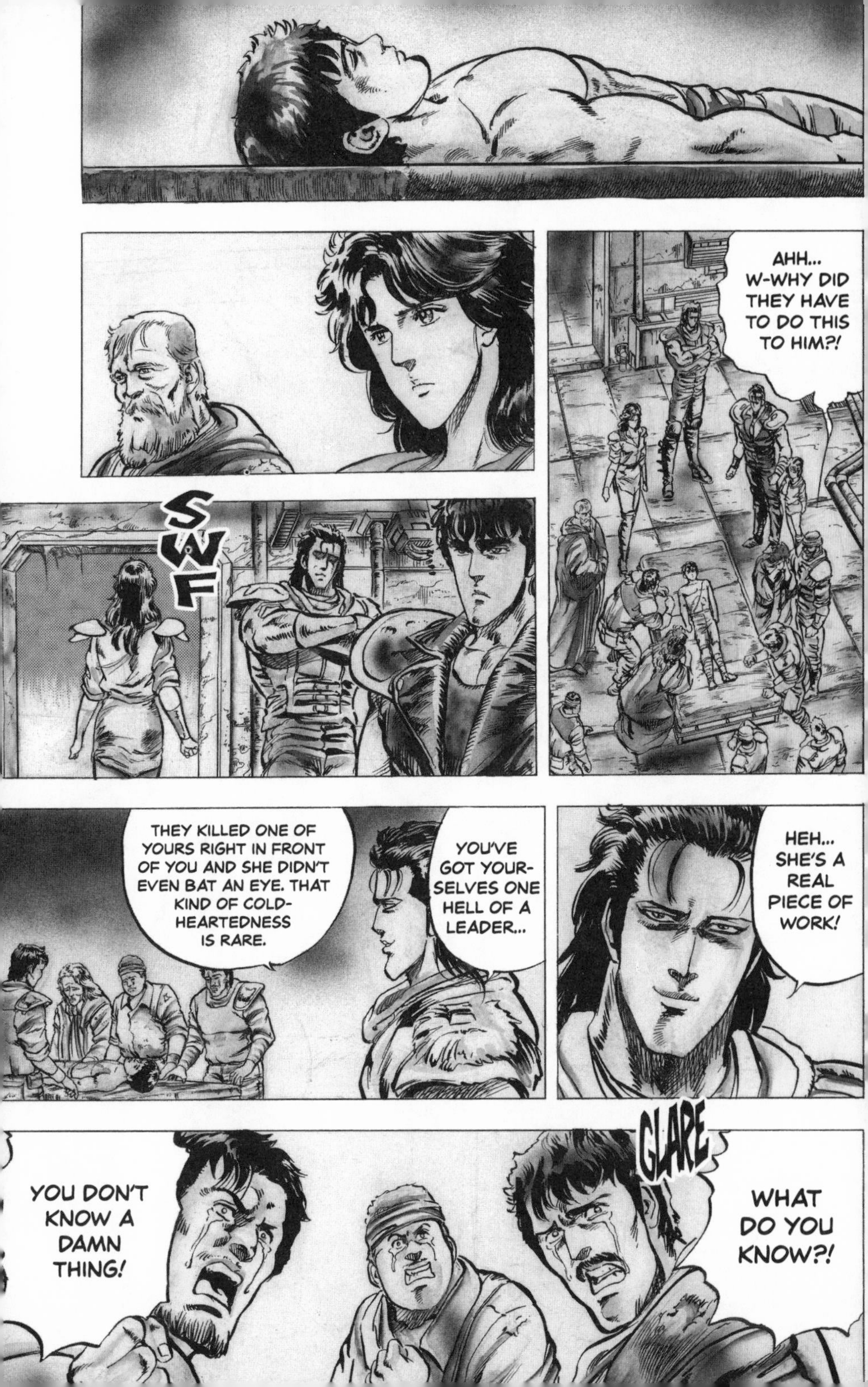
AHH... W-WHY DID THEY HAVE TO DO THIS TO HIM?!
SWF
HEH... SHE'S A REAL PIECE OF WORK!
THEY KILLED ONE OF YOURS RIGHT IN FRONT OF YOU AND SHE DIDN'T EVEN BAT AN EYE. THAT KIND OF COLD-HEARTEDNESS IS RARE.
YOU'VE GOT YOURSELVES ONE HELL OF A LEADER...
GLARE
WHAT DO YOU KNOW?!
YOU DON'T KNOW A DAMN THING!

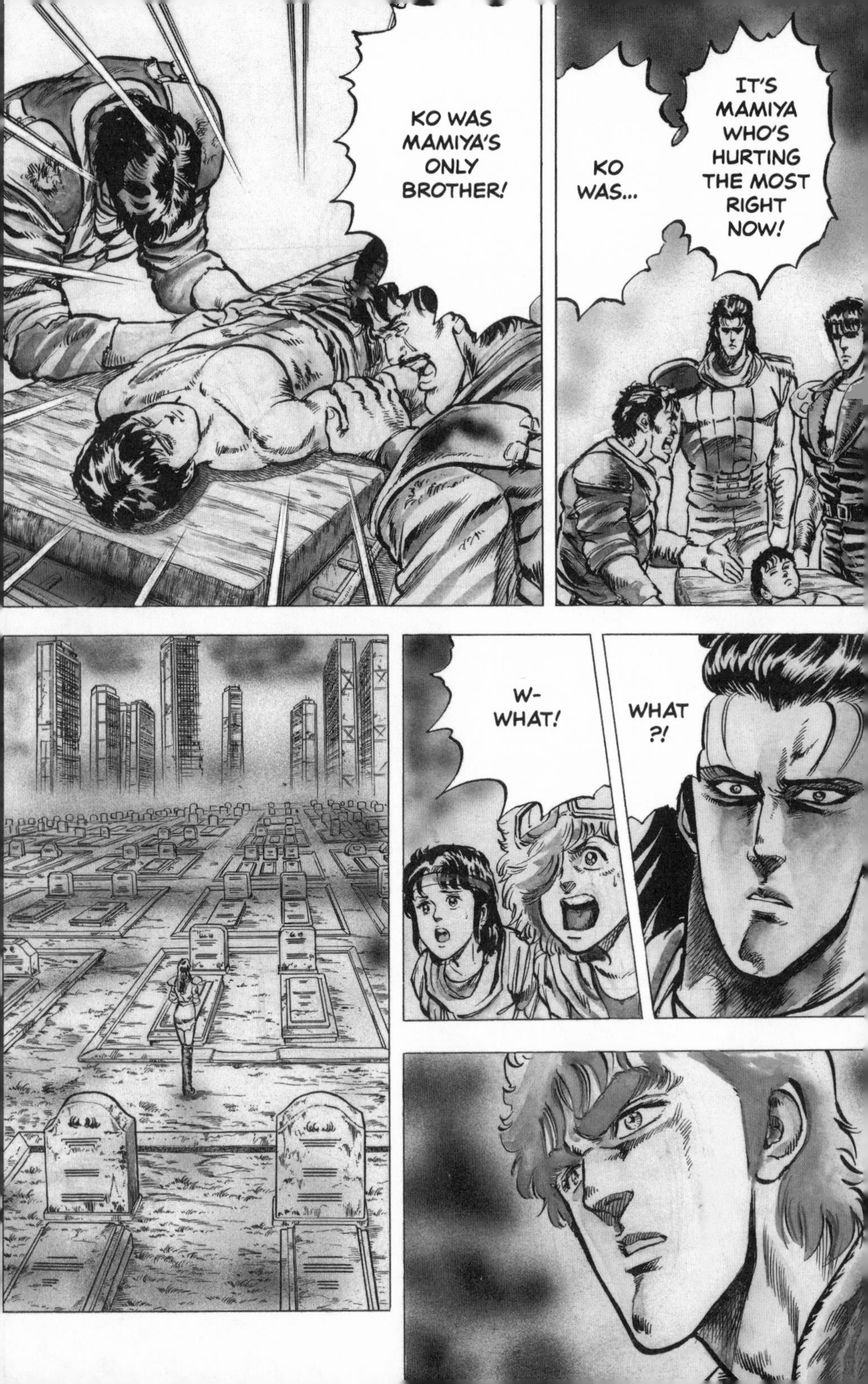
IT'S MAMIYA WHO'S HURTING THE MOST RIGHT NOW!
KO WAS...
KO WAS MAMIYA'S ONLY BROTHER!
WHAT ?!
W- WHAT!

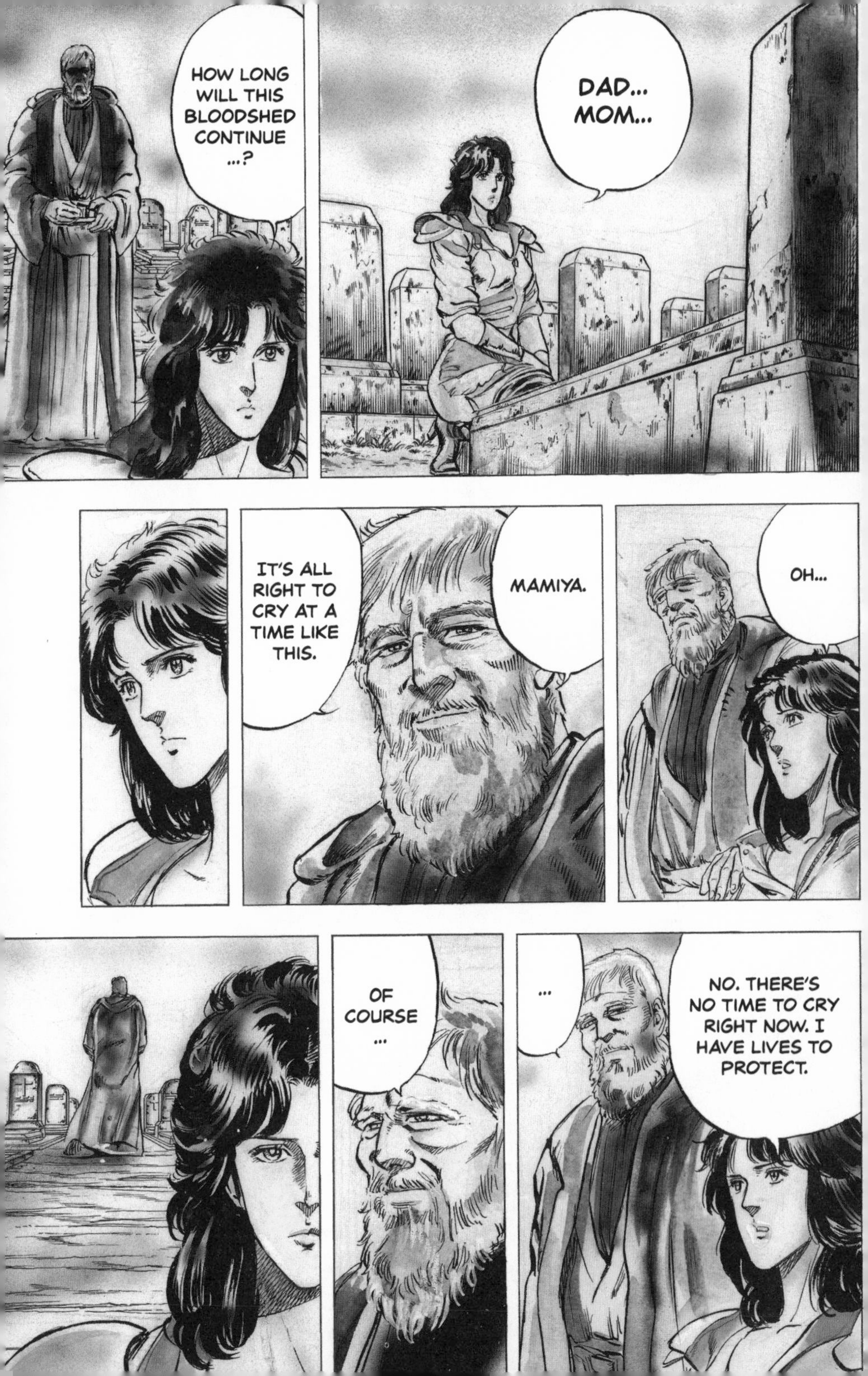
DAD... MOM...
HOW LONG WILL THIS BLOODSHED CONTINUE ...?
OH...
MAMIYA.
IT'S ALL RIGHT TO CRY AT A TIME LIKE THIS.
NO. THERE'S NO TIME TO CRY RIGHT NOW. I HAVE LIVES TO PROTECT.
...
OF COURSE ...

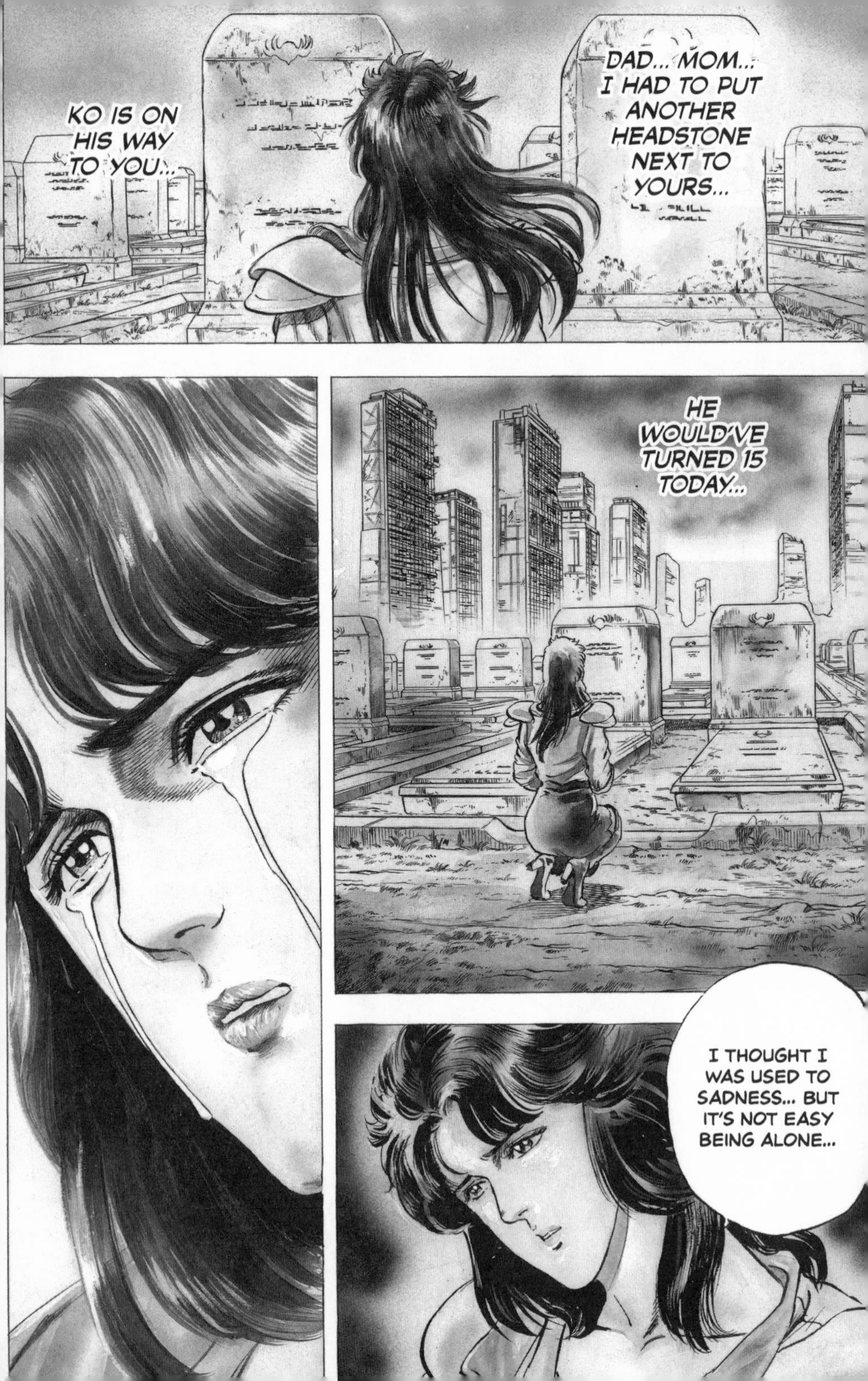
DAD... MOM... I HAD TO PUT ANOTHER HEADSTONE NEXT TO YOURS...
KO IS ON HIS WAY TO YOU...
HE WOULD'VE TURNED 15 TODAY...
I THOUGHT I WAS USED TO SADNESS... BUT IT'S NOT EASY BEING ALONE...

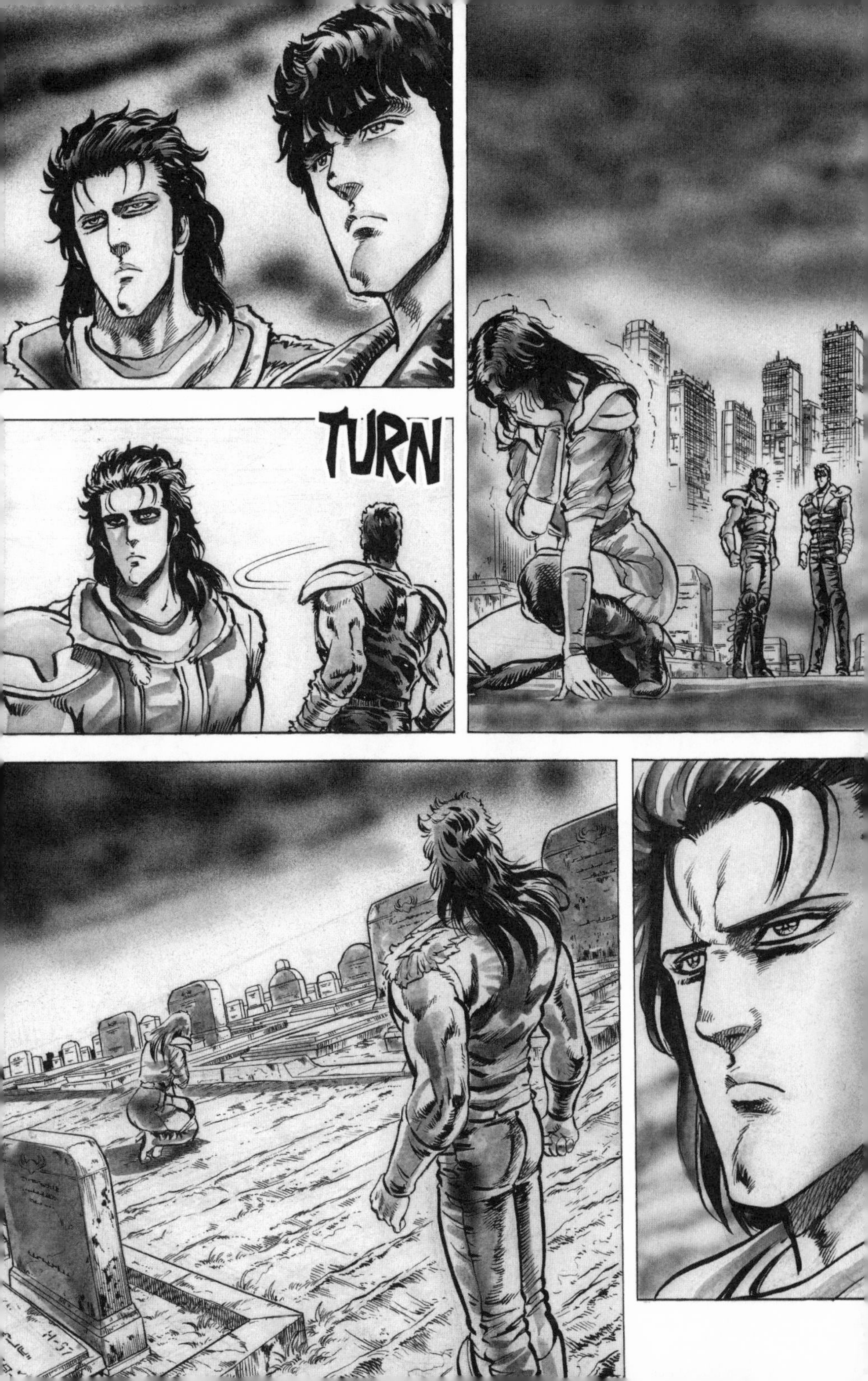
TURN

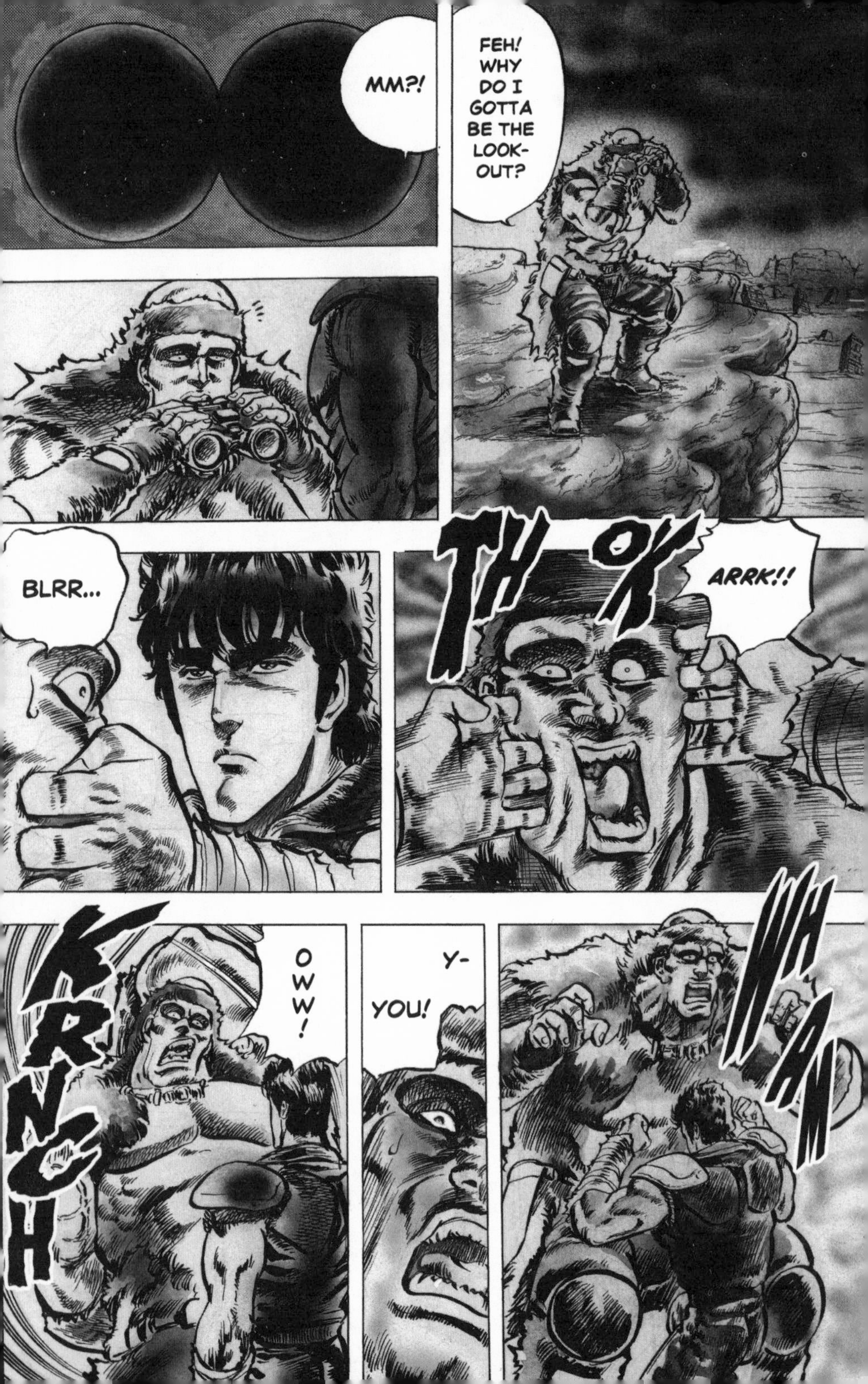
FEH! WHY DO I GOTTA BE THE LOOK-OUT?
MM?!
THOK
ARRK!!
BLRR...
WHAM
Y- YOU!
OWW!
KRNCH

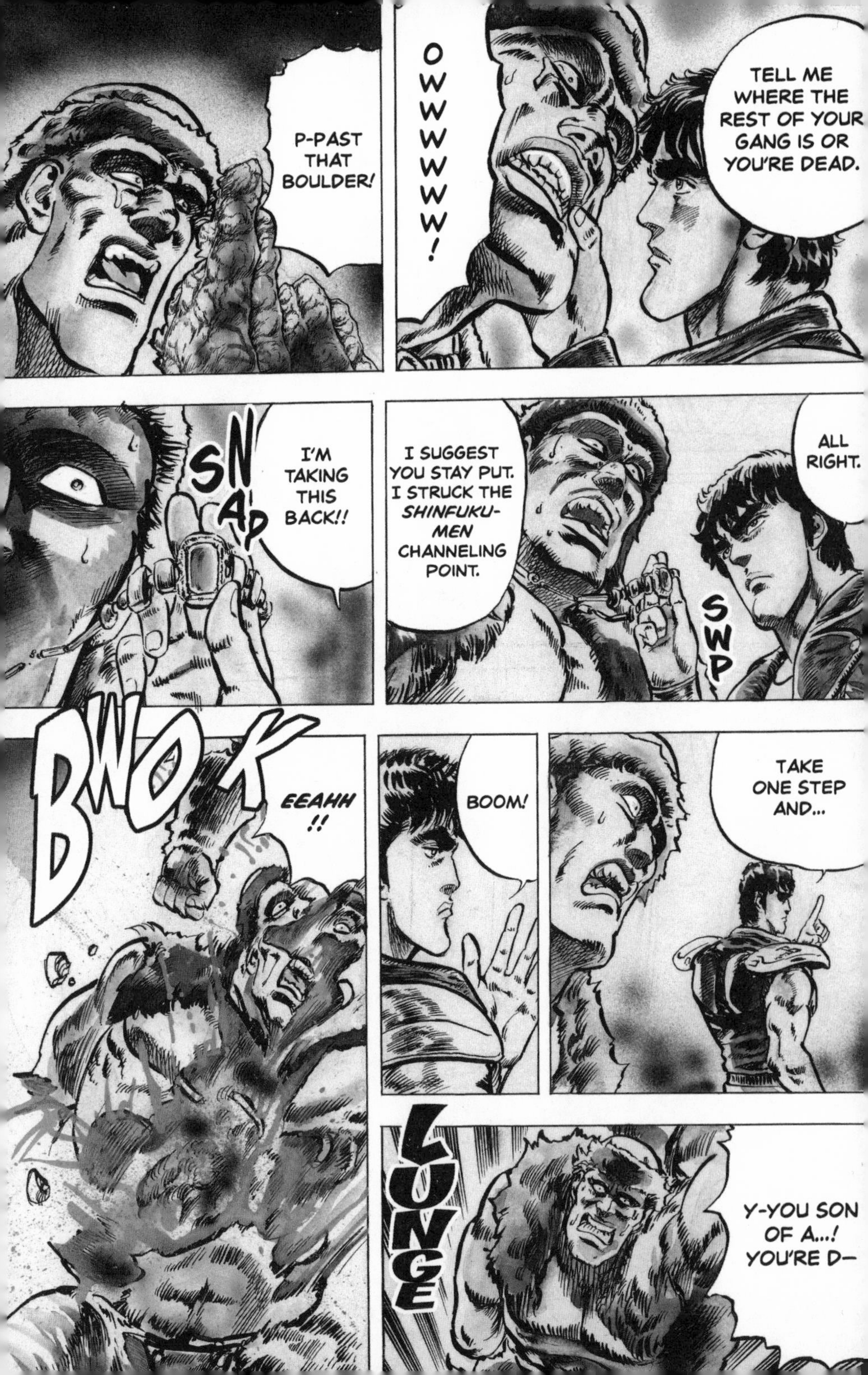
TELL ME WHERE THE REST OF YOUR GANG IS OR YOU'RE DEAD.
OWWWWWW!
P-PAST THAT BOULDER!
ALL RIGHT.
SWP
I SUGGEST YOU STAY PUT. I STRUCK THE *SHINFUKU-MEN* CHANNELING POINT.
I'M TAKING THIS BACK!!
SNAP
TAKE ONE STEP AND...
BOOM!
LUNGE
Y-YOU SON OF A...! YOU'RE D—
BWOK
EEAHH!!

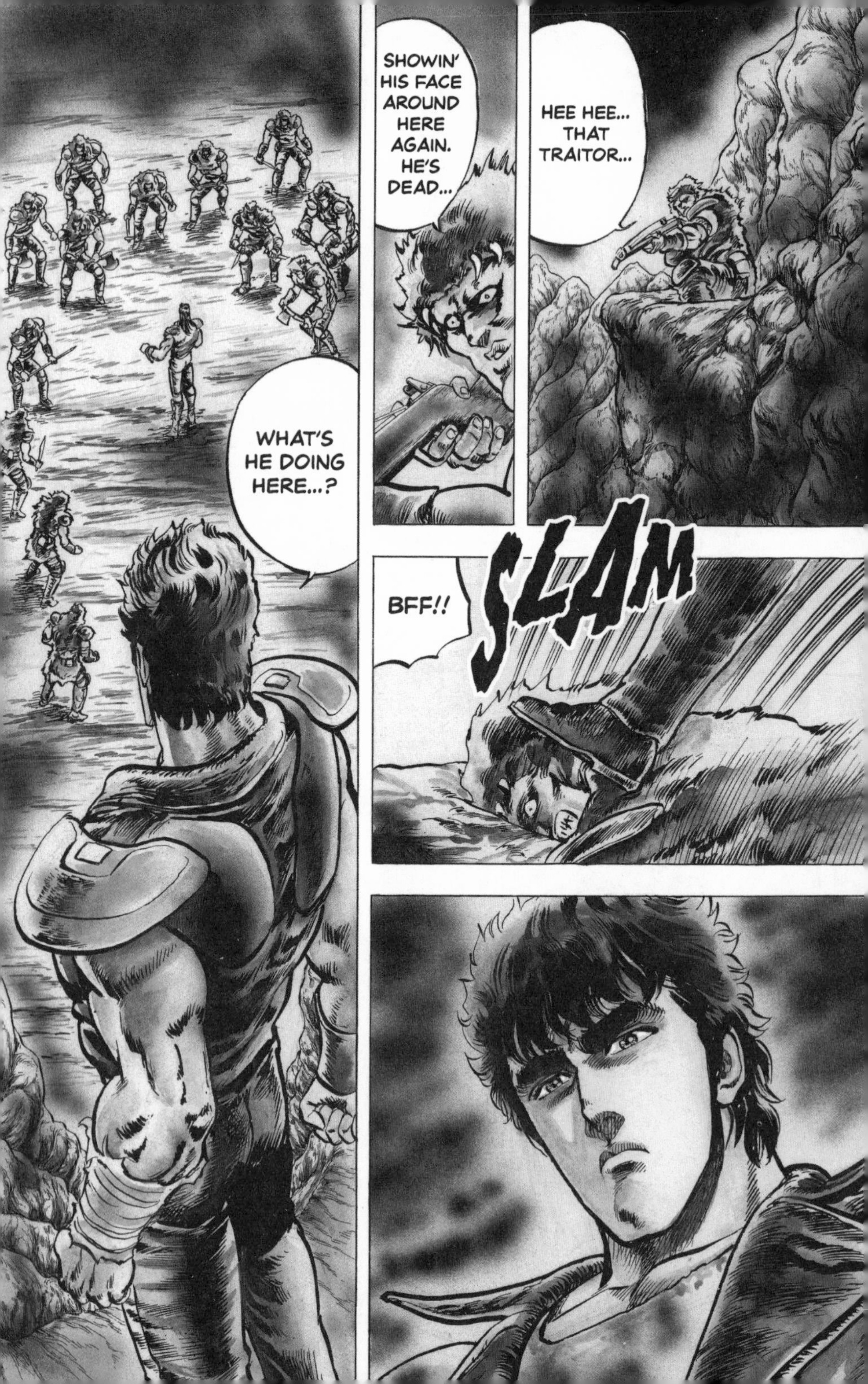
HEE HEE... THAT TRAITOR...
SHOWIN' HIS FACE AROUND HERE AGAIN. HE'S DEAD...
BFF!!
SLAM
WHAT'S HE DOING HERE...?

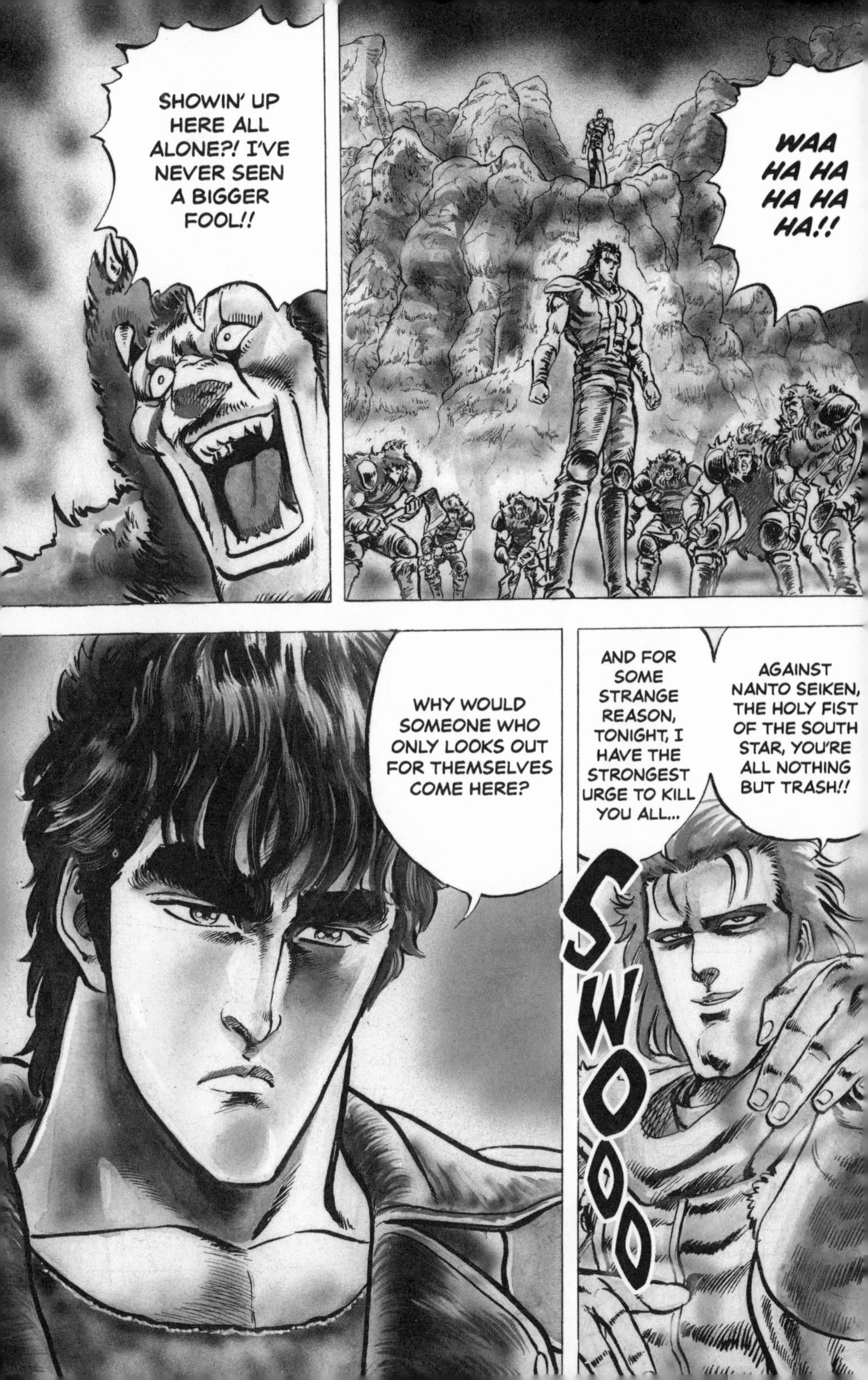
WAA HA HA HA HA HA!!
SHOWIN' UP HERE ALL ALONE?! I'VE NEVER SEEN A BIGGER FOOL!!
AGAINST NANTO SEIKEN, THE HOLY FIST OF THE SOUTH STAR, YOU'RE ALL NOTHING BUT TRASH!!
AND FOR SOME STRANGE REASON, TONIGHT, I HAVE THE STRONGEST URGE TO KILL YOU ALL...
SWOOOO
WHY WOULD SOMEONE WHO ONLY LOOKS OUT FOR THEMSELVES COME HERE?

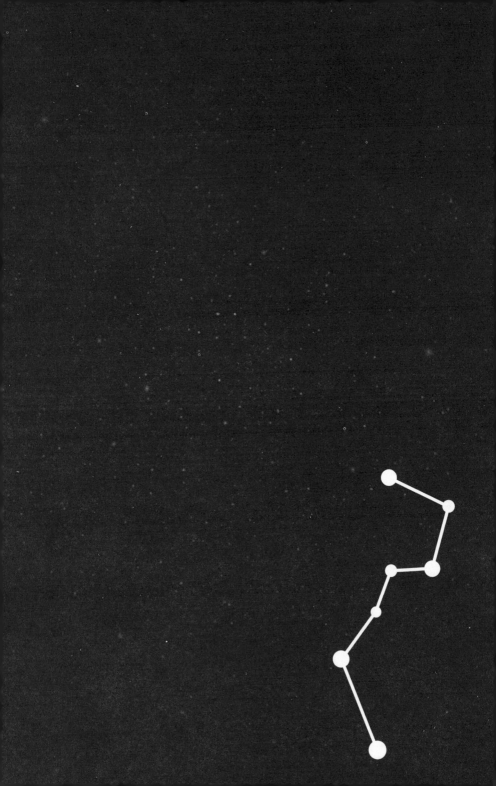

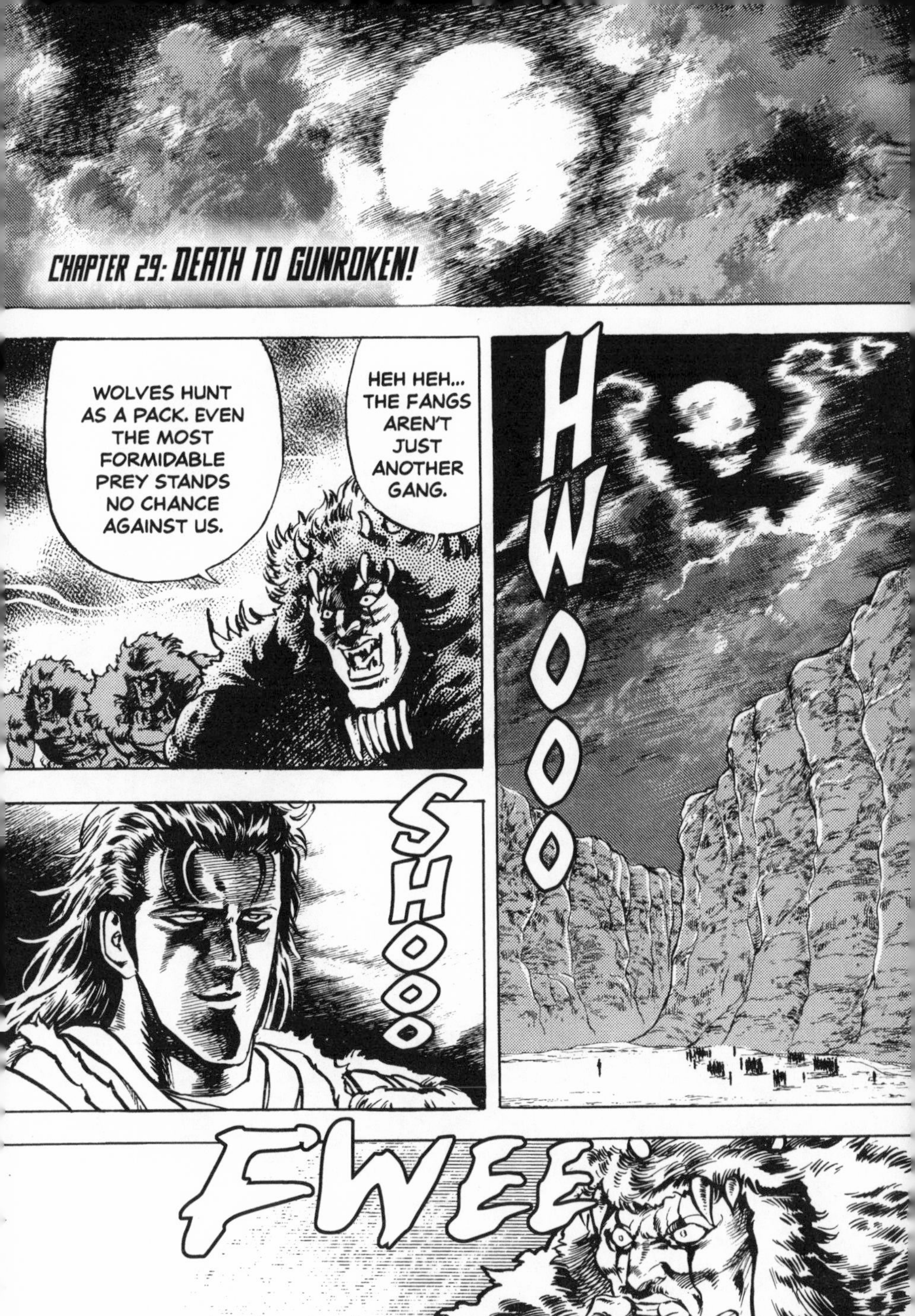
CHAPTER 29: DEATH TO GUNROKEN!
HWOOO
HEH HEH... THE FANGS AREN'T JUST ANOTHER GANG.
WOLVES HUNT AS A PACK. EVEN THE MOST FORMIDABLE PREY STANDS NO CHANCE AGAINST US.
SHOOOO
FWEE

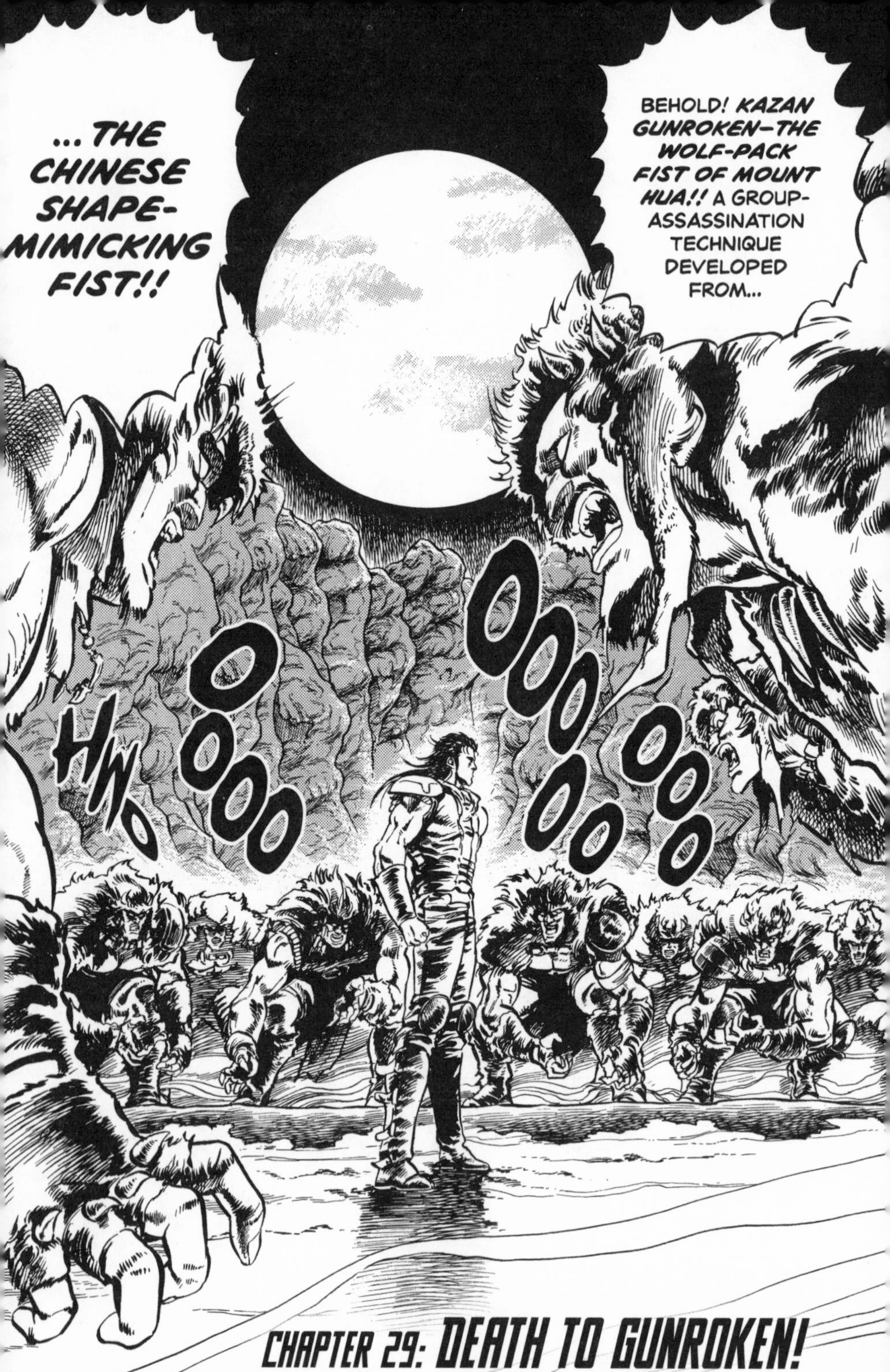
BEHOLD! KAZAN GUNROKEN—THE WOLF-PACK FIST OF MOUNT HUA!! A GROUP-ASSASSINATION TECHNIQUE DEVELOPED FROM...
...THE CHINESE SHAPE-MIMICKING FIST!!
HWOOOOO
OOOOOOOOO

CHAPTER 29: DEATH TO GUNROKEN!

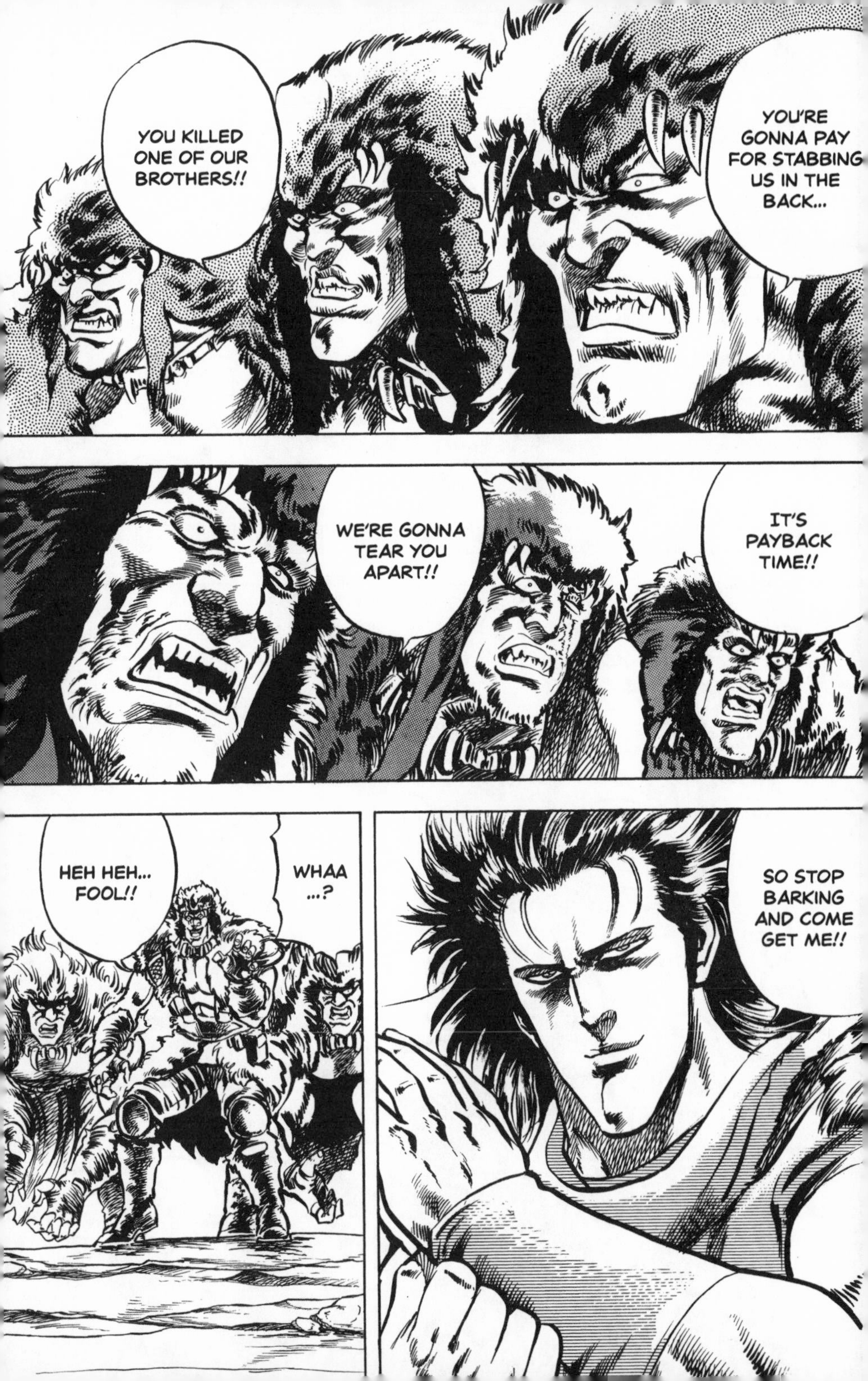
YOU'RE GONNA PAY FOR STABBING US IN THE BACK...
YOU KILLED ONE OF OUR BROTHERS!!
IT'S PAYBACK TIME!!
WE'RE GONNA TEAR YOU APART!!
SO STOP BARKING AND COME GET ME!!
WHAA ...?
HEH HEH... FOOL!!

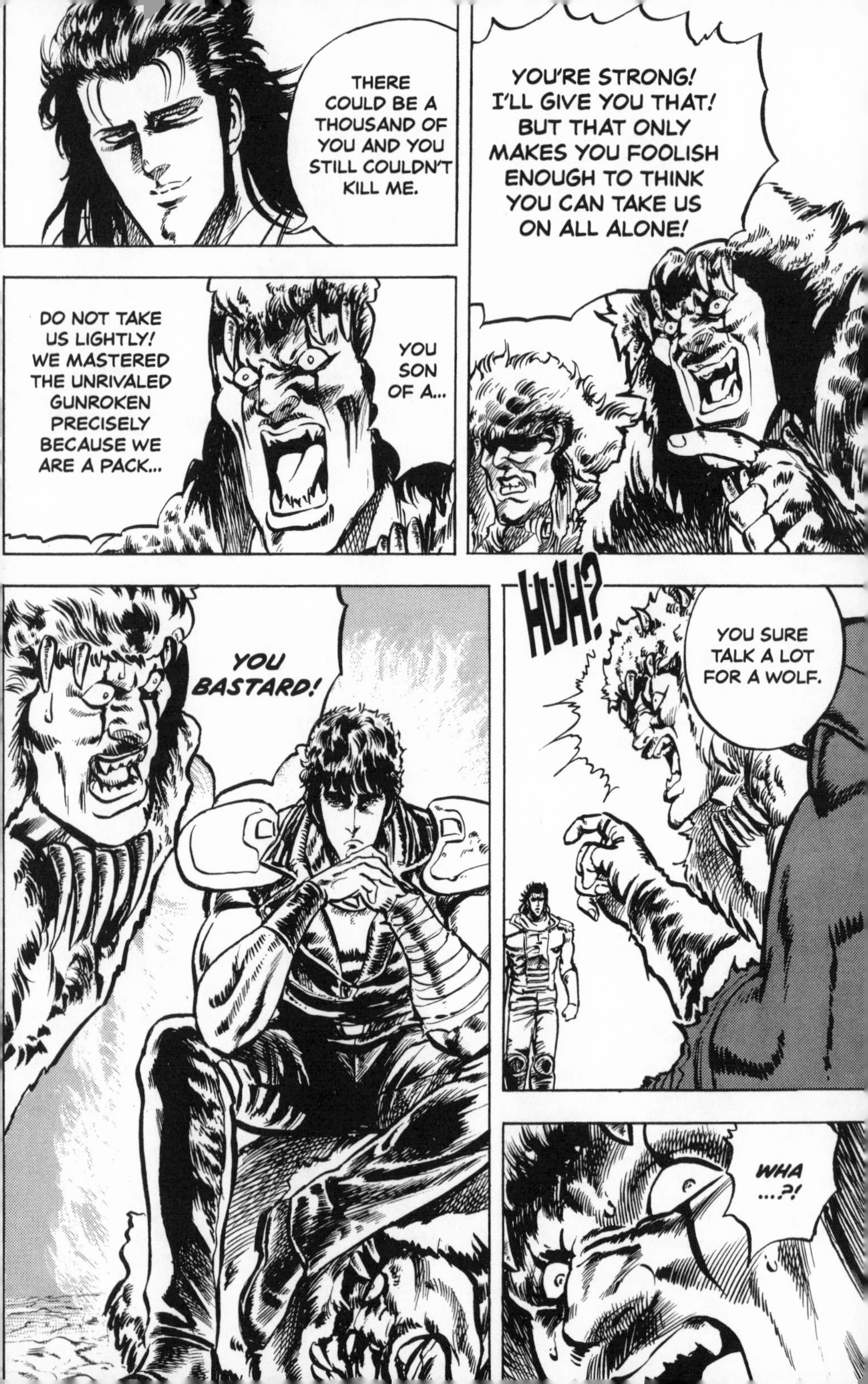
YOU'RE STRONG! I'LL GIVE YOU THAT! BUT THAT ONLY MAKES YOU FOOLISH ENOUGH TO THINK YOU CAN TAKE US ON ALL ALONE!
THERE COULD BE A THOUSAND OF YOU AND YOU STILL COULDN'T KILL ME.
YOU SON OF A...
DO NOT TAKE US LIGHTLY! WE MASTERED THE UNRIVALED GUNROKEN PRECISELY BECAUSE WE ARE A PACK...
YOU SURE TALK A LOT FOR A WOLF.
HUH?
WHA ...?!
YOU BASTARD!

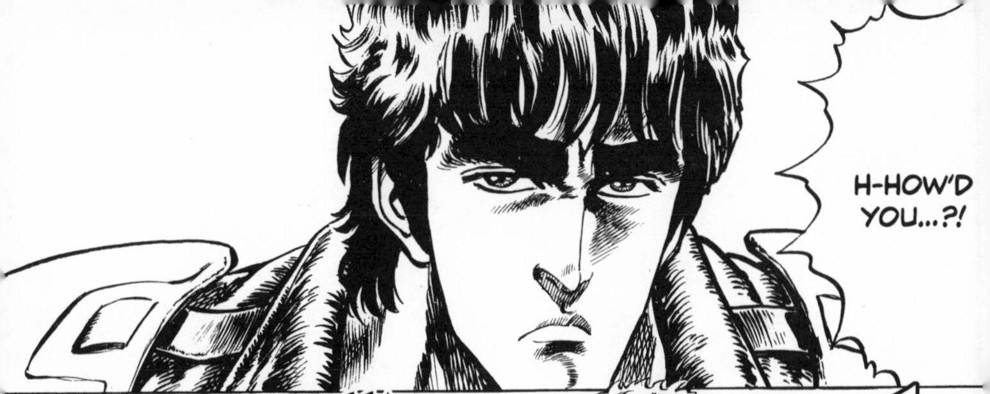
H-HOW'D YOU...?!

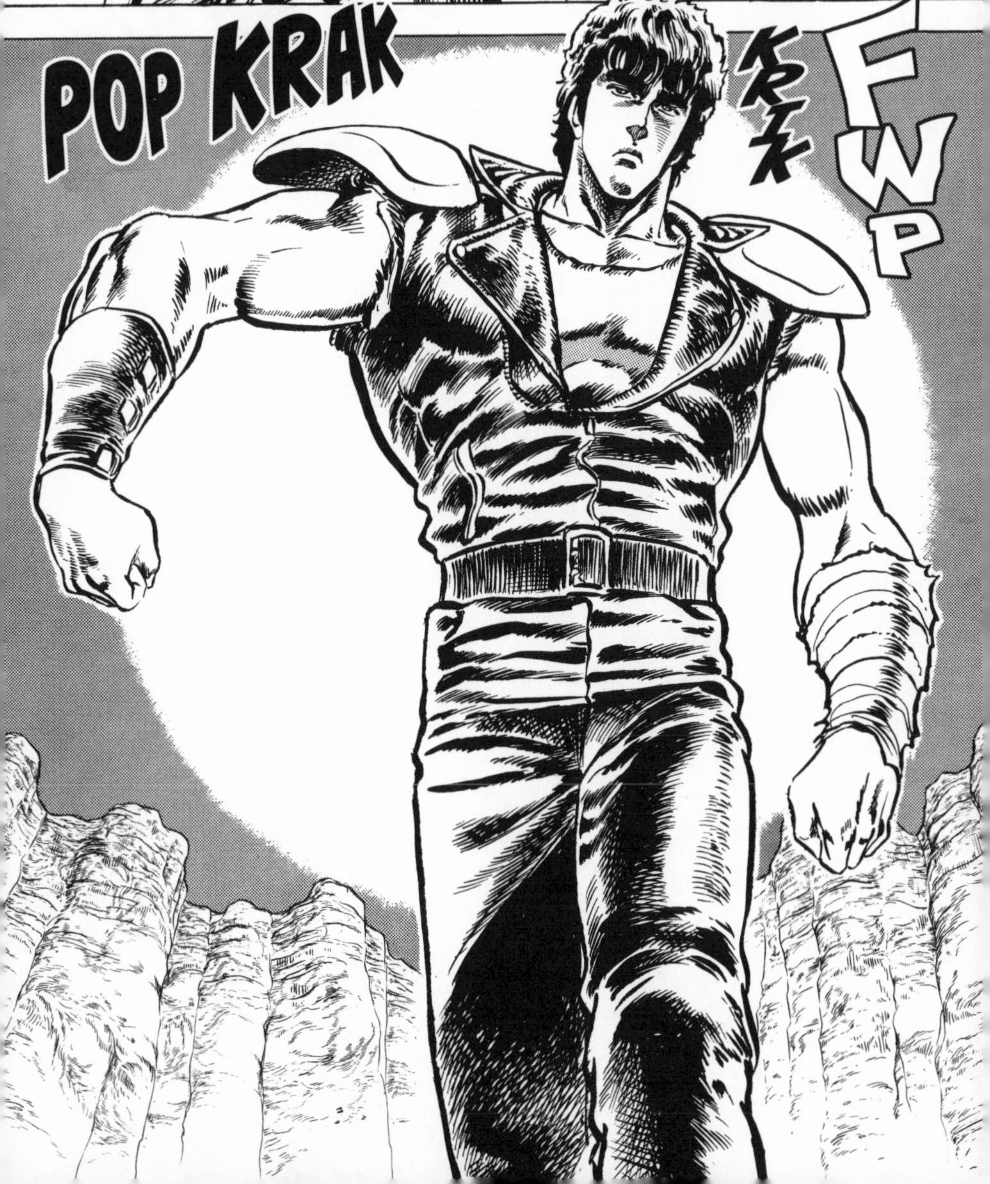
FWP
KRIK
POP KRAK

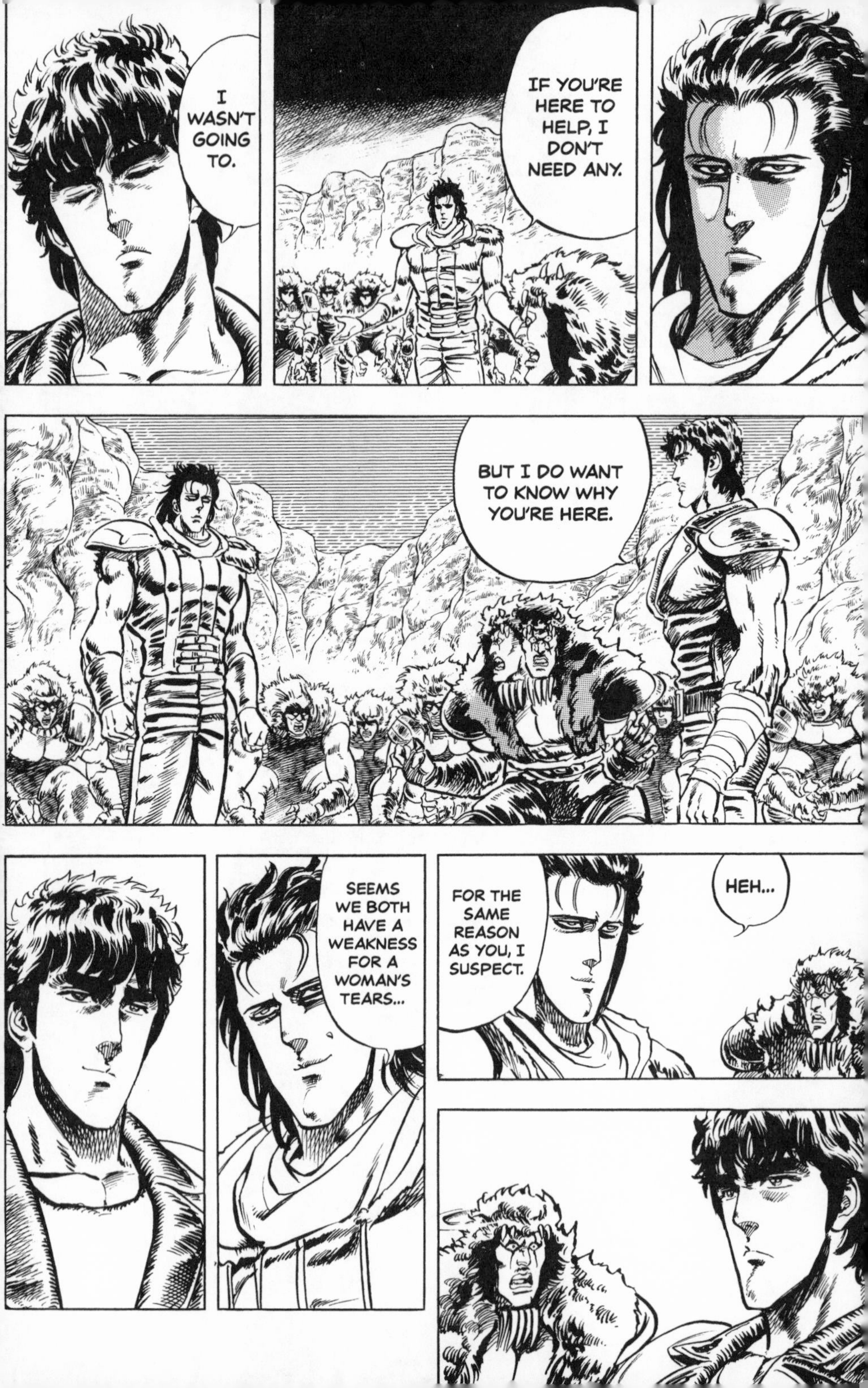
IF YOU'RE HERE TO HELP, I DON'T NEED ANY.
I WASN'T GOING TO.
BUT I DO WANT TO KNOW WHY YOU'RE HERE.
HEH...
FOR THE SAME REASON AS YOU, I SUSPECT.
SEEMS WE BOTH HAVE A WEAKNESS FOR A WOMAN'S TEARS...

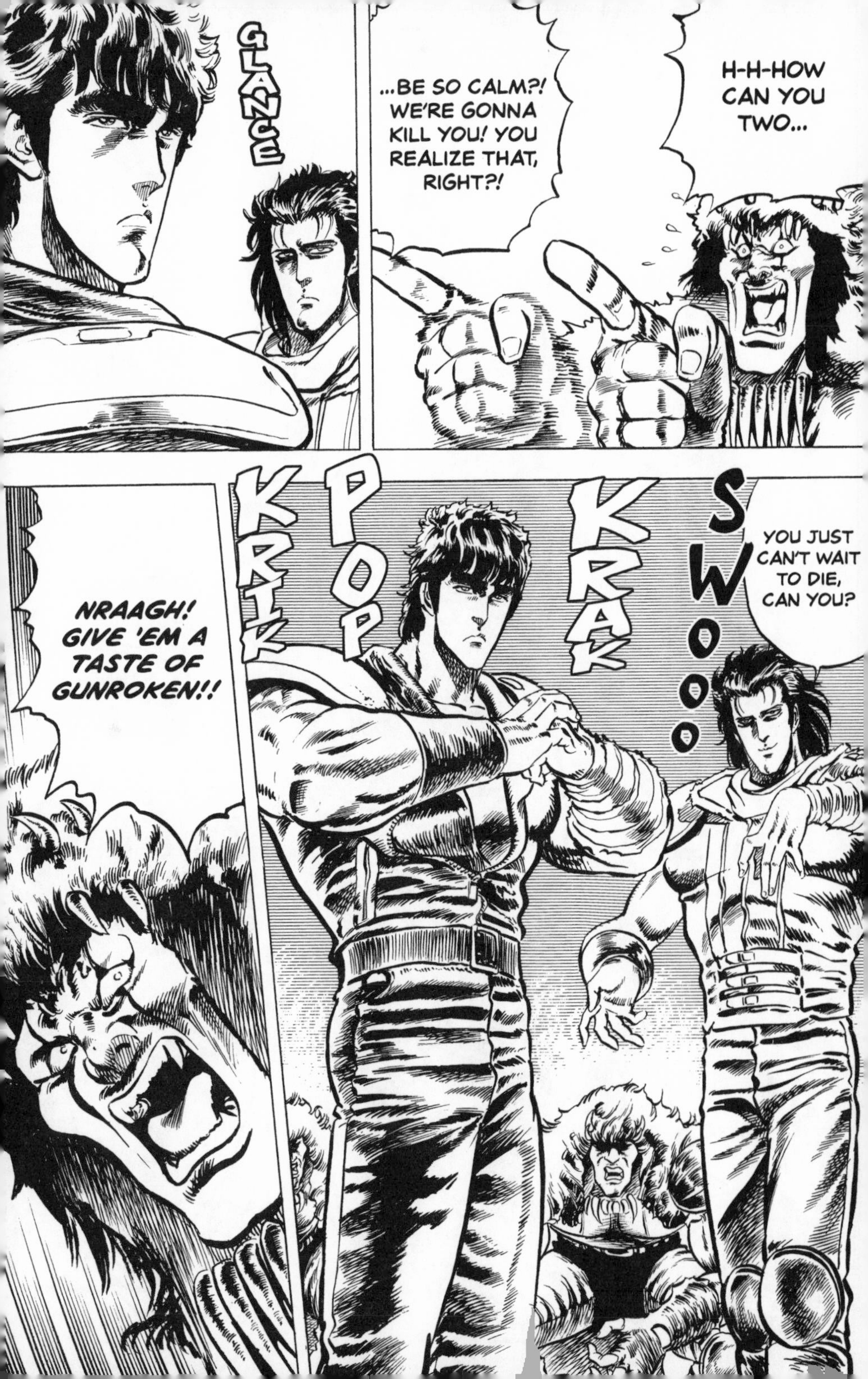
H-H-HOW CAN YOU TWO...
...BE SO CALM?! WE'RE GONNA KILL YOU! YOU REALIZE THAT, RIGHT?!
GLANCE
SWOOO
YOU JUST CAN'T WAIT TO DIE, CAN YOU?
KRAK
POP
KRIK
NRAAGH! GIVE 'EM A TASTE OF GUNROKEN!!

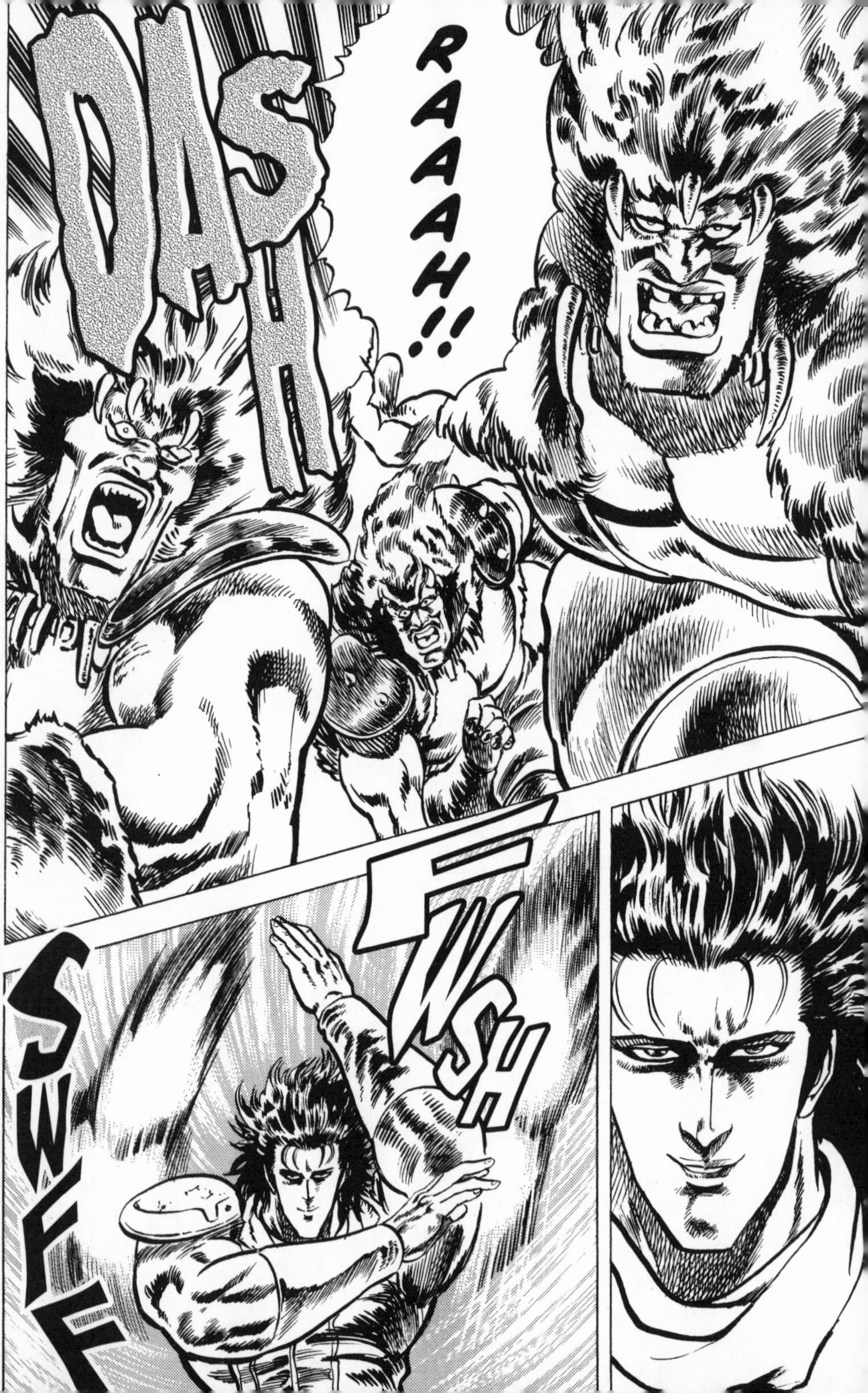
RAAAAH!!
DASH
FWSH
SWFF

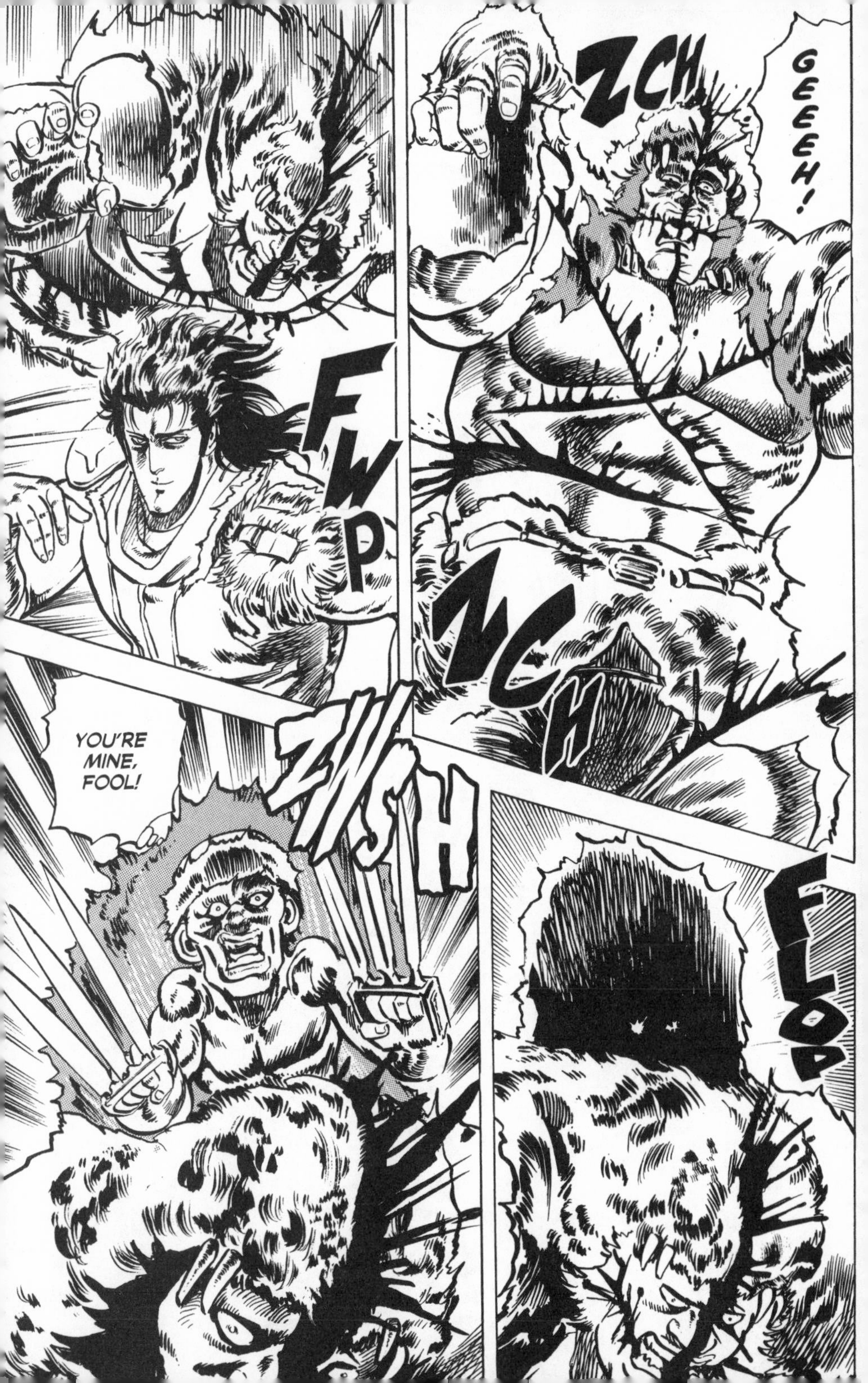
ZCH
GEEEEH!
NCH
FWP
FLOP
YOU'RE MINE, FOOL!
ZWSH

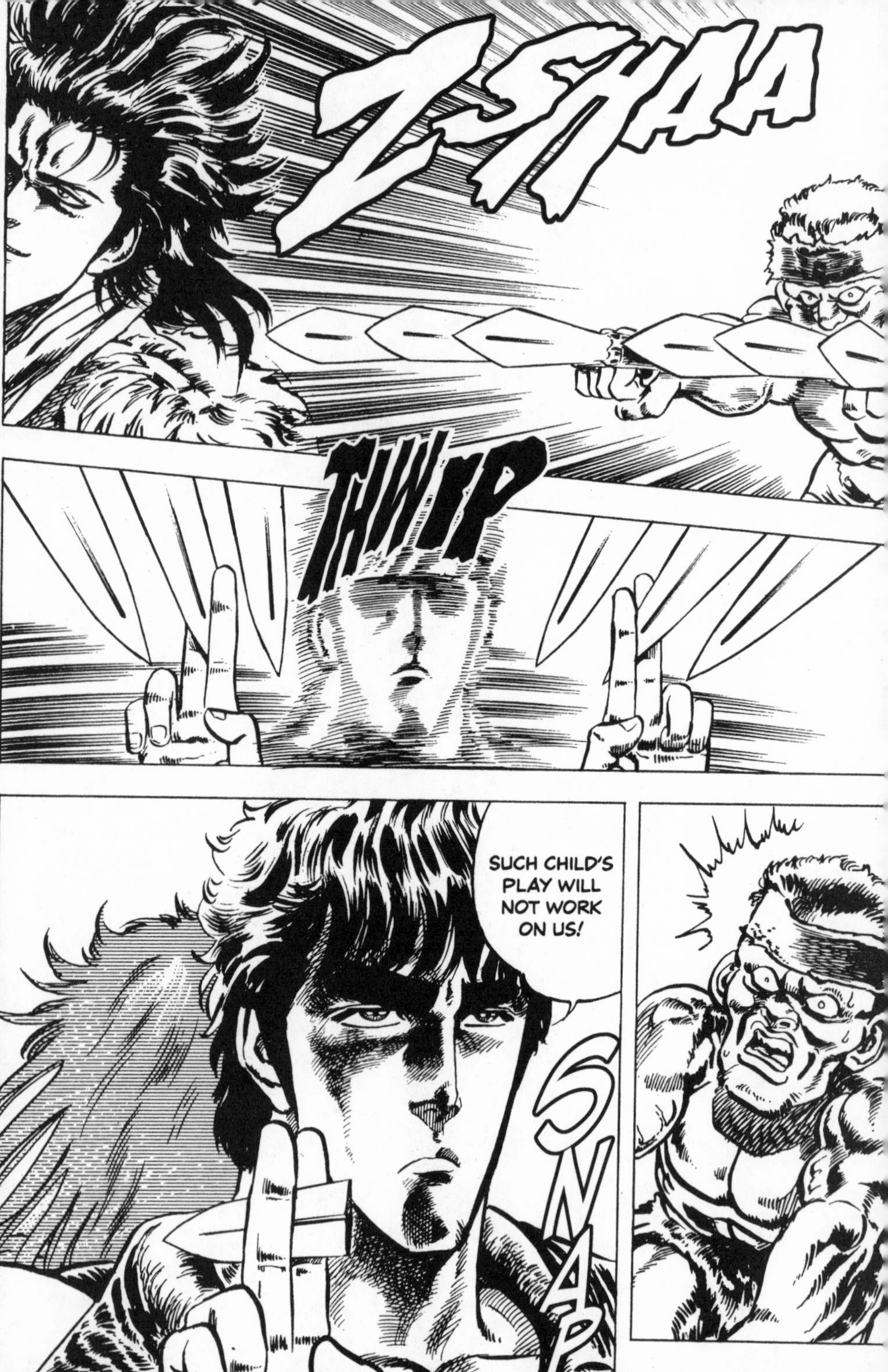
Z-SHAA
THWIP
SUCH CHILD'S PLAY WILL NOT WORK ON US!
SNAP

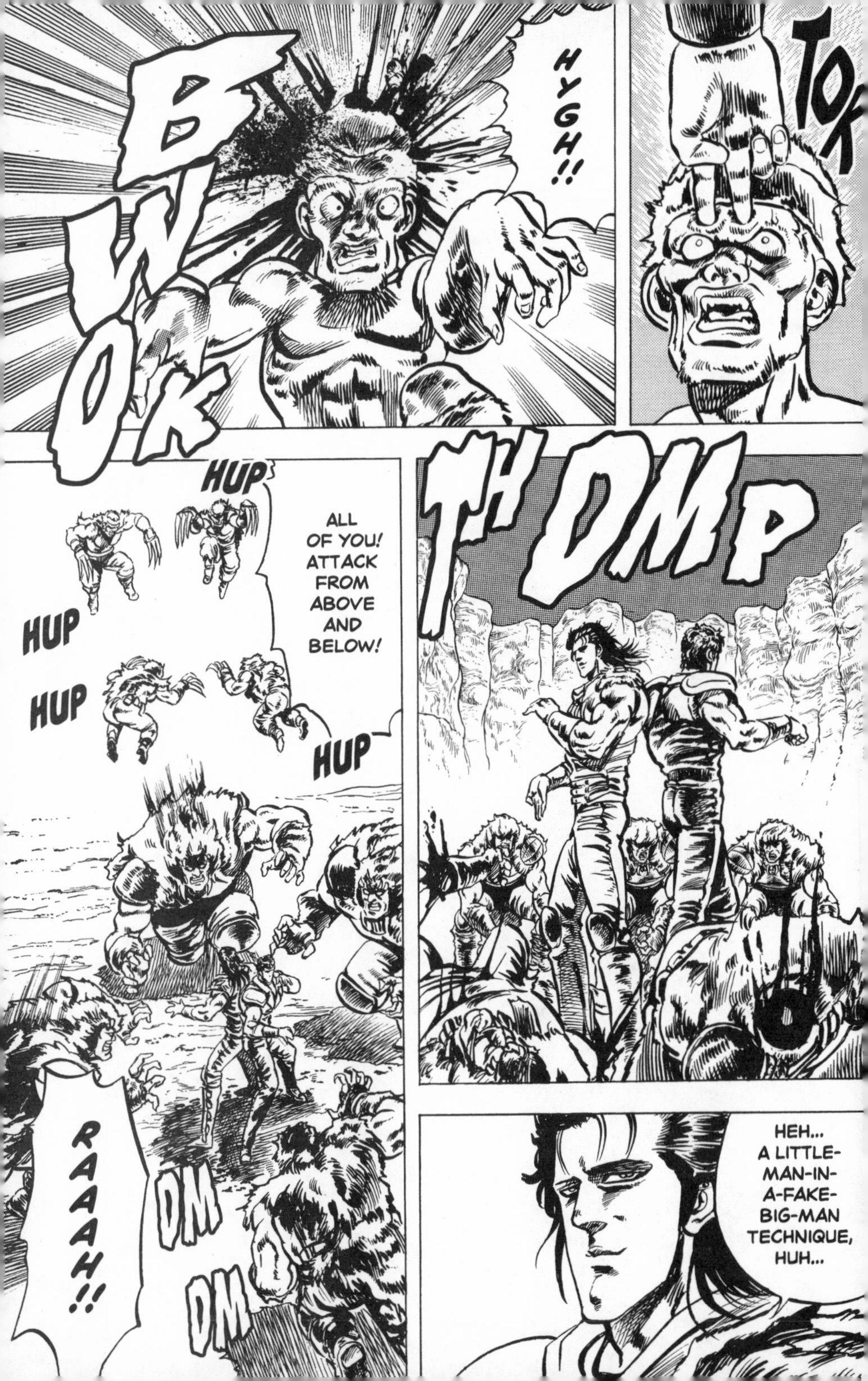
TOK
BWOK
HYGH!!
THDMP
HEH... A LITTLE-MAN-IN-A-FAKE-BIG-MAN TECHNIQUE, HUH...
HUP
ALL OF YOU! ATTACK FROM ABOVE AND BELOW!
HUP
HUP
HUP
RAAAAH!!
DM
DM

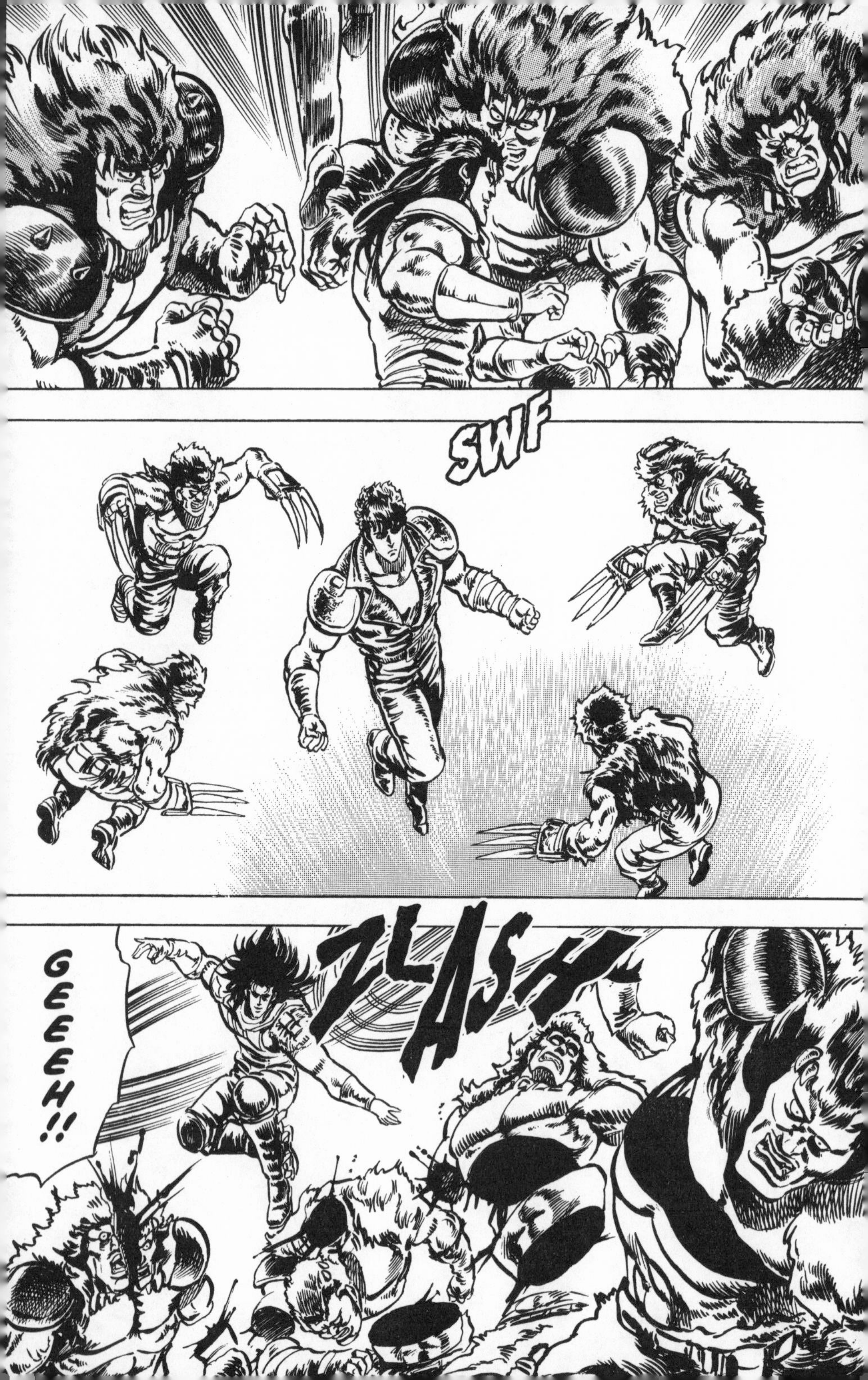
SWF
ZLASH
GEEEEH!!

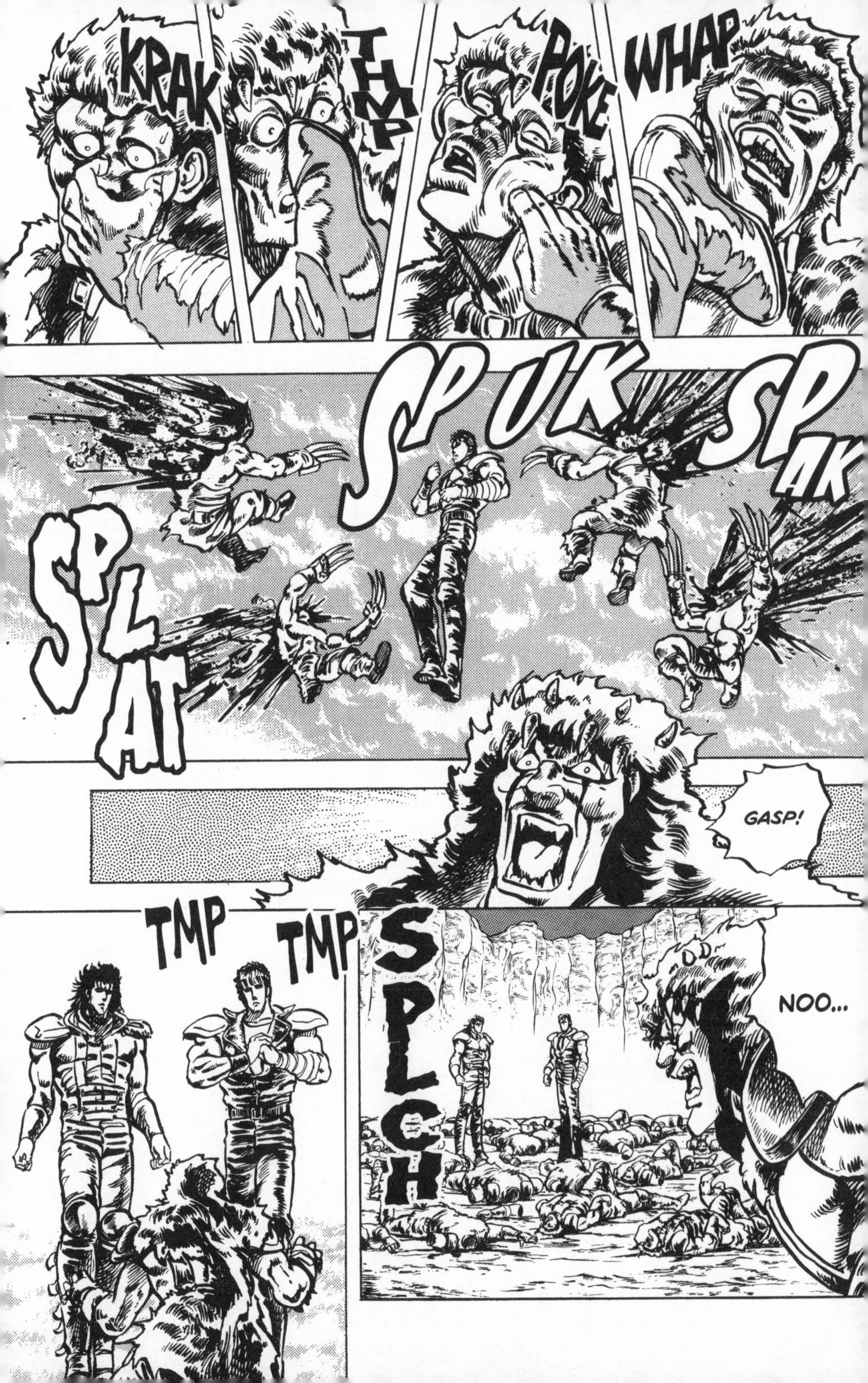
WHAP
POKE
THMP
KRAK
SPAK
SPUK
SPLAT
GASP!
NOO...
SPLCH
TMP
TMP

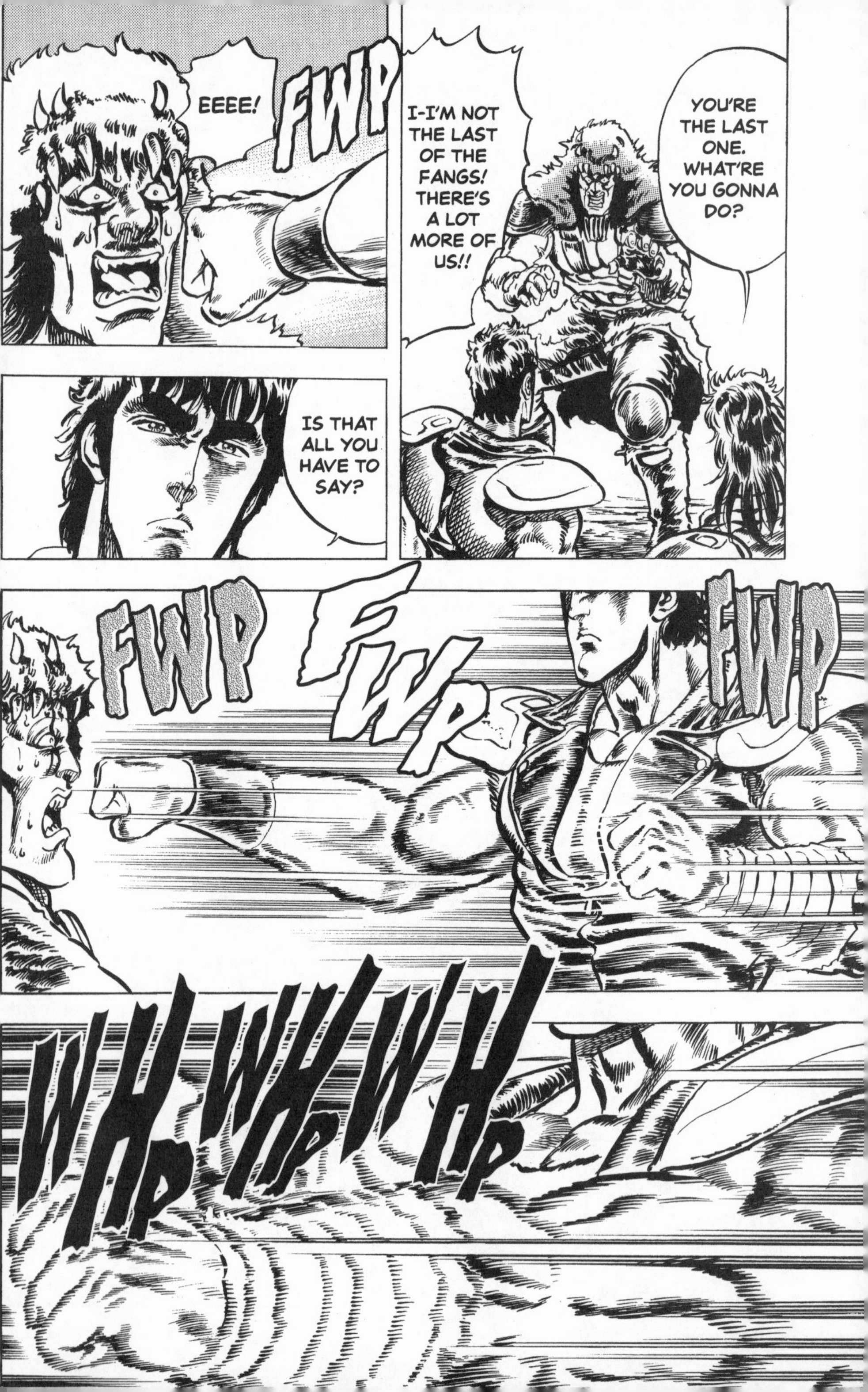
YOU'RE THE LAST ONE. WHAT'RE YOU GONNA DO?
I-I'M NOT THE LAST OF THE FANGS! THERE'S A LOT MORE OF US!!
IS THAT ALL YOU HAVE TO SAY?
FWP
EEEE!
FWP
FWP
FWP
WHP
WHP
WHP

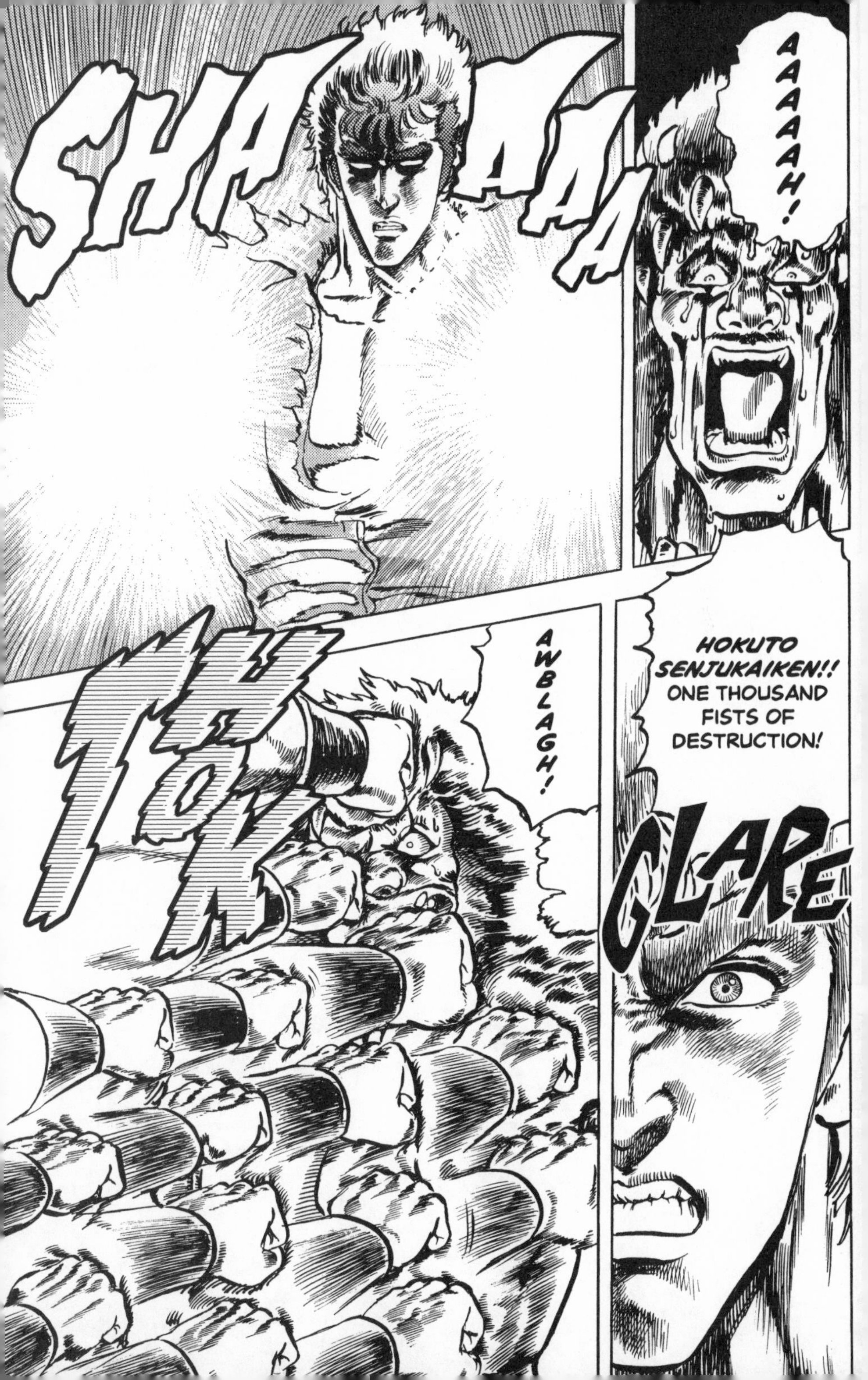
AAAAAAH!
SHAAAA
HOKUTO SENJUKAIKEN!! ONE THOUSAND FISTS OF DESTRUCTION!
GLARE
AWBLAGH!
THOK

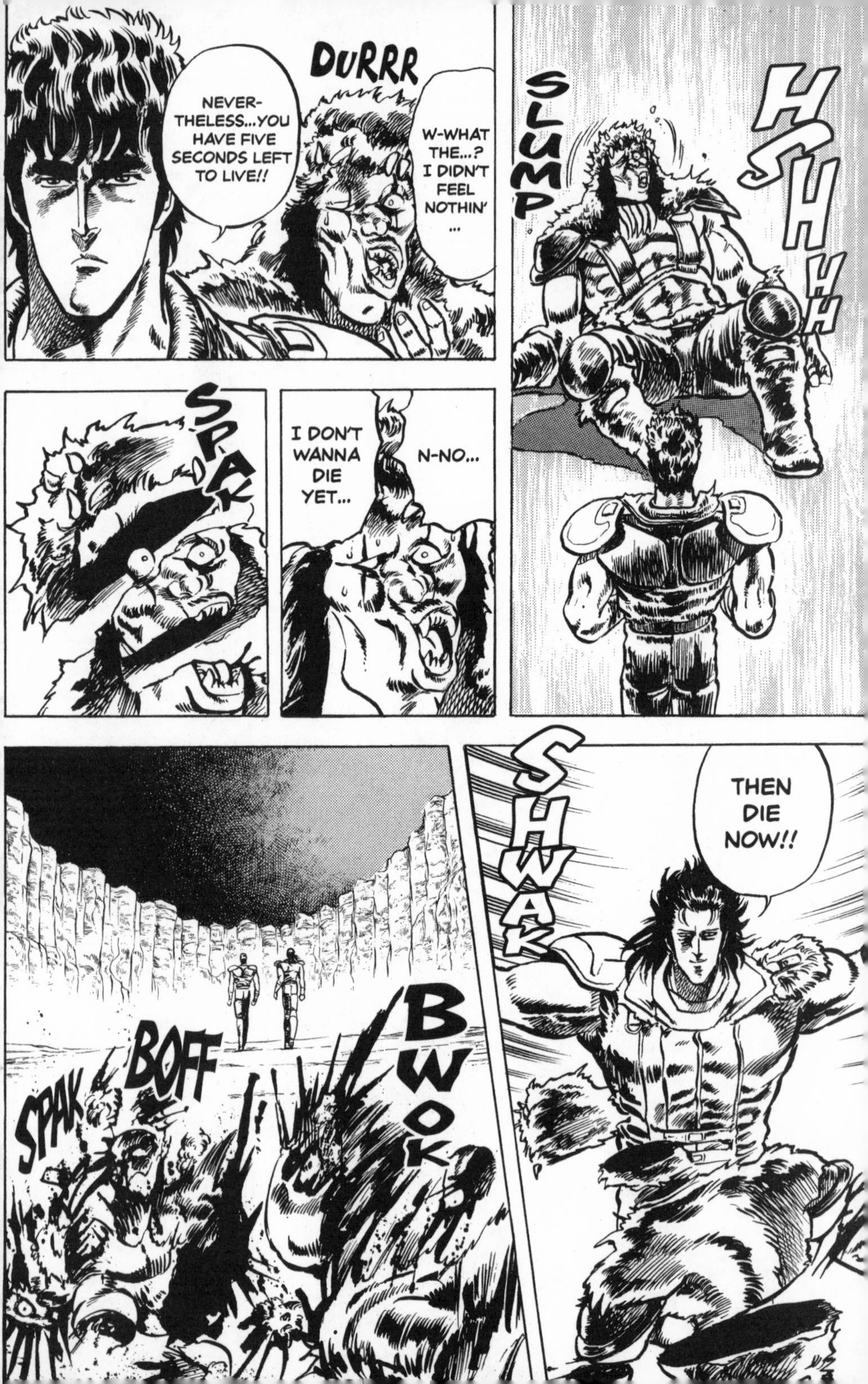
SLUMP
HSHHHH
DURRR
W-WHAT THE...? I DIDN'T FEEL NOTHIN' ...
NEVER-THELESS...YOU HAVE FIVE SECONDS LEFT TO LIVE!!
N-NO...
I DON'T WANNA DIE YET...
SPAK
SHWAK
THEN DIE NOW!!
BWOK
BOFF
SPAK

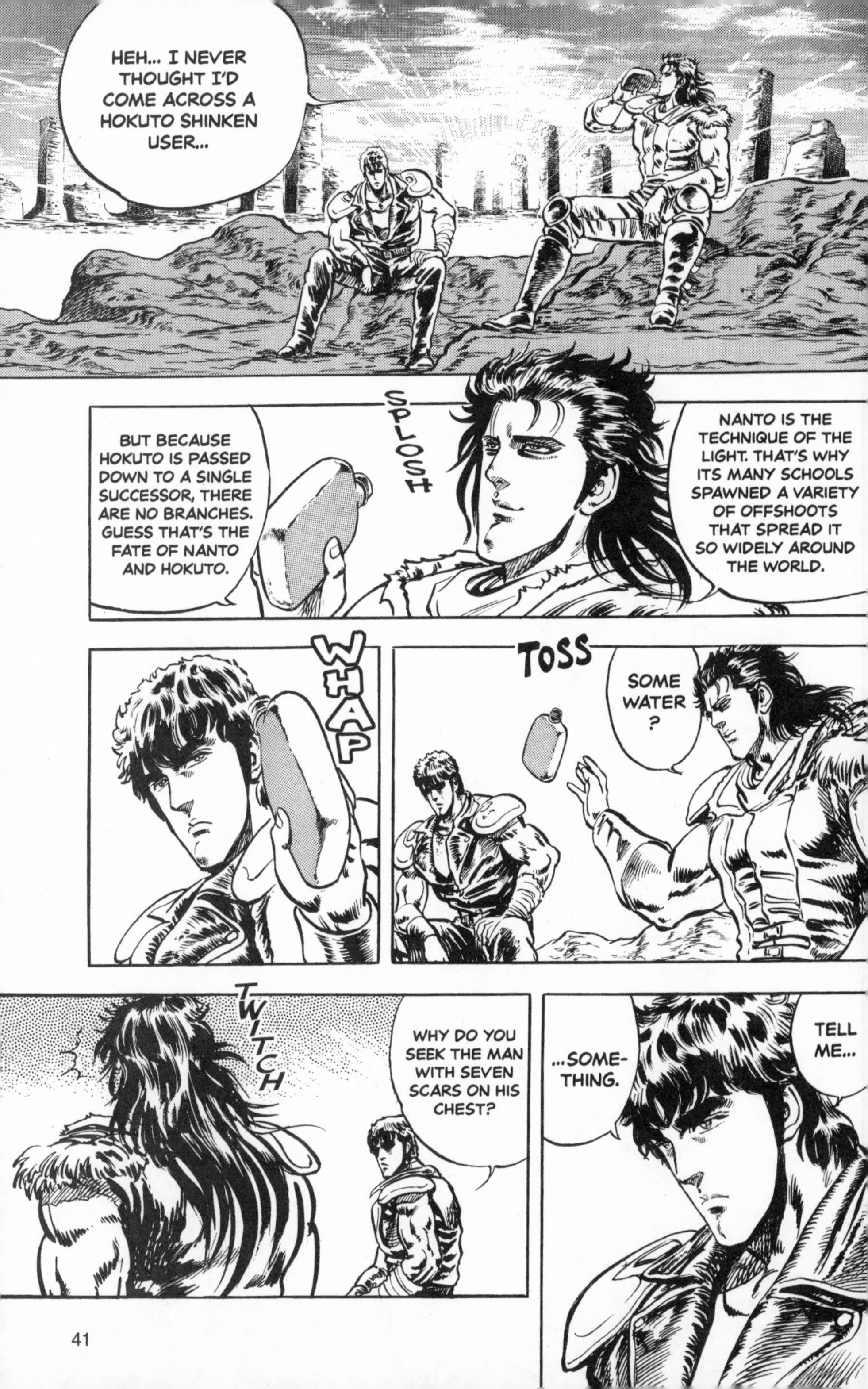
HEH... I NEVER THOUGHT I'D COME ACROSS A HOKUTO SHINKEN USER...
NANTO IS THE TECHNIQUE OF THE LIGHT. THAT'S WHY ITS MANY SCHOOLS SPAWNED A VARIETY OF OFFSHOOTS THAT SPREAD IT SO WIDELY AROUND THE WORLD.
SPLOSH
BUT BECAUSE HOKUTO IS PASSED DOWN TO A SINGLE SUCCESSOR, THERE ARE NO BRANCHES. GUESS THAT'S THE FATE OF NANTO AND HOKUTO.
TOSS
SOME WATER ?
WHAP
TELL ME...
...SOME-THING.
WHY DO YOU SEEK THE MAN WITH SEVEN SCARS ON HIS CHEST?
TWITCH

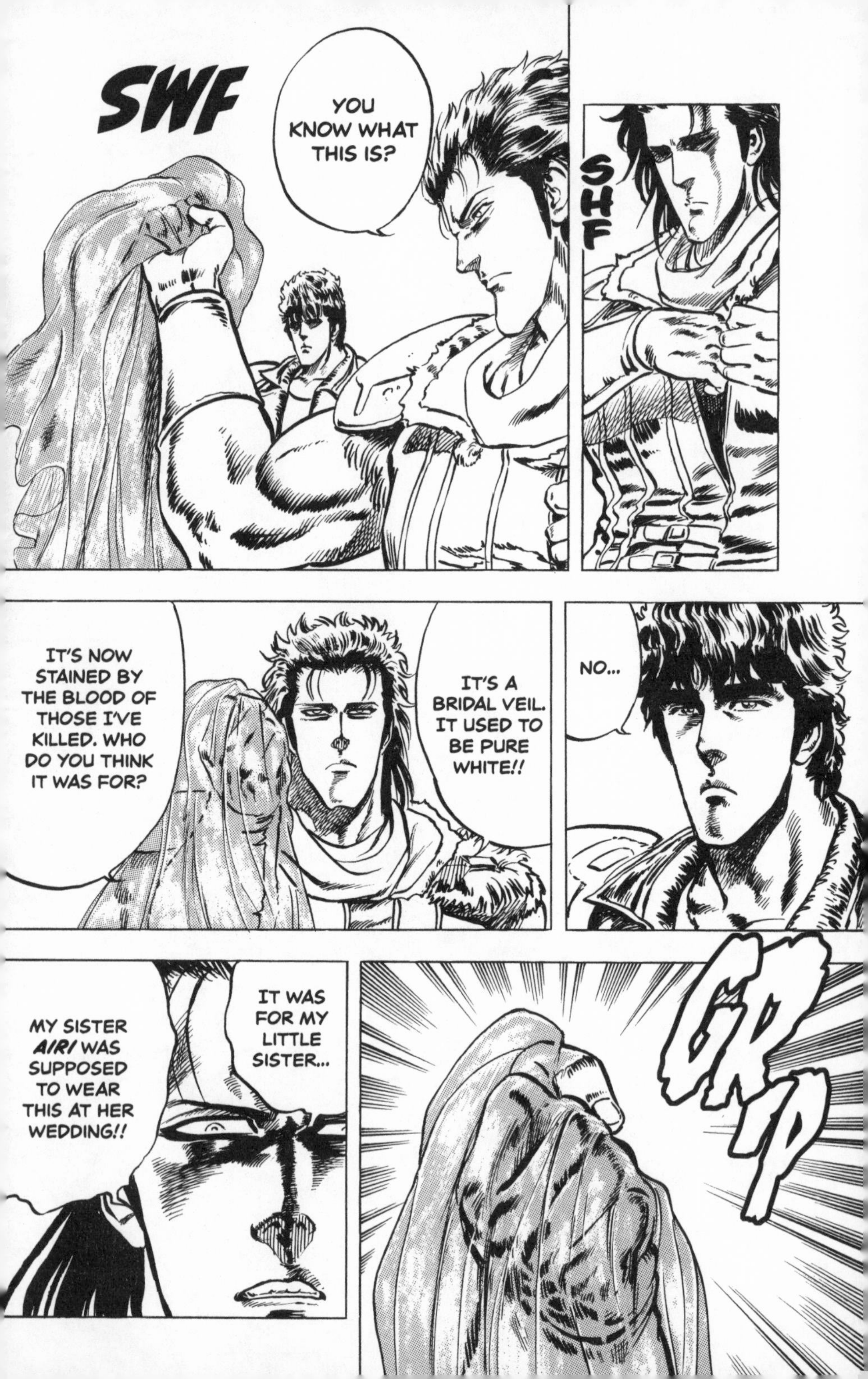
SHF
YOU KNOW WHAT THIS IS?
SWF
NO...
IT'S A BRIDAL VEIL. IT USED TO BE PURE WHITE!!
IT'S NOW STAINED BY THE BLOOD OF THOSE I'VE KILLED. WHO DO YOU THINK IT WAS FOR?
GRIP
IT WAS FOR MY LITTLE SISTER...
MY SISTER *AIRI* WAS SUPPOSED TO WEAR THIS AT HER WEDDING!!

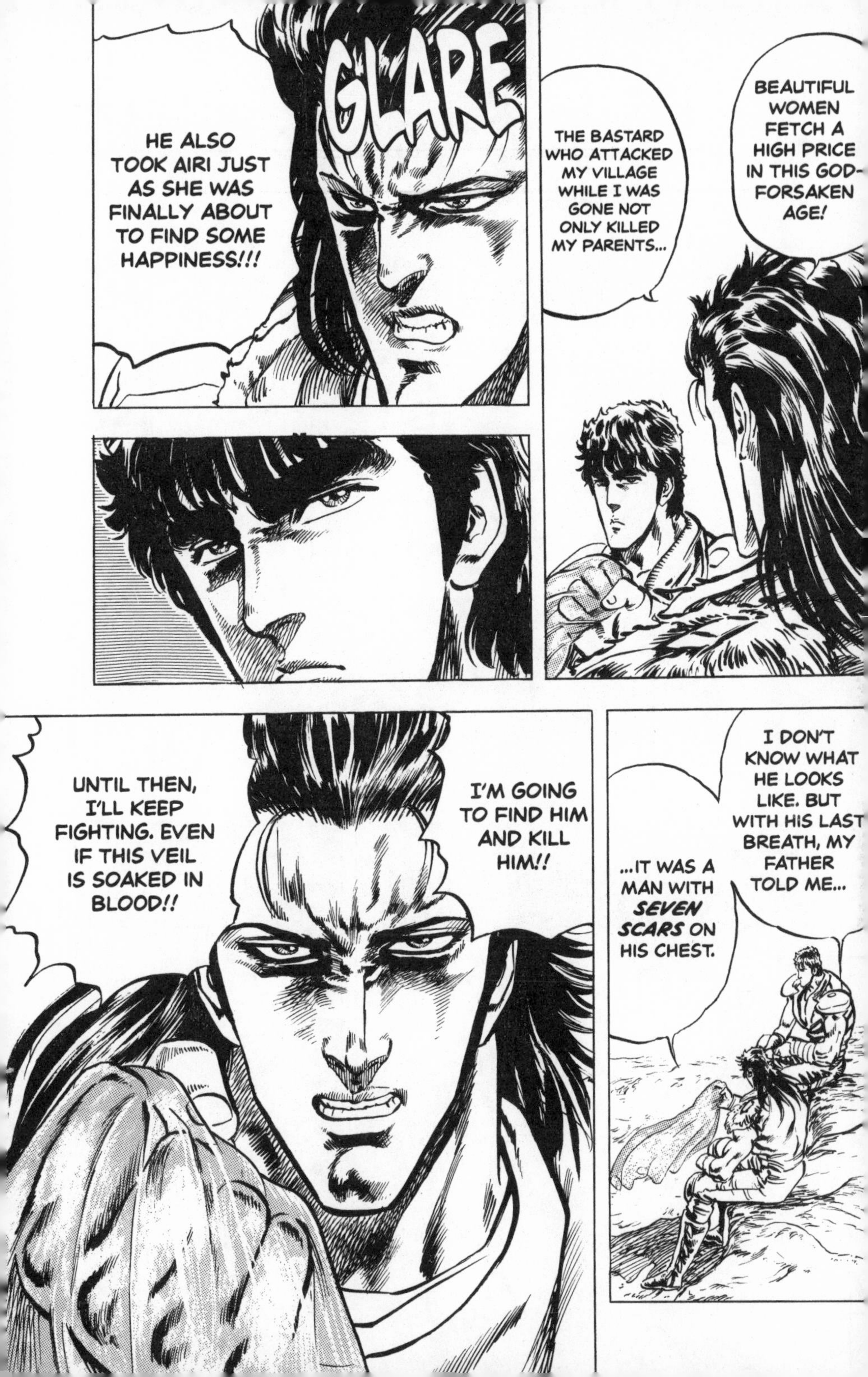
BEAUTIFUL WOMEN FETCH A HIGH PRICE IN THIS GOD-FORSAKEN AGE!
THE BASTARD WHO ATTACKED MY VILLAGE WHILE I WAS GONE NOT ONLY KILLED MY PARENTS...
GLARE
HE ALSO TOOK AIRI JUST AS SHE WAS FINALLY ABOUT TO FIND SOME HAPPINESS!!!
I DON'T KNOW WHAT HE LOOKS LIKE. BUT WITH HIS LAST BREATH, MY FATHER TOLD ME...
...IT WAS A MAN WITH ***SEVEN SCARS*** ON HIS CHEST.
I'M GOING TO FIND HIM AND KILL HIM!!
UNTIL THEN, I'LL KEEP FIGHTING. EVEN IF THIS VEIL IS SOAKED IN BLOOD!!

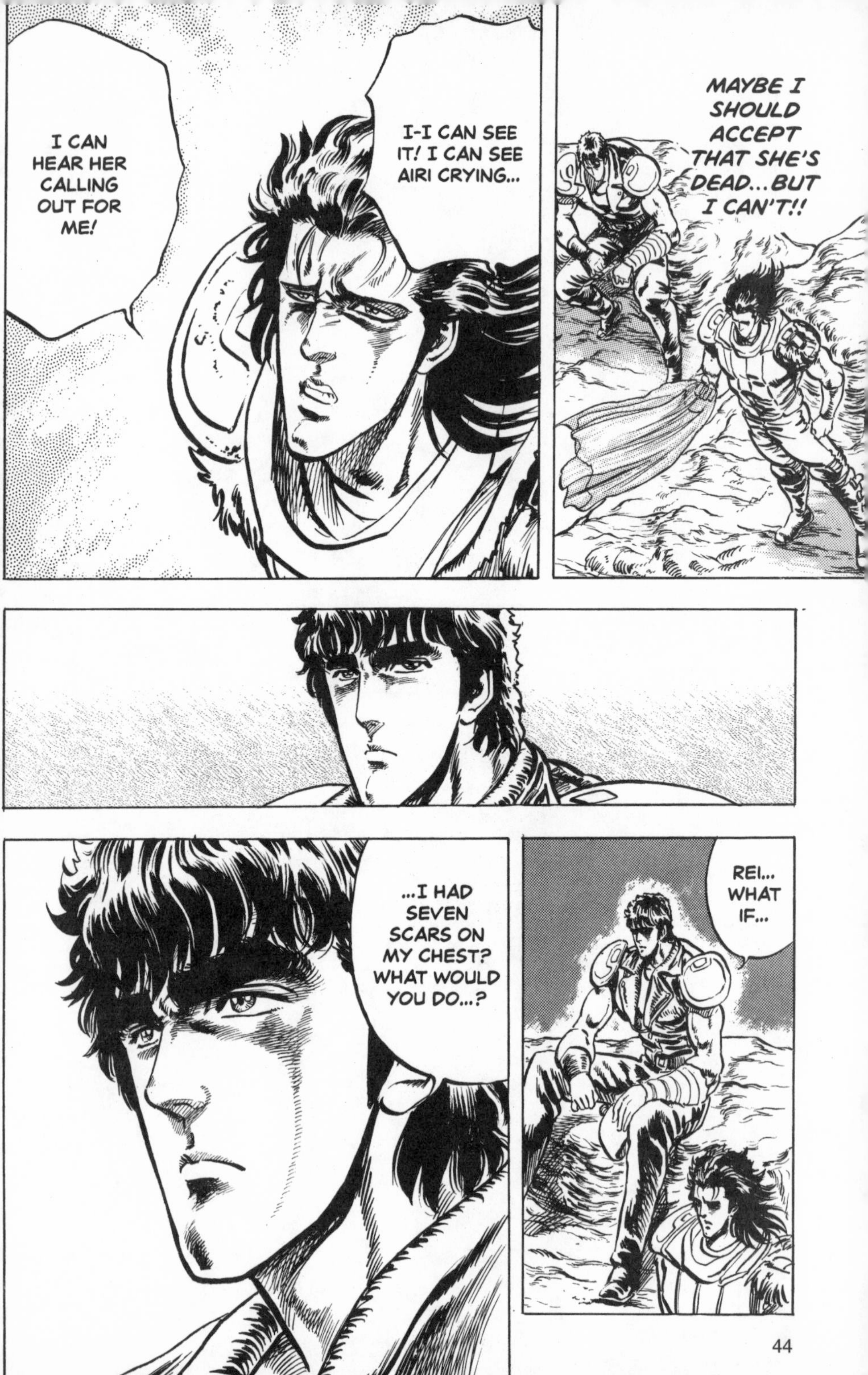
MAYBE I SHOULD ACCEPT THAT SHE'S DEAD...BUT I CAN'T!!
I-I CAN SEE IT! I CAN SEE AIRI CRYING...
I CAN HEAR HER CALLING OUT FOR ME!
REI... WHAT IF...
...I HAD SEVEN SCARS ON MY CHEST? WHAT WOULD YOU DO...?

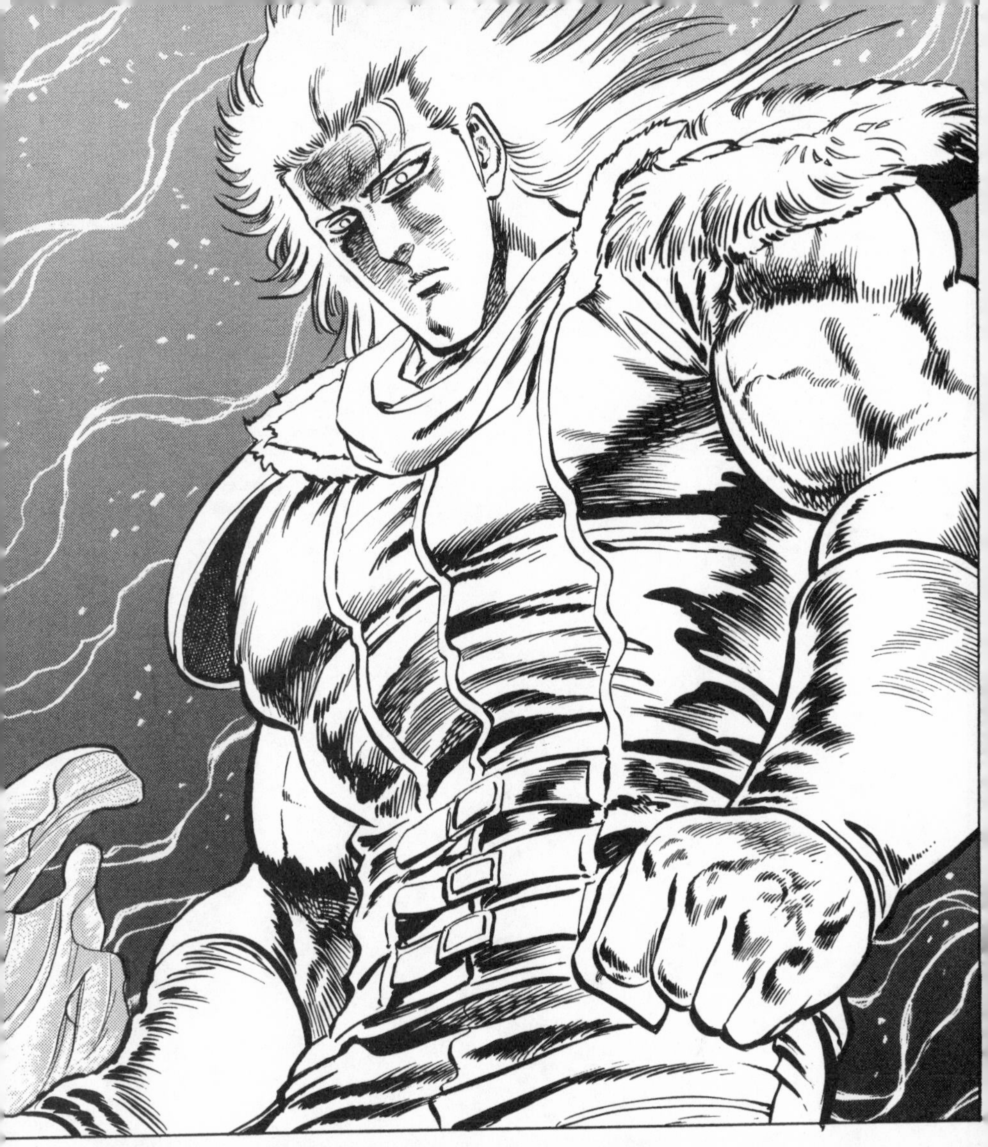

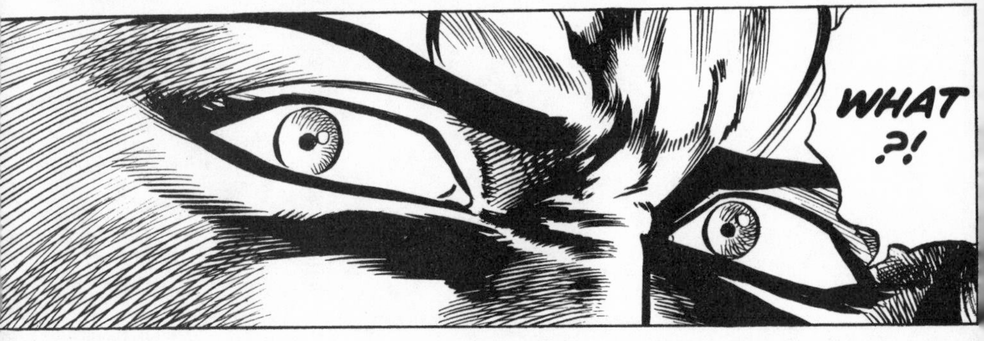
WHAT ?!

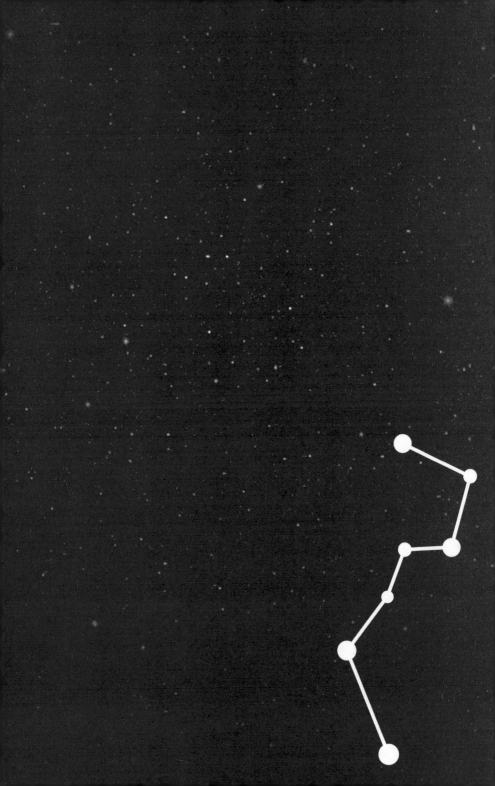

CHAPTER 30: YOU ARE A WOMAN!

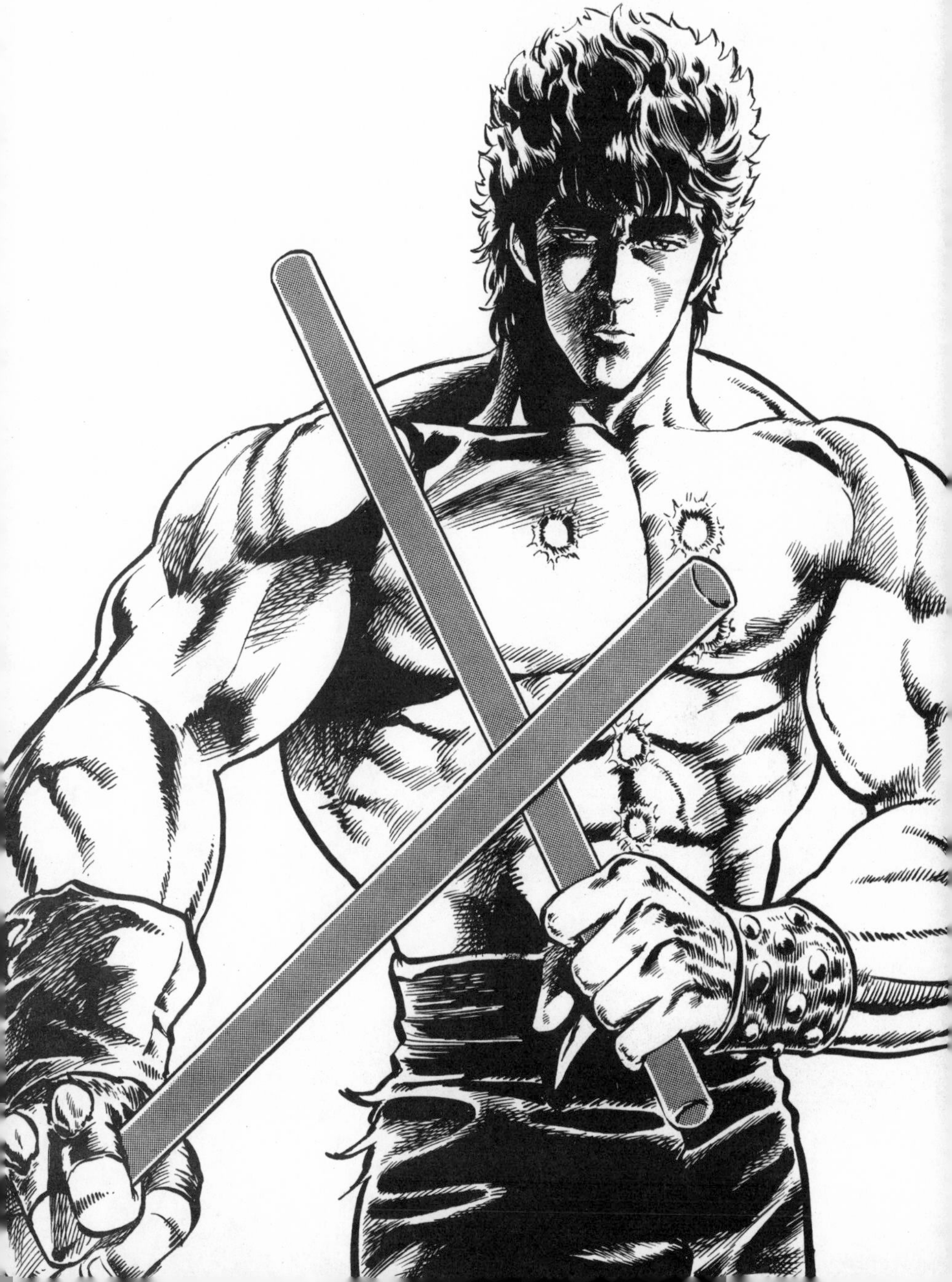

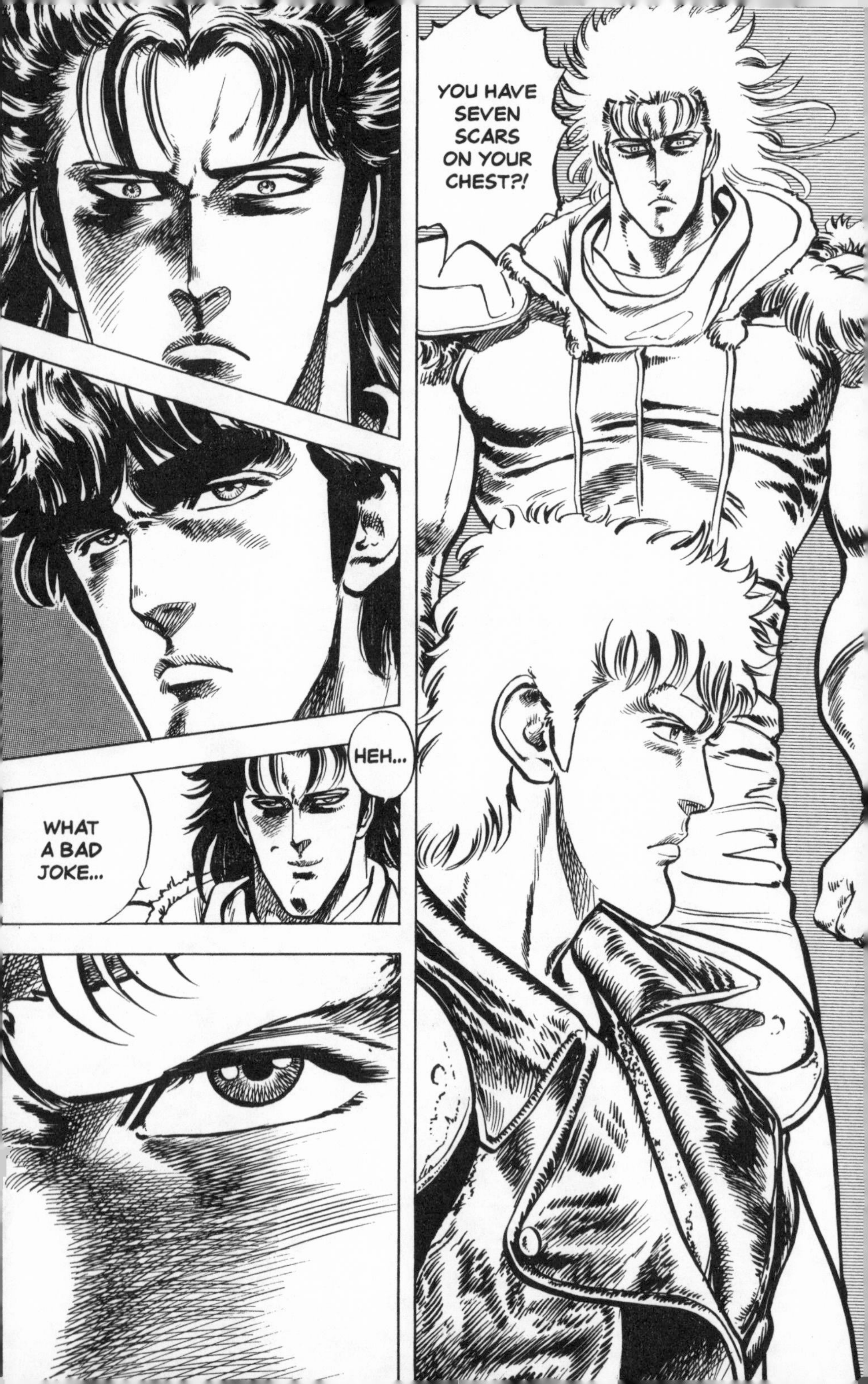
YOU HAVE SEVEN SCARS ON YOUR CHEST?!
HEH...
WHAT A BAD JOKE...

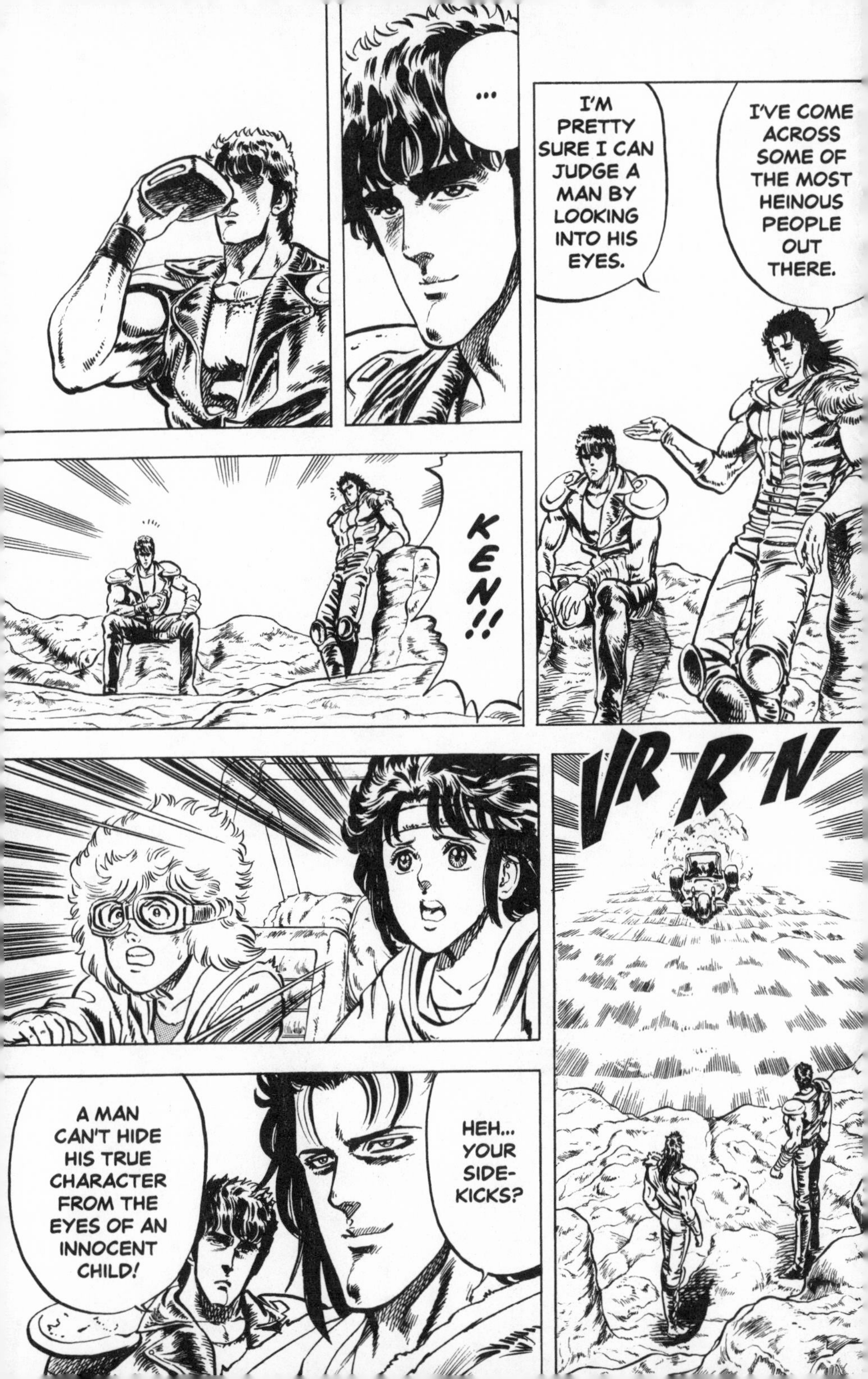
I'VE COME ACROSS SOME OF THE MOST HEINOUS PEOPLE OUT THERE.
I'M PRETTY SURE I CAN JUDGE A MAN BY LOOKING INTO HIS EYES.
...
KEN!!
VRRN
HEH... YOUR SIDE-KICKS?
A MAN CAN'T HIDE HIS TRUE CHARACTER FROM THE EYES OF AN INNOCENT CHILD!

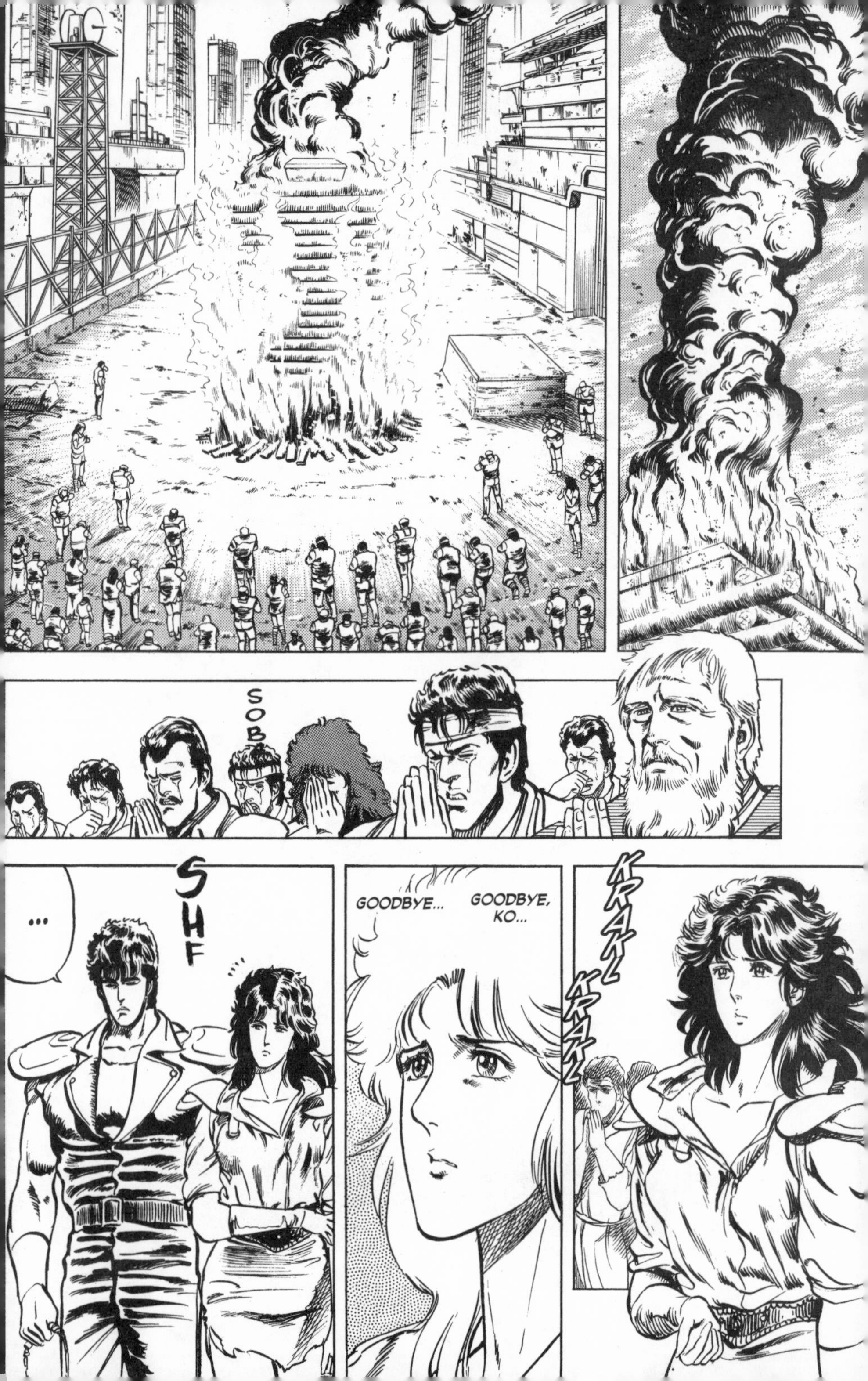
SOB
KRAK
KRAK
GOODBYE...
GOODBYE, KO...
SHF
...

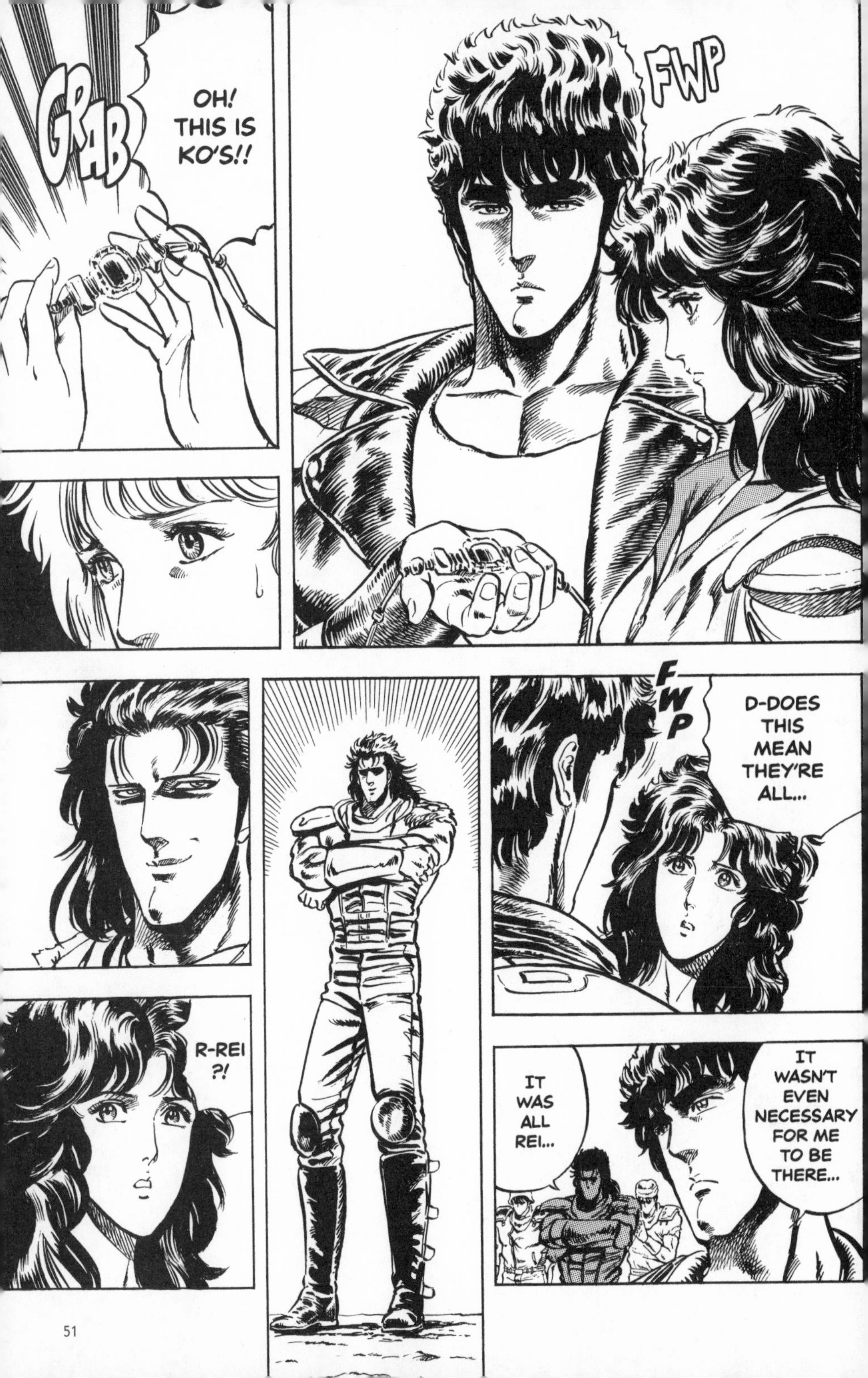
FWP
GRAB
OH! THIS IS KO'S!!
FWP
D-DOES THIS MEAN THEY'RE ALL...
IT WASN'T EVEN NECESSARY FOR ME TO BE THERE...
IT WAS ALL REI...
R-REI ?!

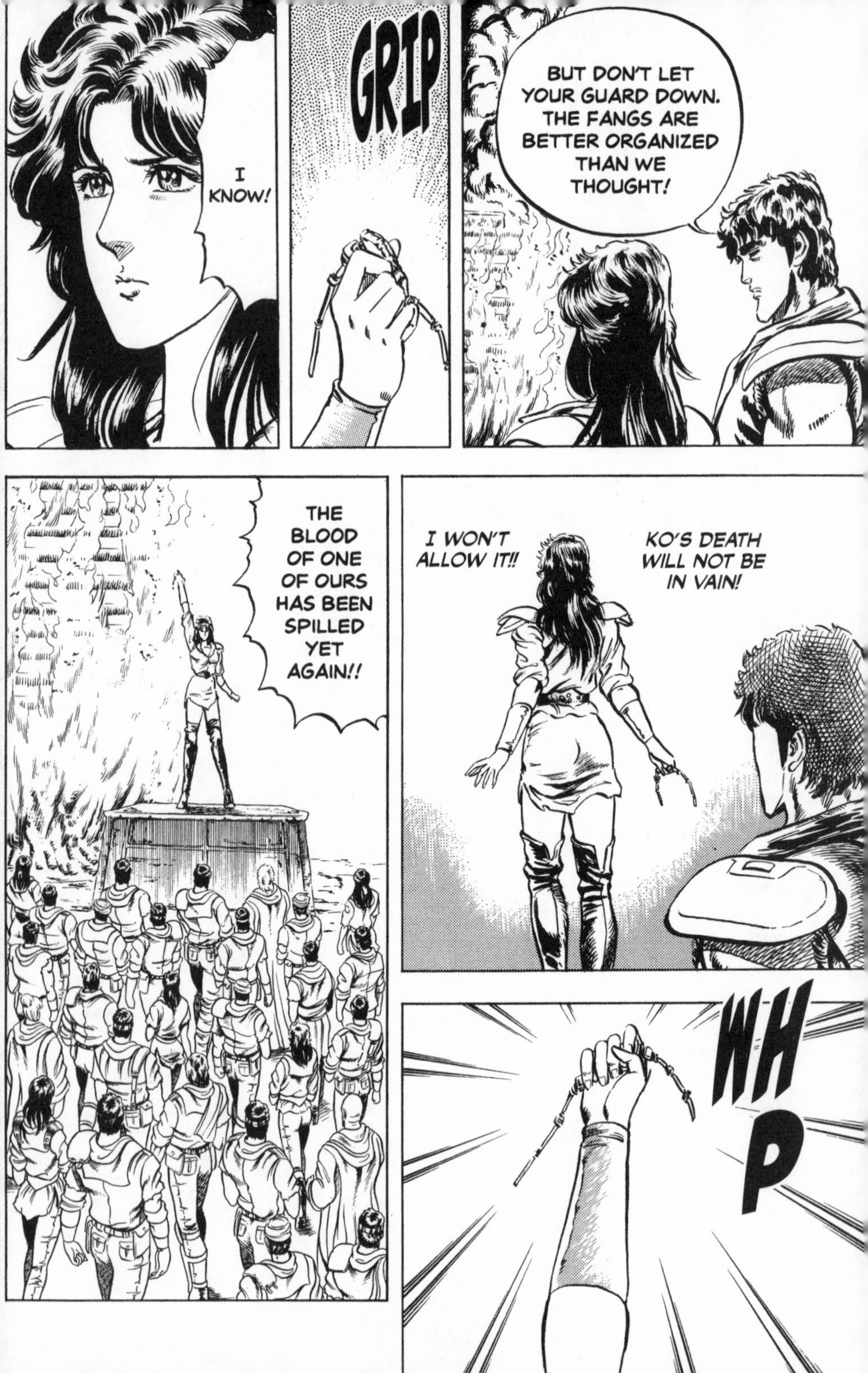
BUT DON'T LET YOUR GUARD DOWN. THE FANGS ARE BETTER ORGANIZED THAN WE THOUGHT!
GRIP
I KNOW!
KO'S DEATH WILL NOT BE IN VAIN!
I WON'T ALLOW IT!!
WHP
THE BLOOD OF ONE OF OURS HAS BEEN SPILLED YET AGAIN!!

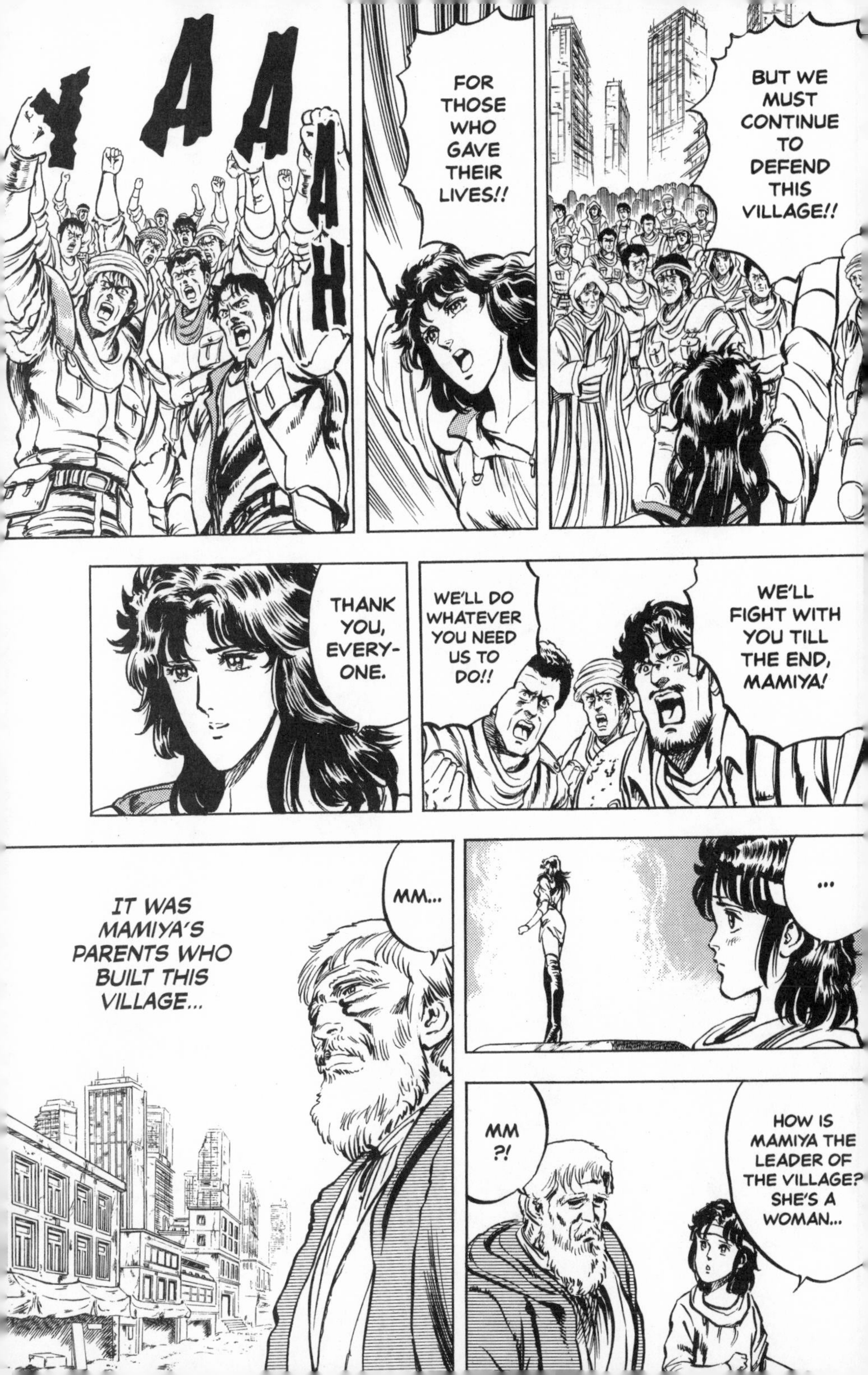
BUT WE MUST CONTINUE TO DEFEND THIS VILLAGE!!
FOR THOSE WHO GAVE THEIR LIVES!!
YAAAH
WE'LL FIGHT WITH YOU TILL THE END, MAMIYA!
WE'LL DO WHATEVER YOU NEED US TO DO!!
THANK YOU, EVERY-ONE.
...
HOW IS MAMIYA THE LEADER OF THE VILLAGE? SHE'S A WOMAN...
MM ?!
MM...
IT WAS MAMIYA'S PARENTS WHO BUILT THIS VILLAGE...

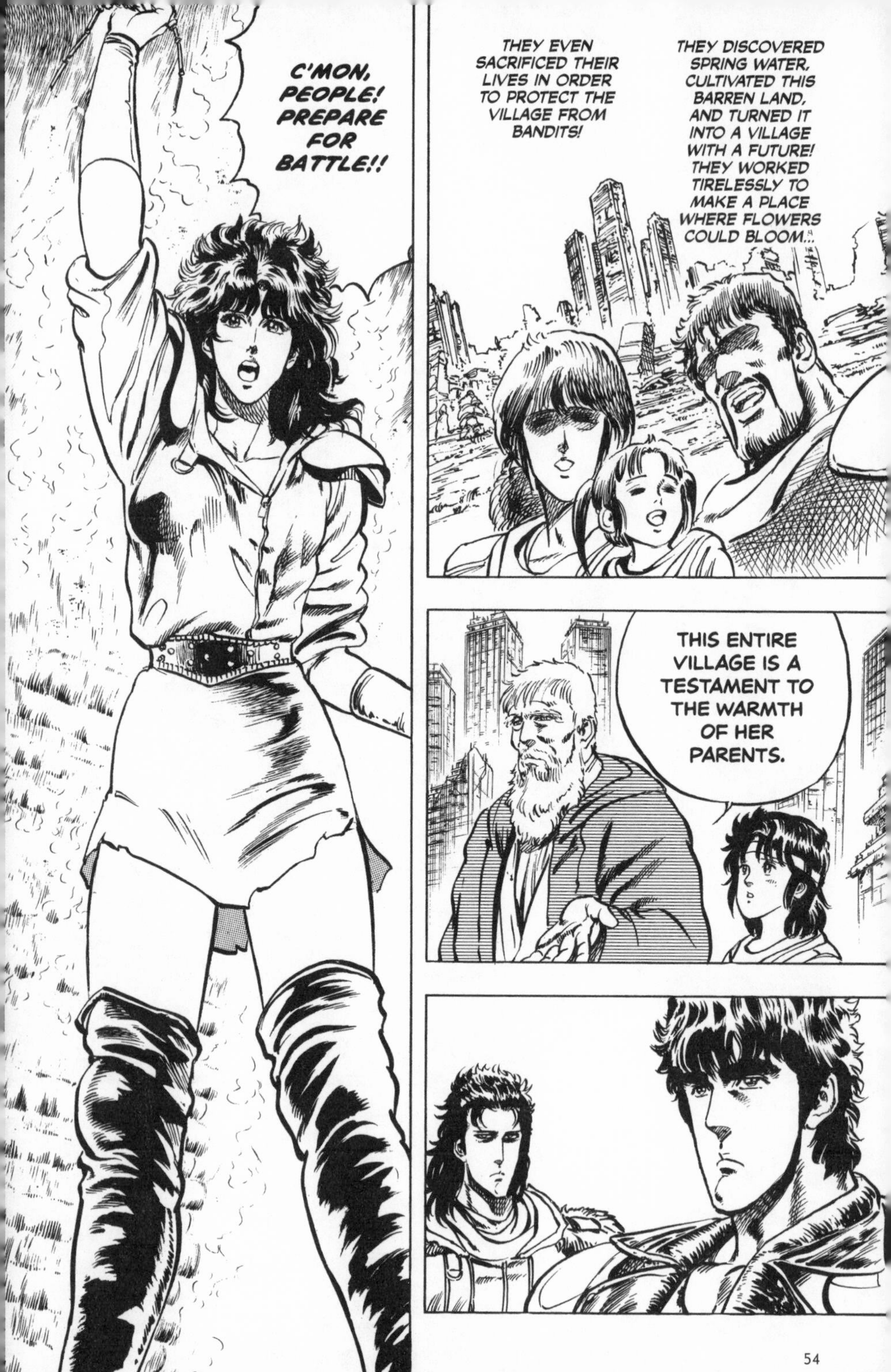
THEY DISCOVERED SPRING WATER, CULTIVATED THIS BARREN LAND, AND TURNED IT INTO A VILLAGE WITH A FUTURE! THEY WORKED TIRELESSLY TO MAKE A PLACE WHERE FLOWERS COULD BLOOM...
THEY EVEN SACRIFICED THEIR LIVES IN ORDER TO PROTECT THE VILLAGE FROM BANDITS!
THIS ENTIRE VILLAGE IS A TESTAMENT TO THE WARMTH OF HER PARENTS.
C'MON, PEOPLE! PREPARE FOR BATTLE!!

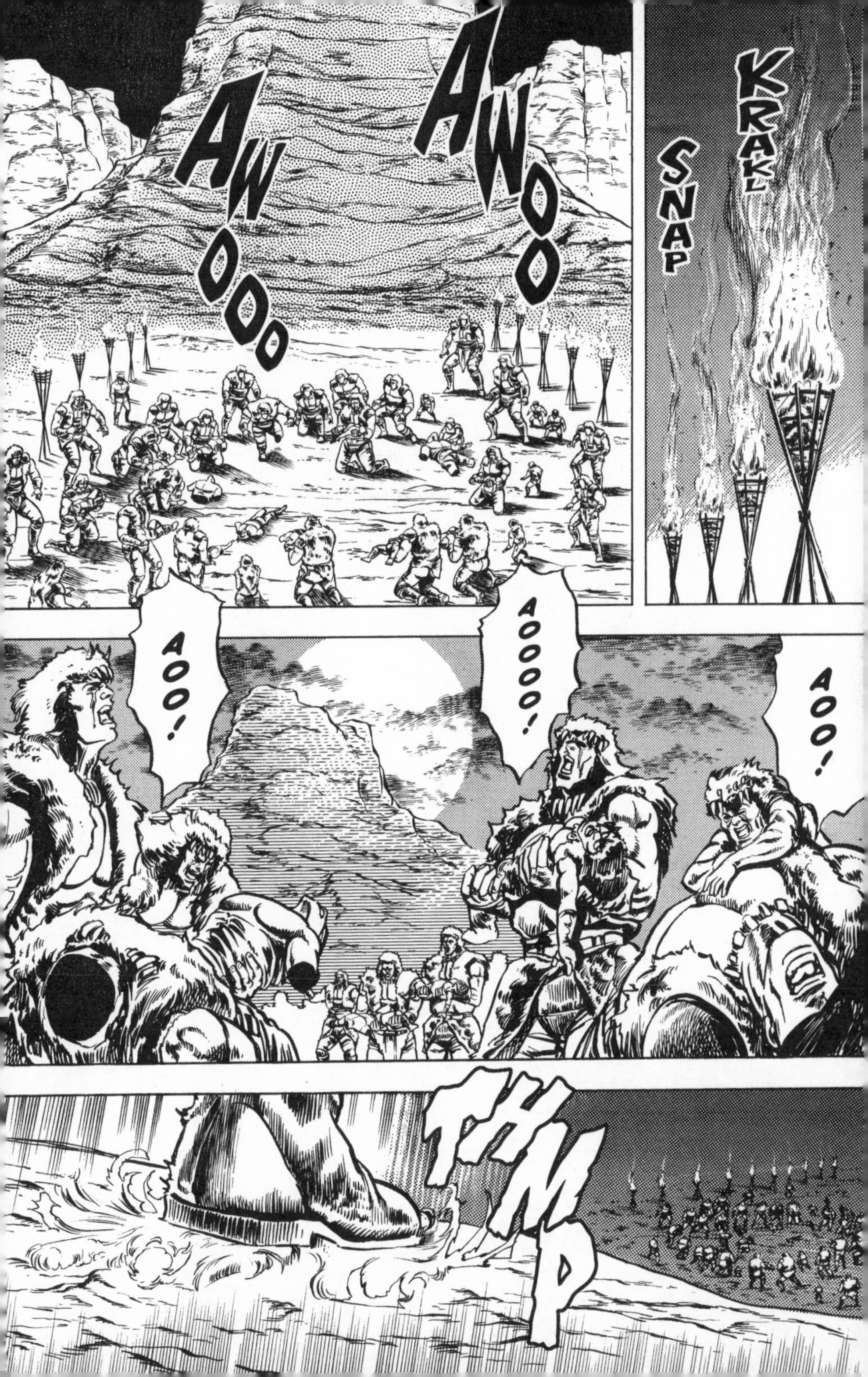
KRAKL
SNAP
AWOO
AWOOO
AOO!
AOOOOO!
AOO!
THMP

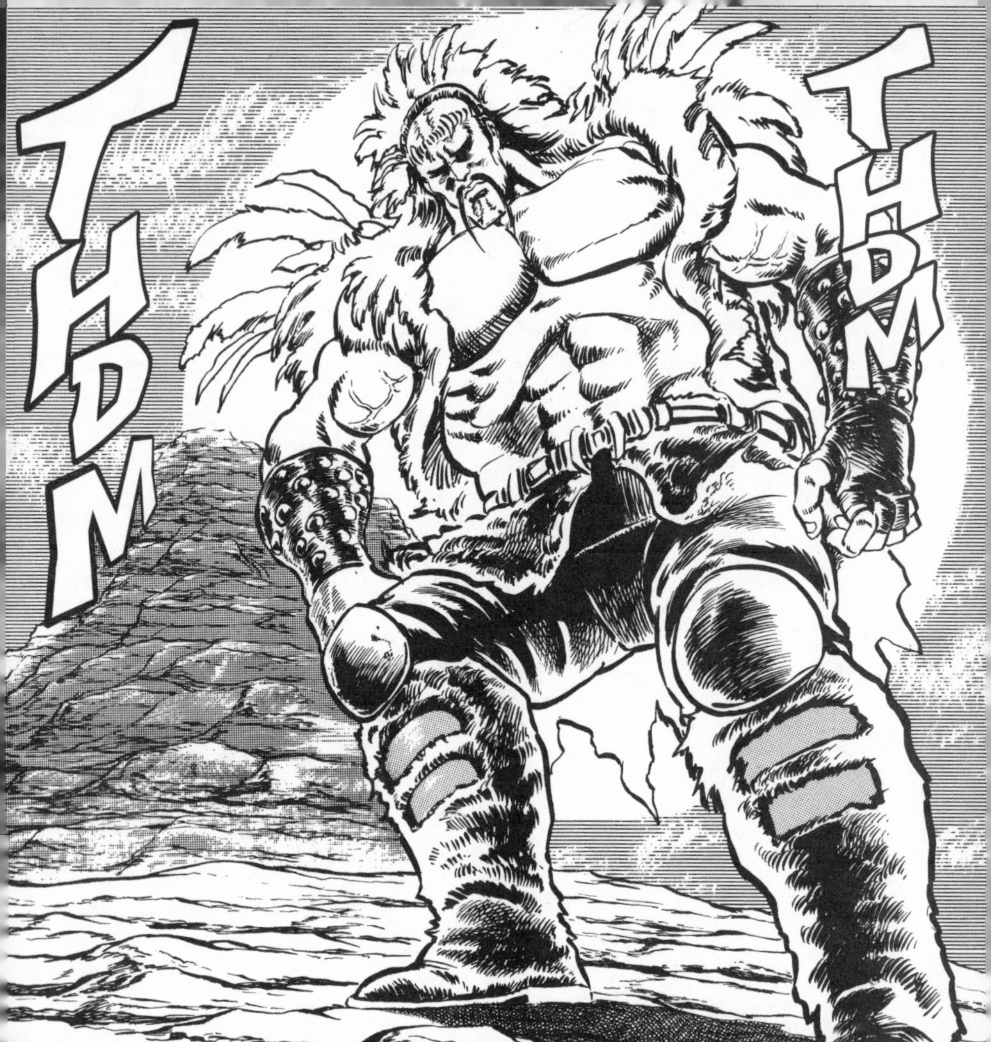
THDM
THDM
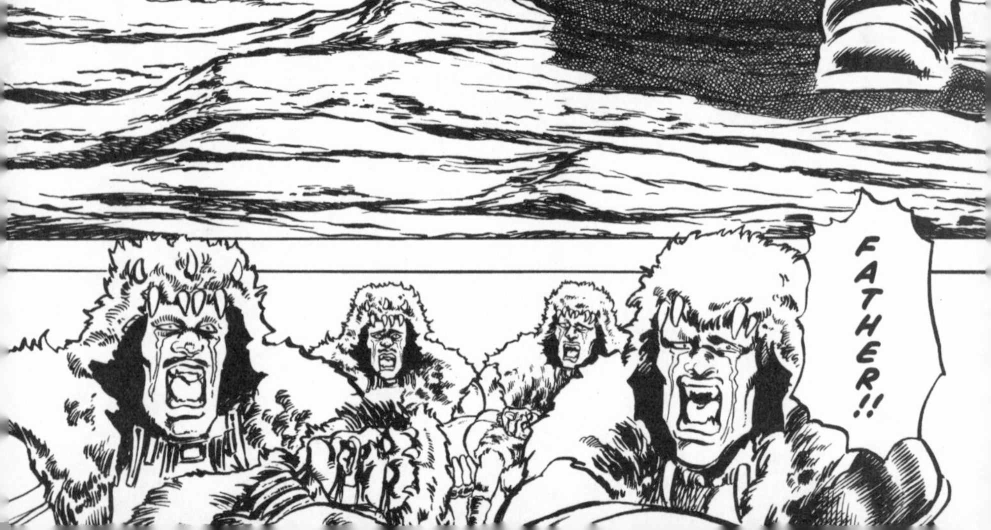
FATHER!!

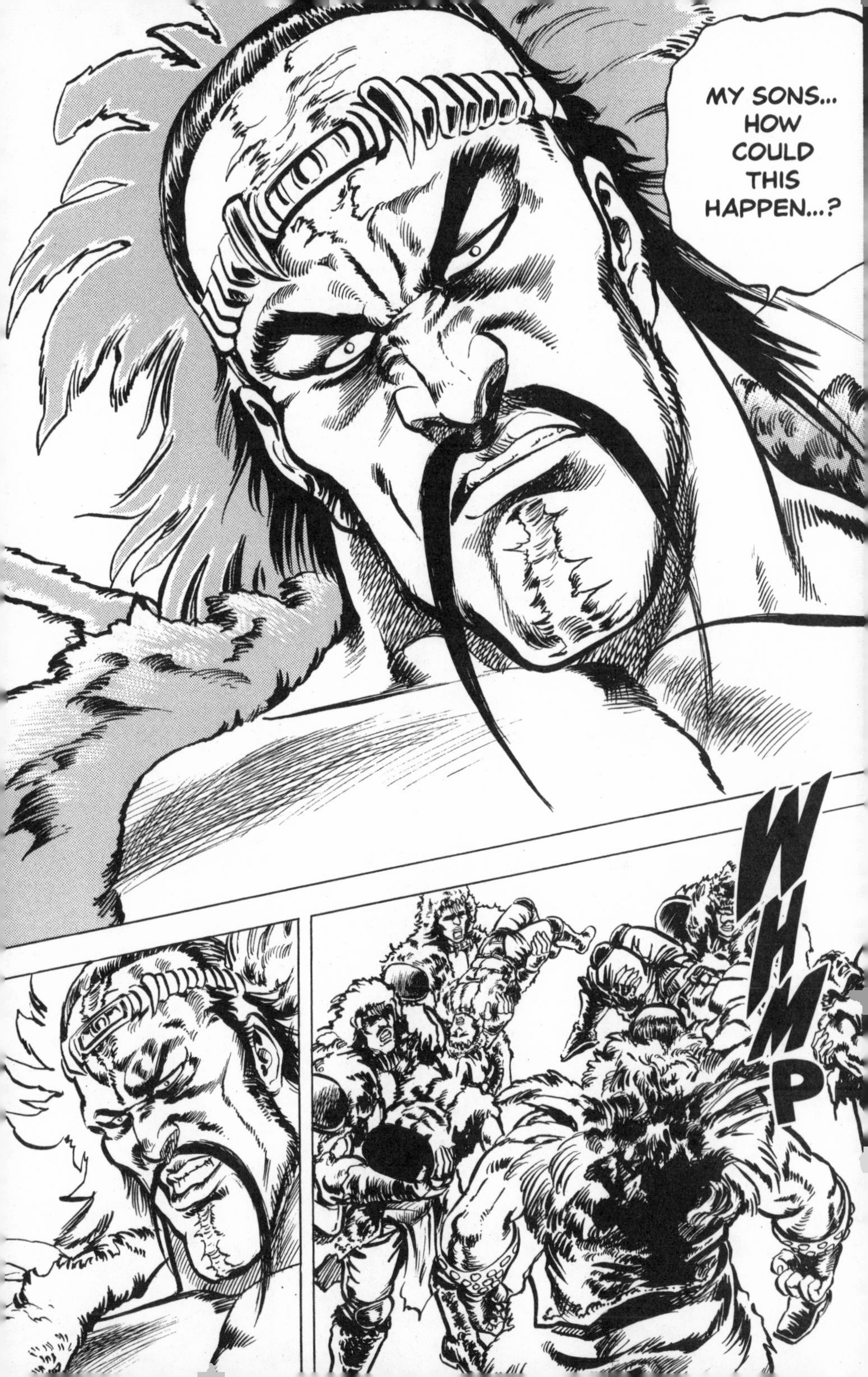
MY SONS... HOW COULD THIS HAPPEN...?
WHMP

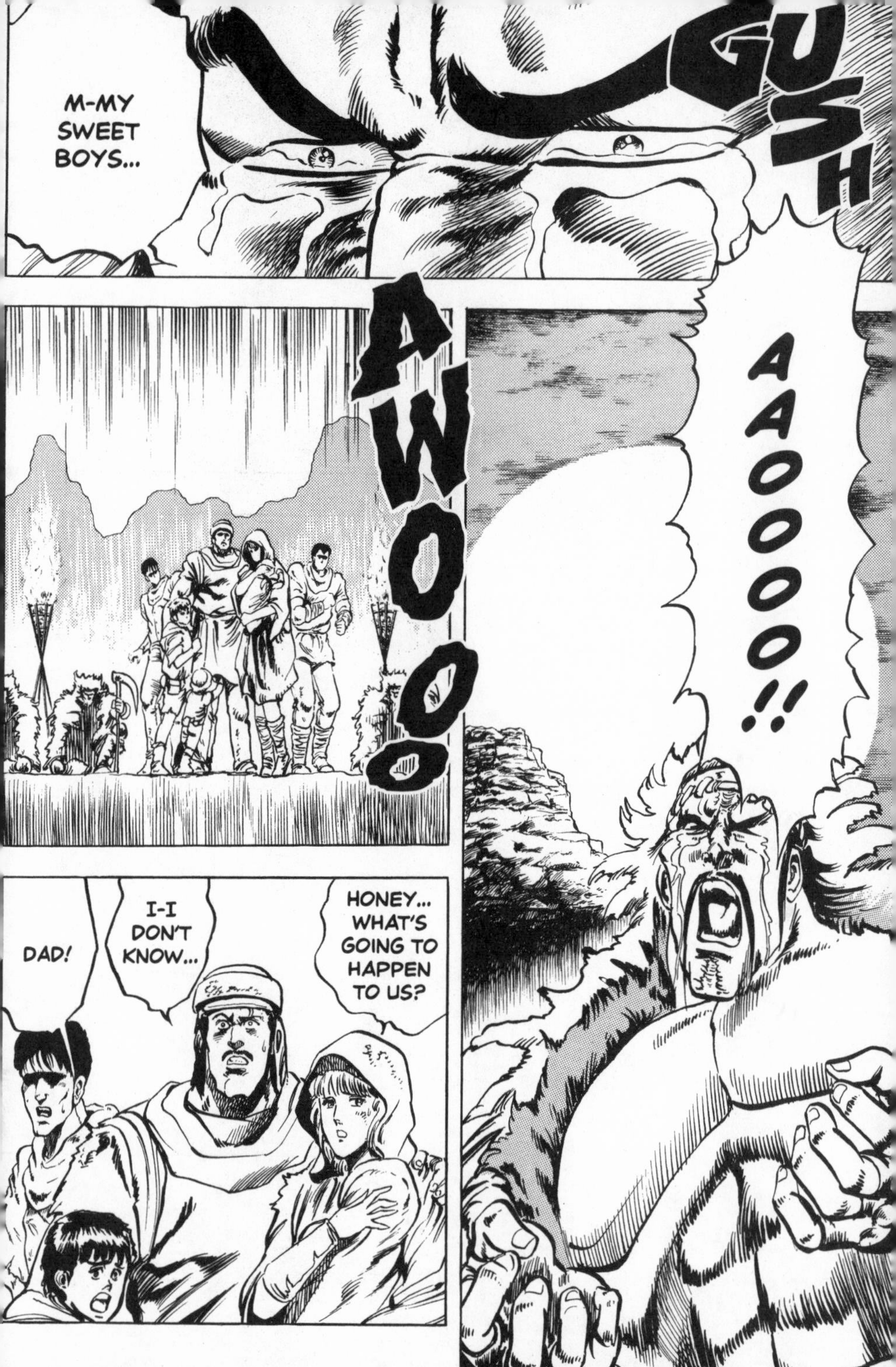
GUSH
M-MY SWEET BOYS...
AAOOOOO!!
AWOOOO
HONEY... WHAT'S GOING TO HAPPEN TO US?
I-I DON'T KNOW...
DAD!

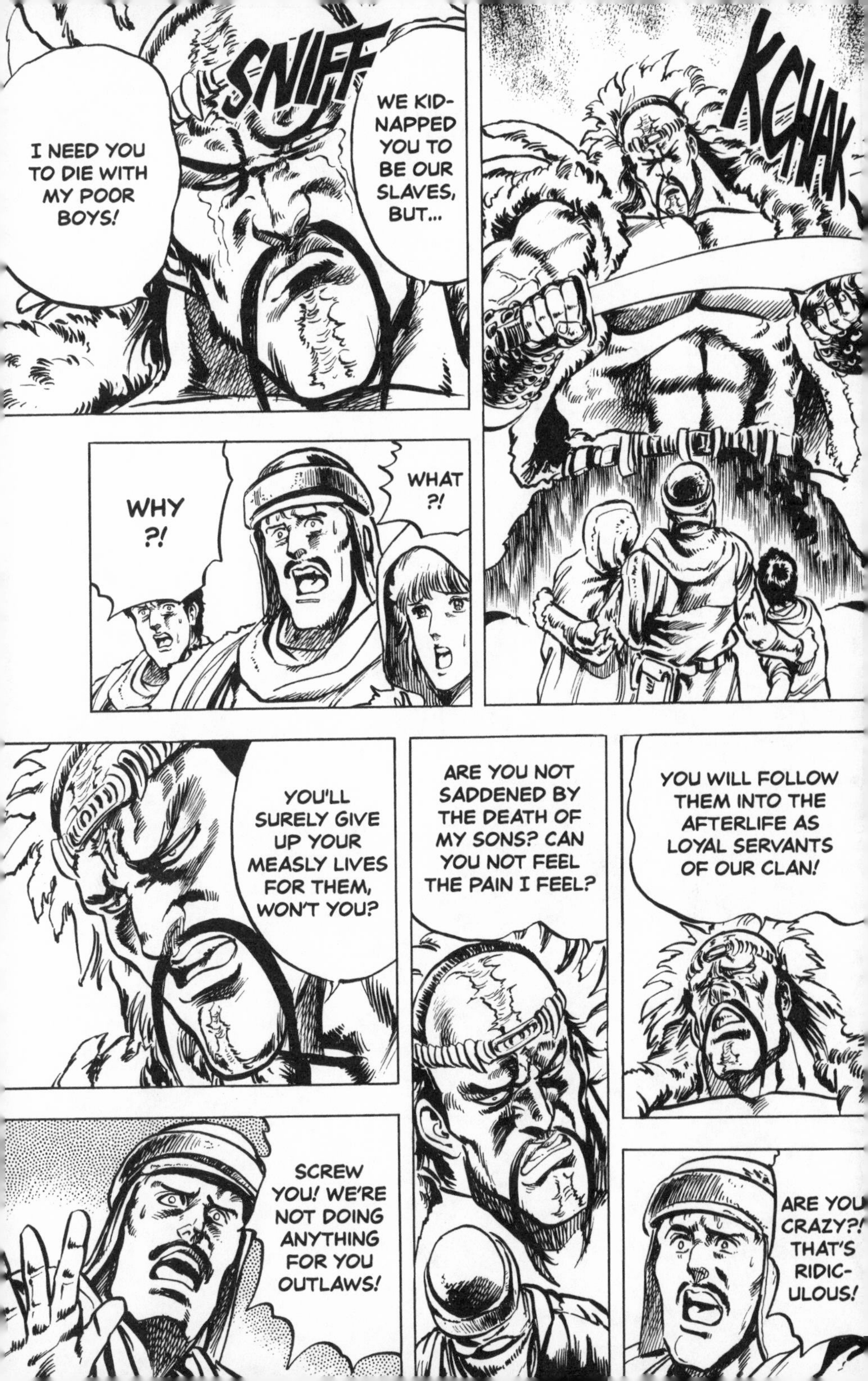
KCHAK
SNIFF
WE KID-NAPPED YOU TO BE OUR SLAVES, BUT...
I NEED YOU TO DIE WITH MY POOR BOYS!
WHAT ?!
WHY ?!
YOU WILL FOLLOW THEM INTO THE AFTERLIFE AS LOYAL SERVANTS OF OUR CLAN!
ARE YOU CRAZY?! THAT'S RIDIC-ULOUS!
ARE YOU NOT SADDENED BY THE DEATH OF MY SONS? CAN YOU NOT FEEL THE PAIN I FEEL?
YOU'LL SURELY GIVE UP YOUR MEASLY LIVES FOR THEM, WON'T YOU?
SCREW YOU! WE'RE NOT DOING ANYTHING FOR YOU OUTLAWS!

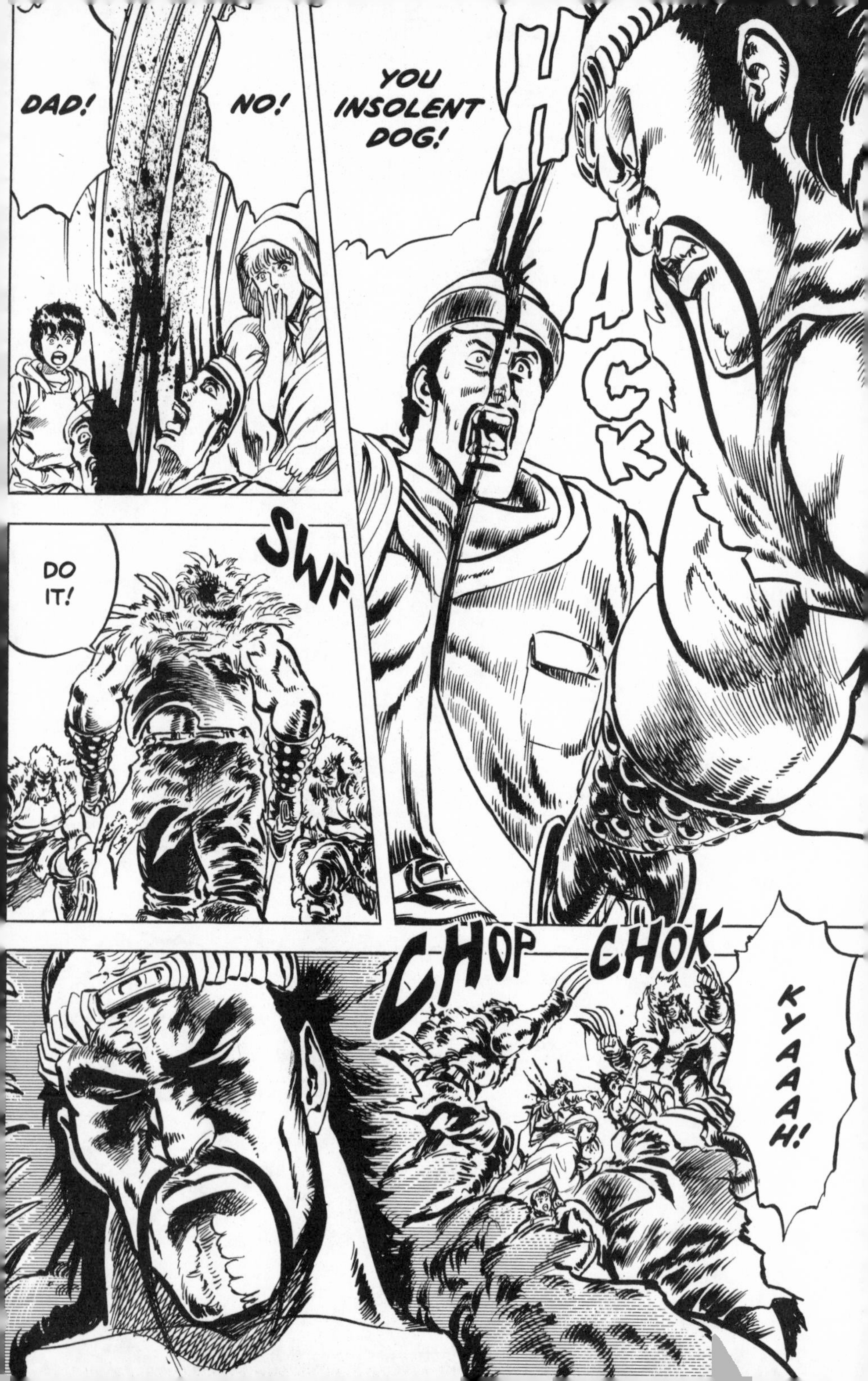
YOU INSOLENT DOG!
HACK
DAD!
NO!
SWF
DO IT!
CHOP
CHOK
KYAAAAH!

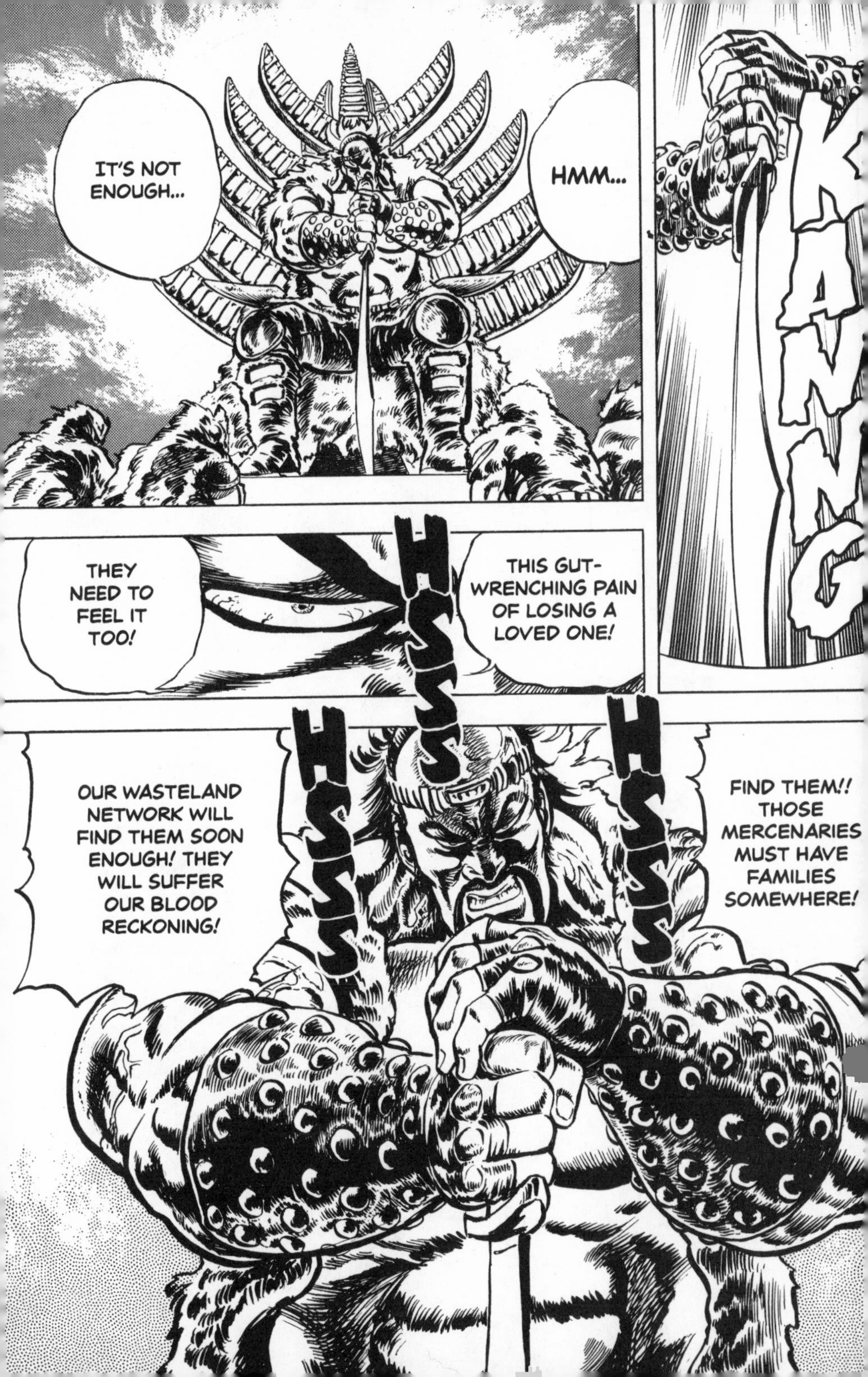
KANNG
HMM...
IT'S NOT ENOUGH...
THIS GUT-WRENCHING PAIN OF LOSING A LOVED ONE!
HSSS
THEY NEED TO FEEL IT TOO!
FIND THEM!! THOSE MERCENARIES MUST HAVE FAMILIES SOMEWHERE!
HSSS
HSSS
OUR WASTELAND NETWORK WILL FIND THEM SOON ENOUGH! THEY WILL SUFFER OUR BLOOD RECKONING!

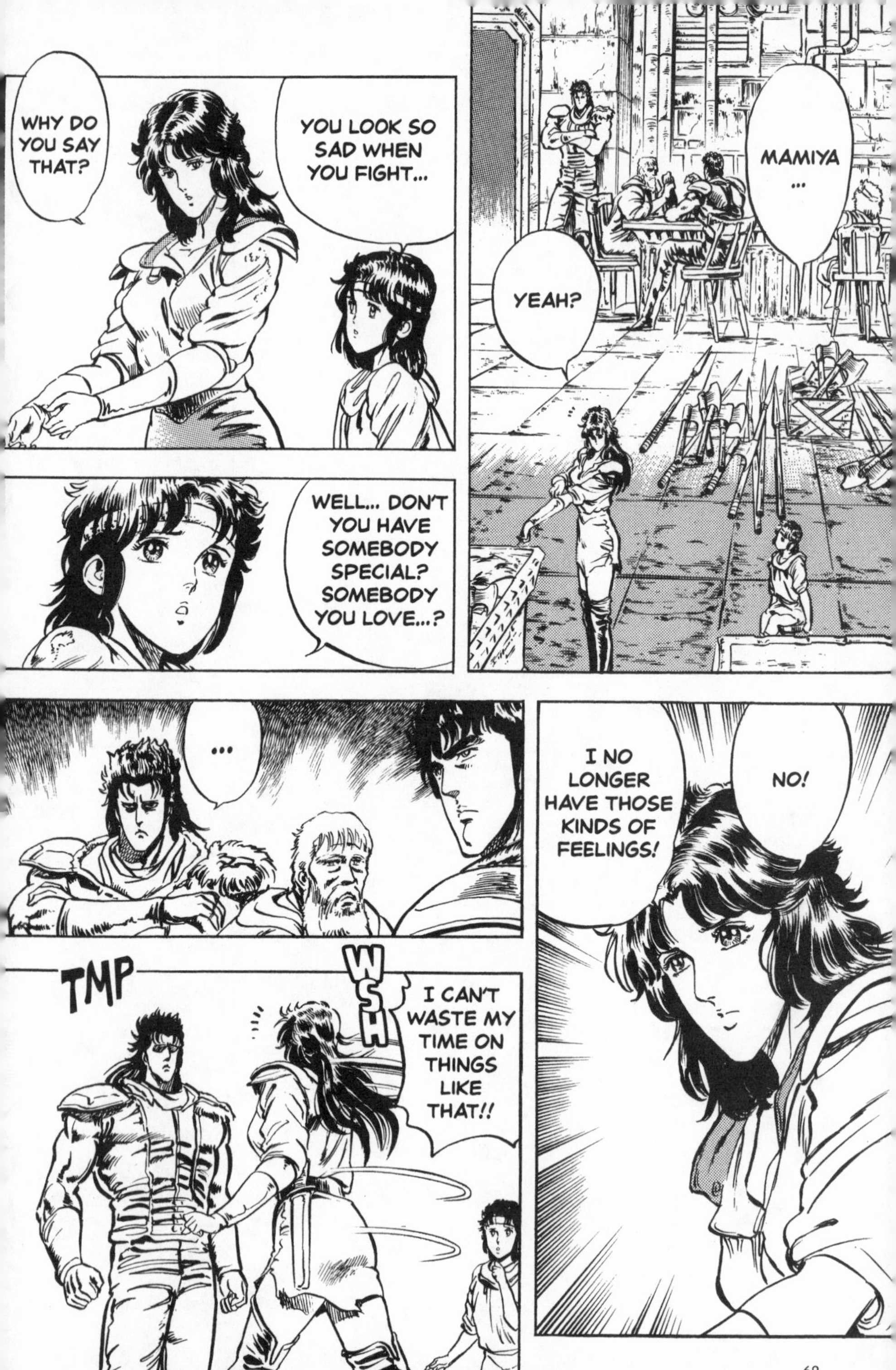
MAMIYA ...
YEAH?
YOU LOOK SO SAD WHEN YOU FIGHT...
WHY DO YOU SAY THAT?
WELL... DON'T YOU HAVE SOMEBODY SPECIAL? SOMEBODY YOU LOVE...?
NO!
I NO LONGER HAVE THOSE KINDS OF FEELINGS!
...
WSH
I CAN'T WASTE MY TIME ON THINGS LIKE THAT!!
TMP

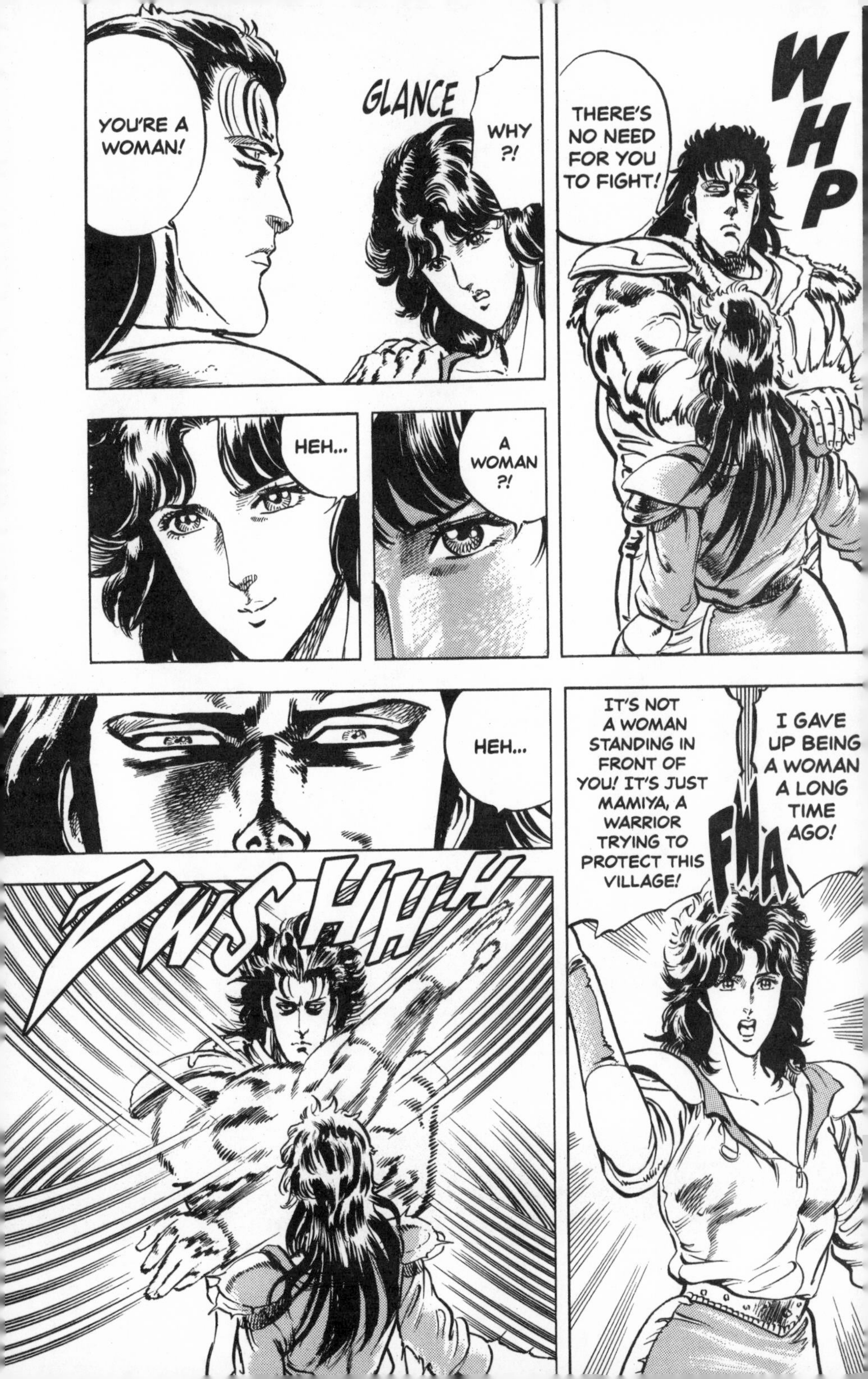
WHP
THERE'S NO NEED FOR YOU TO FIGHT!
WHY ?!
GLANCE
YOU'RE A WOMAN!
A WOMAN ?!
HEH...
I GAVE UP BEING A WOMAN A LONG TIME AGO!
IT'S NOT A WOMAN STANDING IN FRONT OF YOU! IT'S JUST MAMIYA, A WARRIOR TRYING TO PROTECT THIS VILLAGE!
FWA
HEH...
ZWSHHH

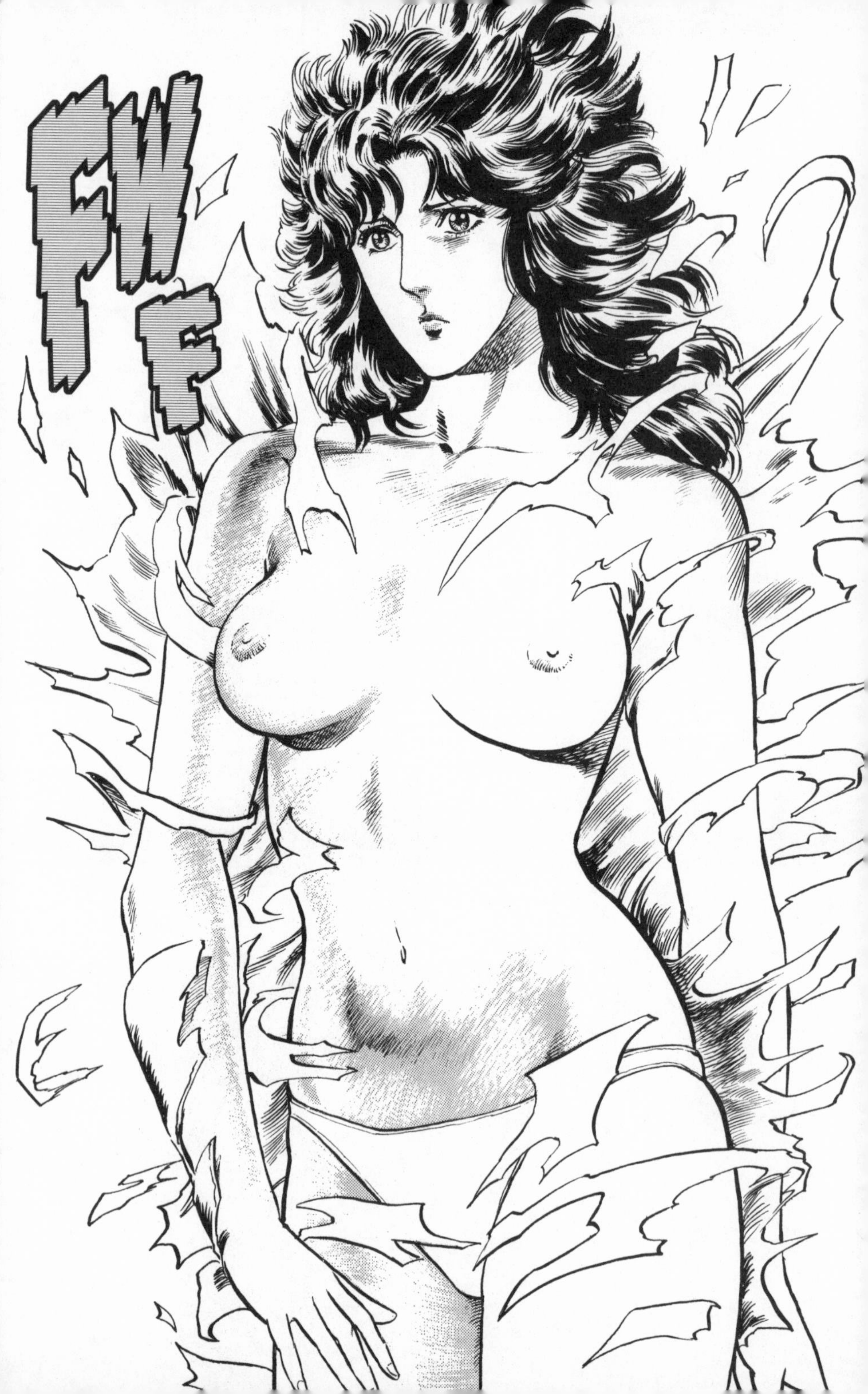
FWF

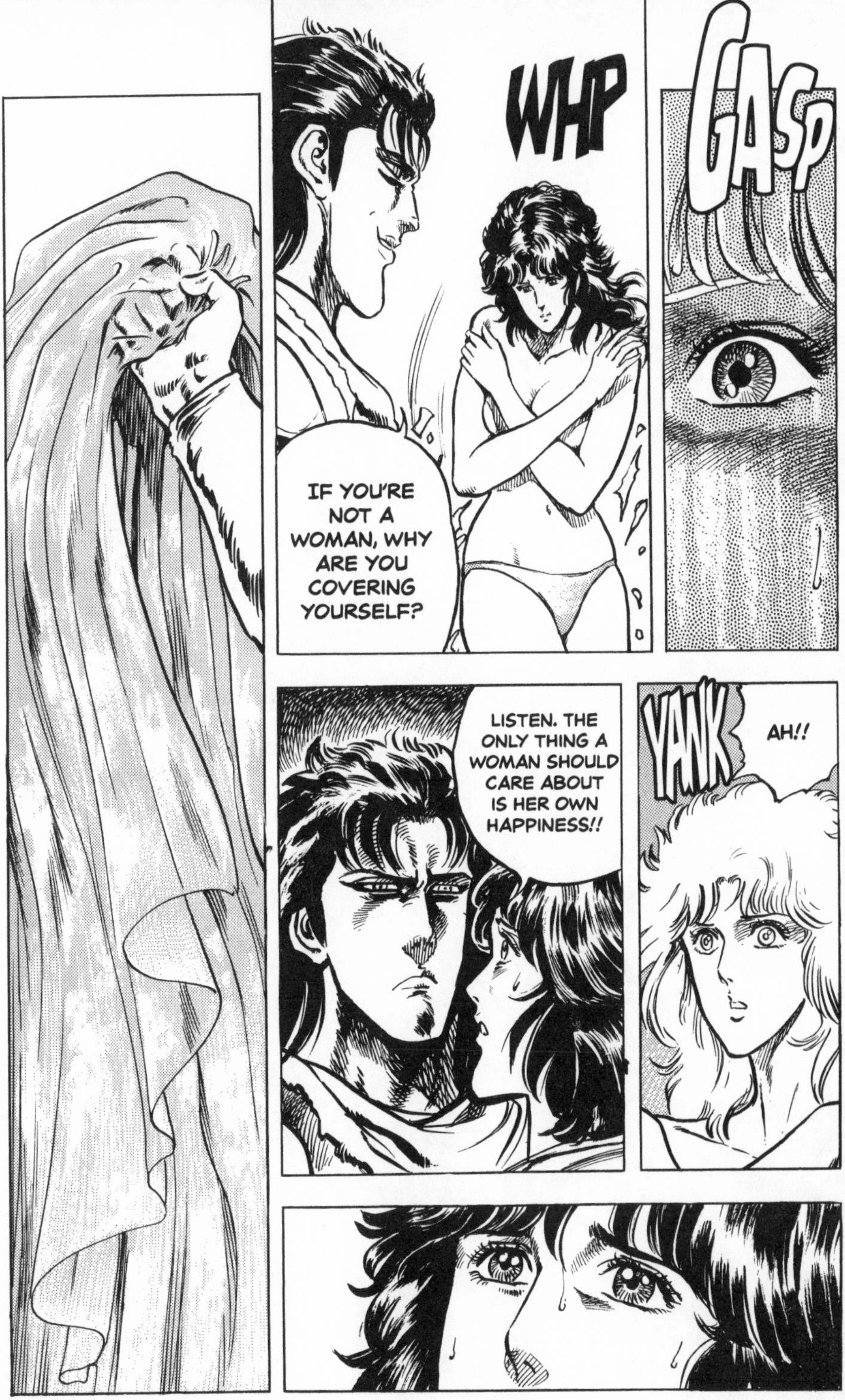
GASP
WHP
IF YOU'RE NOT A WOMAN, WHY ARE YOU COVERING YOURSELF?
YANK
AH!!
LISTEN. THE ONLY THING A WOMAN SHOULD CARE ABOUT IS HER OWN HAPPINESS!!

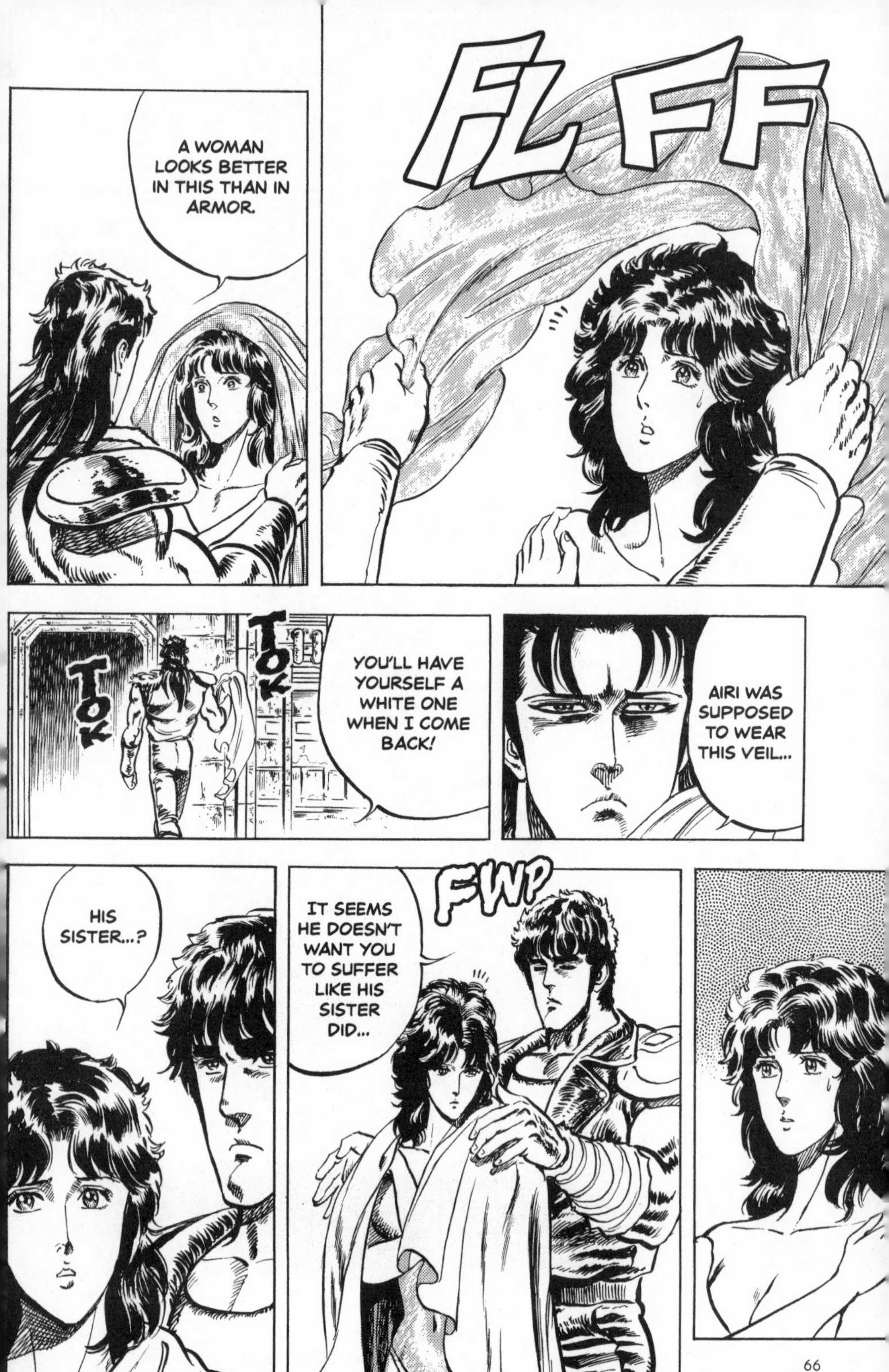
FL FF
A WOMAN LOOKS BETTER IN THIS THAN IN ARMOR.
AIRI WAS SUPPOSED TO WEAR THIS VEIL...
YOU'LL HAVE YOURSELF A WHITE ONE WHEN I COME BACK!
TOK
TOK
FWP
IT SEEMS HE DOESN'T WANT YOU TO SUFFER LIKE HIS SISTER DID...
HIS SISTER...?

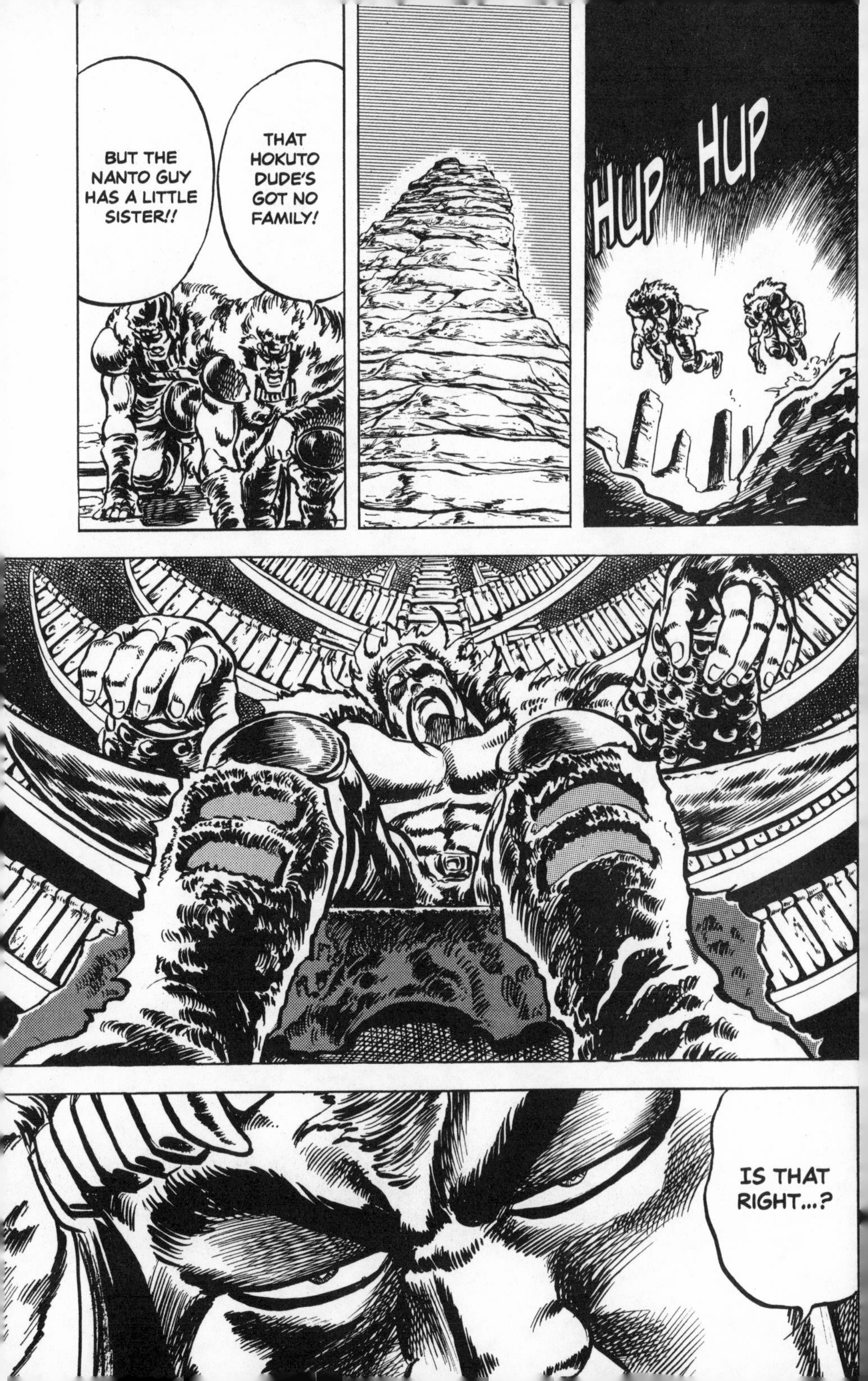
HUP HUP
THAT HOKUTO DUDE'S GOT NO FAMILY!
BUT THE NANTO GUY HAS A LITTLE SISTER!!
IS THAT RIGHT...?

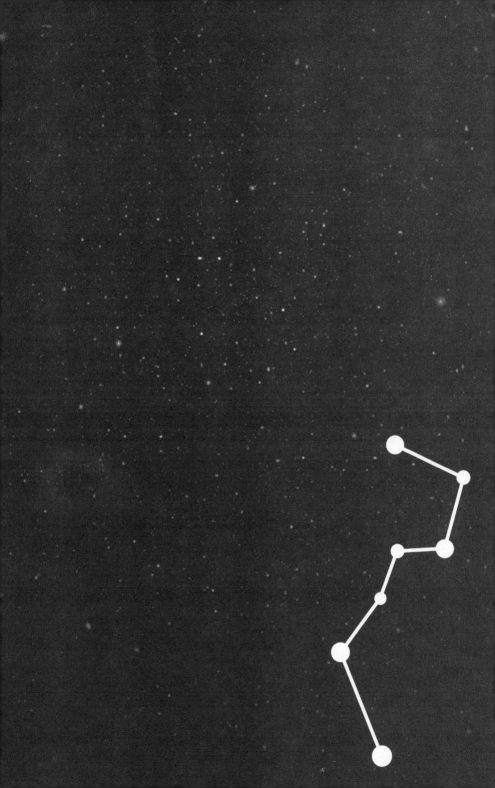

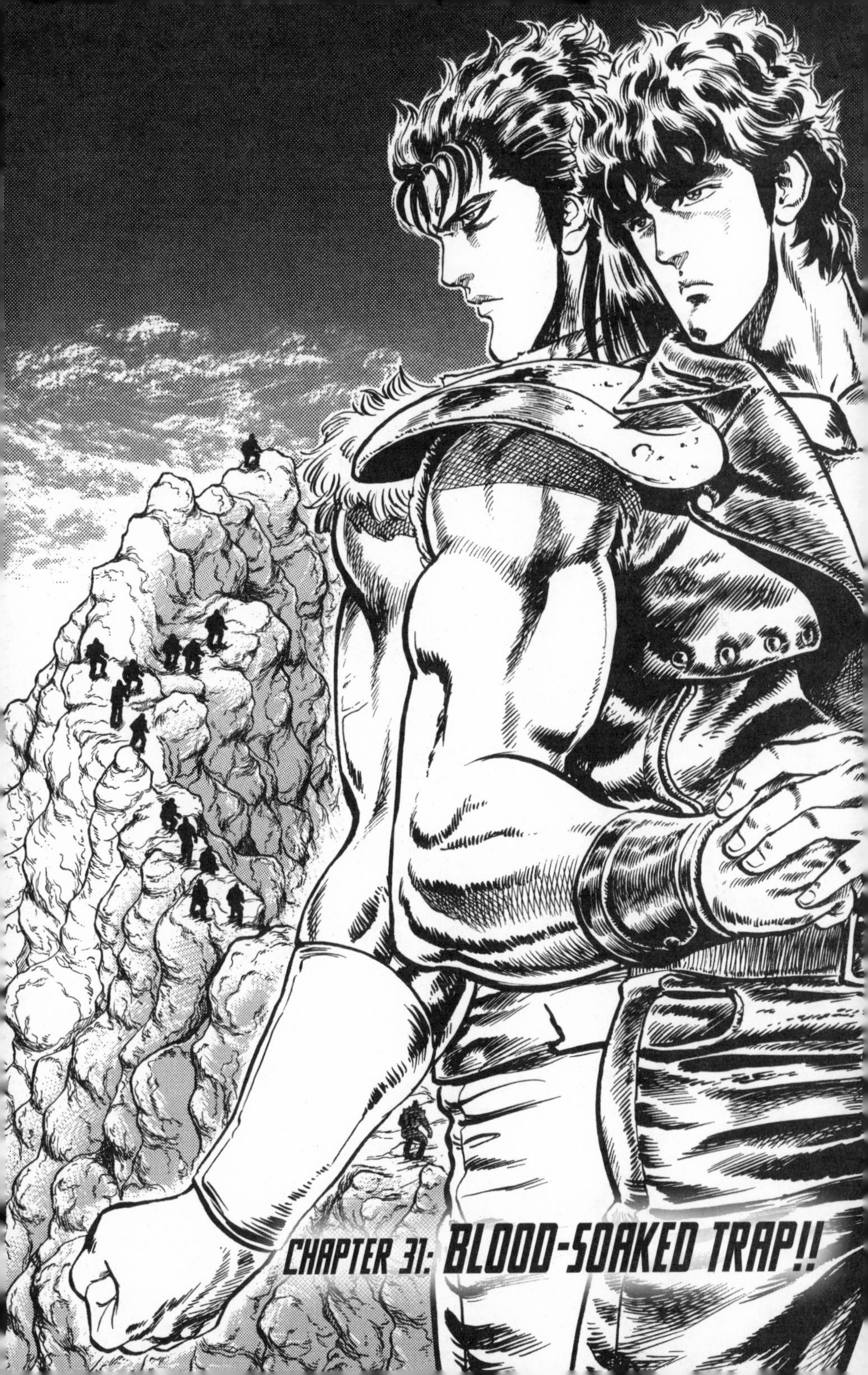
CHAPTER 31: BLOOD-SOAKED TRAP!!

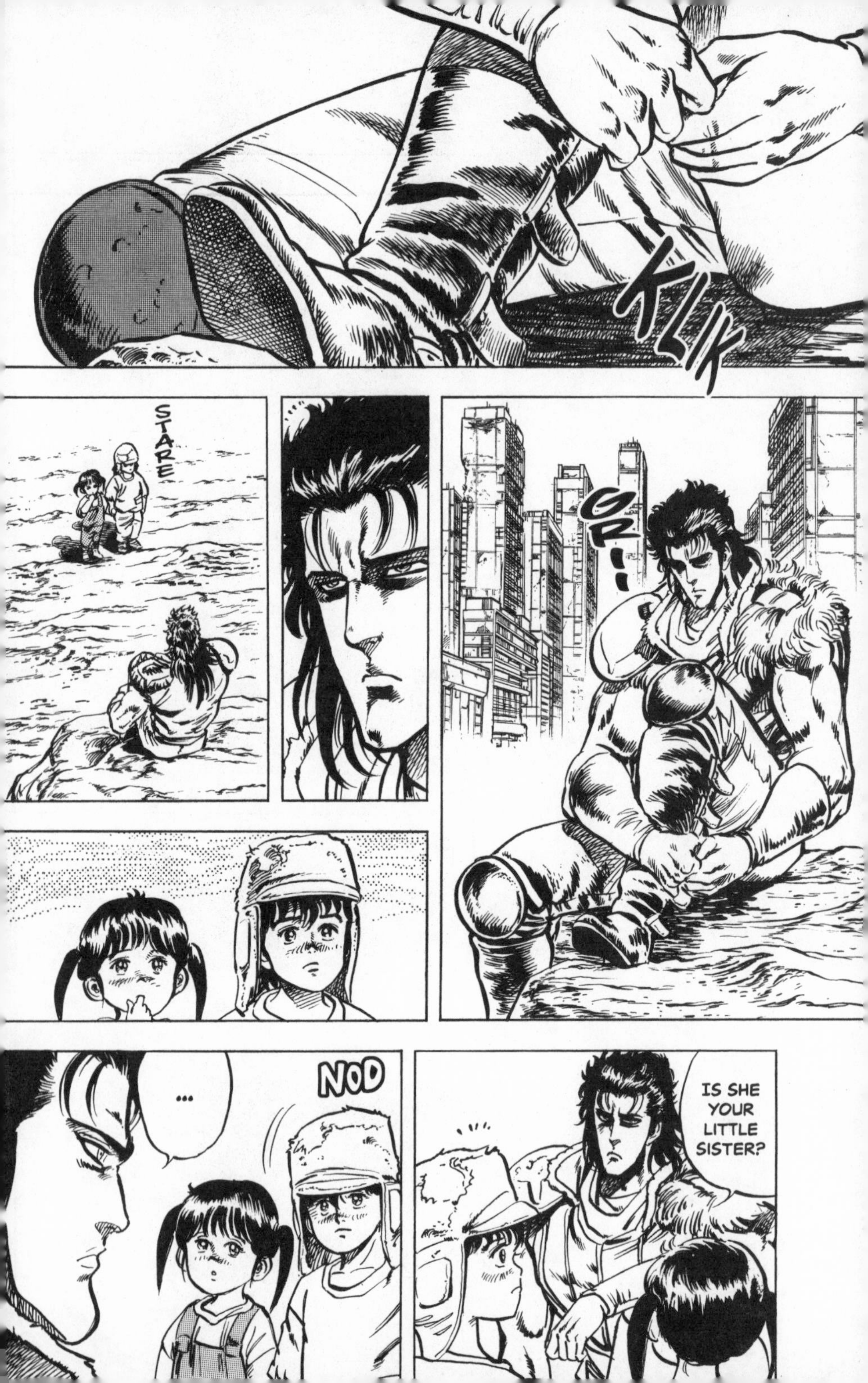

KLIK
GR!!
STARE
IS SHE YOUR LITTLE SISTER?
NOD
...

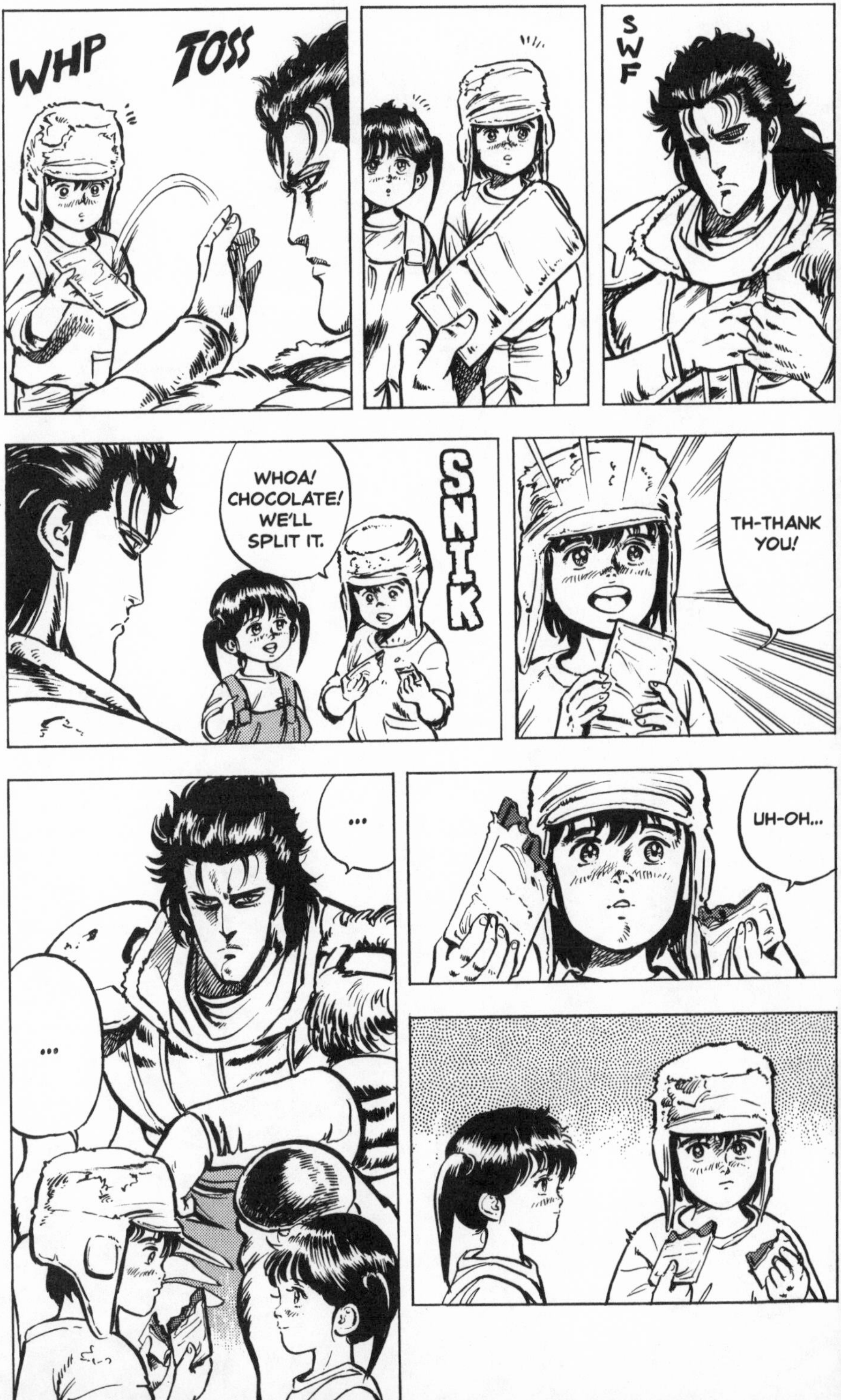
SWF
TOSS
WHP
TH-THANK YOU!
SNIK
WHOA! CHOCOLATE! WE'LL SPLIT IT.
UH-OH...
...
...

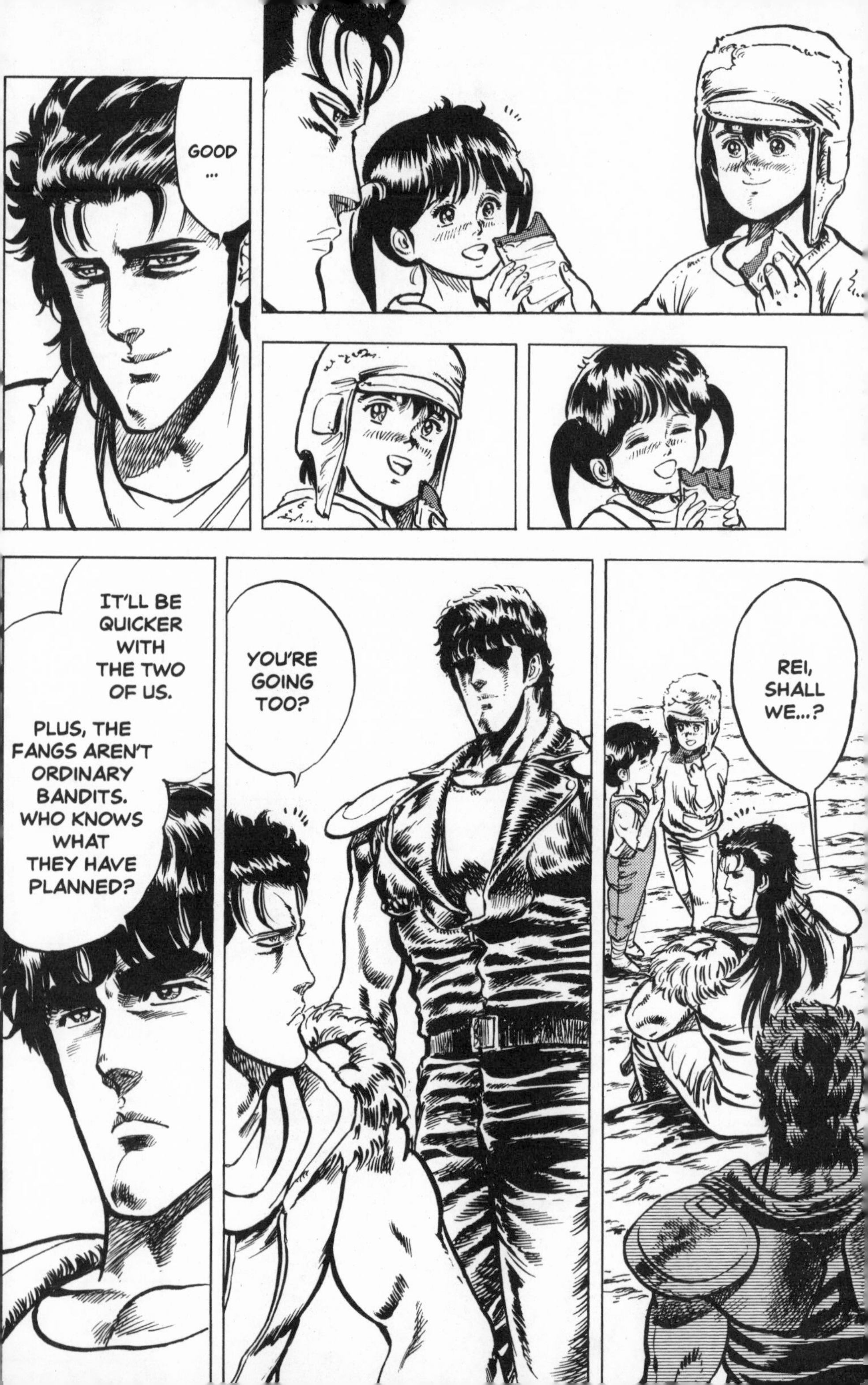
GOOD ...
REI, SHALL WE...?
YOU'RE GOING TOO?
IT'LL BE QUICKER WITH THE TWO OF US.
PLUS, THE FANGS AREN'T ORDINARY BANDITS. WHO KNOWS WHAT THEY HAVE PLANNED?

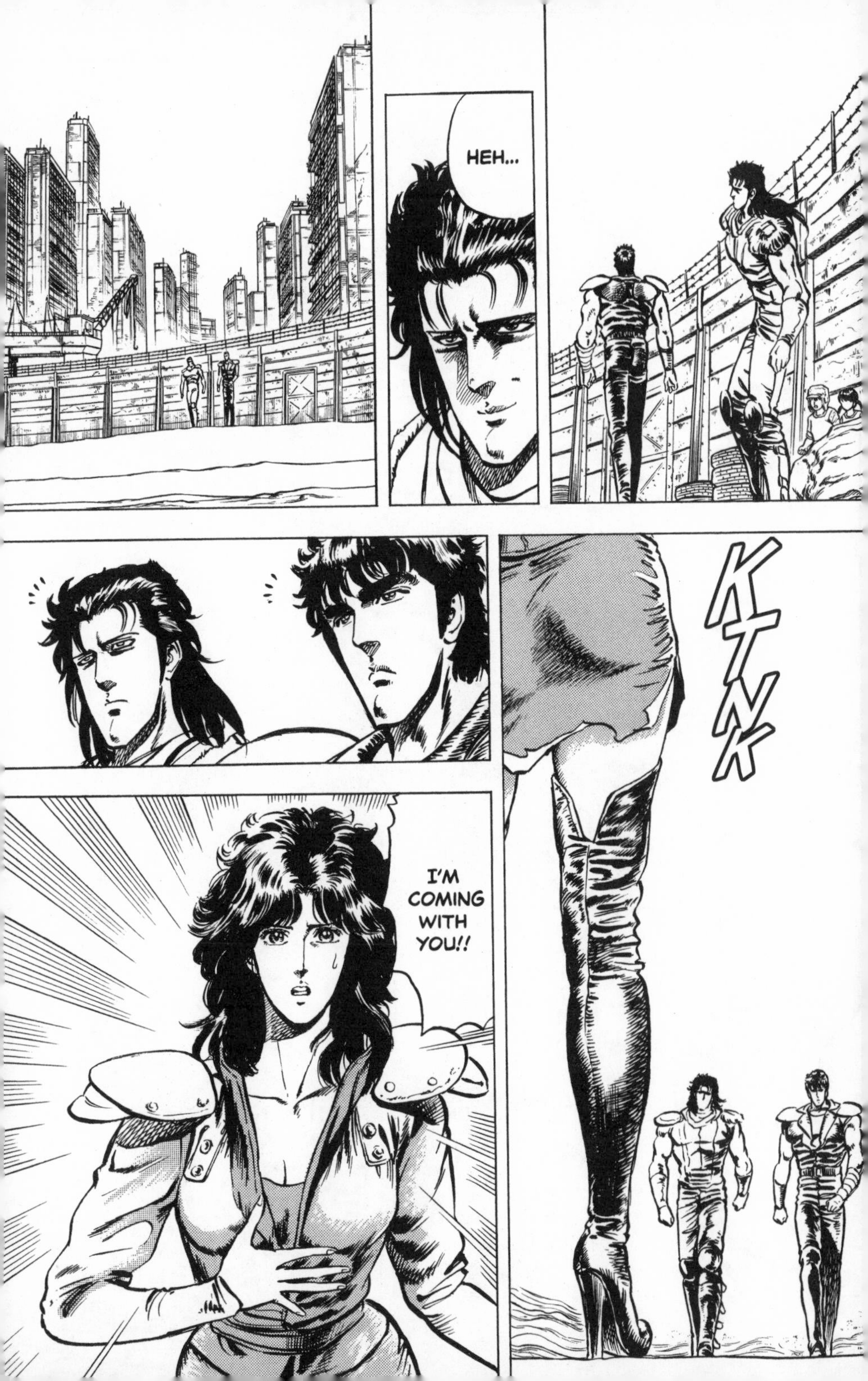
HEH...
KTNK
I'M COMING WITH YOU!!

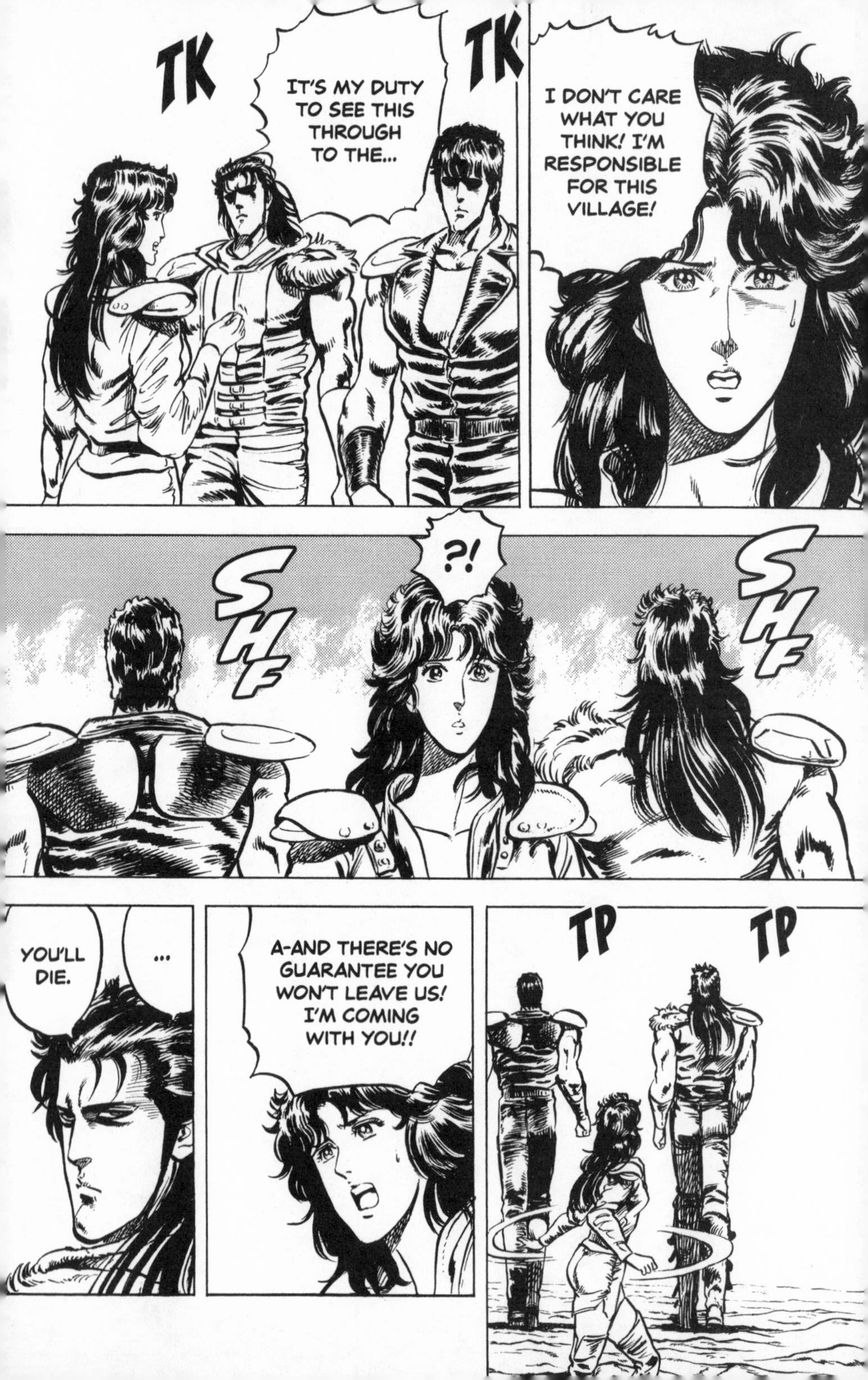
TK
IT'S MY DUTY TO SEE THIS THROUGH TO THE...
TK
I DON'T CARE WHAT YOU THINK! I'M RESPONSIBLE FOR THIS VILLAGE!
SHF
?!
SHF
YOU'LL DIE.
...
A-AND THERE'S NO GUARANTEE YOU WON'T LEAVE US! I'M COMING WITH YOU!!
TP
TP

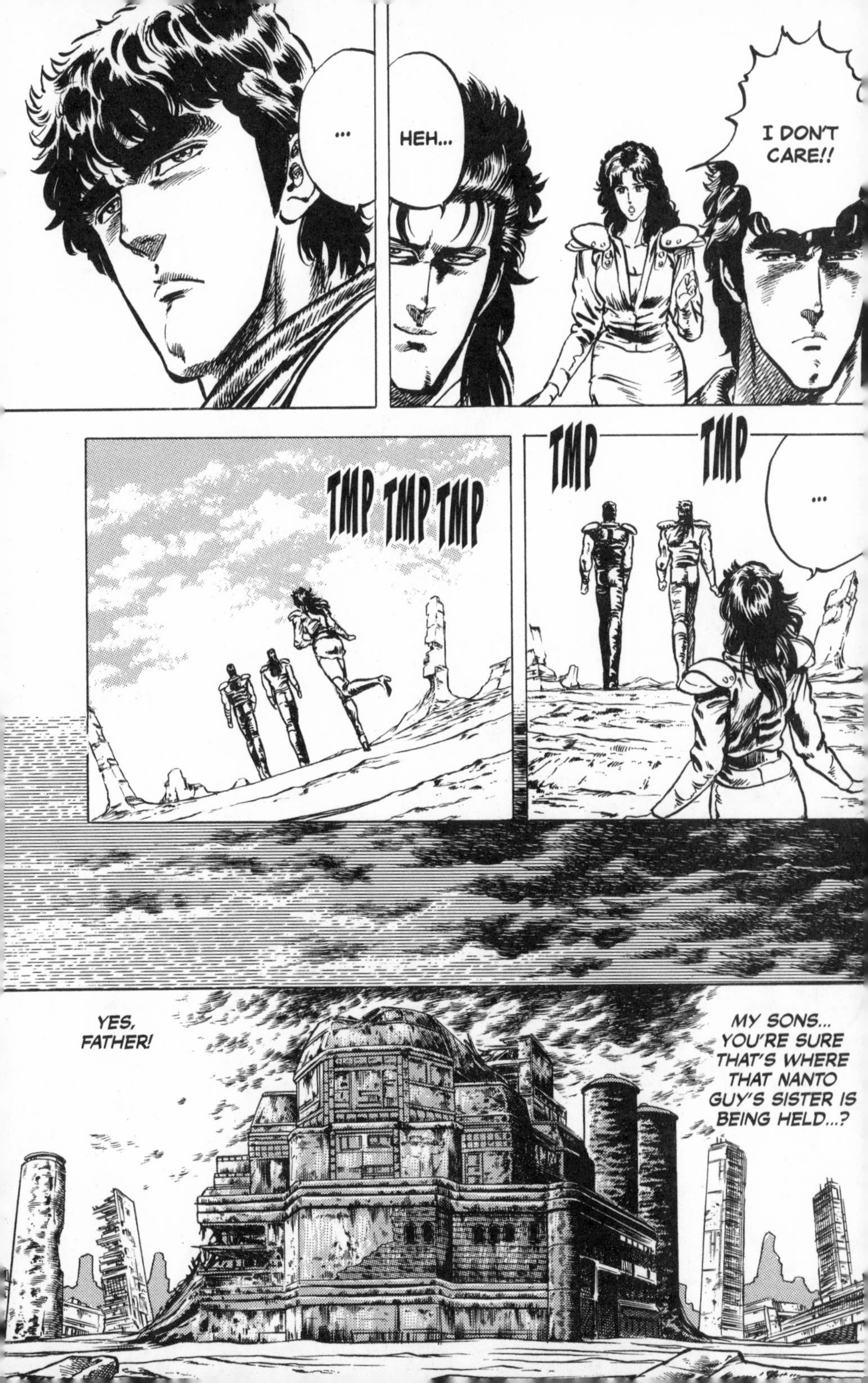
I DON'T CARE!!
HEH...
...
TMP
TMP
...
TMP TMP TMP
MY SONS... YOU'RE SURE THAT'S WHERE THAT NANTO GUY'S SISTER IS BEING HELD...?
YES, FATHER!

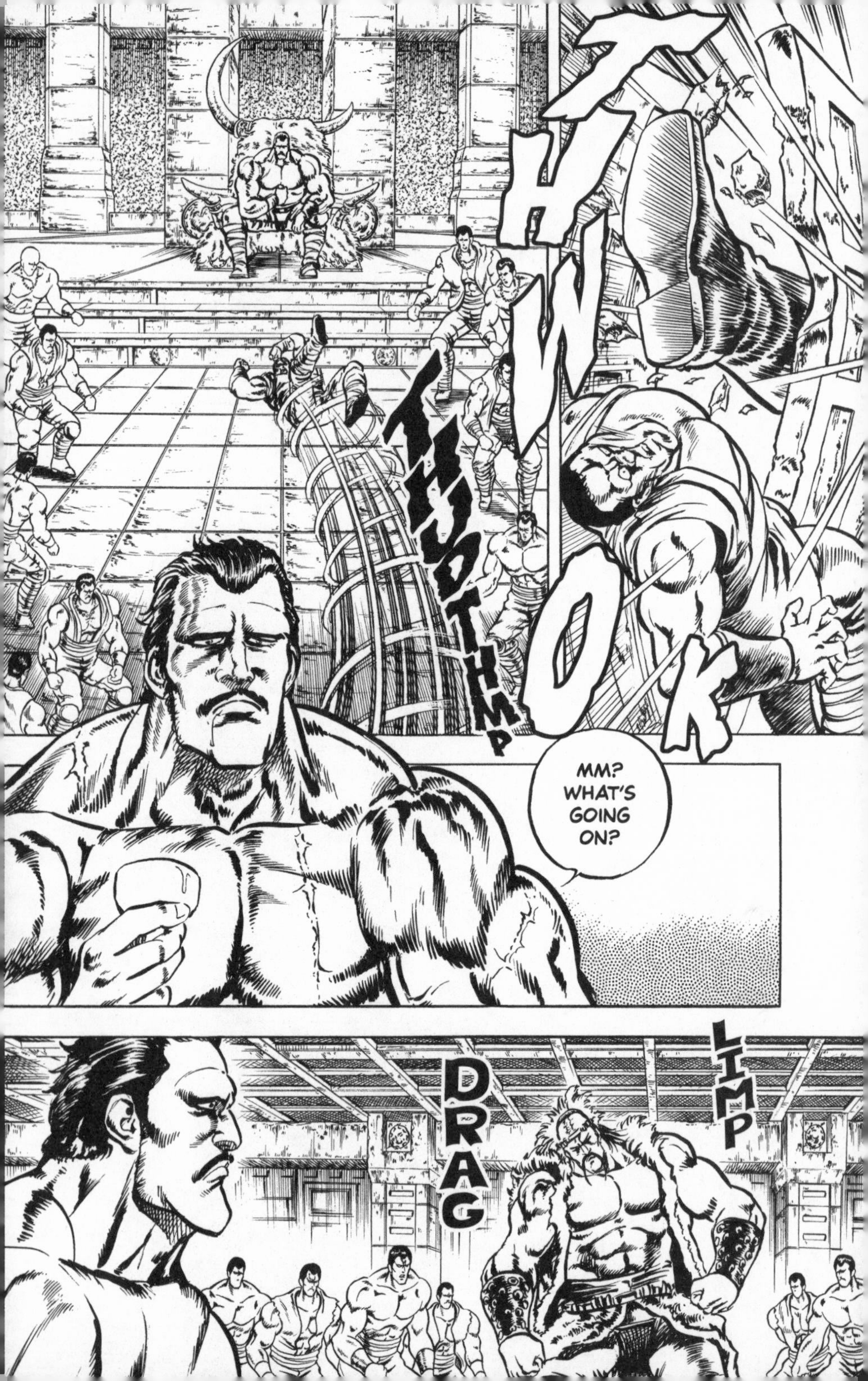
THWOK
THUDTHMP
MM? WHAT'S GOING ON?
LIMP
DRAG

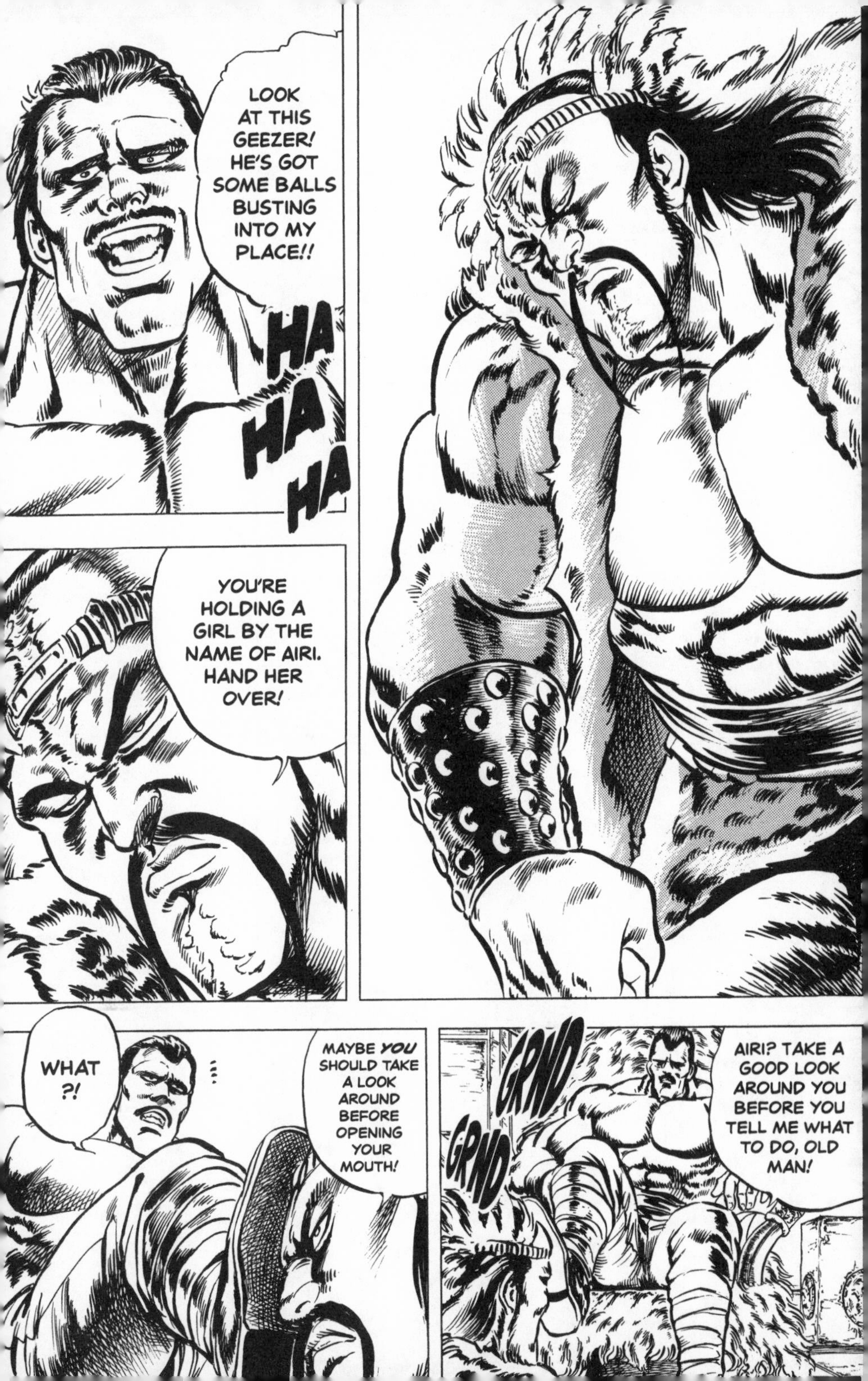
LOOK AT THIS GEEZER! HE'S GOT SOME BALLS BUSTING INTO MY PLACE!!
HA HA HA HA
YOU'RE HOLDING A GIRL BY THE NAME OF AIRI. HAND HER OVER!
AIRI? TAKE A GOOD LOOK AROUND YOU BEFORE YOU TELL ME WHAT TO DO, OLD MAN!
GRND GRND
MAYBE *YOU* SHOULD TAKE A LOOK AROUND BEFORE OPENING YOUR MOUTH!
...
WHAT ?!

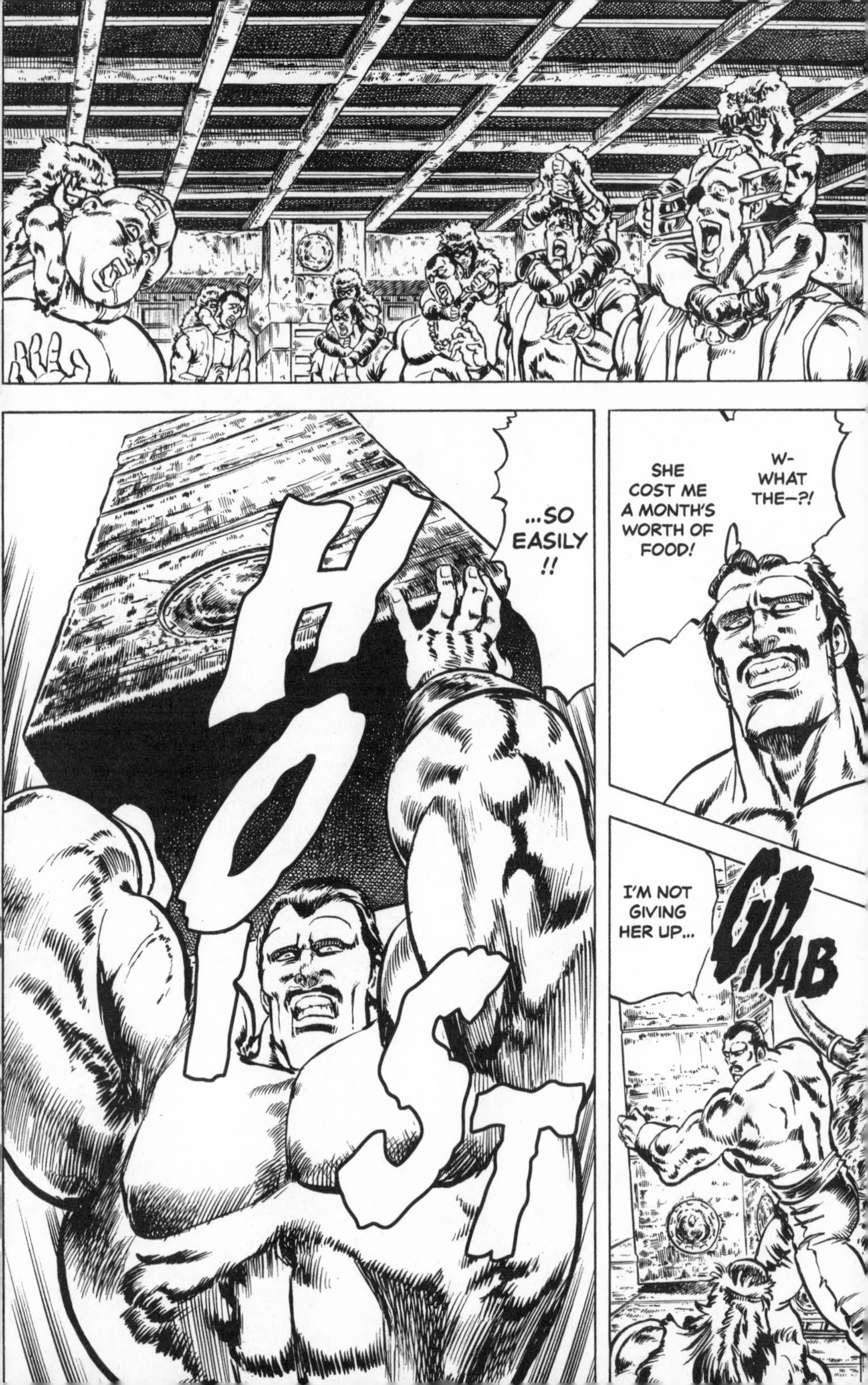
W- WHAT THE–?!
SHE COST ME A MONTH'S WORTH OF FOOD!
I'M NOT GIVING HER UP...
GRAB
...SO EASILY!!
HOIST

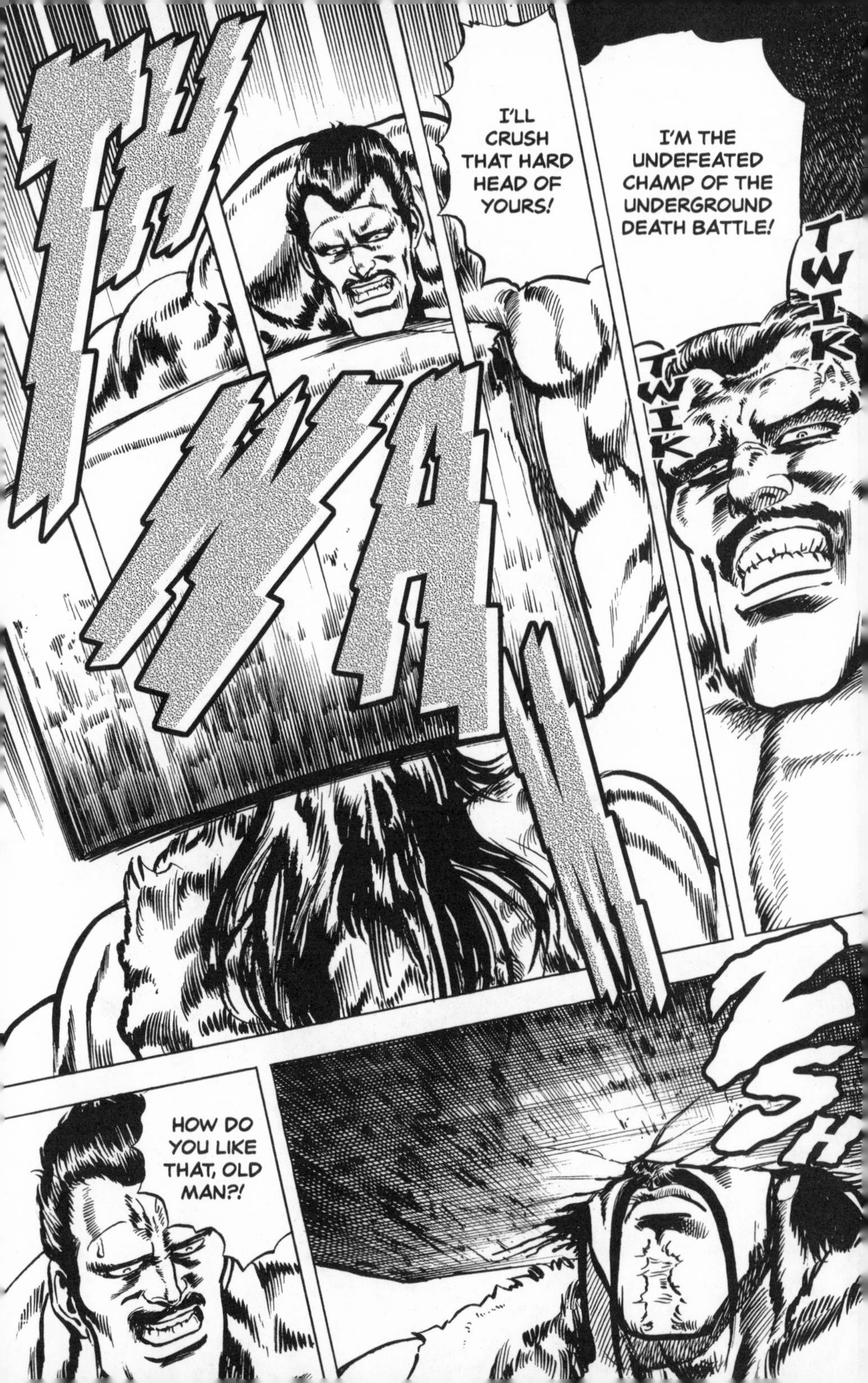
I'M THE UNDEFEATED CHAMP OF THE UNDERGROUND DEATH BATTLE!
TWIK
TWIK
I'LL CRUSH THAT HARD HEAD OF YOURS!
ZSH
HOW DO YOU LIKE THAT, OLD MAN?!

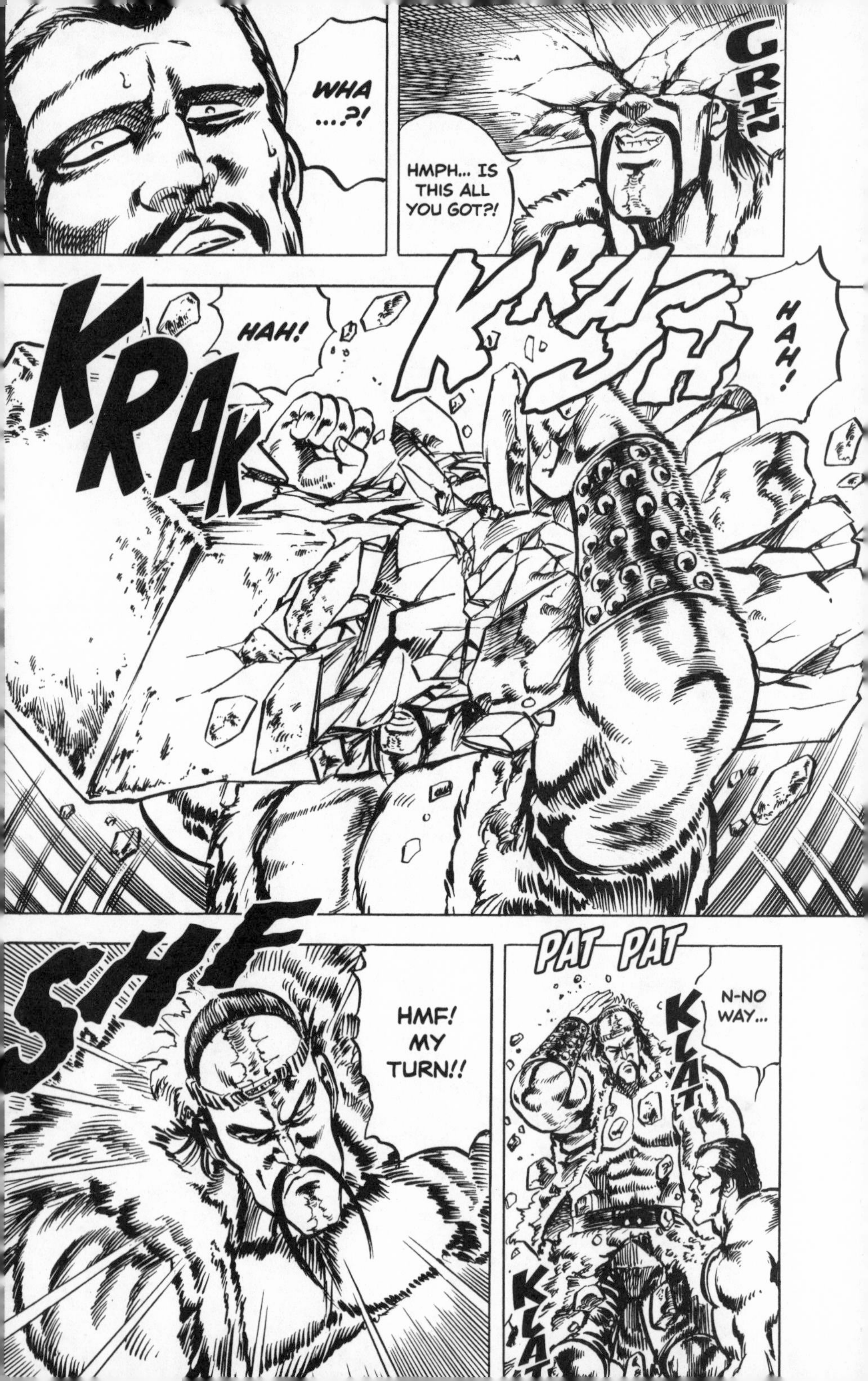
GRIN
HMPH... IS THIS ALL YOU GOT?!
WHA ...?!
KRAAH
HAH!
HAH!
KRAK
PAT PAT
N-NO WAY...
KLAT
KLAT
SHF
HMF! MY TURN!!

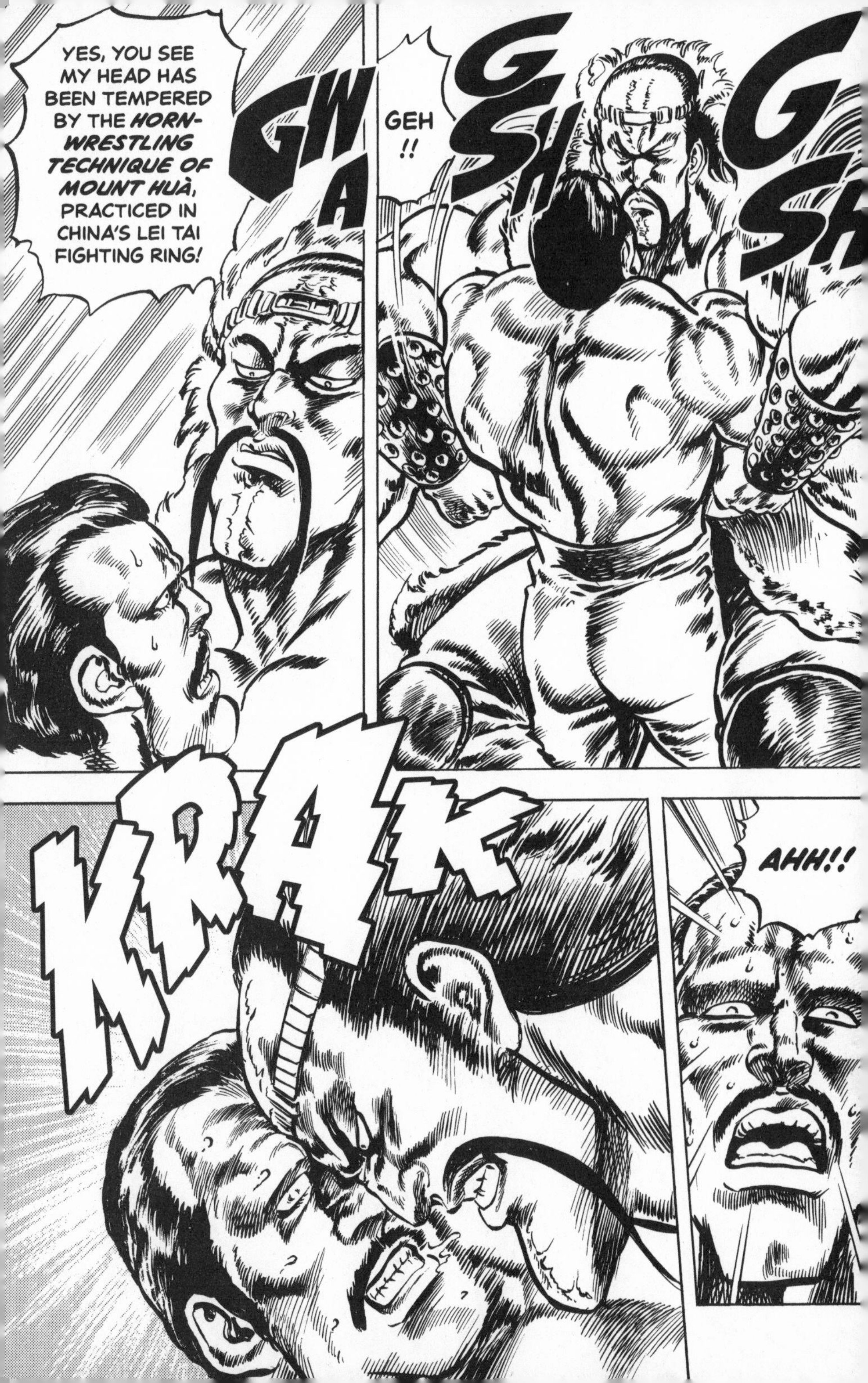

GASH
GASH
GEH !!
YES, YOU SEE MY HEAD HAS BEEN TEMPERED BY THE *HORN-WRESTLING TECHNIQUE OF MOUNT HUÀ*, PRACTICED IN CHINA'S LEI TAI FIGHTING RING!
GWA
AHH!!
KRAK

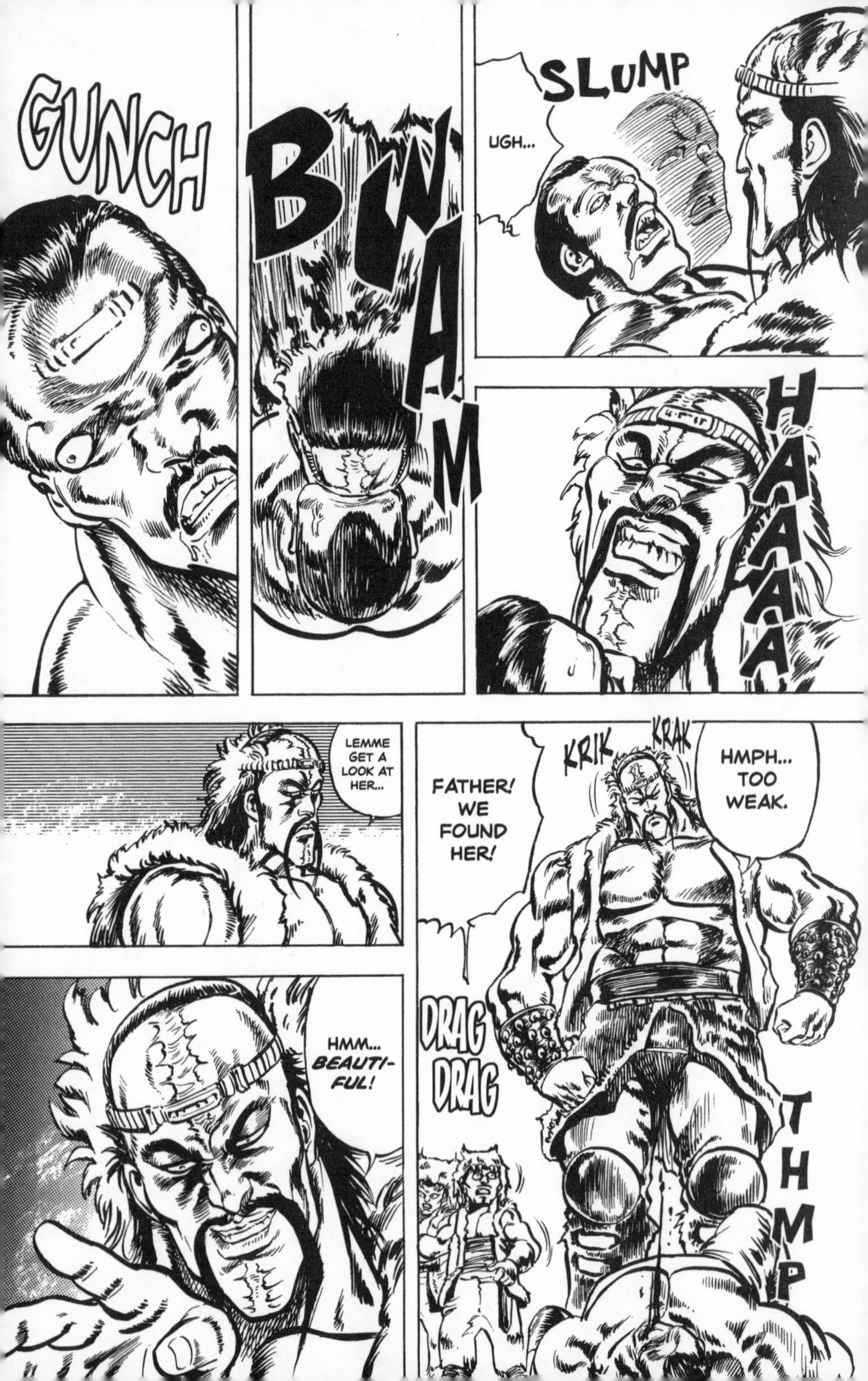
SLUMP
UGH...
HAAAAAA
BWAM
GUNCH
KRAK
KRIK
HMPH... TOO WEAK.
FATHER! WE FOUND HER!
THMP
DRAG DRAG
LEMME GET A LOOK AT HER...
HMM... *BEAUTI-FUL!*

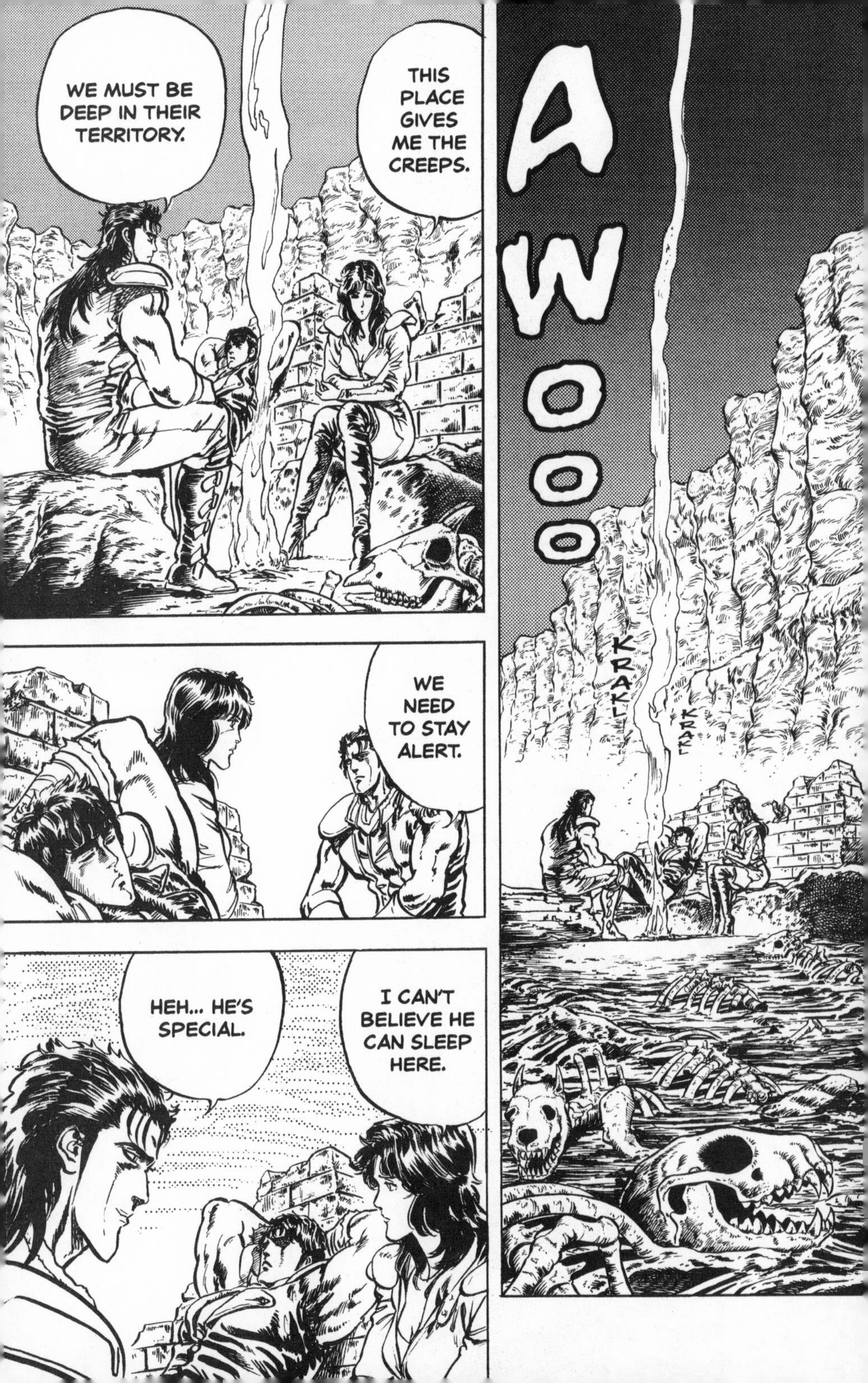
AWOOOO
KRAKL
KRAKL
THIS PLACE GIVES ME THE CREEPS.
WE MUST BE DEEP IN THEIR TERRITORY.
WE NEED TO STAY ALERT.
I CAN'T BELIEVE HE CAN SLEEP HERE.
HEH... HE'S SPECIAL.

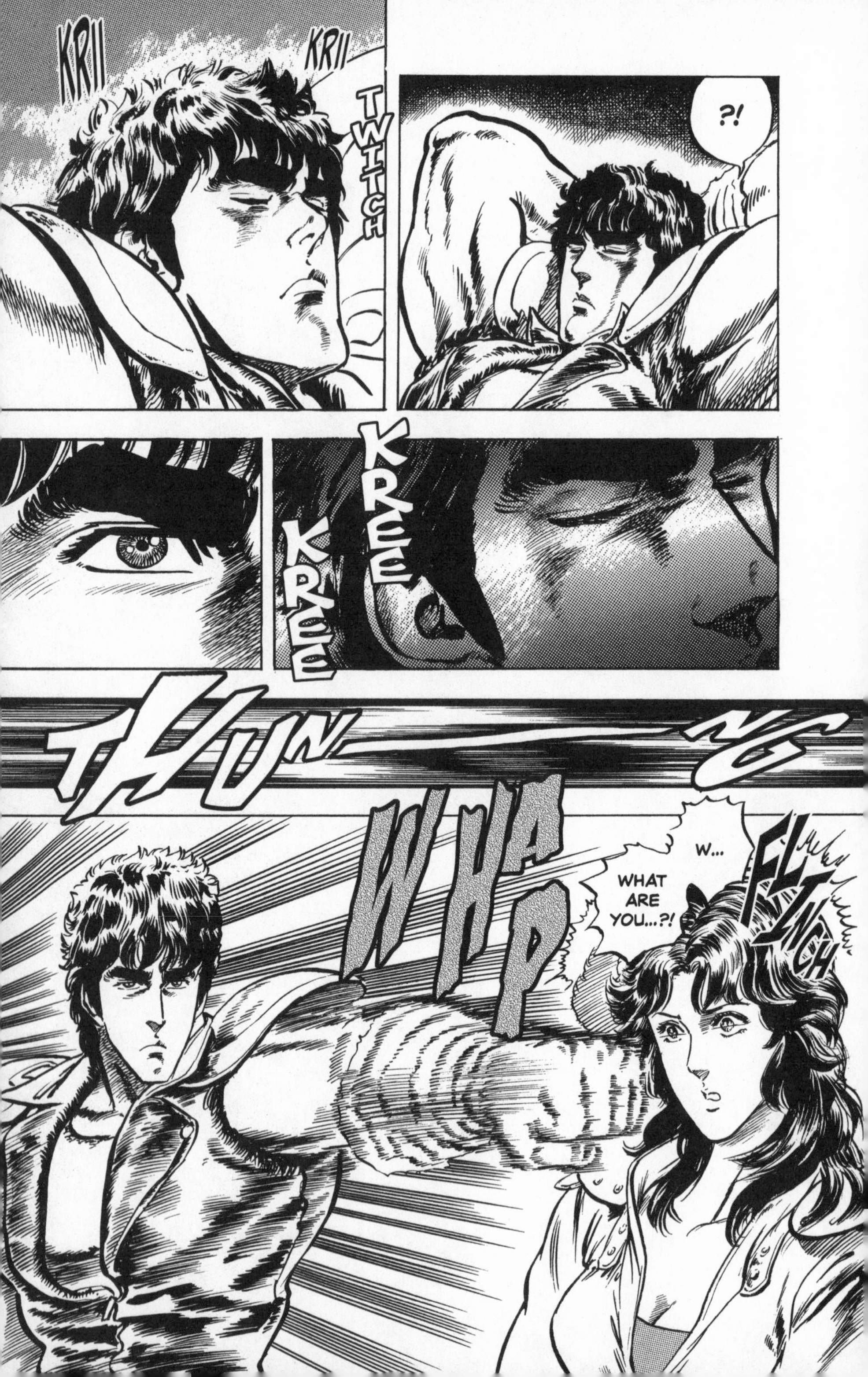
?!
TWITCH
KRII
KRII
KREE
KREE
THUNNG
FLINCH
W...
WHAT ARE YOU...?!
WHAP

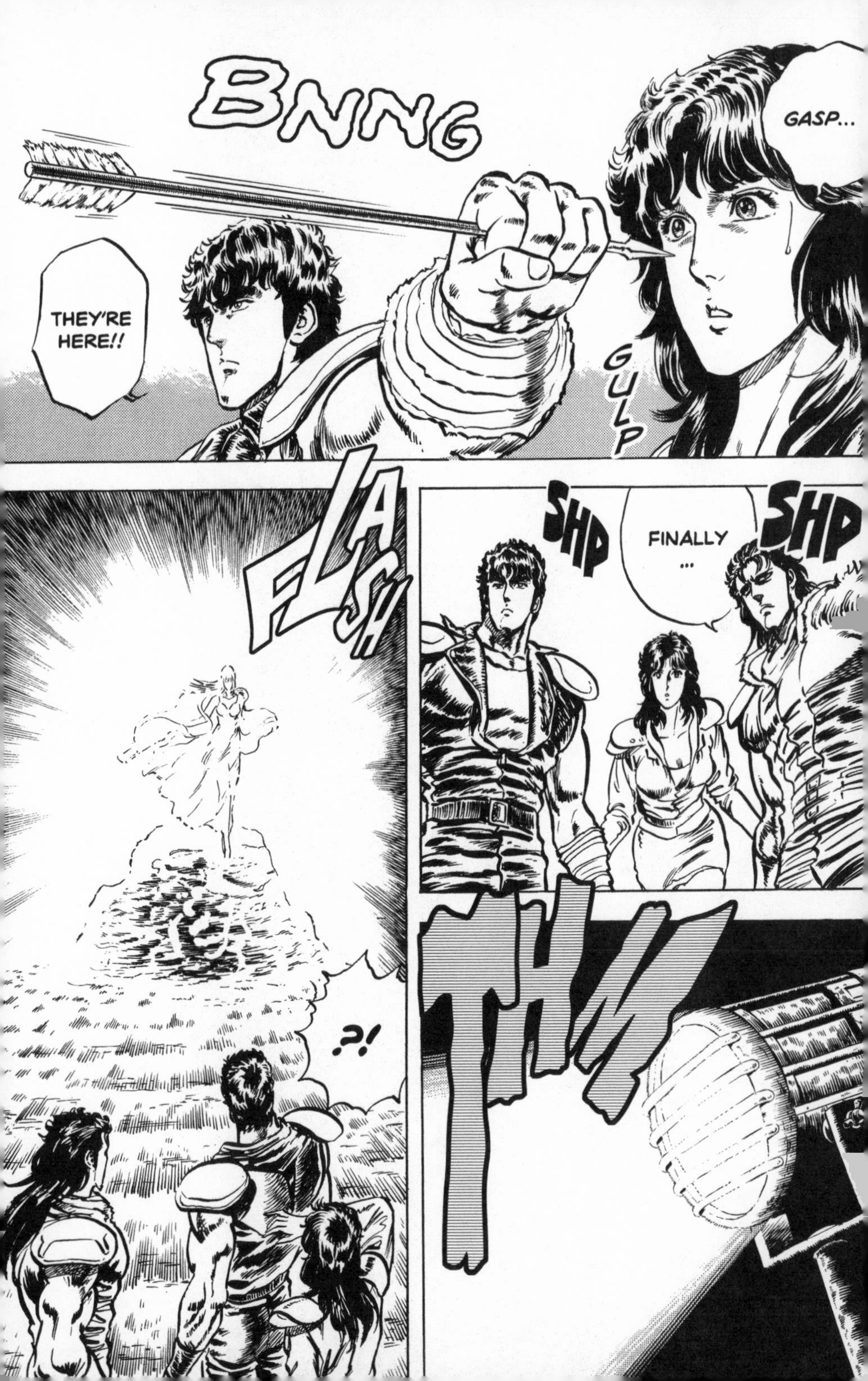
GASP...
BNNG
GULP
THEY'RE HERE!!
SHP
FINALLY ...
SHP
THM
FLASH
?!

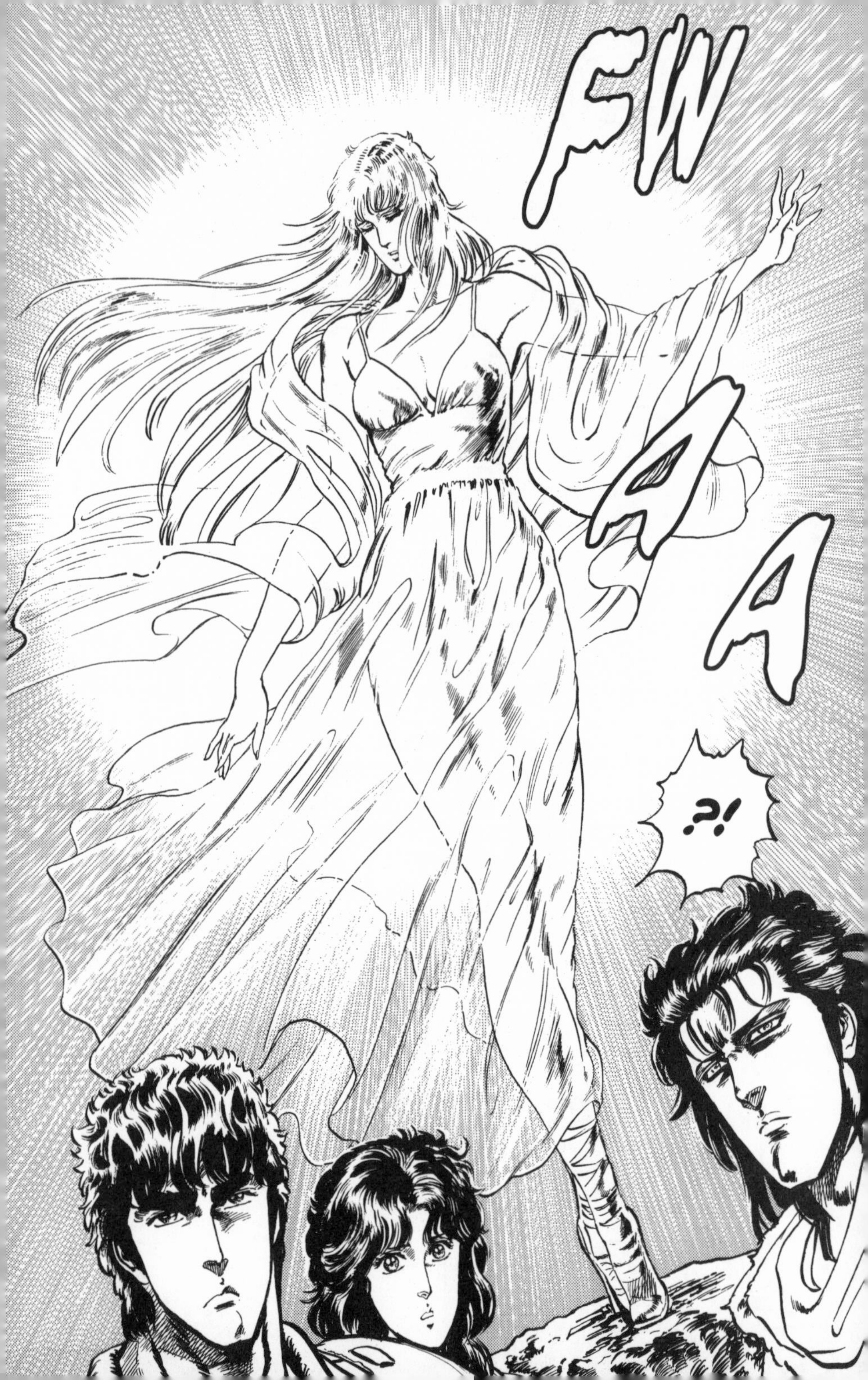
FWAA
?!

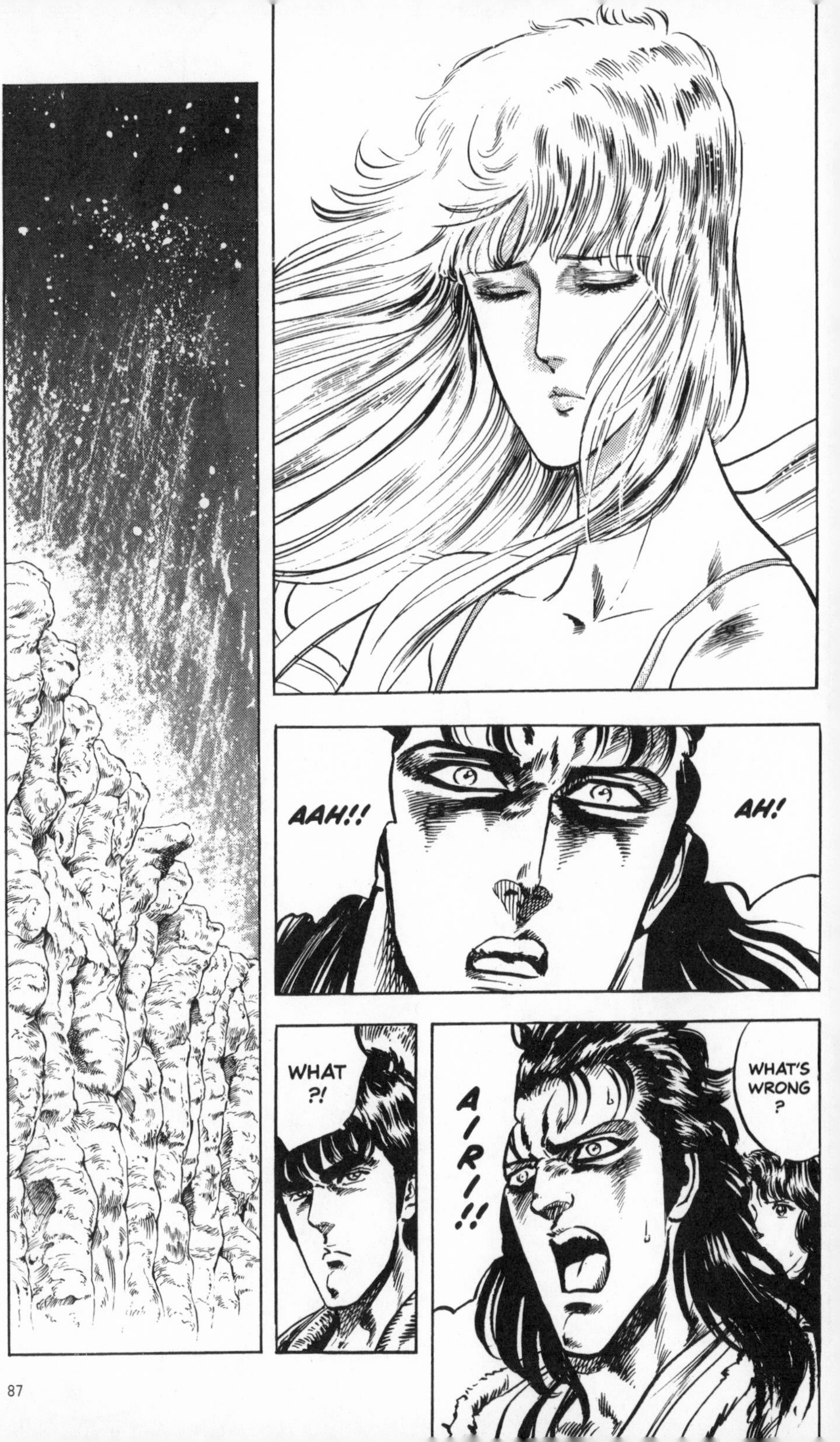
AH!
AAH!!
WHAT'S WRONG ?
AIRI!!
WHAT ?!

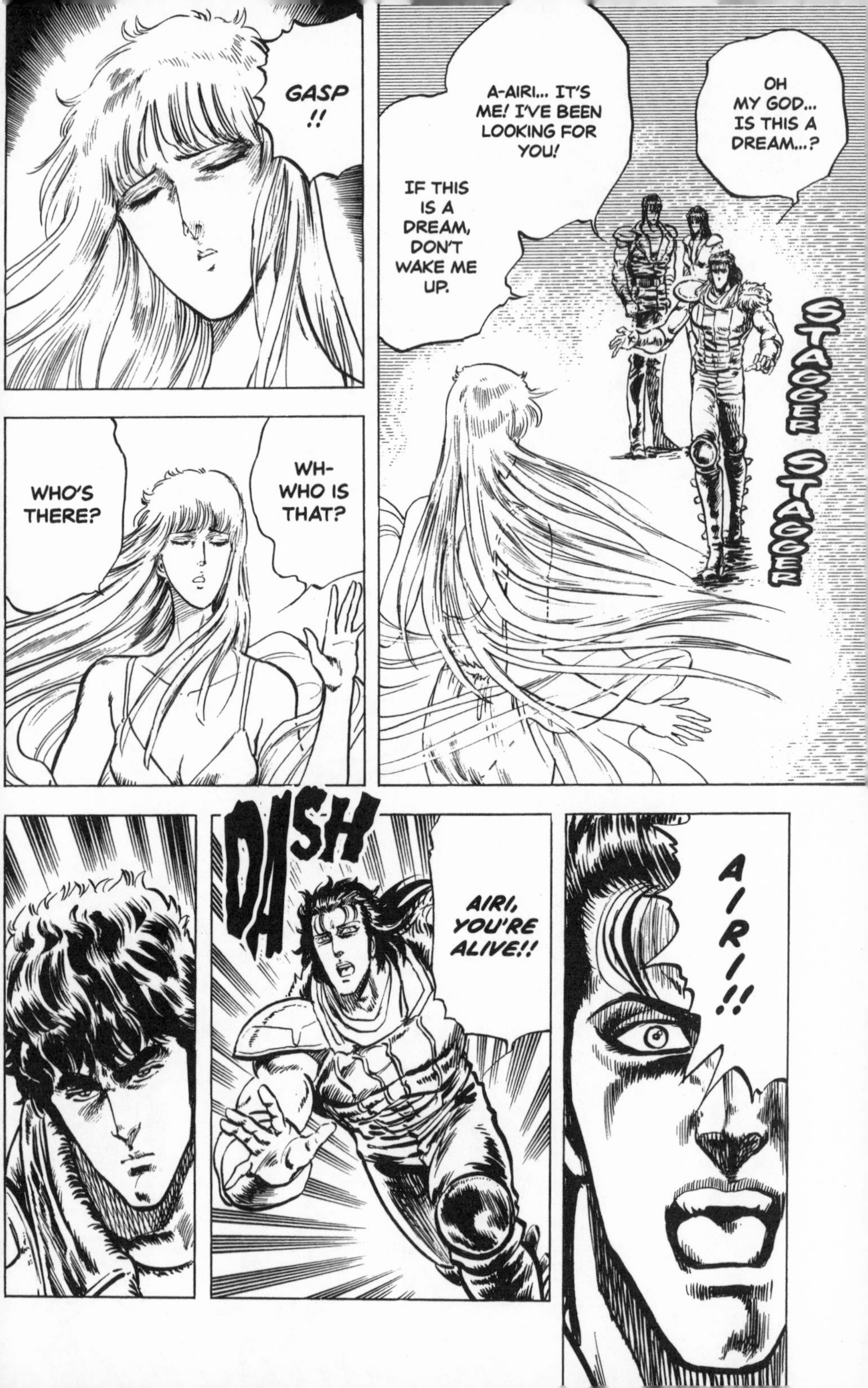
OH MY GOD... IS THIS A DREAM...?
A-AIRI... IT'S ME! I'VE BEEN LOOKING FOR YOU!
IF THIS IS A DREAM, DON'T WAKE ME UP.
STAGGER STAGGER
GASP!!
WH- WHO IS THAT?
WHO'S THERE?
AIRI!!
DASH
AIRI, YOU'RE ALIVE!!

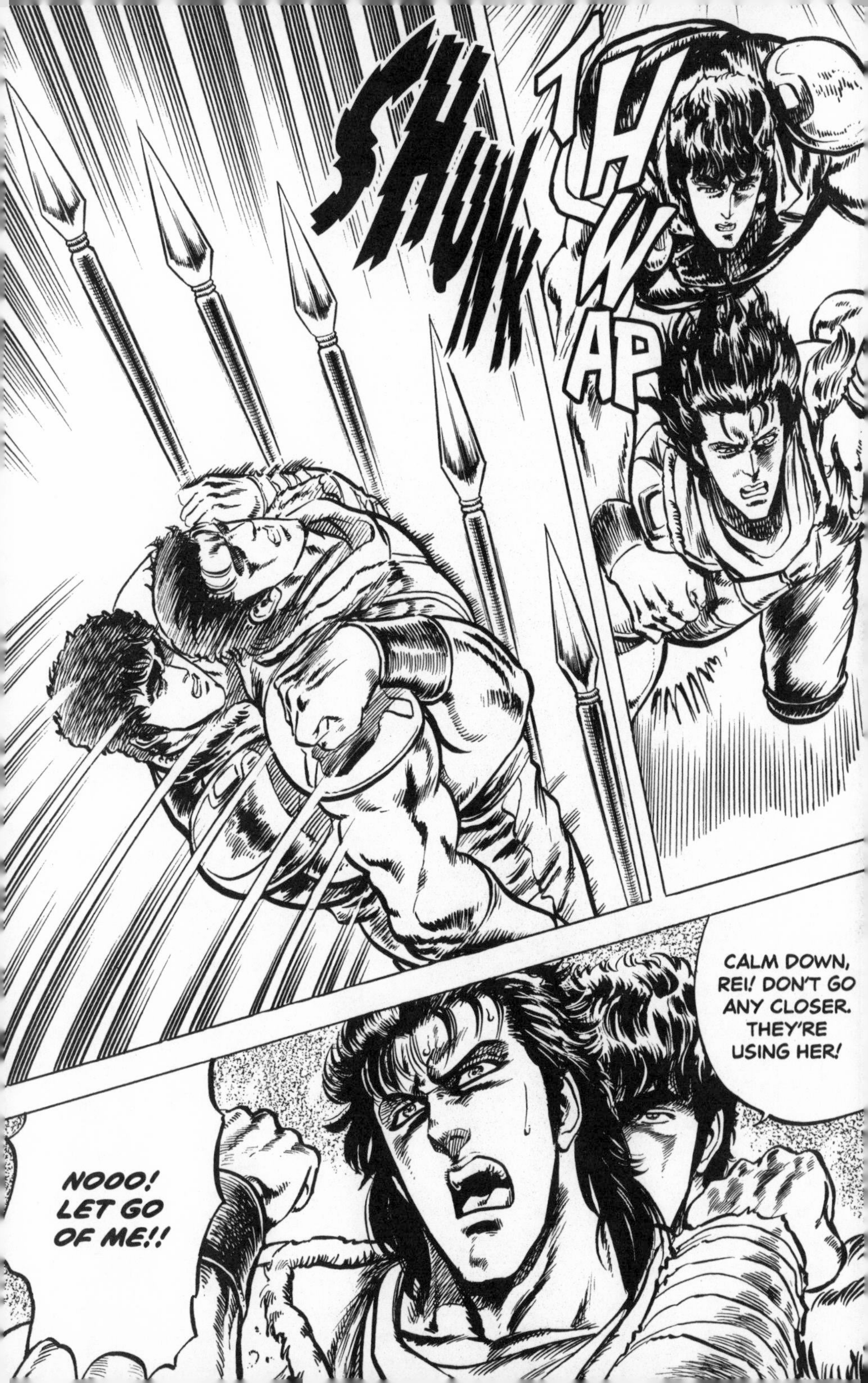
THWAP
SHUNK
CALM DOWN, REI! DON'T GO ANY CLOSER. THEY'RE USING HER!
NOOO! LET GO OF ME!!

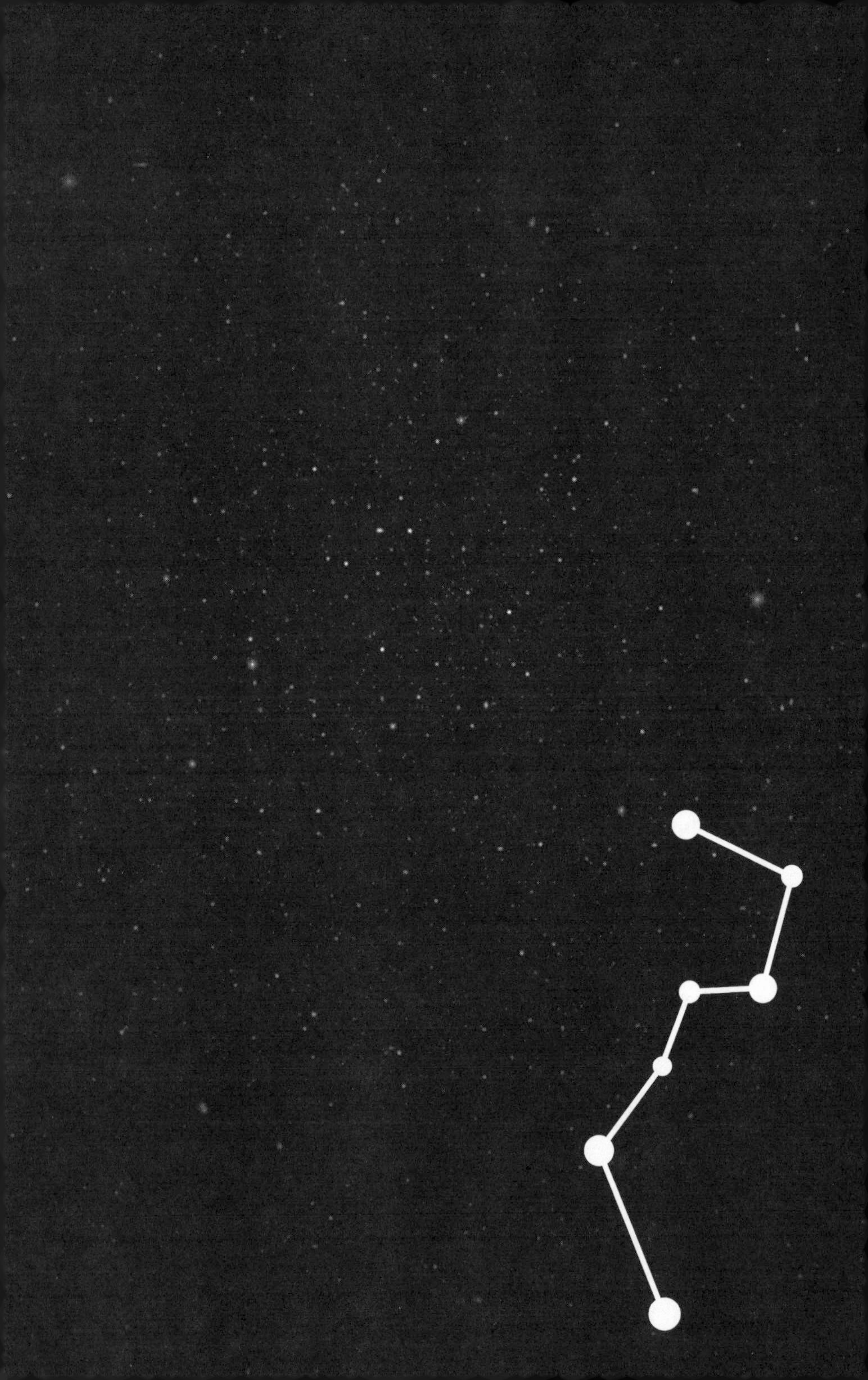

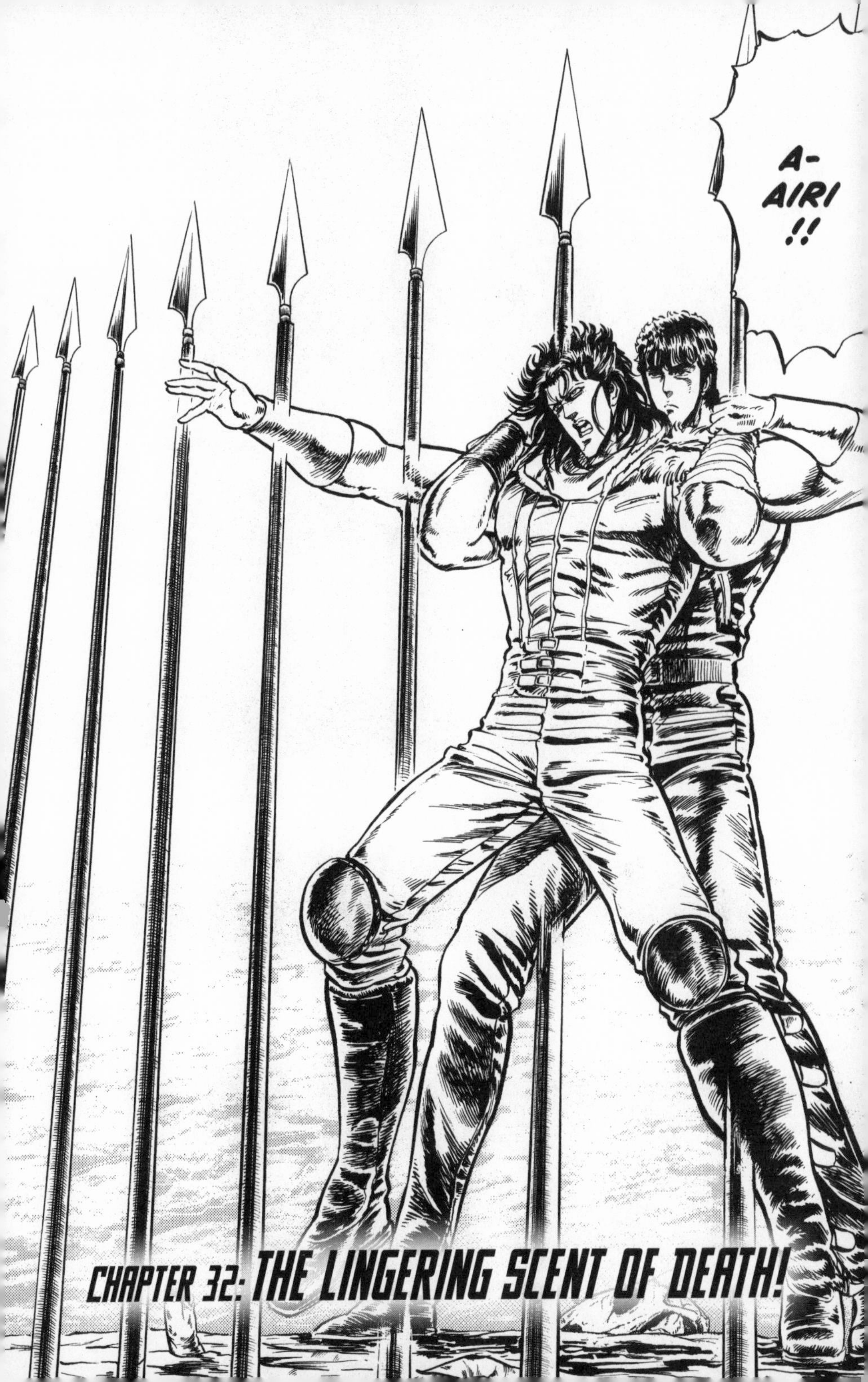
A-AIRI!!

CHAPTER 32: THE LINGERING SCENT OF DEATH!

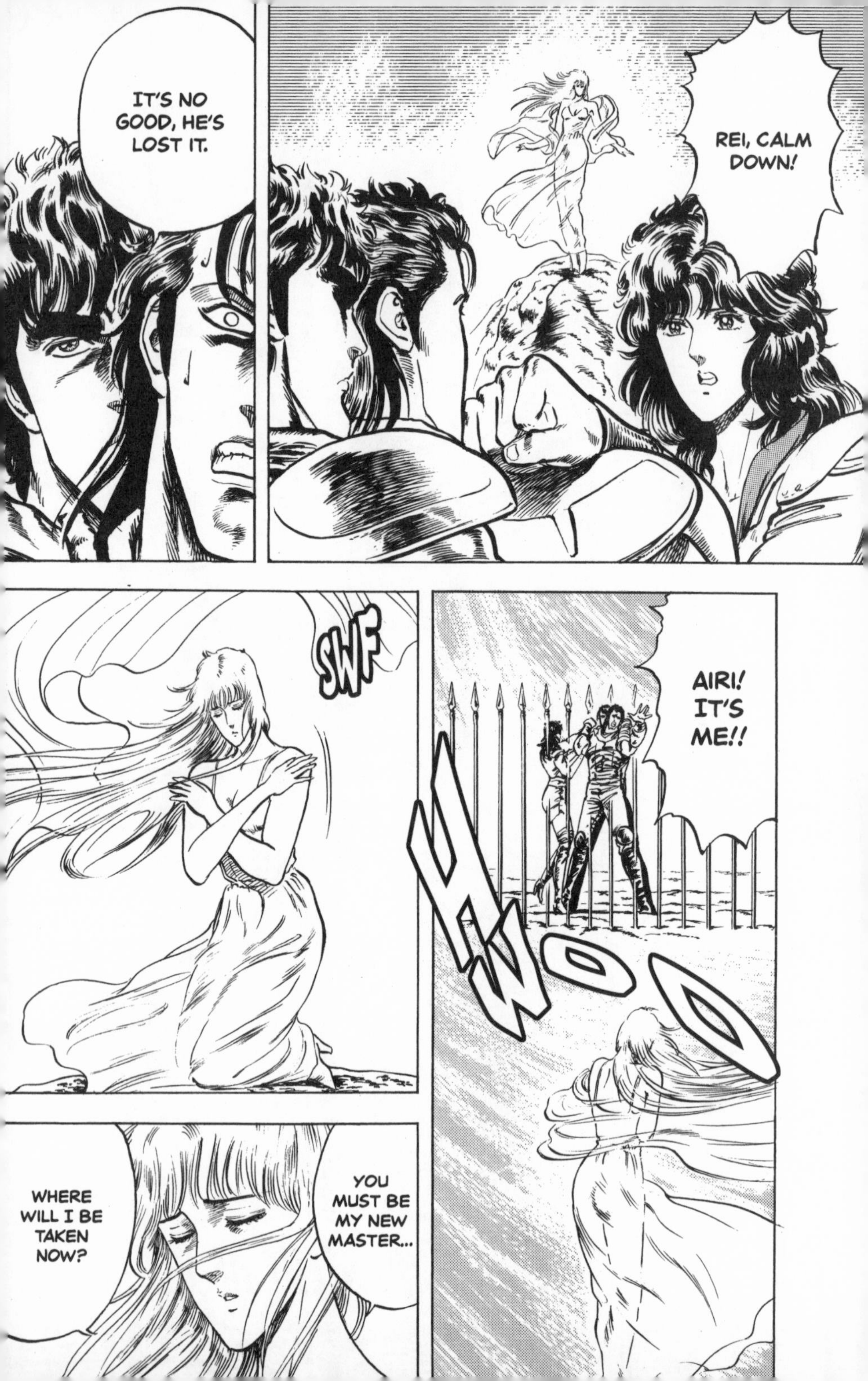
REI, CALM DOWN!
IT'S NO GOOD, HE'S LOST IT.
AIRI! IT'S ME!!
SWF
YOU MUST BE MY NEW MASTER...
WHERE WILL I BE TAKEN NOW?

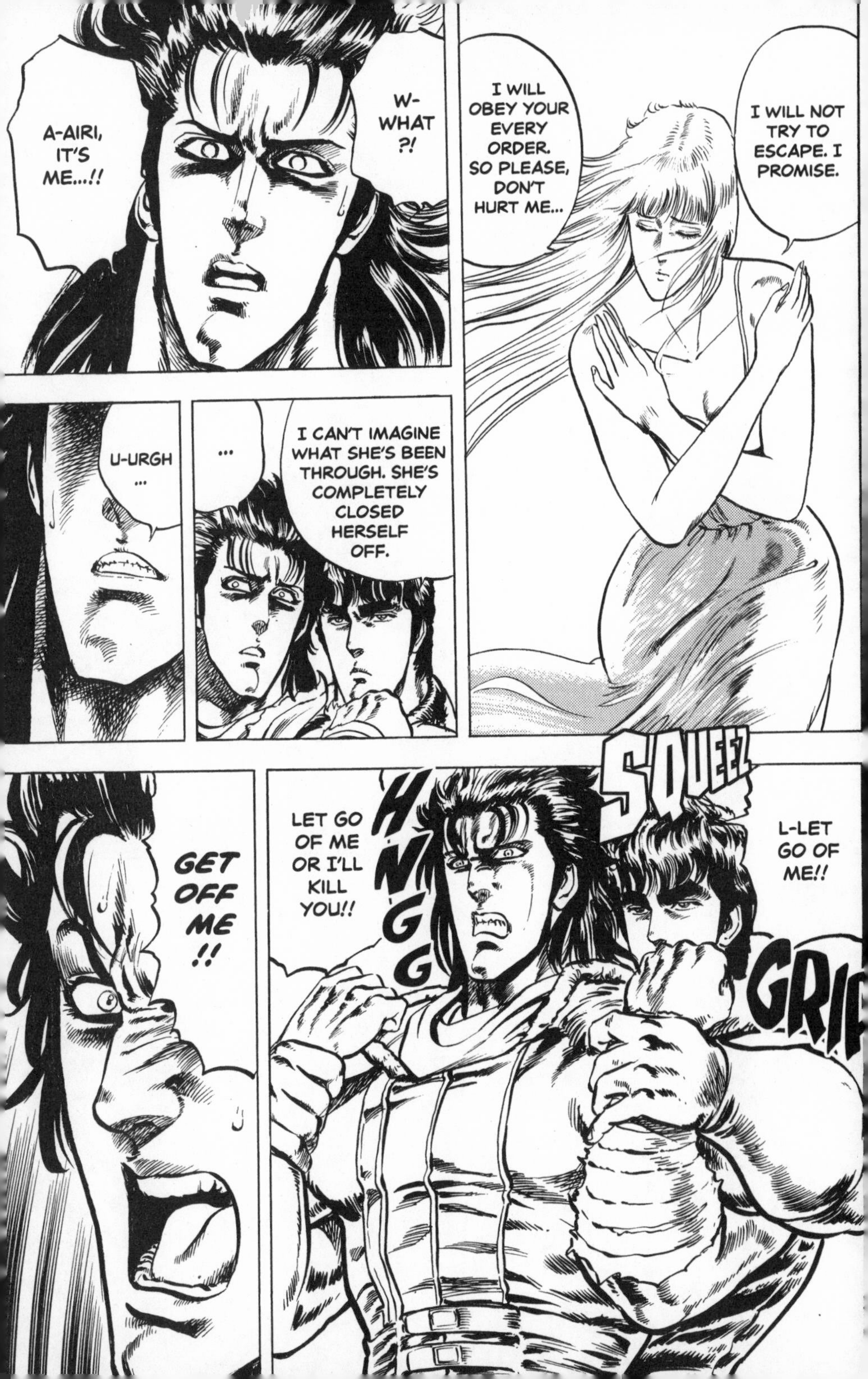
I WILL NOT TRY TO ESCAPE. I PROMISE.
I WILL OBEY YOUR EVERY ORDER. SO PLEASE, DON'T HURT ME...
W-WHAT ?!
A-AIRI, IT'S ME...!!
I CAN'T IMAGINE WHAT SHE'S BEEN THROUGH. SHE'S COMPLETELY CLOSED HERSELF OFF.
...
U-URGH ...
L-LET GO OF ME!!
GRIP
SQUEEZ
LET GO OF ME OR I'LL KILL YOU!!
HNGG
GET OFF ME !!

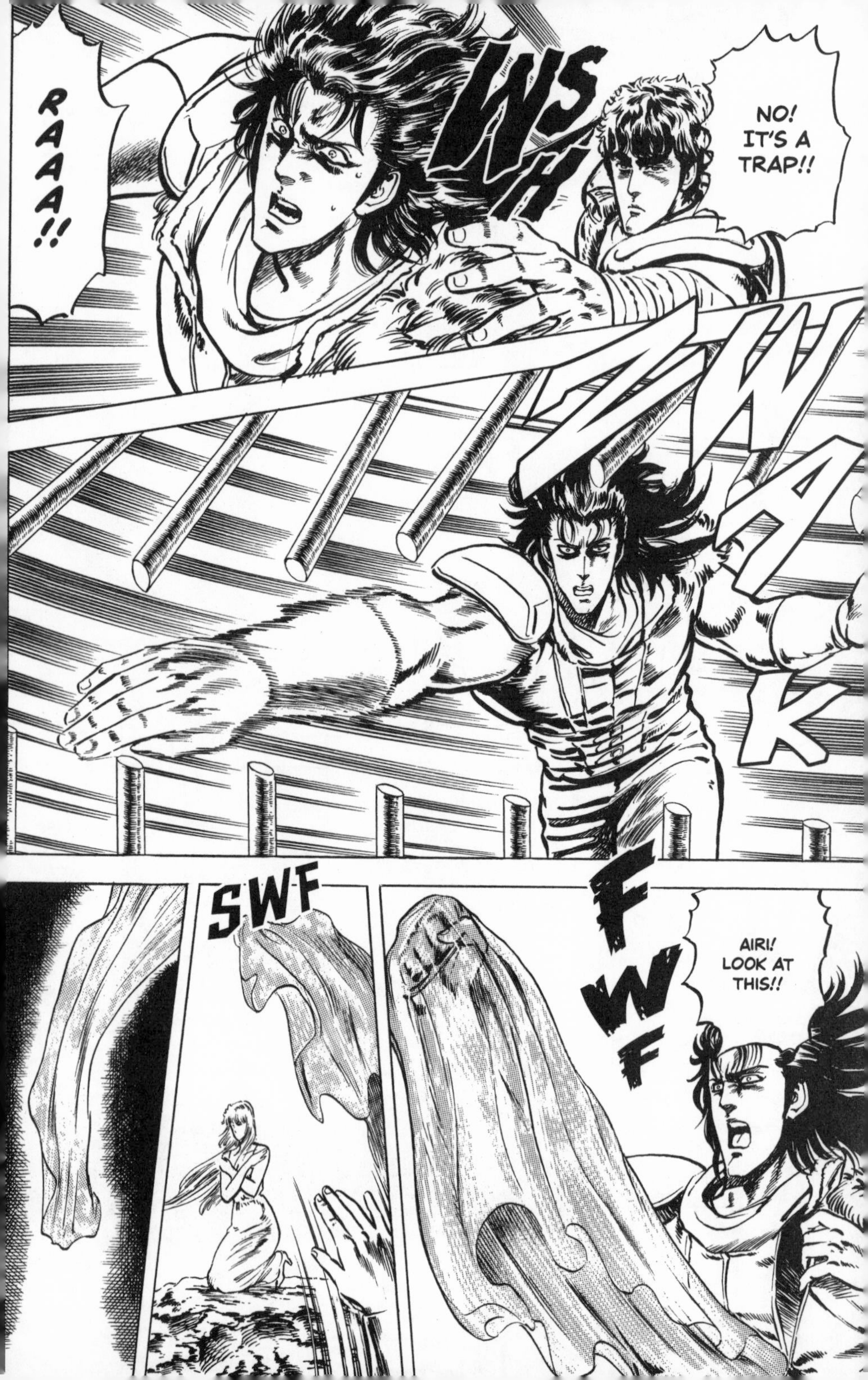
NO! IT'S A TRAP!!
WSH
RAAAA!!
AIRI! LOOK AT THIS!!
FWF
SWF

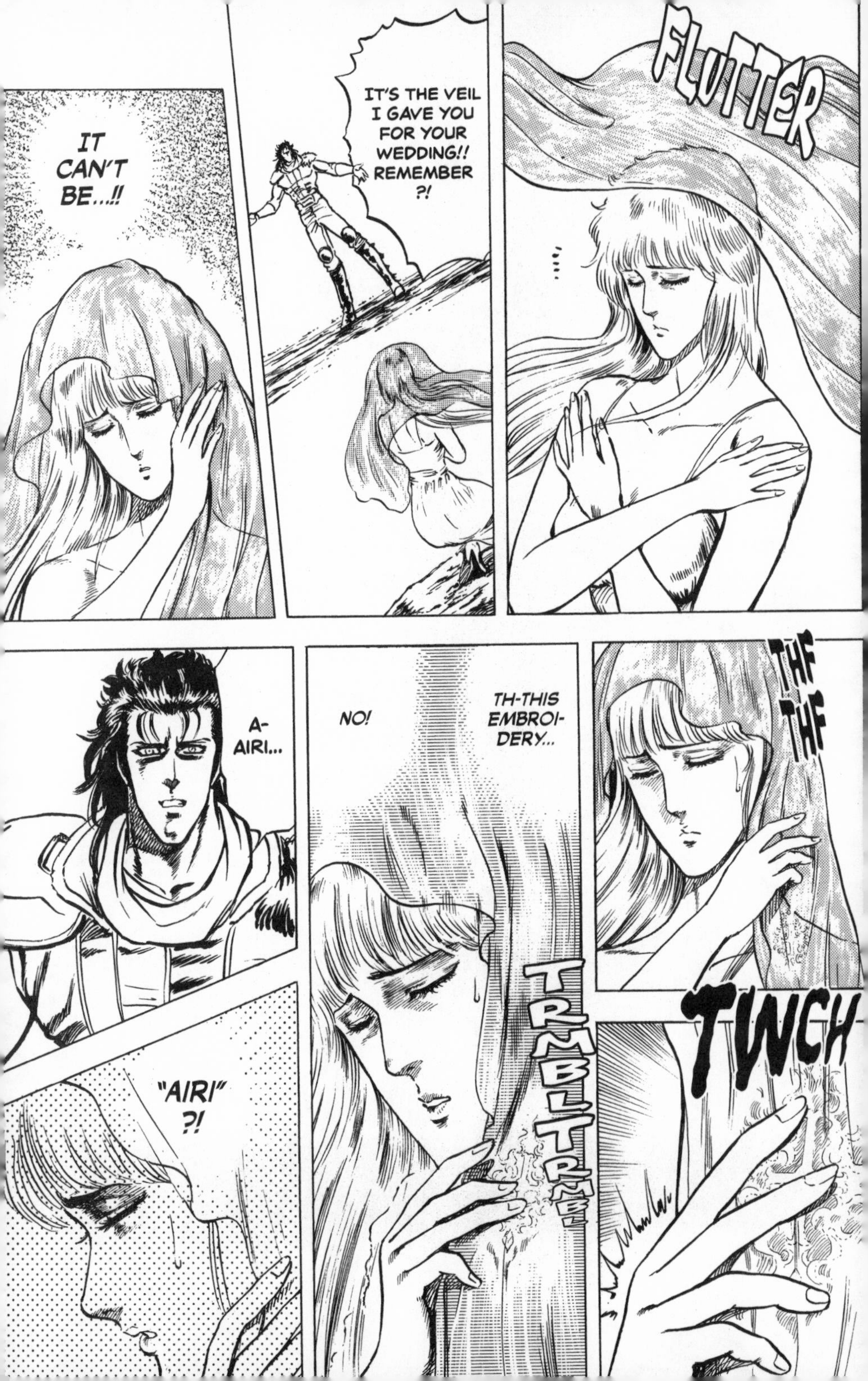
FLUTTER
....
IT'S THE VEIL I GAVE YOU FOR YOUR WEDDING!! REMEMBER ?!
IT CAN'T BE...!!
THF THF
TWCH
TH-THIS EMBROIDERY...
NO!
TRMBL TRMBL
A- AIRI...
"AIRI" ?!

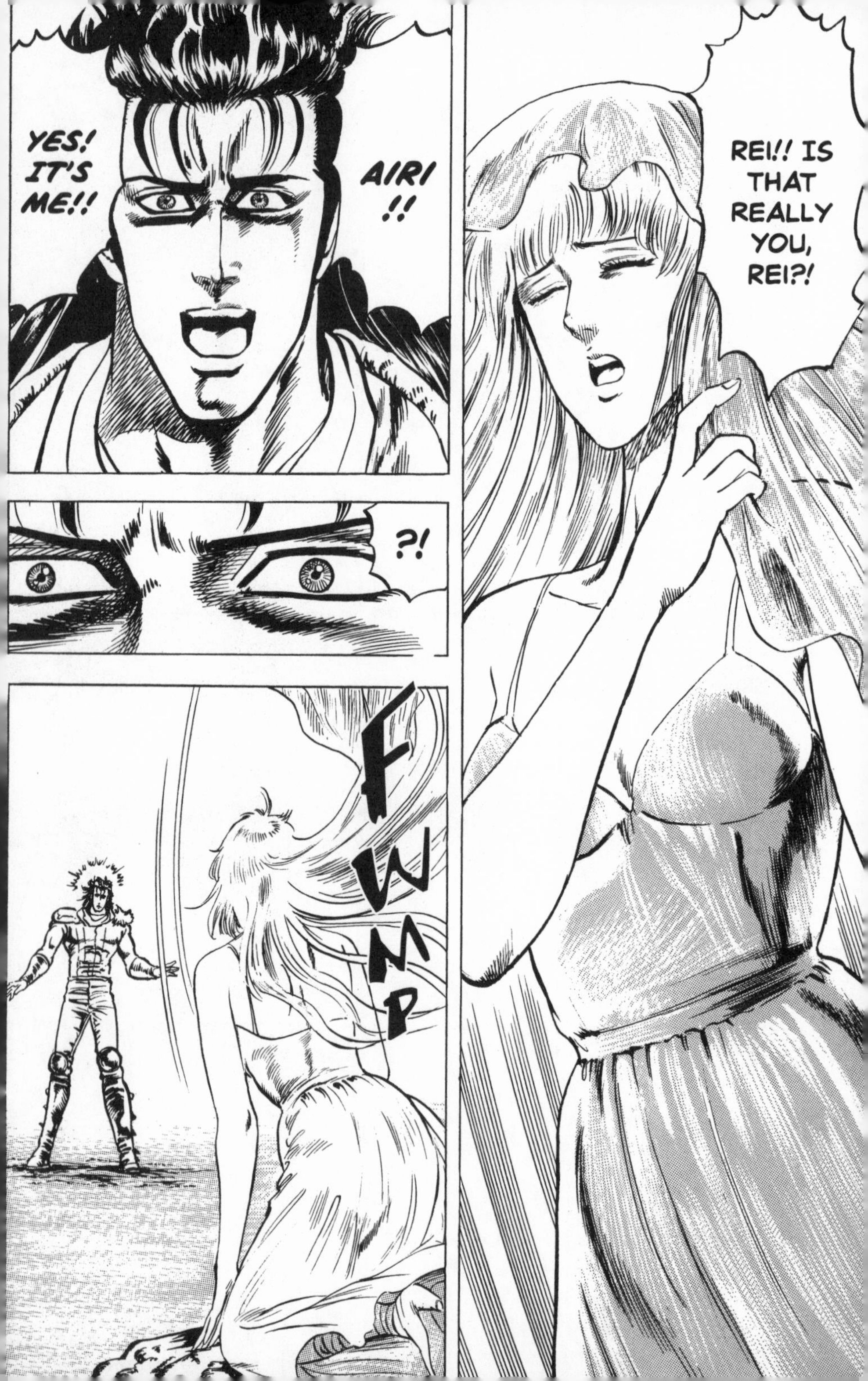
REI!! IS THAT REALLY YOU, REI?!
AIRI!!
YES! IT'S ME!!
?!
FWMP

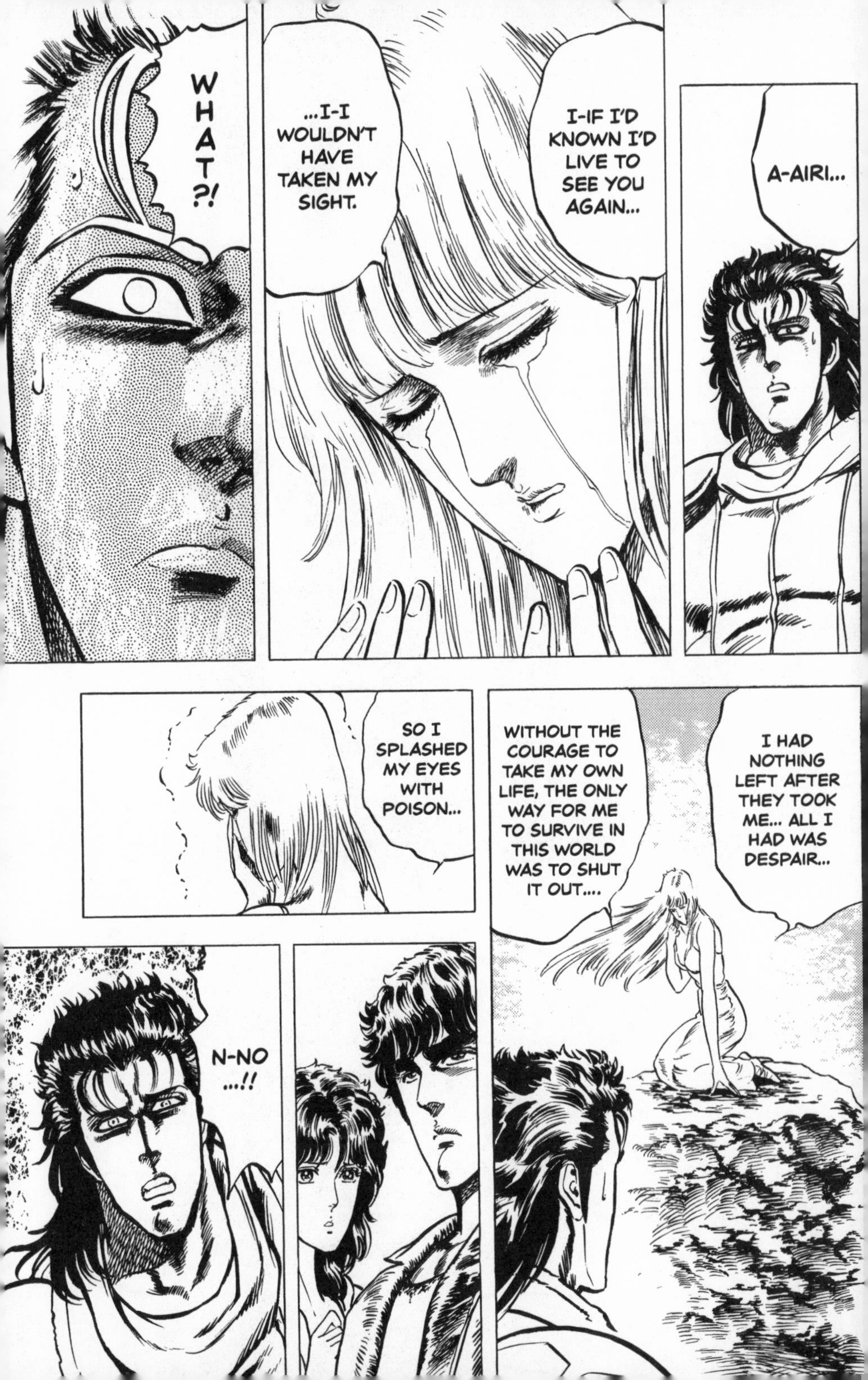
A-AIRI...
I-IF I'D KNOWN I'D LIVE TO SEE YOU AGAIN...
...I-I WOULDN'T HAVE TAKEN MY SIGHT.
WHAT?!
I HAD NOTHING LEFT AFTER THEY TOOK ME... ALL I HAD WAS DESPAIR...
WITHOUT THE COURAGE TO TAKE MY OWN LIFE, THE ONLY WAY FOR ME TO SURVIVE IN THIS WORLD WAS TO SHUT IT OUT....
SO I SPLASHED MY EYES WITH POISON...
N-NO ...!!

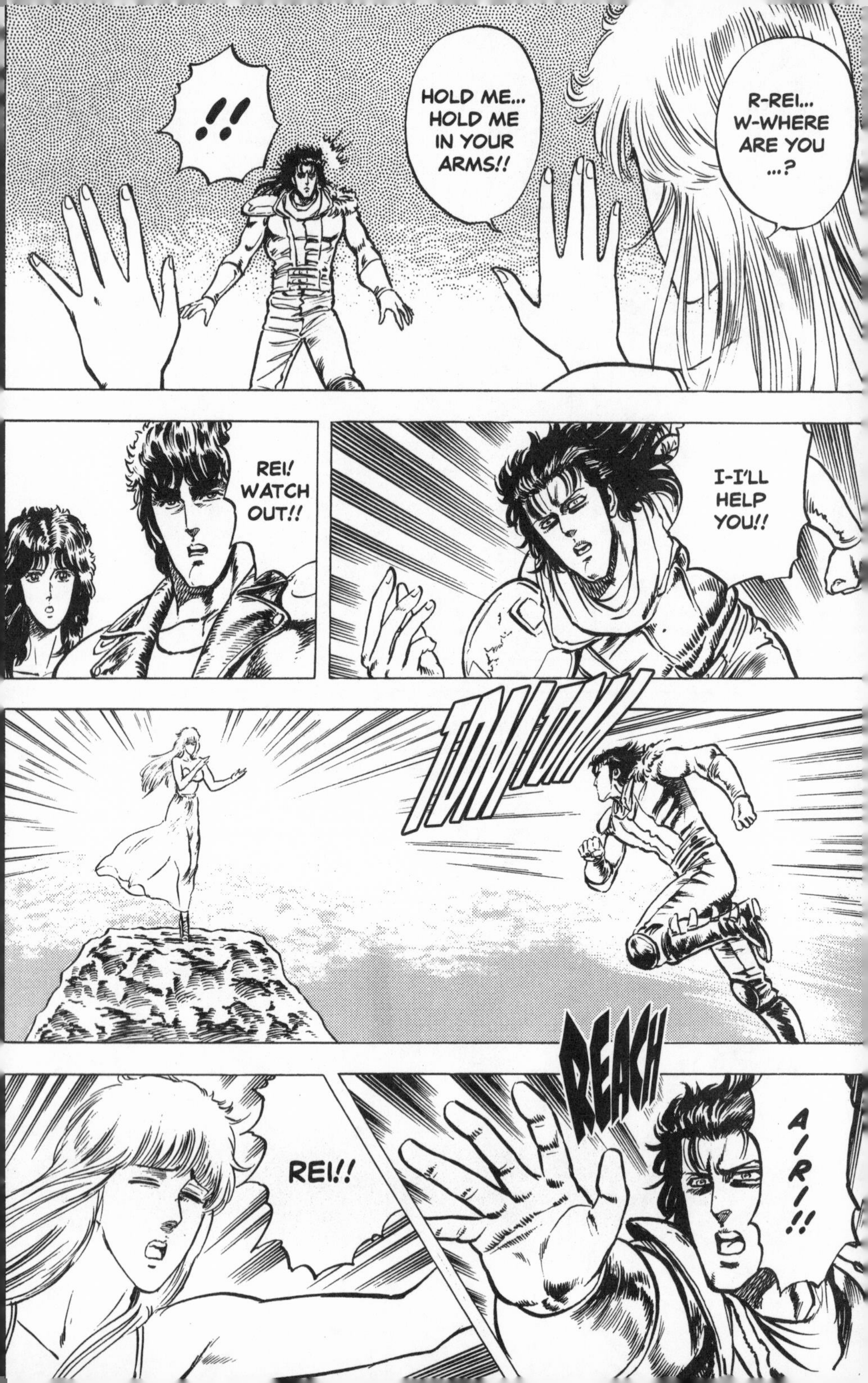
R-REI...
W-WHERE
ARE YOU
...?
HOLD ME...
HOLD ME
IN YOUR
ARMS!!
!!
I-I'LL
HELP
YOU!!
REI!
WATCH
OUT!!
TOM TOM
REACH
AIRI!!
REI!!

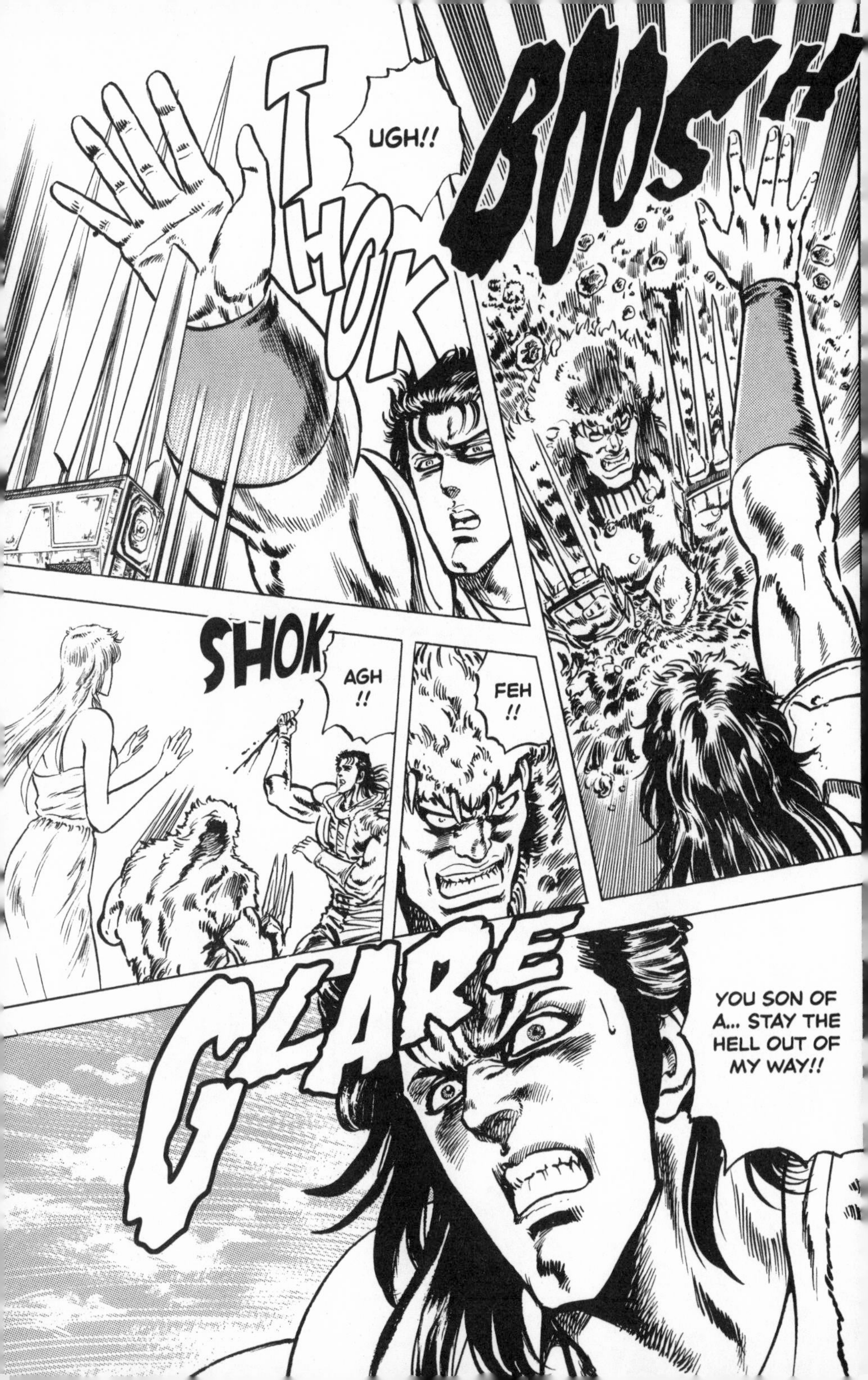
BOOSH
THOK
UGH!!
FEH!!
SHOK
AGH!!
GLARE
YOU SON OF A... STAY THE HELL OUT OF MY WAY!!

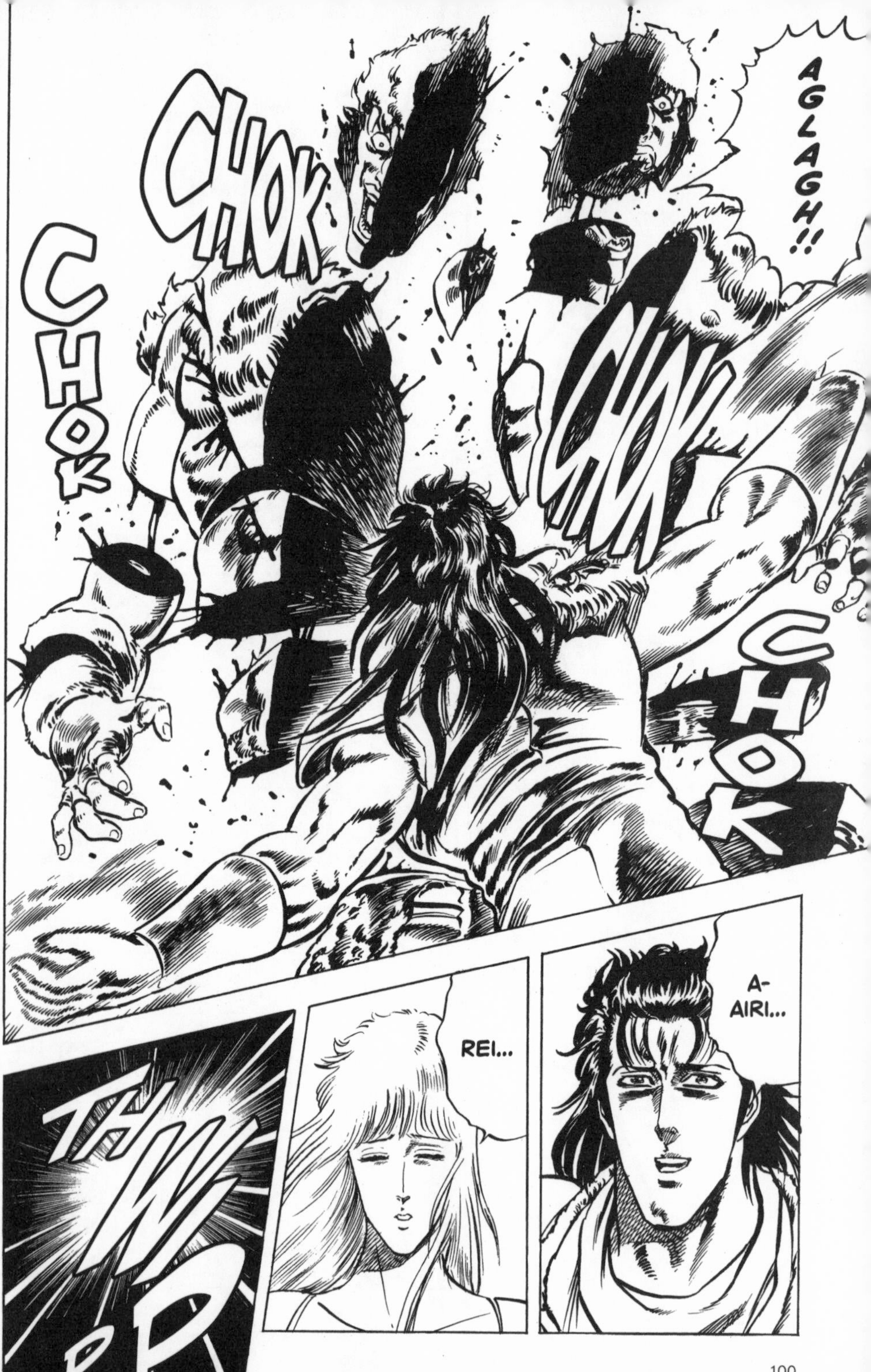
AGLAGH!!
CHOK
CHOK
CHOK
CHOK
A-AIRI...
REI...
THWIPP

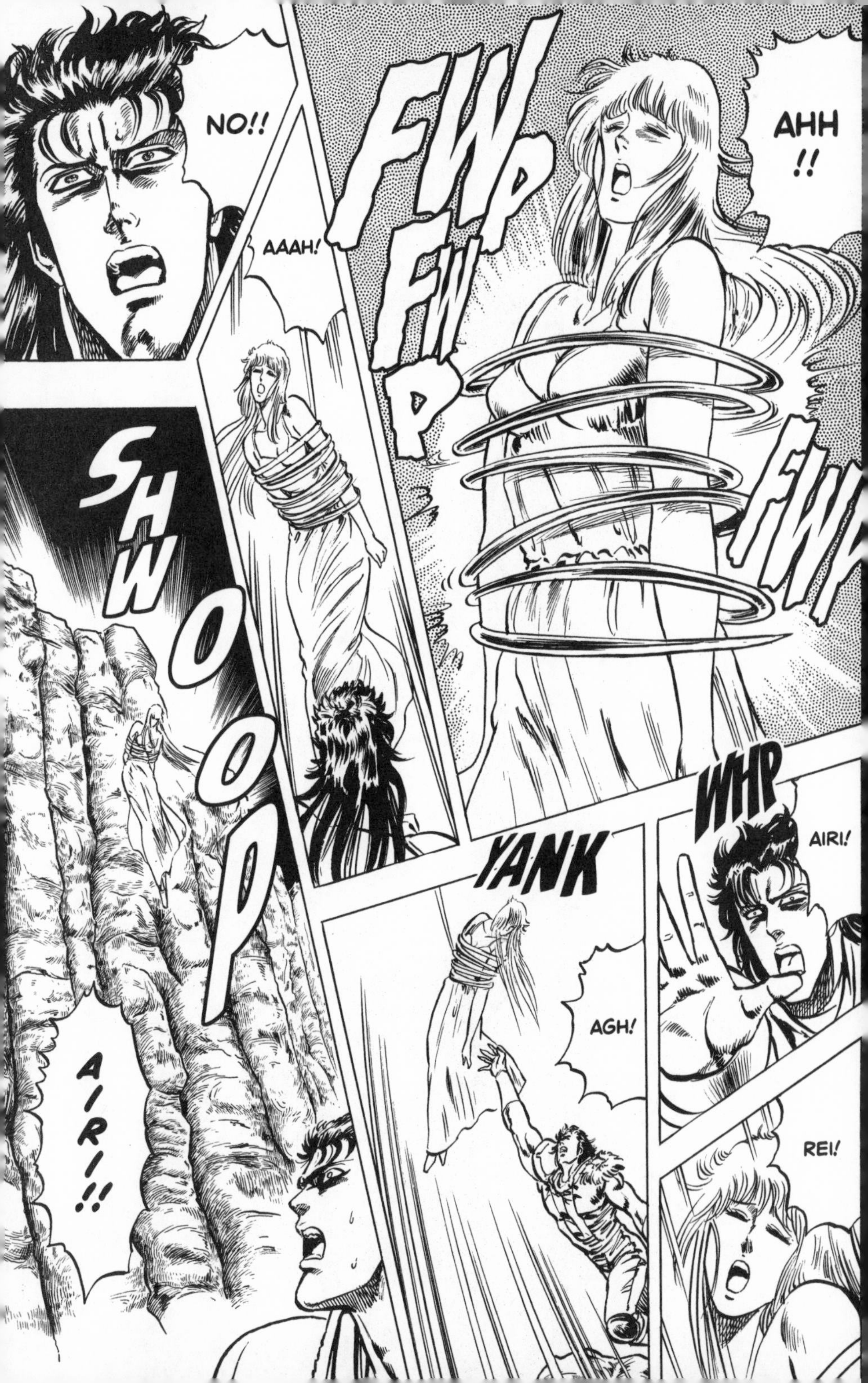
FWP
FWP
AHH!!
AAAH!
NO!!
WHP
AIRI!
YANK
AGH!
REI!
SHWOOP
AIRI!!

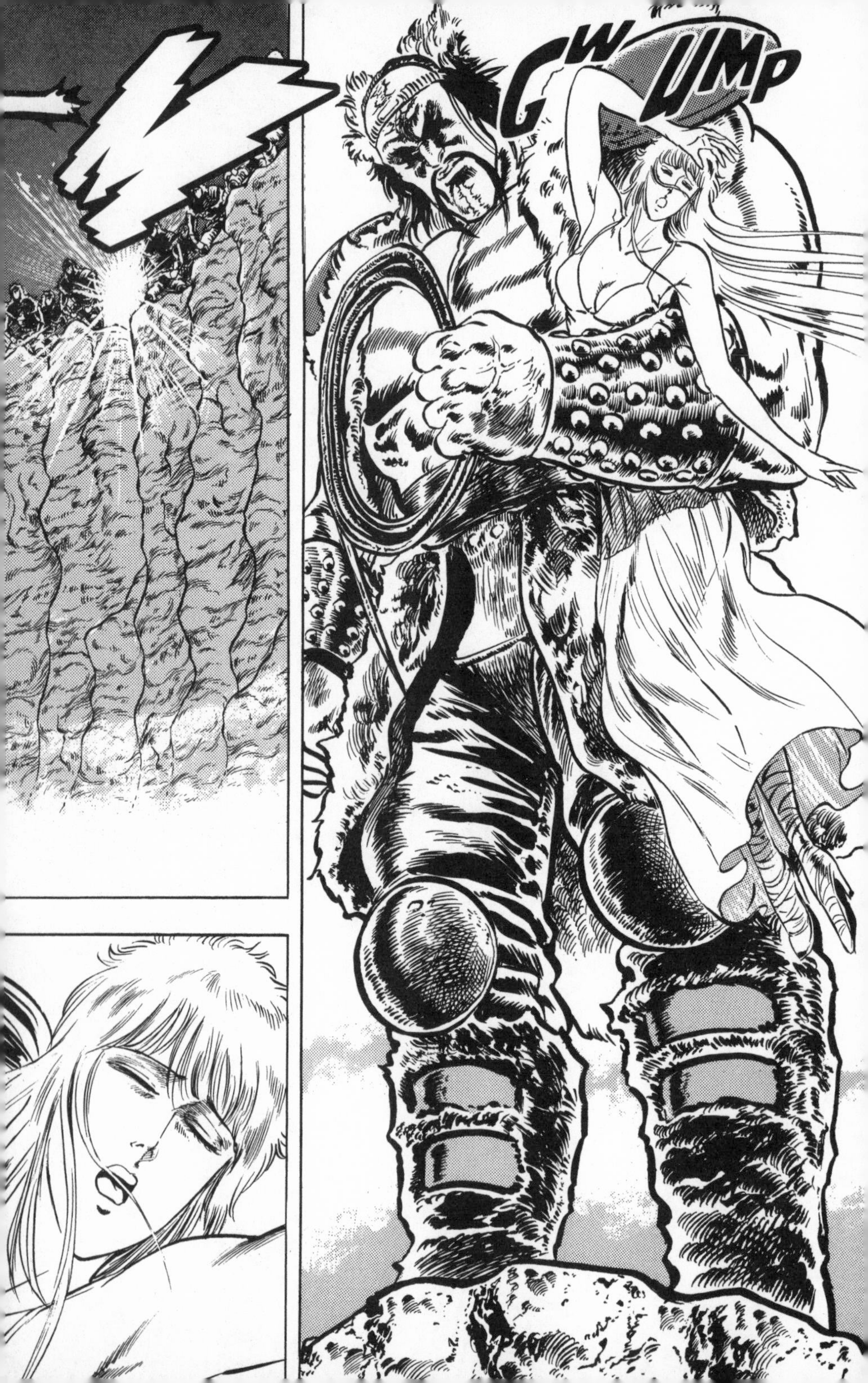
GWUMP

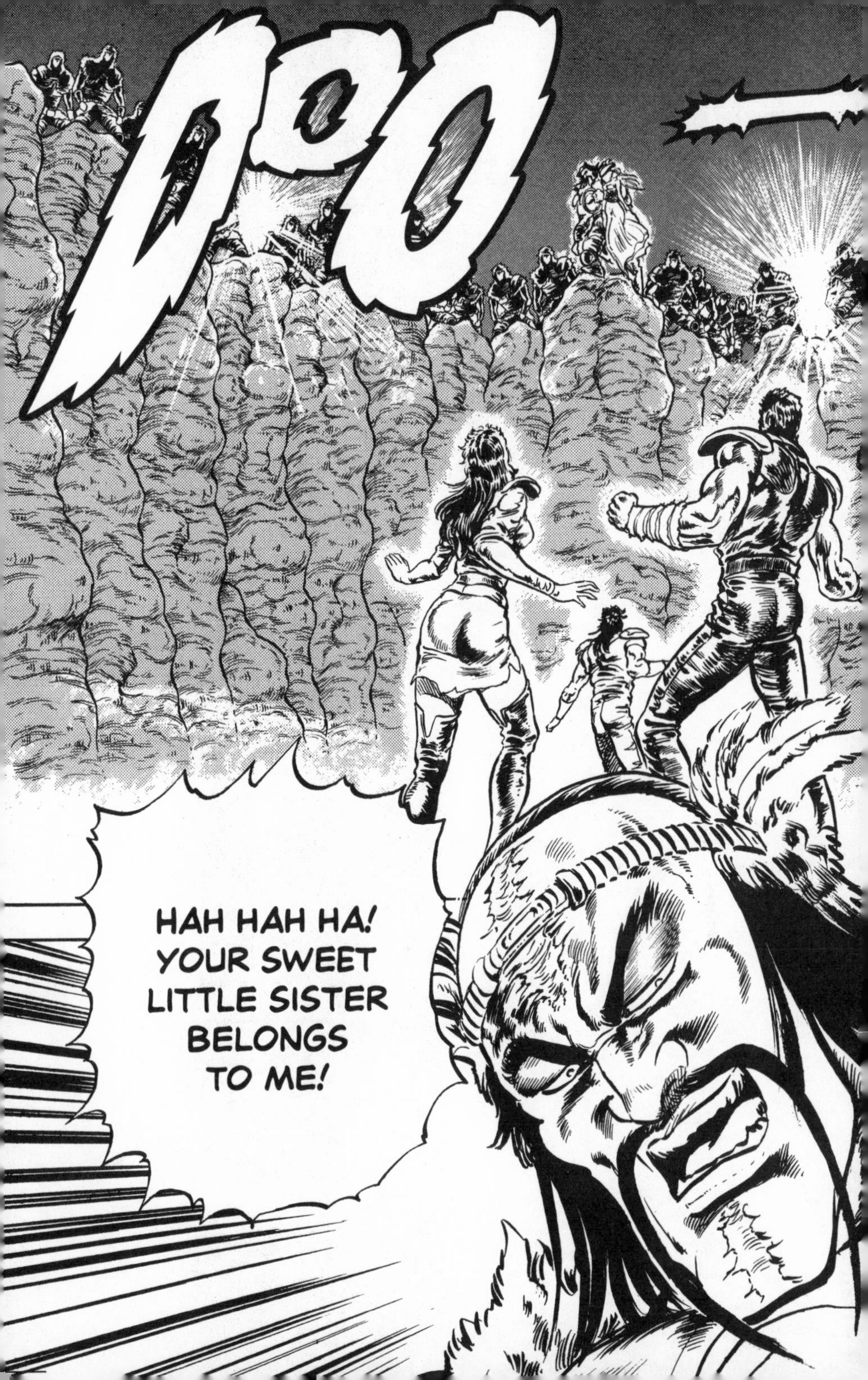
DOO
HAH HAH HA! YOUR SWEET LITTLE SISTER BELONGS TO ME!

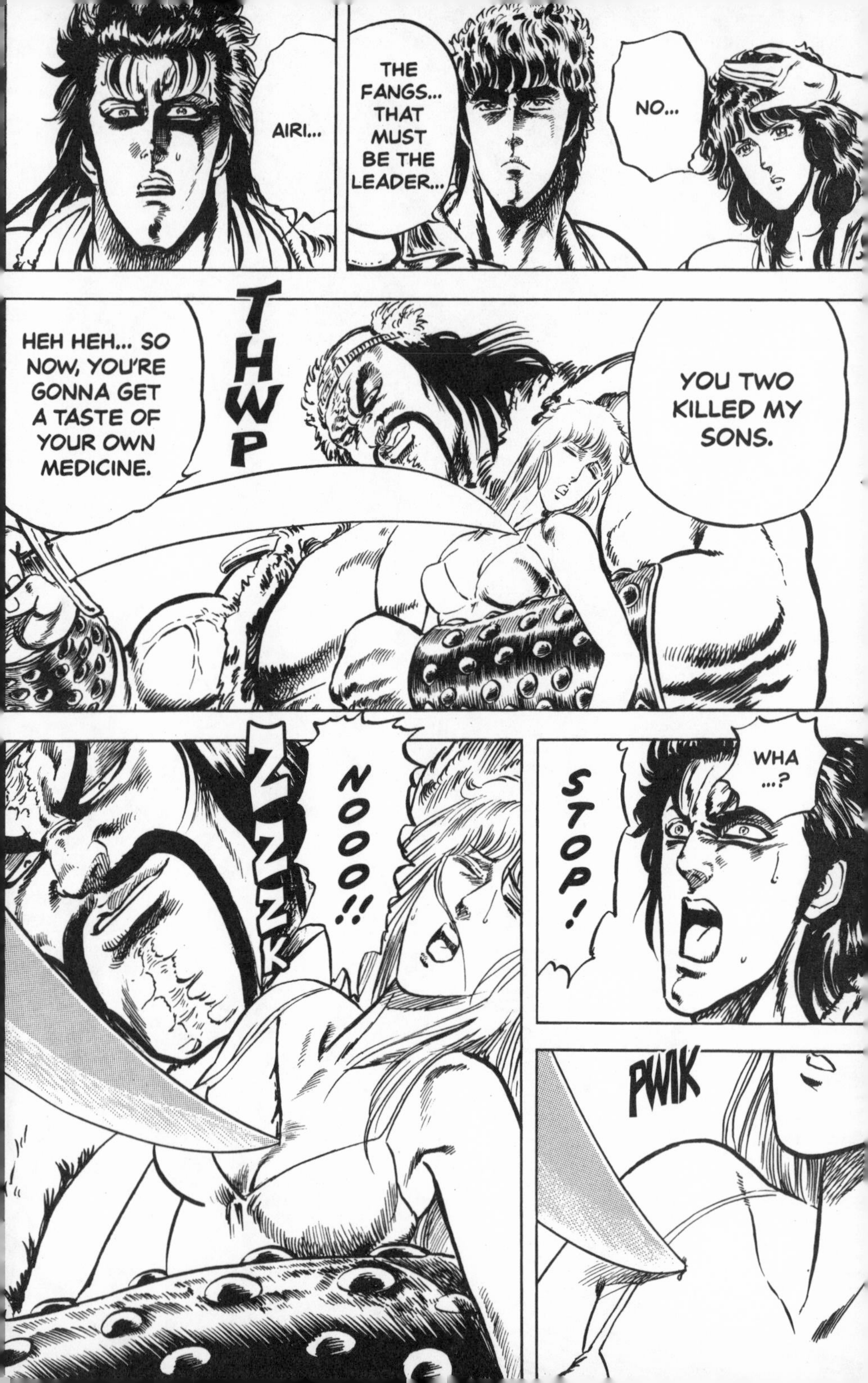
NO...
THE FANGS... THAT MUST BE THE LEADER...
AIRI...
YOU TWO KILLED MY SONS.
THWP
HEH HEH... SO NOW, YOU'RE GONNA GET A TASTE OF YOUR OWN MEDICINE.
WHA ...?
STOP!
PWIK
NOOOO!!
ZNZK

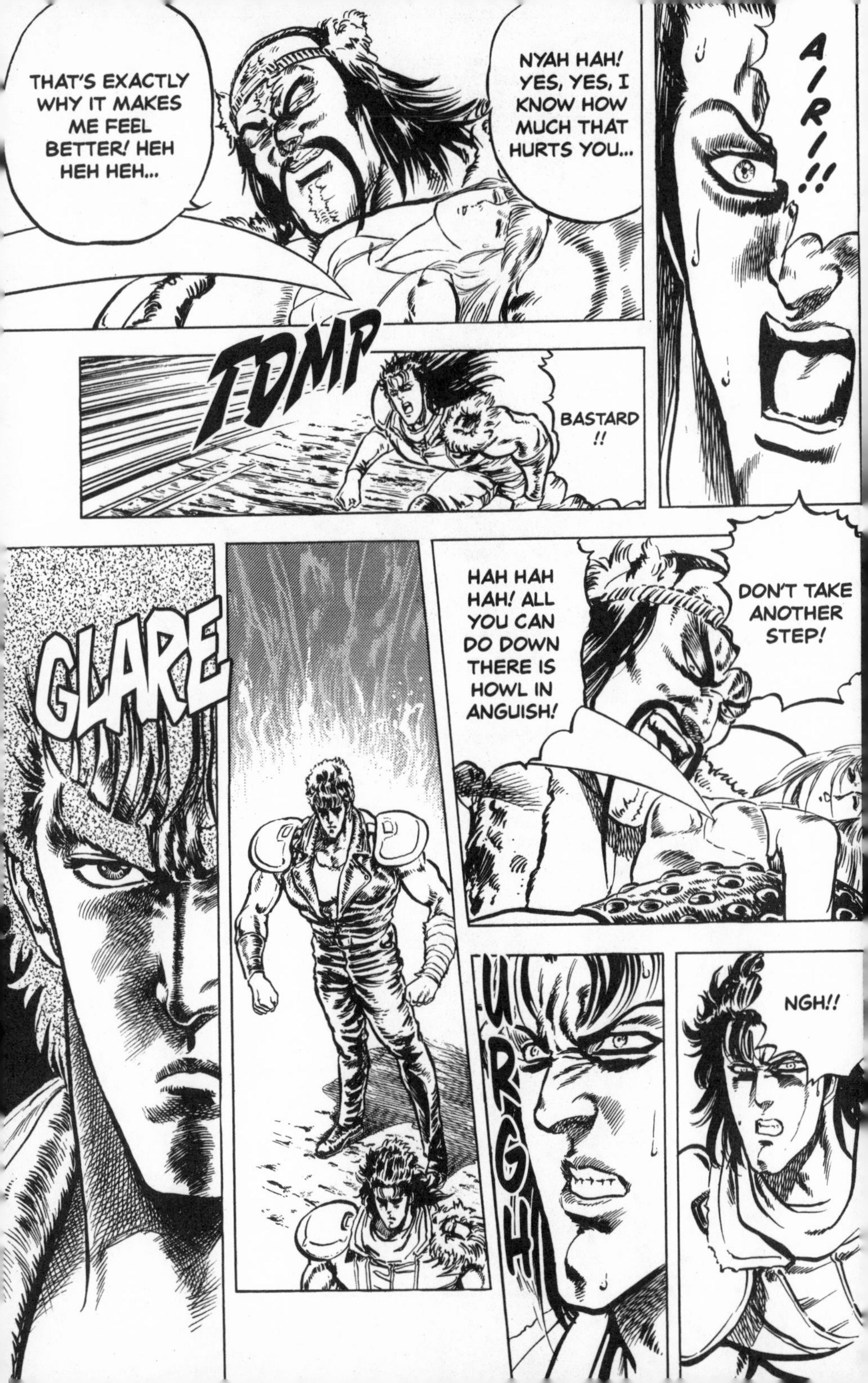
NYAH HAH! YES, YES, I KNOW HOW MUCH THAT HURTS YOU...
THAT'S EXACTLY WHY IT MAKES ME FEEL BETTER! HEH HEH HEH...
AIRI!!
TOMP
BASTARD !!
DON'T TAKE ANOTHER STEP!
HAH HAH HAH! ALL YOU CAN DO DOWN THERE IS HOWL IN ANGUISH!
NGH!!
URRGH
GLARE

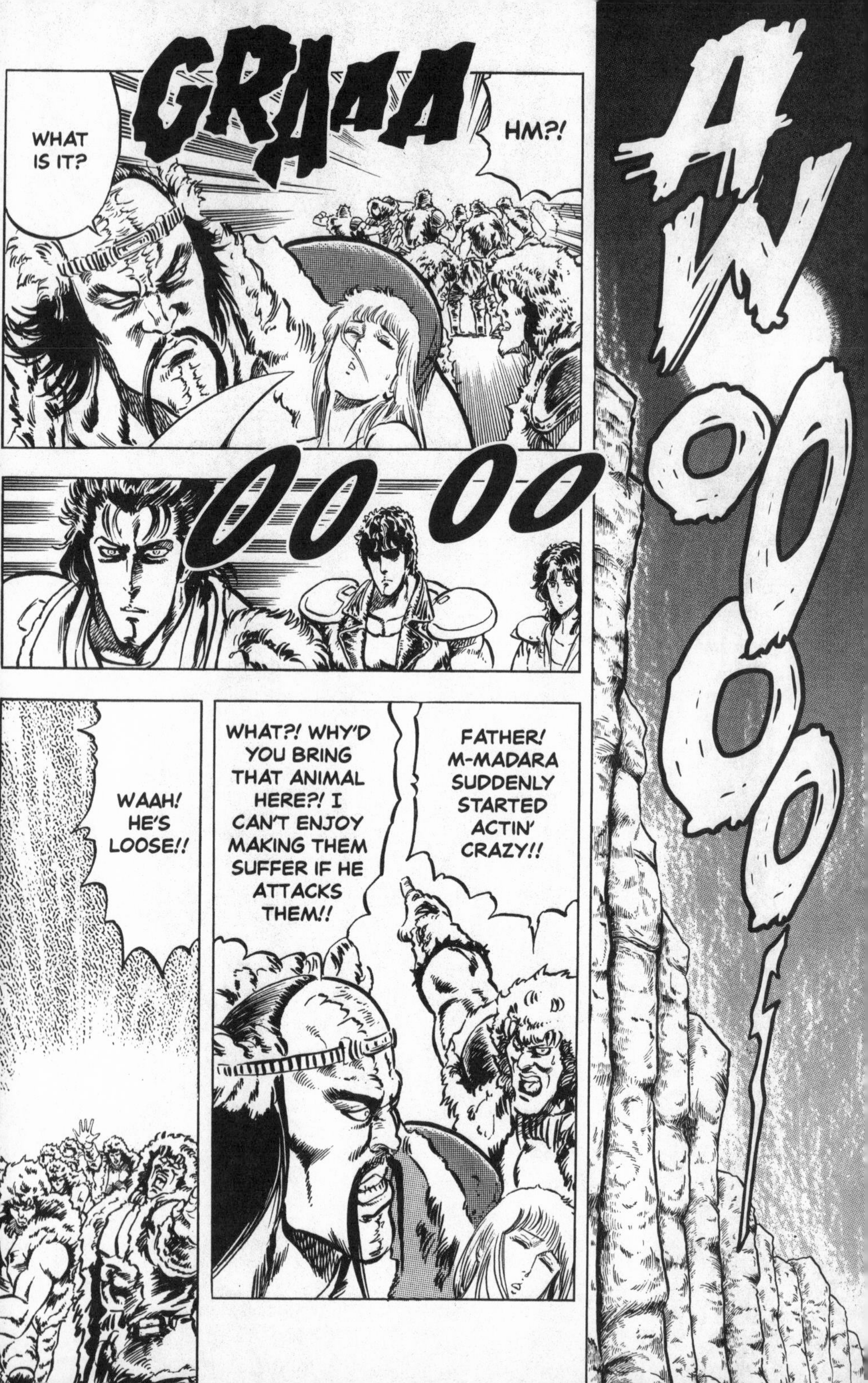
GRAAA
HM?!
WHAT IS IT?
AWOOOO
OO OO
FATHER! M-MADARA SUDDENLY STARTED ACTIN' CRAZY!!
WHAT?! WHY'D YOU BRING THAT ANIMAL HERE?! I CAN'T ENJOY MAKING THEM SUFFER IF HE ATTACKS THEM!!
WAAH! HE'S LOOSE!!

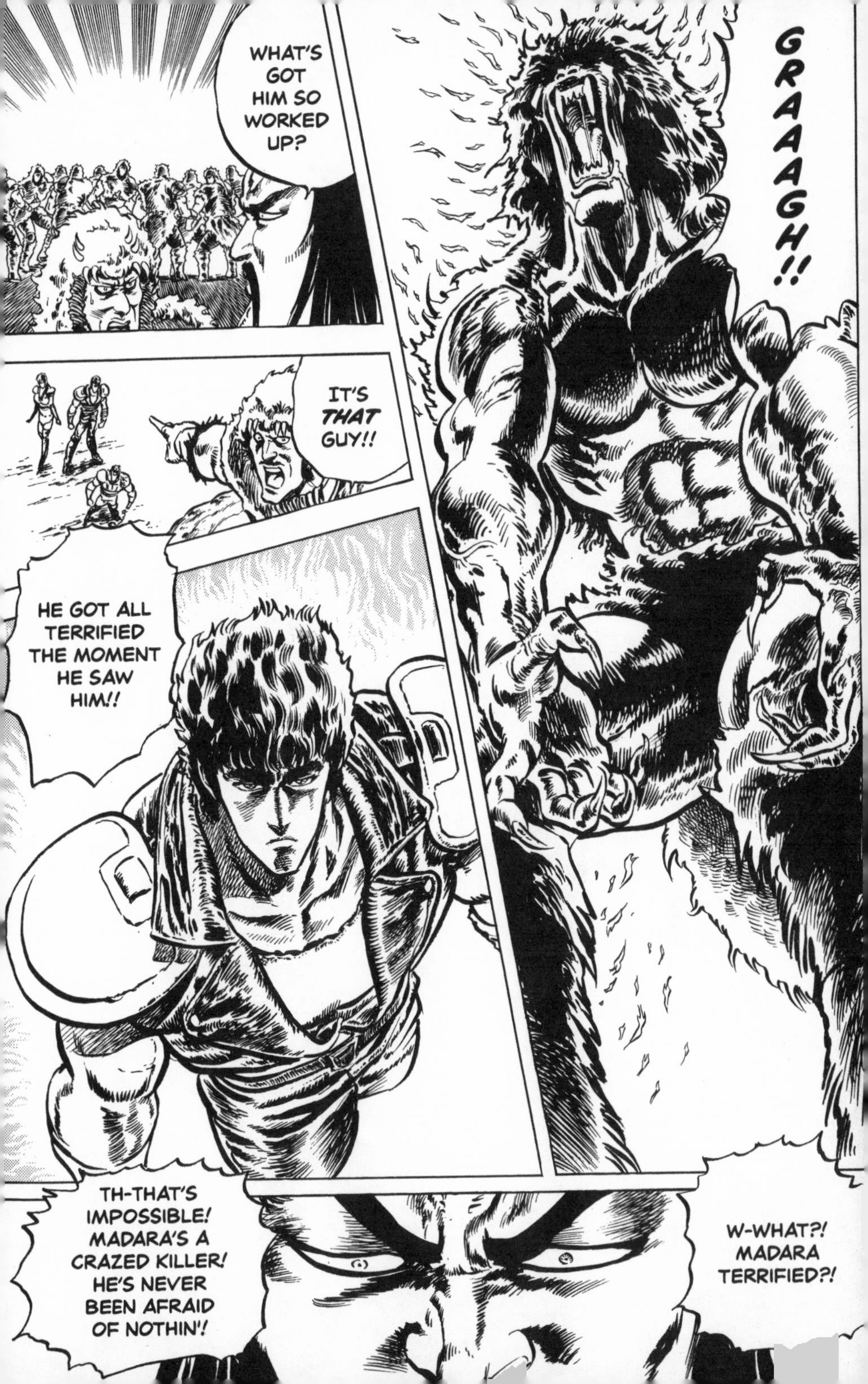
GRAAAAGH!!
WHAT'S GOT HIM SO WORKED UP?
IT'S *THAT* GUY!!
HE GOT ALL TERRIFIED THE MOMENT HE SAW HIM!!
W-WHAT?! MADARA TERRIFIED?!
TH-THAT'S IMPOSSIBLE! MADARA'S A CRAZED KILLER! HE'S NEVER BEEN AFRAID OF NOTHIN'!

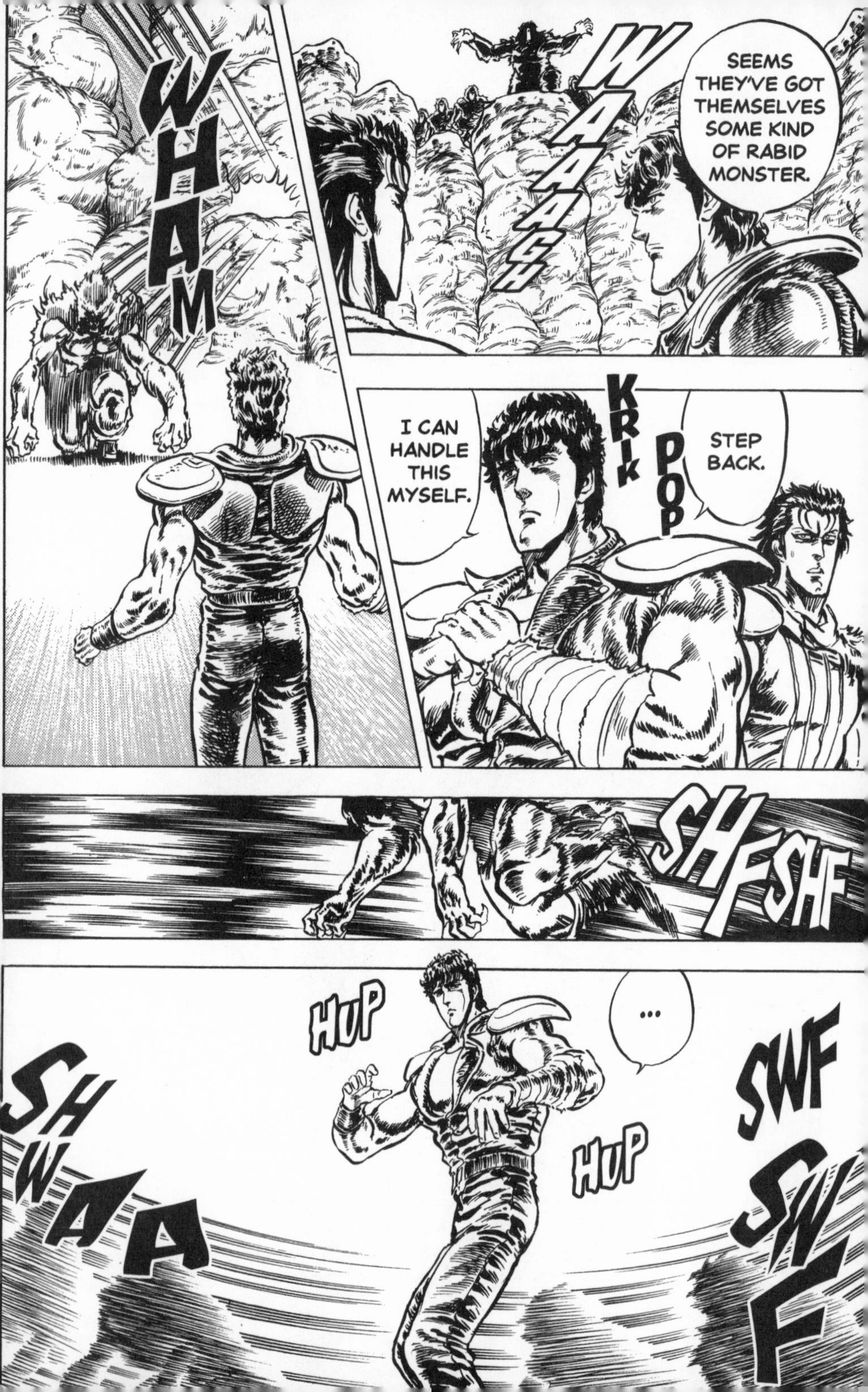
SEEMS THEY'VE GOT THEMSELVES SOME KIND OF RABID MONSTER.
WAAAAGH
STEP BACK.
KRIK
POP
I CAN HANDLE THIS MYSELF.
WHAM
SHFSHF
SWF
SWF
...
HUP
HUP
SHWAA

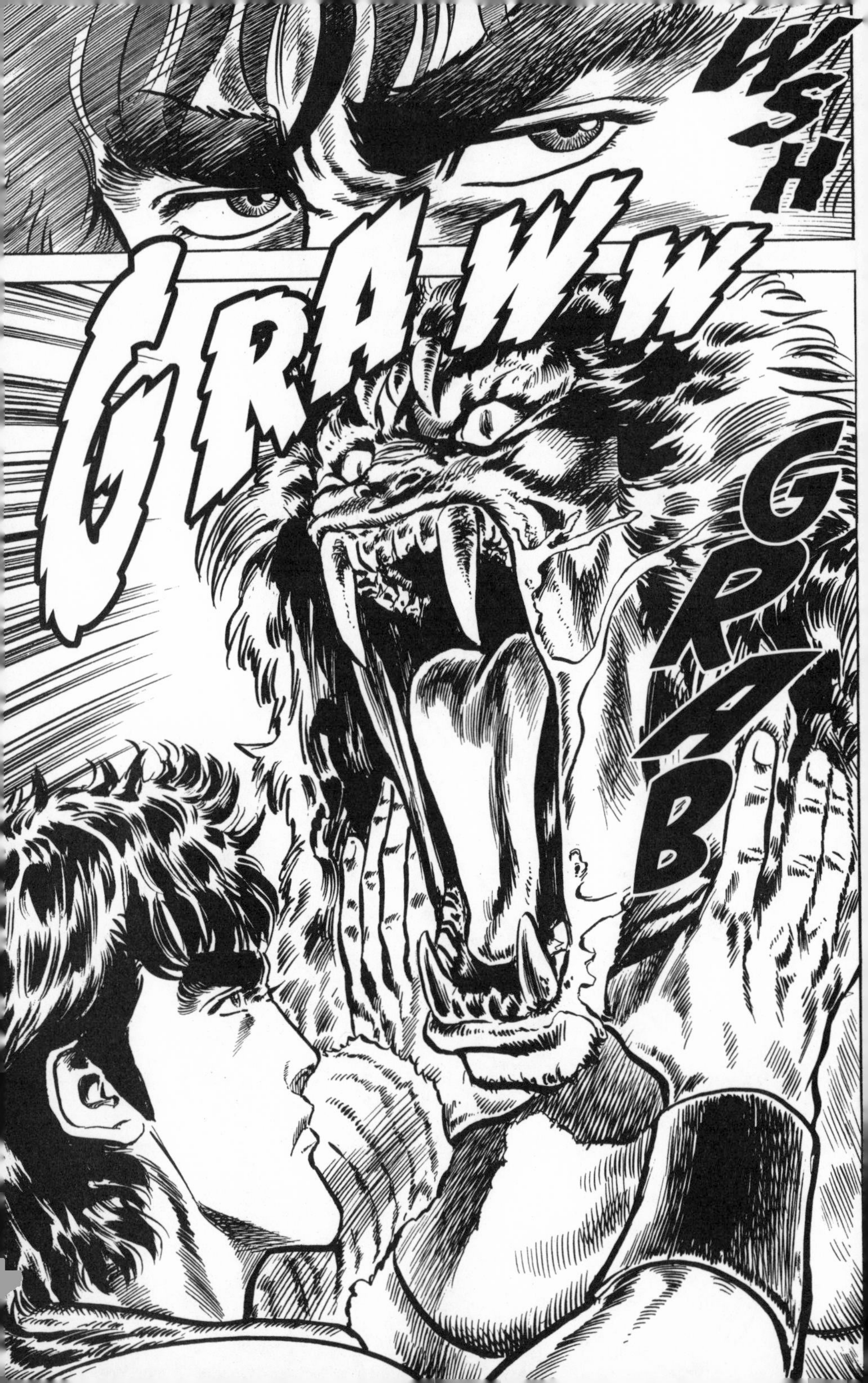
WSH
GRAWW
GRAB

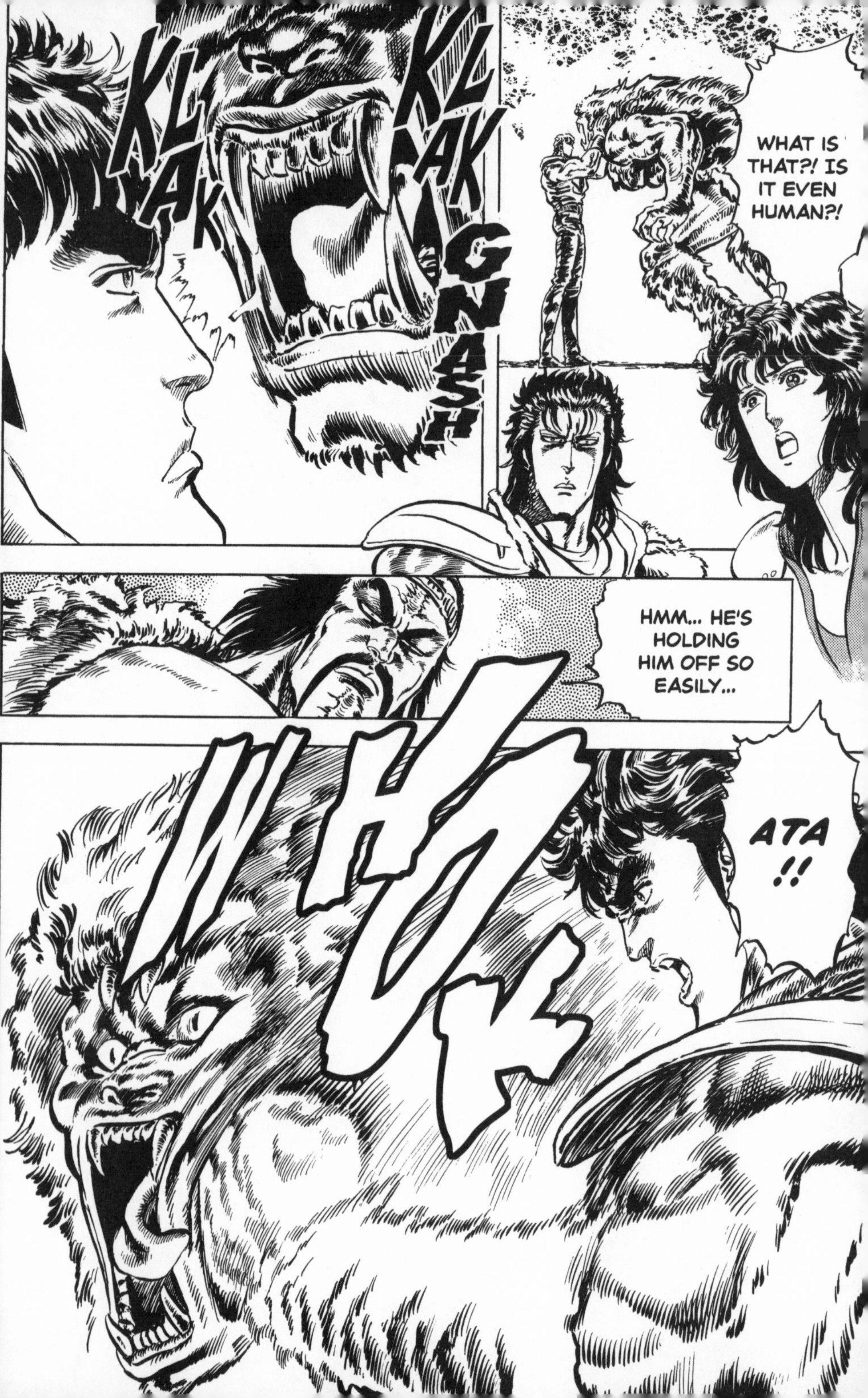
WHAT IS THAT?! IS IT EVEN HUMAN?!
KLAK KLAK
KLAK KLAK
GNASH
HMM... HE'S HOLDING HIM OFF SO EASILY...
ATA !!
WHUK

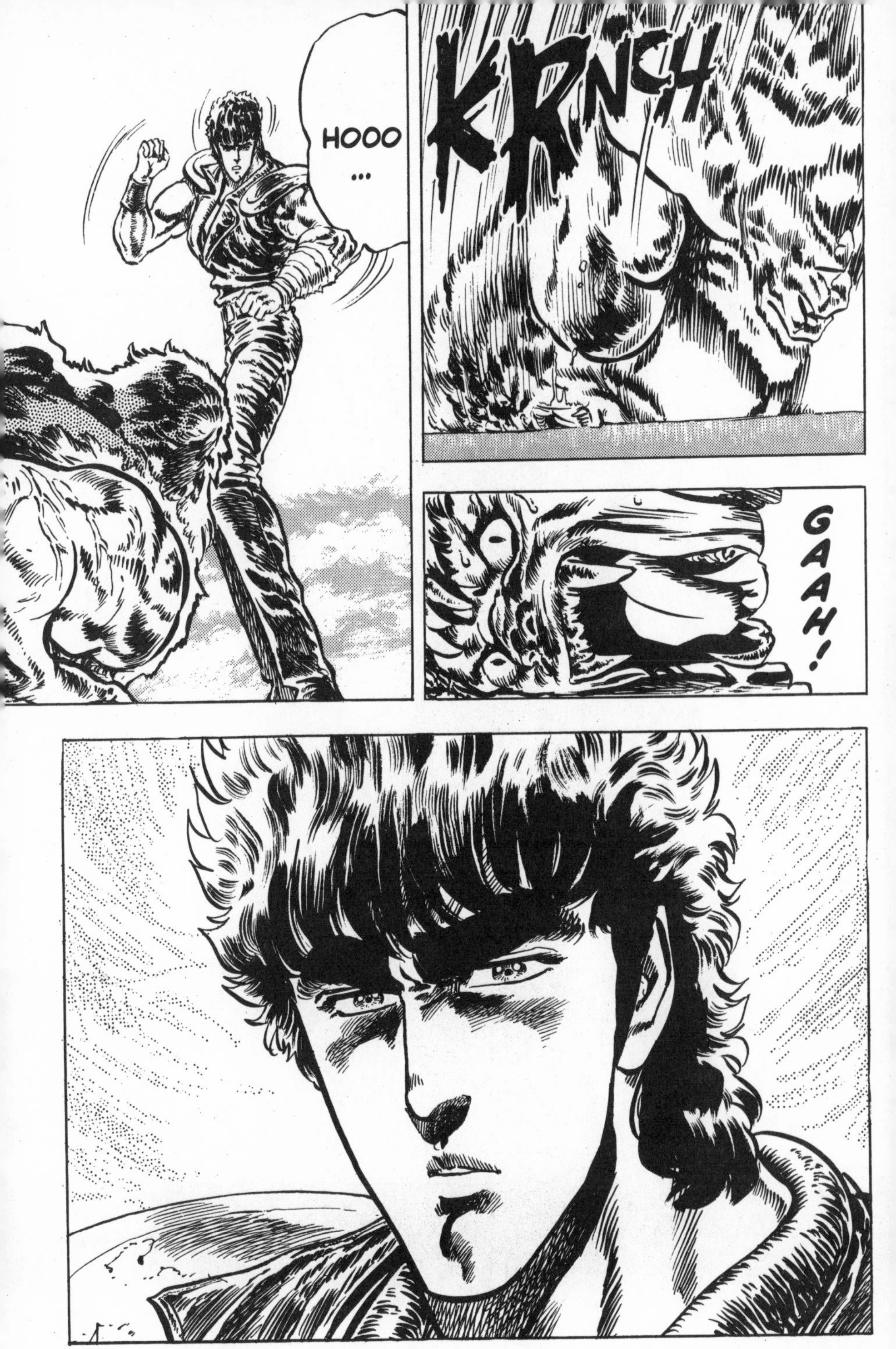
KRNCH
GAAH!
HOOO
...

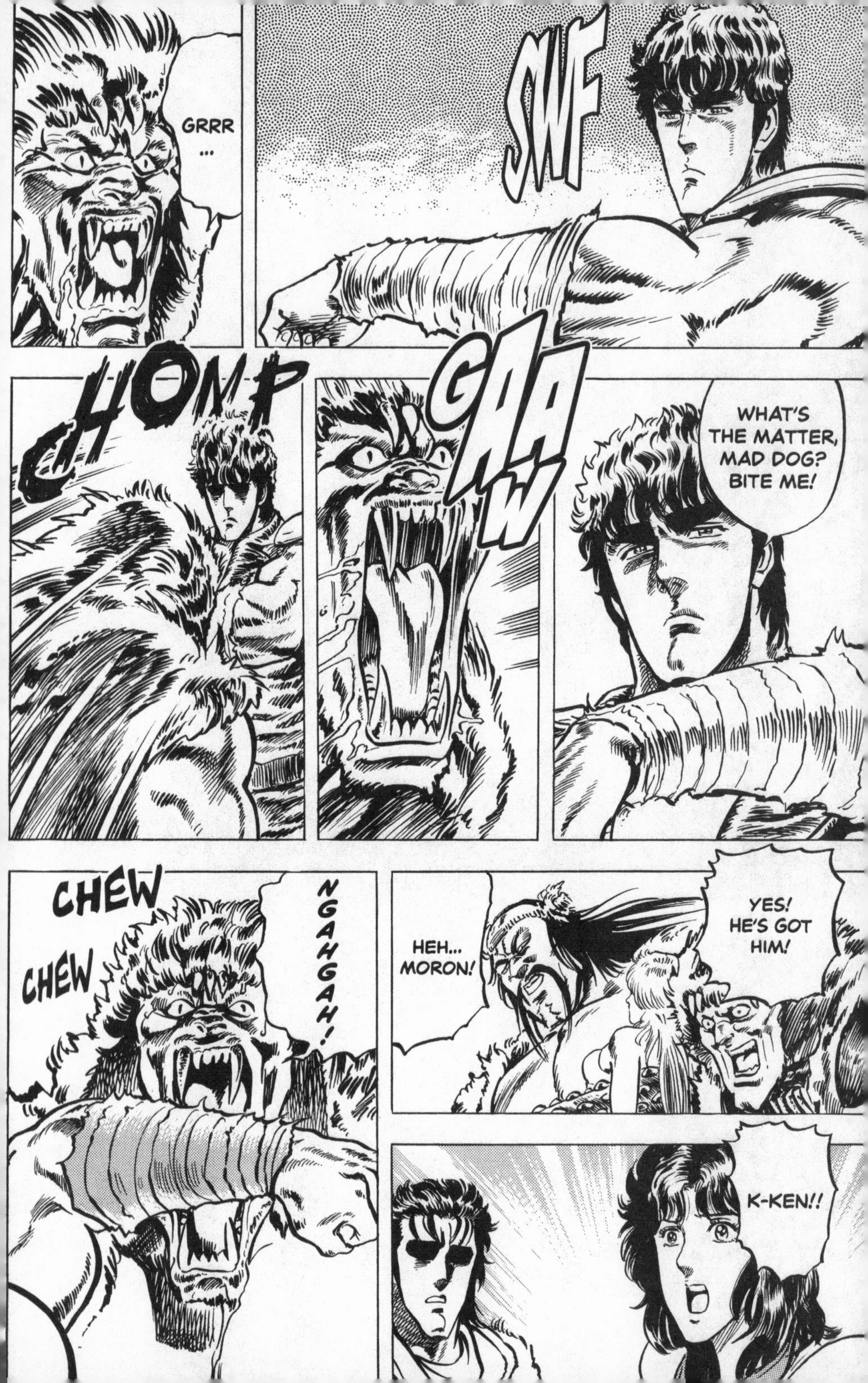
SWF
GRRR ...
WHAT'S THE MATTER, MAD DOG? BITE ME!
GAAAW
CHOMP
YES! HE'S GOT HIM!
HEH... MORON!
K-KEN!!
NGAHGAH!
CHEW
CHEW

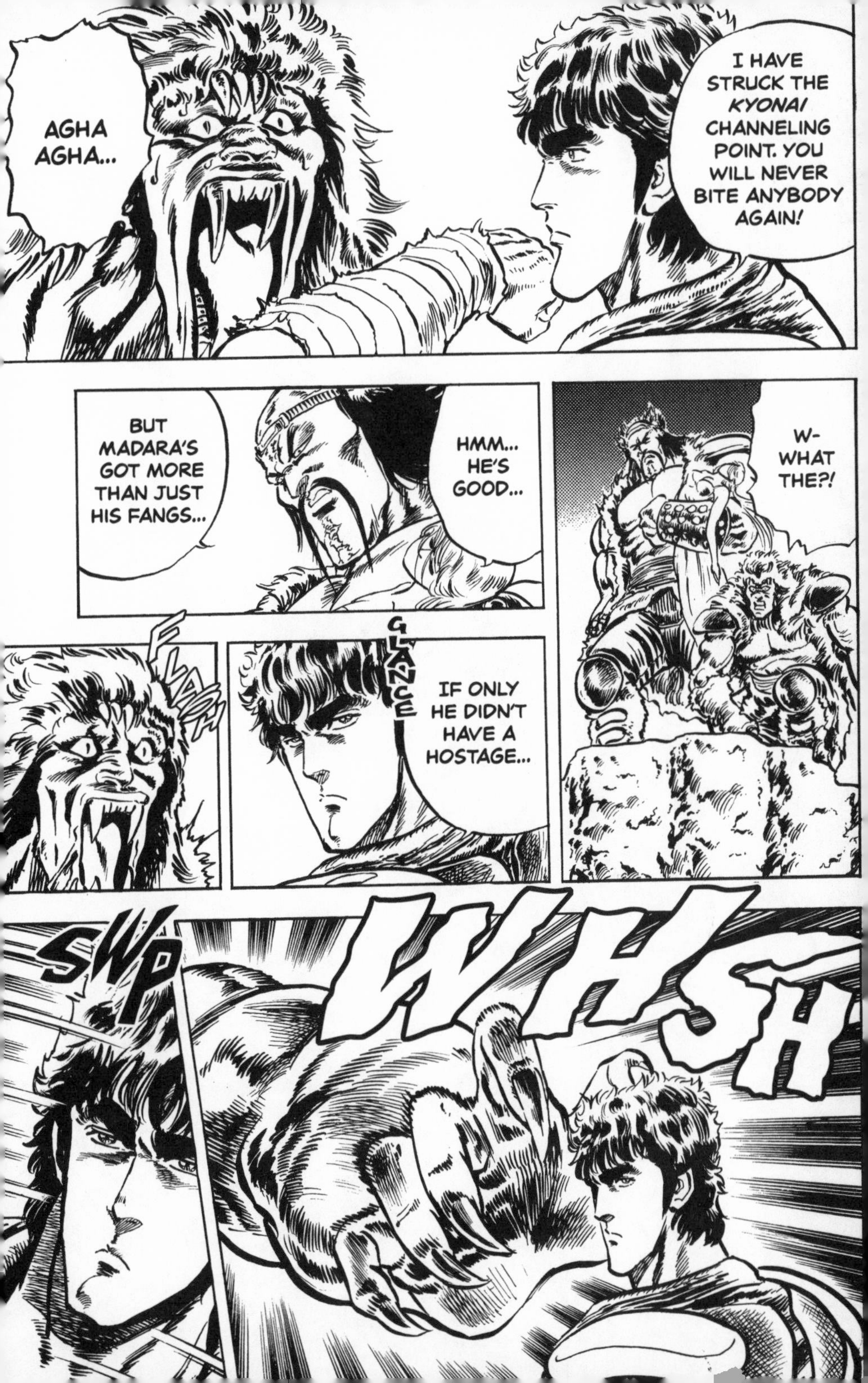
I HAVE STRUCK THE *KYONAI* CHANNELING POINT. YOU WILL NEVER BITE ANYBODY AGAIN!
AGHA AGHA...
W- WHAT THE?!
HMM... HE'S GOOD...
BUT MADARA'S GOT MORE THAN JUST HIS FANGS...
GLANCE
IF ONLY HE DIDN'T HAVE A HOSTAGE...
FLASH
WHSH
SWP

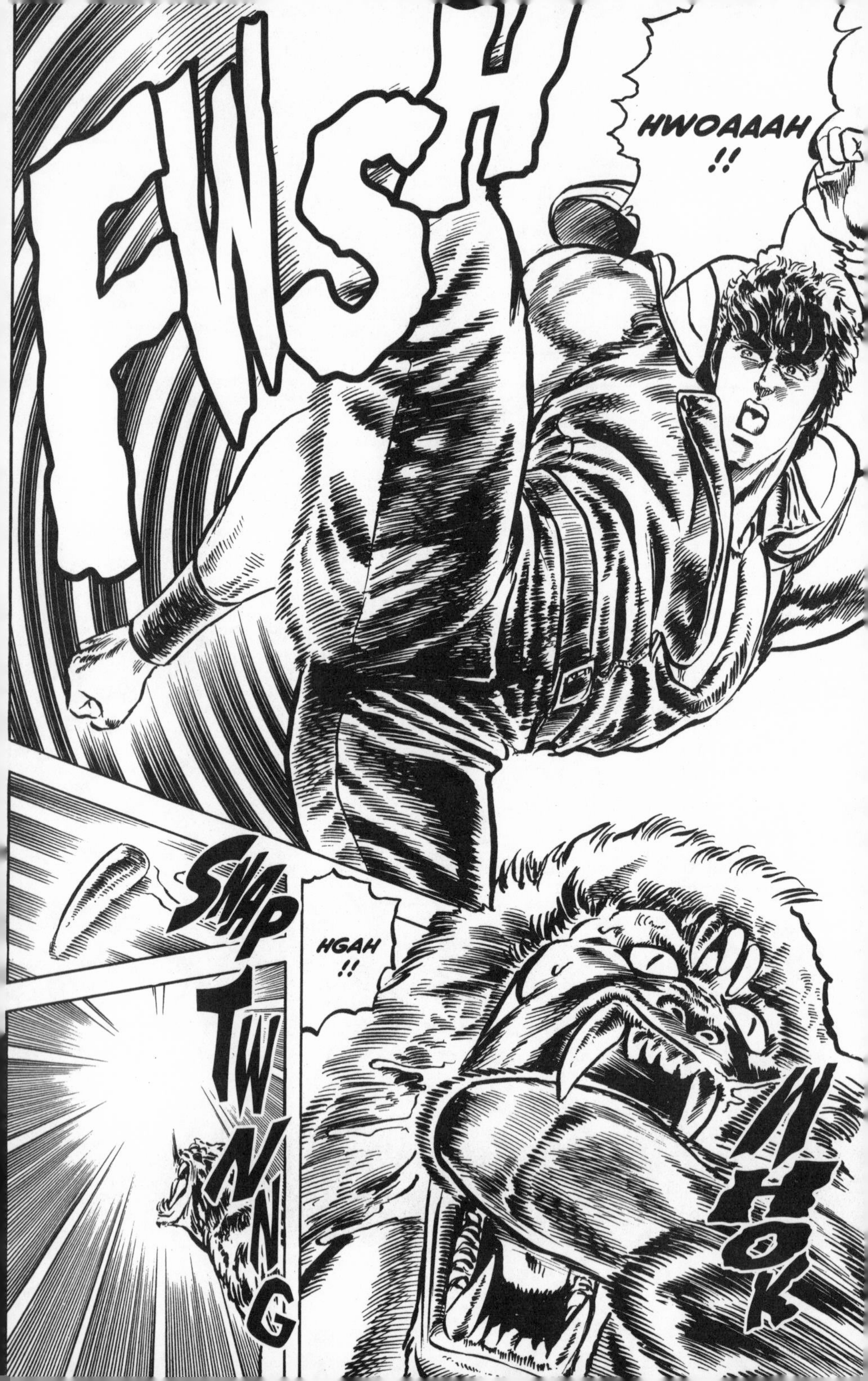
HWOAAAH !!
FWSH
HGAH !!
WHOK
SNAP
TWNNG

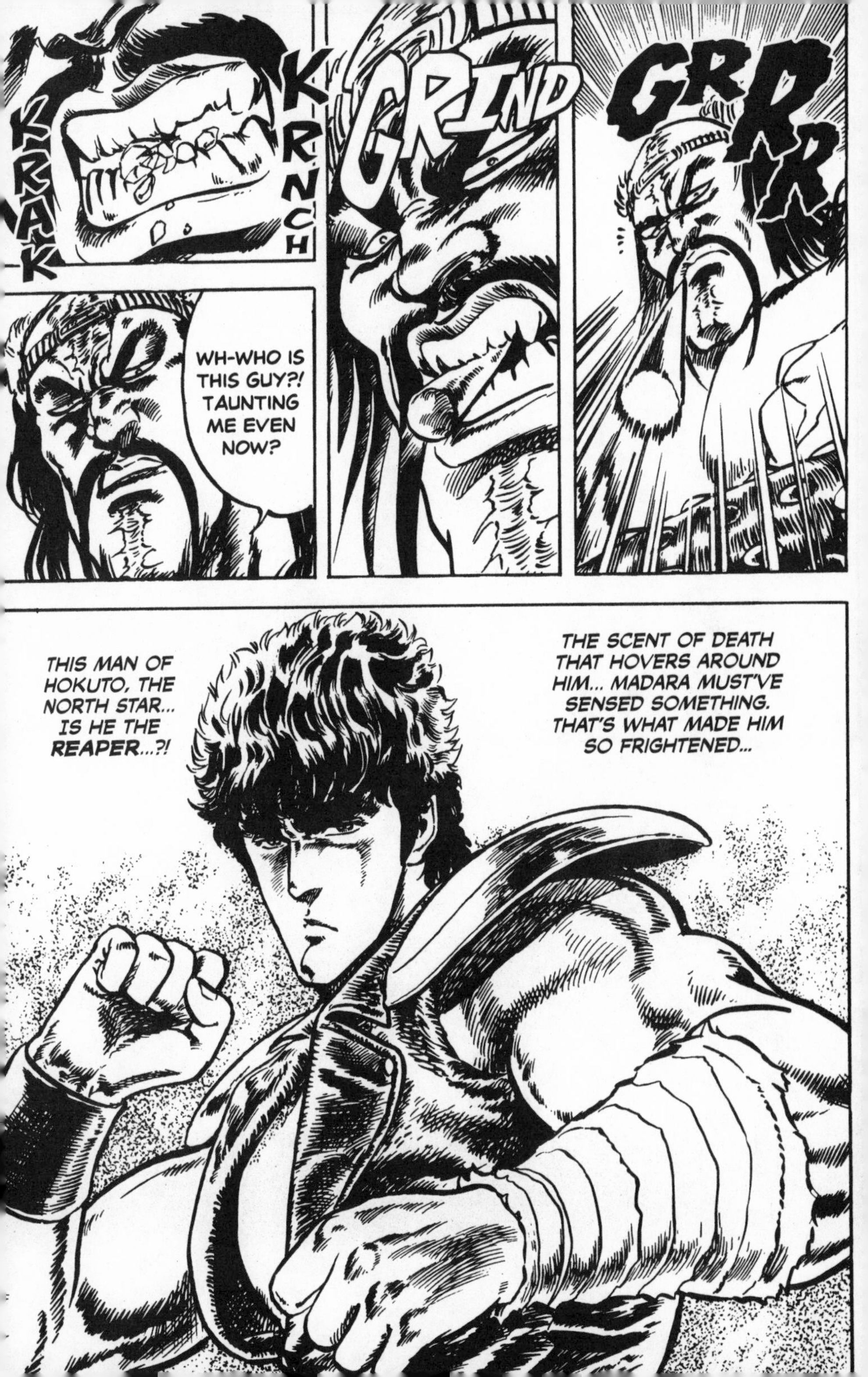
GRRR
GRIND
KRNCH
KRAK
WH-WHO IS THIS GUY?! TAUNTING ME EVEN NOW?
THE SCENT OF DEATH THAT HOVERS AROUND HIM... MADARA MUST'VE SENSED SOMETHING. THAT'S WHAT MADE HIM SO FRIGHTENED...
THIS MAN OF HOKUTO, THE NORTH STAR... IS HE THE **REAPER**...?!

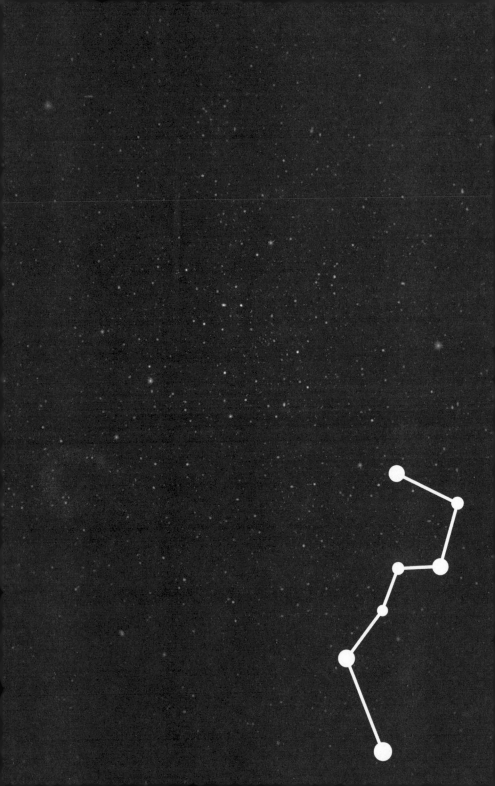

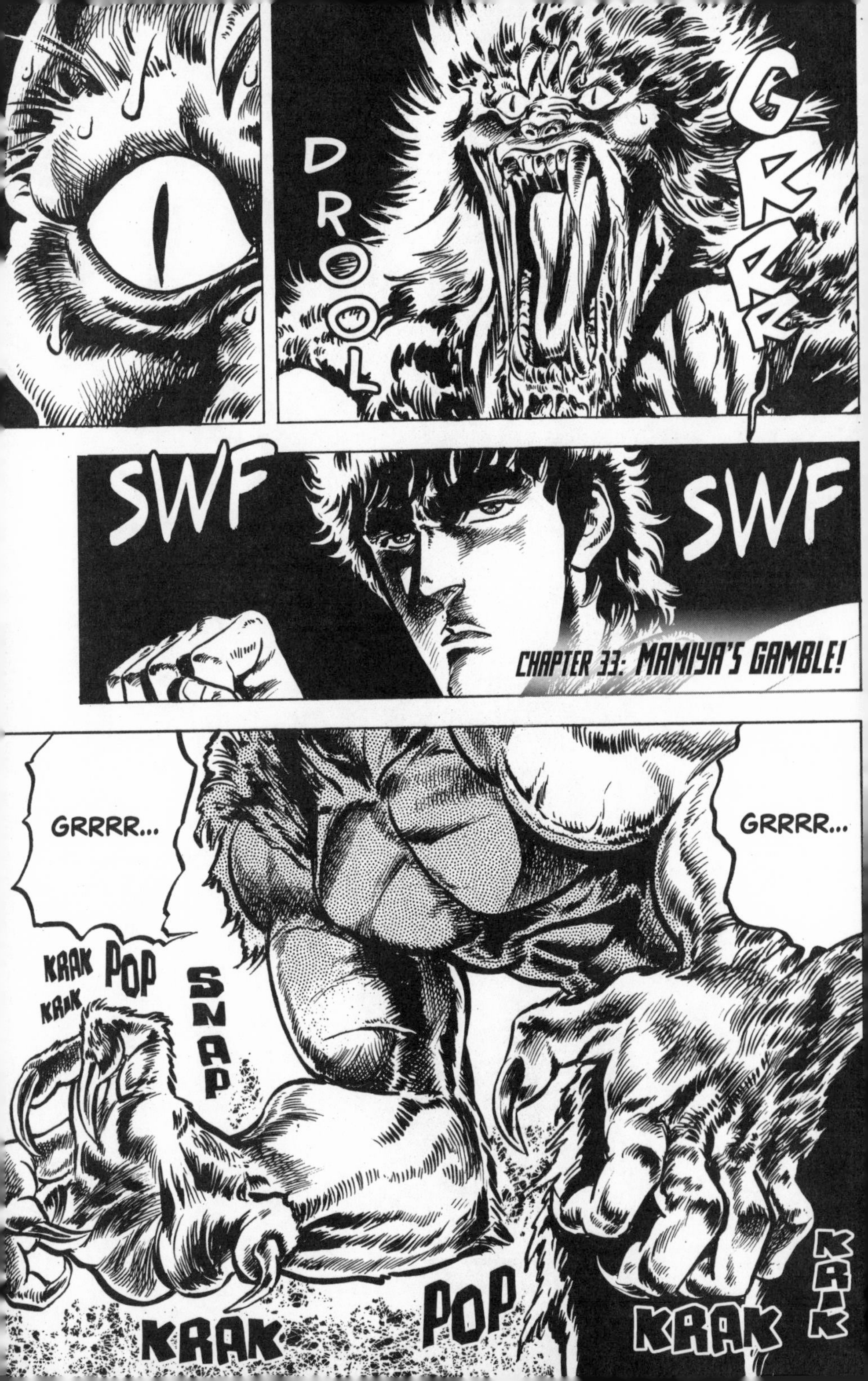
GRRR
DROOL
SWF
SWF
CHAPTER 33: MAMIYA'S GAMBLE!
GRRRR...
GRRRR...
KRAK
KRAK
KRAK
POP
KRAK
SNAP
POP
KRAK
KRAK

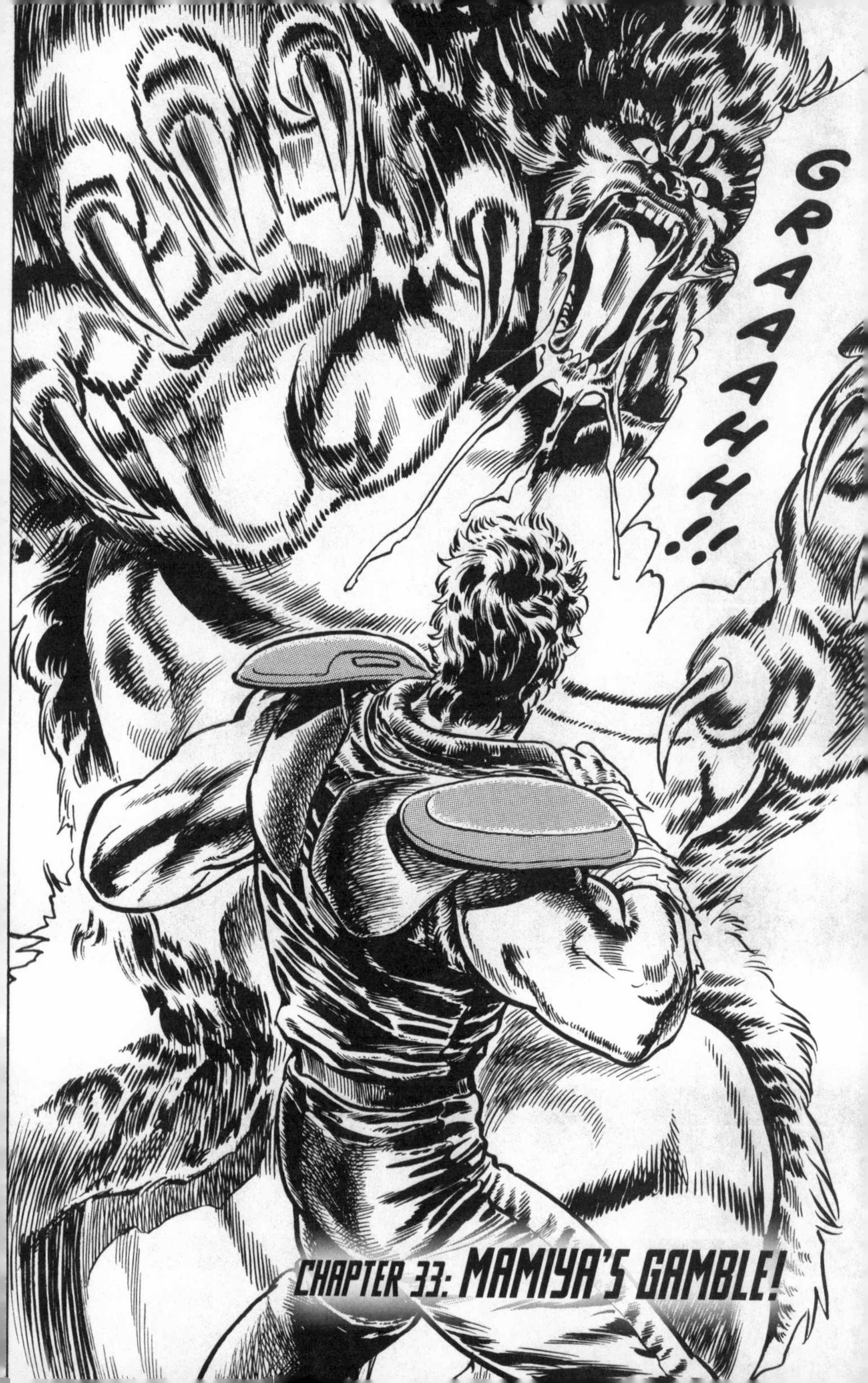
GRAAAAHHH!!!
CHAPTER 33: MAMIYA'S GAMBLE!

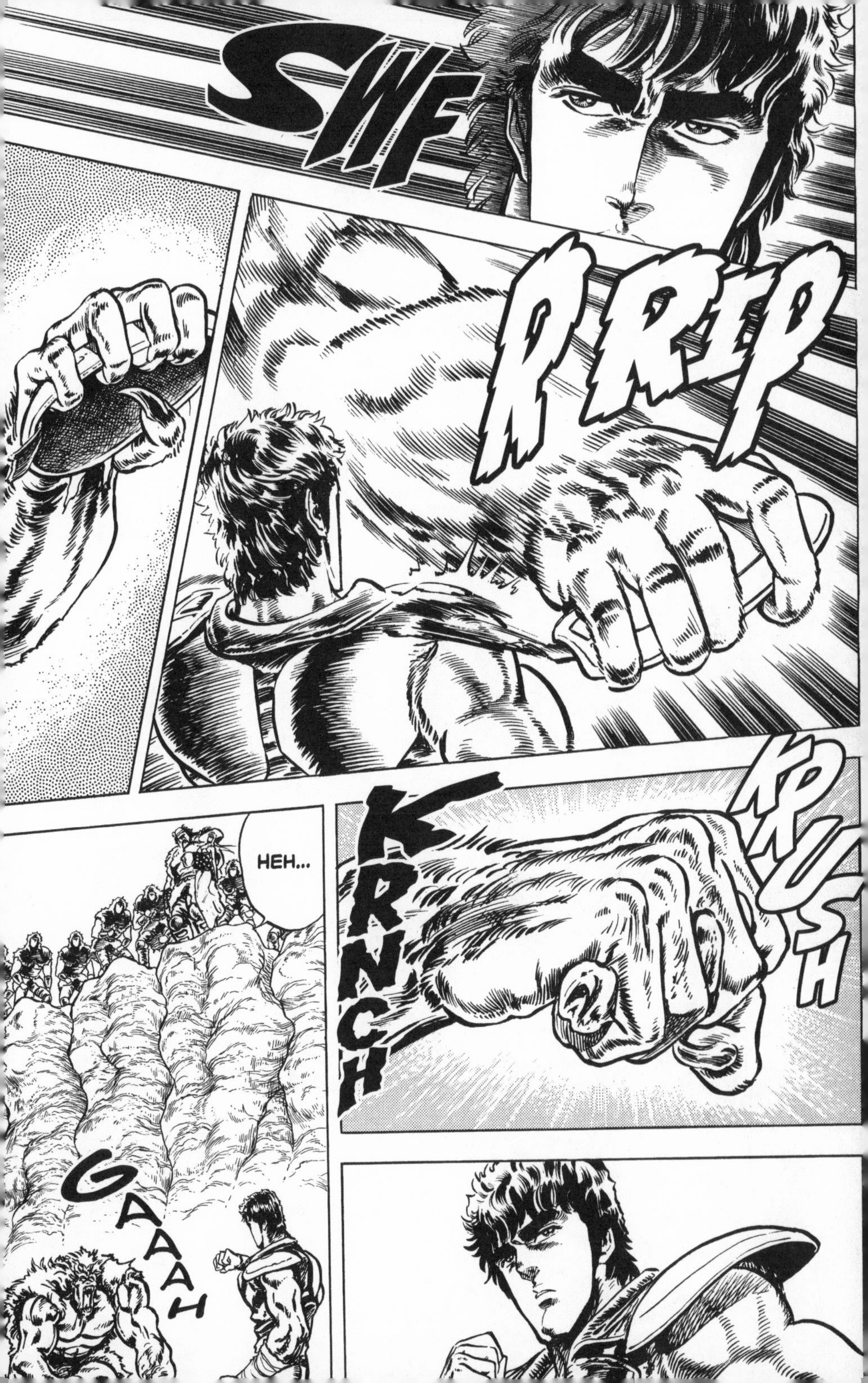
SWF
RRIP
KRUSH
KRNCH
HEH...
GAAAH

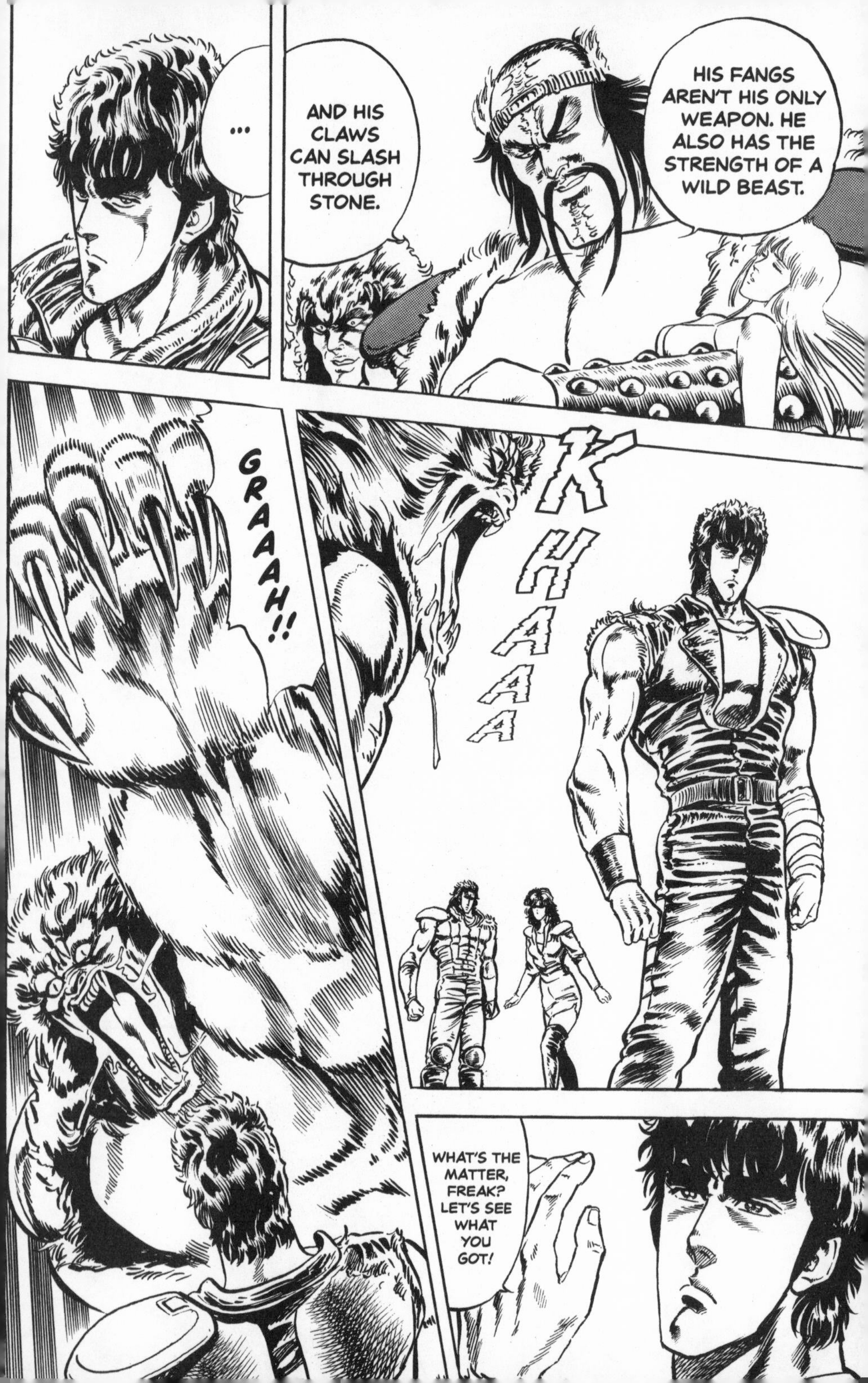
HIS FANGS AREN'T HIS ONLY WEAPON. HE ALSO HAS THE STRENGTH OF A WILD BEAST.
AND HIS CLAWS CAN SLASH THROUGH STONE.
...
KHAAAA
WHAT'S THE MATTER, FREAK? LET'S SEE WHAT YOU GOT!
GRAAAH!!

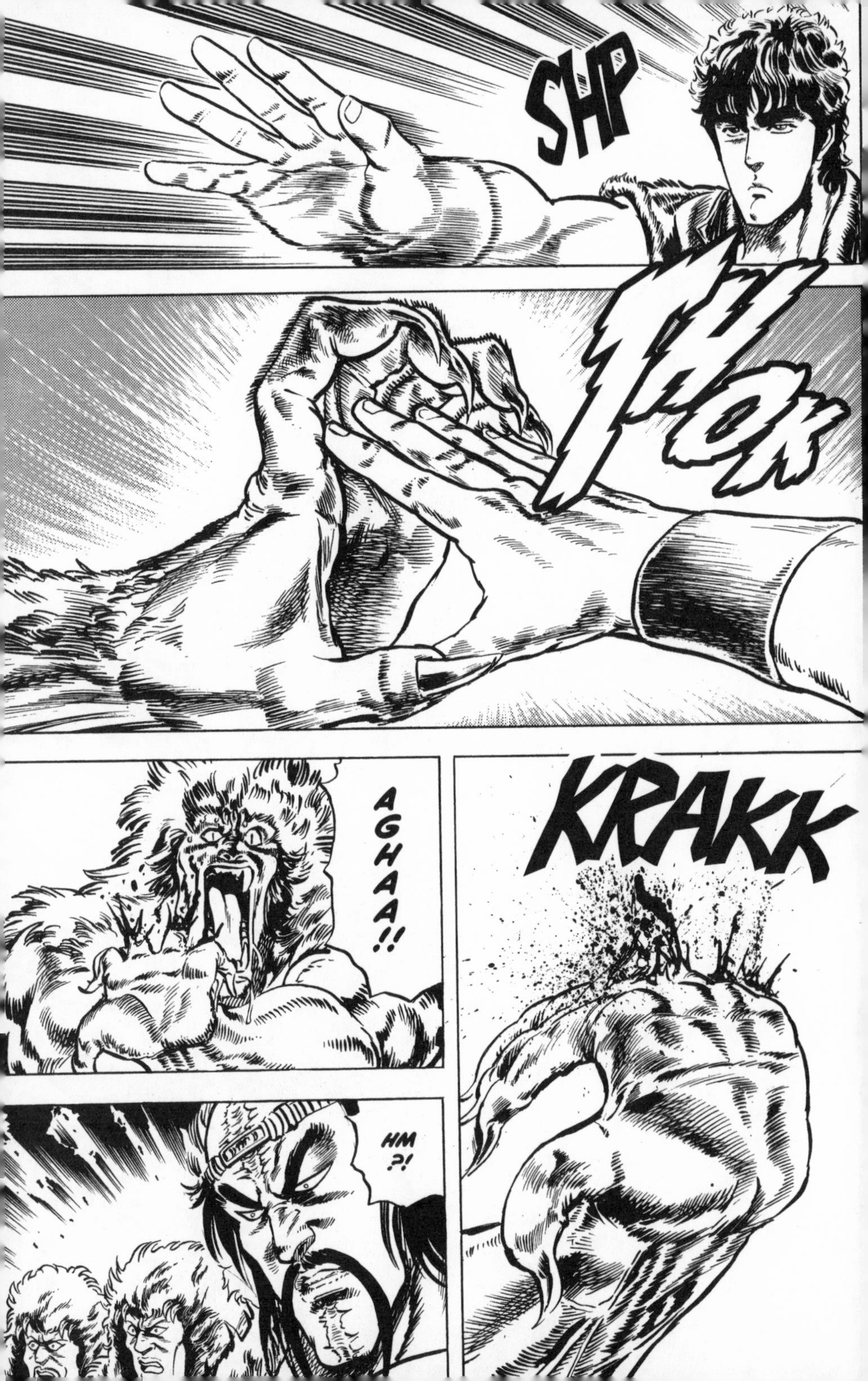
SHP
THOK
KRAKK
AGHAAA!!
HM ?!

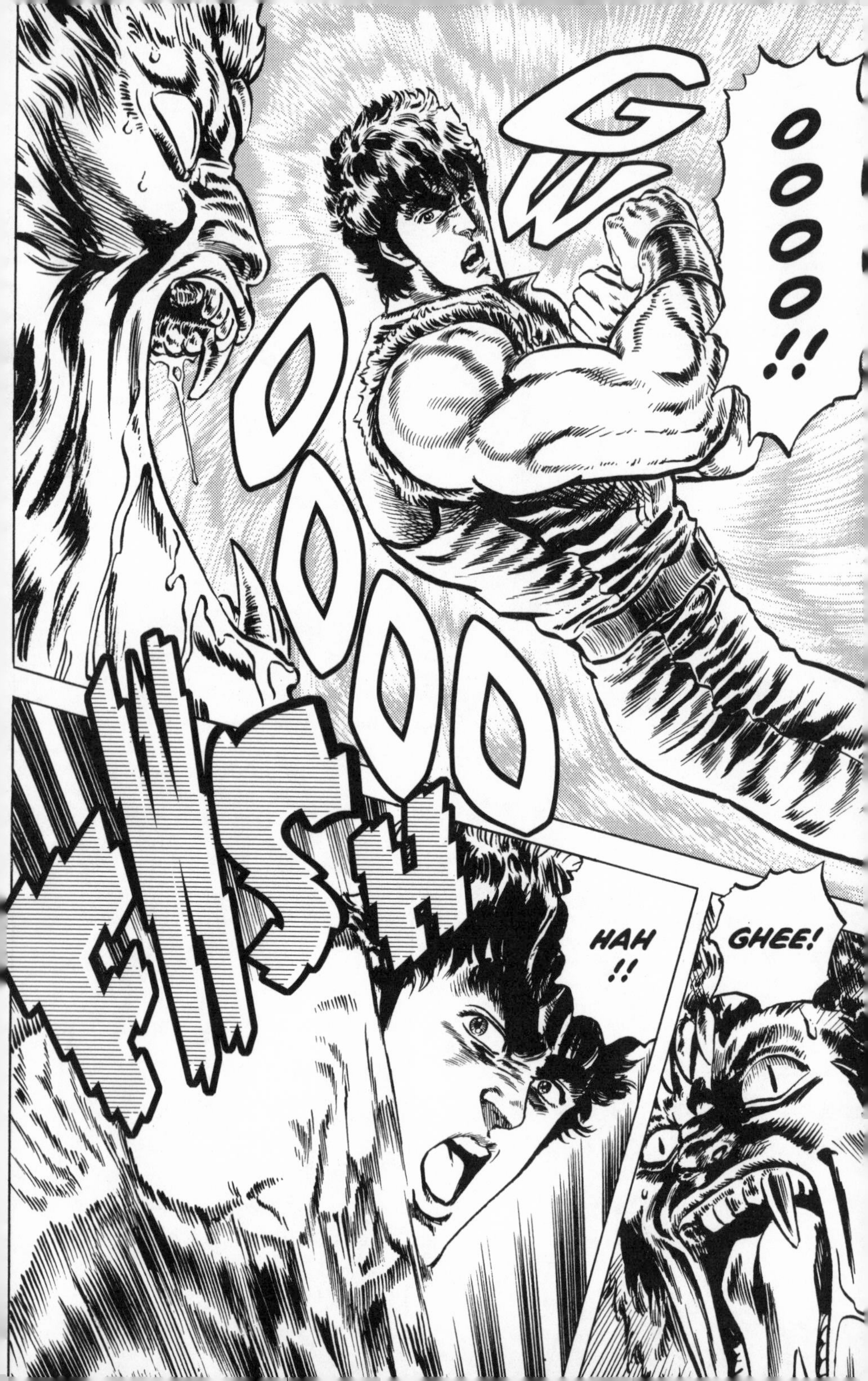
OOOOO!!
GHEE!
HAH !!

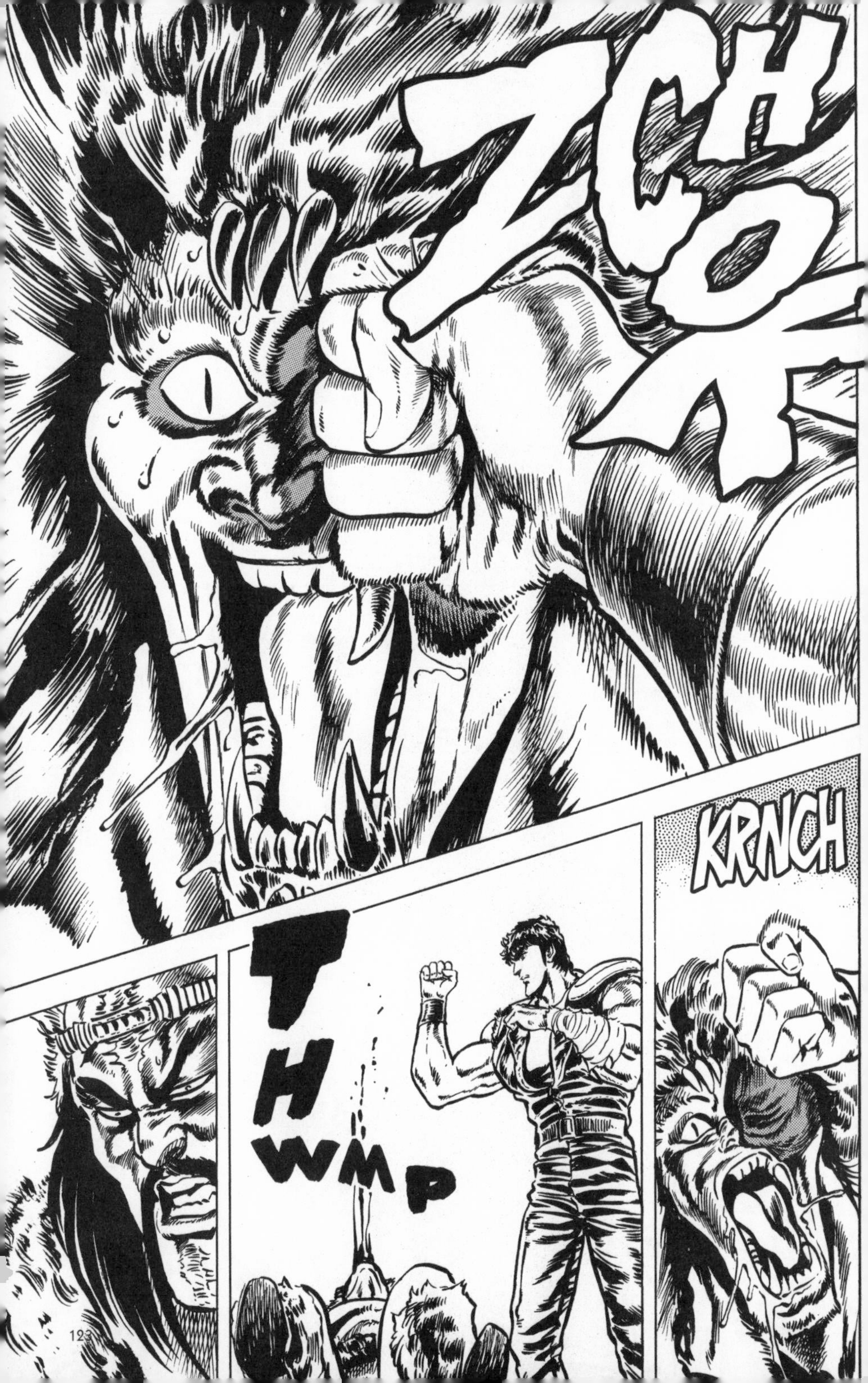
ZCHOK
KRNCH
THWMP

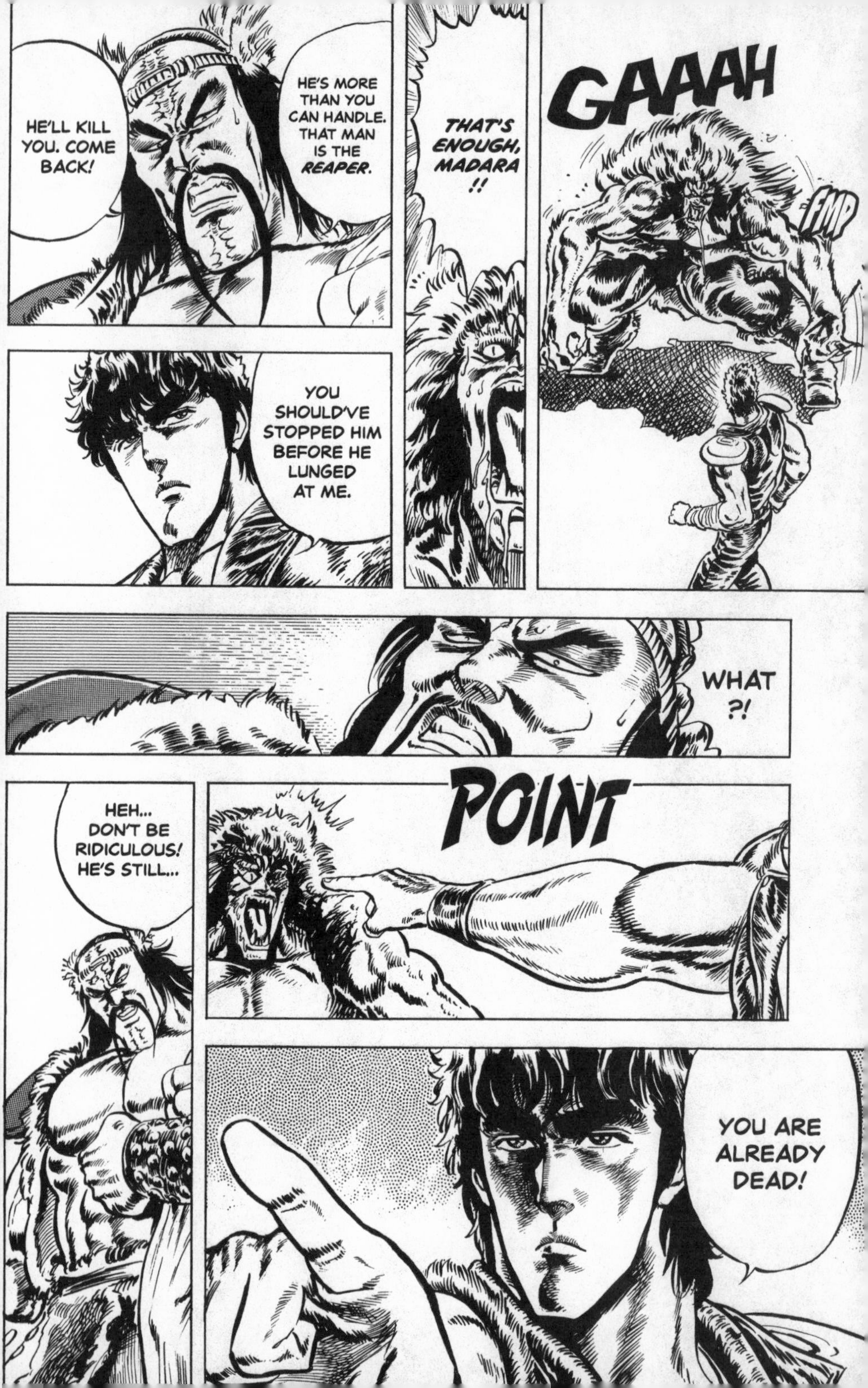
GAAAH
FMP
THAT'S ENOUGH, MADARA!!
HE'S MORE THAN YOU CAN HANDLE. THAT MAN IS THE REAPER.
HE'LL KILL YOU. COME BACK!
YOU SHOULD'VE STOPPED HIM BEFORE HE LUNGED AT ME.
WHAT?!
POINT
HEH... DON'T BE RIDICULOUS! HE'S STILL...
YOU ARE ALREADY DEAD!

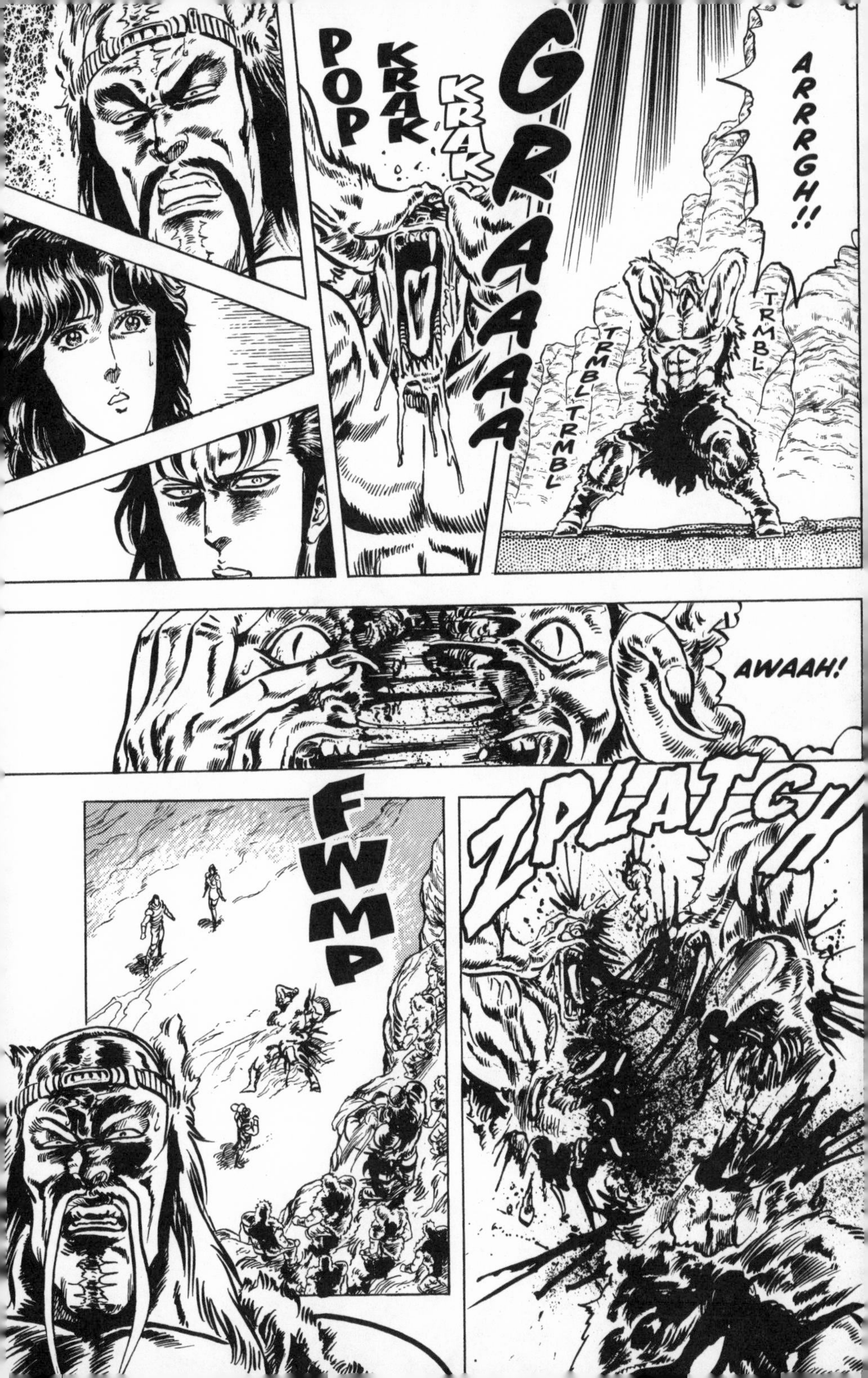
ARRRGH!!
TRMBL
TRMBL TRMBL
GRAAAAAA
KRAK
POP KRAK
AWAAH!
ZPLATCH
FWMP

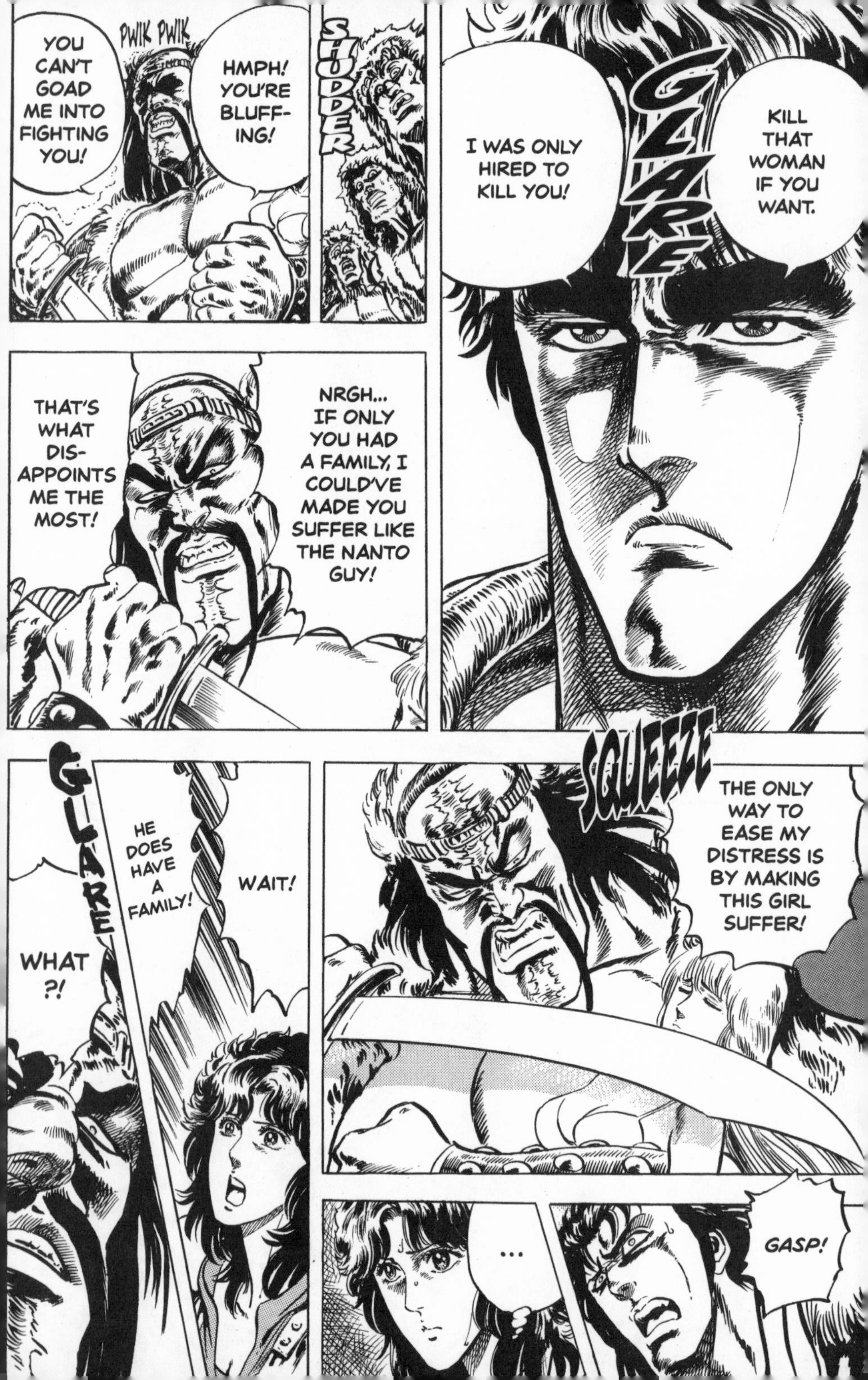
GLARE
KILL THAT WOMAN IF YOU WANT.
I WAS ONLY HIRED TO KILL YOU!
SHUDDER
PWIK PWIK
HMPH! YOU'RE BLUFF-ING!
YOU CAN'T GOAD ME INTO FIGHTING YOU!
NRGH... IF ONLY YOU HAD A FAMILY, I COULD'VE MADE YOU SUFFER LIKE THE NANTO GUY!
THAT'S WHAT DIS-APPOINTS ME THE MOST!
SQUEEZE
THE ONLY WAY TO EASE MY DISTRESS IS BY MAKING THIS GIRL SUFFER!
GASP!
...
WAIT!
HE DOES HAVE A FAMILY!
GLARE
WHAT ?!

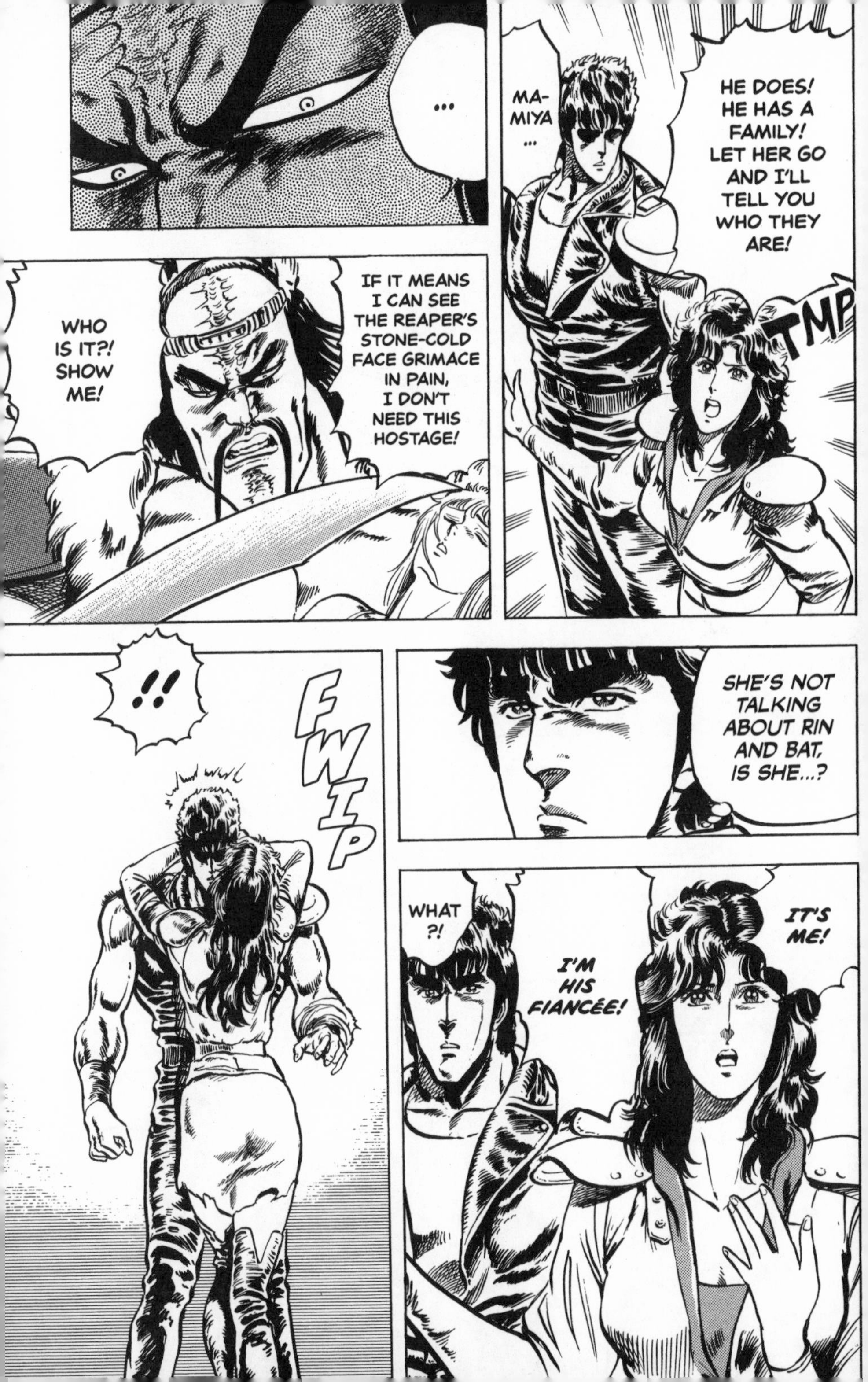
HE DOES! HE HAS A FAMILY! LET HER GO AND I'LL TELL YOU WHO THEY ARE!
TMP
MA-MIYA...
...
IF IT MEANS I CAN SEE THE REAPER'S STONE-COLD FACE GRIMACE IN PAIN, I DON'T NEED THIS HOSTAGE!
WHO IS IT?! SHOW ME!
SHE'S NOT TALKING ABOUT RIN AND BAT, IS SHE...?
IT'S ME!
I'M HIS FIANCÉE!
WHAT?!
FWIP
!!

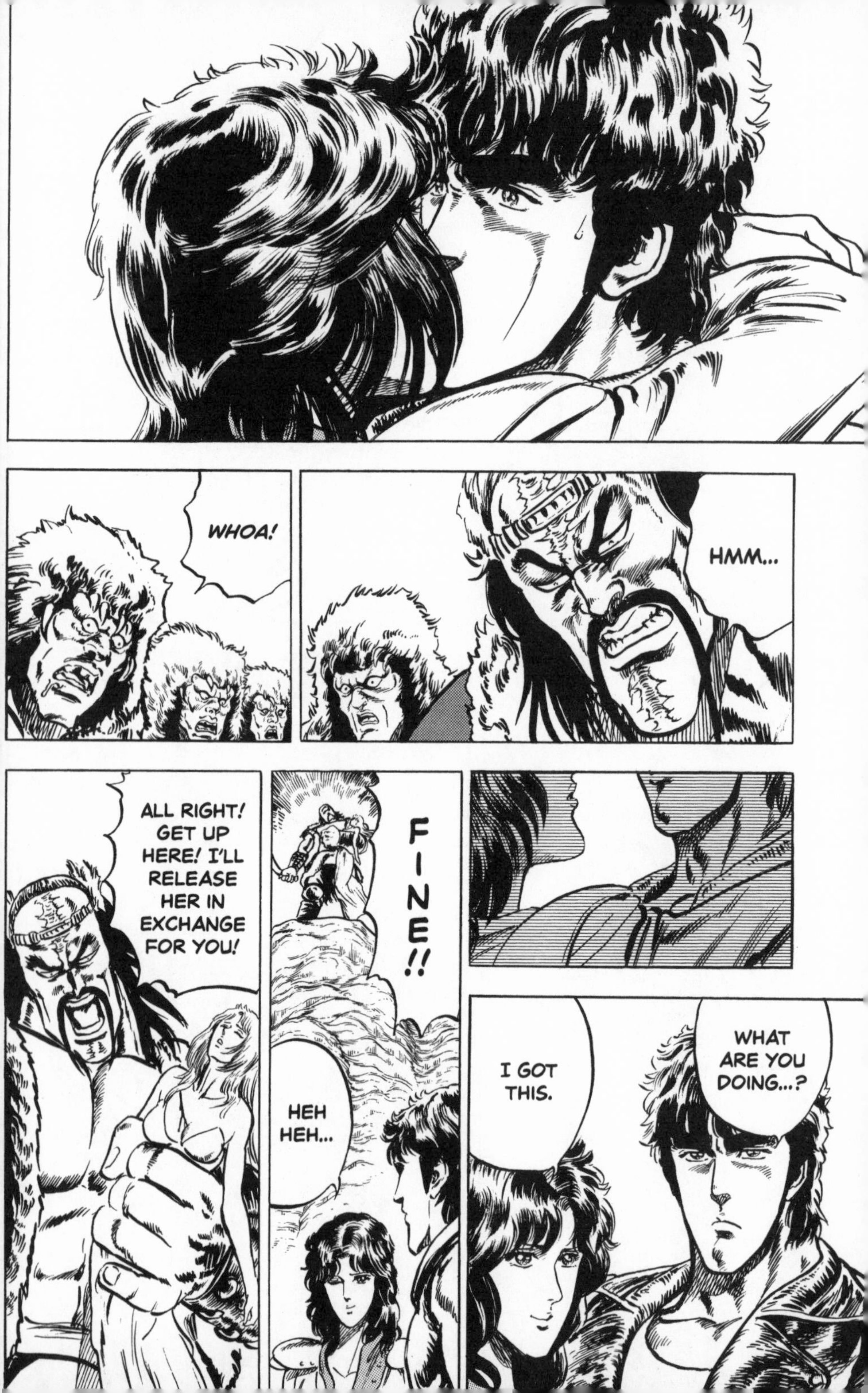
HMM...
WHOA!
WHAT ARE YOU DOING...?
I GOT THIS.
FINE!!
HEH HEH...
ALL RIGHT! GET UP HERE! I'LL RELEASE HER IN EXCHANGE FOR YOU!

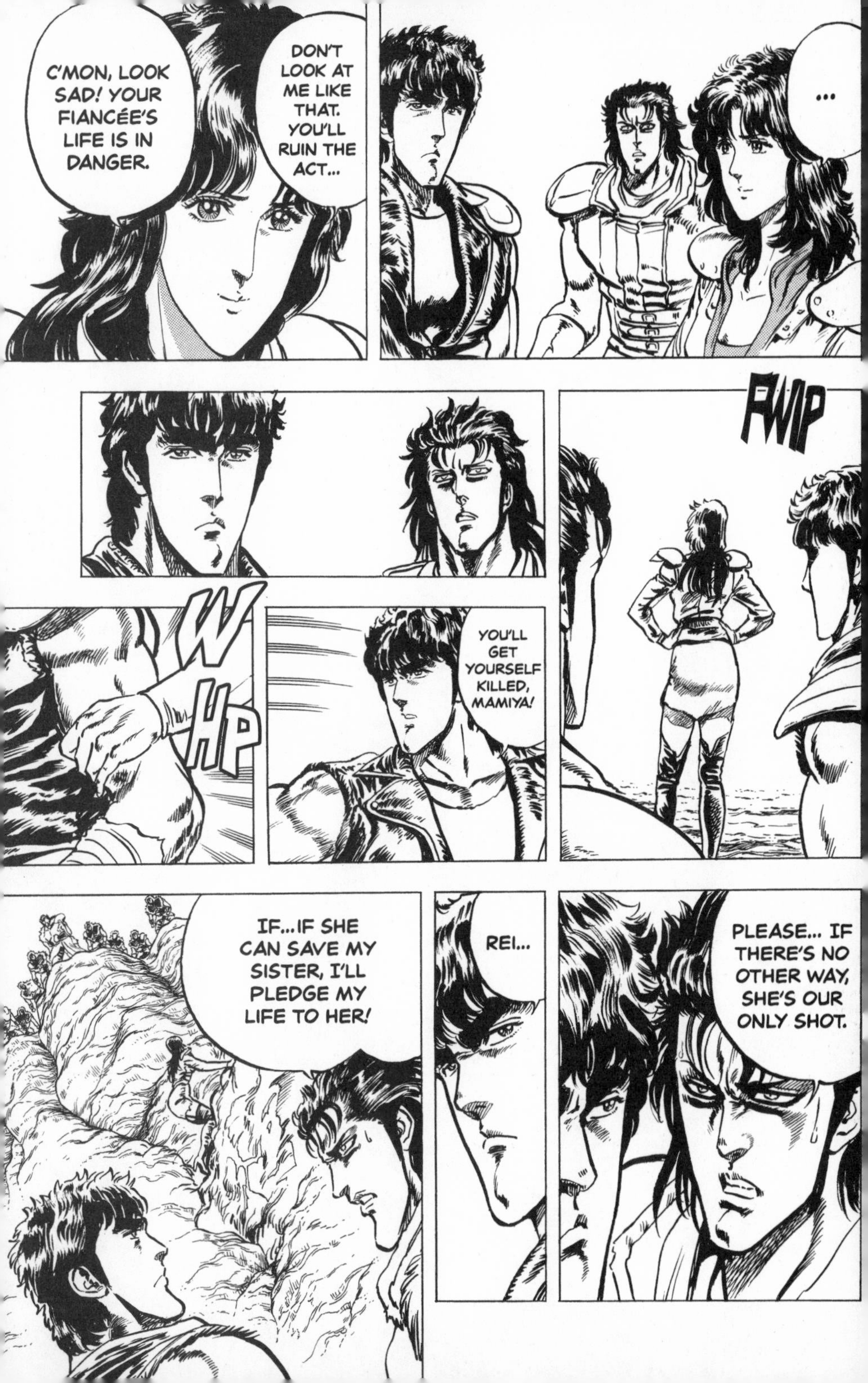
C'MON, LOOK SAD! YOUR FIANCÉE'S LIFE IS IN DANGER.
DON'T LOOK AT ME LIKE THAT. YOU'LL RUIN THE ACT...
...
RWIP
WHIP
YOU'LL GET YOURSELF KILLED, MAMIYA!
IF...IF SHE CAN SAVE MY SISTER, I'LL PLEDGE MY LIFE TO HER!
REI...
PLEASE... IF THERE'S NO OTHER WAY, SHE'S OUR ONLY SHOT.

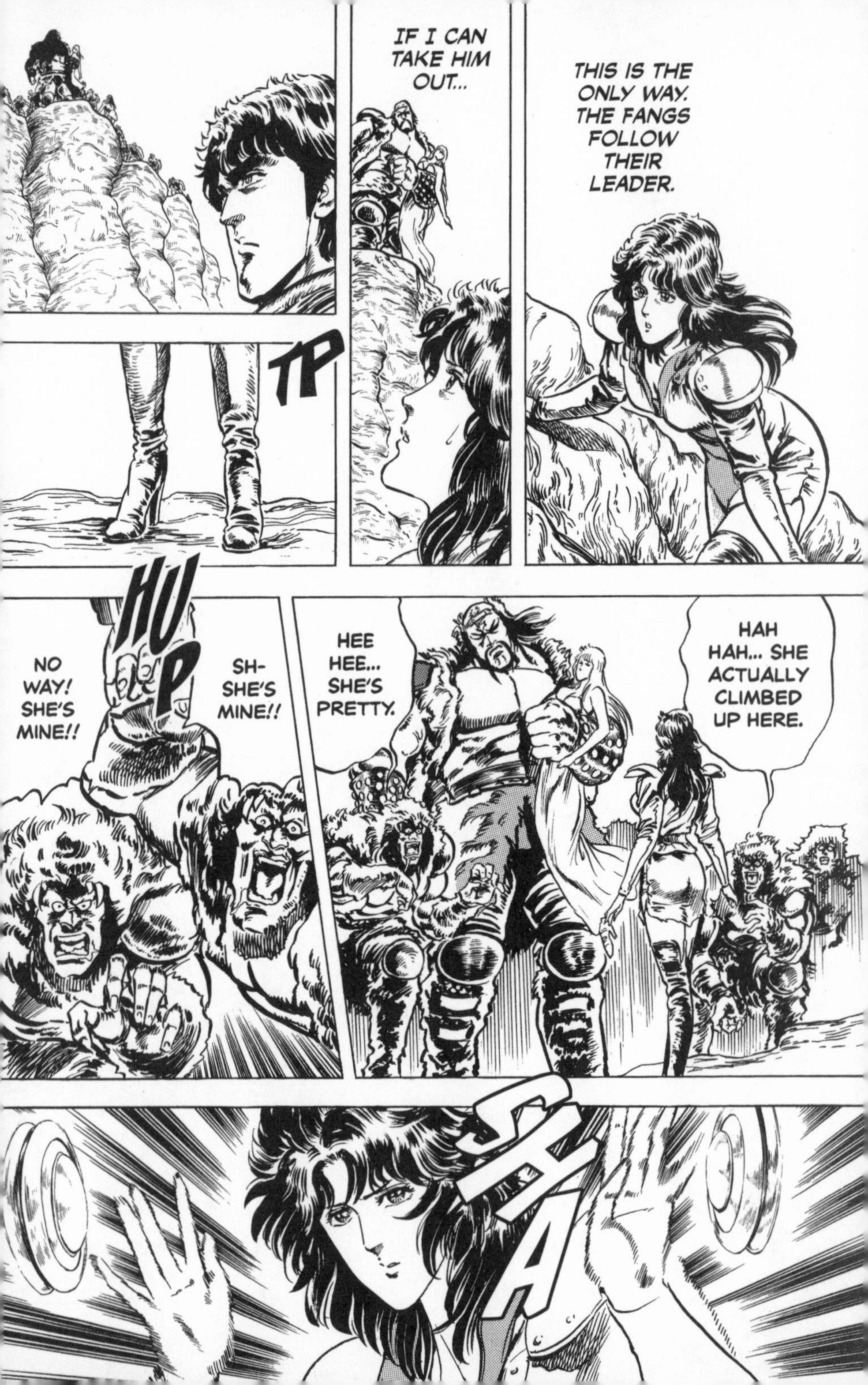
THIS IS THE ONLY WAY. THE FANGS FOLLOW THEIR LEADER.
IF I CAN TAKE HIM OUT...
TP
HAH HAH... SHE ACTUALLY CLIMBED UP HERE.
HEE HEE... SHE'S PRETTY.
SH- SHE'S MINE!!
NO WAY! SHE'S MINE!!
HUP
SHA

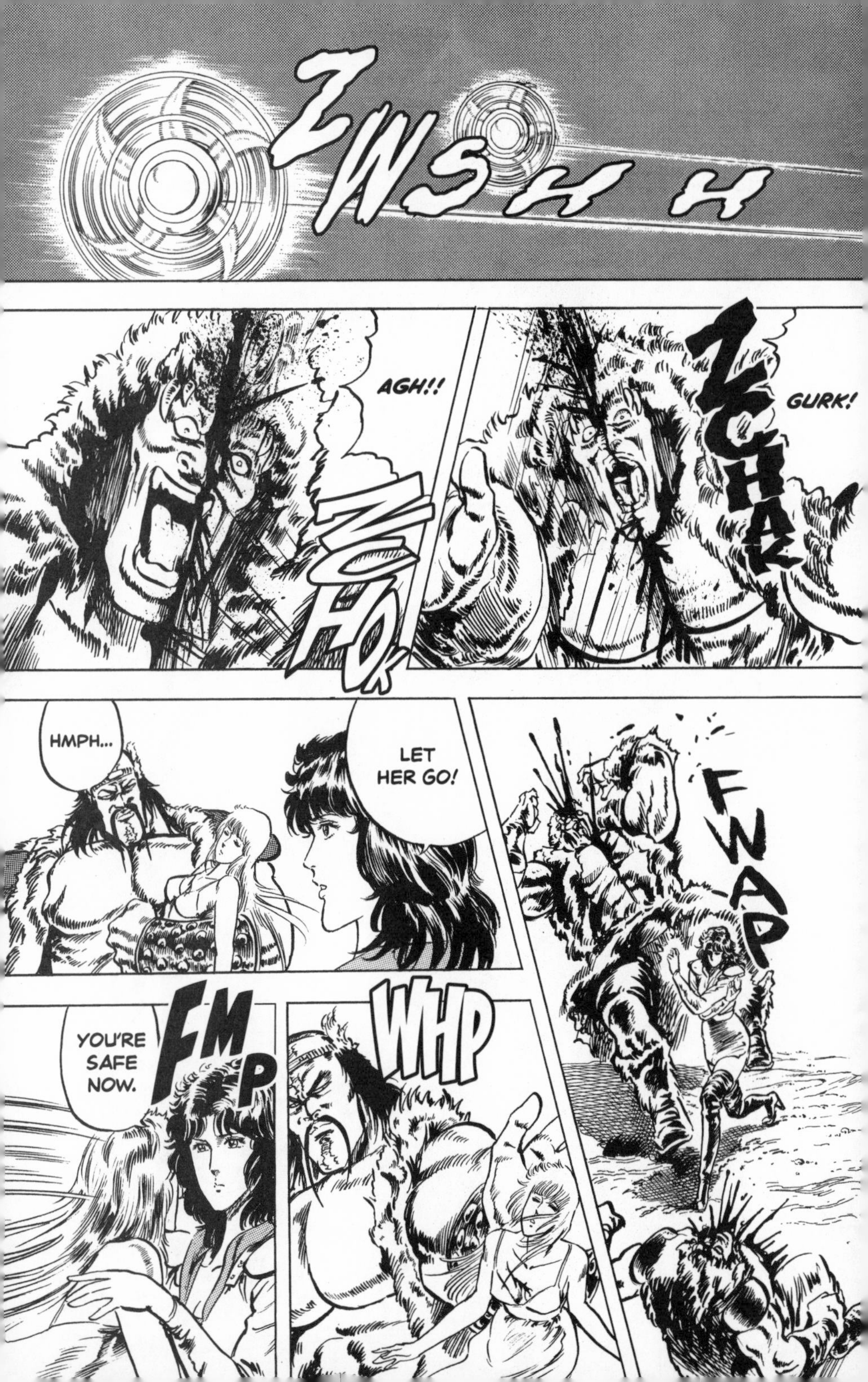
ZWSHHH
GURK!
ZCHAK
AGH!!
ZSHOK
FWAP
LET HER GO!
HMPH...
WHP
FMP
YOU'RE SAFE NOW.

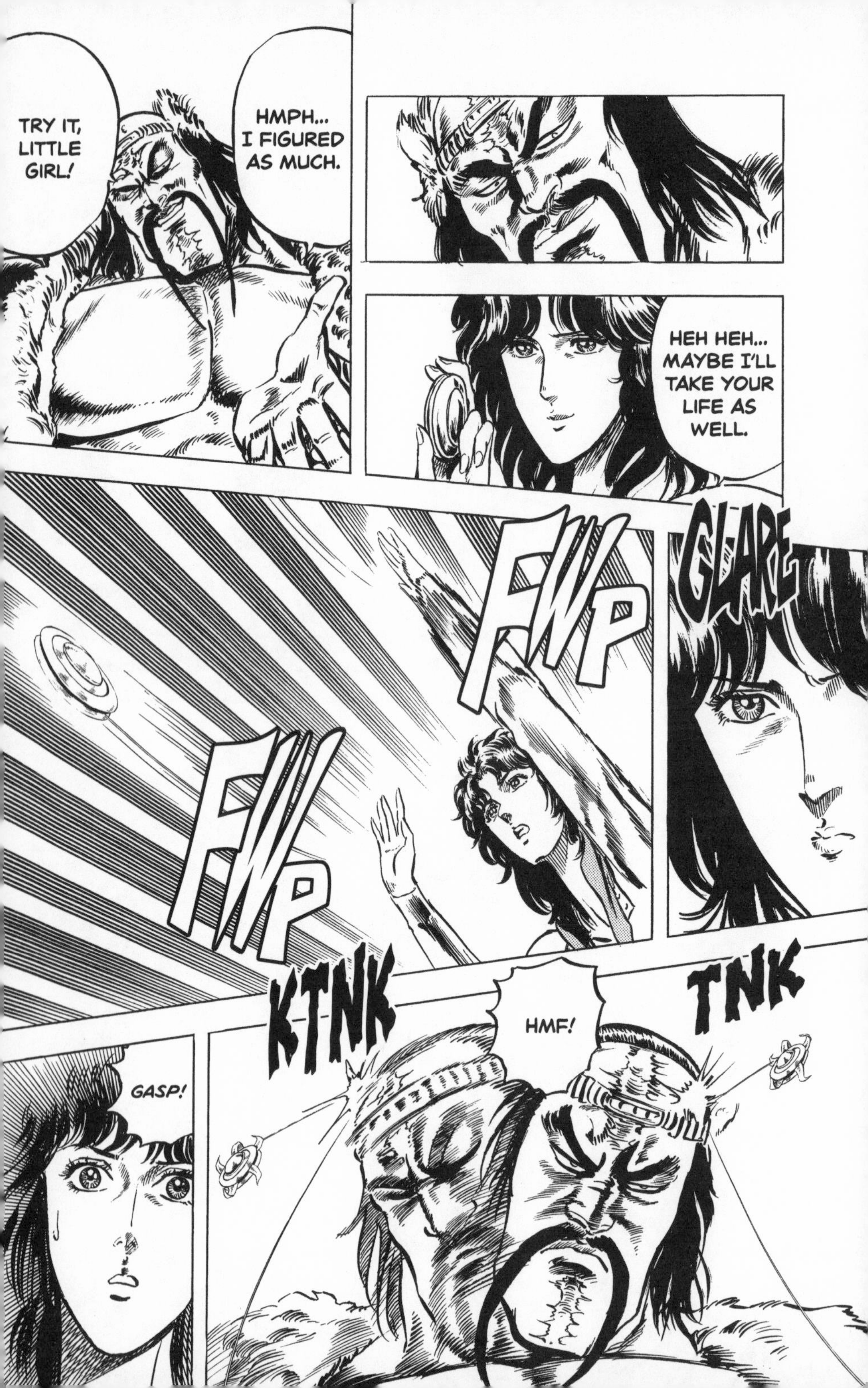
HEH HEH... MAYBE I'LL TAKE YOUR LIFE AS WELL.
HMPH... I FIGURED AS MUCH.
TRY IT, LITTLE GIRL!
GLARE
FWP
FWP
TNK
HMF!
KTNK
GASP!

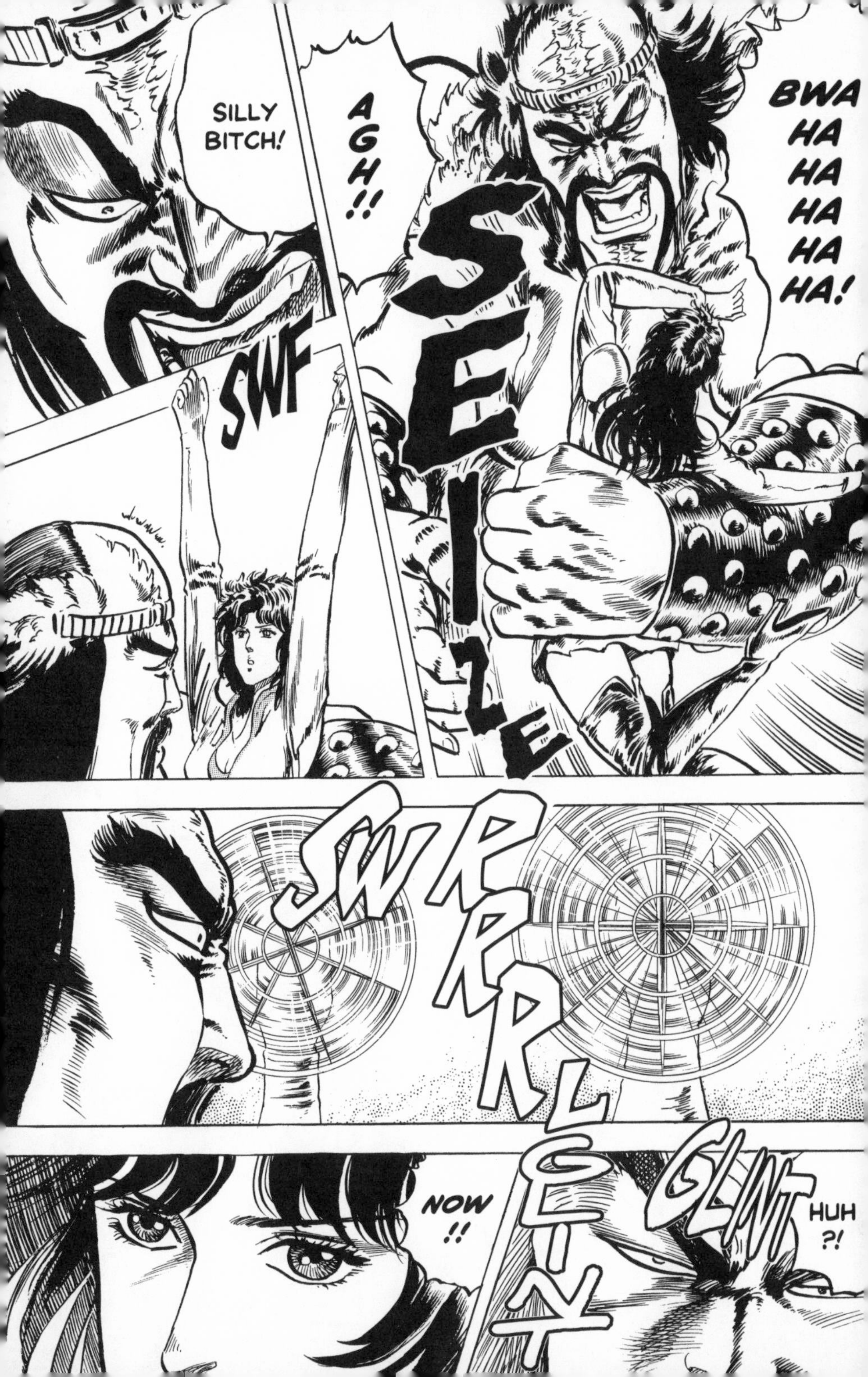
BWA HA HA HA HA HA HA!
SEIZE
AGH!!
SILLY BITCH!
SWF
SWRRRL
HUH ?!
GLINT
GLINT
NOW !!

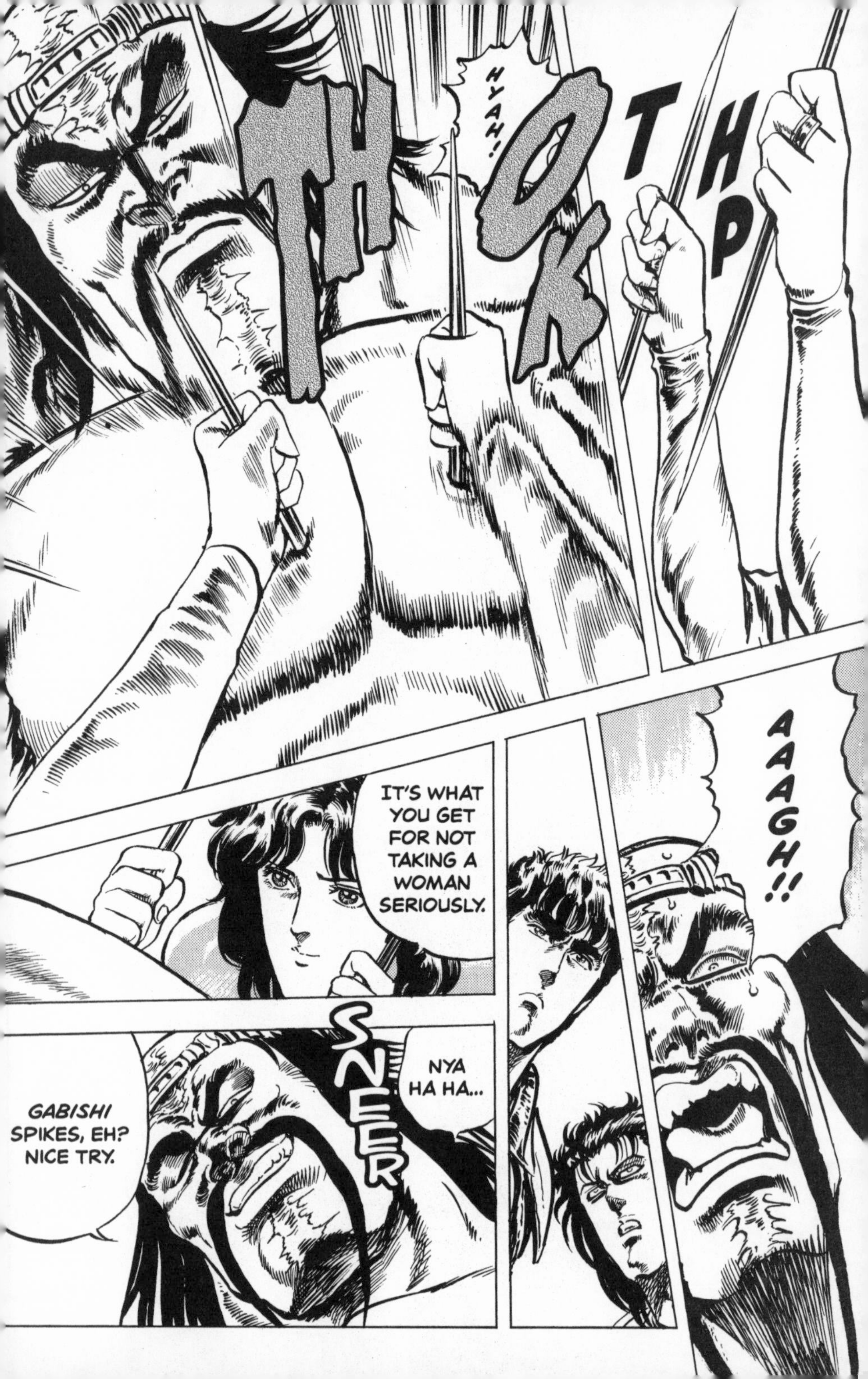
HYAH!
THOK
THP
AAAGH!!
IT'S WHAT YOU GET FOR NOT TAKING A WOMAN SERIOUSLY.
SNEER
NYA HA HA...
GABISHI SPIKES, EH? NICE TRY.

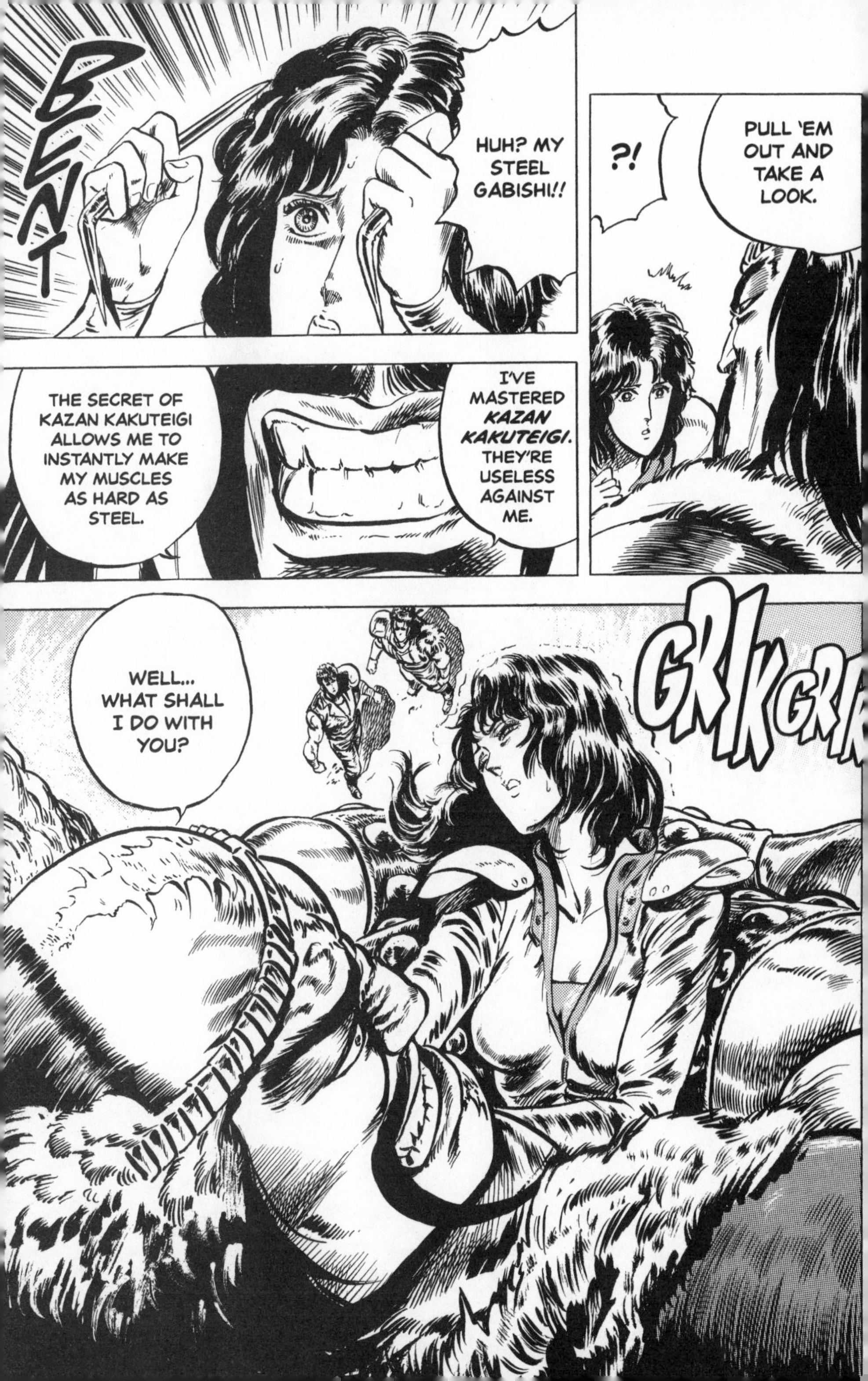
?!
PULL 'EM OUT AND TAKE A LOOK.
BENT
HUH? MY STEEL GABISHI!!
I'VE MASTERED *KAZAN KAKUTEIGI*. THEY'RE USELESS AGAINST ME.
THE SECRET OF KAZAN KAKUTEIGI ALLOWS ME TO INSTANTLY MAKE MY MUSCLES AS HARD AS STEEL.
GRIK GRIK
WELL... WHAT SHALL I DO WITH YOU?

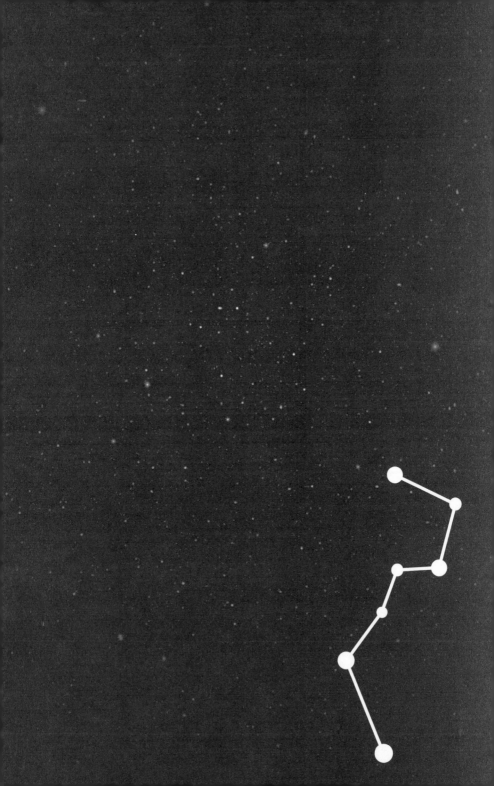

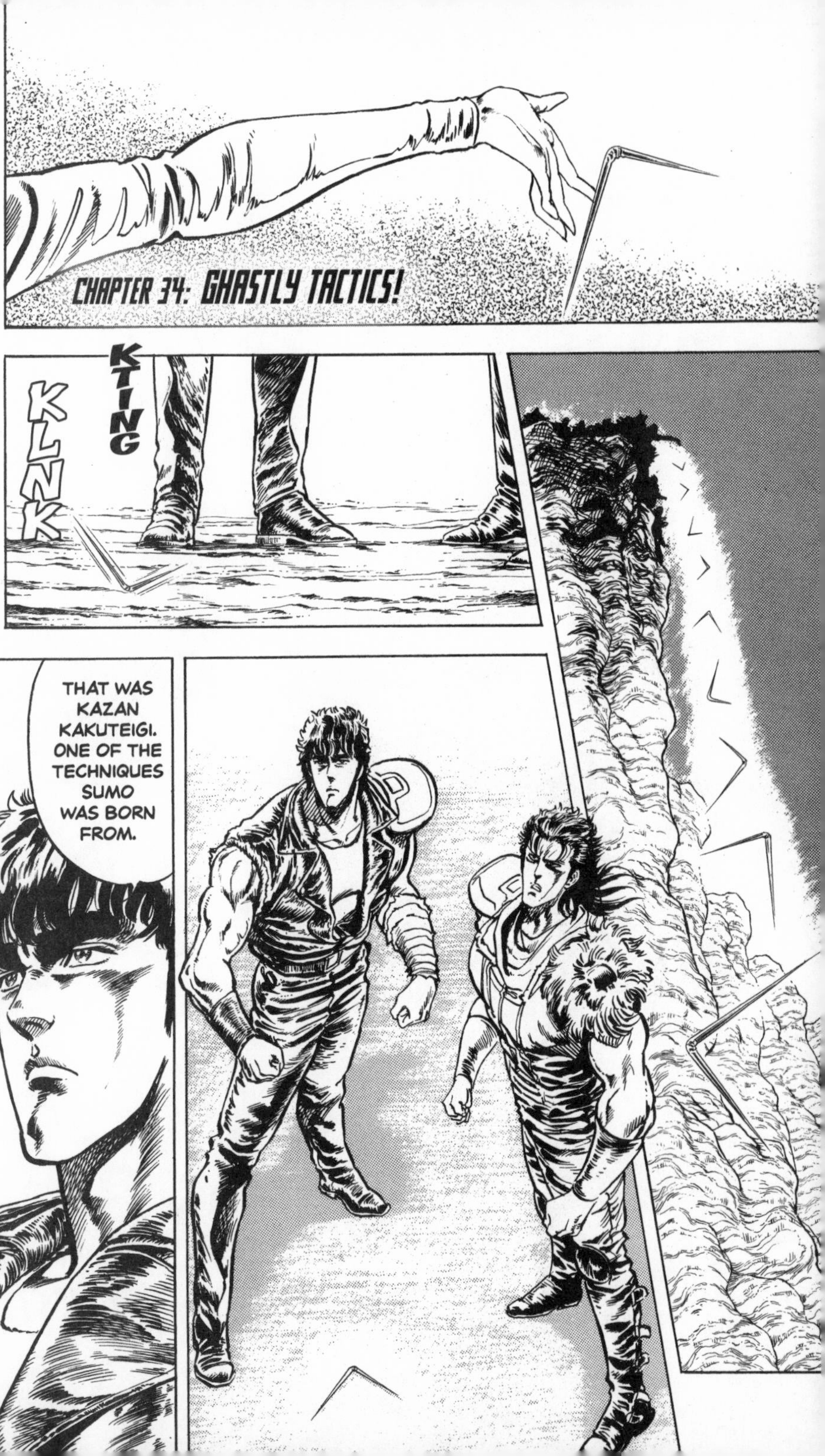
CHAPTER 34: GHASTLY TACTICS!
KTING
KLNK
THAT WAS KAZAN KAKUTEIGI. ONE OF THE TECHNIQUES SUMO WAS BORN FROM.

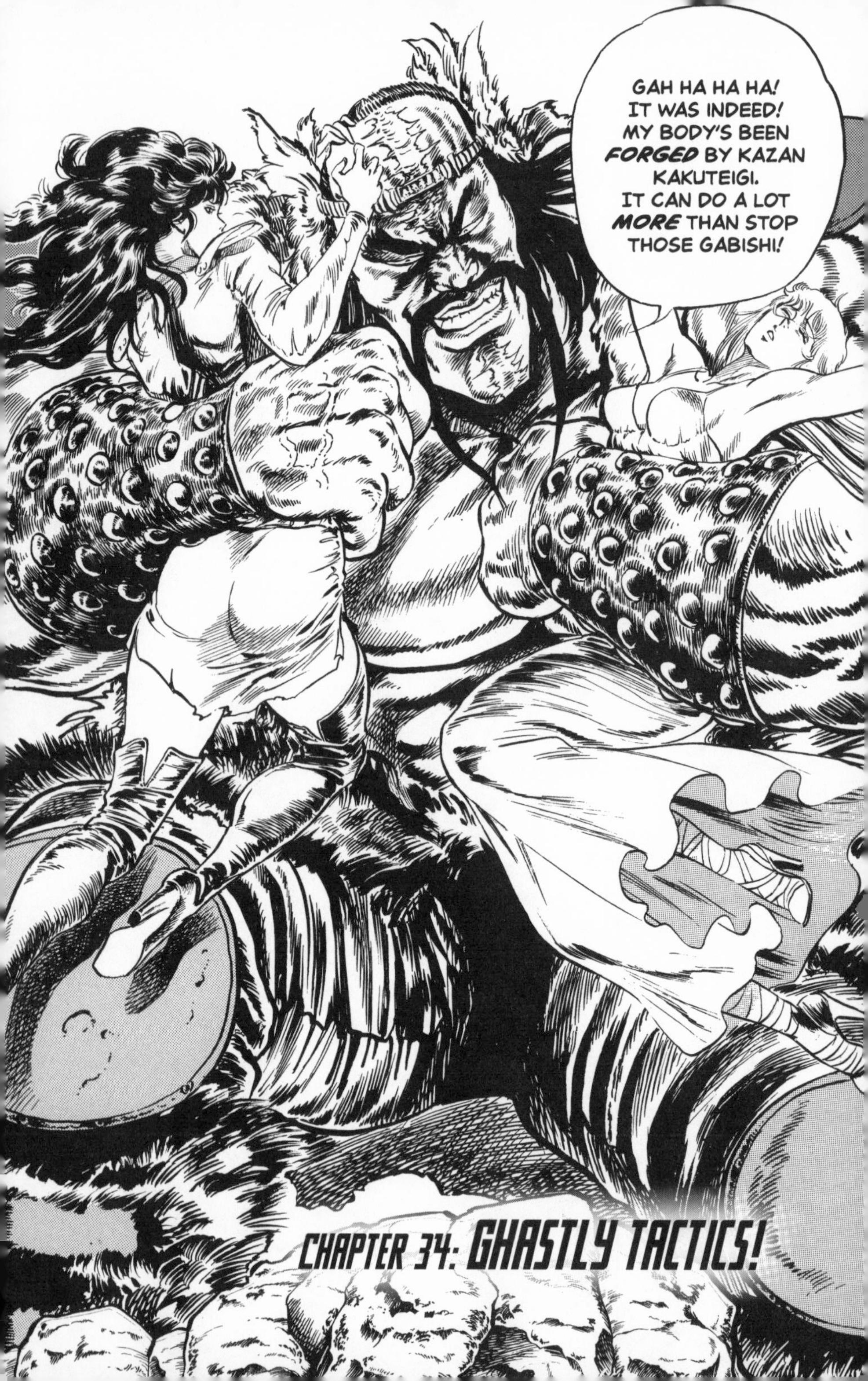
GAH HA HA HA! IT WAS INDEED! MY BODY'S BEEN FORGED BY KAZAN KAKUTEIGI. IT CAN DO A LOT MORE THAN STOP THOSE GABISHI!
CHAPTER 34: GHASTLY TACTICS!

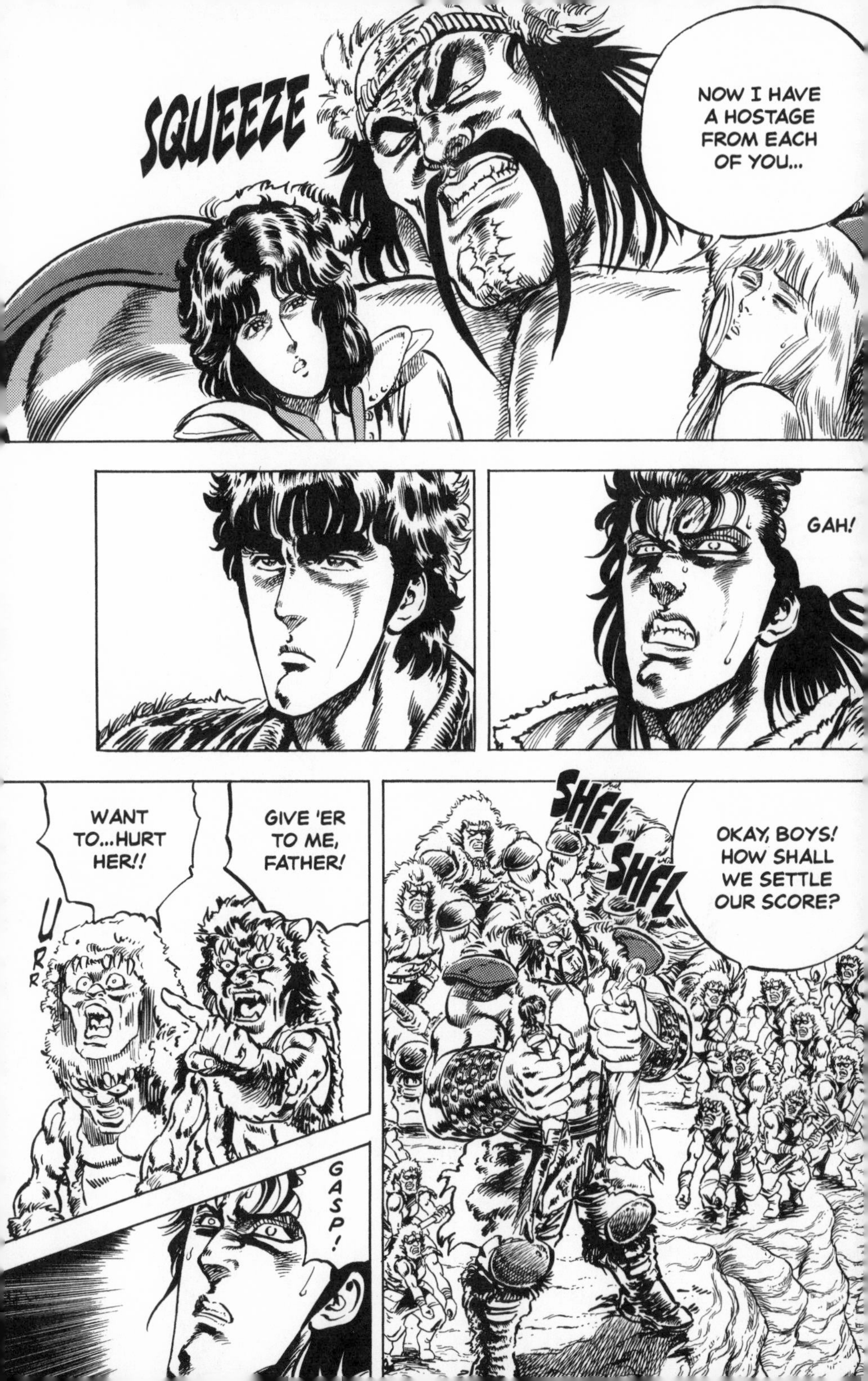
SQUEEZE
NOW I HAVE A HOSTAGE FROM EACH OF YOU...
GAH!
SHFL
SHFL
OKAY, BOYS! HOW SHALL WE SETTLE OUR SCORE?
GIVE 'ER TO ME, FATHER!
WANT TO...HURT HER!!
URR
GASP!

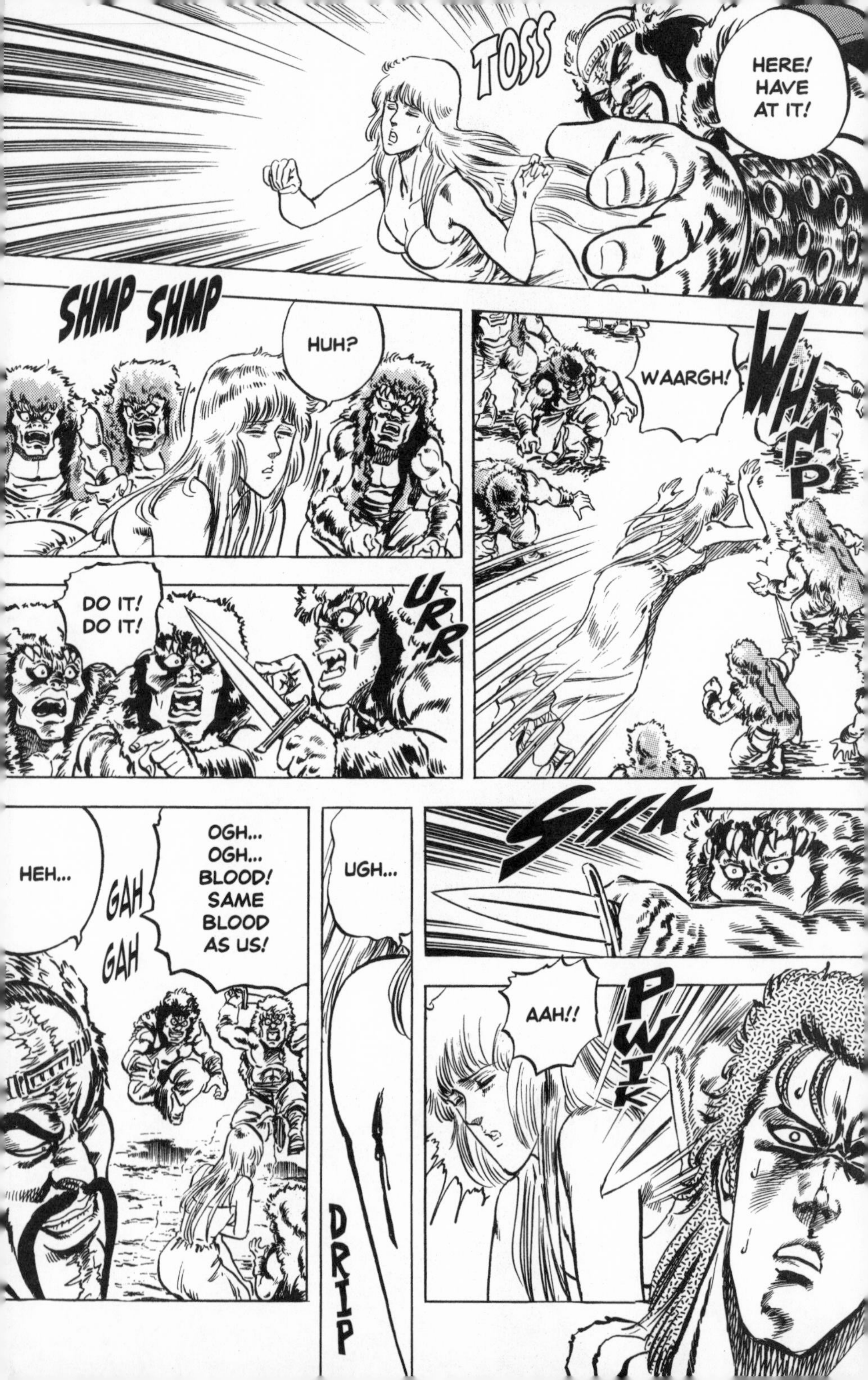
TOSS
HERE! HAVE AT IT!
WAARGH!
WHUMP
SHMP SHMP
HUH?
DO IT! DO IT!
URR
SHK
AAH!!
PWIK
UGH...
DRIP
OGH... OGH... BLOOD! SAME BLOOD AS US!
GAH GAH
HEH...

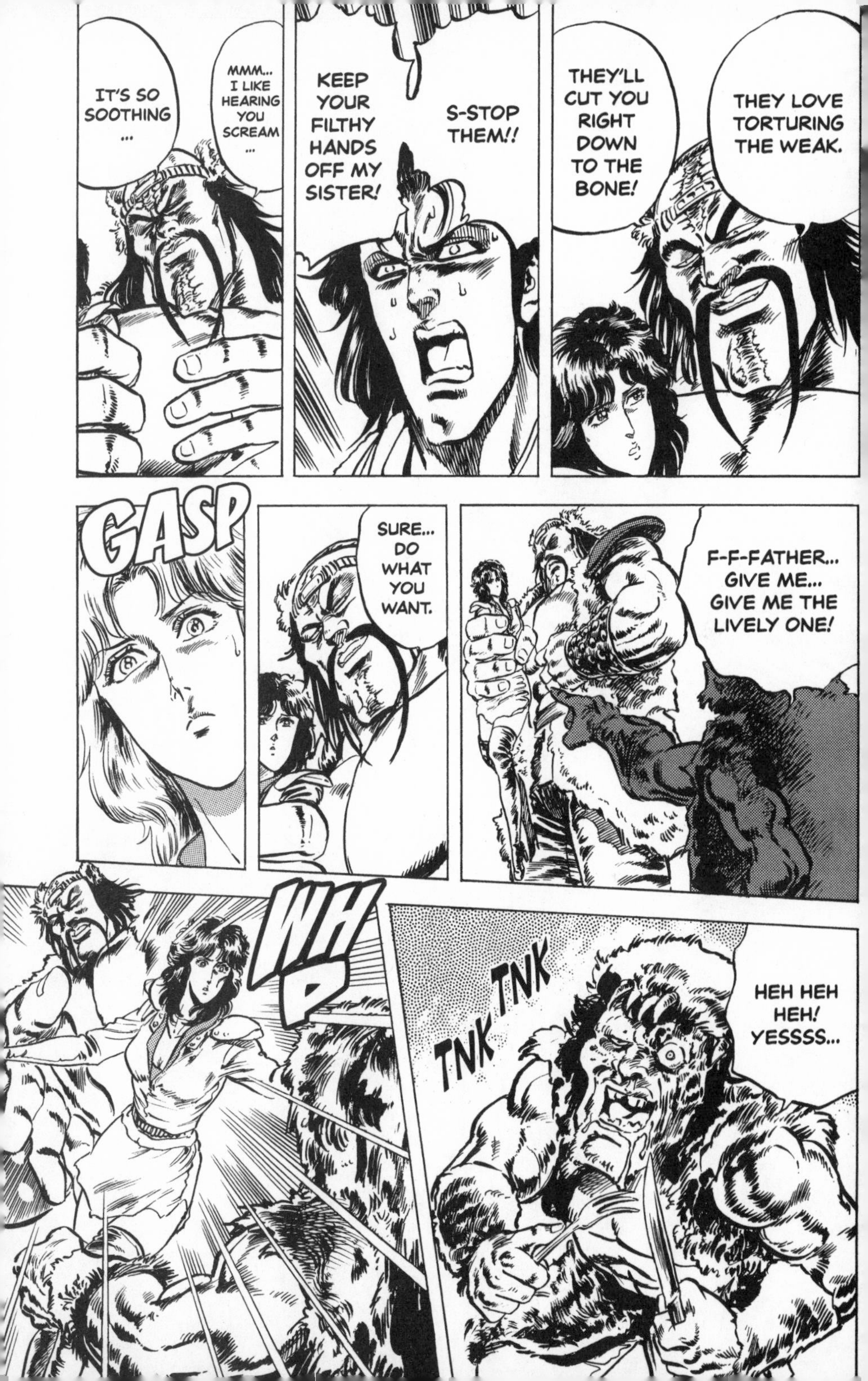
THEY LOVE TORTURING THE WEAK.
THEY'LL CUT YOU RIGHT DOWN TO THE BONE!
S-STOP THEM!!
KEEP YOUR FILTHY HANDS OFF MY SISTER!
MMM... I LIKE HEARING YOU SCREAM ...
IT'S SO SOOTHING ...
F-F-FATHER... GIVE ME... GIVE ME THE LIVELY ONE!
SURE... DO WHAT YOU WANT.
GASP
HEH HEH HEH! YESSSS...
TNK TNK
WHP

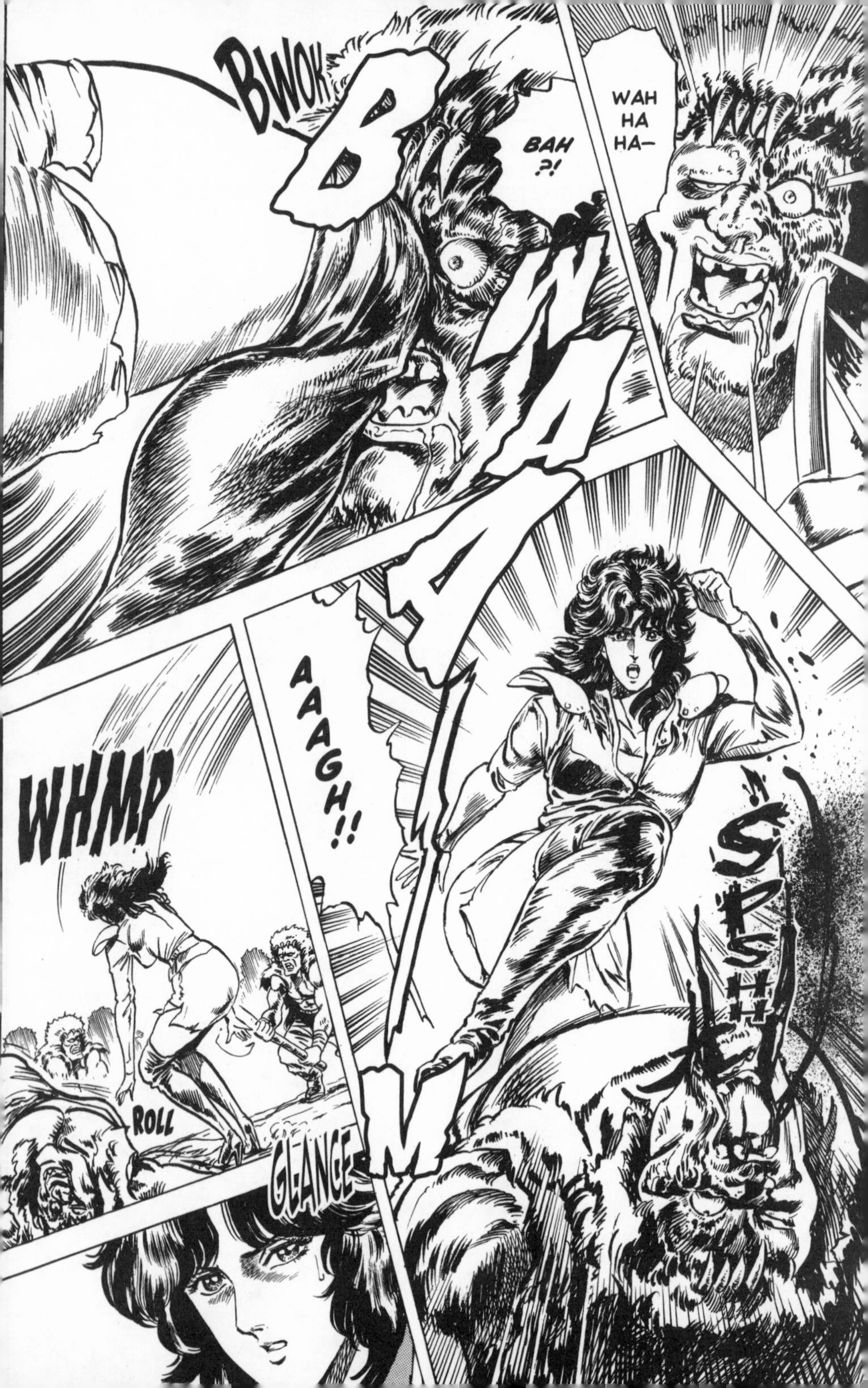
WAH HA HA—
BAH ?!
BWOK
BAM
AAAGH!!
SPSH
WHMP
ROLL
GLANCE

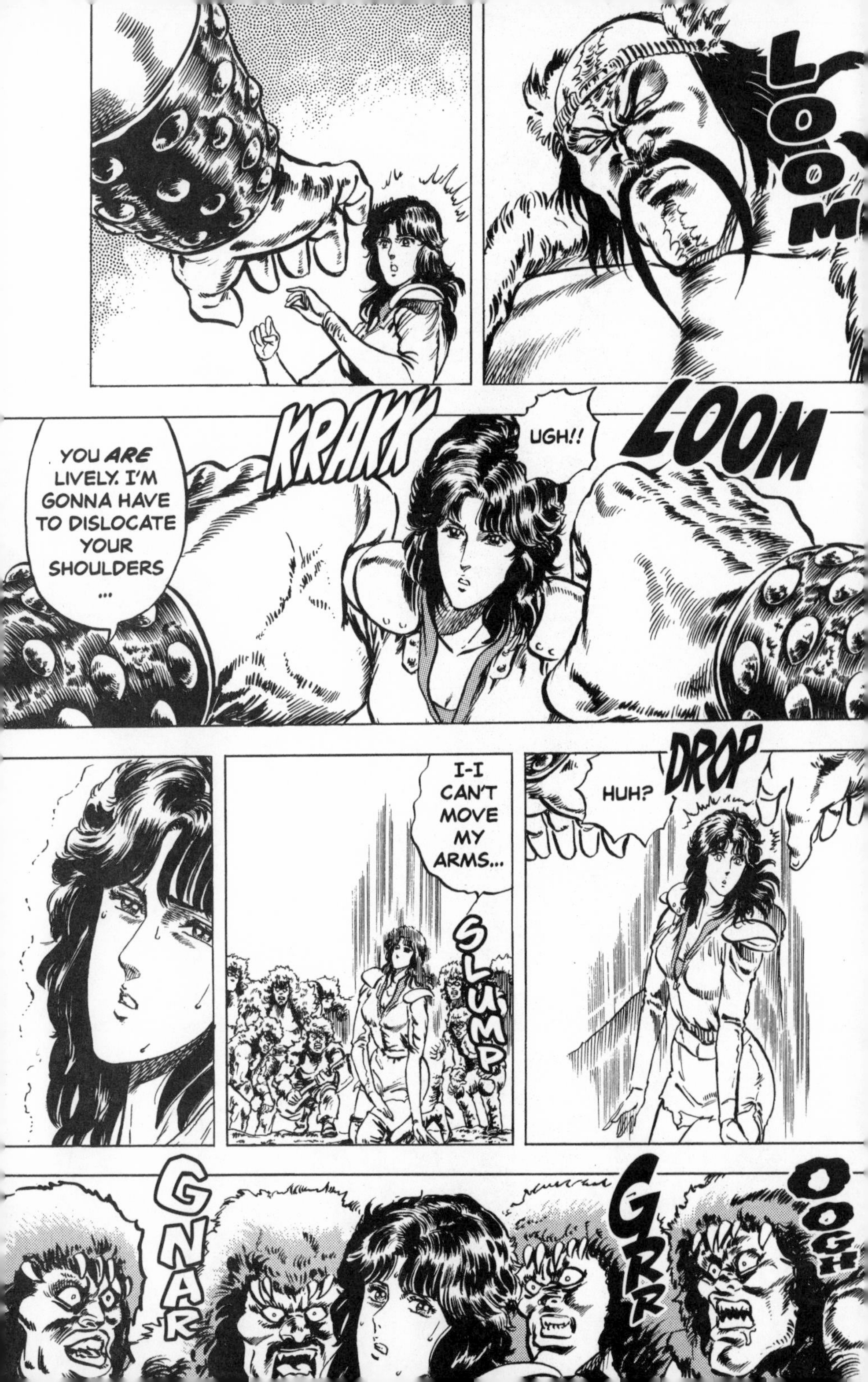
LOOM
LOOM
UGH!!
KRAKK
YOU *ARE* LIVELY. I'M GONNA HAVE TO DISLOCATE YOUR SHOULDERS ...
DROP
HUH?
I-I CAN'T MOVE MY ARMS...
SLUMP
OOGH
GRR
GNAR

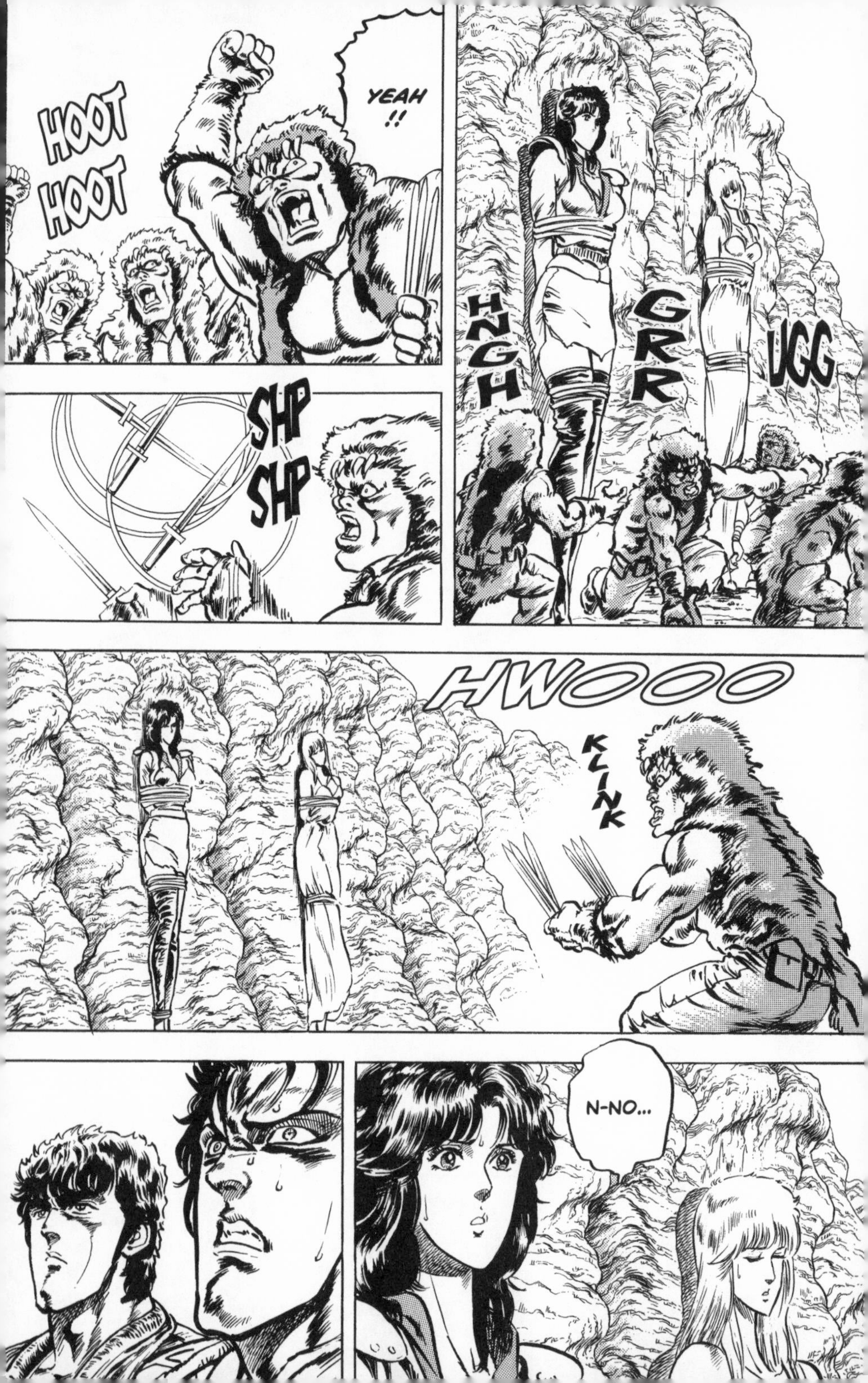
UGG
GRR
HNGH
YEAH!!
HOOT HOOT
SHP SHP
HWOOO
KLINK
N-NO...

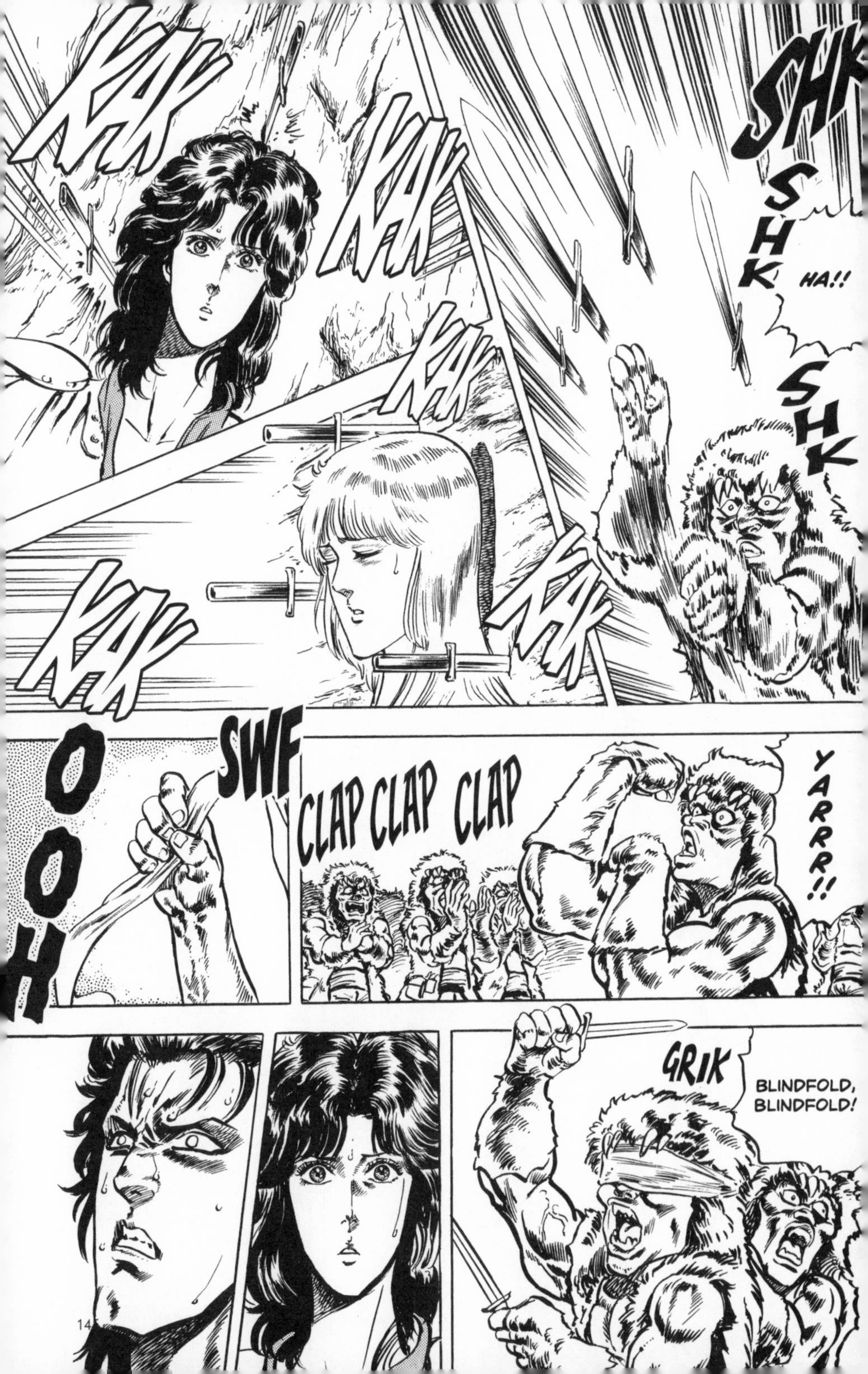
SHK
SHK
HA!!
SHK
KAK
KAK
KAK
KAK
KAK
KAK
YARRR!!
CLAP CLAP CLAP
SWF
OOOH
BLINDFOLD, BLINDFOLD!
GRIK

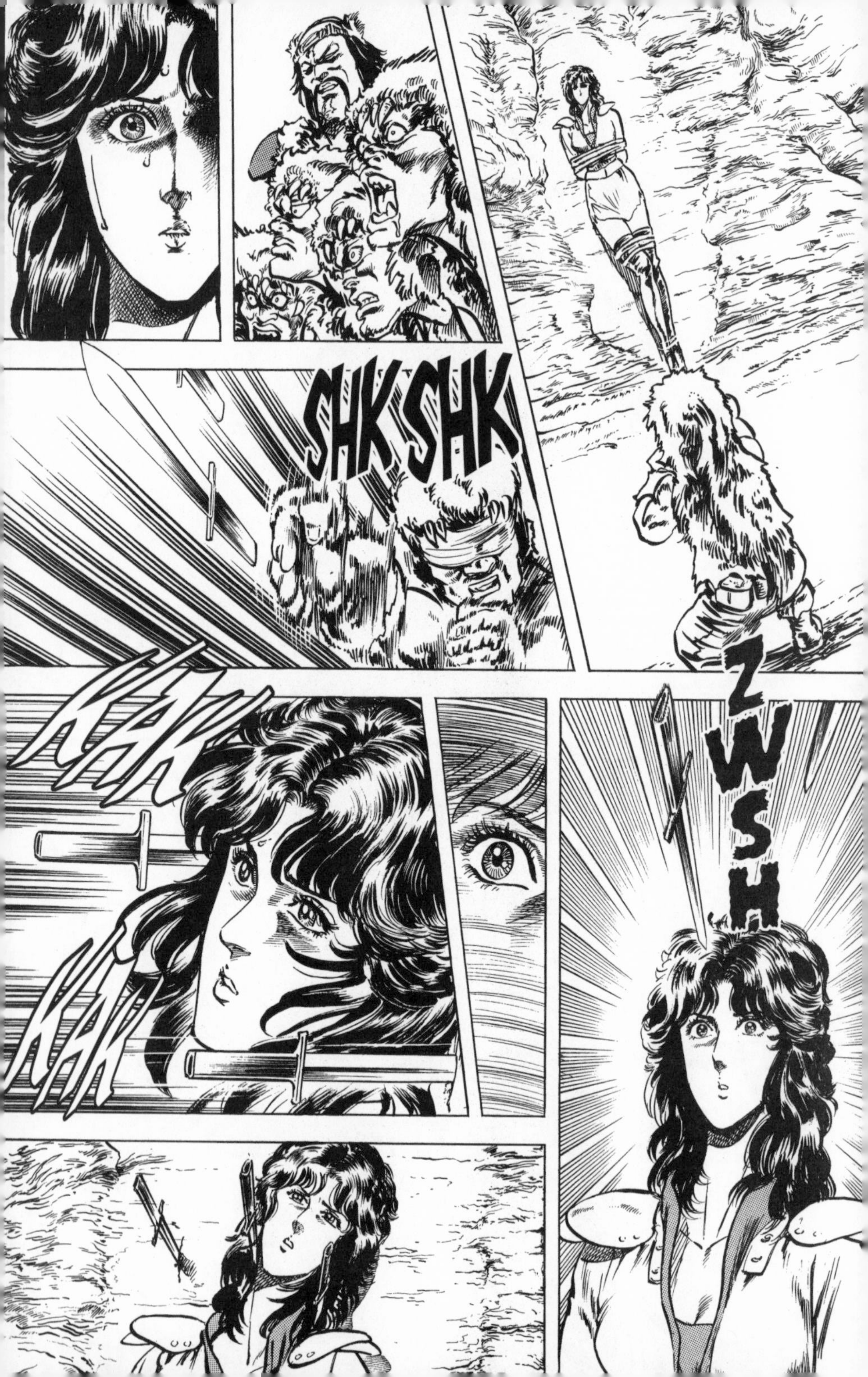
SHK SHK
ZWSH
KAK
KAK

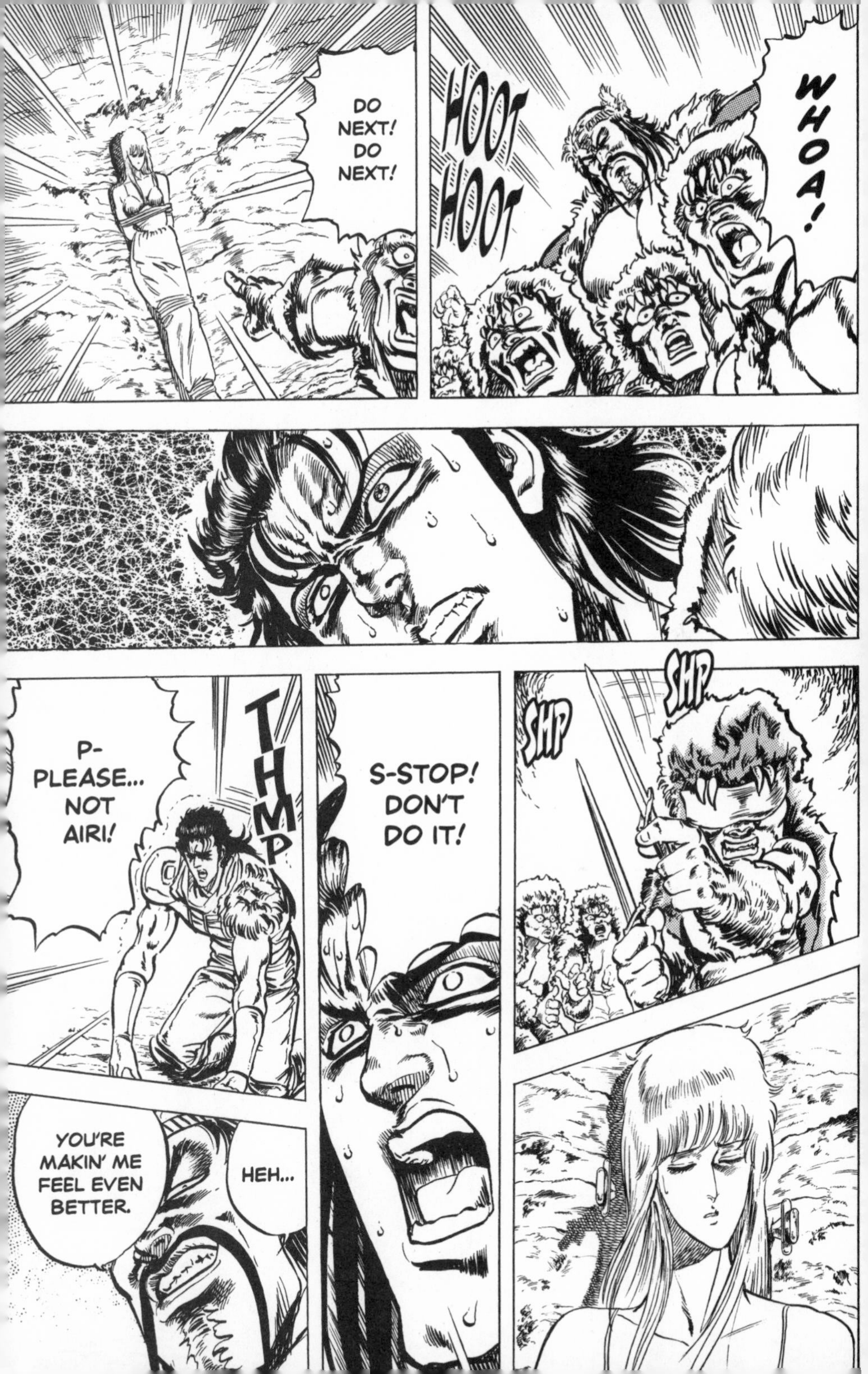
WHOA!
HOOT HOOT
DO NEXT! DO NEXT!
SHP
SHP
S-STOP! DON'T DO IT!
THMP
P-PLEASE... NOT AIRI!
HEH...
YOU'RE MAKIN' ME FEEL EVEN BETTER.

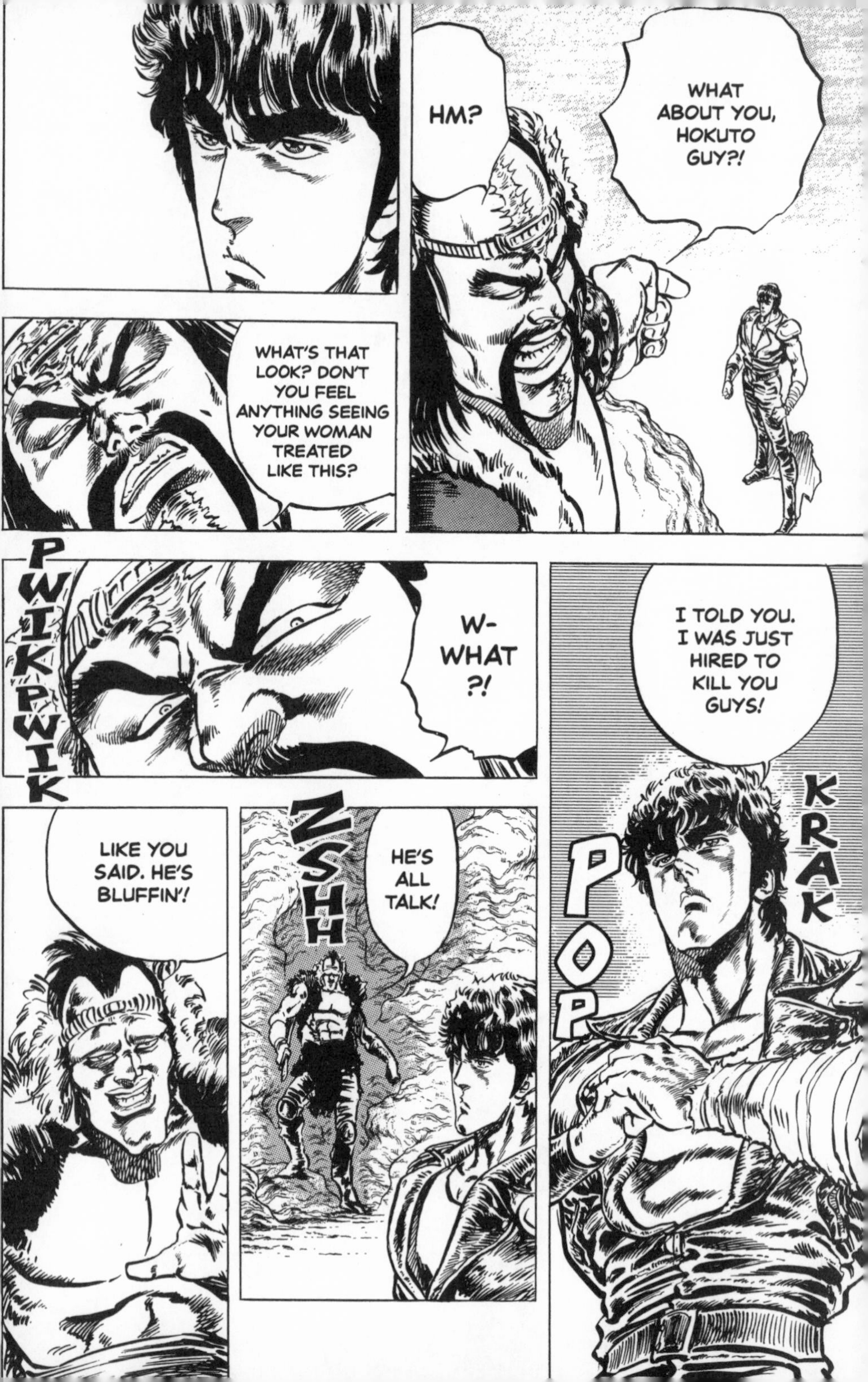
WHAT ABOUT YOU, HOKUTO GUY?!
HM?
WHAT'S THAT LOOK? DON'T YOU FEEL ANYTHING SEEING YOUR WOMAN TREATED LIKE THIS?
KRAK
POP
I TOLD YOU. I WAS JUST HIRED TO KILL YOU GUYS!
W-WHAT?!
PWIK PWIK
HE'S ALL TALK!
ZSHH
LIKE YOU SAID. HE'S BLUFFIN'!

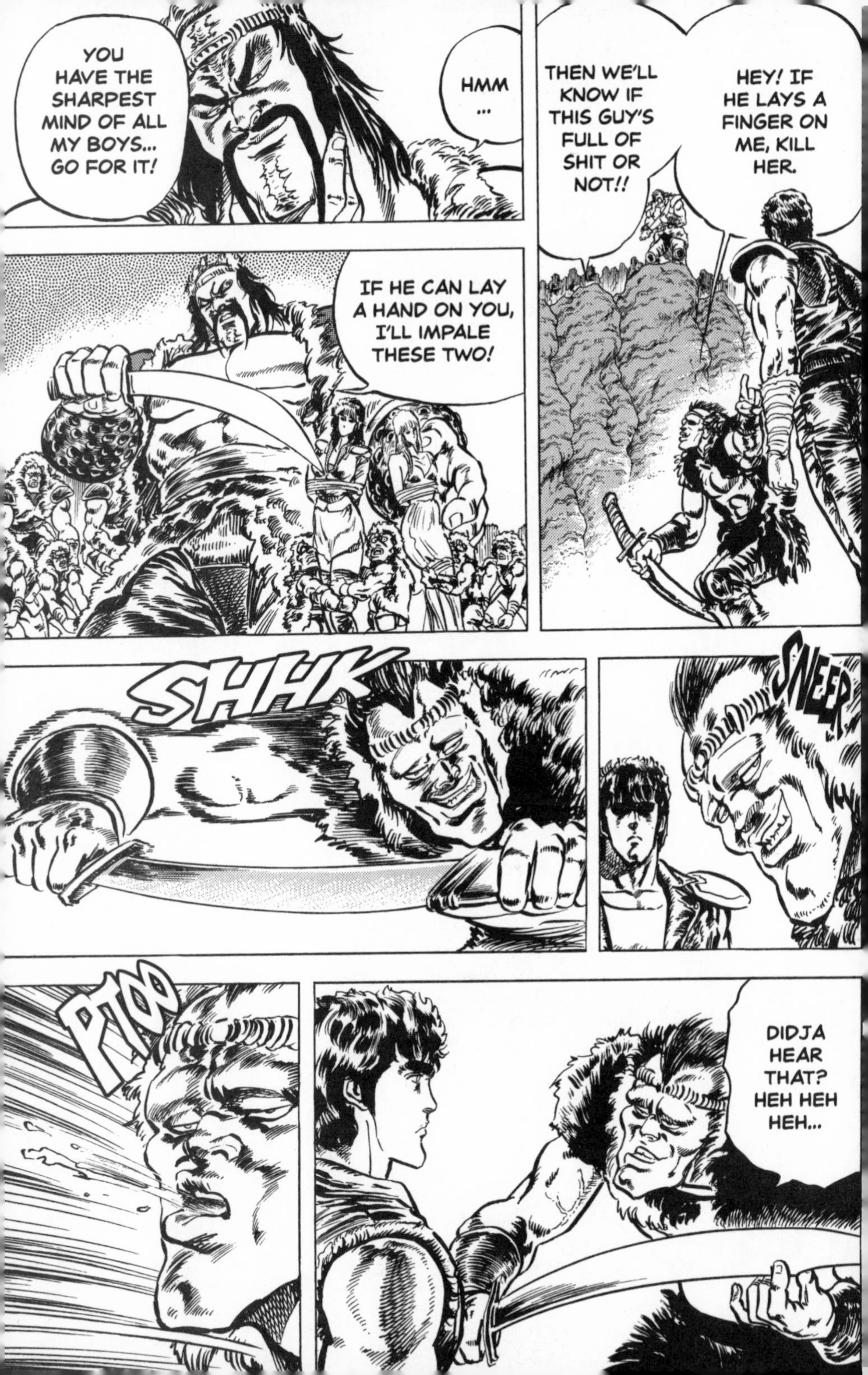
HEY! IF HE LAYS A FINGER ON ME, KILL HER.
THEN WE'LL KNOW IF THIS GUY'S FULL OF SHIT OR NOT!!
HMM ...
YOU HAVE THE SHARPEST MIND OF ALL MY BOYS... GO FOR IT!
IF HE CAN LAY A HAND ON YOU, I'LL IMPALE THESE TWO!
SNEER
SHHK
DIDJA HEAR THAT? HEH HEH HEH...
PTOO

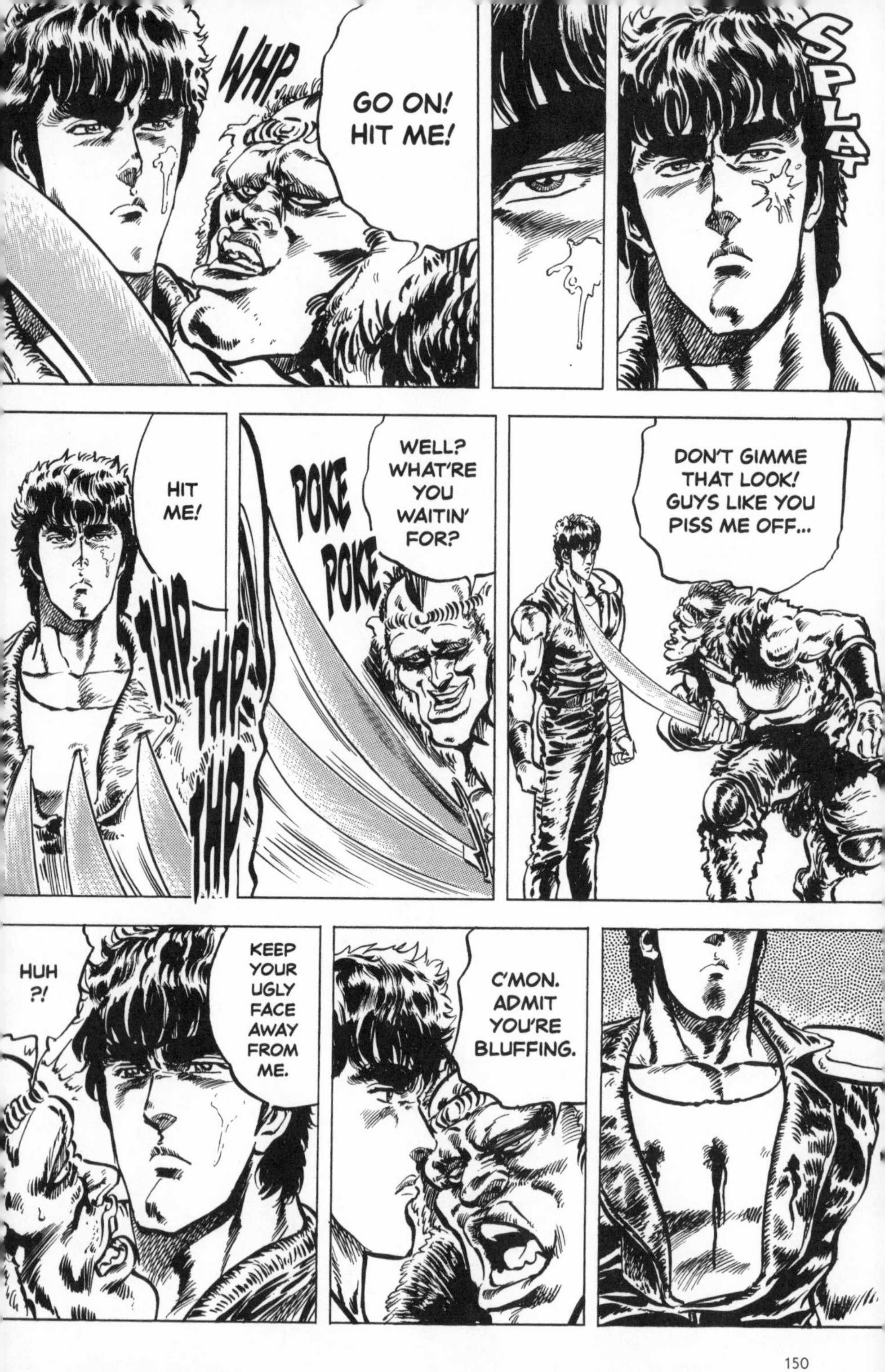
SPLAT
GO ON! HIT ME!
WHP
DON'T GIMME THAT LOOK! GUYS LIKE YOU PISS ME OFF...
WELL? WHAT'RE YOU WAITIN' FOR?
POKE
POKE
HIT ME!
THP THP THP THP
C'MON. ADMIT YOU'RE BLUFFING.
KEEP YOUR UGLY FACE AWAY FROM ME.
HUH?!

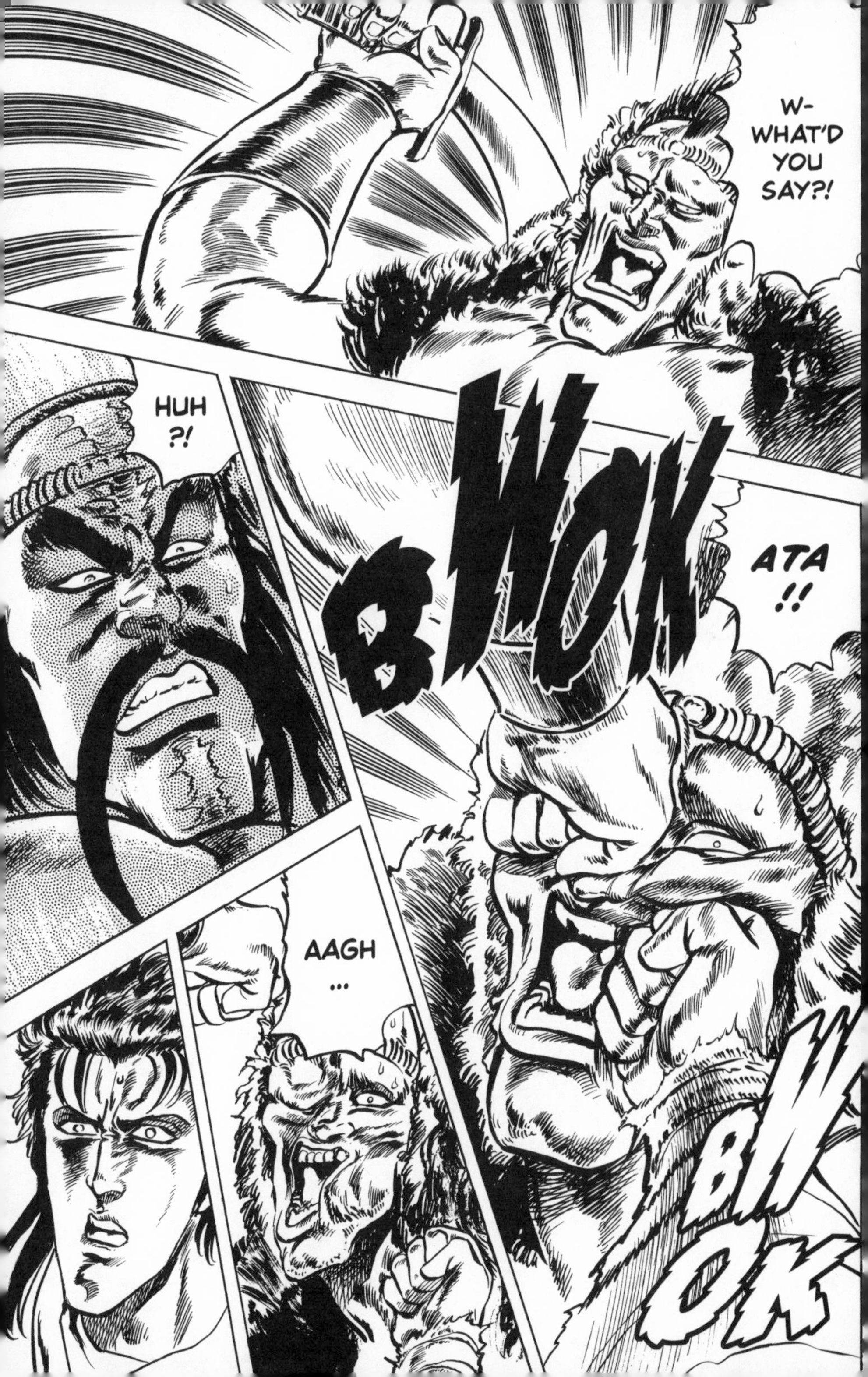
W- WHAT'D YOU SAY?!
BWOK
ATA !!
BWOK
HUH ?!
AAGH ...

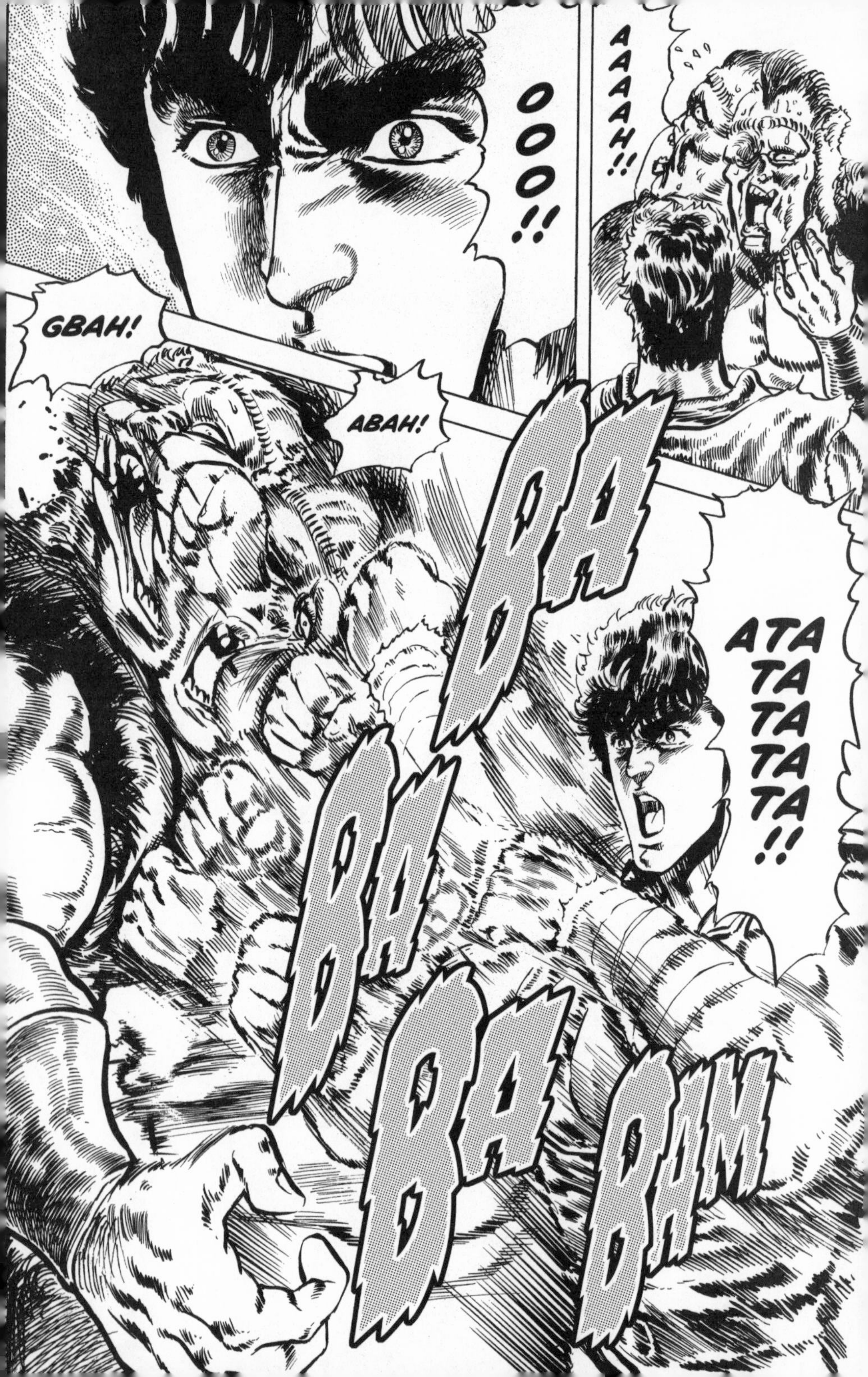
AAAAAH!!
OOOO!!
GBAH!
ABAH!
ATATATATATA!!
BA
BA
BA
BAM

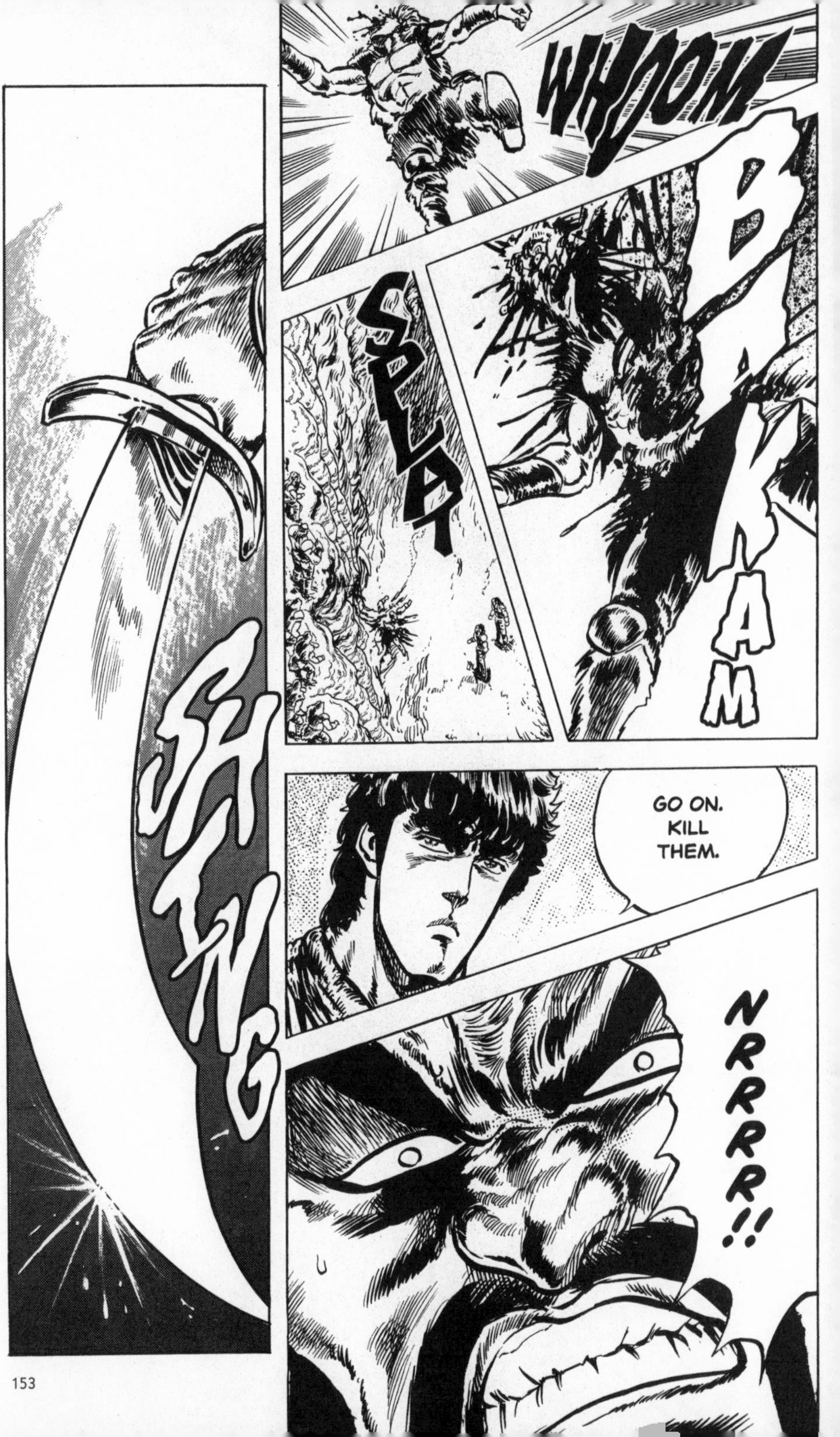
WHOOM
BAKAM
SPLAT
GO ON. KILL THEM.
NRRRR!!
SHING

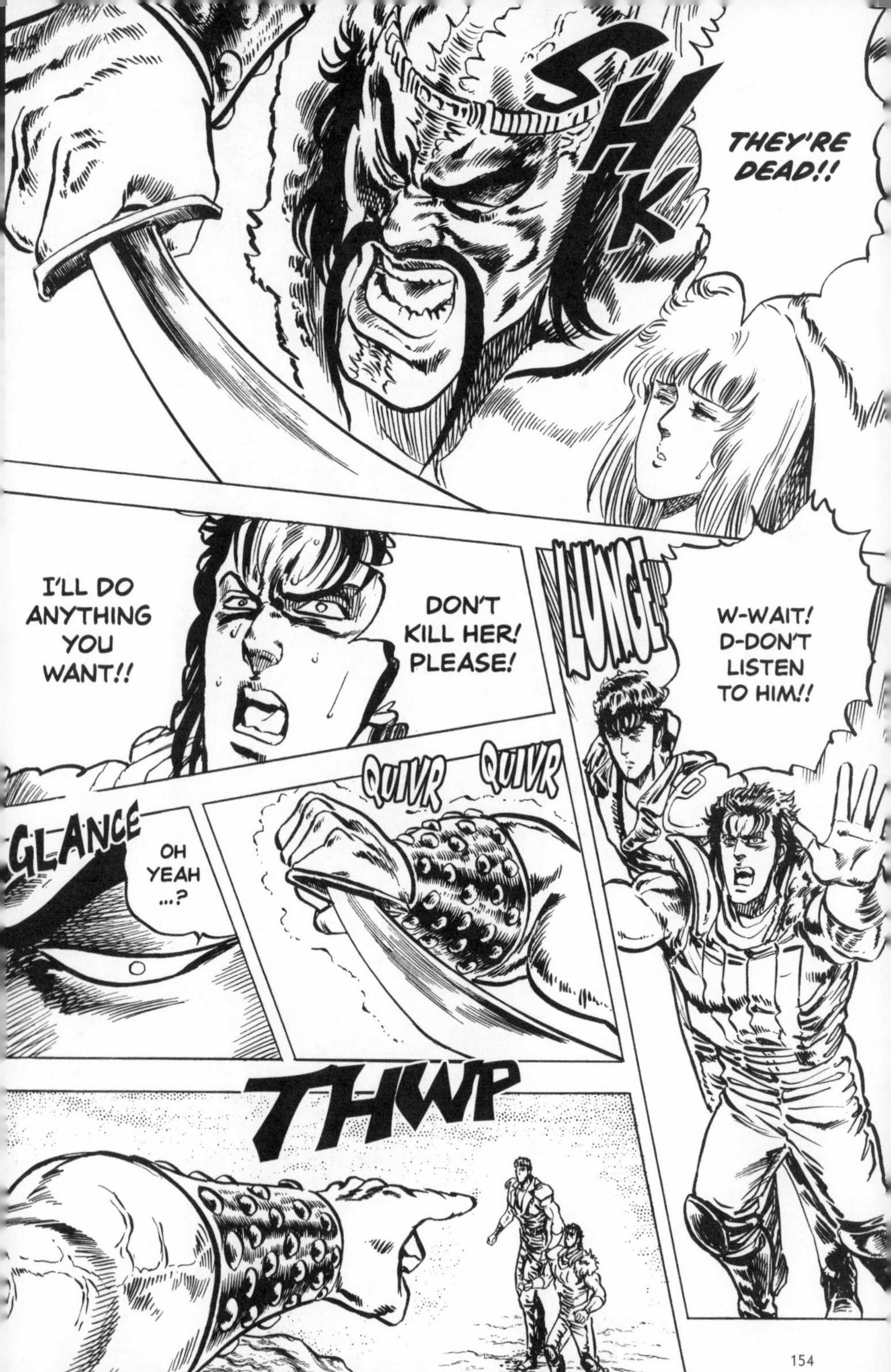
SHK
THEY'RE DEAD!!
LUNGE
W-WAIT! D-DON'T LISTEN TO HIM!!
DON'T KILL HER! PLEASE!
I'LL DO ANYTHING YOU WANT!!
QUIVR QUIVR
GLANCE
OH YEAH ...?
THWP

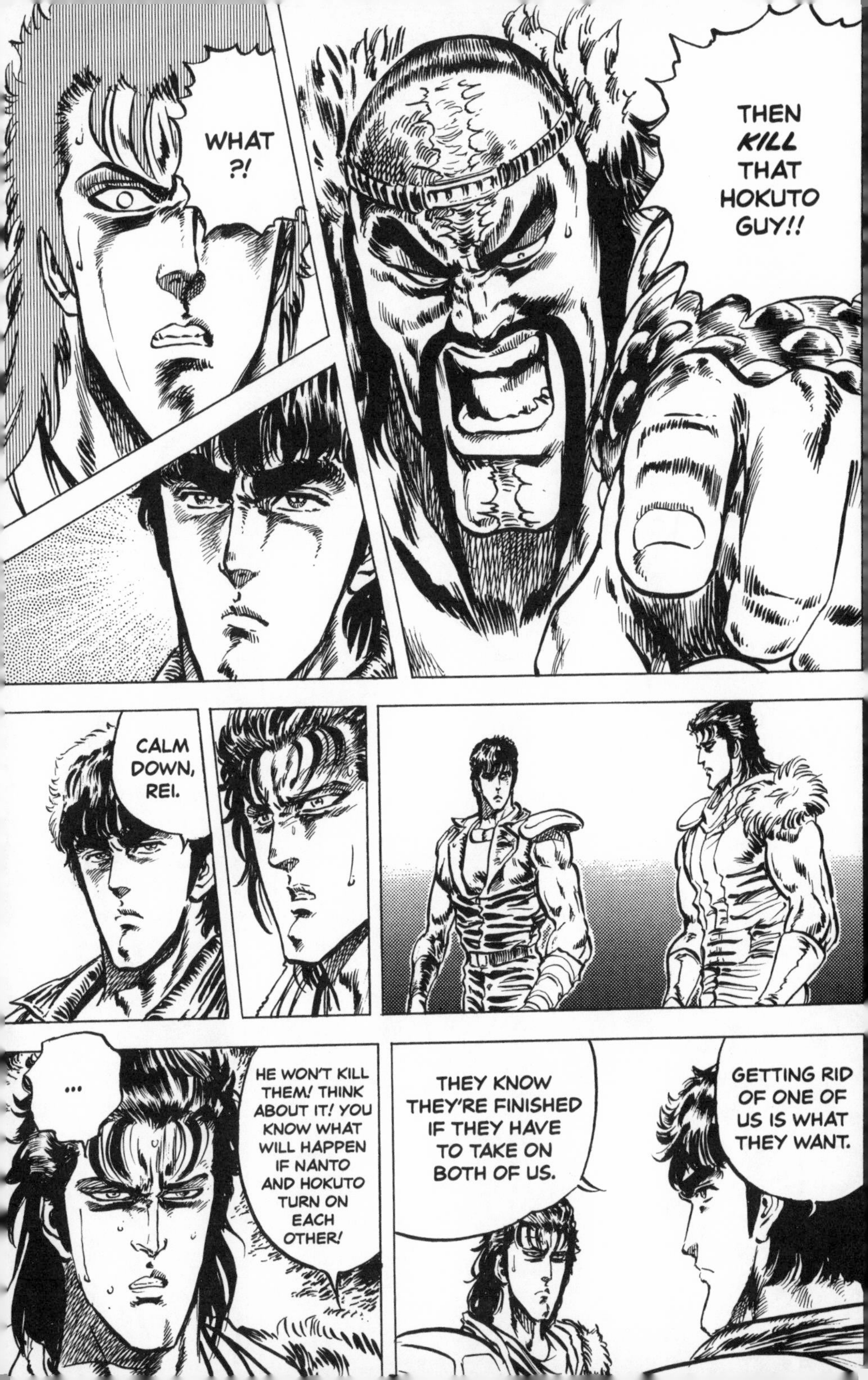
THEN KILL THAT HOKUTO GUY!!
WHAT ?!
CALM DOWN, REI.
THEY KNOW THEY'RE FINISHED IF THEY HAVE TO TAKE ON BOTH OF US.
GETTING RID OF ONE OF US IS WHAT THEY WANT.
...
HE WON'T KILL THEM! THINK ABOUT IT! YOU KNOW WHAT WILL HAPPEN IF NANTO AND HOKUTO TURN ON EACH OTHER!

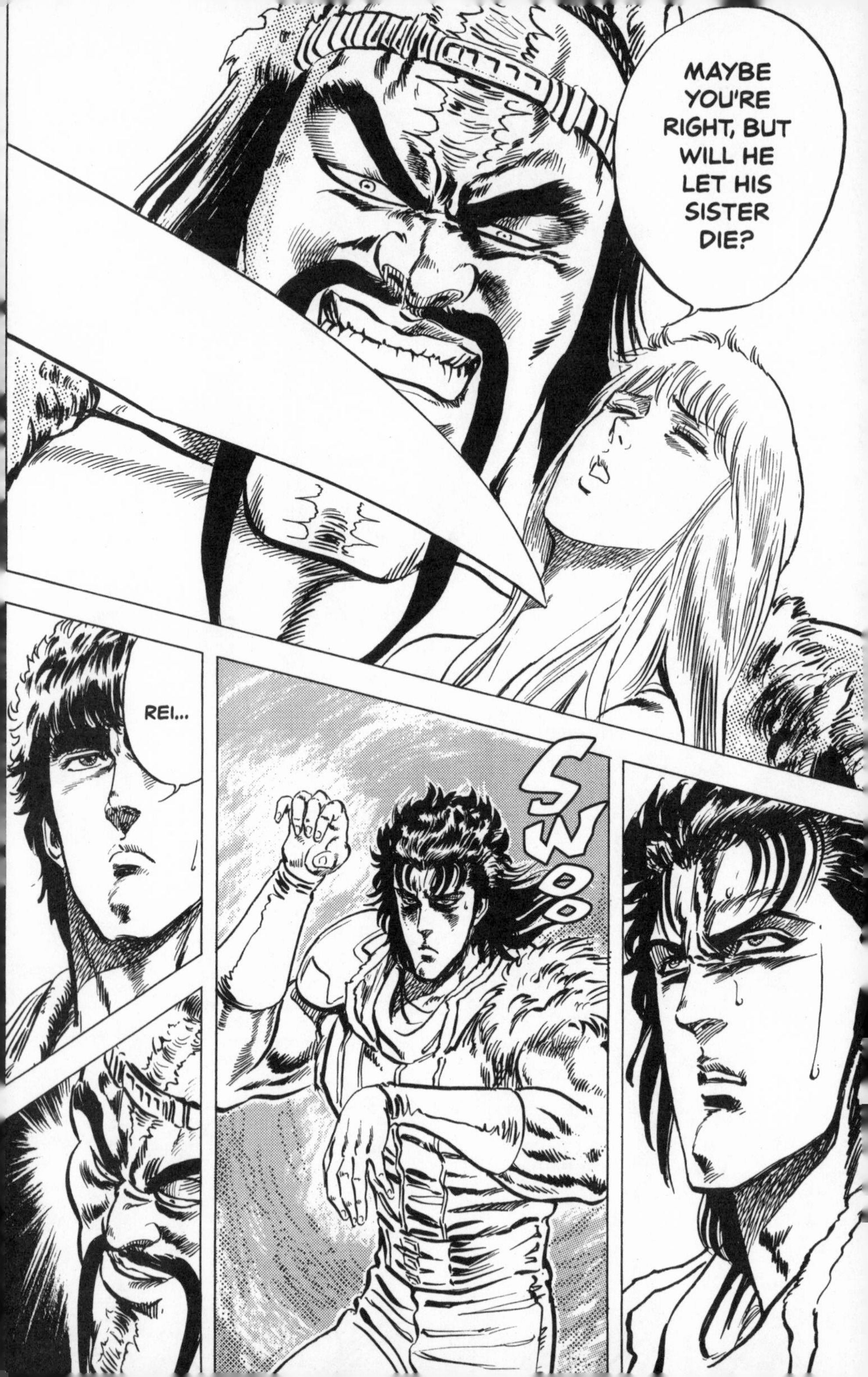
MAYBE YOU'RE RIGHT, BUT WILL HE LET HIS SISTER DIE?
SWOOP
REI...

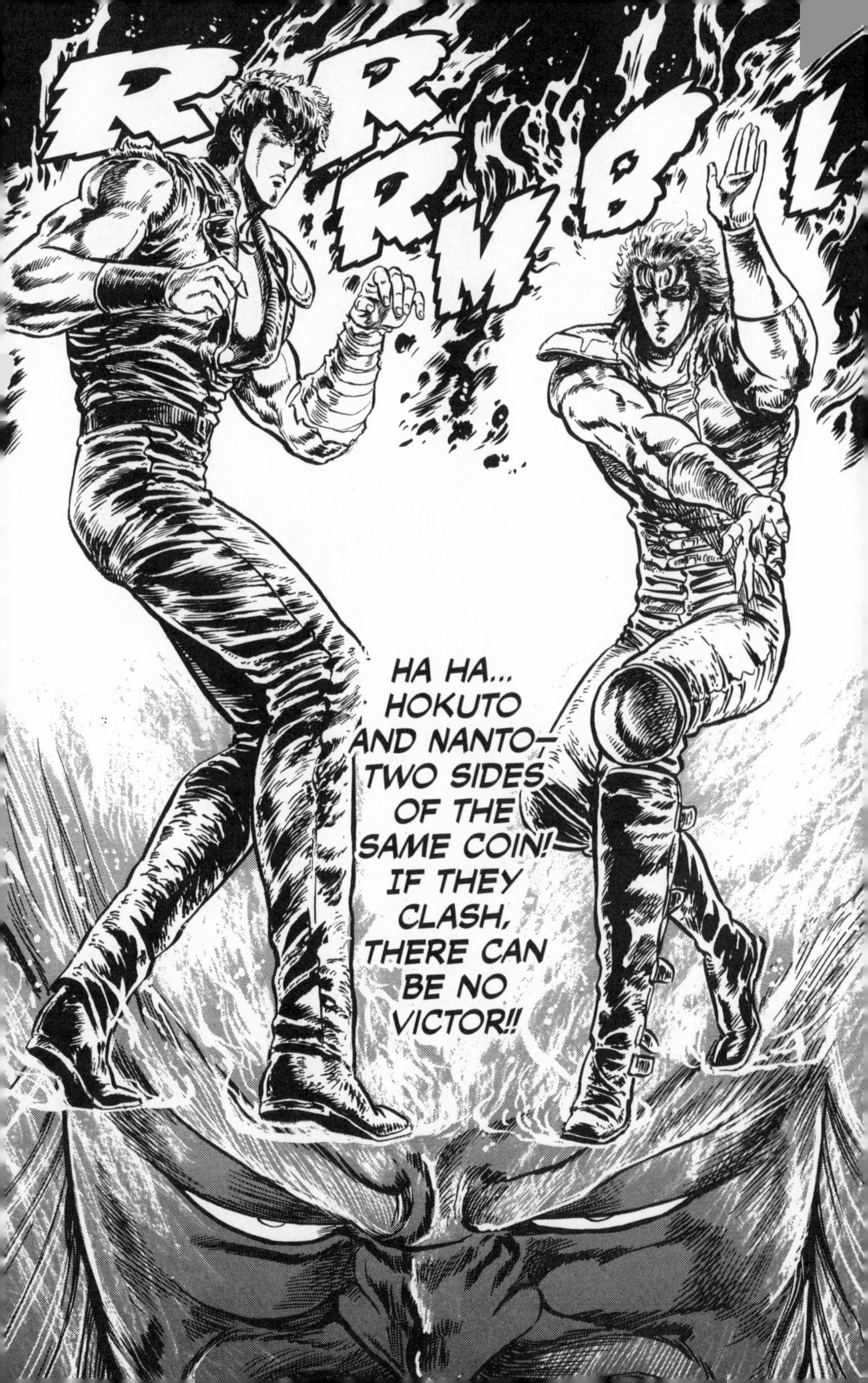
RRRUMBL
HA HA... HOKUTO AND NANTO—TWO SIDES OF THE SAME COIN! IF THEY CLASH, THERE CAN BE NO VICTOR!!

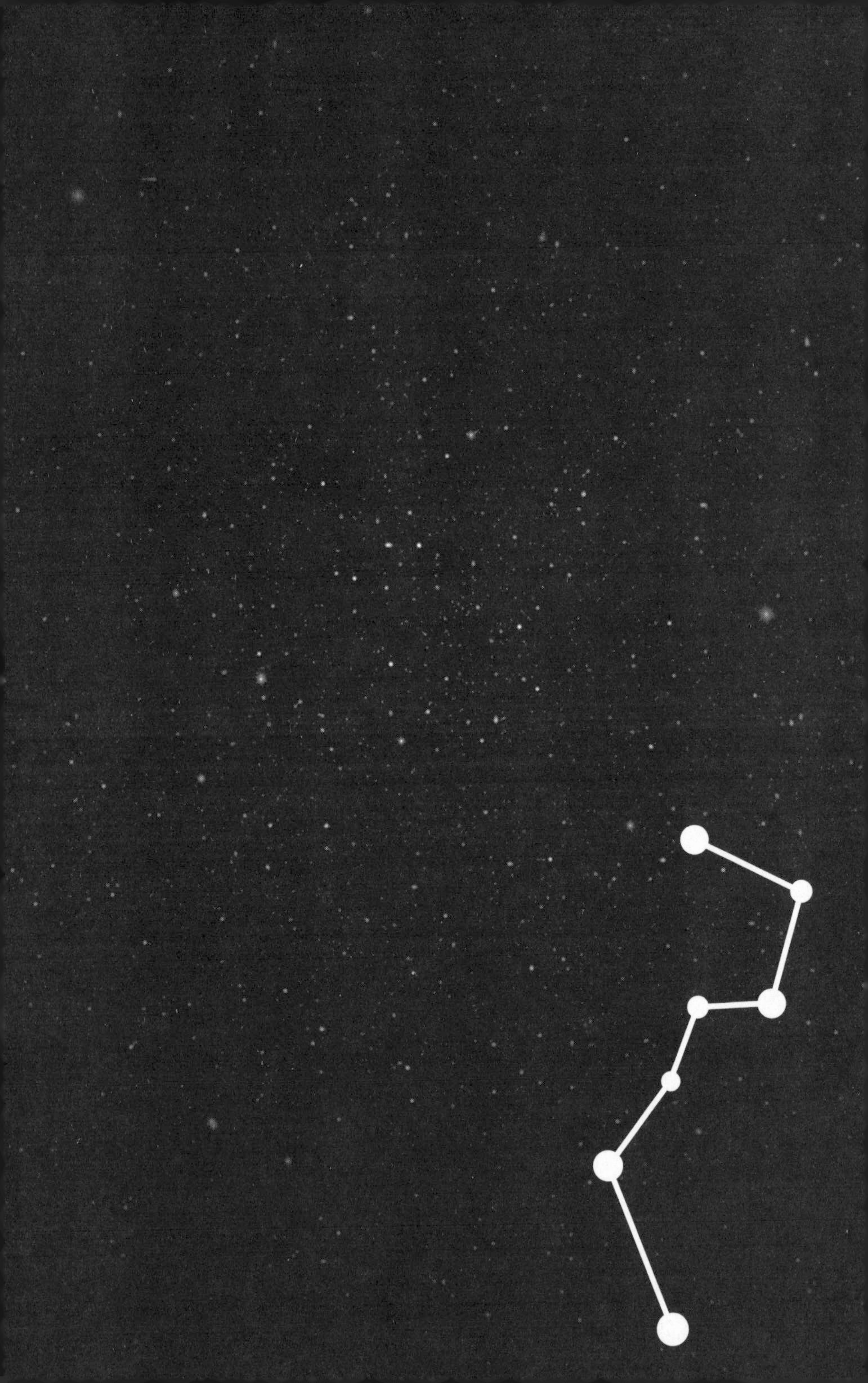

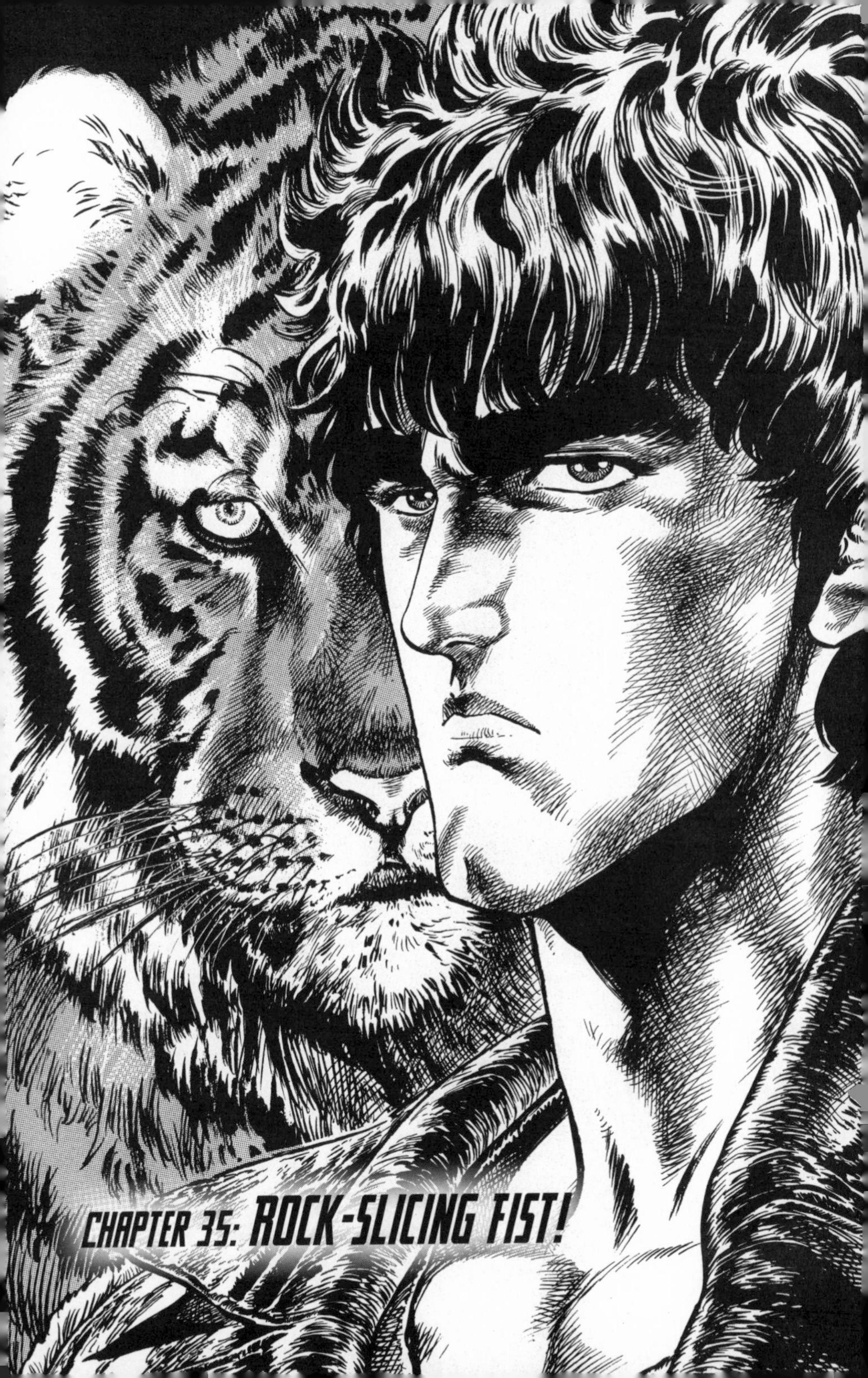
CHAPTER 35: ROCK-SLICING FIST!

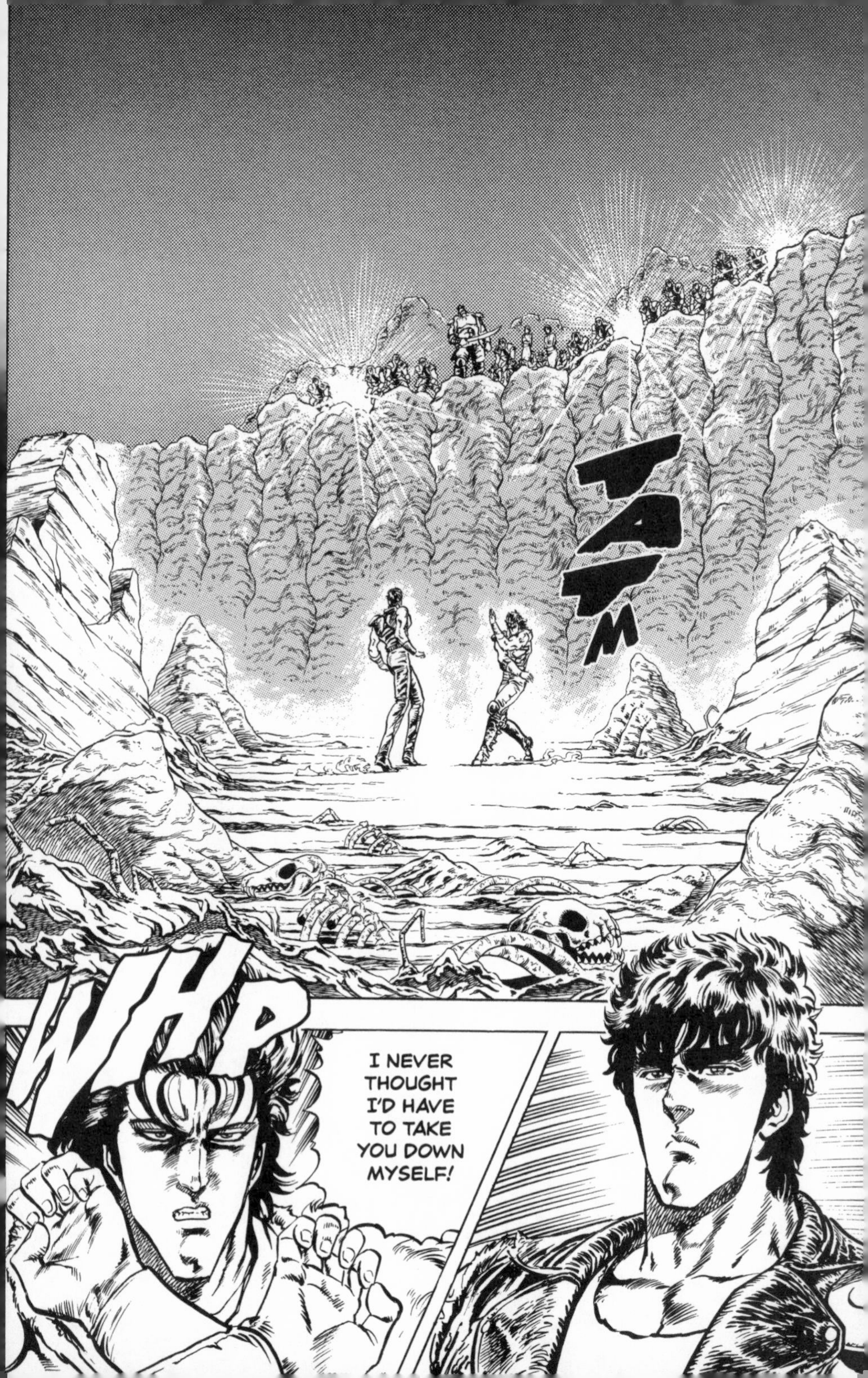
TATM
WHP
I NEVER THOUGHT I'D HAVE TO TAKE YOU DOWN MYSELF!

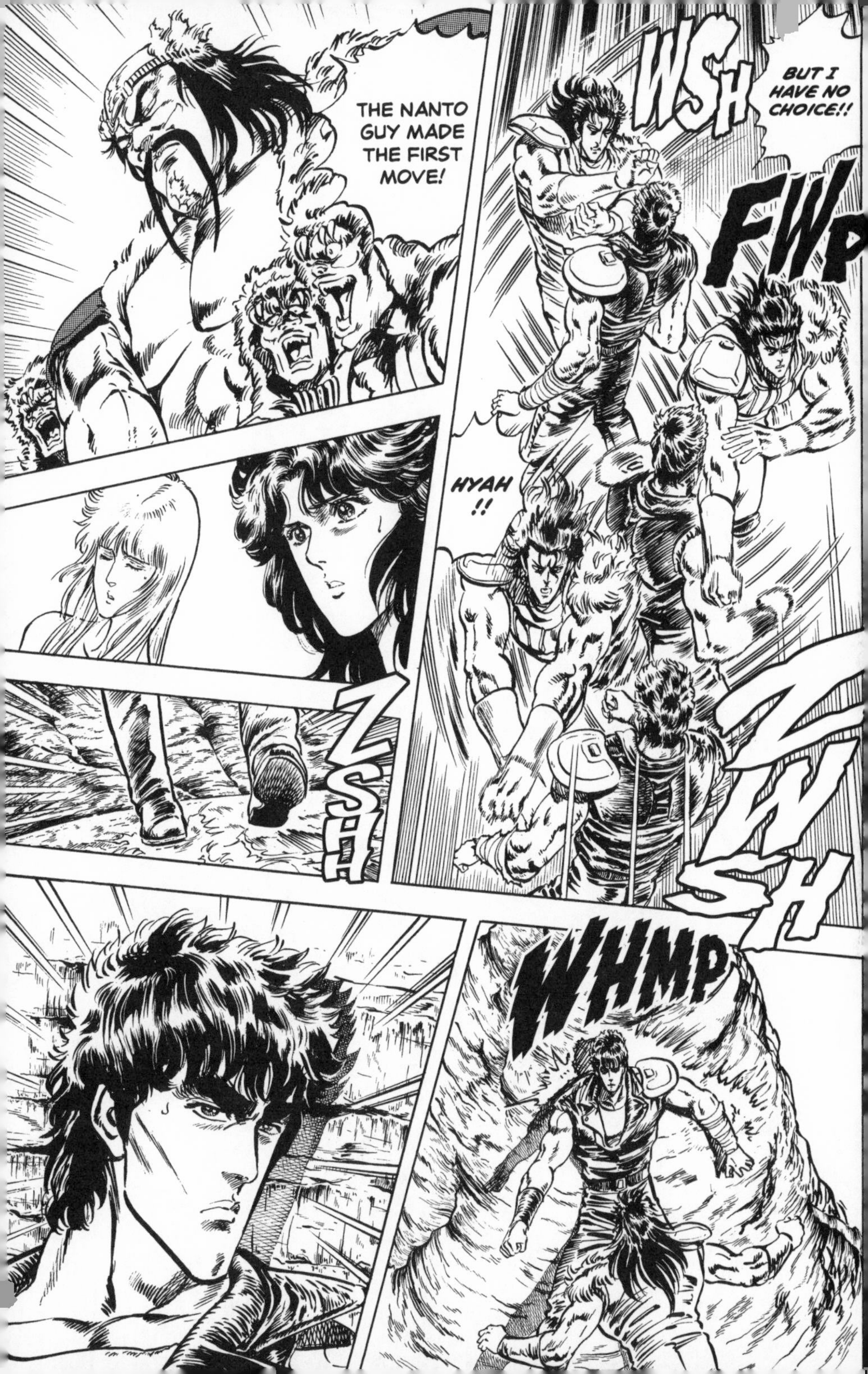
WSH
BUT I HAVE NO CHOICE!!
FWP
HYAH !!
ZWSH
THE NANTO GUY MADE THE FIRST MOVE!
ZSHH
WHMP

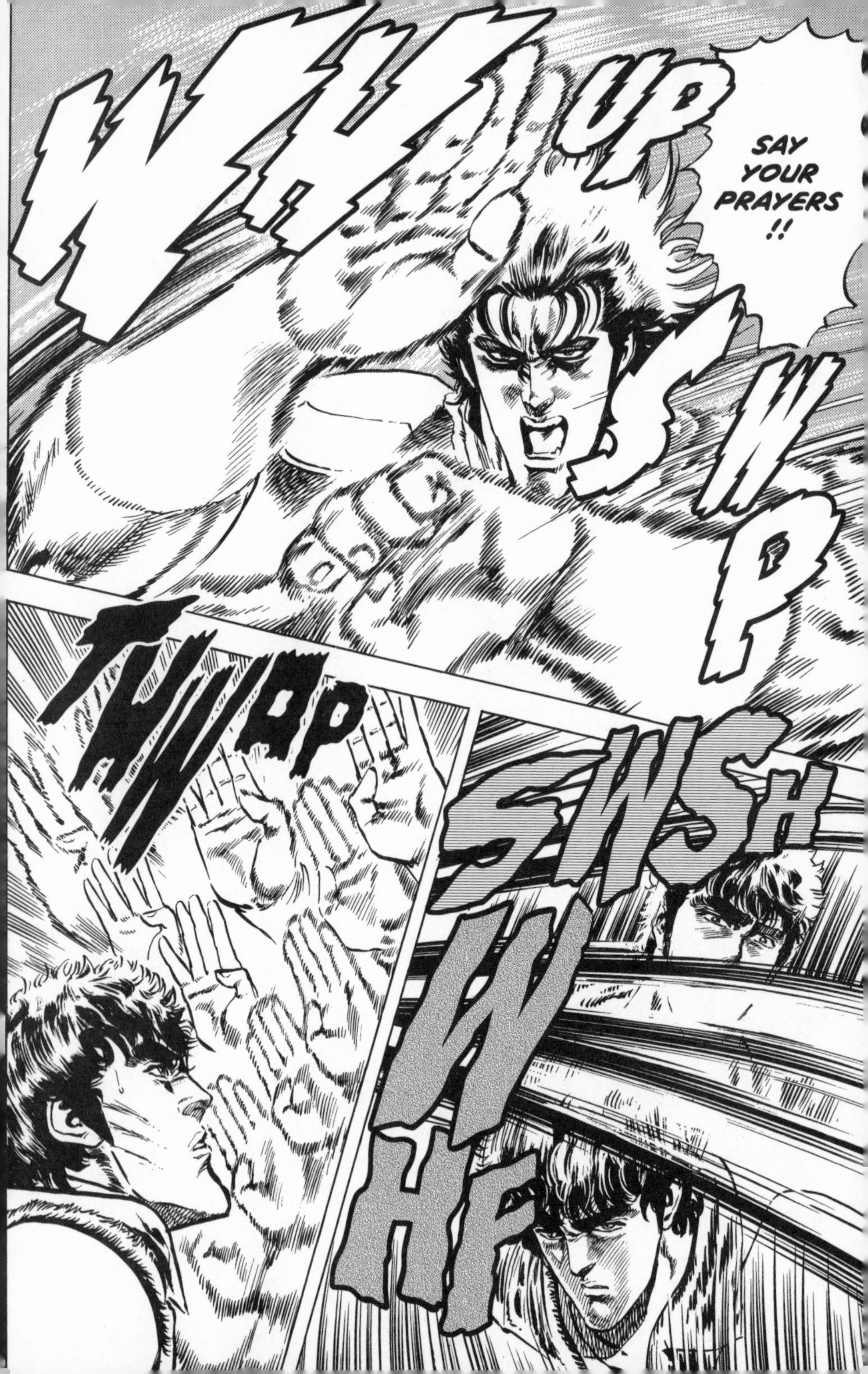
SAY YOUR PRAYERS !!
SWISH
THWAP

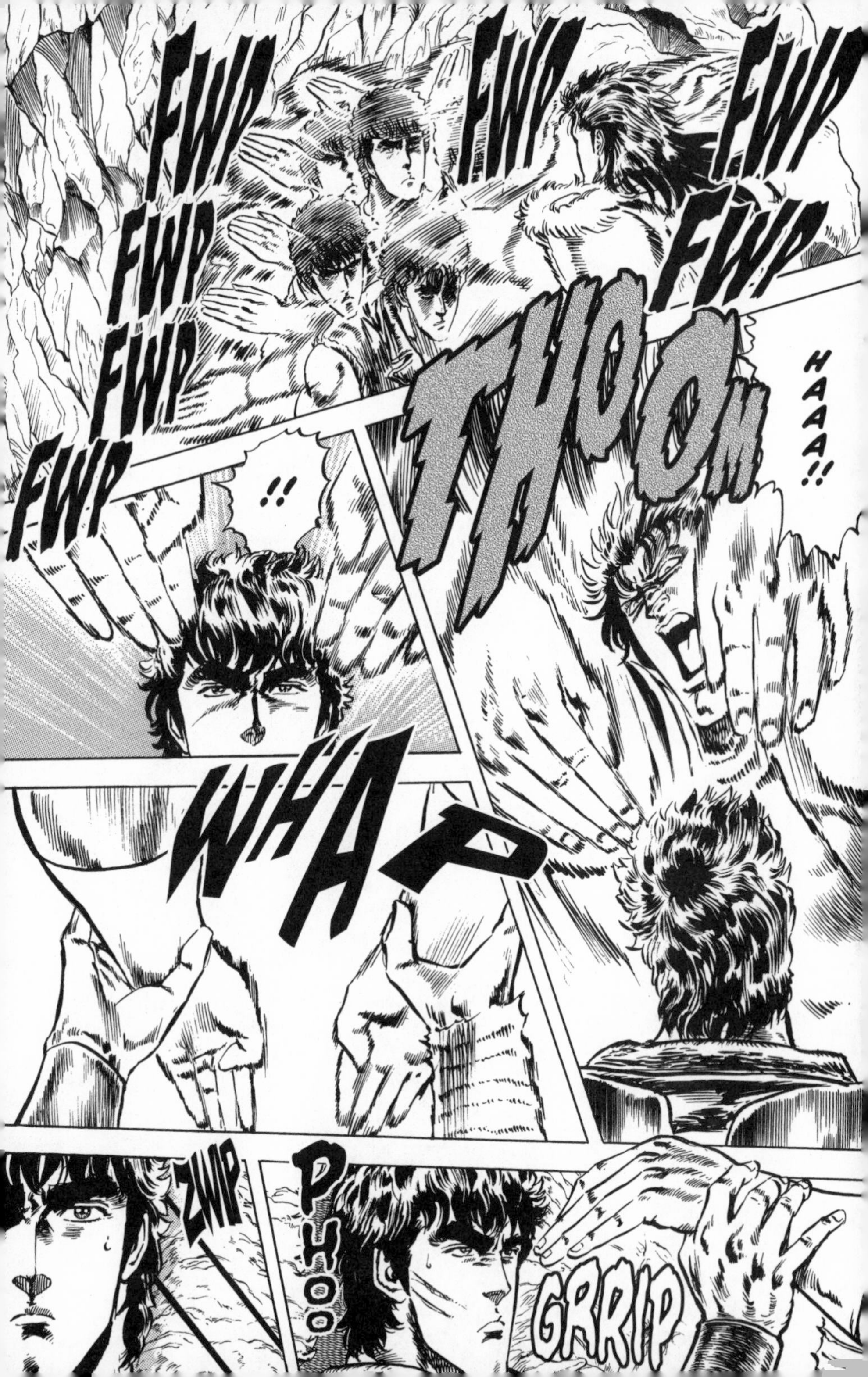
FWP
FWP
FWP
FWP
FWP
FWP
FWP
FWP
THOOM
HAAAA!!
!!
WHAP
GRIP
PHOOO
ZWIP

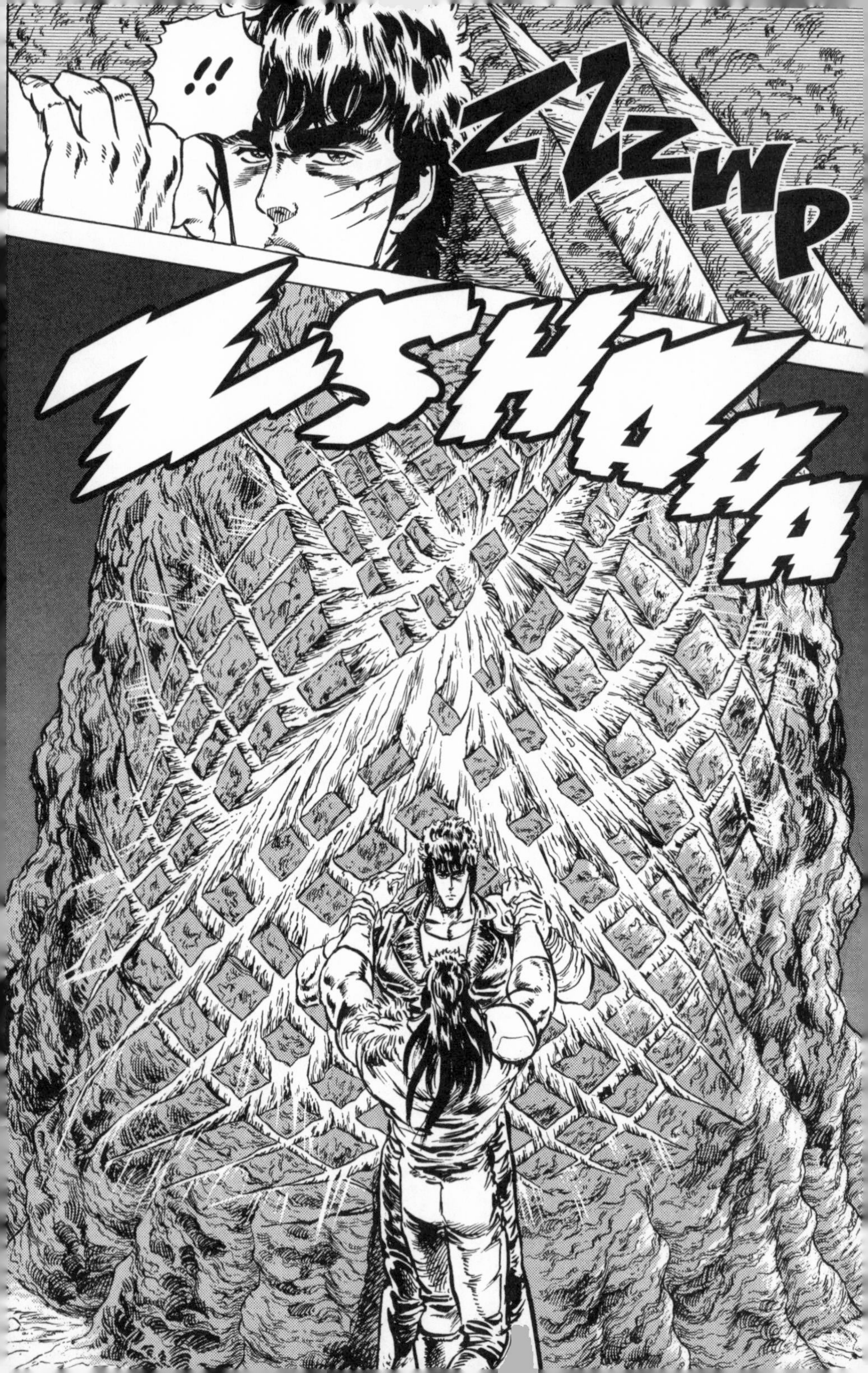
!!
ZZZWP
ZSHAAA

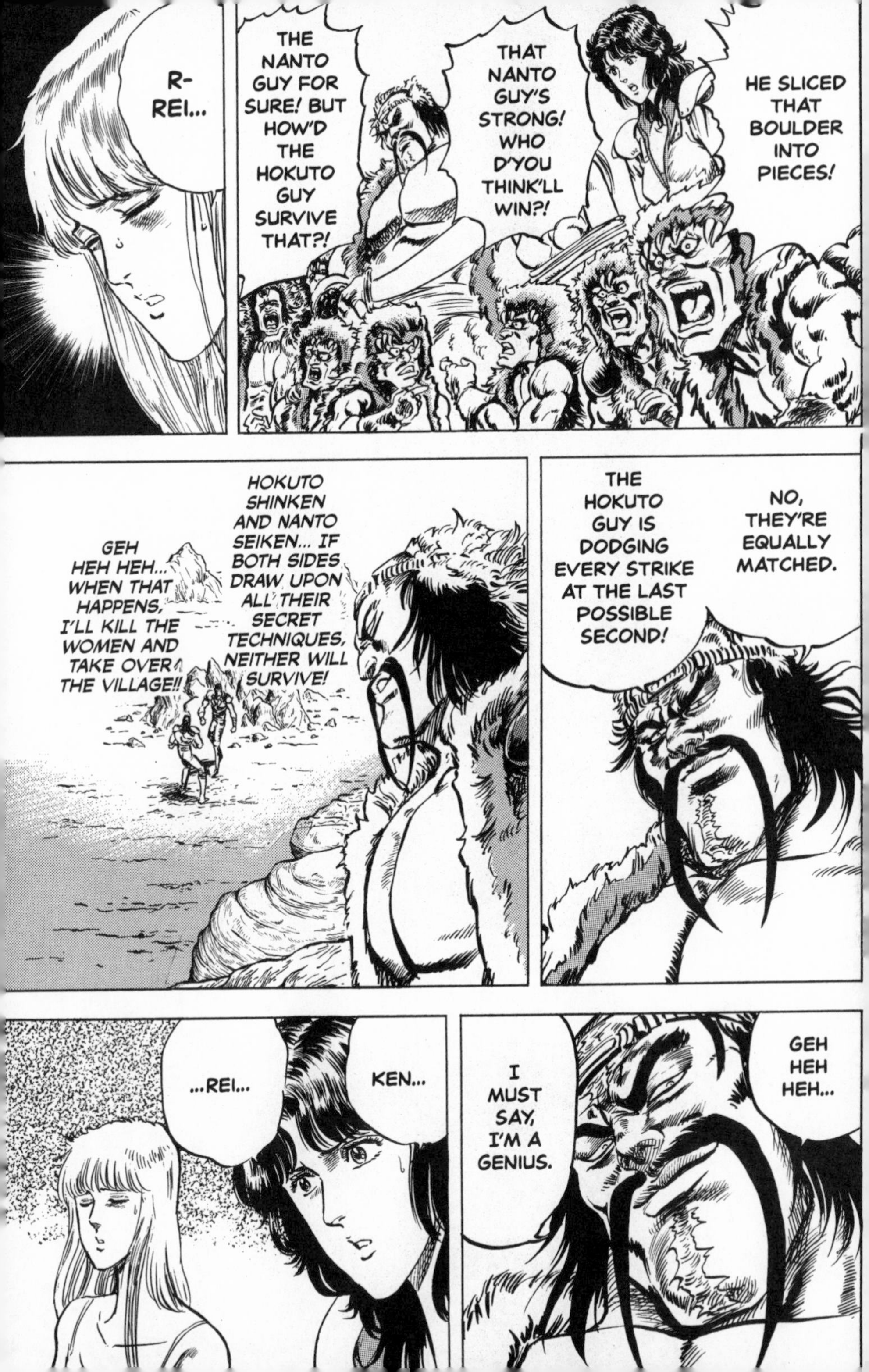
HE SLICED THAT BOULDER INTO PIECES!
THAT NANTO GUY'S STRONG! WHO D'YOU THINK'LL WIN?!
THE NANTO GUY FOR SURE! BUT HOW'D THE HOKUTO GUY SURVIVE THAT?!
R-REI...
NO, THEY'RE EQUALLY MATCHED.
THE HOKUTO GUY IS DODGING EVERY STRIKE AT THE LAST POSSIBLE SECOND!
HOKUTO SHINKEN AND NANTO SEIKEN... IF BOTH SIDES DRAW UPON ALL THEIR SECRET TECHNIQUES, NEITHER WILL SURVIVE!
GEH HEH HEH... WHEN THAT HAPPENS, I'LL KILL THE WOMEN AND TAKE OVER THE VILLAGE!!
GEH HEH HEH...
I MUST SAY, I'M A GENIUS.
KEN...
...REI...

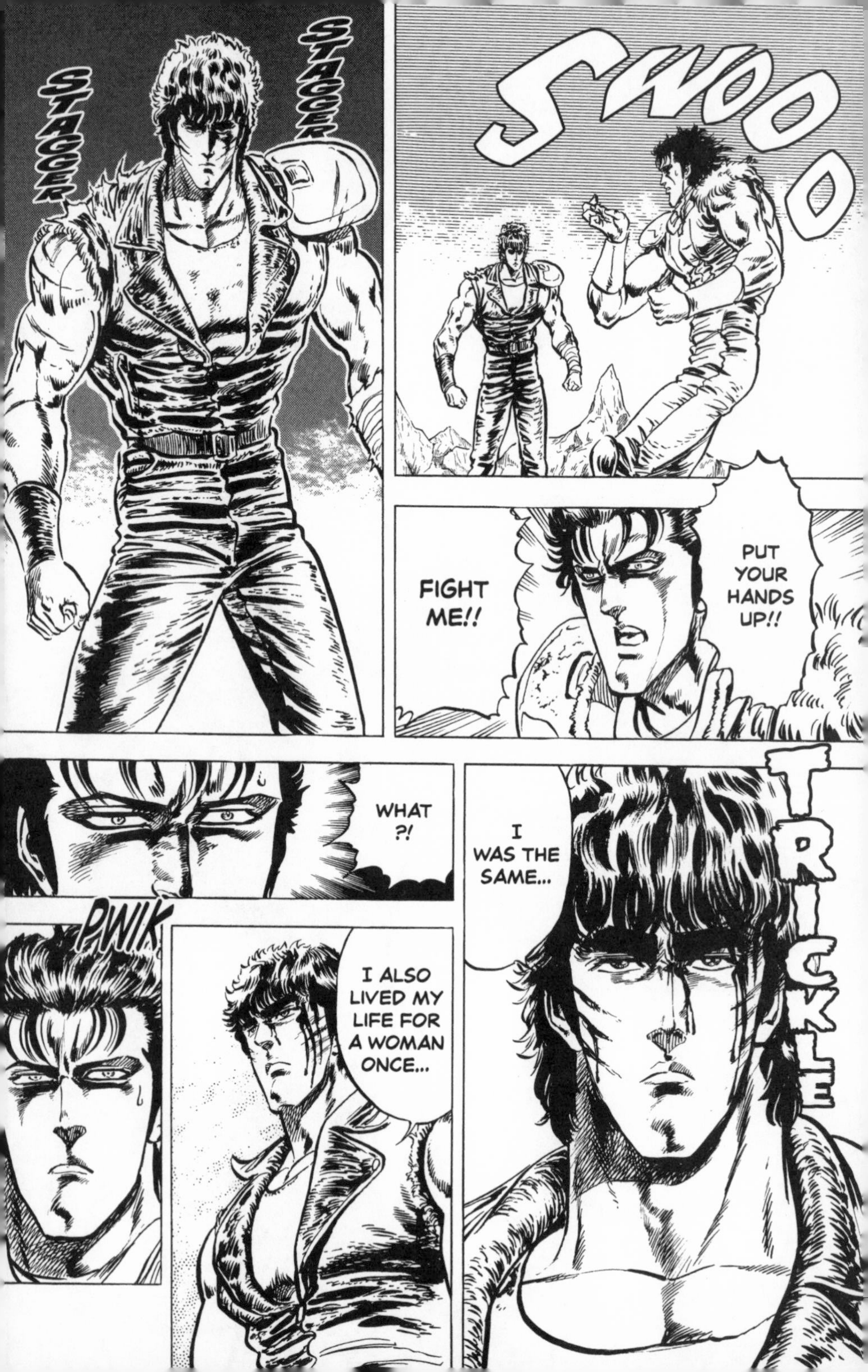
SWOOO
PUT YOUR HANDS UP!!
FIGHT ME!!
STAGGER
STAGGER
TRICKLE
I WAS THE SAME...
WHAT ?!
I ALSO LIVED MY LIFE FOR A WOMAN ONCE...
PWIK

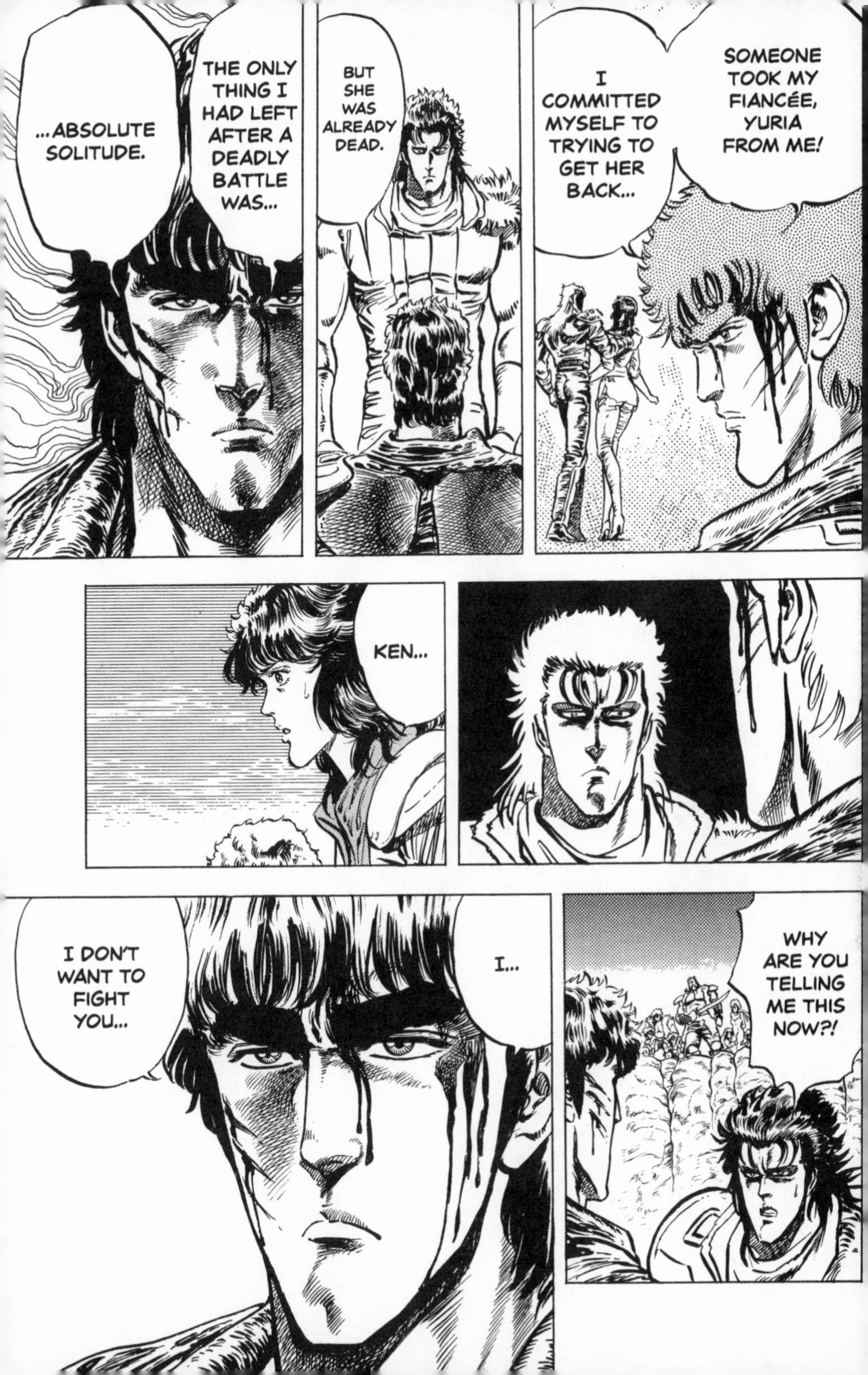
SOMEONE TOOK MY FIANCÉE, YURIA FROM ME!
I COMMITTED MYSELF TO TRYING TO GET HER BACK...
BUT SHE WAS ALREADY DEAD.
THE ONLY THING I HAD LEFT AFTER A DEADLY BATTLE WAS...
...ABSOLUTE SOLITUDE.
KEN...
WHY ARE YOU TELLING ME THIS NOW?!
I...
I DON'T WANT TO FIGHT YOU...

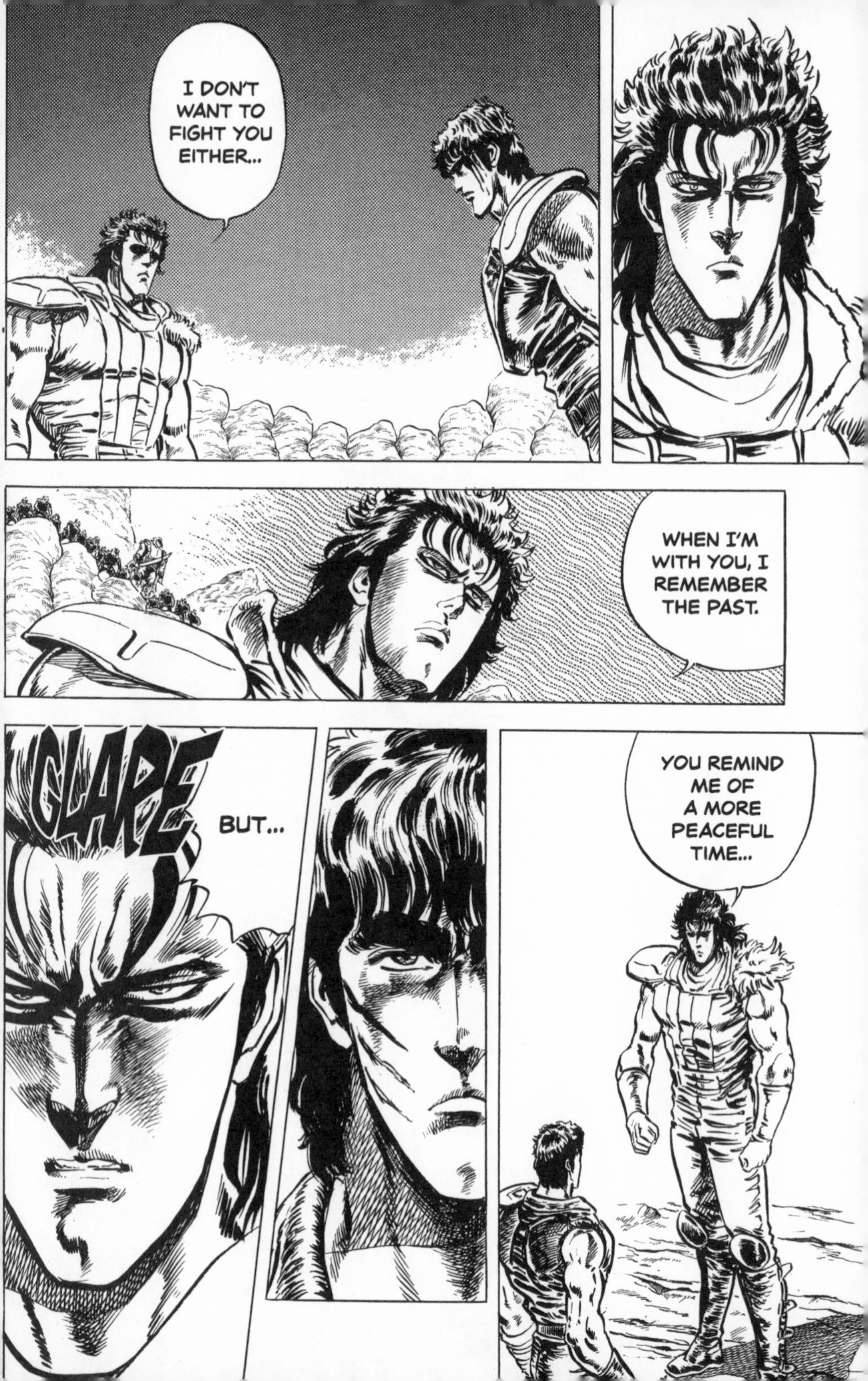
I DON'T WANT TO FIGHT YOU EITHER...
WHEN I'M WITH YOU, I REMEMBER THE PAST.
YOU REMIND ME OF A MORE PEACEFUL TIME...
GLAPE
BUT...

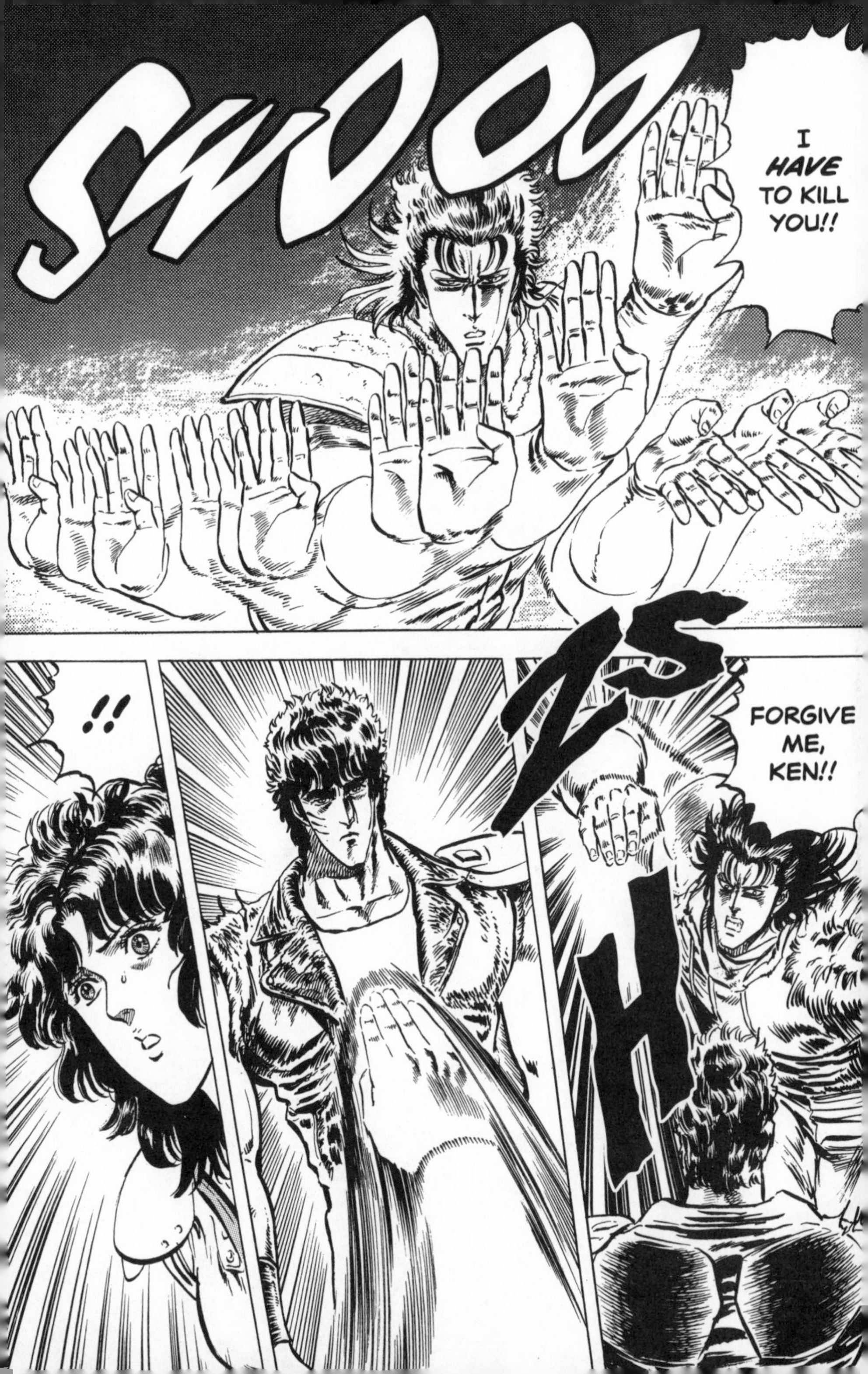
SHOOO
I *HAVE* TO KILL YOU!!
FORGIVE ME, KEN!!
!!

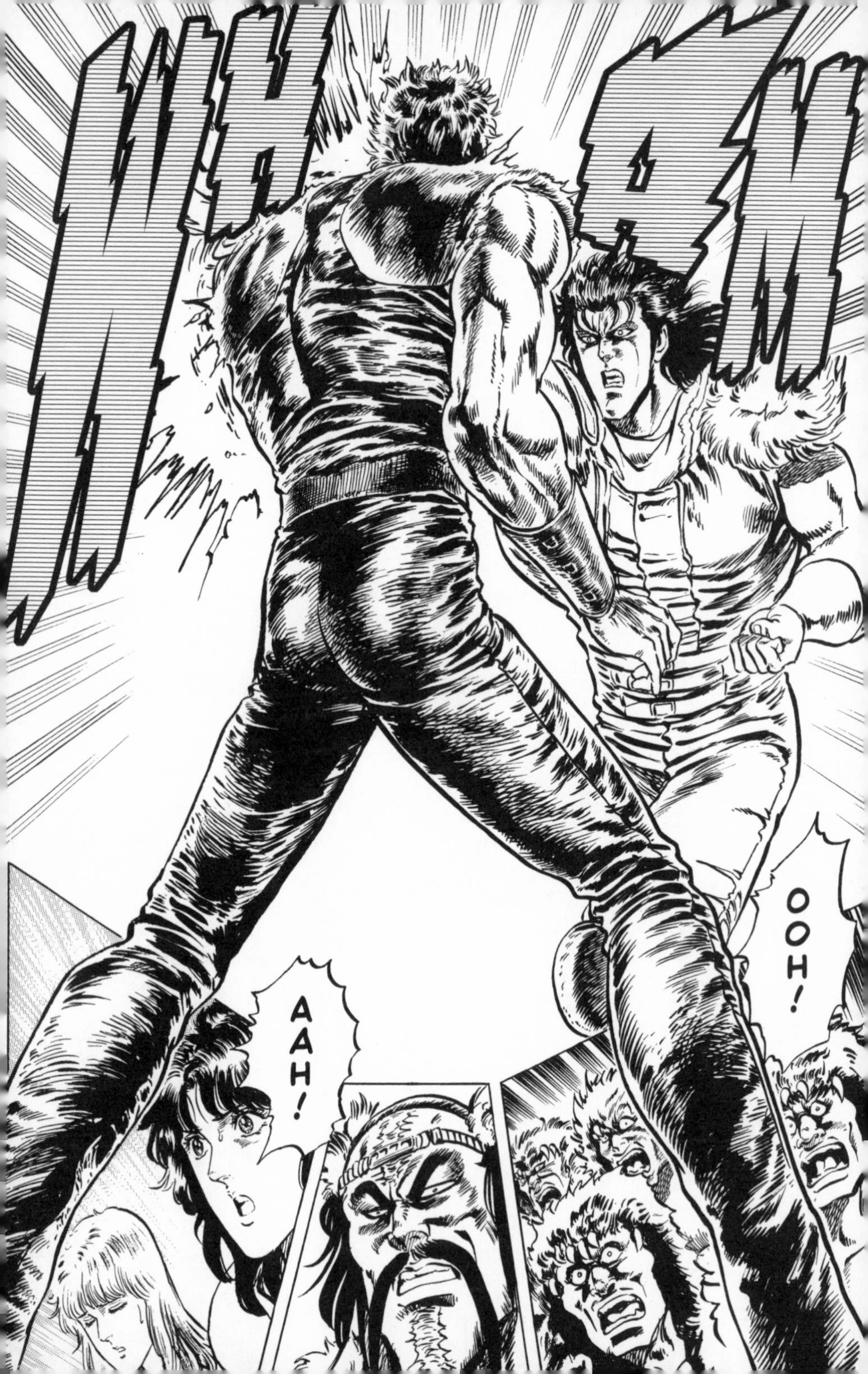
WHAM
OOH!
AAH!

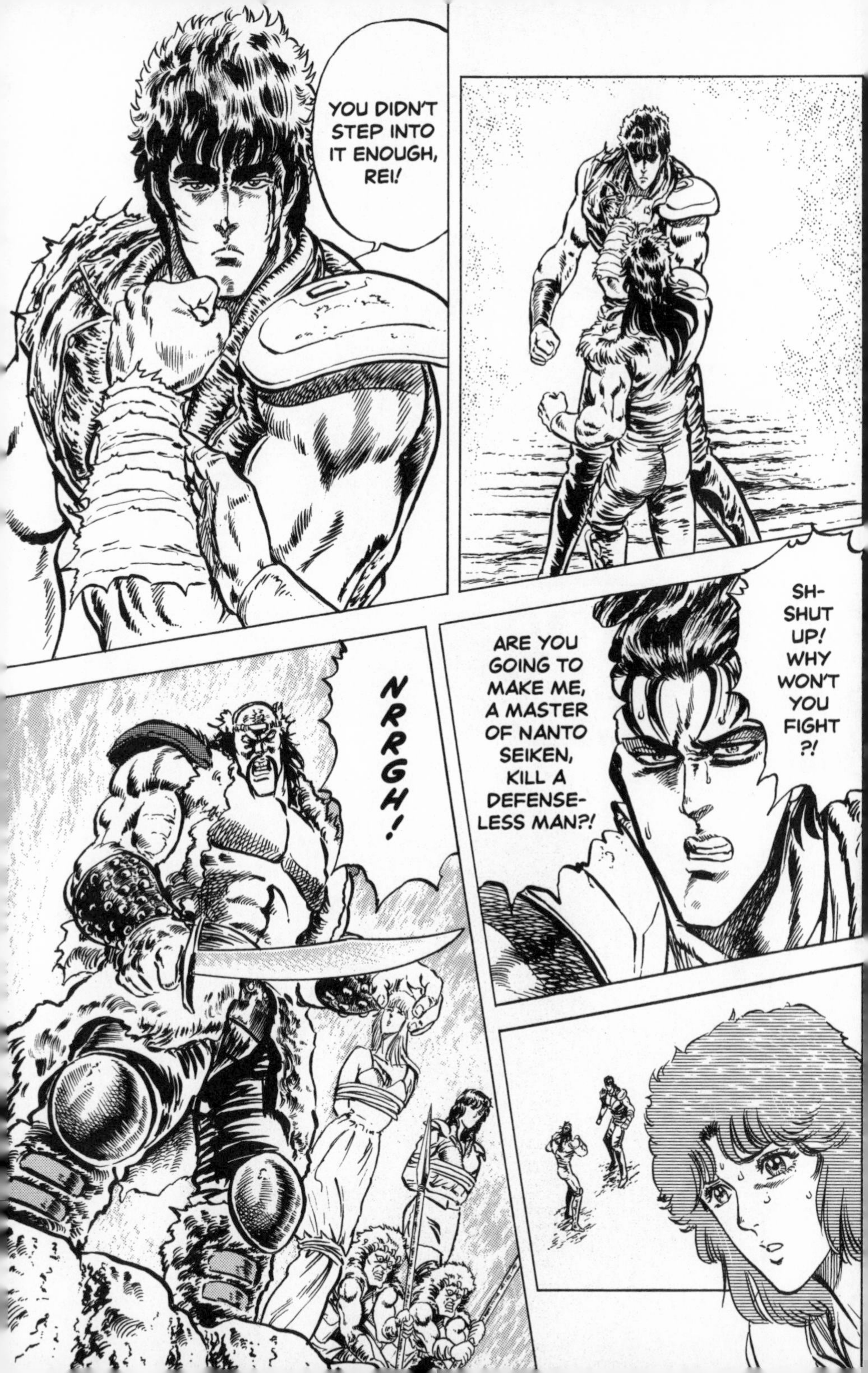
YOU DIDN'T STEP INTO IT ENOUGH, REI!
SH-SHUT UP! WHY WON'T YOU FIGHT?!
ARE YOU GOING TO MAKE ME, A MASTER OF NANTO SEIKEN, KILL A DEFENSELESS MAN?!
NRRGH!

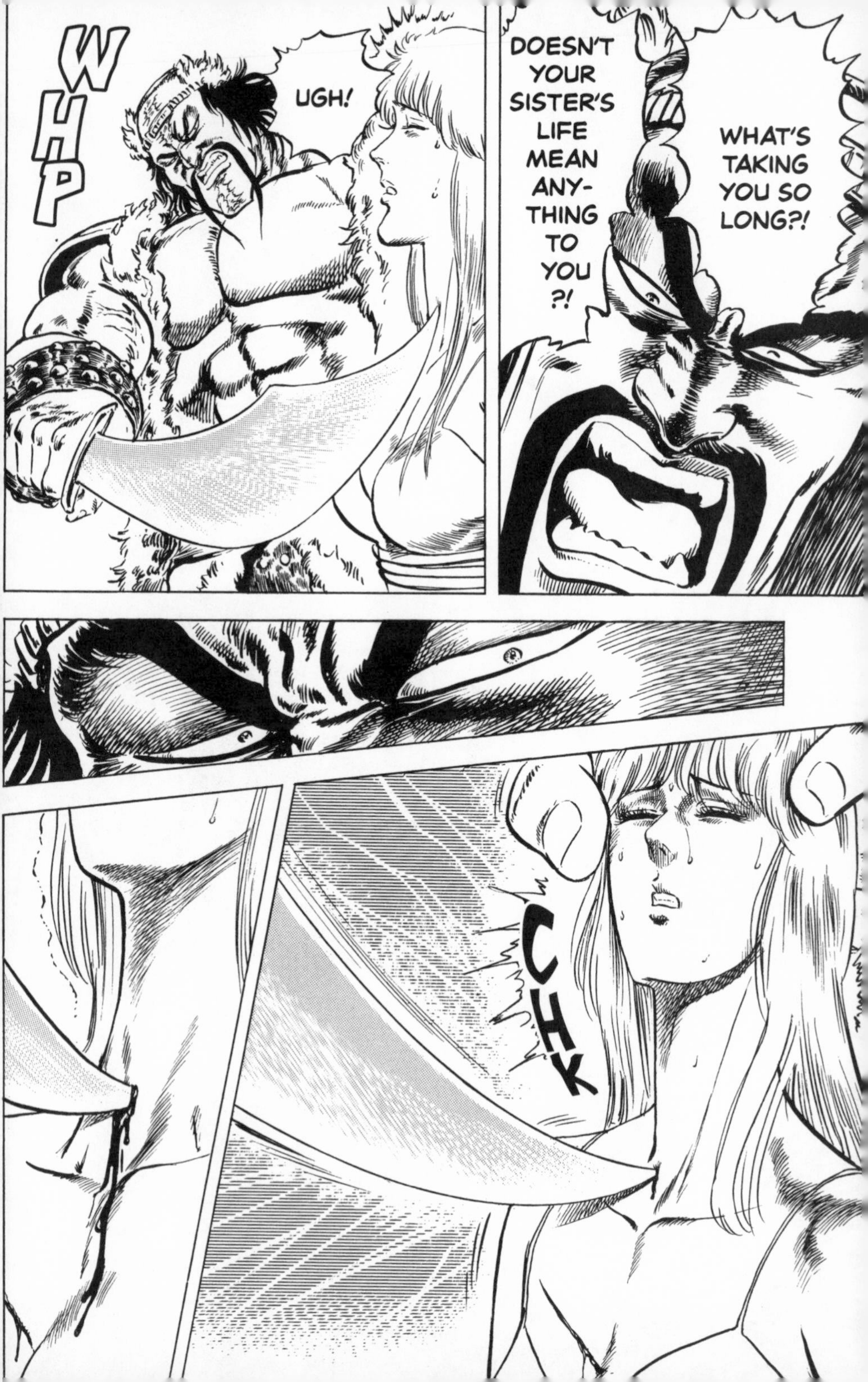
WHAT'S TAKING YOU SO LONG?!
DOESN'T YOUR SISTER'S LIFE MEAN ANYTHING TO YOU ?!
UGH!
WHP
CHK

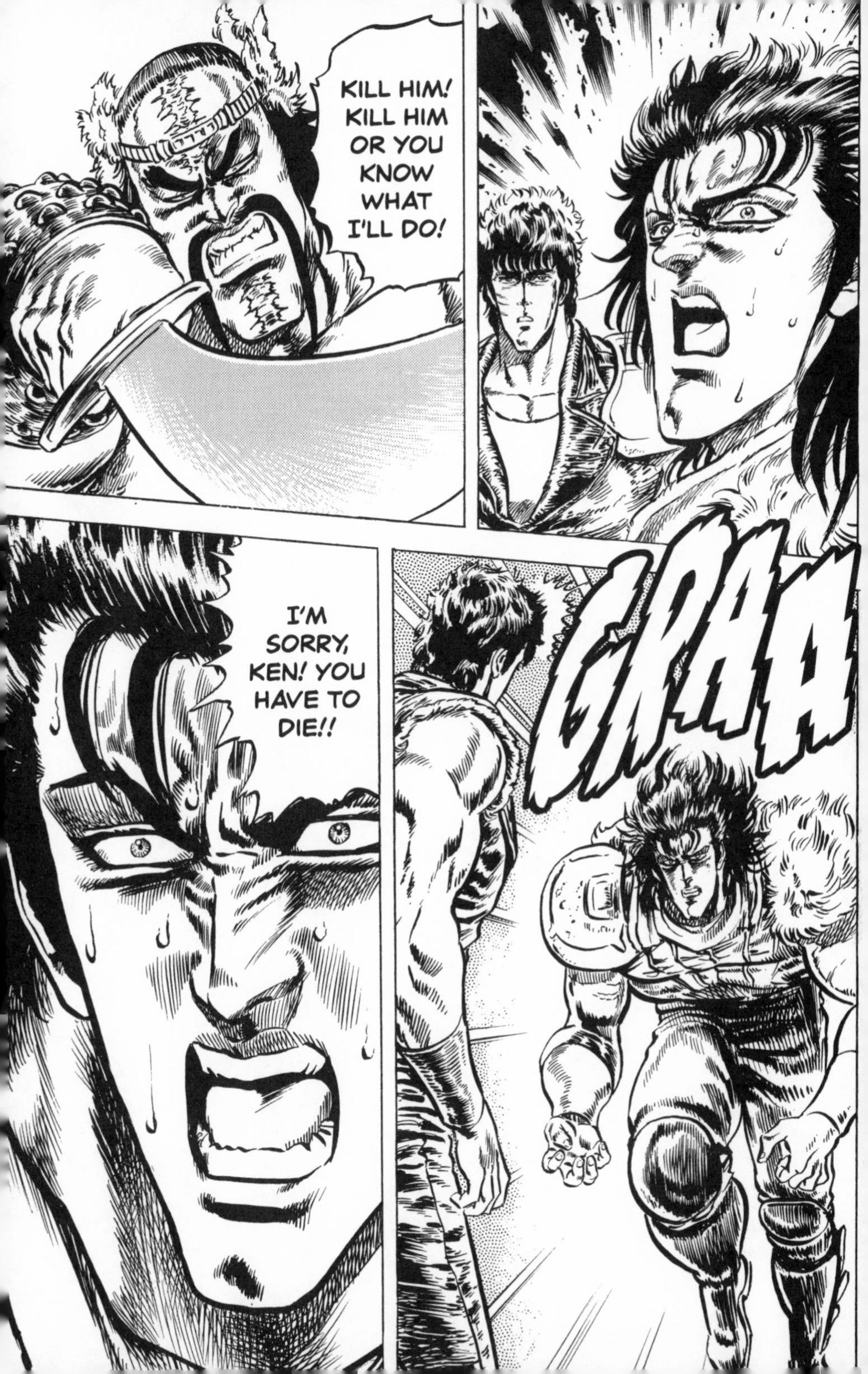
KILL HIM! KILL HIM OR YOU KNOW WHAT I'LL DO!
GRAA
I'M SORRY, KEN! YOU HAVE TO DIE!!

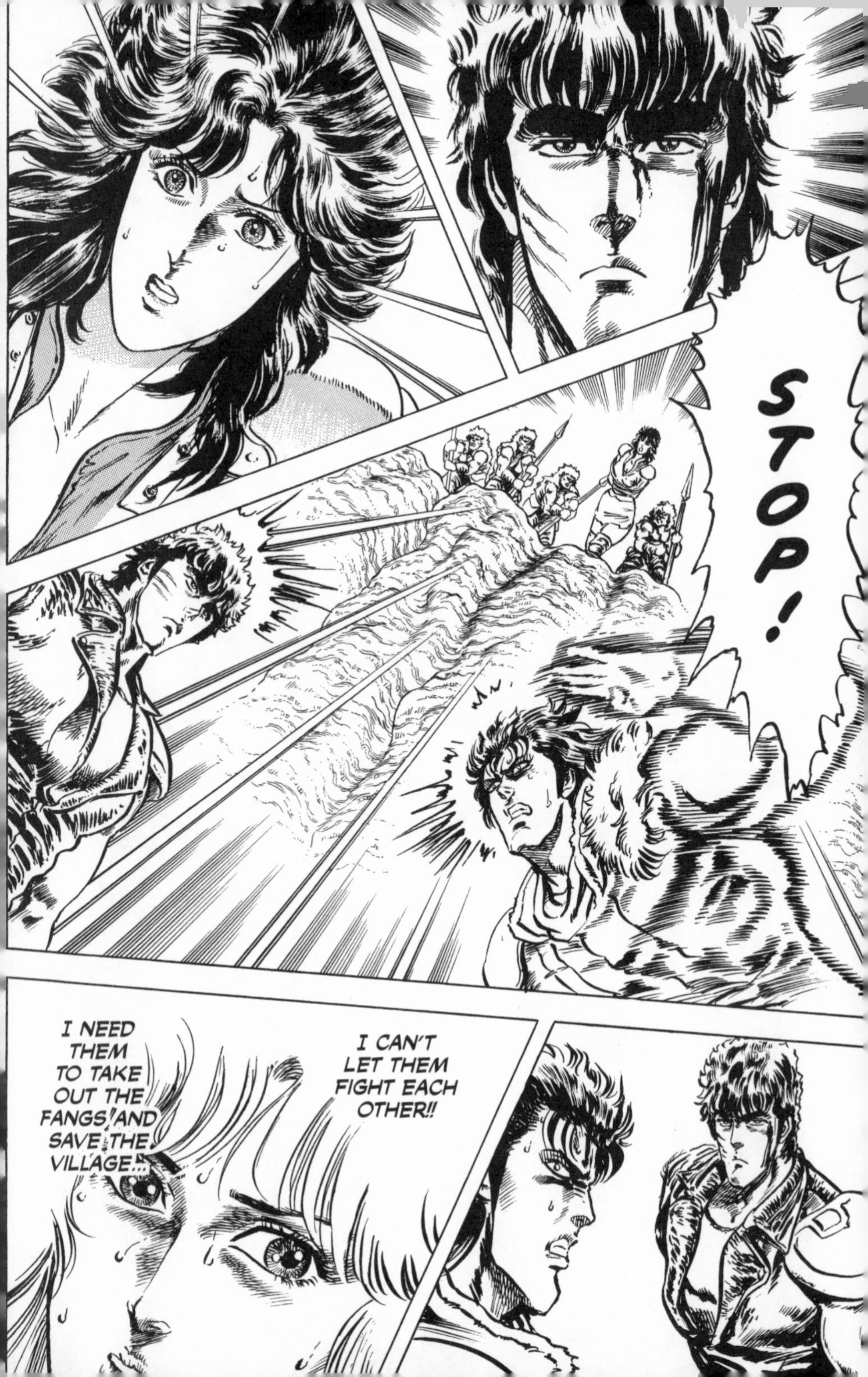
STOP!!
I CAN'T LET THEM FIGHT EACH OTHER!!
I NEED THEM TO TAKE OUT THE FANGS AND SAVE THE VILLAGE...

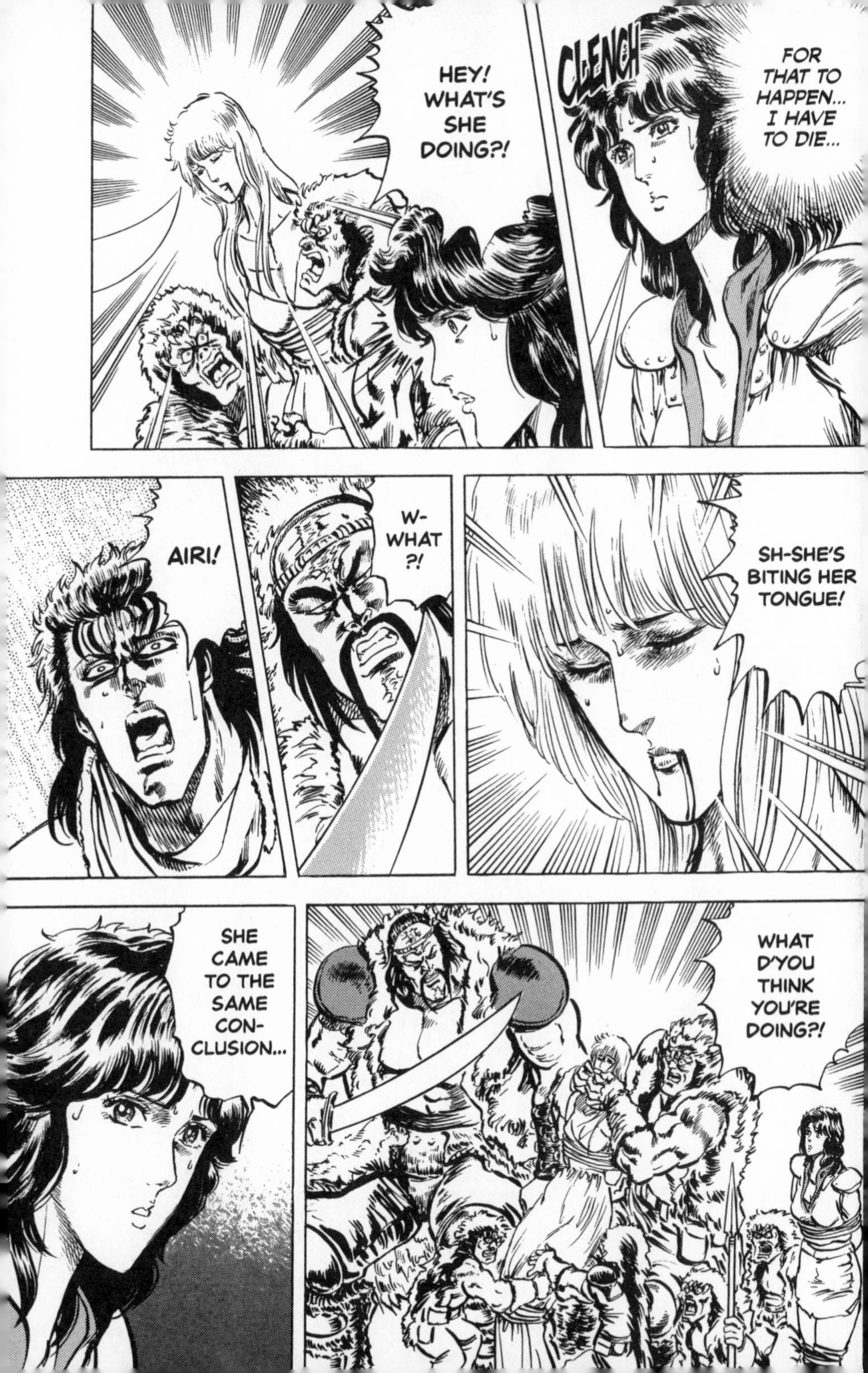

FOR THAT TO HAPPEN... I HAVE TO DIE...
CLENCH
HEY! WHAT'S SHE DOING?!
SH-SHE'S BITING HER TONGUE!
W- WHAT ?!
AIRI!
WHAT D'YOU THINK YOU'RE DOING?!
SHE CAME TO THE SAME CON- CLUSION...

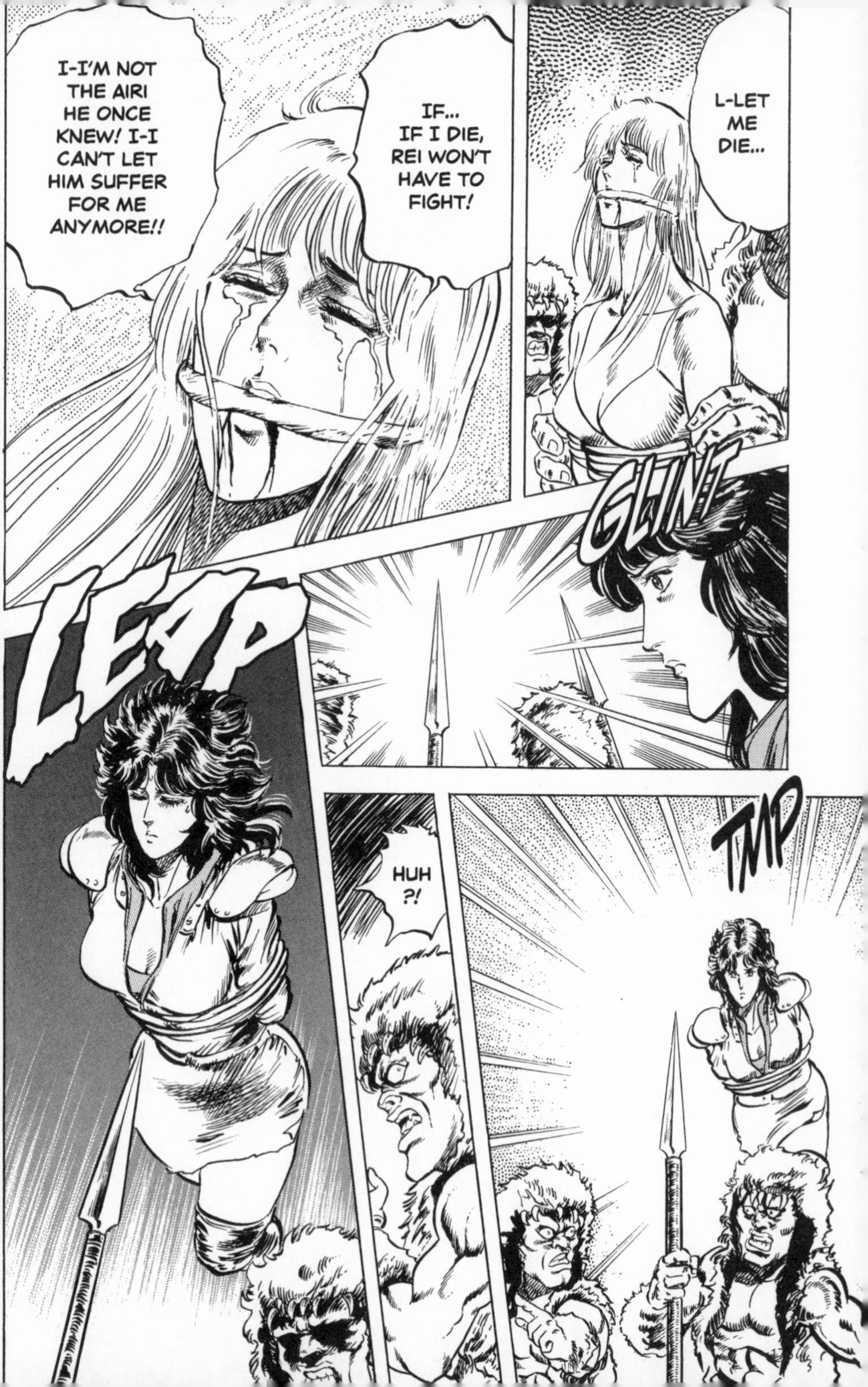
L-LET ME DIE...
IF... IF I DIE, REI WON'T HAVE TO FIGHT!
I-I'M NOT THE AIRI HE ONCE KNEW! I-I CAN'T LET HIM SUFFER FOR ME ANYMORE!!
GLINT
TMP
HUH ?!
LEAP

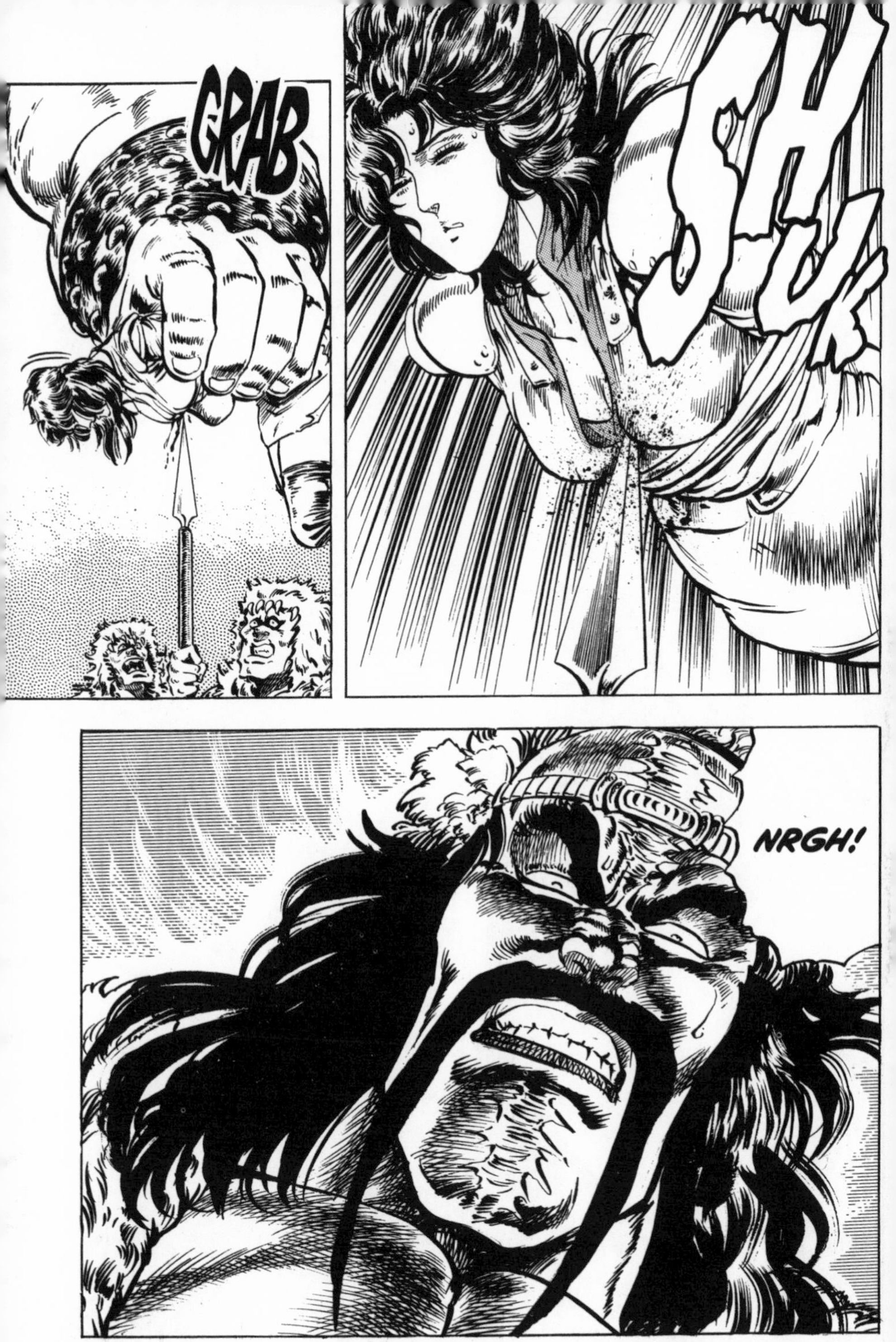
SHUK
GRAB
NRGH!

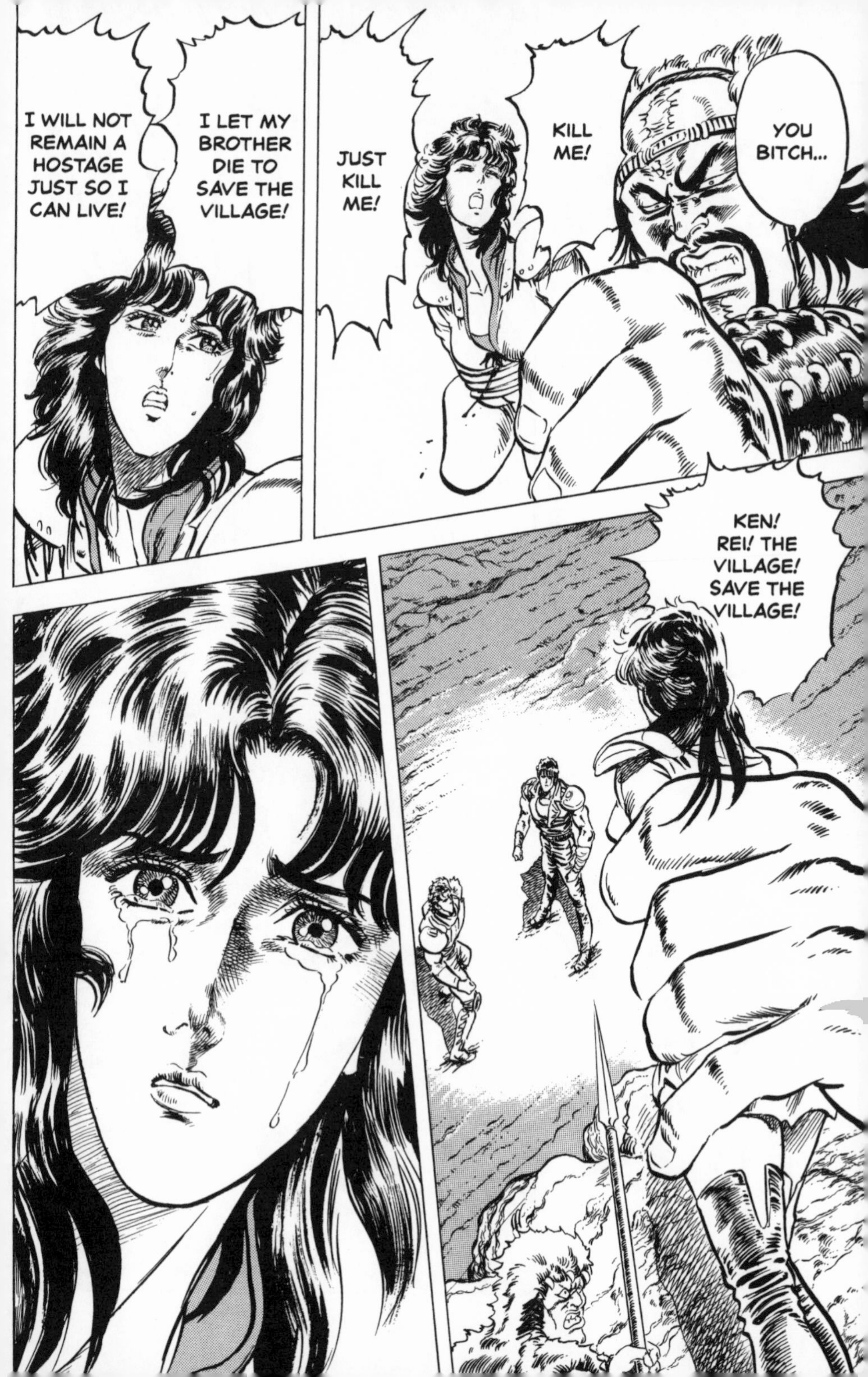
YOU BITCH...
KILL ME!
JUST KILL ME!
I LET MY BROTHER DIE TO SAVE THE VILLAGE!
I WILL NOT REMAIN A HOSTAGE JUST SO I CAN LIVE!
KEN! REI! THE VILLAGE! SAVE THE VILLAGE!

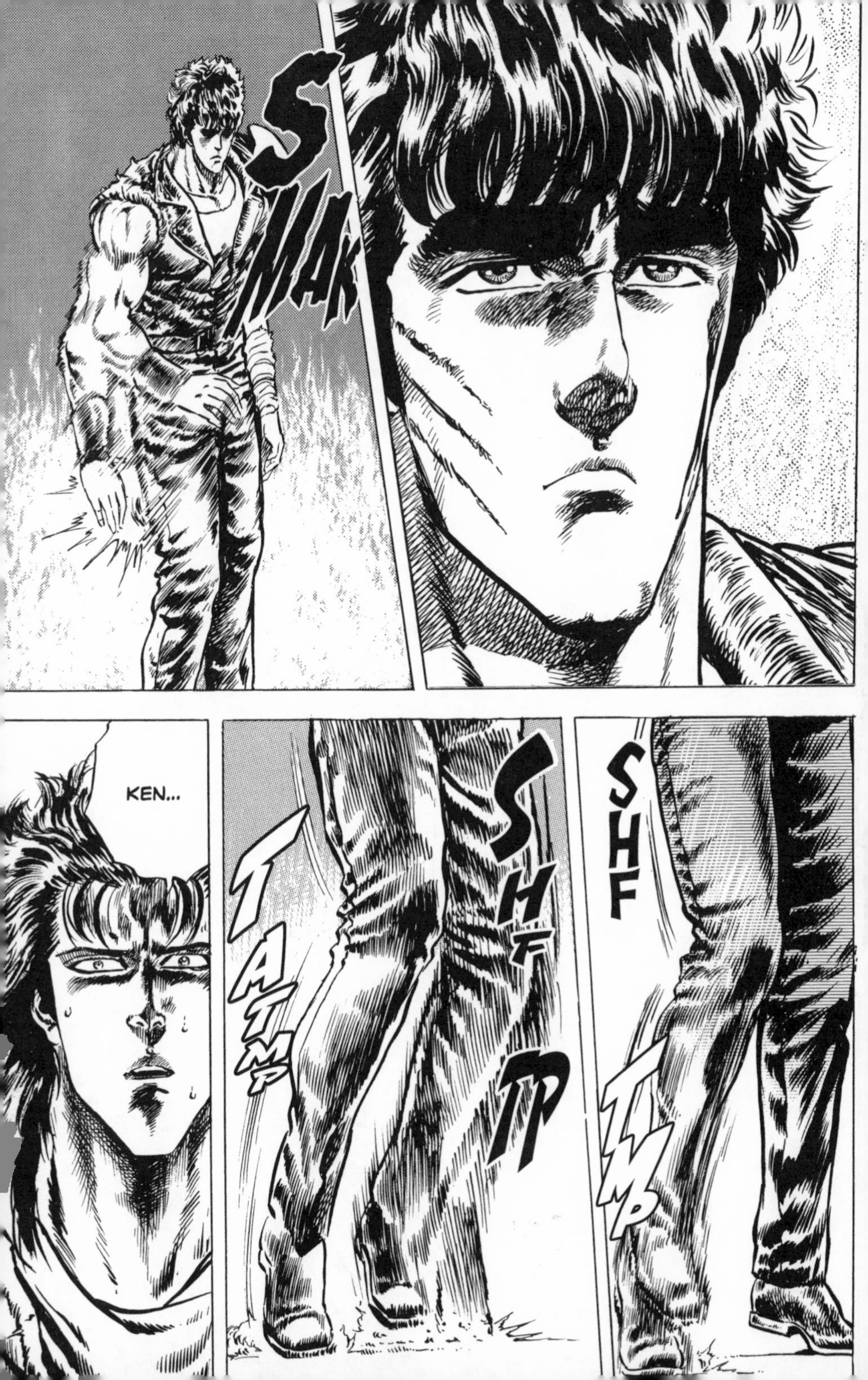
SMAK
SHF
TMP
SHF
TP
TATMP
KEN...

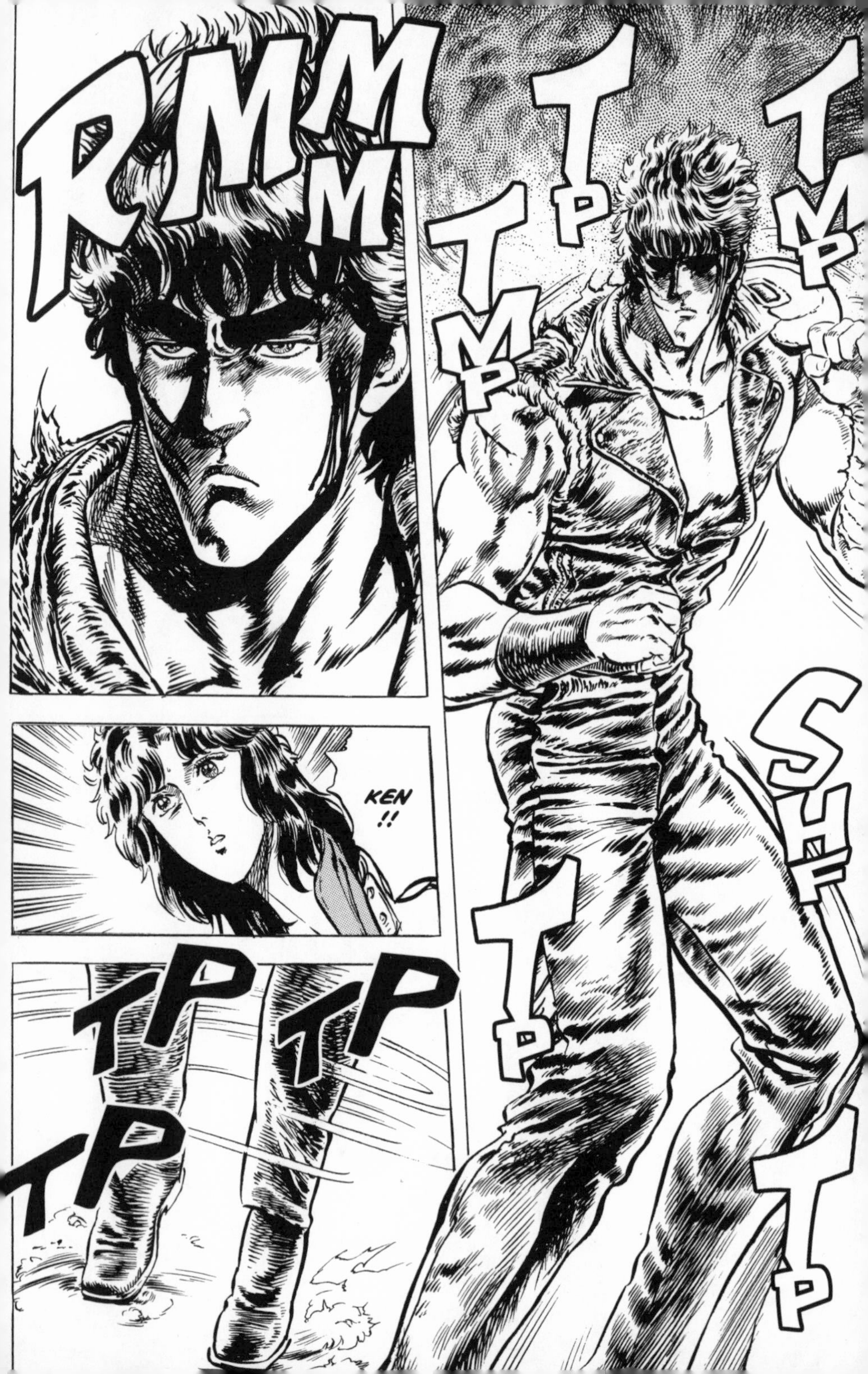
TMP
TP
TMP
SHF
TP
TP
RMMM
KEN !!
TP TP
TP

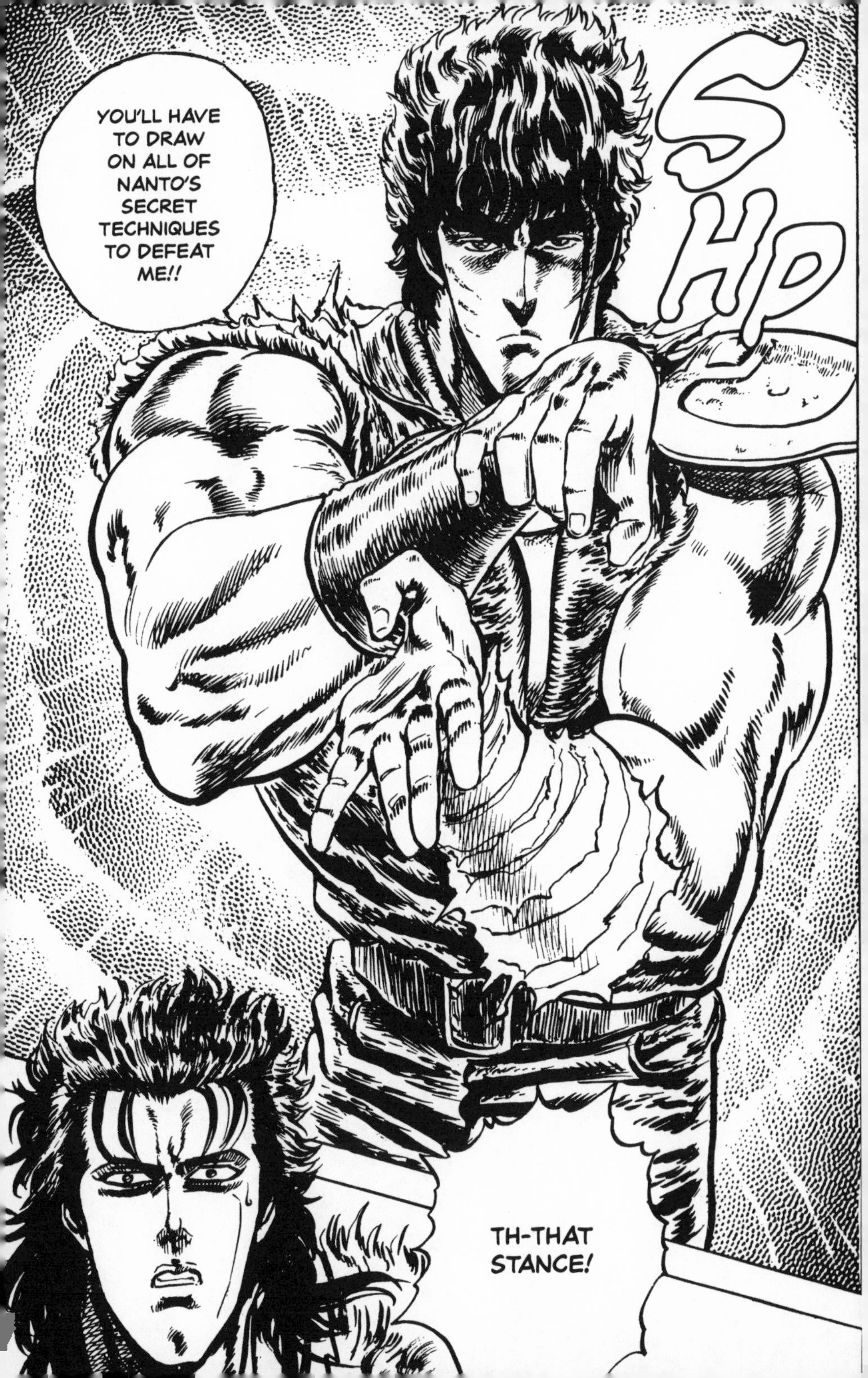
YOU'LL HAVE TO DRAW ON ALL OF NANTO'S SECRET TECHNIQUES TO DEFEAT ME!!
SHP
TH-THAT STANCE!

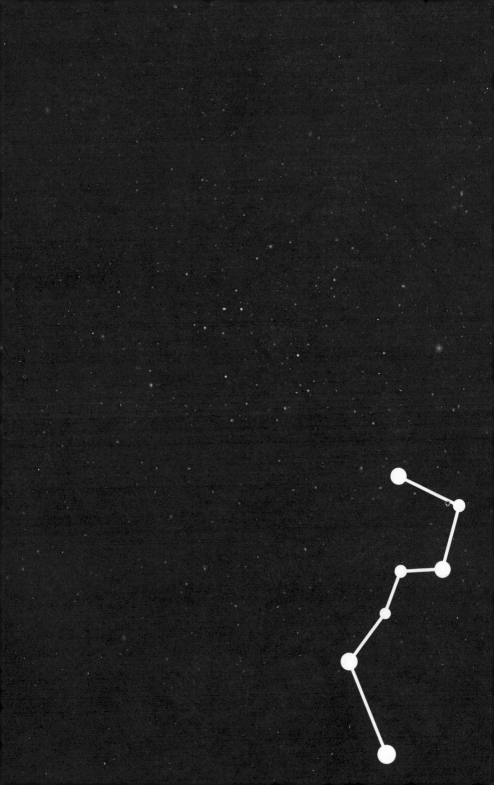

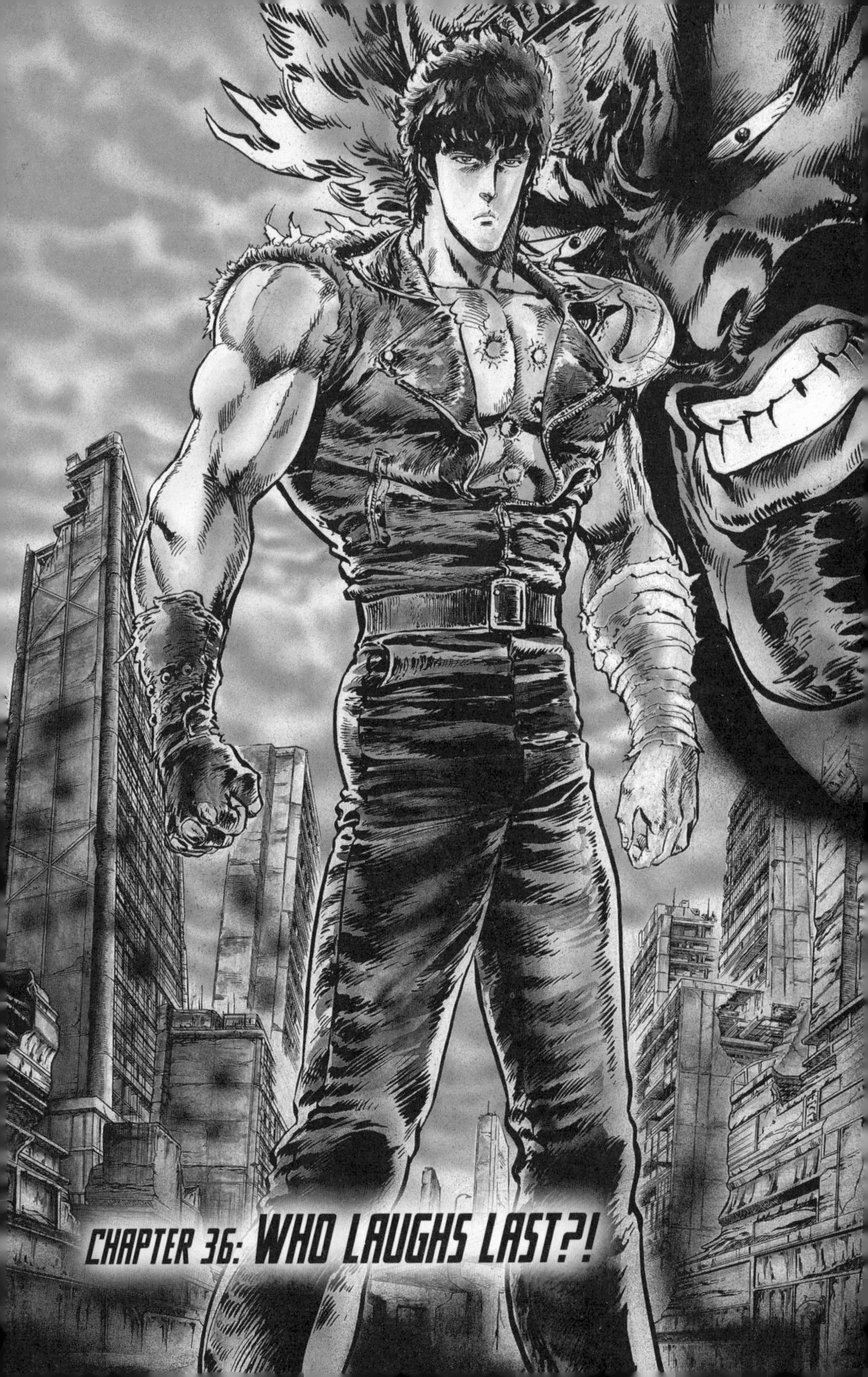
CHAPTER 36: WHO LAUGHS LAST?!

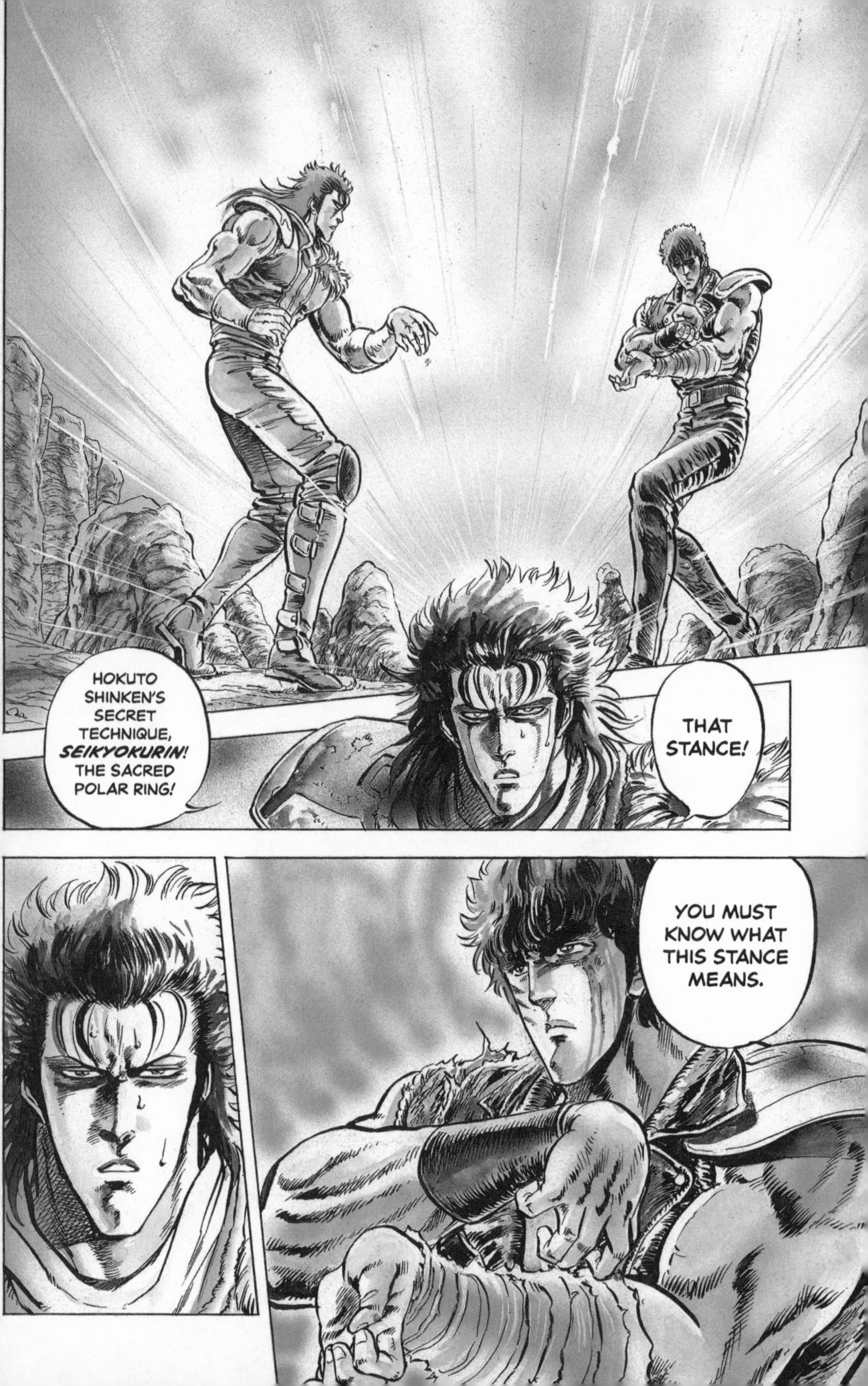
THAT STANCE!
HOKUTO SHINKEN'S SECRET TECHNIQUE, **SEIKYOKURIN!** THE SACRED POLAR RING!
YOU MUST KNOW WHAT THIS STANCE MEANS.

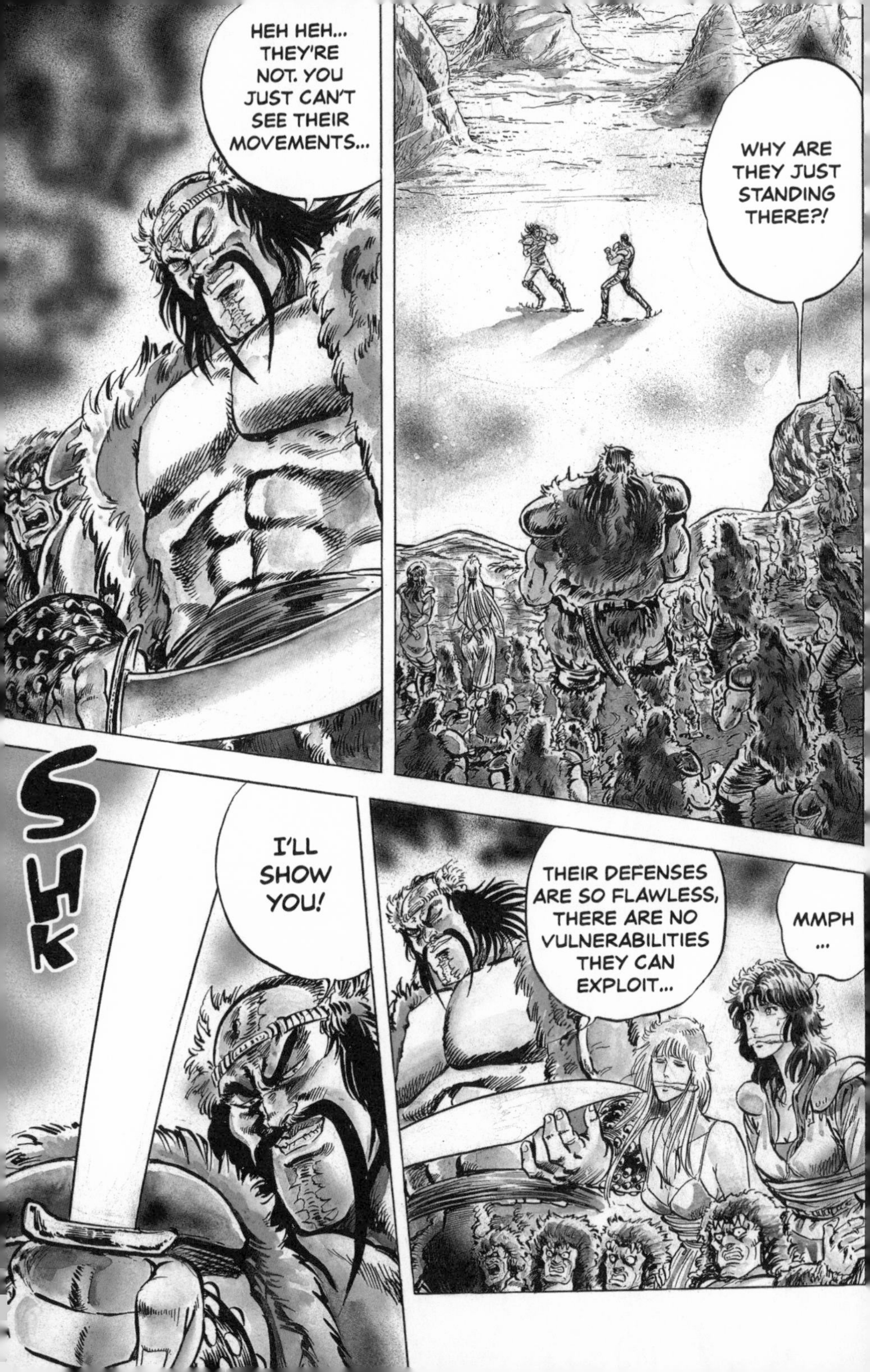
WHY ARE THEY JUST STANDING THERE?!
HEH HEH... THEY'RE NOT. YOU JUST CAN'T SEE THEIR MOVEMENTS...
MMPH ...
THEIR DEFENSES ARE SO FLAWLESS, THERE ARE NO VULNERABILITIES THEY CAN EXPLOIT...
I'LL SHOW YOU!
SHK

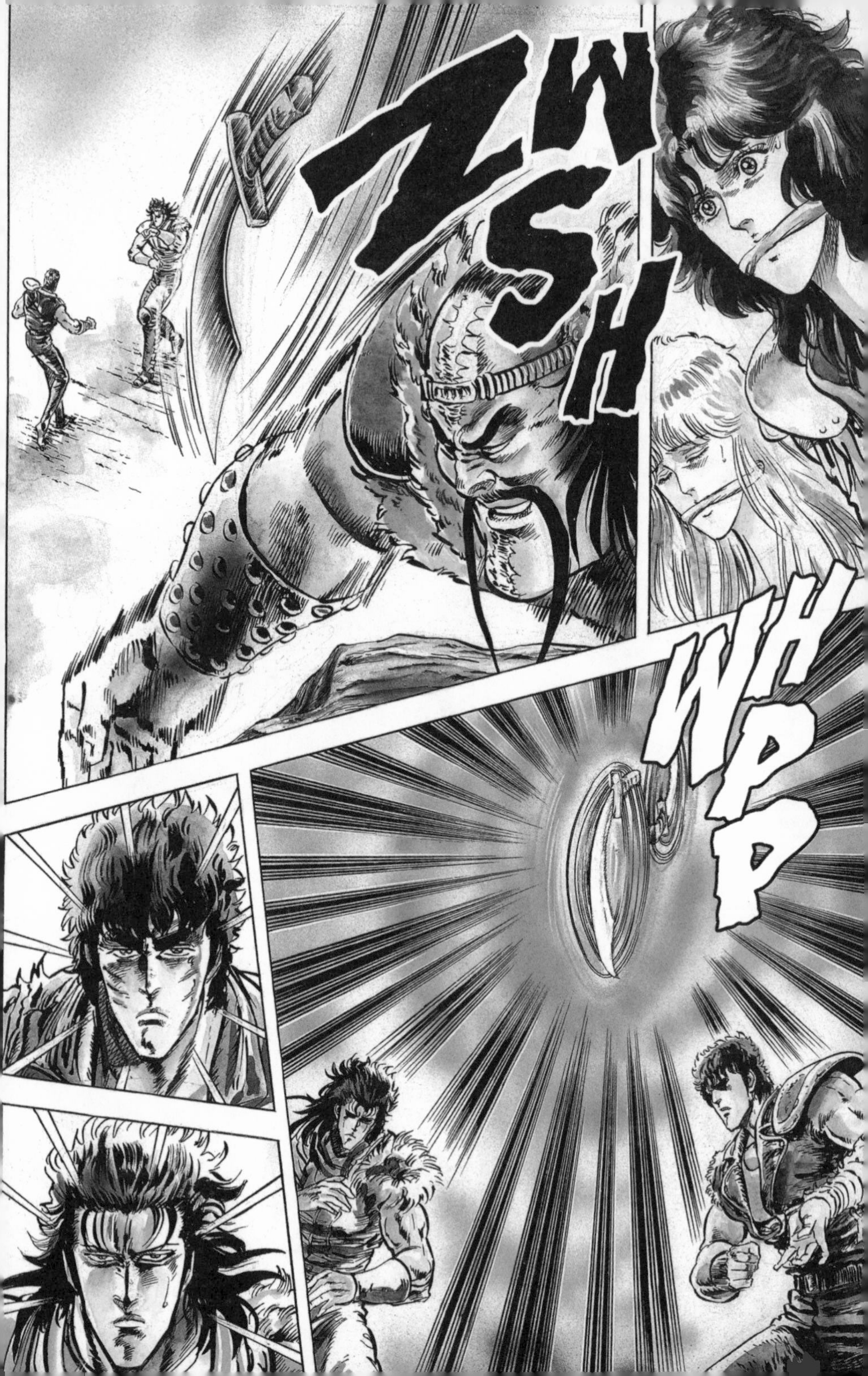
ZWSH
WHPP

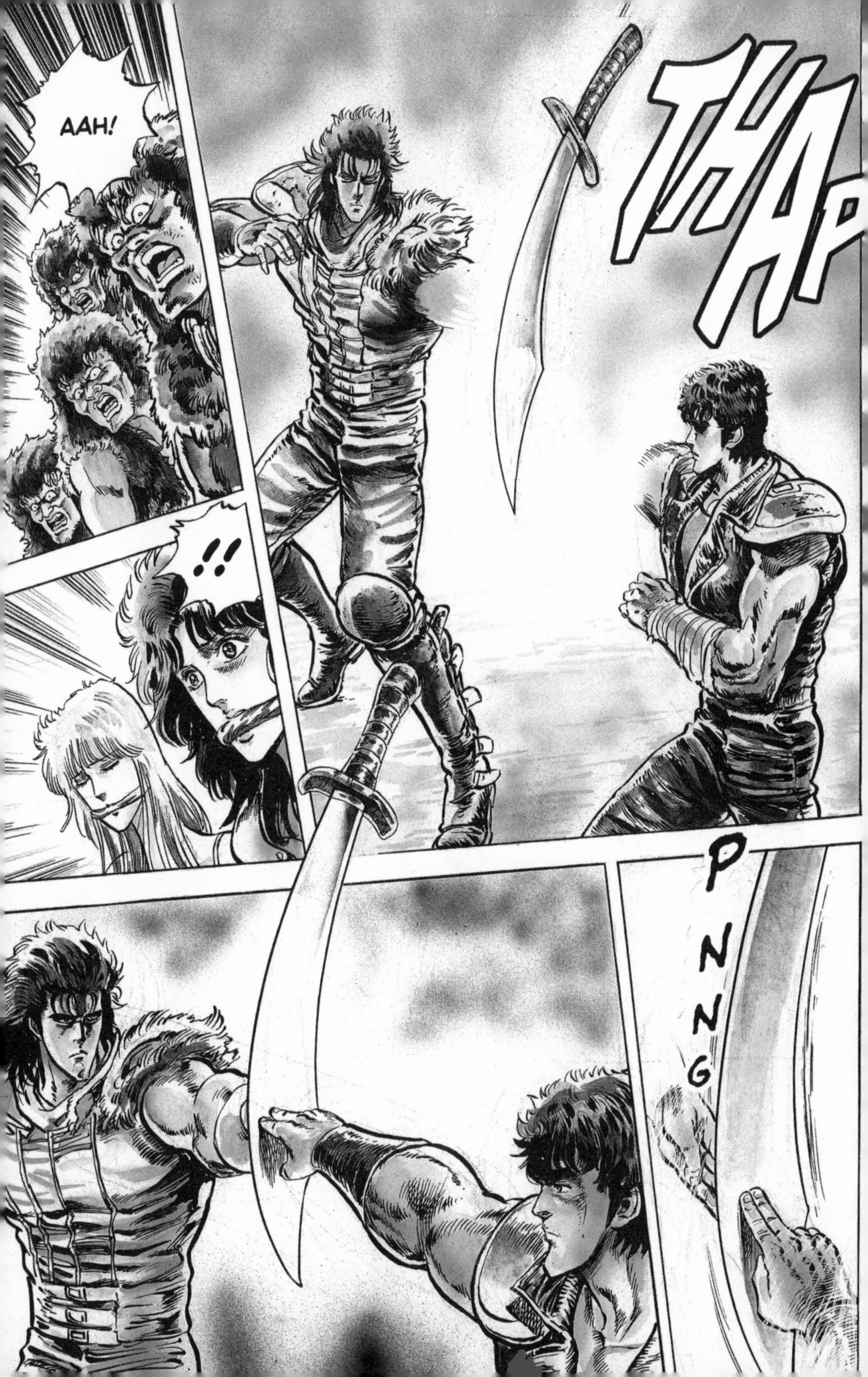
THAP
AAH!
!!
PNNNG

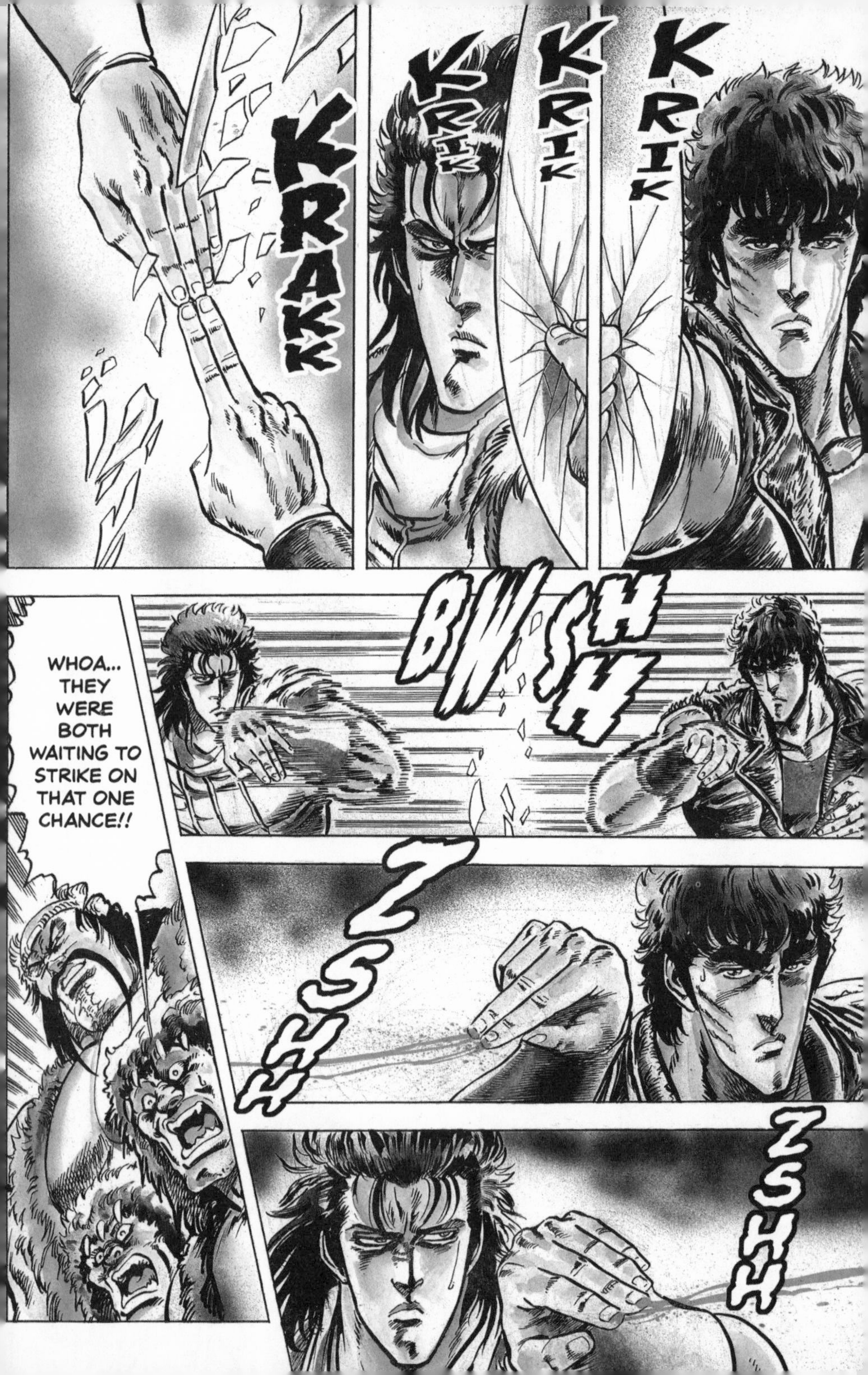
KRIK
KRIK
KRIK
KRAKK
BWSHH
ZSHHH
ZSHHH
WHOA... THEY WERE BOTH WAITING TO STRIKE ON THAT ONE CHANCE!!

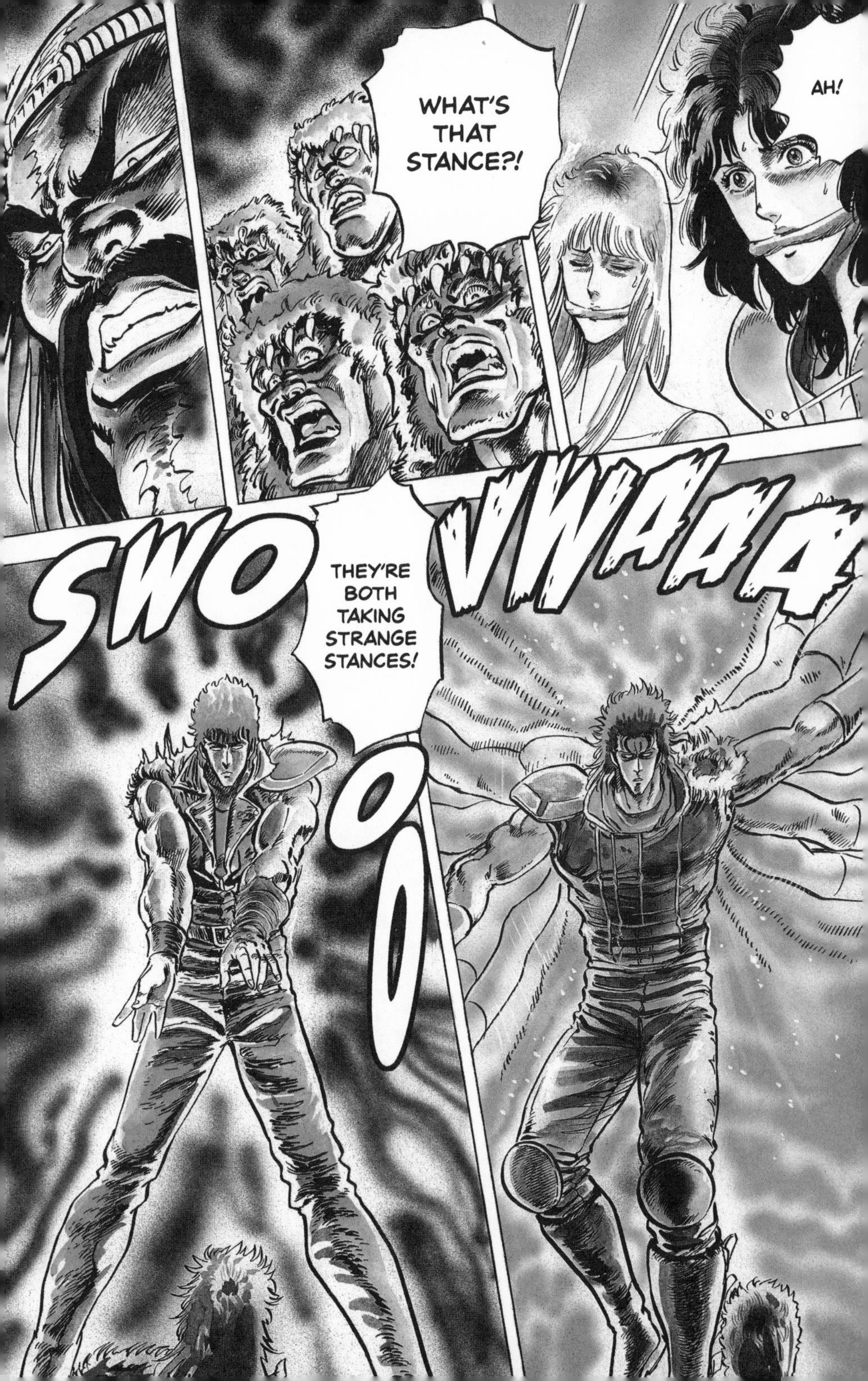
AH!
WHAT'S THAT STANCE?!
THEY'RE BOTH TAKING STRANGE STANCES!
SWOOOO
VWAAAA

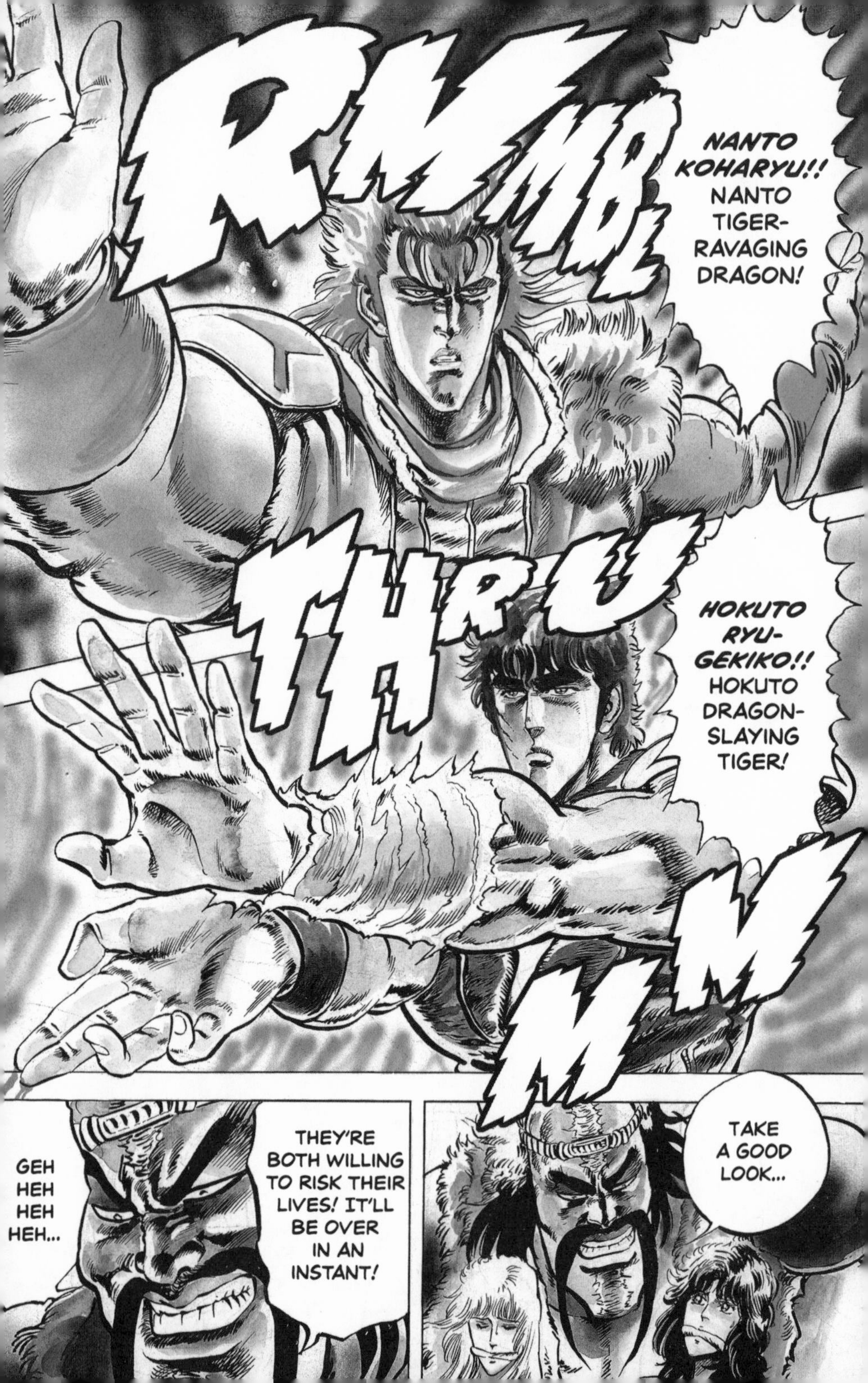
RMMB
NANTO KOHARYU!! NANTO TIGER-RAVAGING DRAGON!
THRU
HOKUTO RYU-GEKIKO!! HOKUTO DRAGON-SLAYING TIGER!
THMM
TAKE A GOOD LOOK...
THEY'RE BOTH WILLING TO RISK THEIR LIVES! IT'LL BE OVER IN AN INSTANT!
GEH HEH HEH HEH...

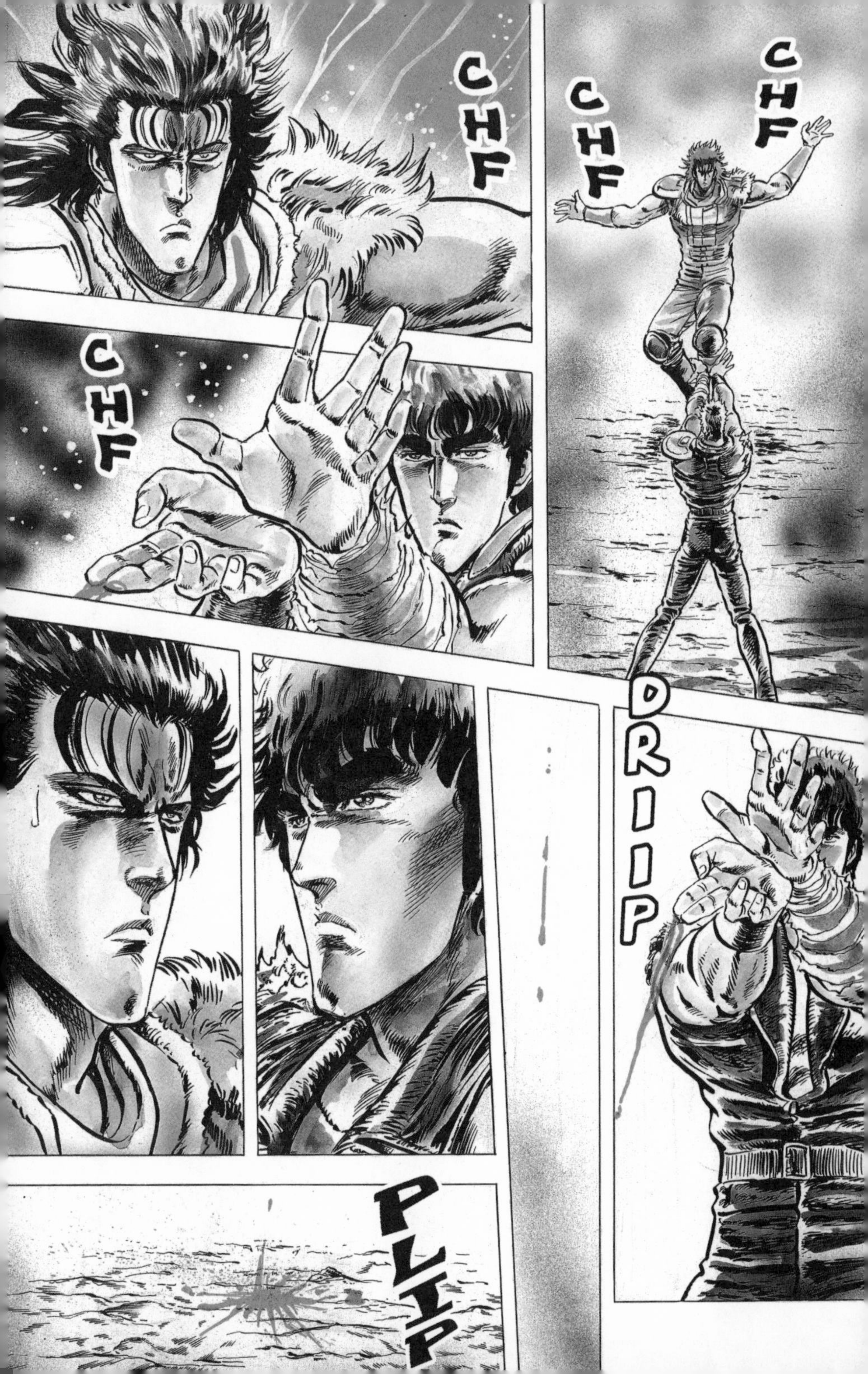
CHF
CHF
CHF
CHF
DRIP
PLIP

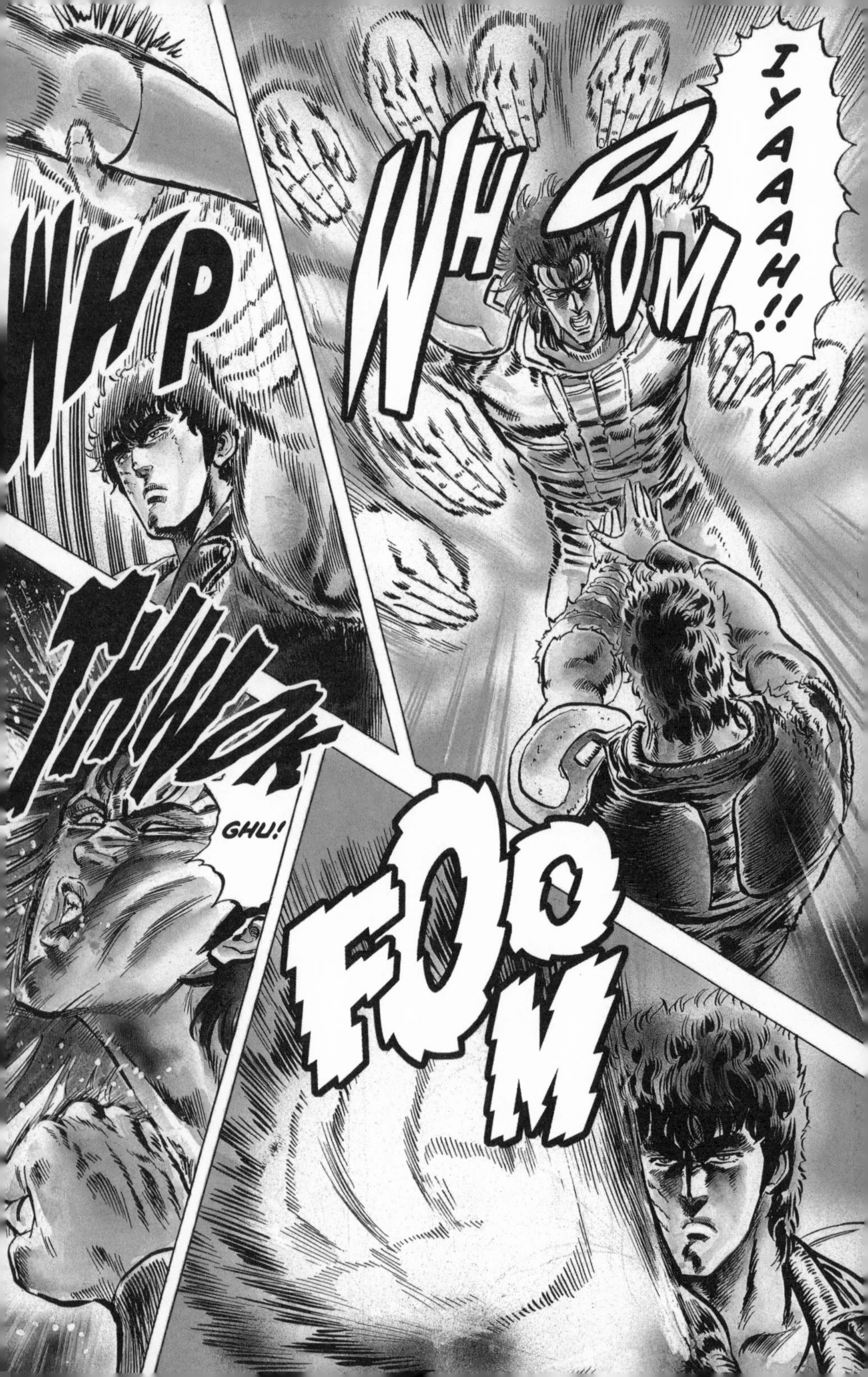
IYAAAAH!!
WHOOM
WHP
THWOK
GHU!
FOOM

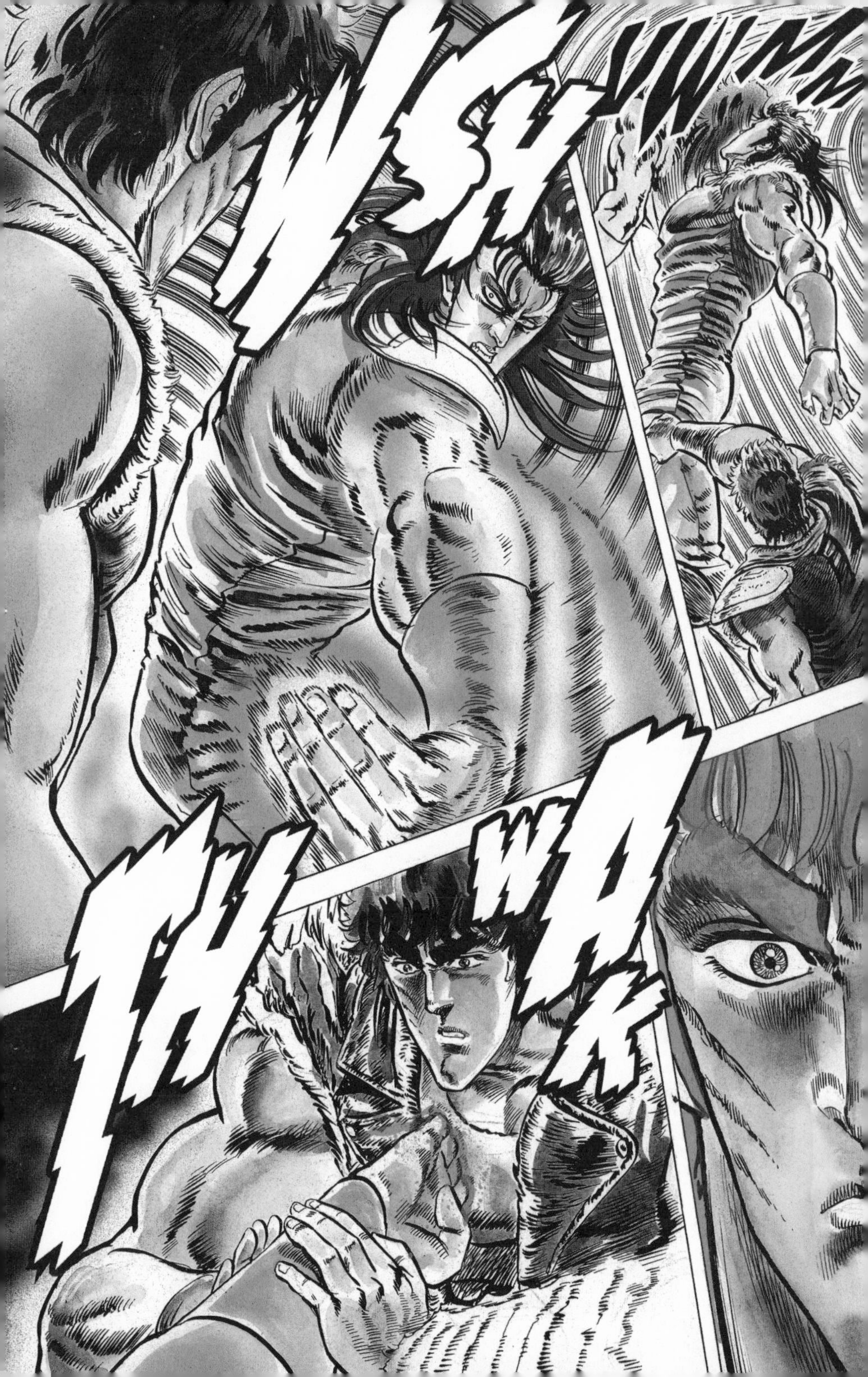
WSH
THWAK

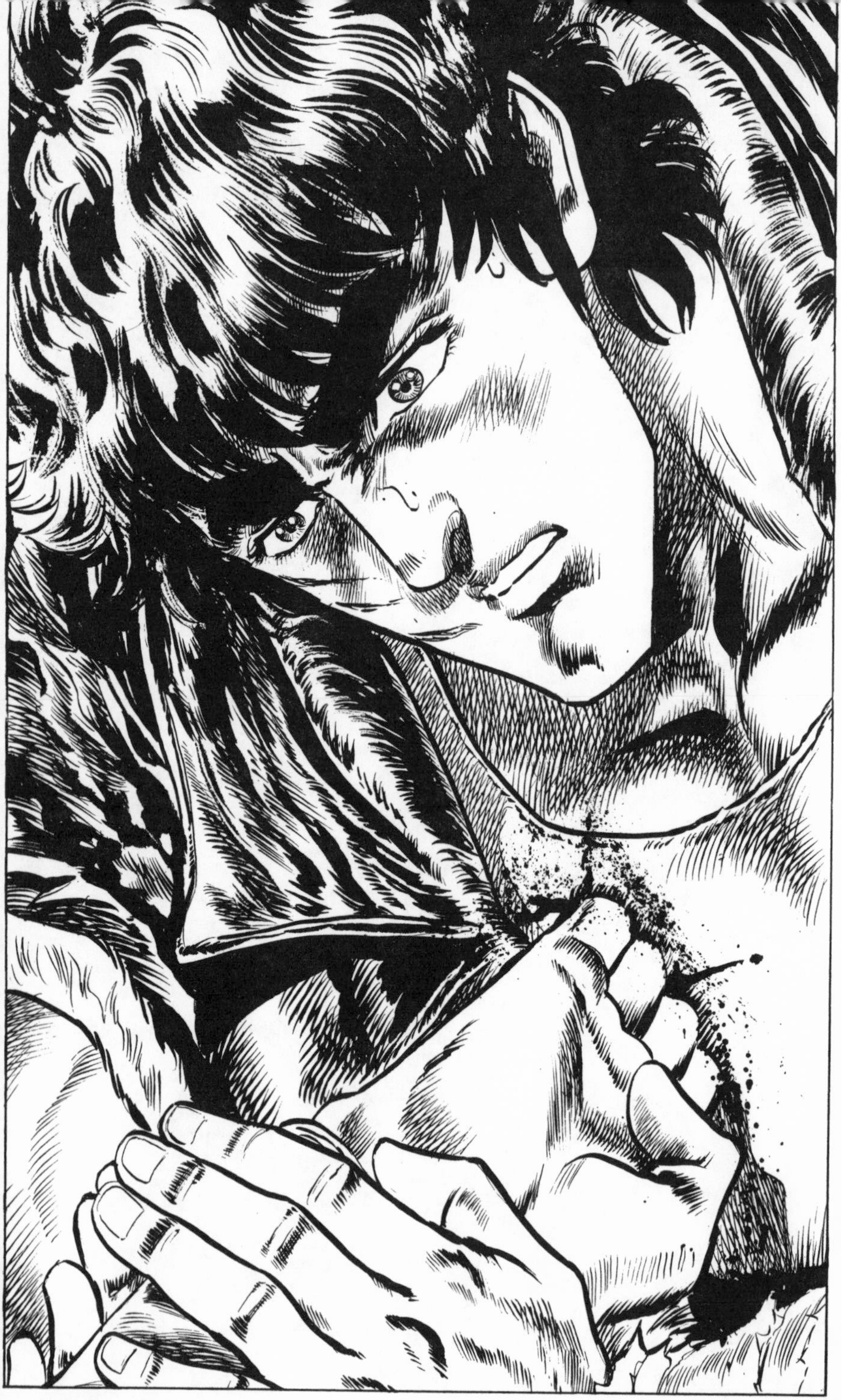

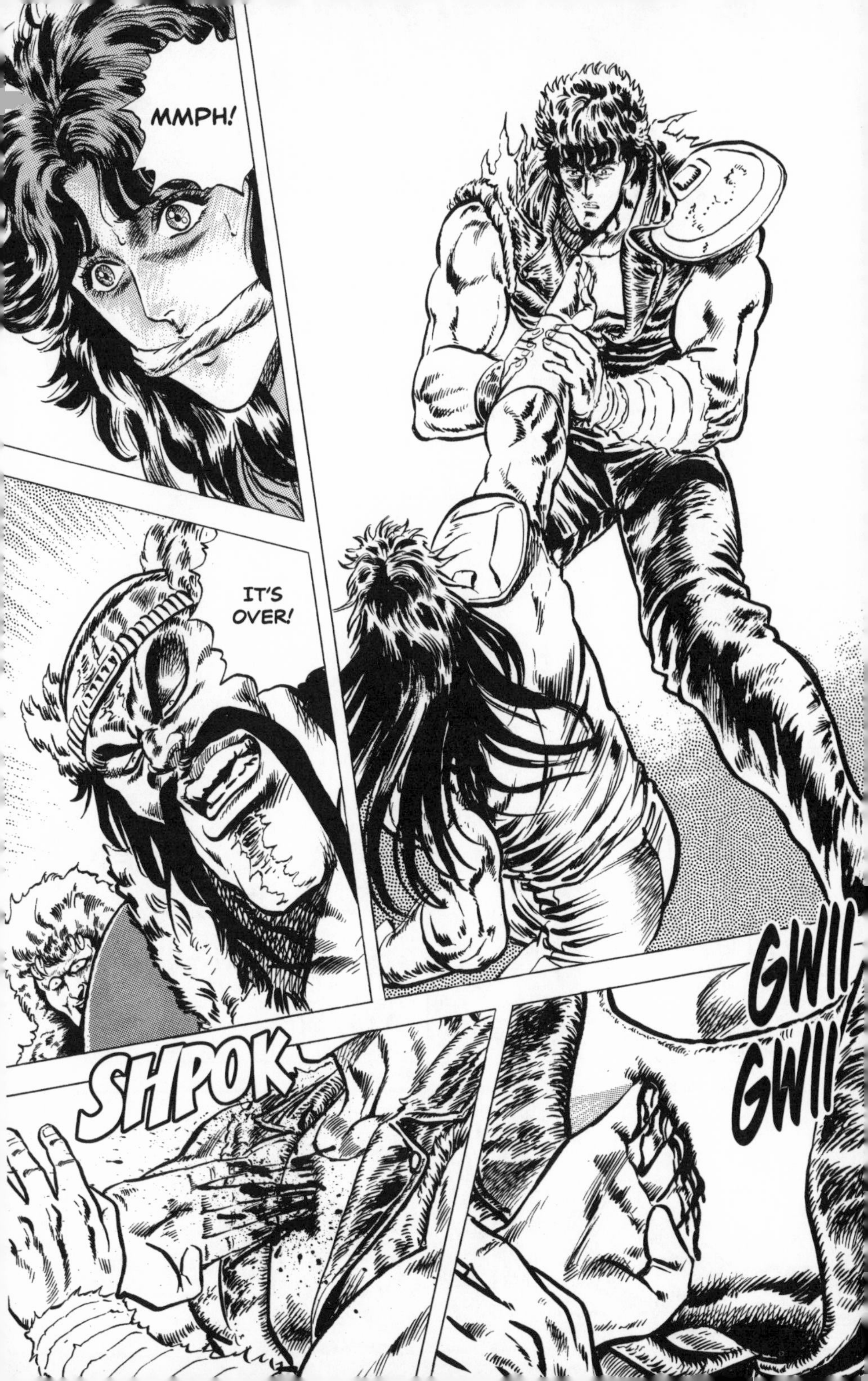
MMPH!
IT'S OVER!
GWII
GWII
SHPOK

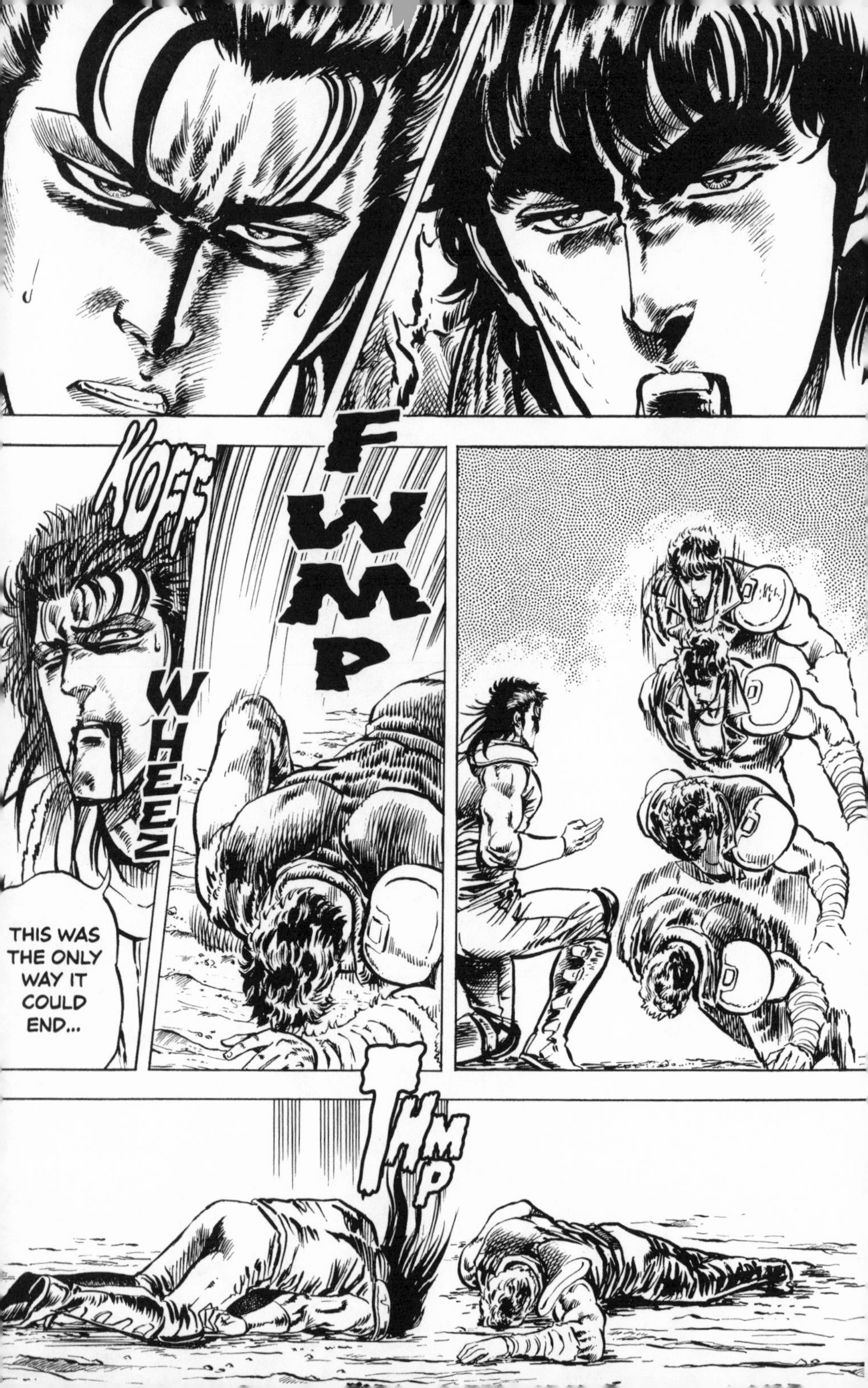
FWMP
KOFF
WHEEZ
THIS WAS THE ONLY WAY IT COULD END...
THMP

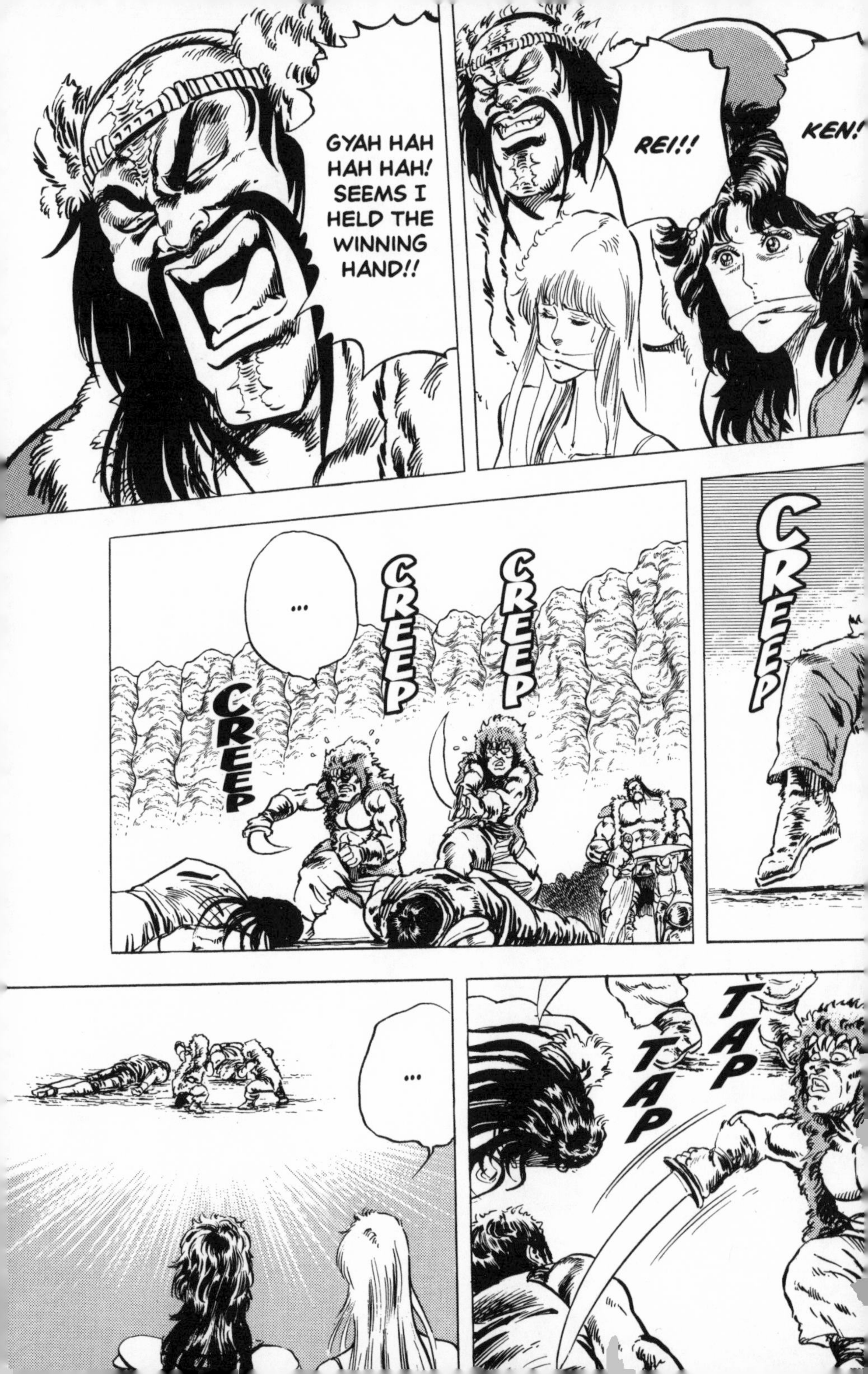
KEN!
REI!!
GYAH HAH HAH HAH! SEEMS I HELD THE WINNING HAND!!
CREEP
...
CREEP
CREEP
CREEP
TAP
TAP
TAP
TAP
...

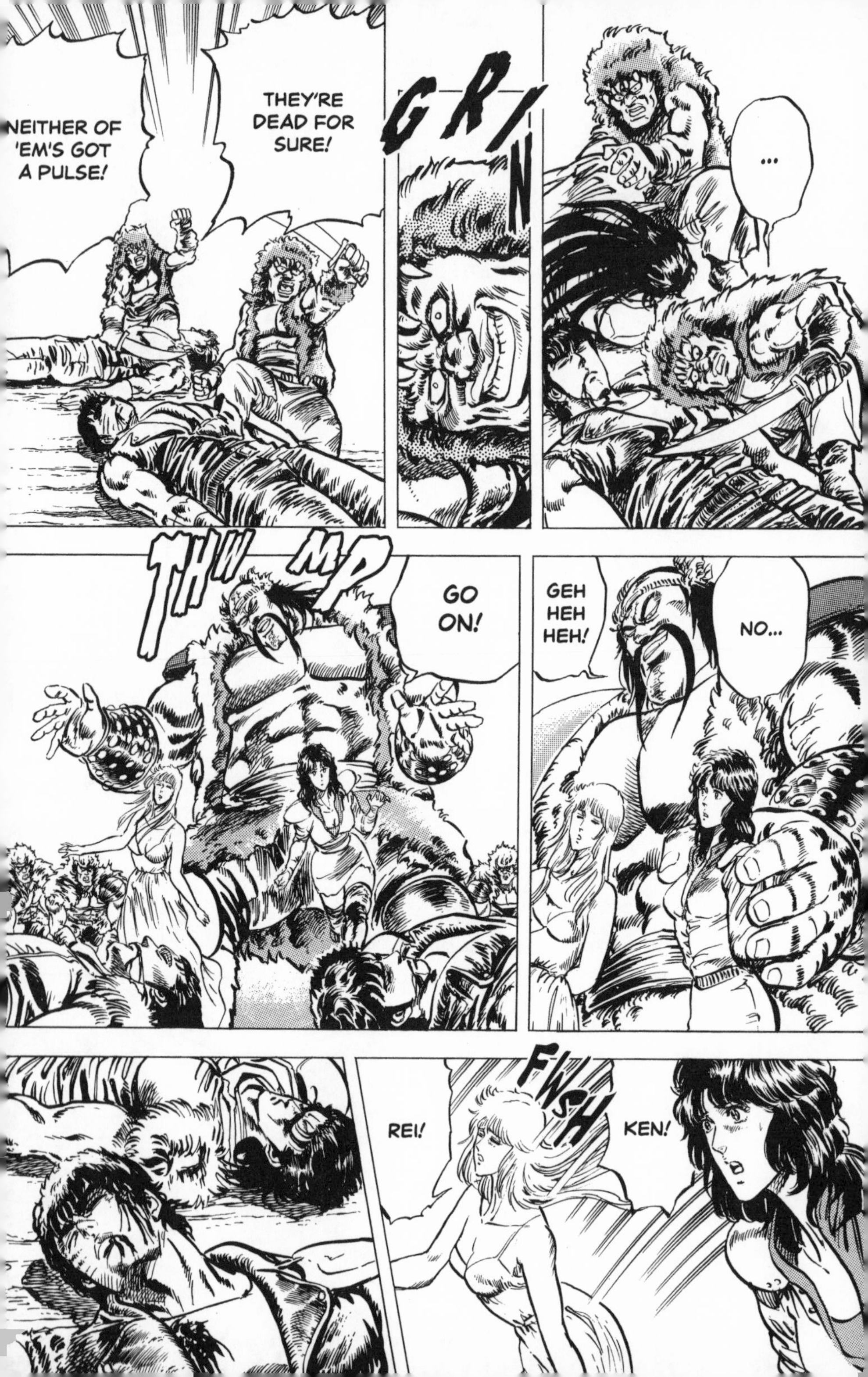
...
GRIN
THEY'RE DEAD FOR SURE!
NEITHER OF 'EM'S GOT A PULSE!
NO...
GEH HEH HEH!
GO ON!
THWMP
KEN!
FWSH
REI!

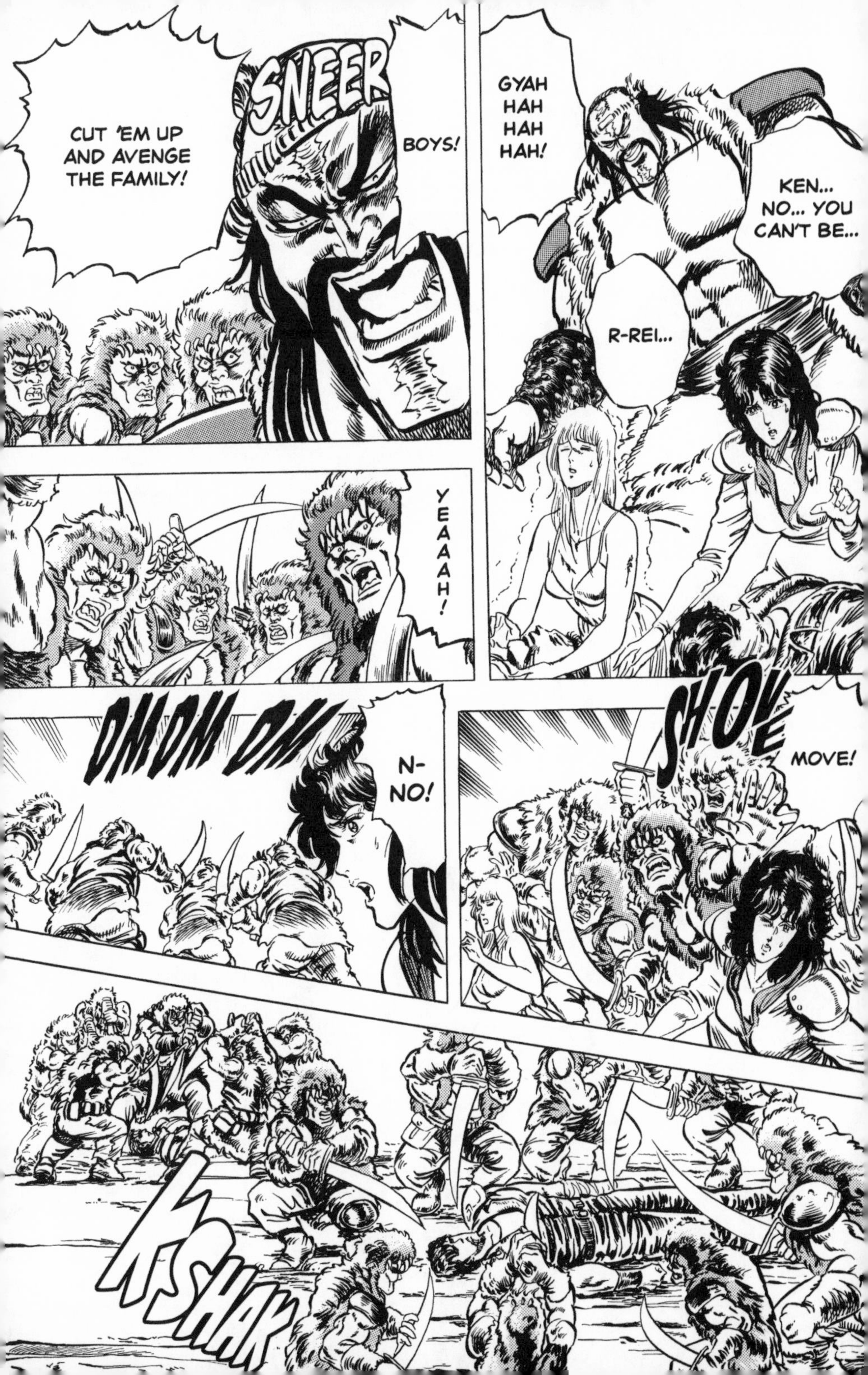
GYAH HAH HAH HAH!
KEN... NO... YOU CAN'T BE...
R-REI...
SNEER
BOYS!
CUT 'EM UP AND AVENGE THE FAMILY!
YEAAAAH!
SHOVE
MOVE!
N- NO!
KSHAK

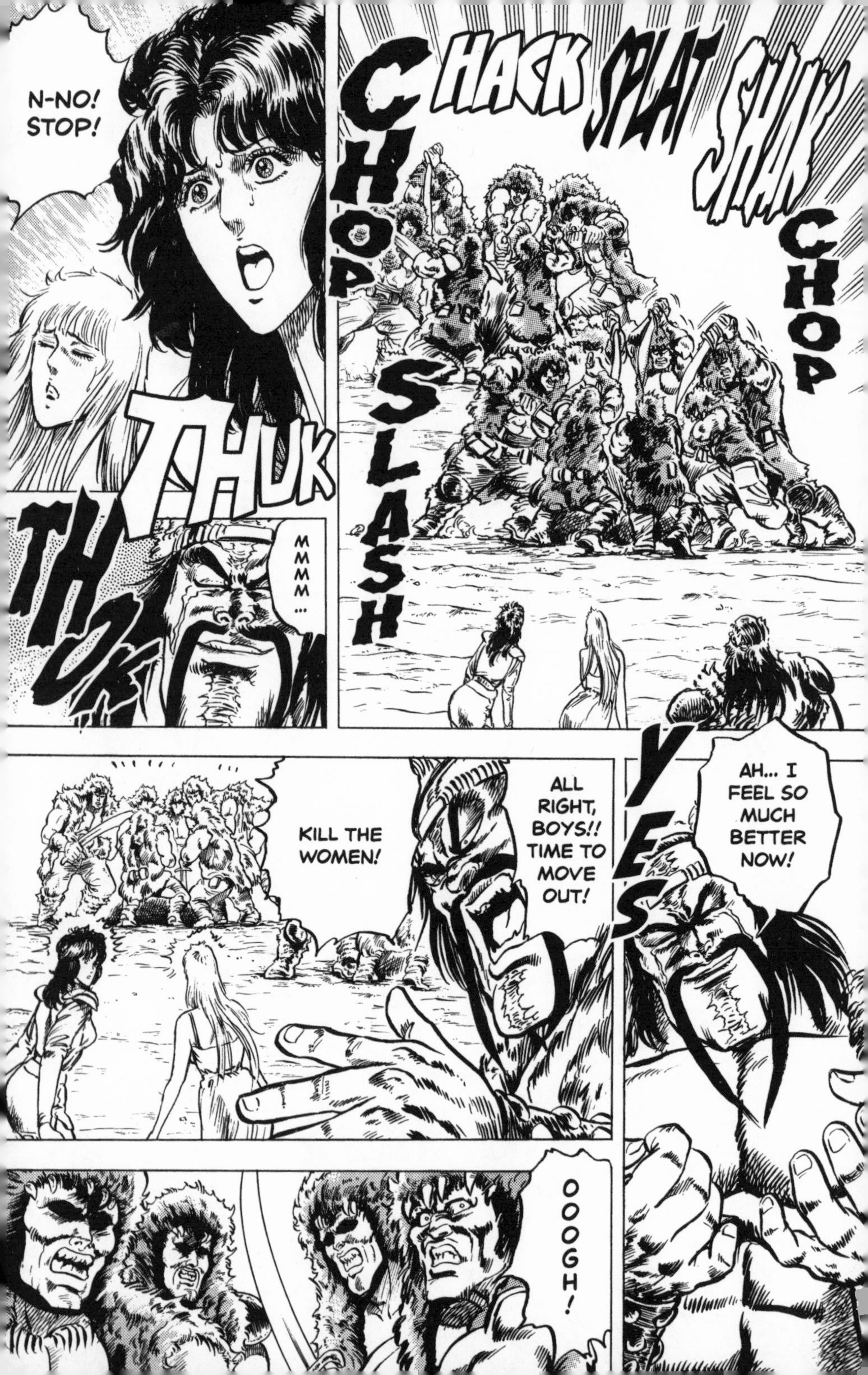

HACK
SPLAT
SHAK
CHOP
CHOP
SLASH
N-NO! STOP!
THUK
THOK
MMMM...
YES
AH... I FEEL SO MUCH BETTER NOW!
ALL RIGHT, BOYS!! TIME TO MOVE OUT!
KILL THE WOMEN!
OOOGH!

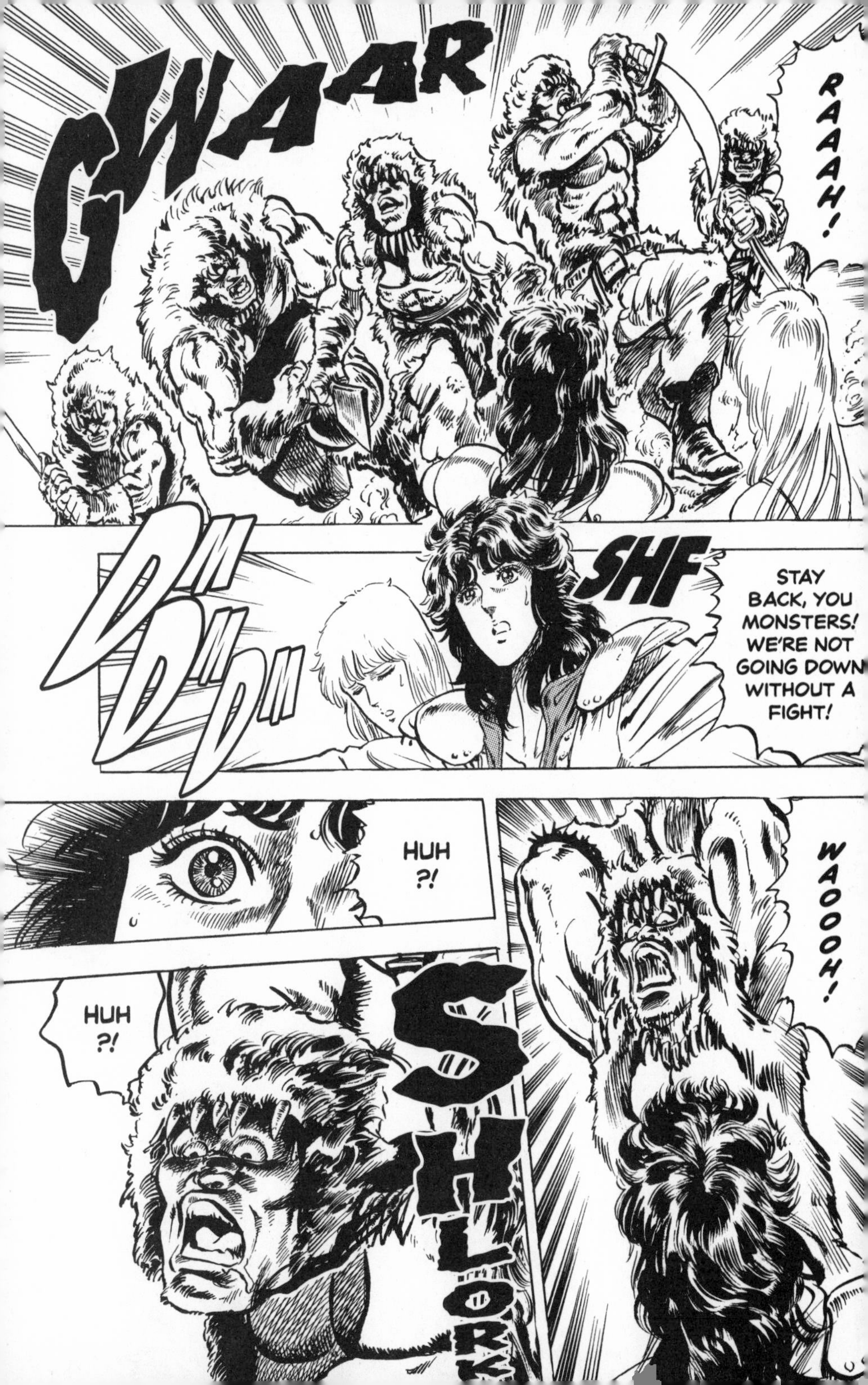
RAAAAH!
GWAAAR
SHF
STAY BACK, YOU MONSTERS! WE'RE NOT GOING DOWN WITHOUT A FIGHT!
DDDD
WAOOOH!
HUH ?!
SHLORK
HUH ?!

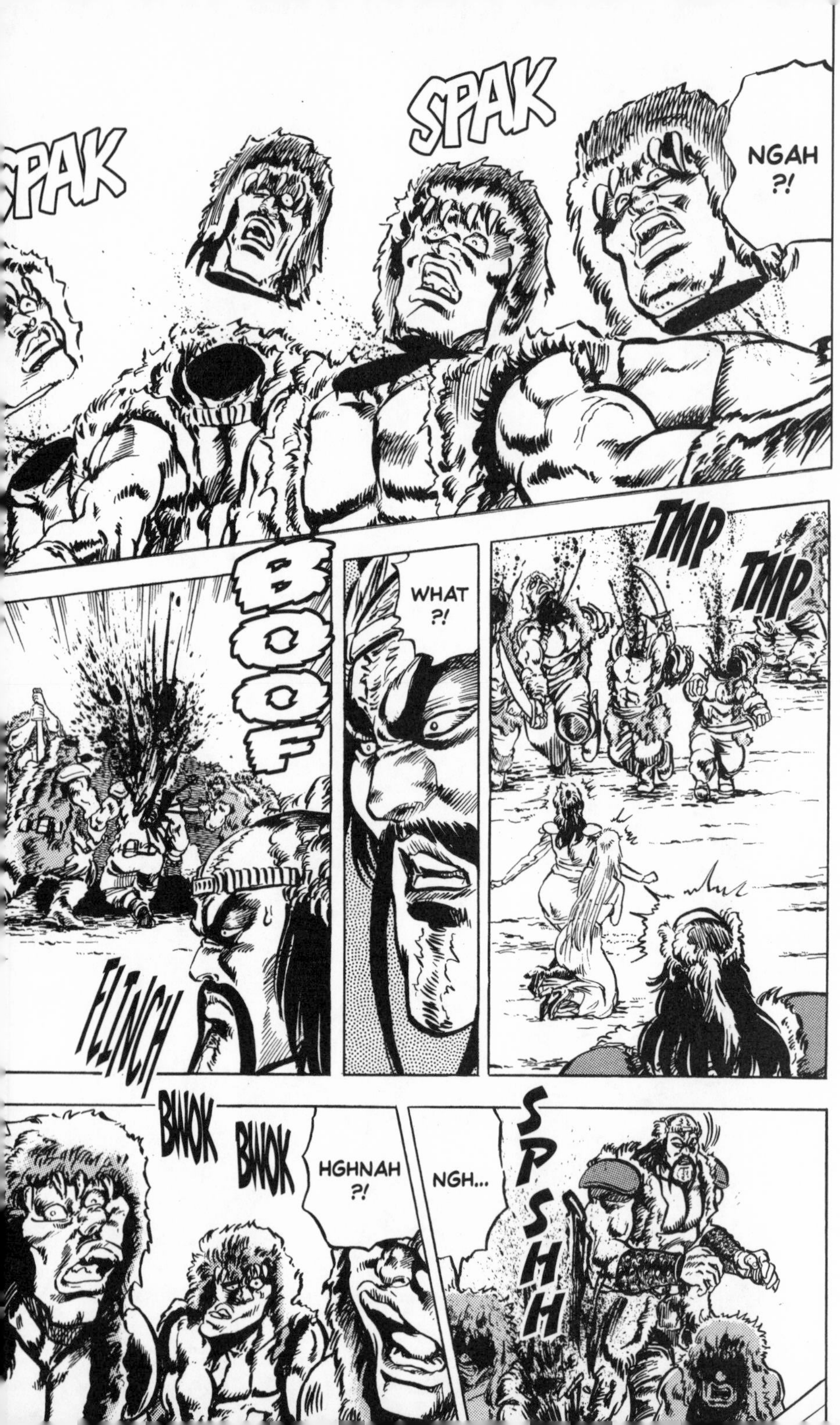
NGAH ?!
SPAK
SPAK
TMP
TMP
WHAT ?!
BOOOF
FLINCH
SPSHH
NGH...
HGHNAH ?!
BWOK
BWOK

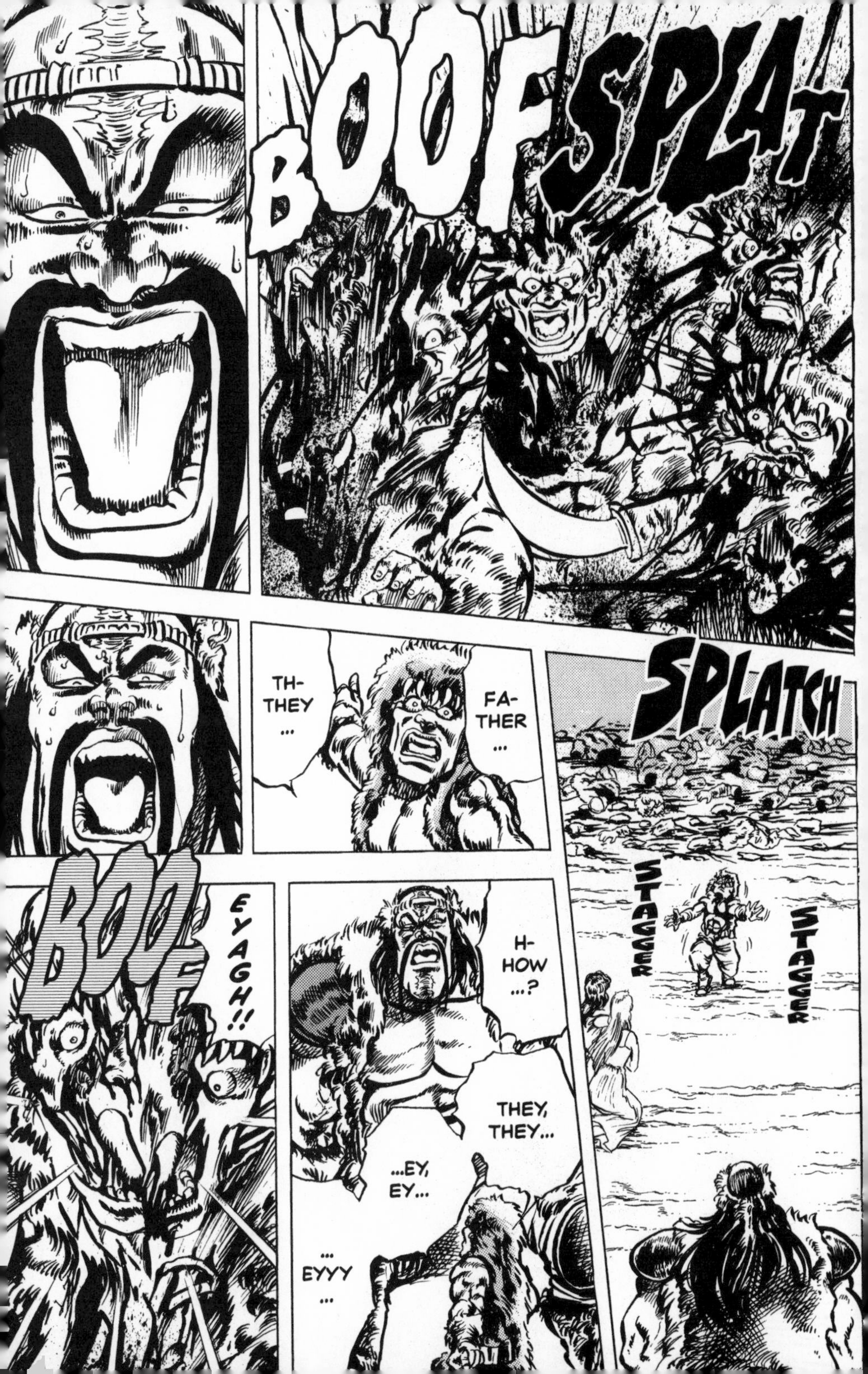
BOOF
SPLAT
SPLATCH
STAGGER
STAGGER
FA-THER...
TH-THEY...
H-HOW...?
THEY, THEY...
...EY, EY...
...EYYY...
BOOF
EYAGH!!

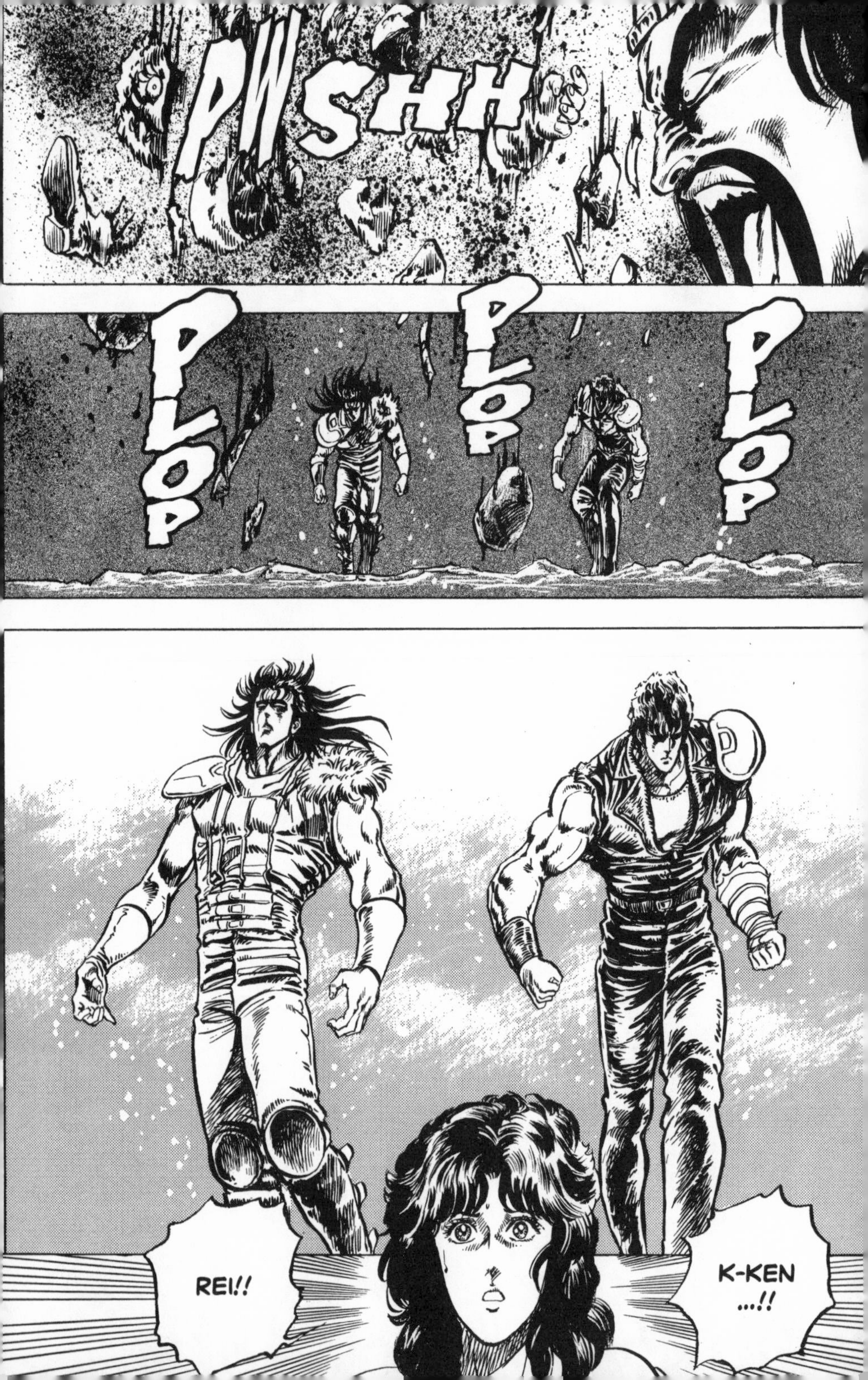
PWSHH
PLOP
PLOP
PLOP
K-KEN ...!!
REI!!

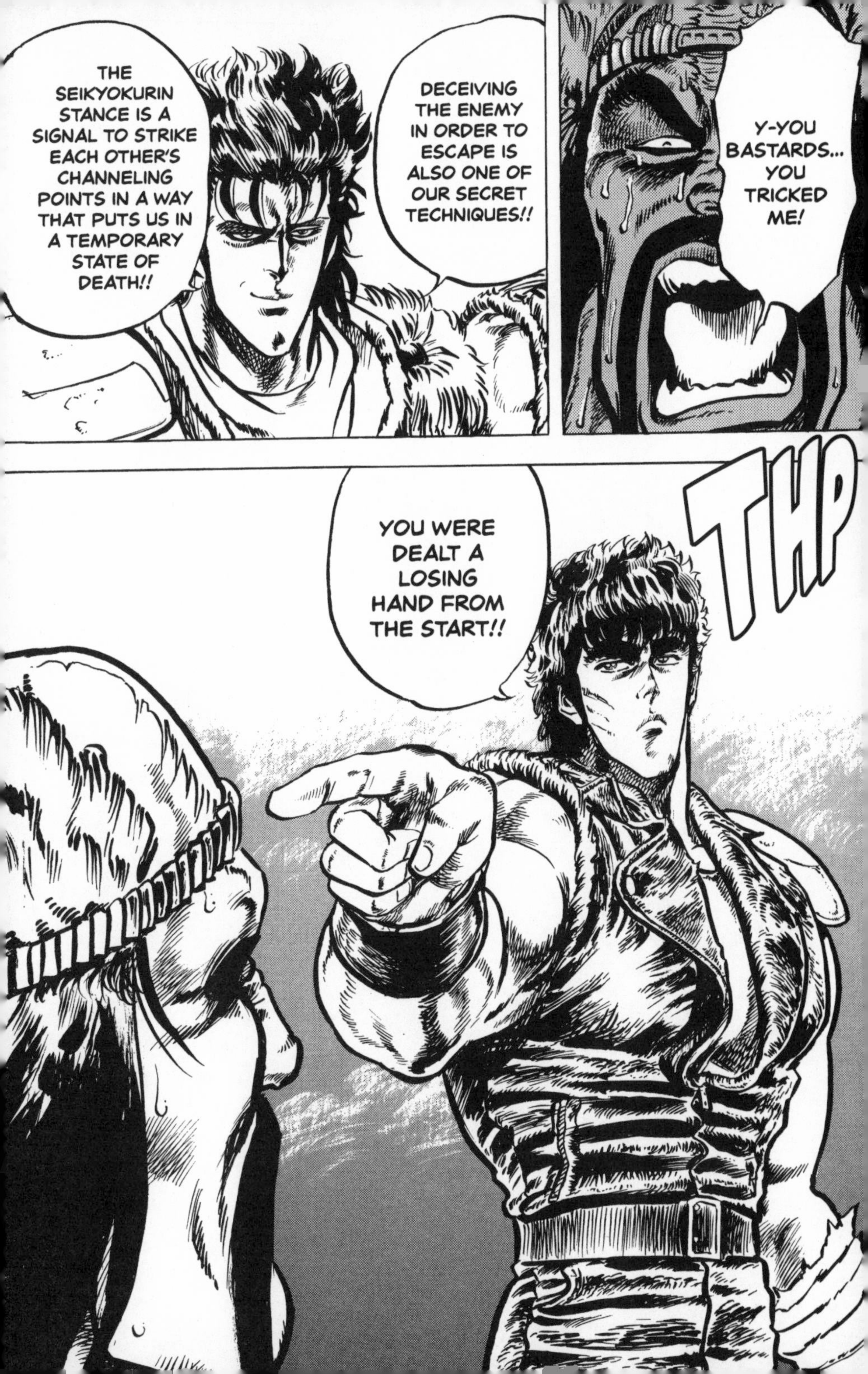
THE SEIKYOKURIN STANCE IS A SIGNAL TO STRIKE EACH OTHER'S CHANNELING POINTS IN A WAY THAT PUTS US IN A TEMPORARY STATE OF DEATH!!
DECEIVING THE ENEMY IN ORDER TO ESCAPE IS ALSO ONE OF OUR SECRET TECHNIQUES!!
Y-YOU BASTARDS... YOU TRICKED ME!
THP
YOU WERE DEALT A LOSING HAND FROM THE START!!

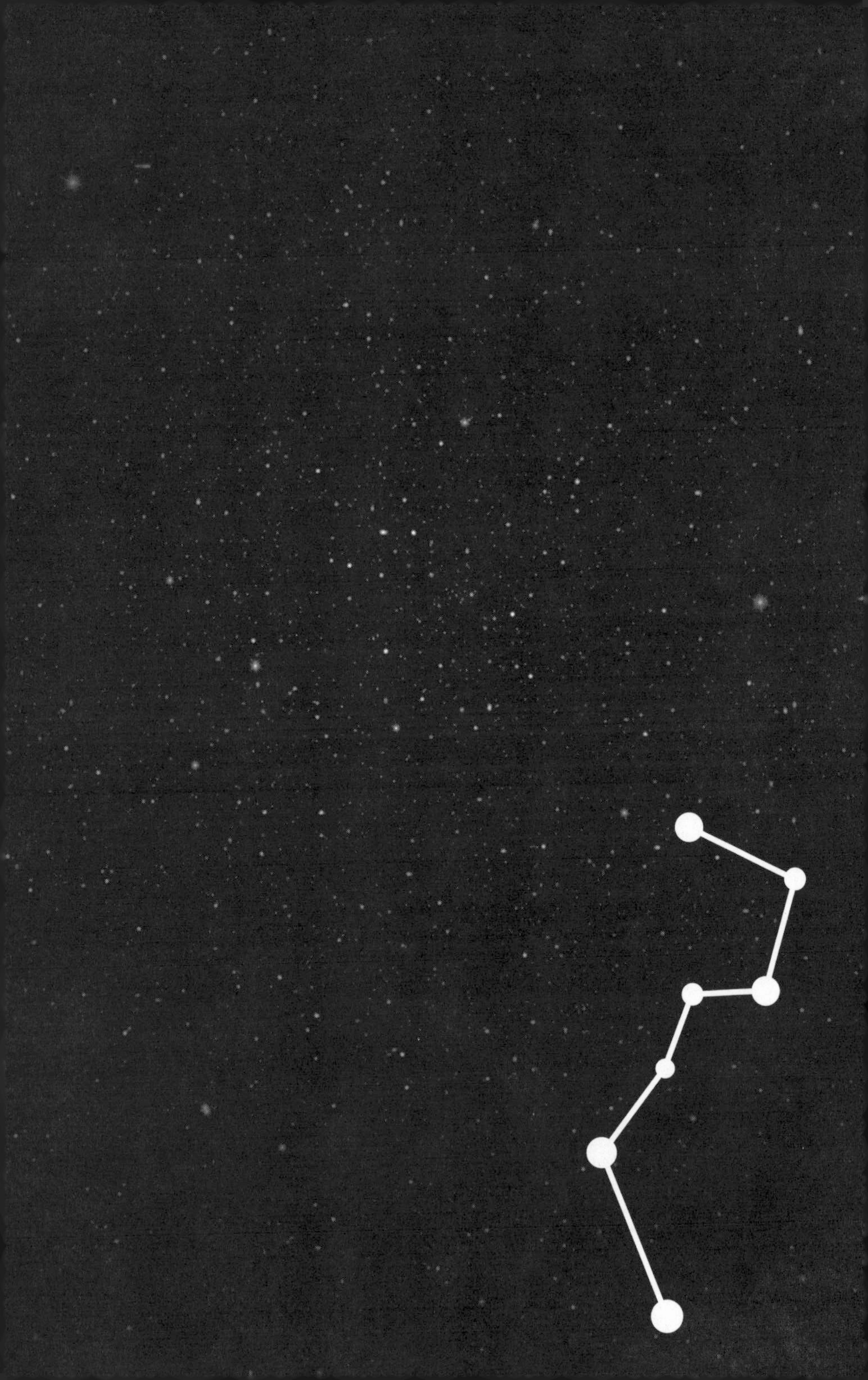

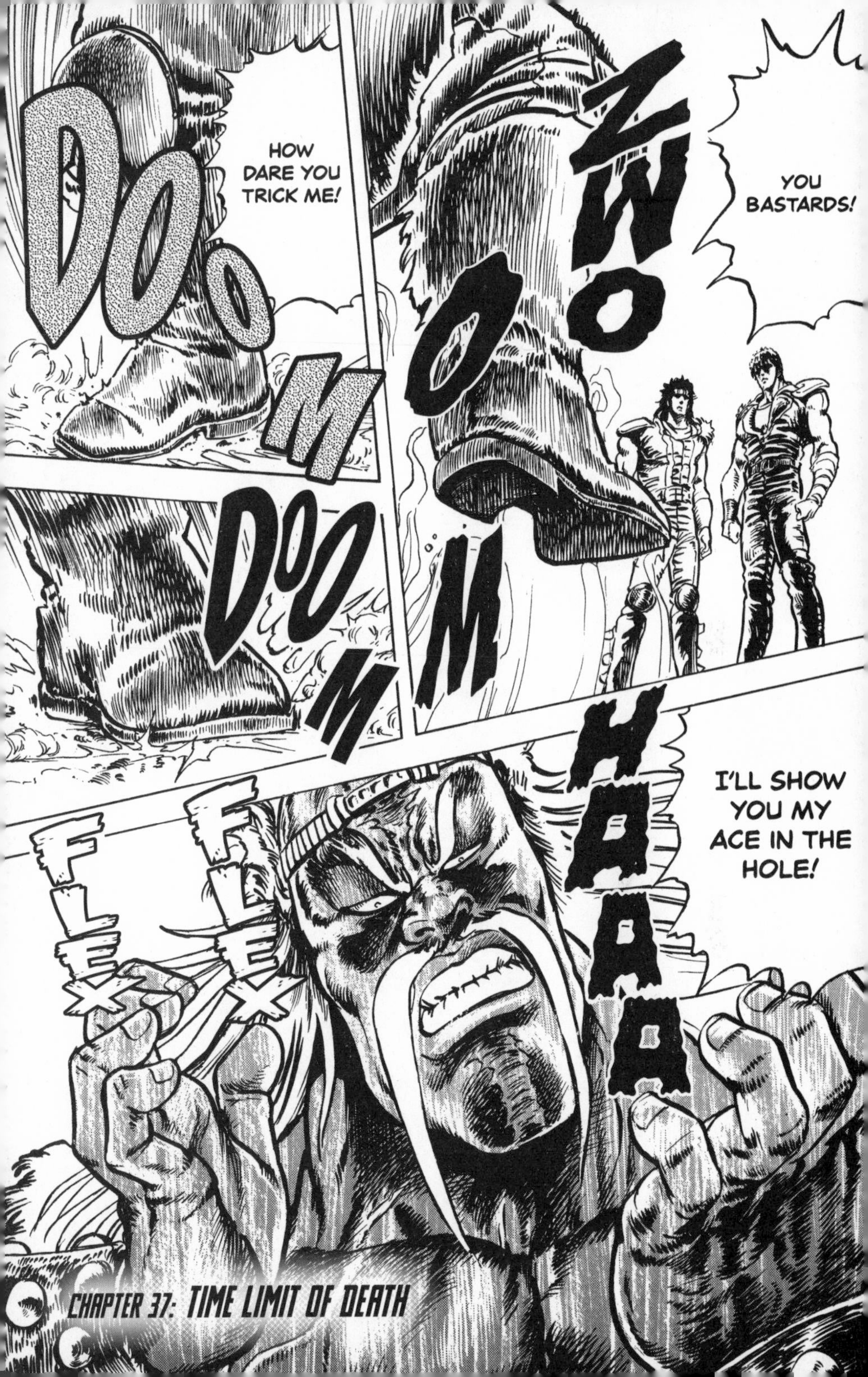
YOU BASTARDS!
WOOOMM
HOW DARE YOU TRICK ME!
DOOOM
DOOMM
I'LL SHOW YOU MY ACE IN THE HOLE!
HAAAA
FLEX
FLEX
CHAPTER 37: TIME LIMIT OF DEATH

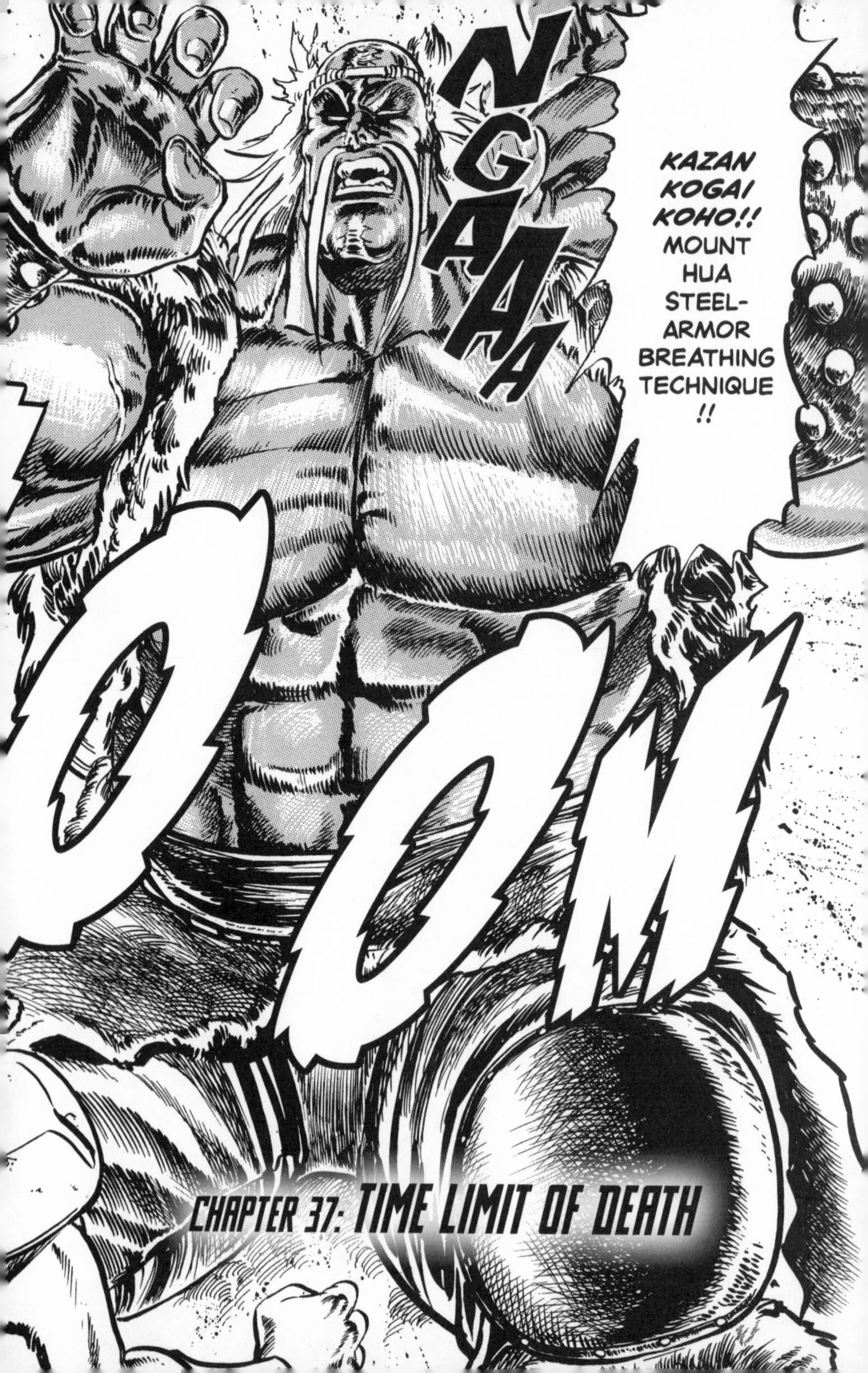
NGAAA
KAZAN KOGAI KOHO!! MOUNT HUA STEEL-ARMOR BREATHING TECHNIQUE !!
BOOM
CHAPTER 37: TIME LIMIT OF DEATH

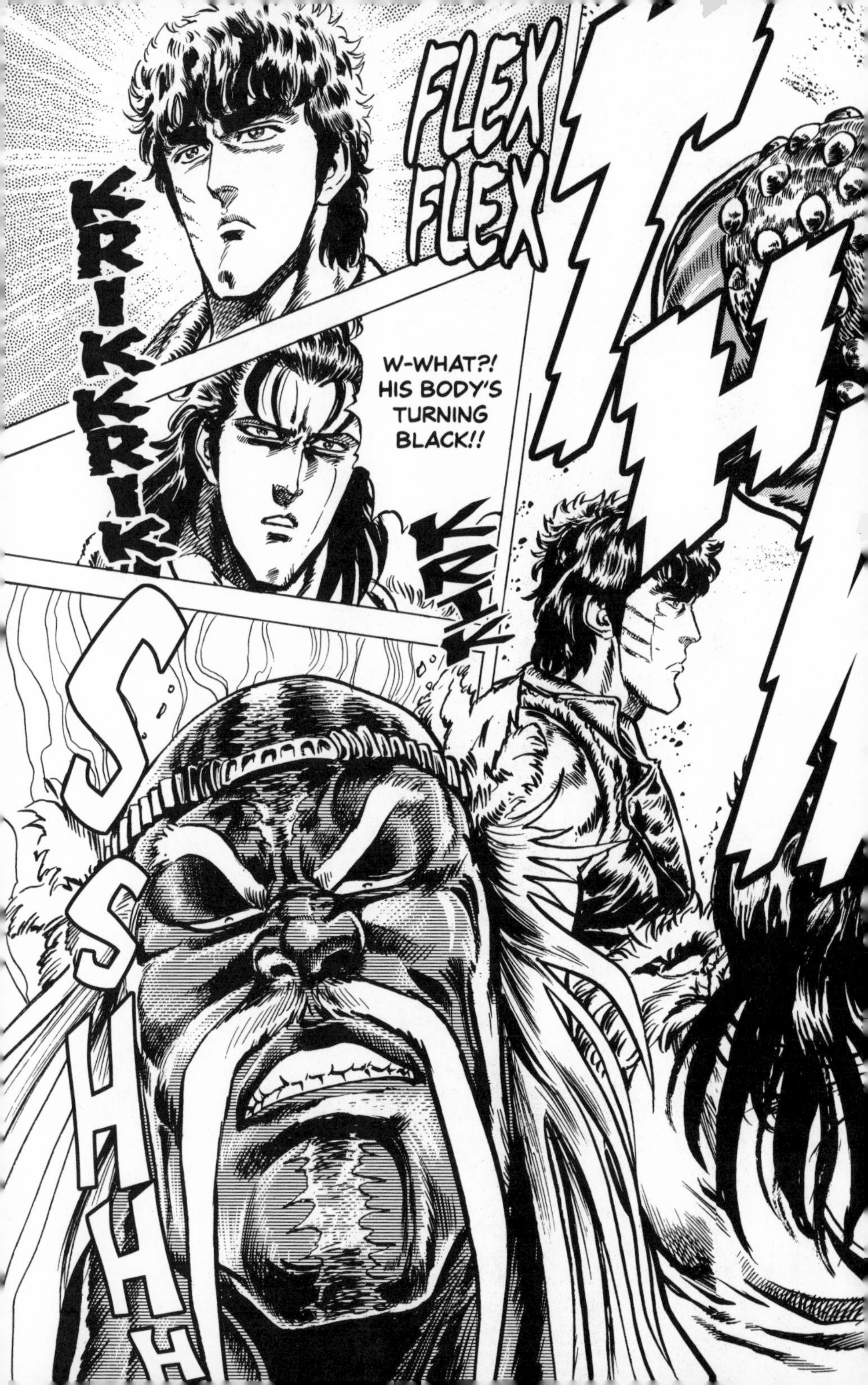
FLEX FLEX
KRIK KRIK
W-WHAT?! HIS BODY'S TURNING BLACK!!
KRIK
SSSHHH

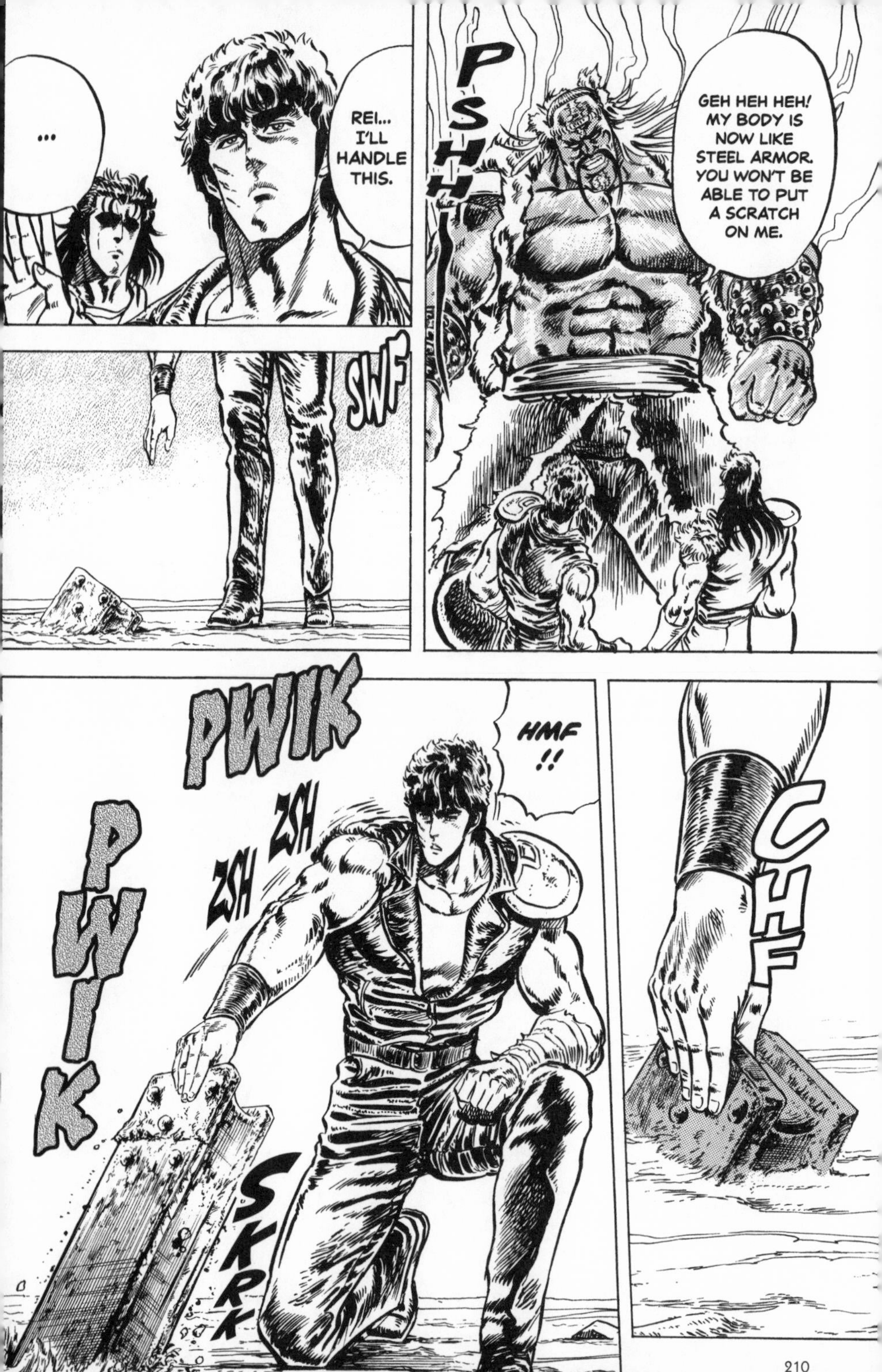
PSHH
GEH HEH HEH! MY BODY IS NOW LIKE STEEL ARMOR. YOU WON'T BE ABLE TO PUT A SCRATCH ON ME.
REI... I'LL HANDLE THIS.
...
SWF
CHHF
HMF !!
PWIK
ZSH
ZSH
PWIK
SKRK

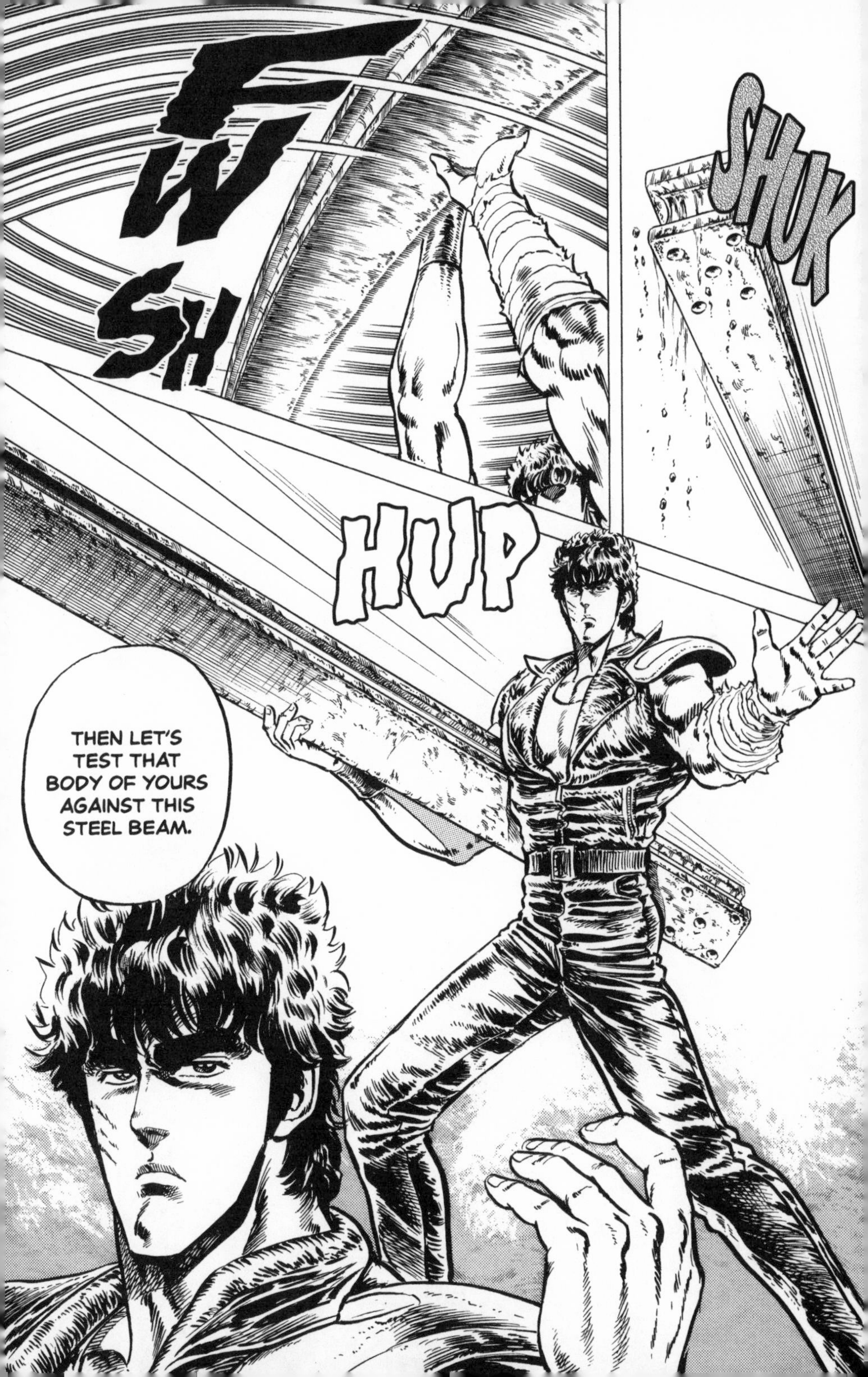
SHUK
FWSH
HUP
THEN LET'S TEST THAT BODY OF YOURS AGAINST THIS STEEL BEAM.

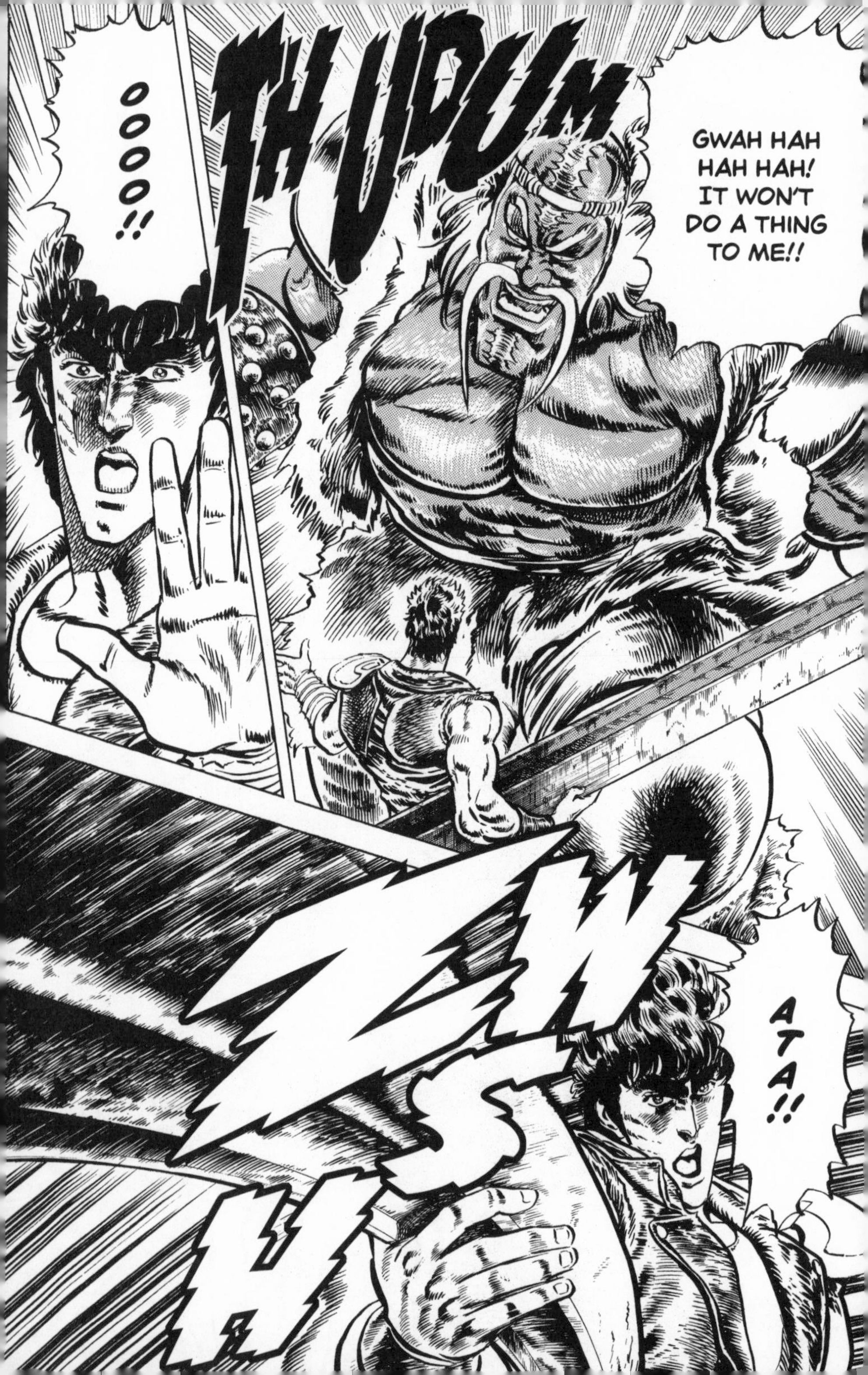
GWAH HAH HAH HAH! IT WON'T DO A THING TO ME!!
THUDUM
OOOOO!!
ZWSH
ATA!!

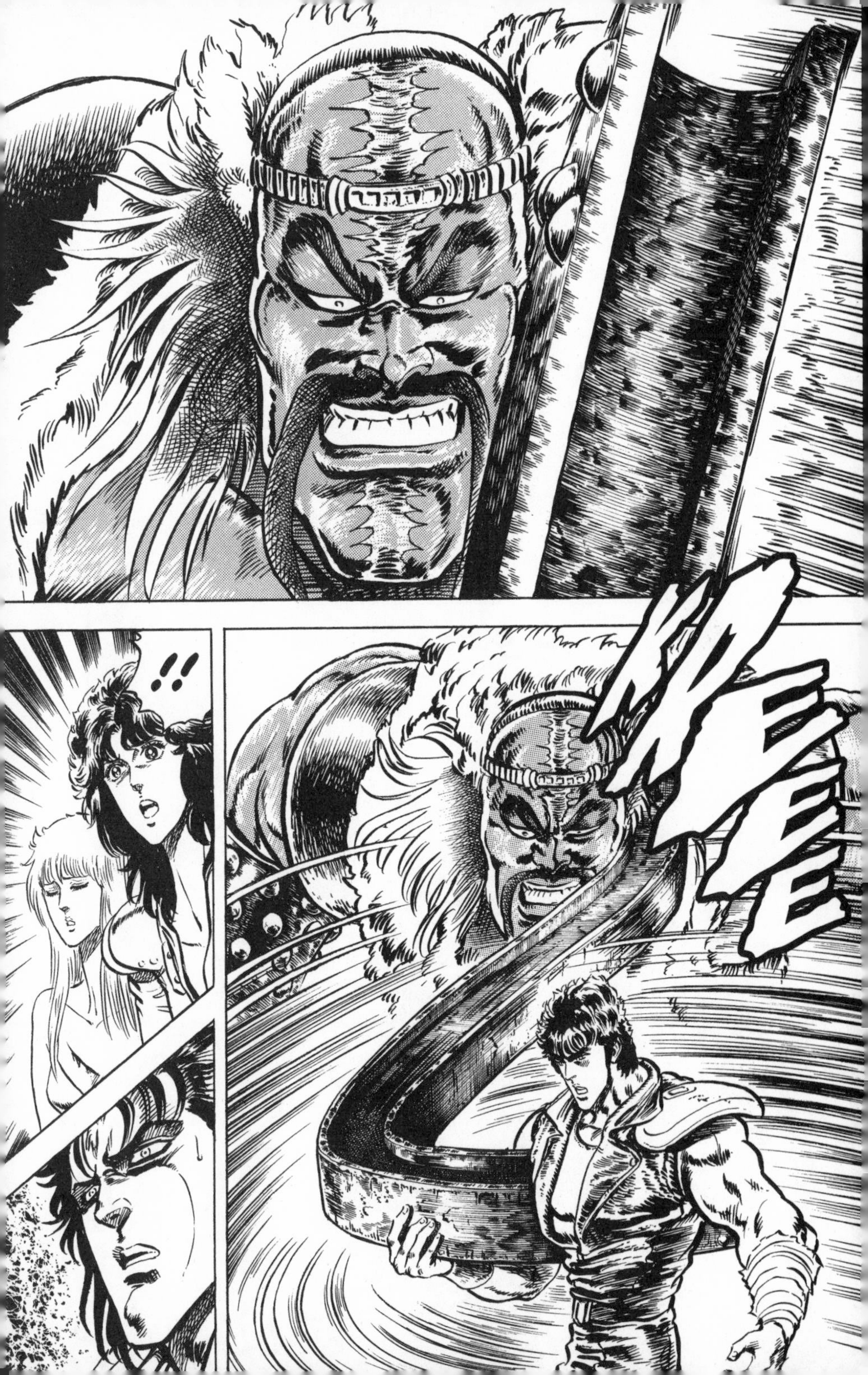
!!

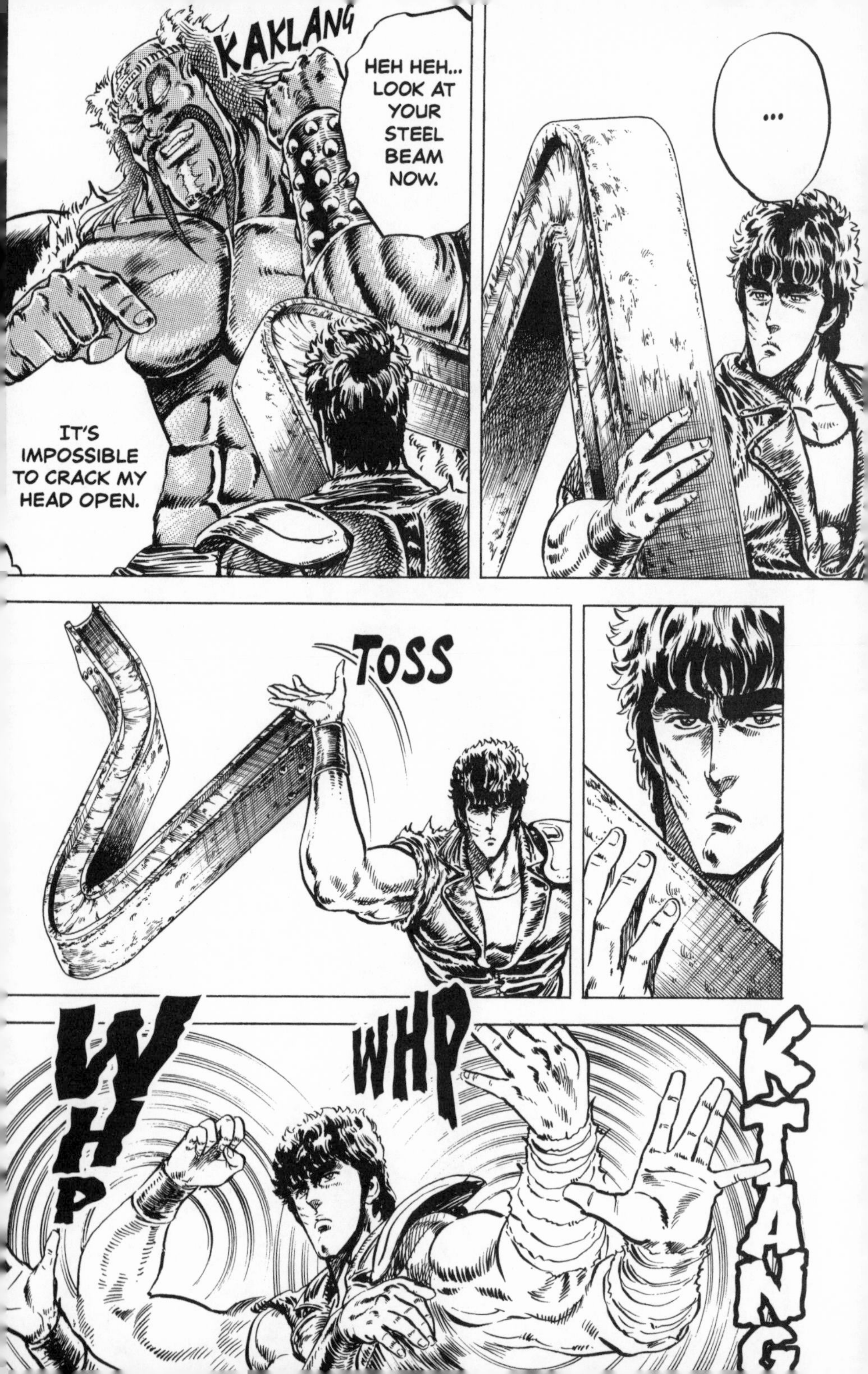
...
KAKLANG
HEH HEH... LOOK AT YOUR STEEL BEAM NOW.
IT'S IMPOSSIBLE TO CRACK MY HEAD OPEN.
TOSS
KTANG
WHP
WHP

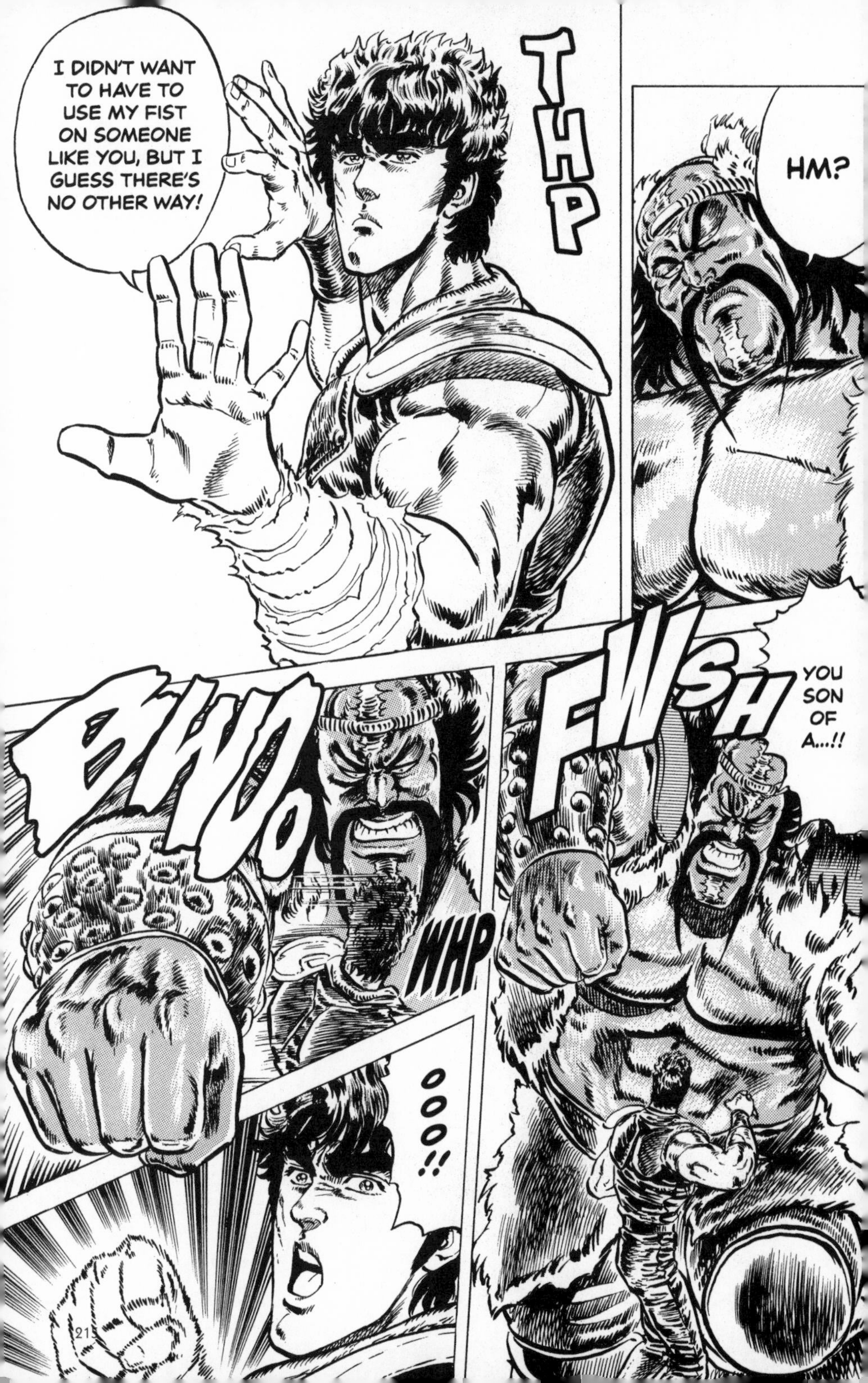
HM?
THP
I DIDN'T WANT TO HAVE TO USE MY FIST ON SOMEONE LIKE YOU, BUT I GUESS THERE'S NO OTHER WAY!
YOU SON OF A...!!
F-WSH
BWOO
WHP
OOO!!

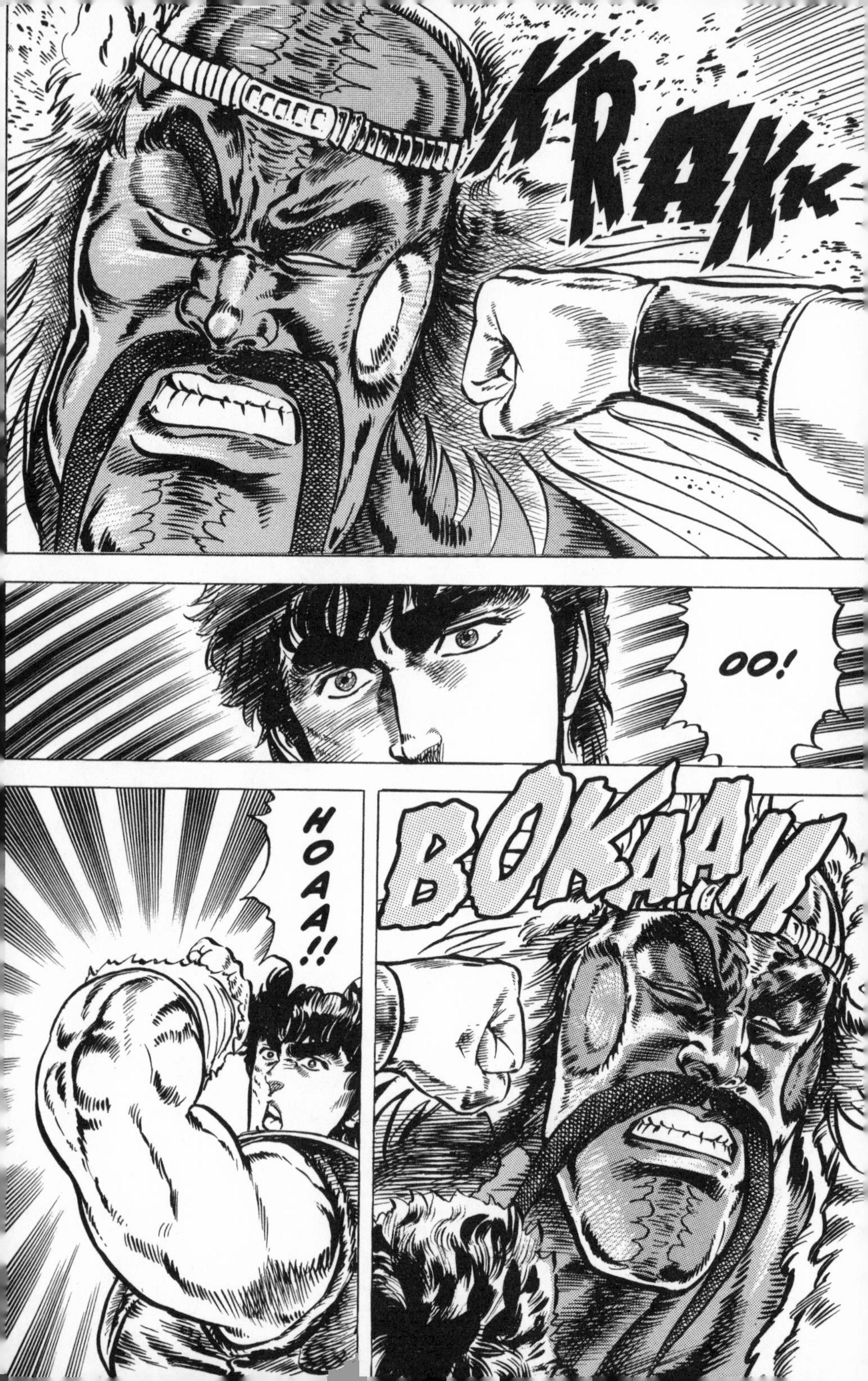
KRAKK
OO!
BOKAAM
HOAAA!!

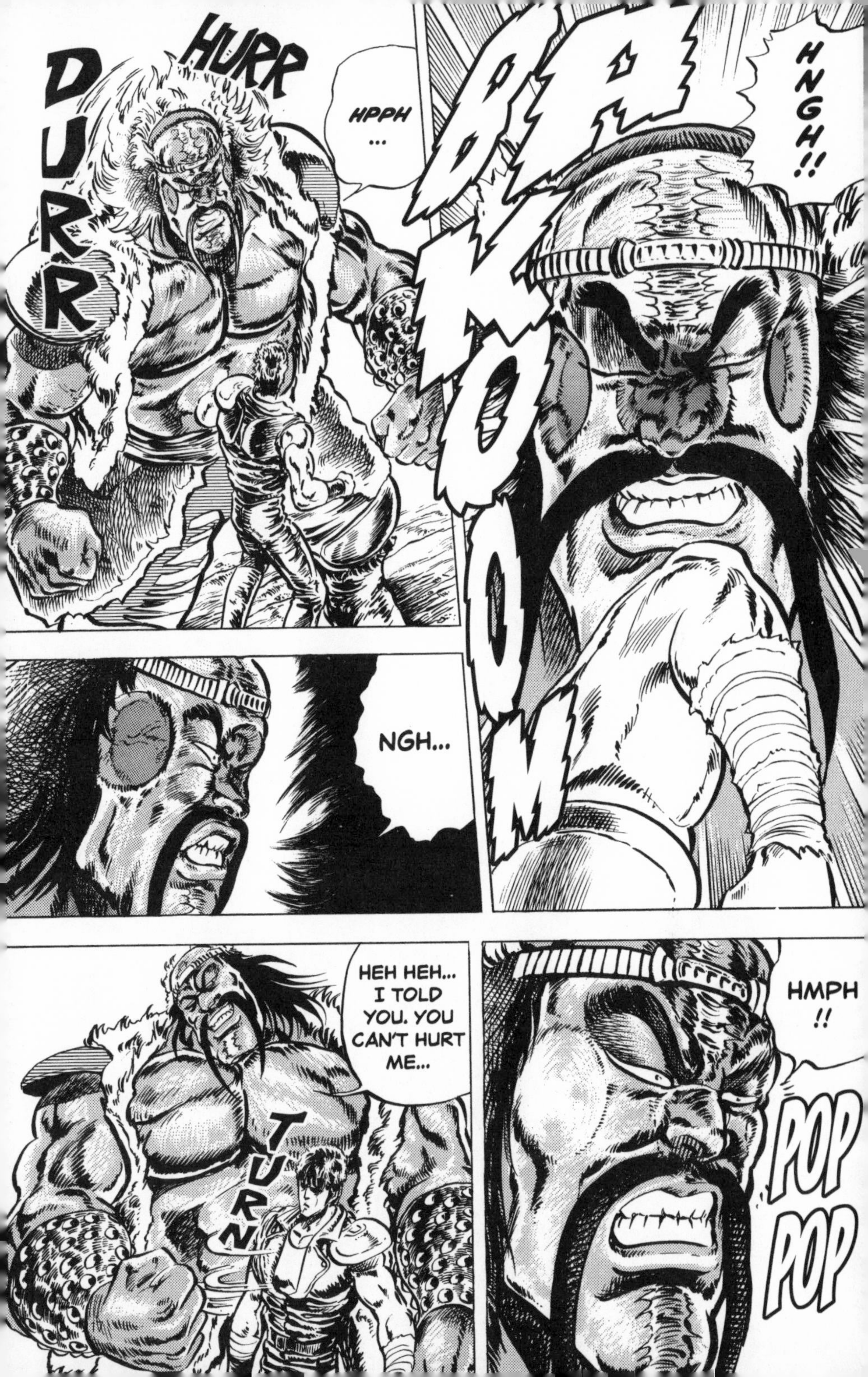
BAKOOM
HNGH!!
HURR
DURR
HPPH ...
NGH...
HMPH !!
POP POP
HEH HEH... I TOLD YOU. YOU CAN'T HURT ME...
TURN

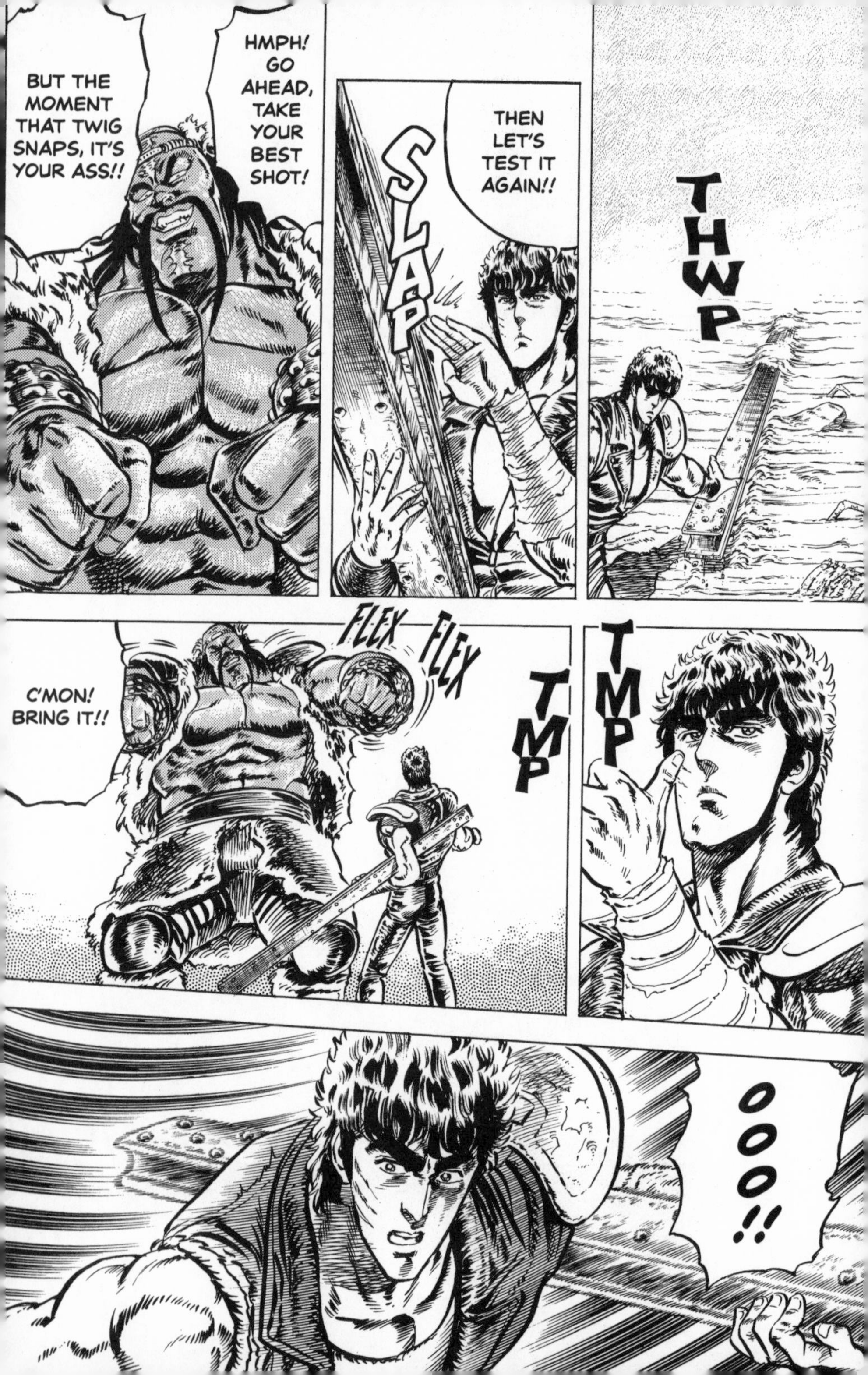
THWP
THEN LET'S TEST IT AGAIN!!
SLAP
HMPH! GO AHEAD, TAKE YOUR BEST SHOT!
BUT THE MOMENT THAT TWIG SNAPS, IT'S YOUR ASS!!
TMP TMP
FLEX FLEX
C'MON! BRING IT!!
OOOO!!

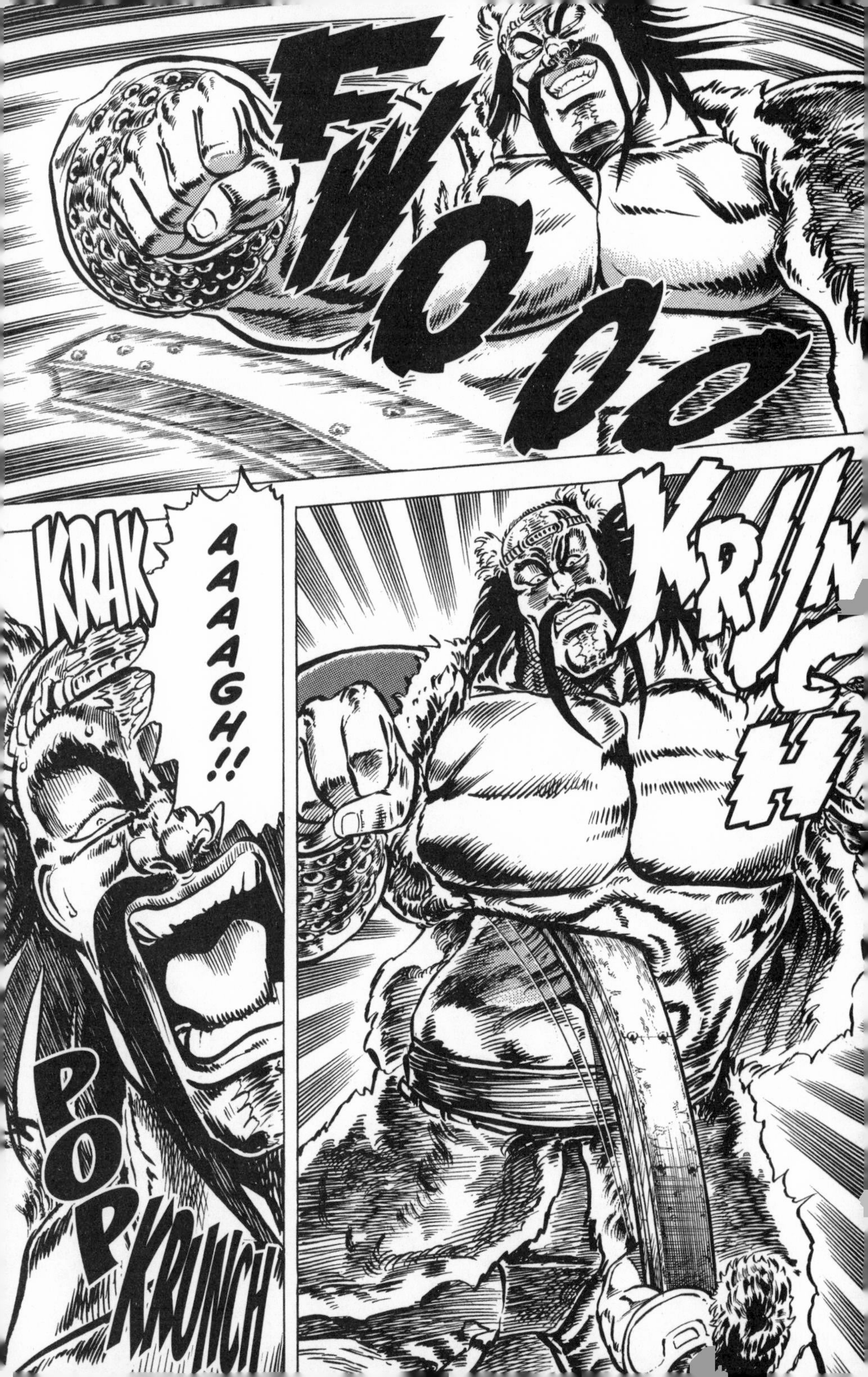
FWOOOO
KRUNCH
KRAK
AAAAAGH!!
POP
KRUNCH

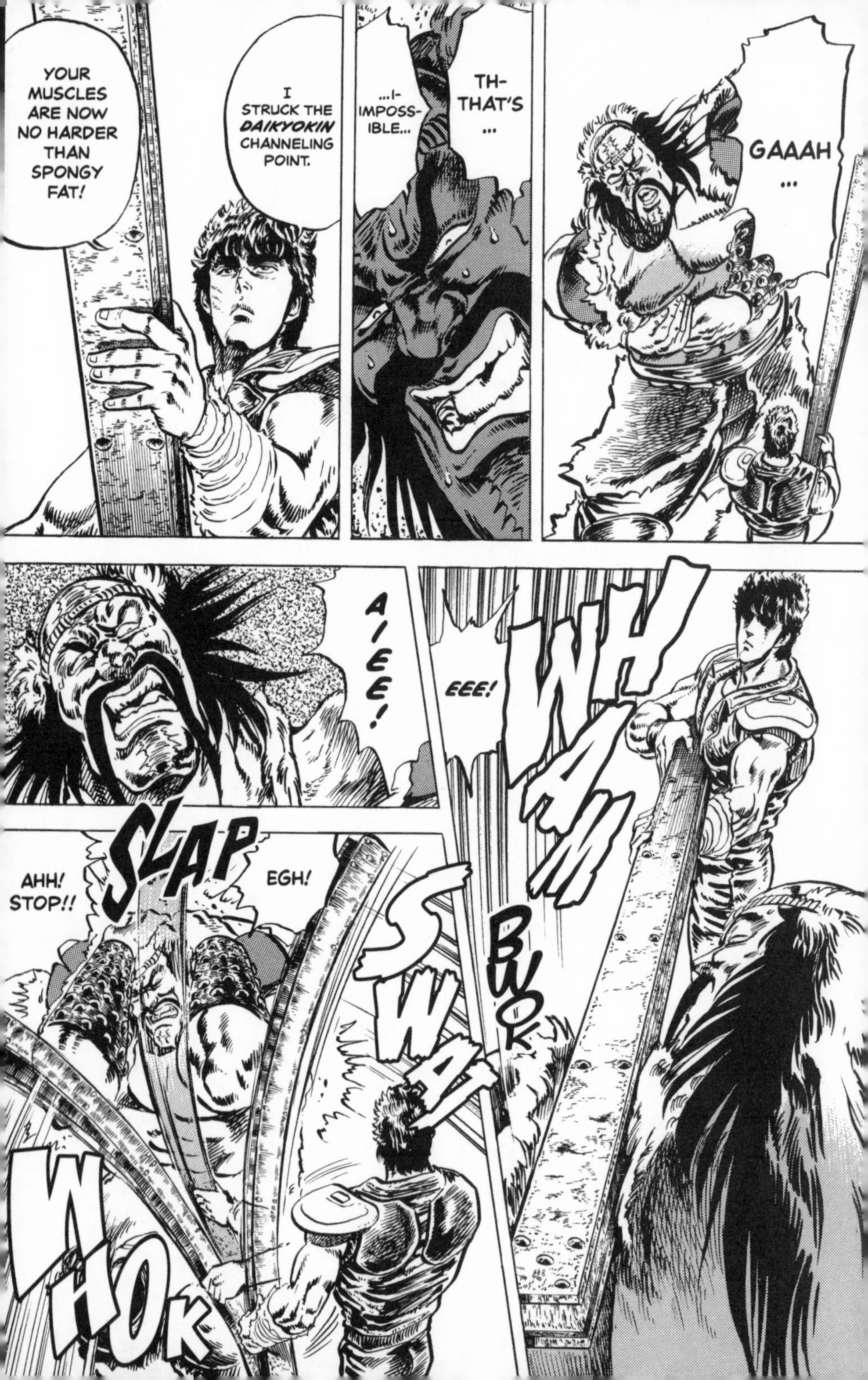

GAAAH ...
TH- THAT'S ...
...I- IMPOSSIBLE...
I STRUCK THE *DAIKYOKIN* CHANNELING POINT.
YOUR MUSCLES ARE NOW NO HARDER THAN SPONGY FAT!
WHAM
EEE!
BWOK
AIEE!
SLAP
EGH!
AHH! STOP!!
SWAT
WHOK

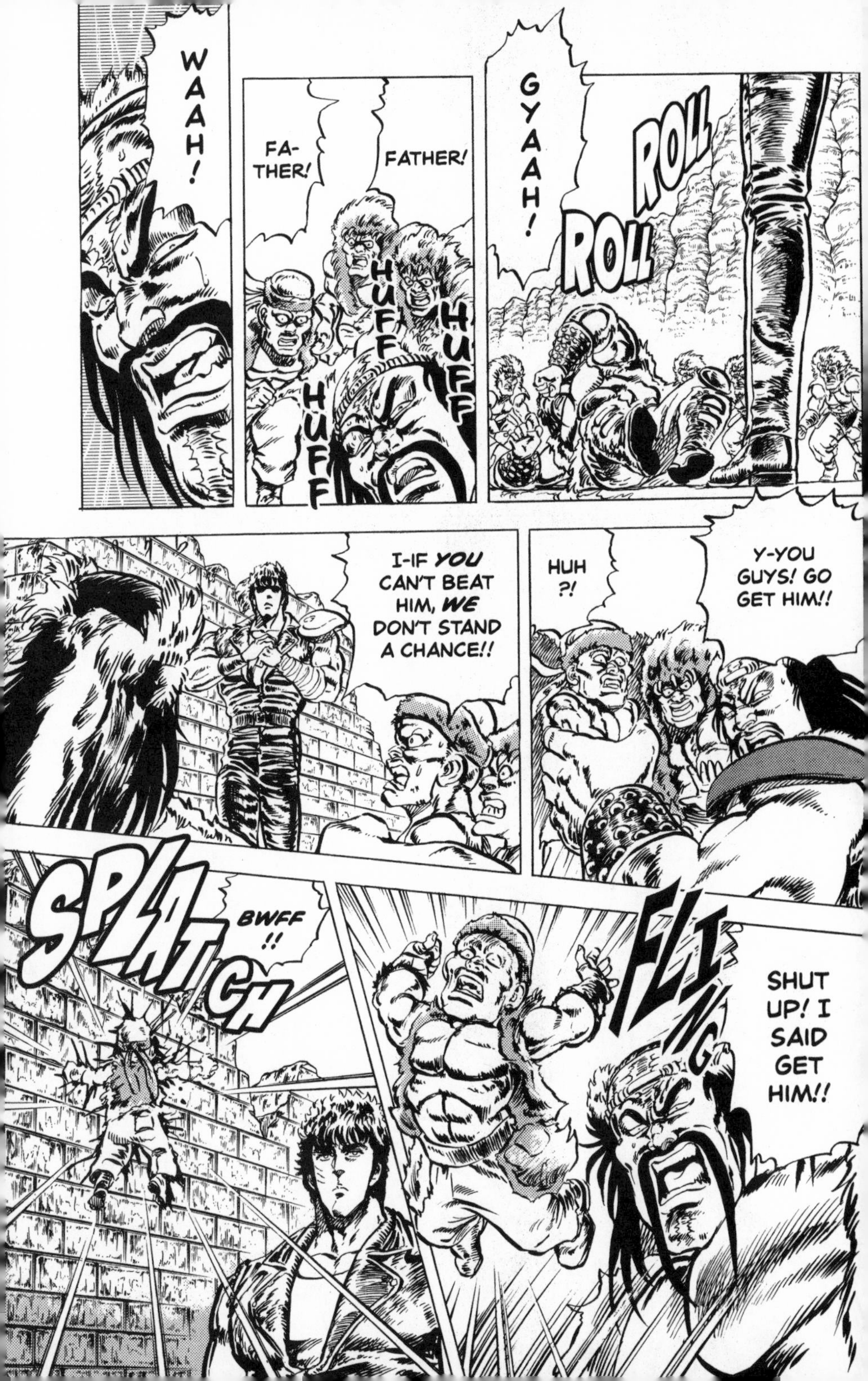
ROLL
ROLL
GYAAH!
FATHER!
FA-THER!
HUFF
HUFF
HUFF
WAAH!
Y-YOU GUYS! GO GET HIM!!
HUH ?!
I-IF YOU CAN'T BEAT HIM, WE DON'T STAND A CHANCE!!
SHUT UP! I SAID GET HIM!!
FLING
BWFF !!
SPLATCH

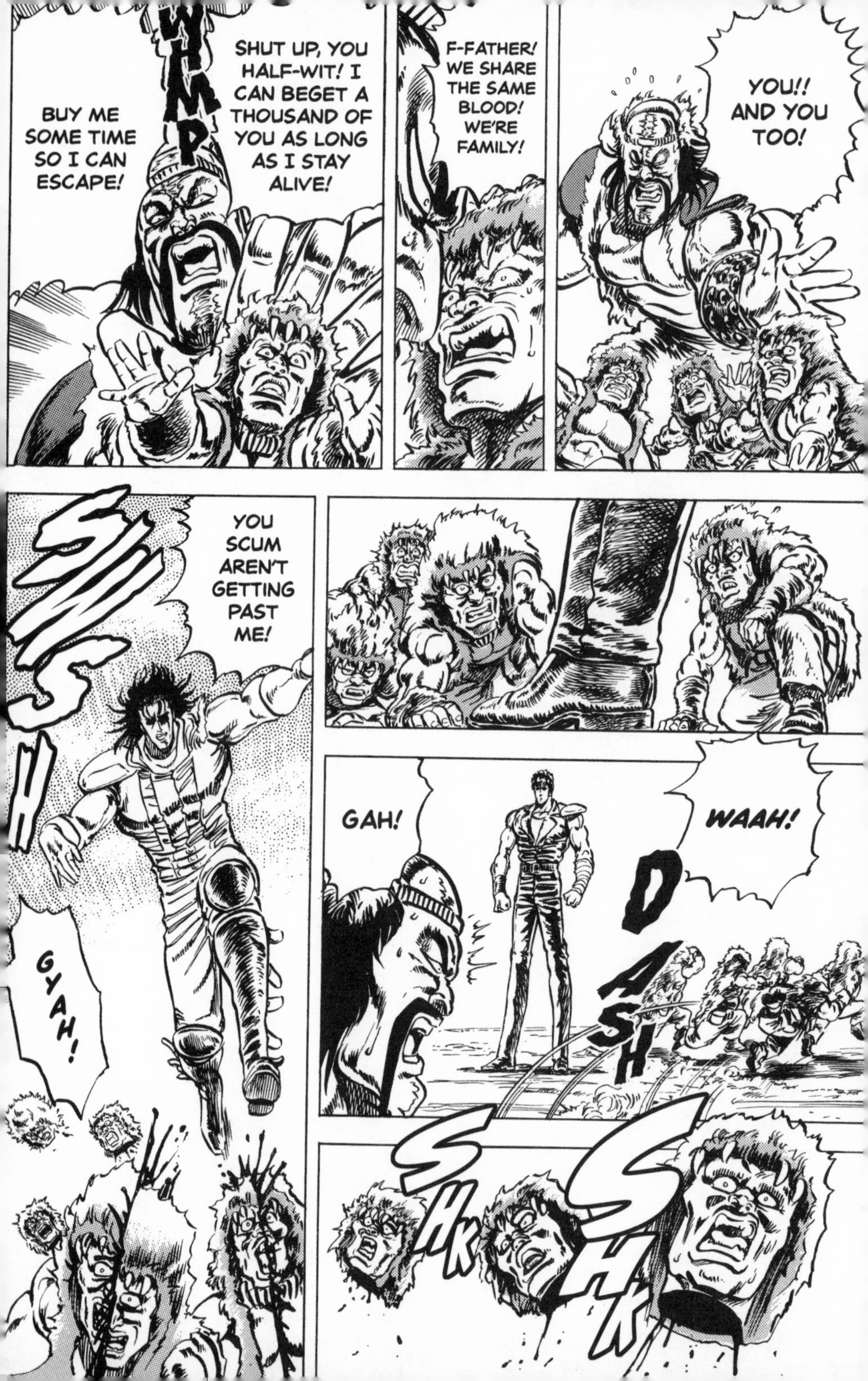
YOU!! AND YOU TOO!
F-FATHER! WE SHARE THE SAME BLOOD! WE'RE FAMILY!
SHUT UP, YOU HALF-WIT! I CAN BEGET A THOUSAND OF YOU AS LONG AS I STAY ALIVE!
WHMP
BUY ME SOME TIME SO I CAN ESCAPE!
WAAH!
GAH!
DASH
SHK
SHK
YOU SCUM AREN'T GETTING PAST ME!
SHHH
GYAH!

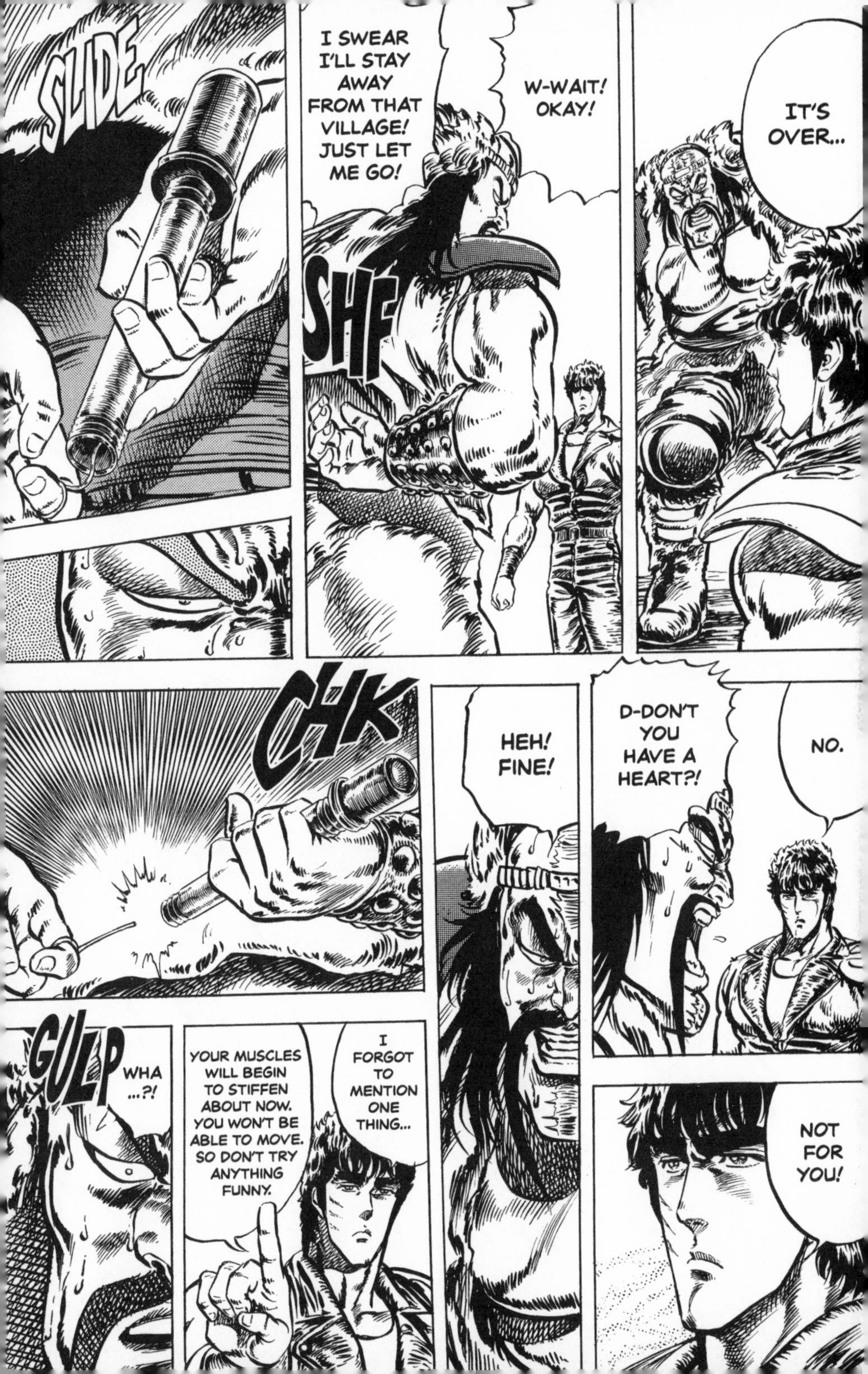
IT'S OVER...
W-WAIT! OKAY!
I SWEAR I'LL STAY AWAY FROM THAT VILLAGE! JUST LET ME GO!
SHF
SLIDE
NO.
D-DON'T YOU HAVE A HEART?!
HEH! FINE!
CHK
NOT FOR YOU!
I FORGOT TO MENTION ONE THING...
YOUR MUSCLES WILL BEGIN TO STIFFEN ABOUT NOW. YOU WON'T BE ABLE TO MOVE. SO DON'T TRY ANYTHING FUNNY.
GULP
WHA ...?!

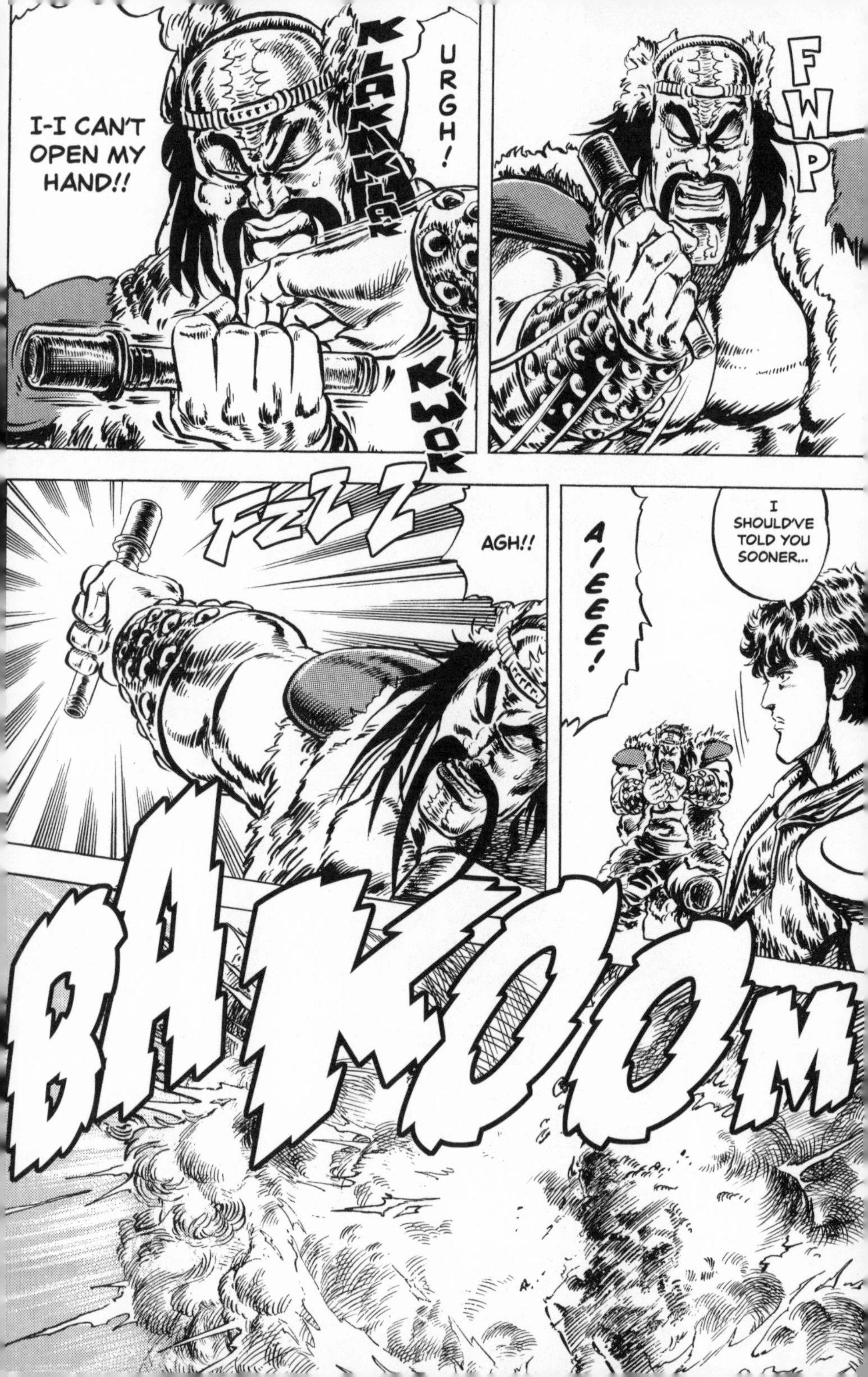
FWP
URGH!
KLAKKLAK
I-I CAN'T OPEN MY HAND!!
KWOK
I SHOULD'VE TOLD YOU SOONER...
AIEEE!
AGH!!
FZZZ
BAKOOM

THERE'S NO PAIN...

W-WAIT...

AWGH!!

AH!

WHAT?!

RIGHT. THAT'S BECAUSE YOUR BODY HAS BEGUN TO DIE.

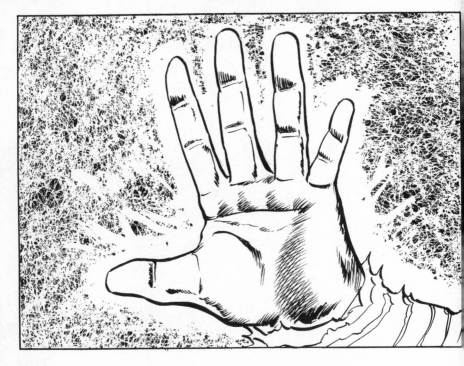

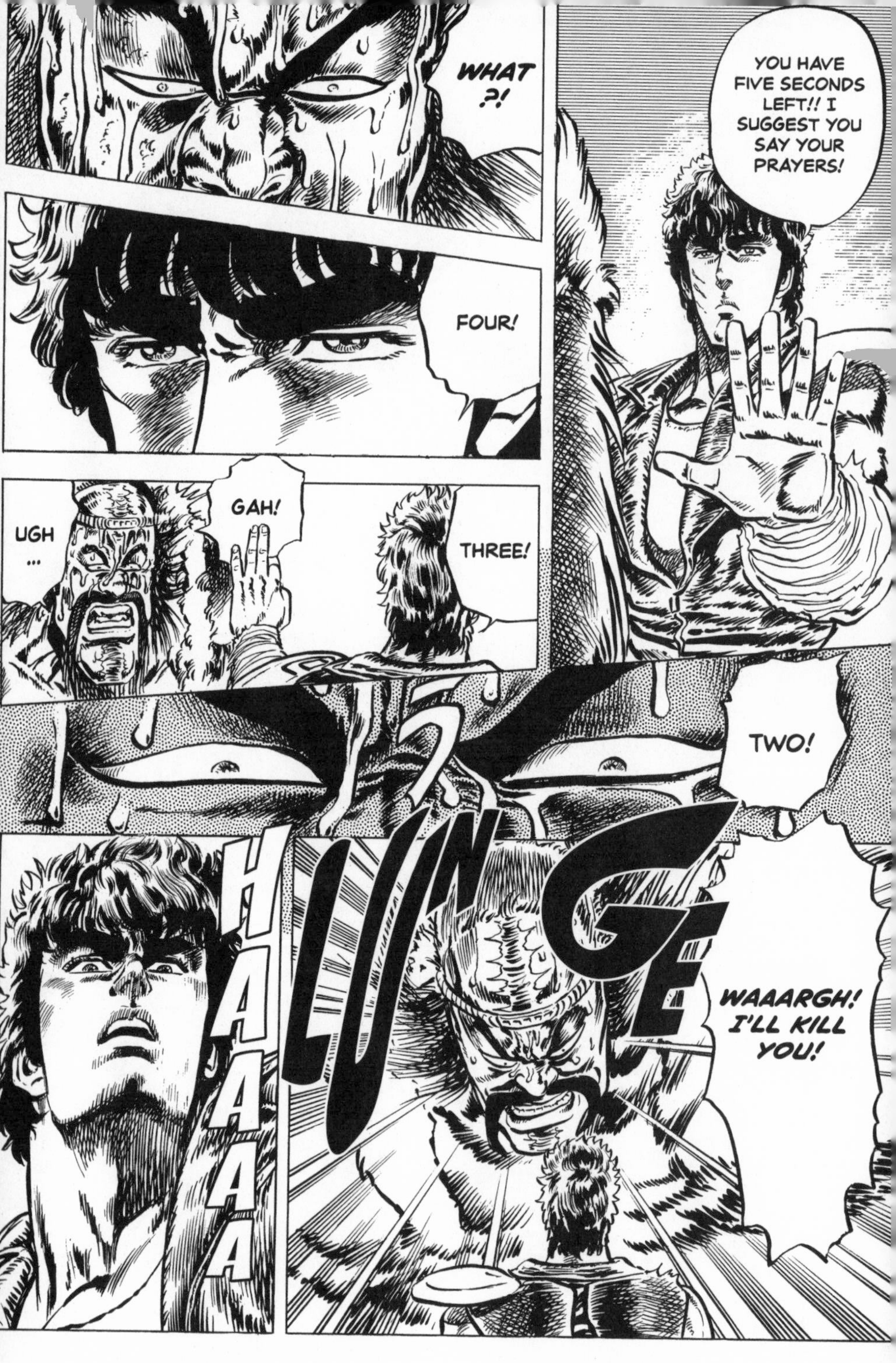
YOU HAVE FIVE SECONDS LEFT!! I SUGGEST YOU SAY YOUR PRAYERS!
WHAT ?!
FOUR!
THREE!
GAH!
UGH ...
TWO!
WAAARGH! I'LL KILL YOU!
LUNGE
HAAAAAA

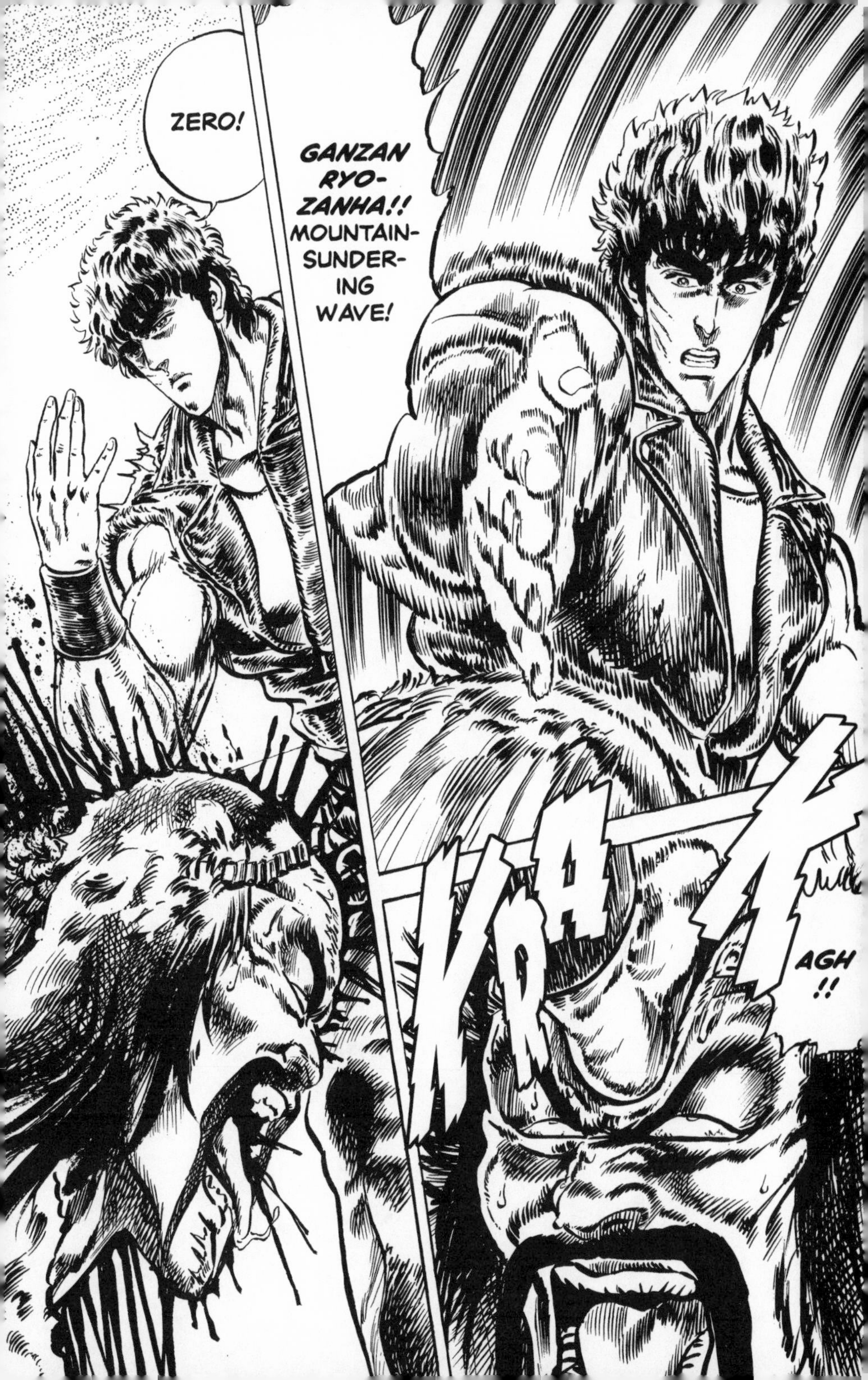
GANZAN RYO-ZANHA!! MOUNTAIN-SUNDER-ING WAVE!
KRAK
AGH !!
ZERO!

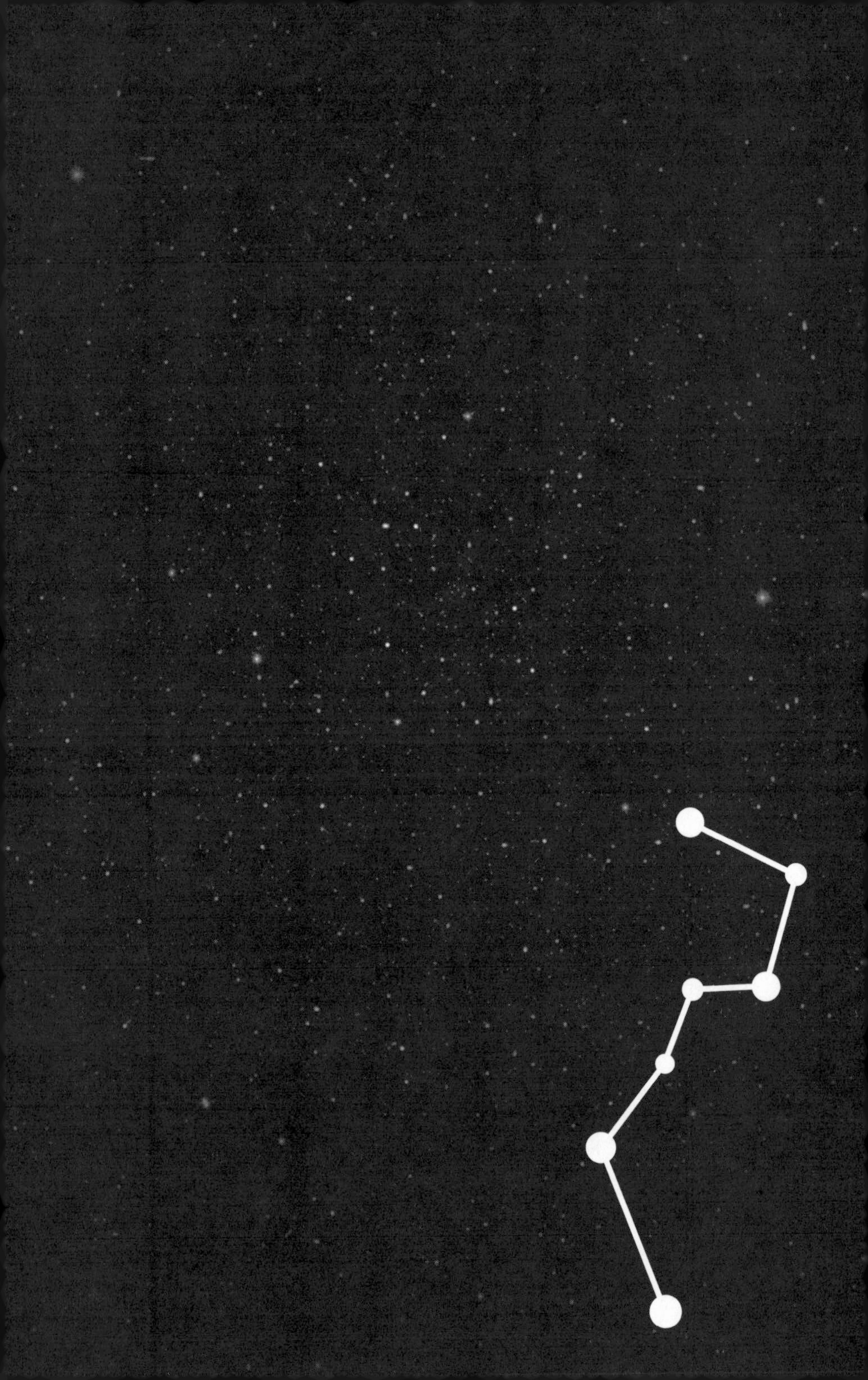

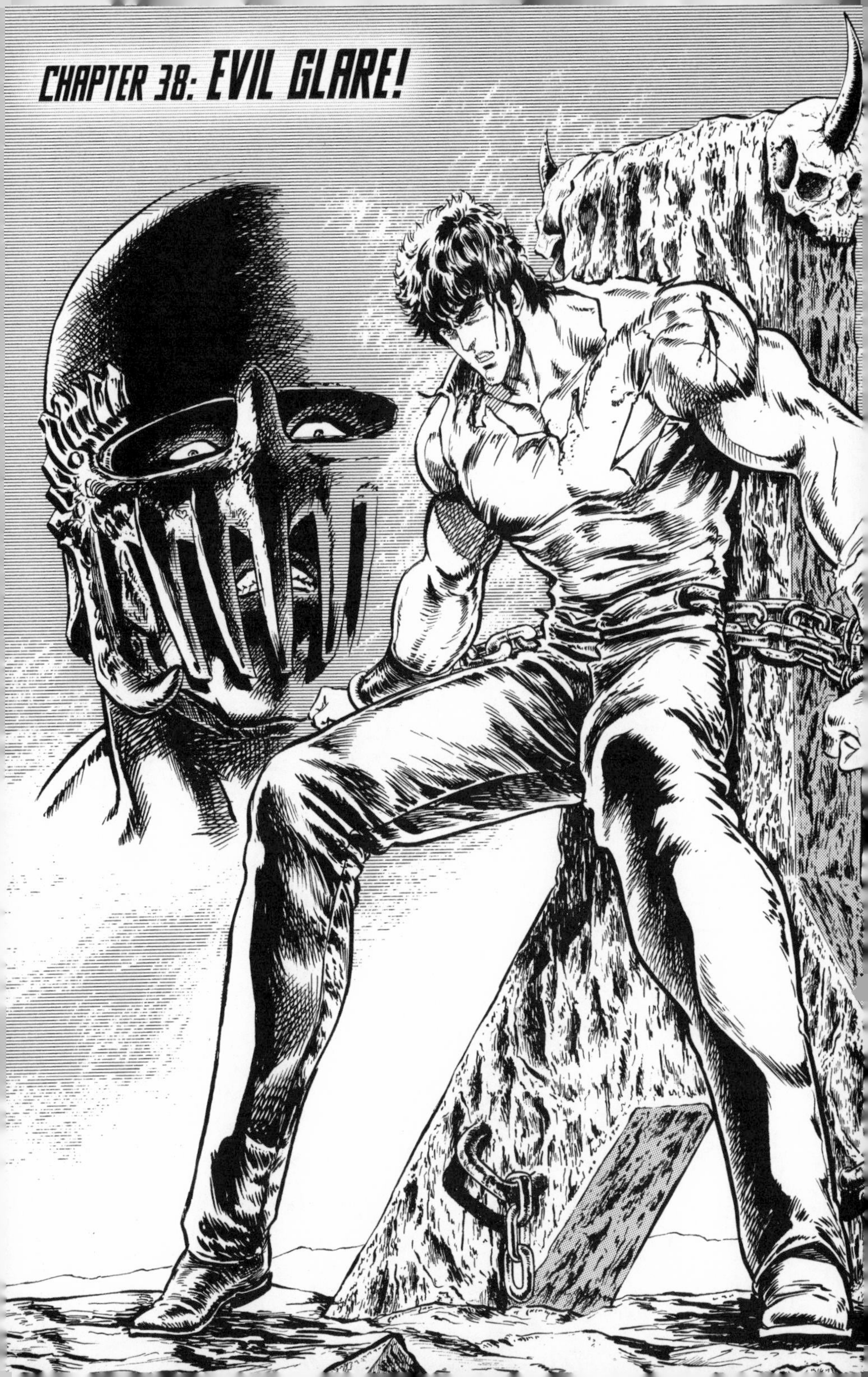
CHAPTER 38: EVIL GLARE!

SHHHH

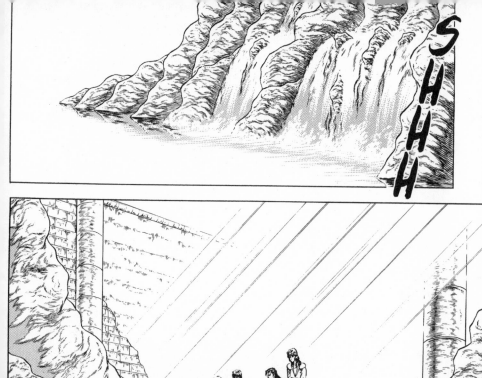

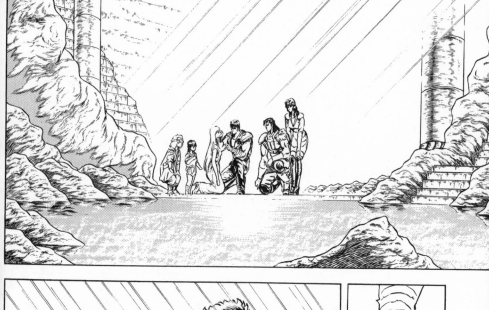

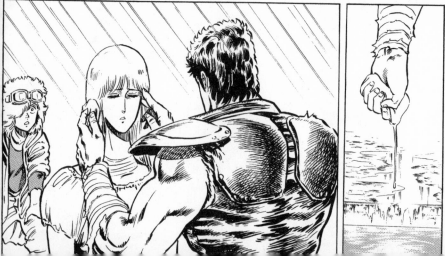

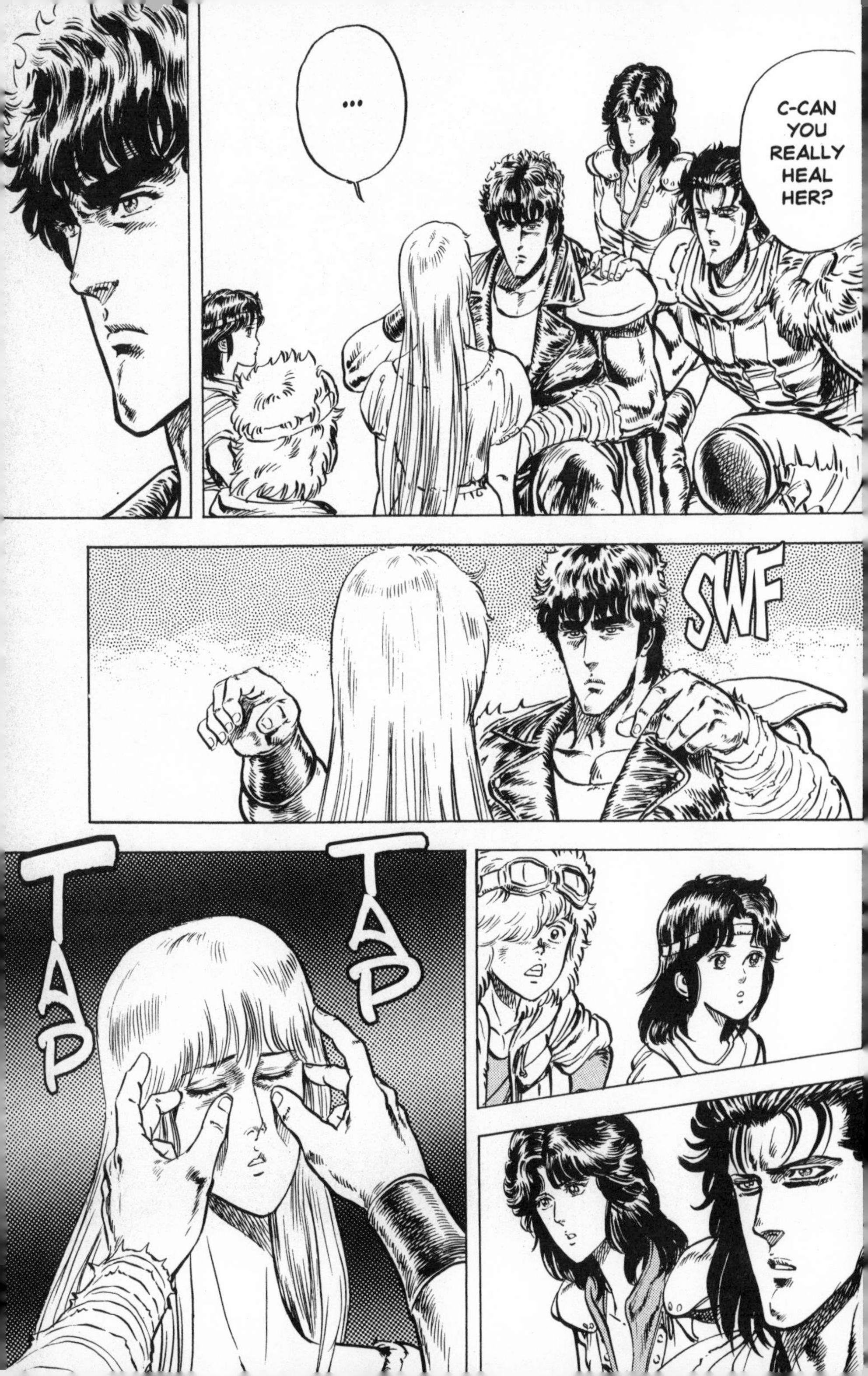
C-CAN YOU REALLY HEAL HER?
...
SWF
TAP
TAP

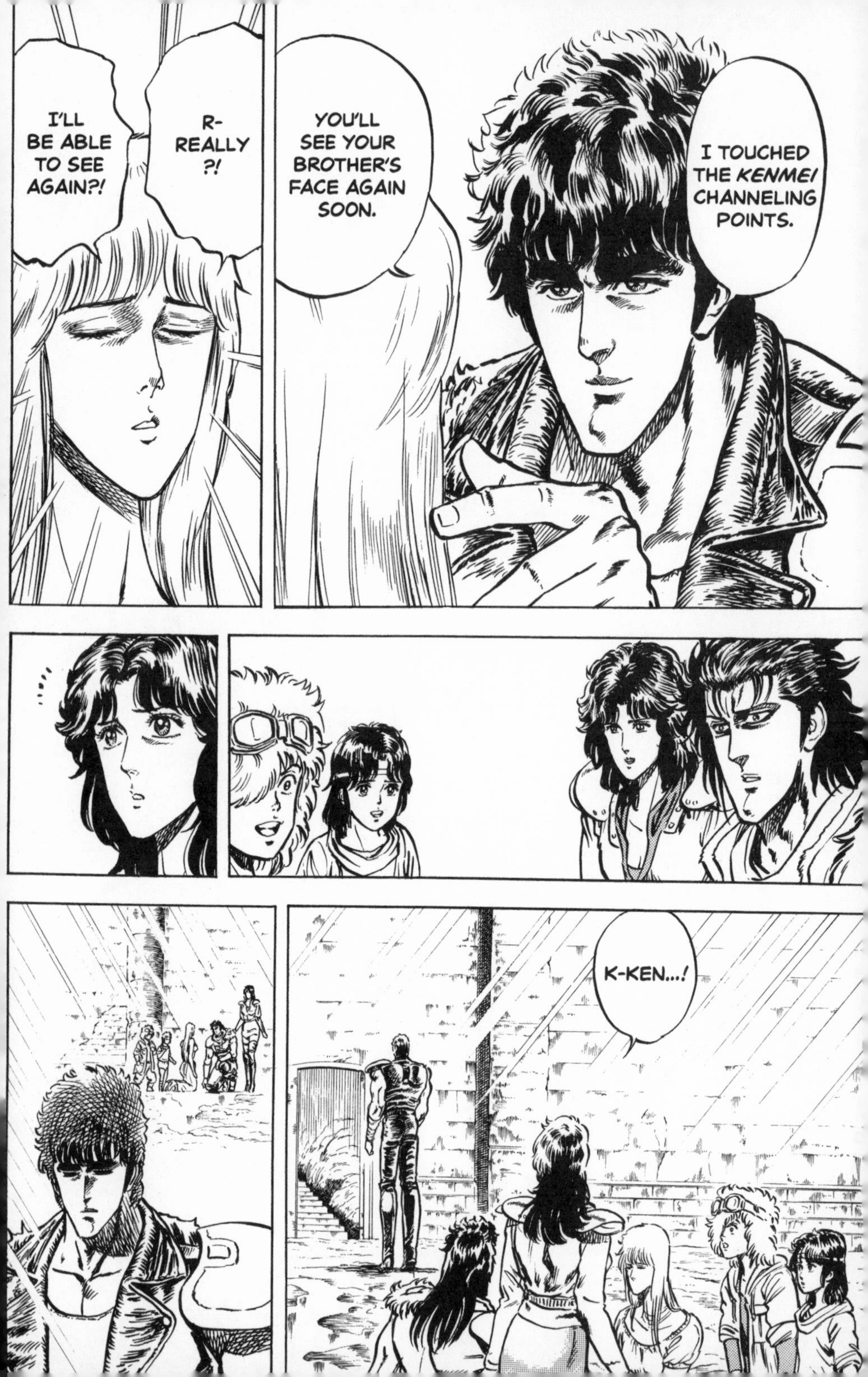
I TOUCHED THE *KENMEI* CHANNELING POINTS.
YOU'LL SEE YOUR BROTHER'S FACE AGAIN SOON.
R- REALLY ?!
I'LL BE ABLE TO SEE AGAIN?!
K-KEN...!

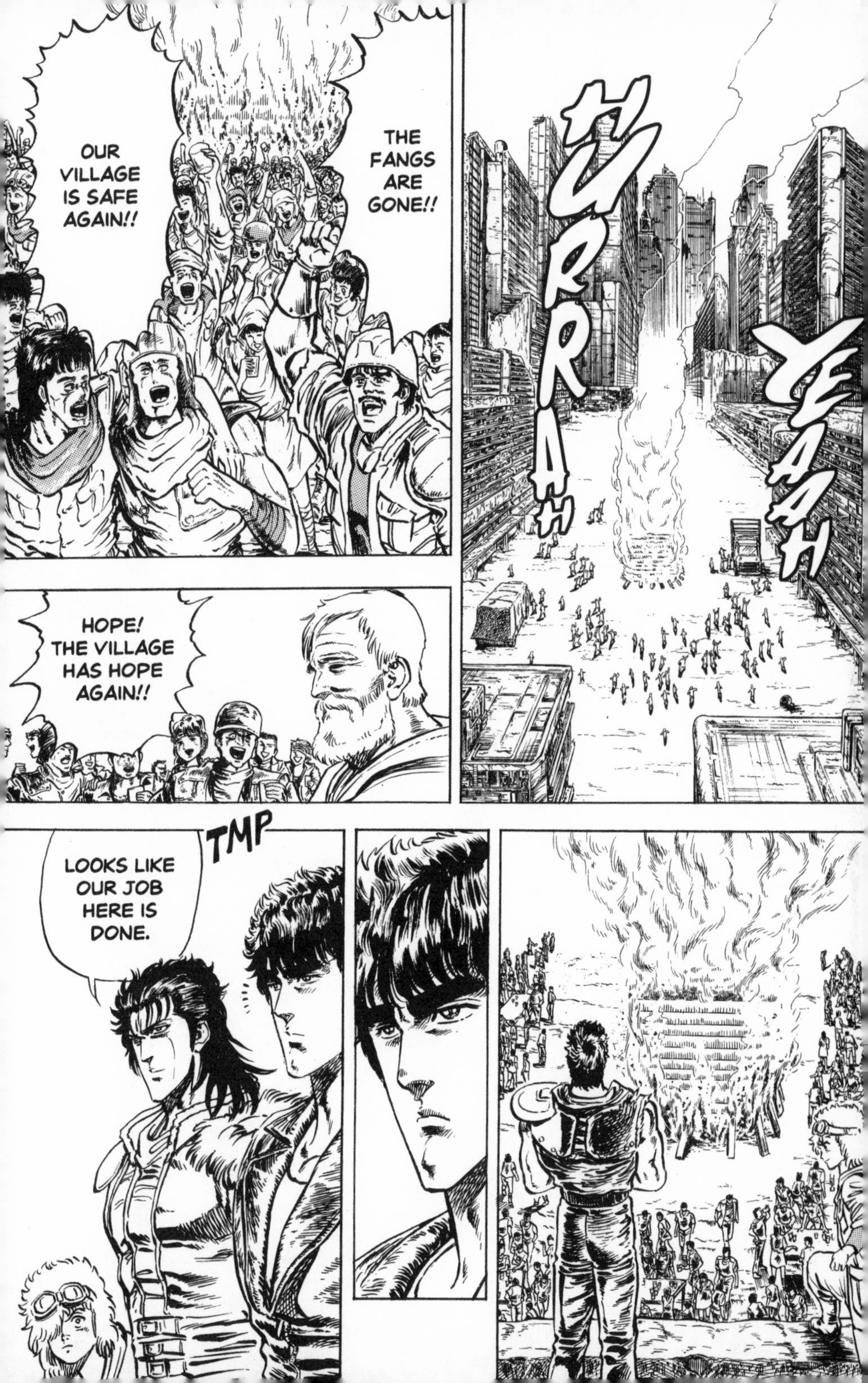
YEAAAH
HURRAH
THE FANGS ARE GONE!!
OUR VILLAGE IS SAFE AGAIN!!
HOPE! THE VILLAGE HAS HOPE AGAIN!!
TMP
LOOKS LIKE OUR JOB HERE IS DONE.

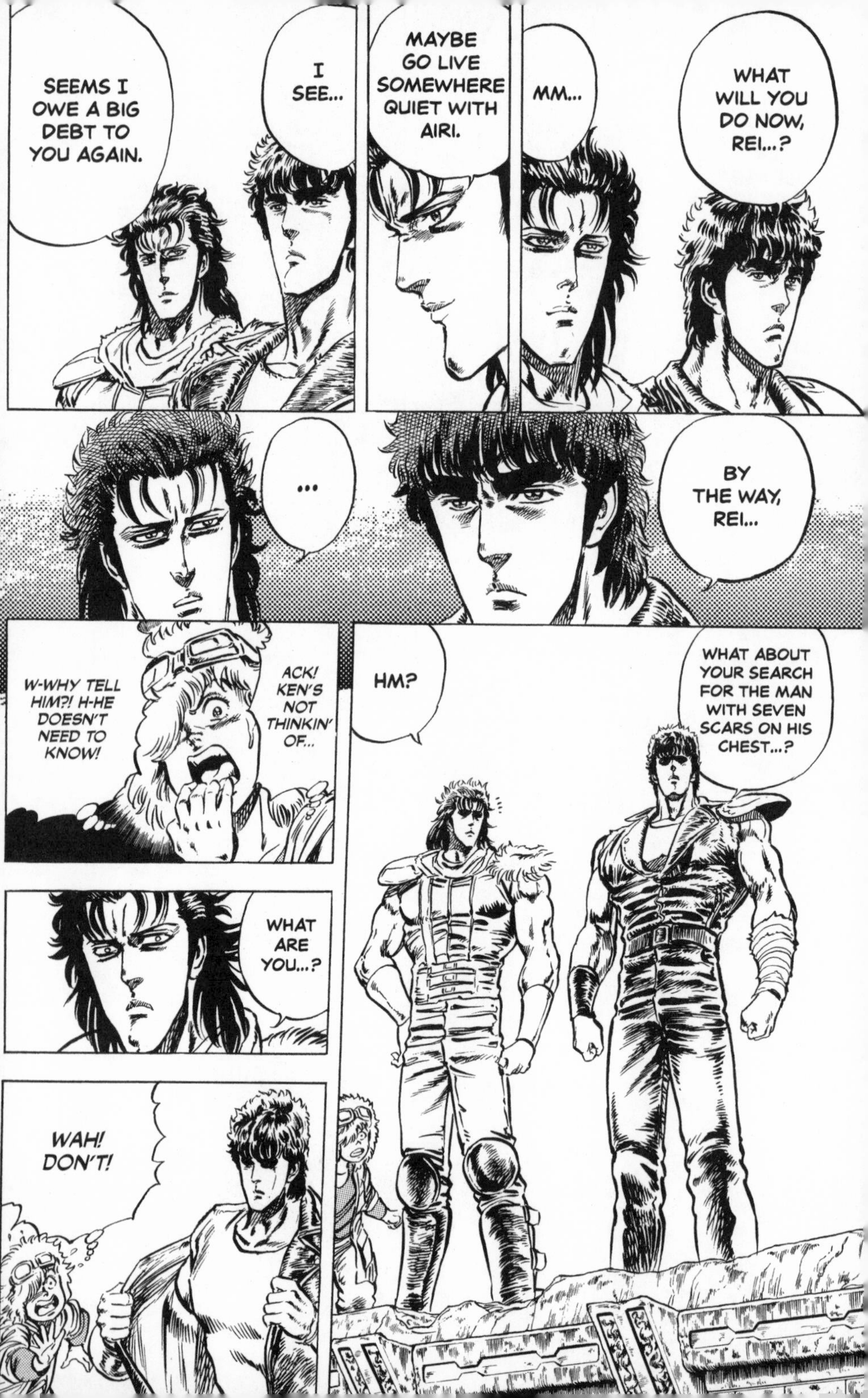
WHAT WILL YOU DO NOW, REI...?
MM...
MAYBE GO LIVE SOMEWHERE QUIET WITH AIRI.
I SEE...
SEEMS I OWE A BIG DEBT TO YOU AGAIN.
BY THE WAY, REI...
...
WHAT ABOUT YOUR SEARCH FOR THE MAN WITH SEVEN SCARS ON HIS CHEST...?
HM?
ACK! KEN'S NOT THINKIN' OF...
W-WHY TELL HIM?! H-HE DOESN'T NEED TO KNOW!
WHAT ARE YOU...?
WAH! DON'T!

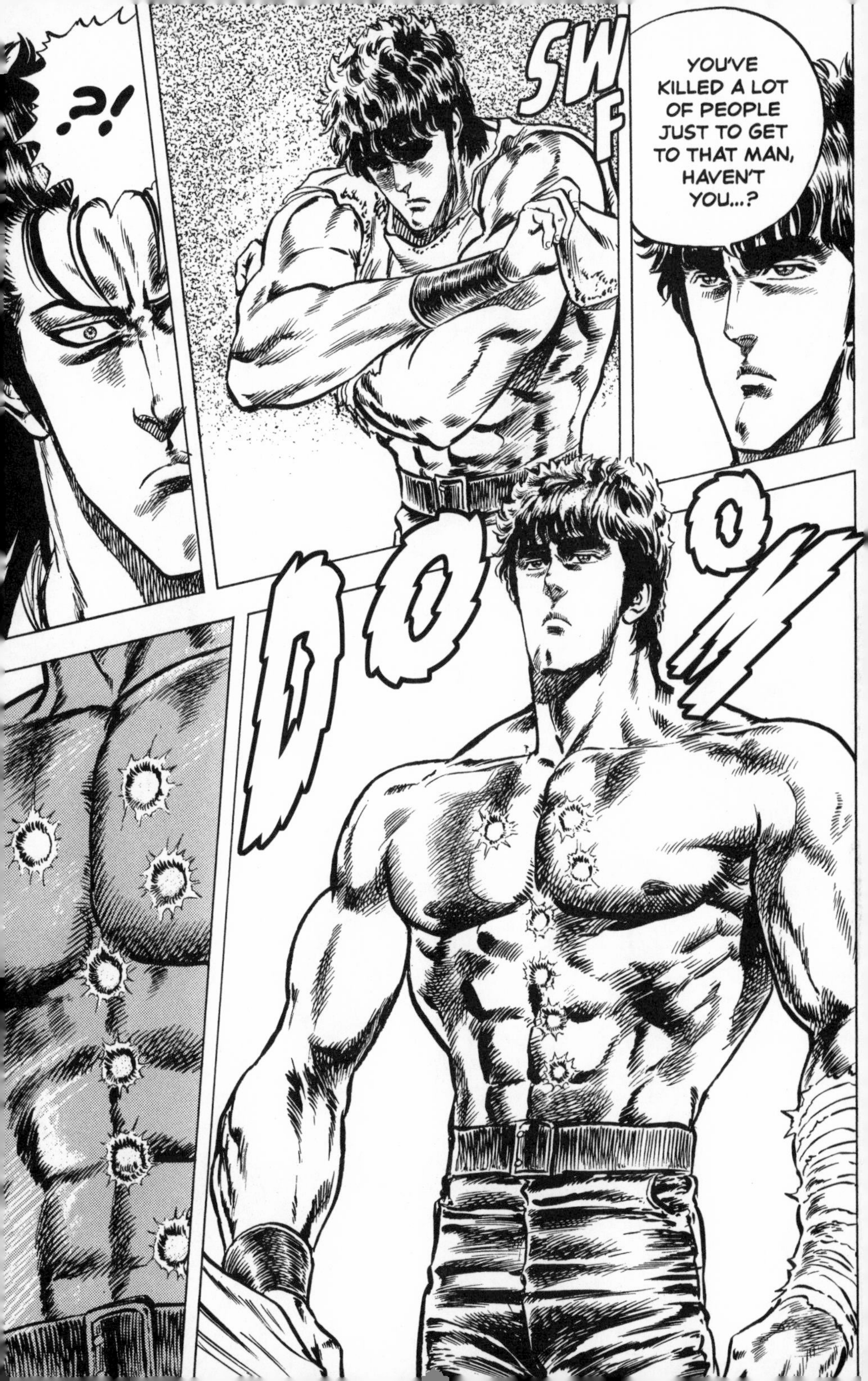
YOU'VE KILLED A LOT OF PEOPLE JUST TO GET TO THAT MAN, HAVEN'T YOU...?
SWF
?!
DOOM

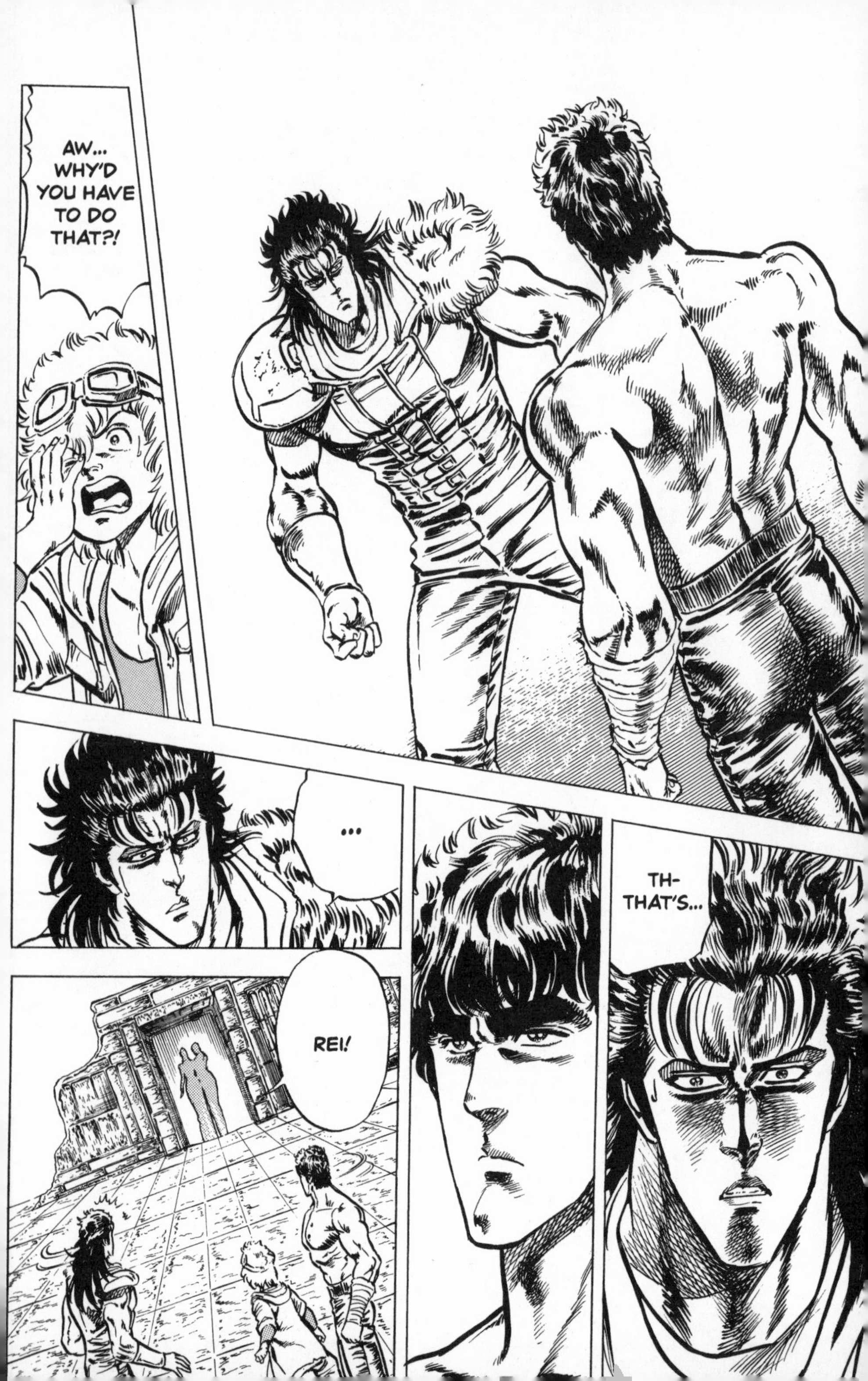
AW... WHY'D YOU HAVE TO DO THAT?!
TH- THAT'S...
...
REI!

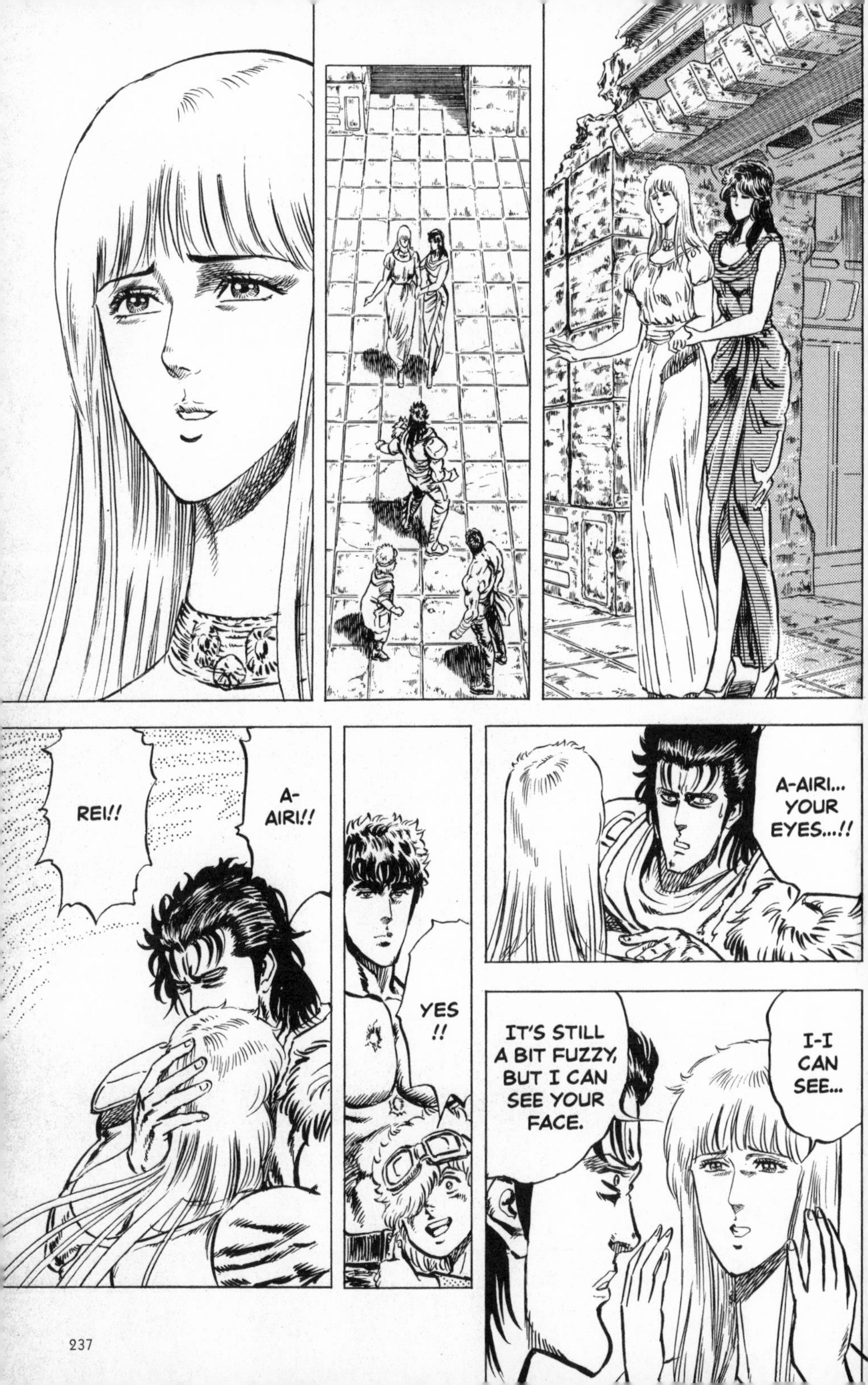
A-AIRI... YOUR EYES...!!
I-I CAN SEE...
IT'S STILL A BIT FUZZY, BUT I CAN SEE YOUR FACE.
YES !!
A-AIRI!!
REI!!

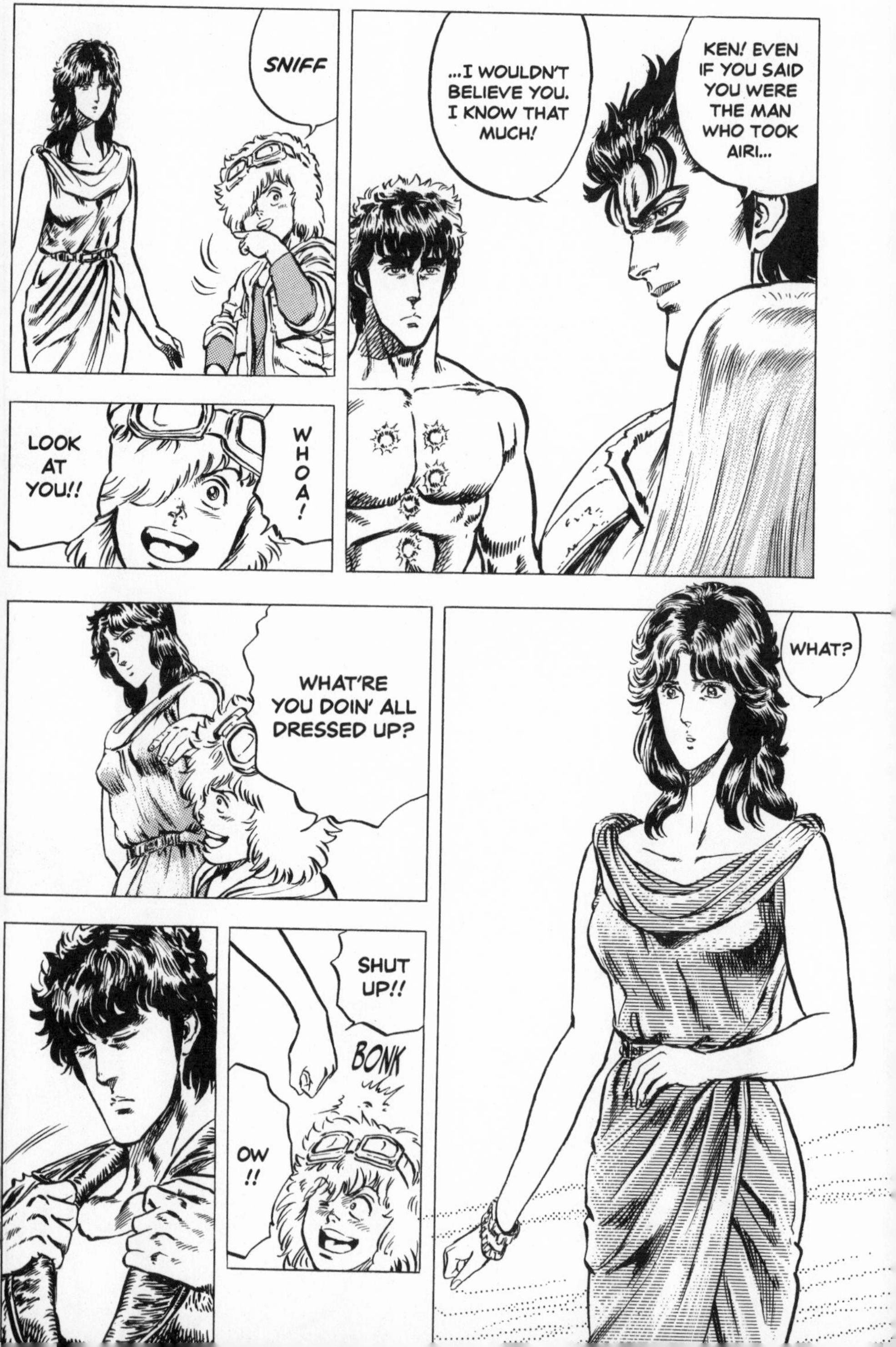
KEN! EVEN IF YOU SAID YOU WERE THE MAN WHO TOOK AIRI...
...I WOULDN'T BELIEVE YOU. I KNOW THAT MUCH!
SNIFF
WHOA!
LOOK AT YOU!!
WHAT?
WHAT'RE YOU DOIN' ALL DRESSED UP?
SHUT UP!!
BONK
OW!!

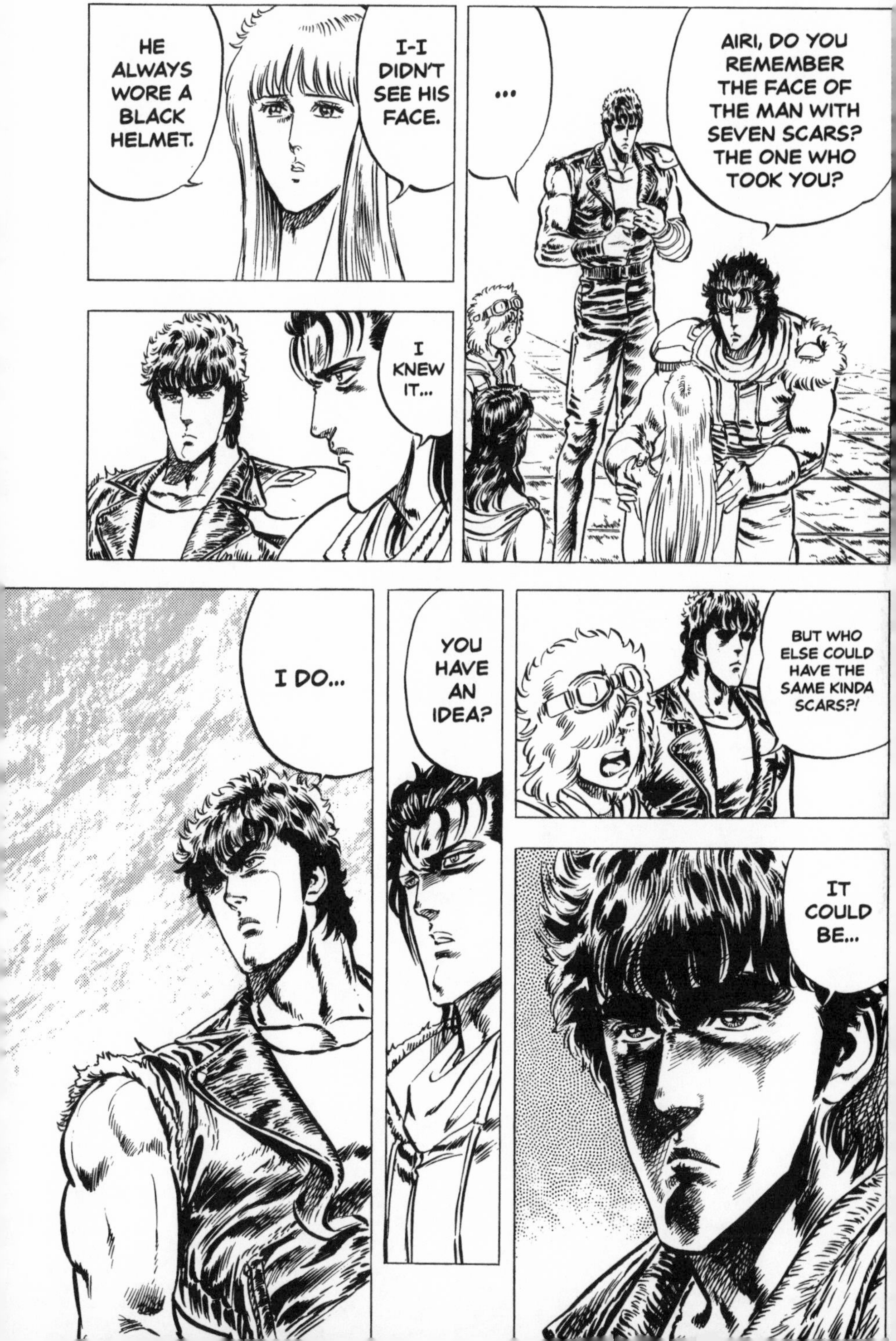
AIRI, DO YOU REMEMBER THE FACE OF THE MAN WITH SEVEN SCARS? THE ONE WHO TOOK YOU?
...
I-I DIDN'T SEE HIS FACE.
HE ALWAYS WORE A BLACK HELMET.
I KNEW IT...
BUT WHO ELSE COULD HAVE THE SAME KINDA SCARS?!
IT COULD BE...
YOU HAVE AN IDEA?
I DO...

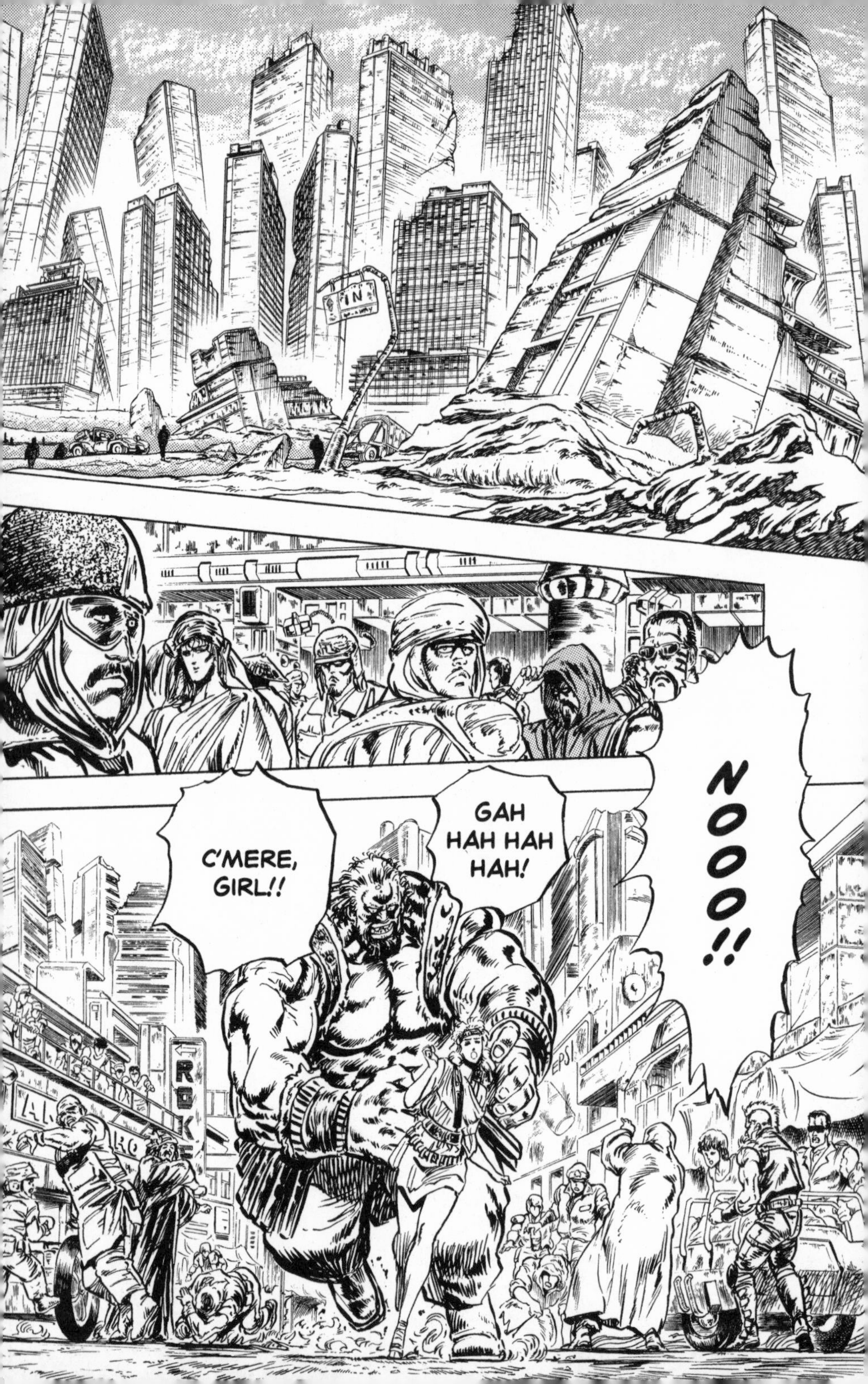
NOOOO!!
GAH HAH HAH HAH!
C'MERE, GIRL!!

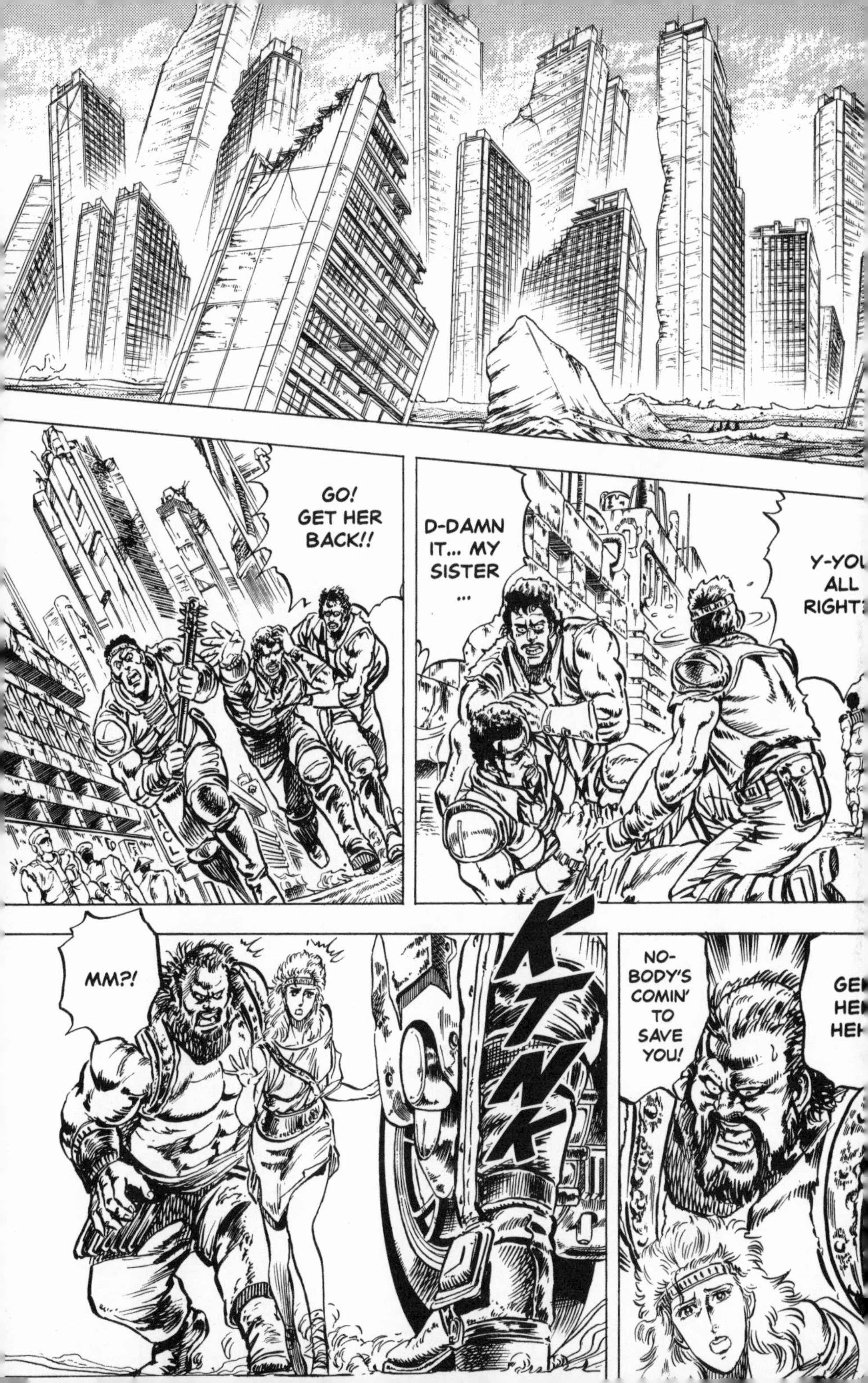
GO! GET HER BACK!!
Y-YOU ALL RIGHT?
D-DAMN IT... MY SISTER ...
MM?!
NO-BODY'S COMIN' TO SAVE YOU!
GEH HEH HEH

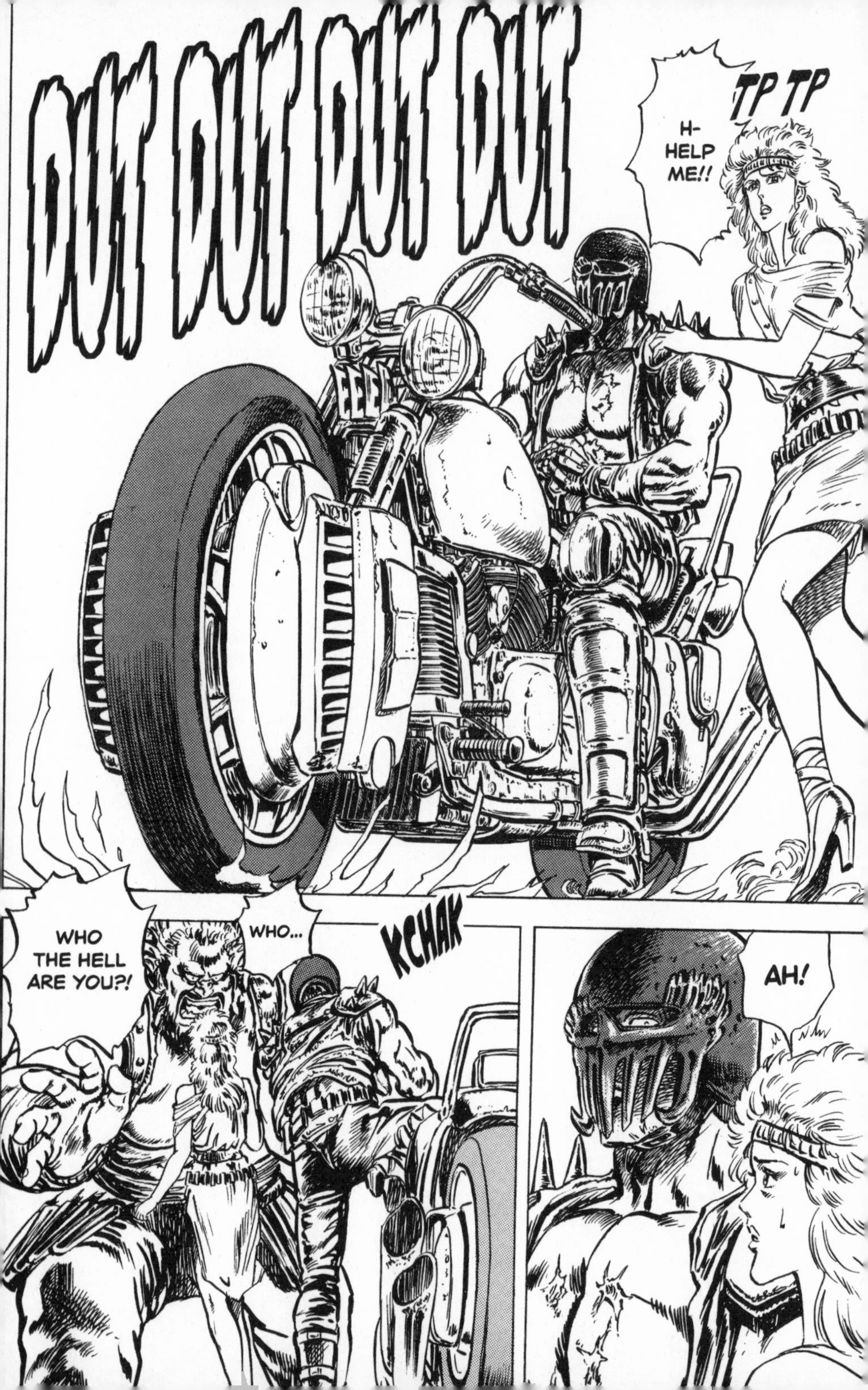
TP TP
H-HELP ME!!
DUT DUT DUT DUT
AH!
KCHAK
WHO...
WHO THE HELL ARE YOU?!

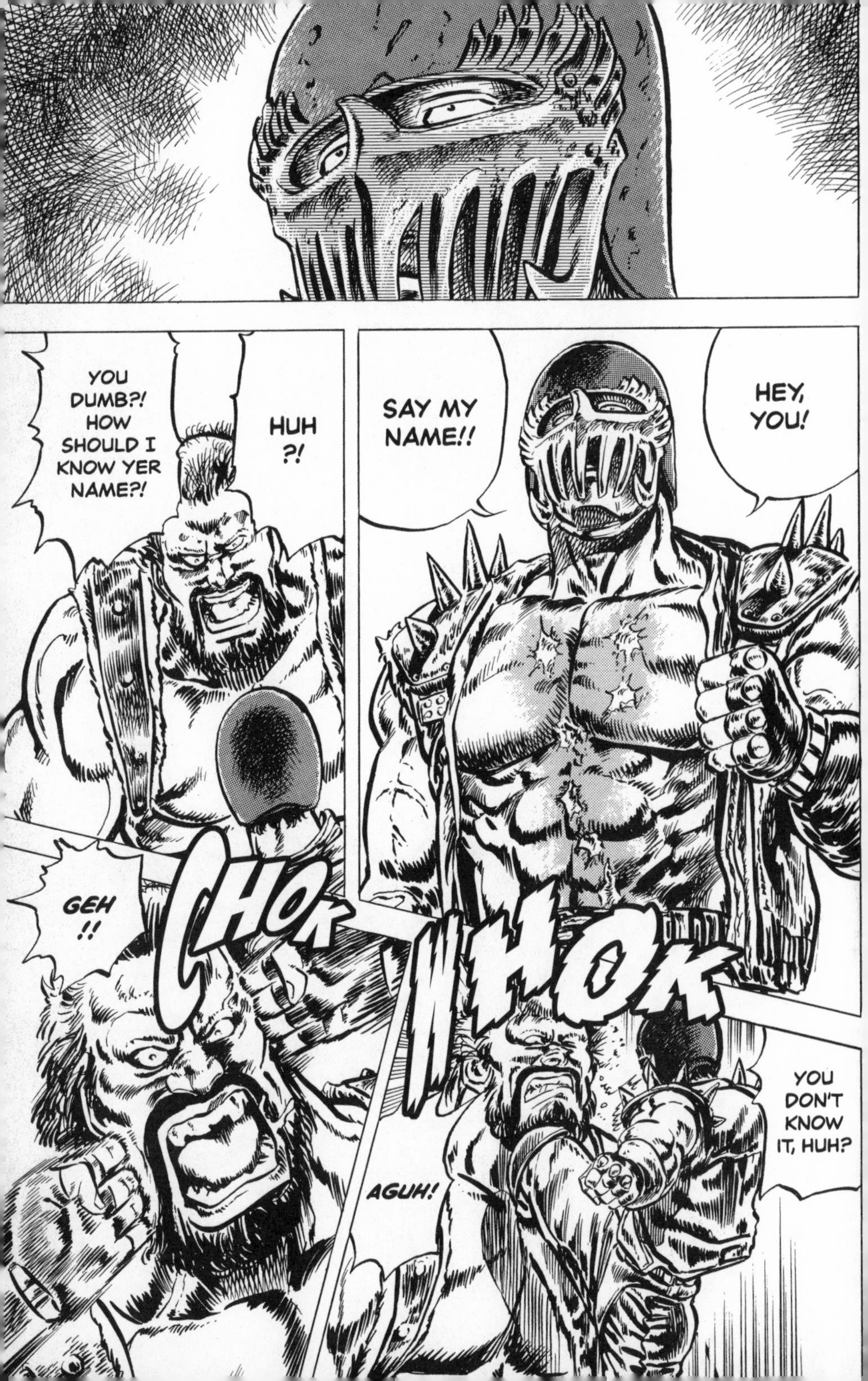
HEY, YOU!
SAY MY NAME!!
HUH ?!
YOU DUMB?! HOW SHOULD I KNOW YER NAME?!
YOU DON'T KNOW IT, HUH?
AGUH!
HOK
CHOK
GEH !!

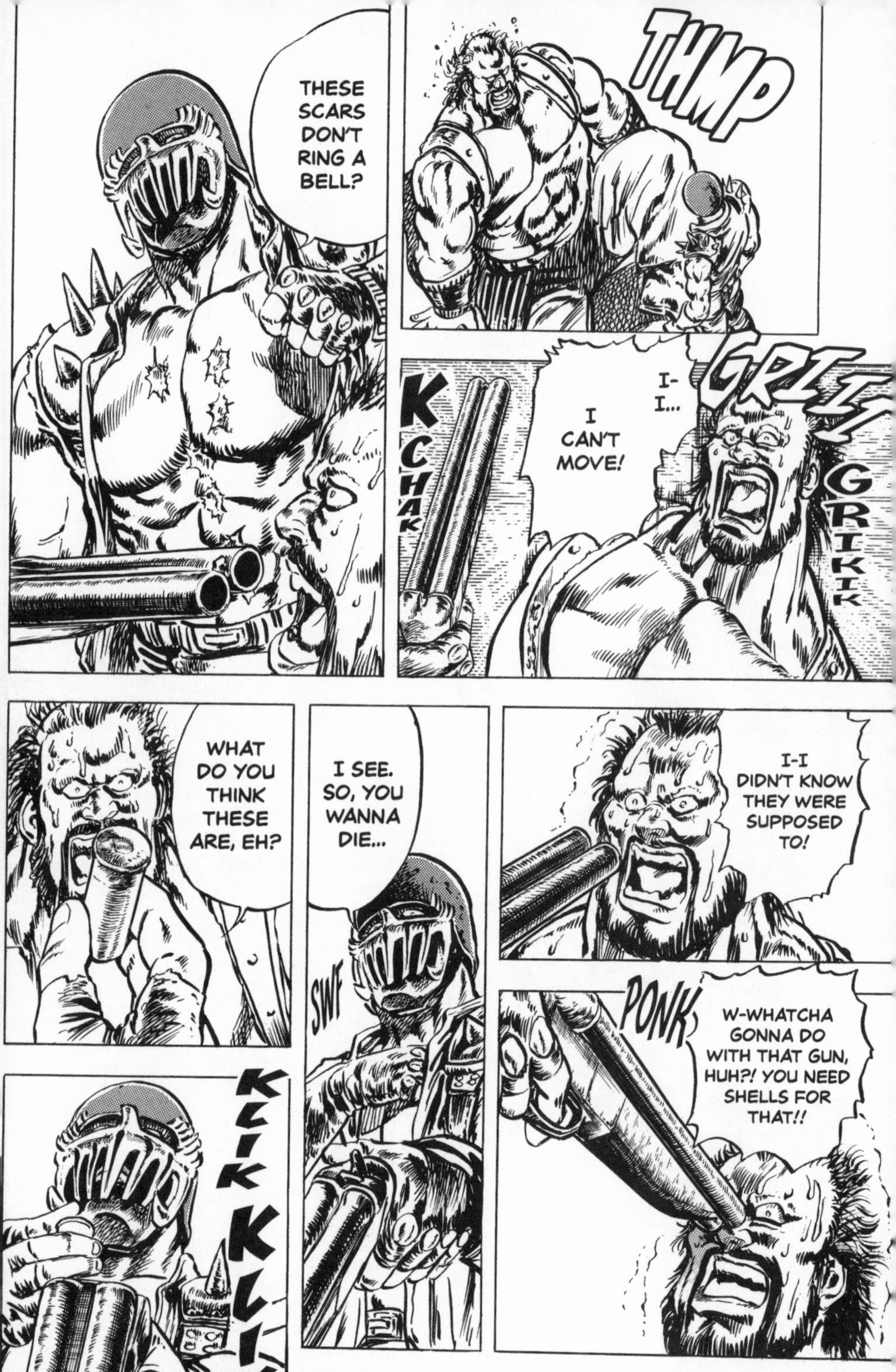
THMP
I-
I...
I CAN'T MOVE!
KCHAK
GRIII
GRIKIK
THESE SCARS DON'T RING A BELL?
I-I DIDN'T KNOW THEY WERE SUPPOSED TO!
PONK
W-WHATCHA GONNA DO WITH THAT GUN, HUH?! YOU NEED SHELLS FOR THAT!!
I SEE. SO, YOU WANNA DIE...
SWF
WHAT DO YOU THINK THESE ARE, EH?
KLIK
KLIK

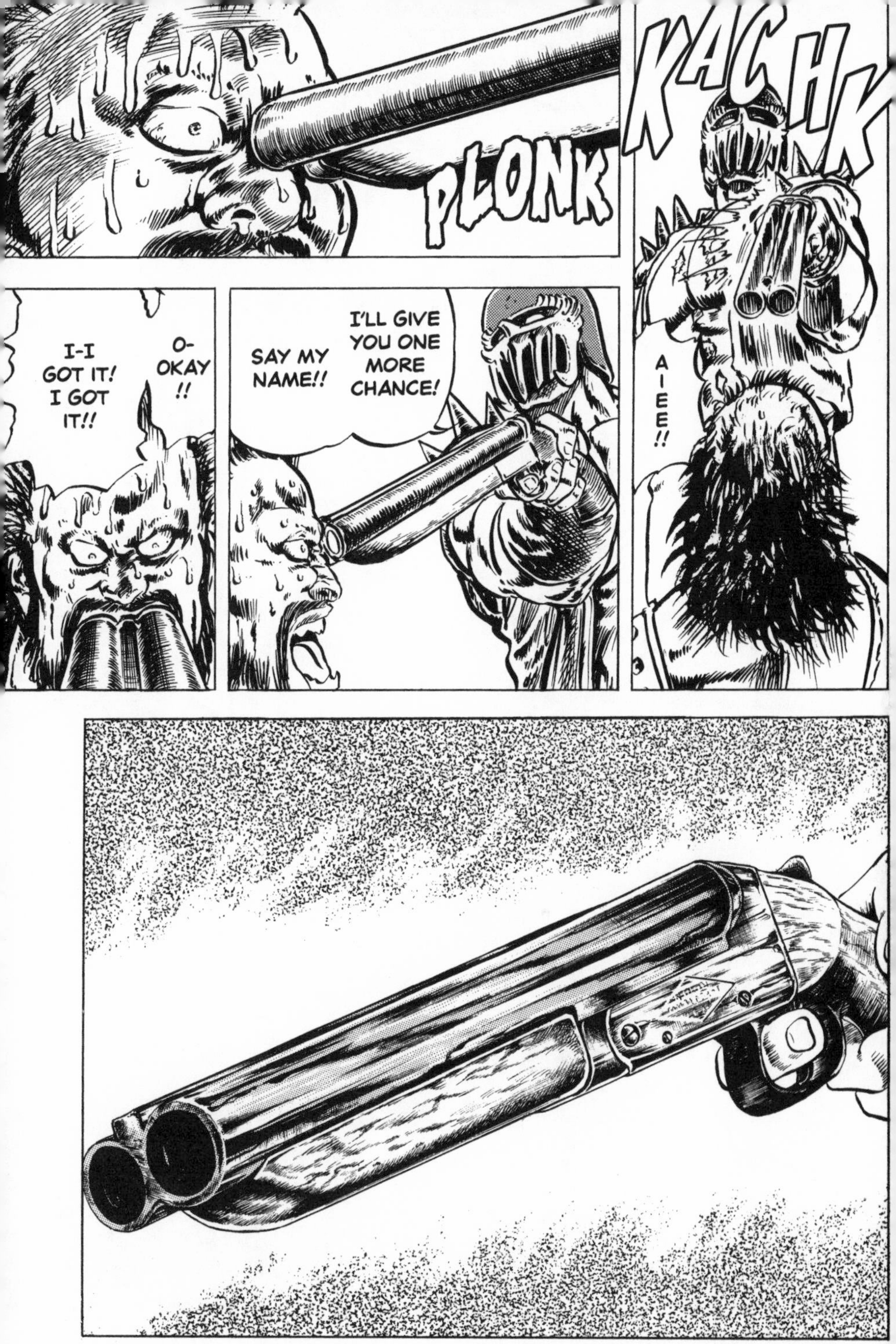
KACHK
AIEE!!
PLONK
I'LL GIVE YOU ONE MORE CHANCE!
SAY MY NAME!!
O-OKAY!!
I-I GOT IT! I GOT IT!!

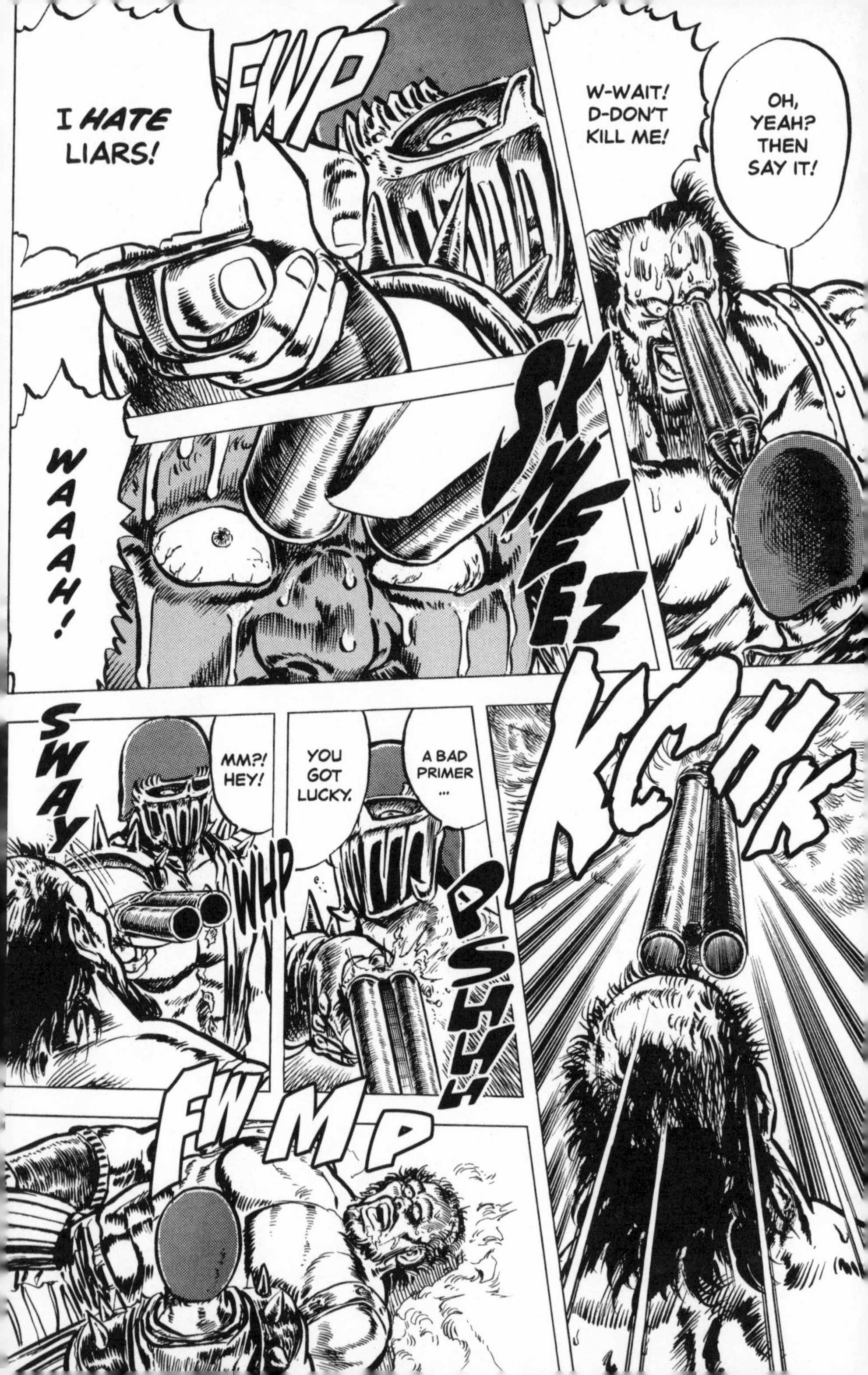
OH, YEAH? THEN SAY IT!
W-WAIT! D-DON'T KILL ME!
FWP
I HATE LIARS!
SKWEEZ
WAAAAH!
KCHK
A BAD PRIMER ...
YOU GOT LUCKY.
PSHHH
SWAY
MM?! HEY!
WHP
FWMP

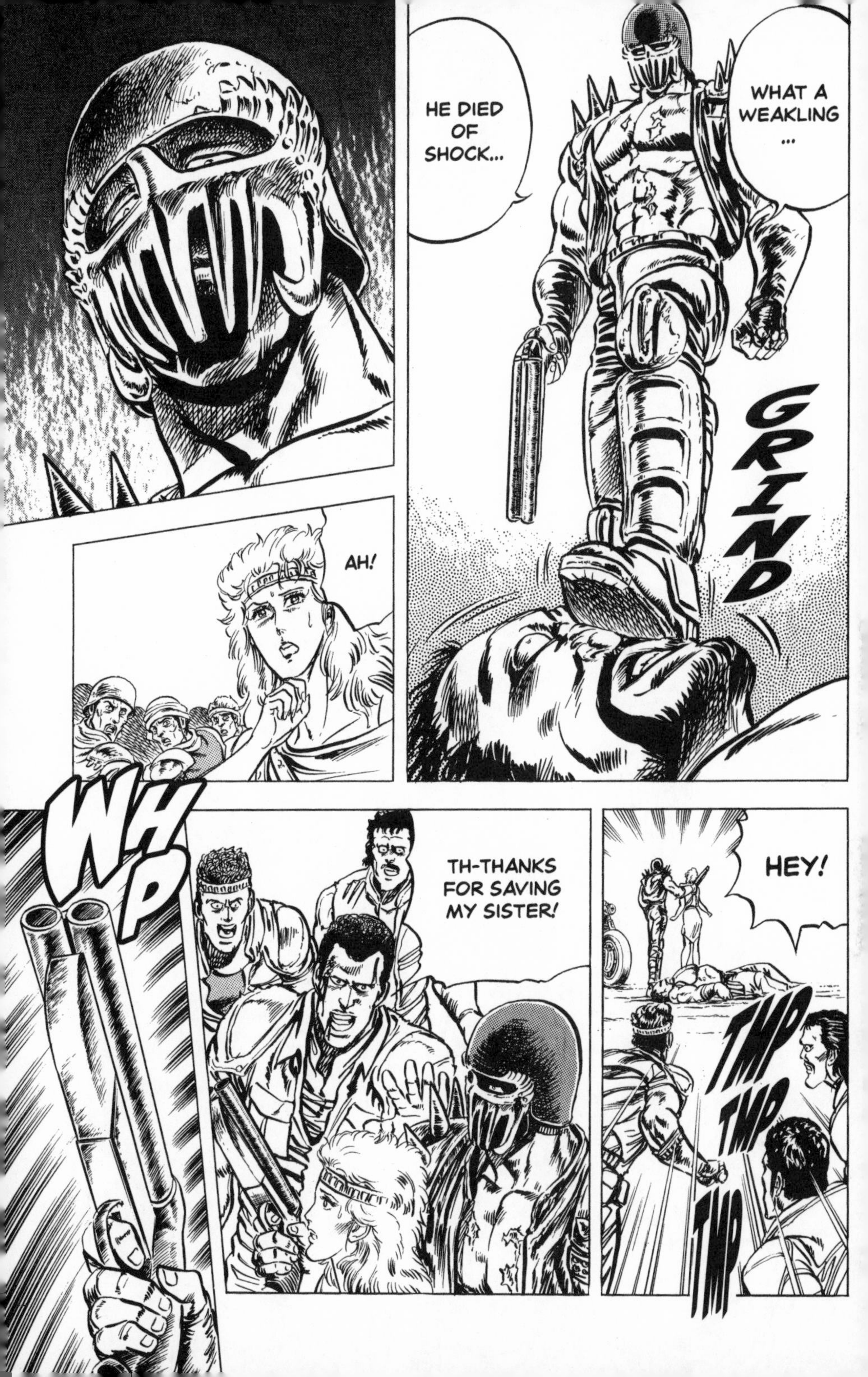

WHAT A WEAKLING...
HE DIED OF SHOCK...
GRIND
AH!
HEY!
THMP THMP THMP
TH-THANKS FOR SAVING MY SISTER!
WHP

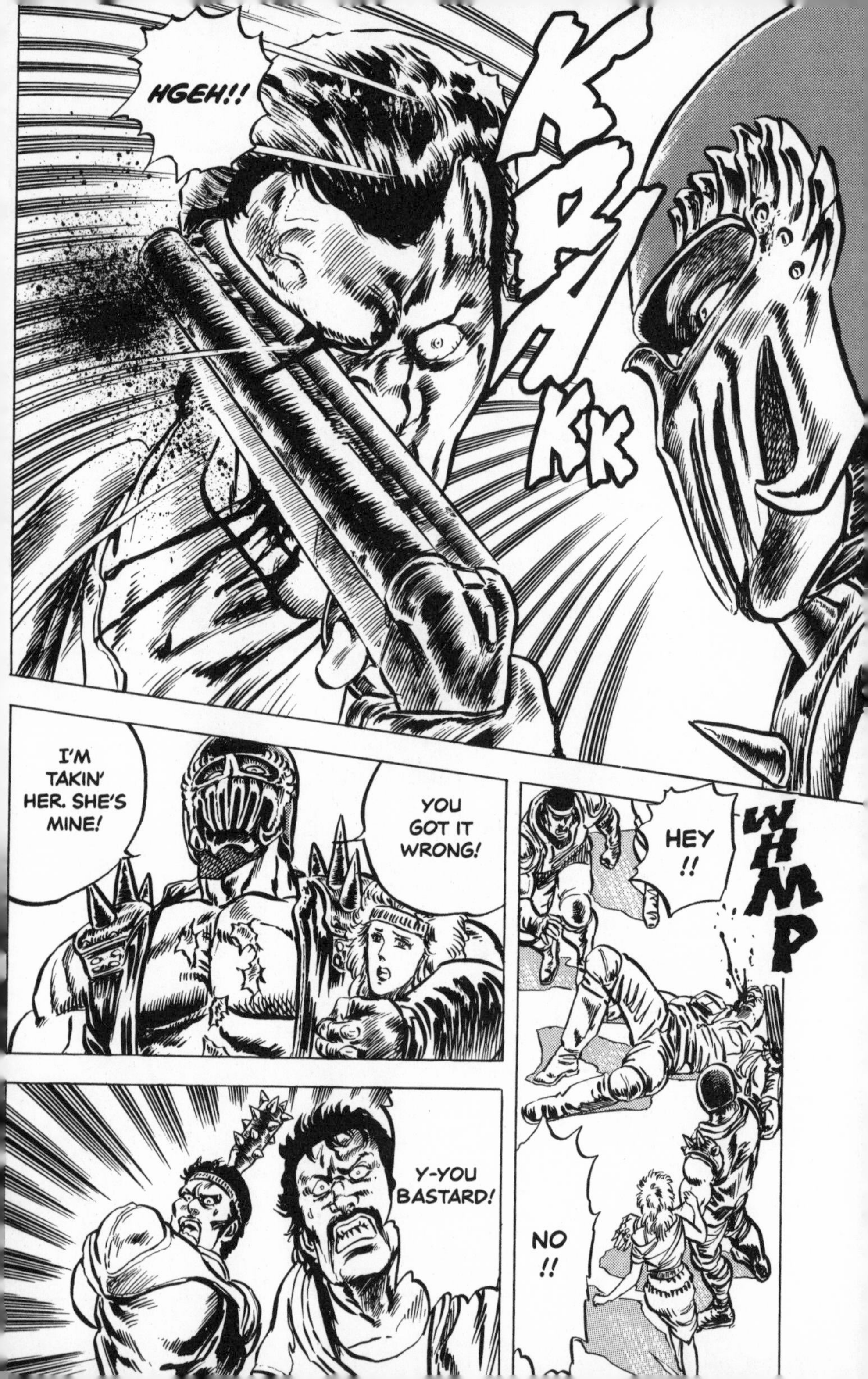
HGEH!!
KRAKK
HEY !!
WHMP
NO !!
I'M TAKIN' HER. SHE'S MINE!
YOU GOT IT WRONG!
Y-YOU BASTARD!

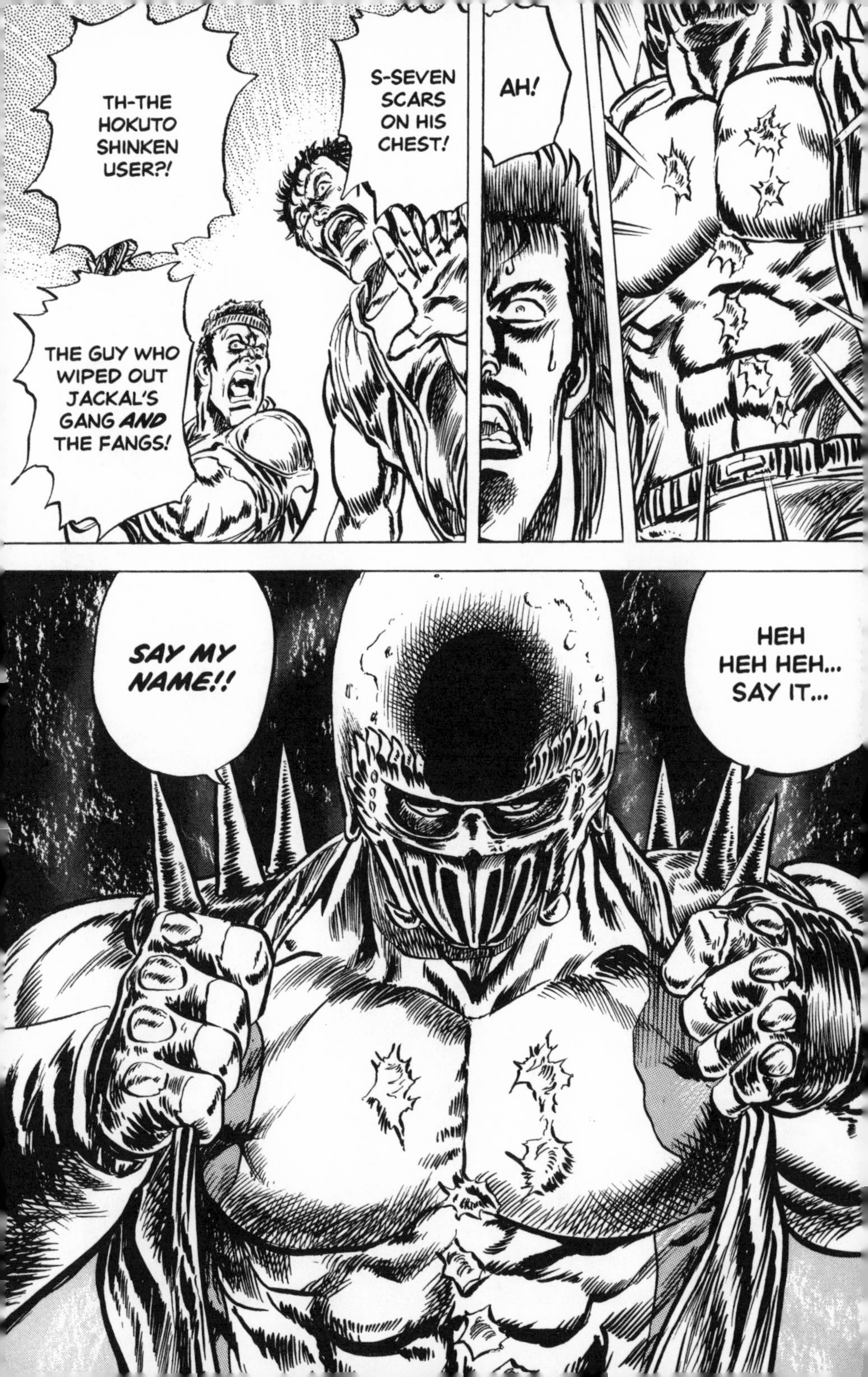
AH!
S-SEVEN SCARS ON HIS CHEST!
TH-THE HOKUTO SHINKEN USER?!
THE GUY WHO WIPED OUT JACKAL'S GANG AND THE FANGS!
HEH HEH HEH... SAY IT...
SAY MY NAME!!

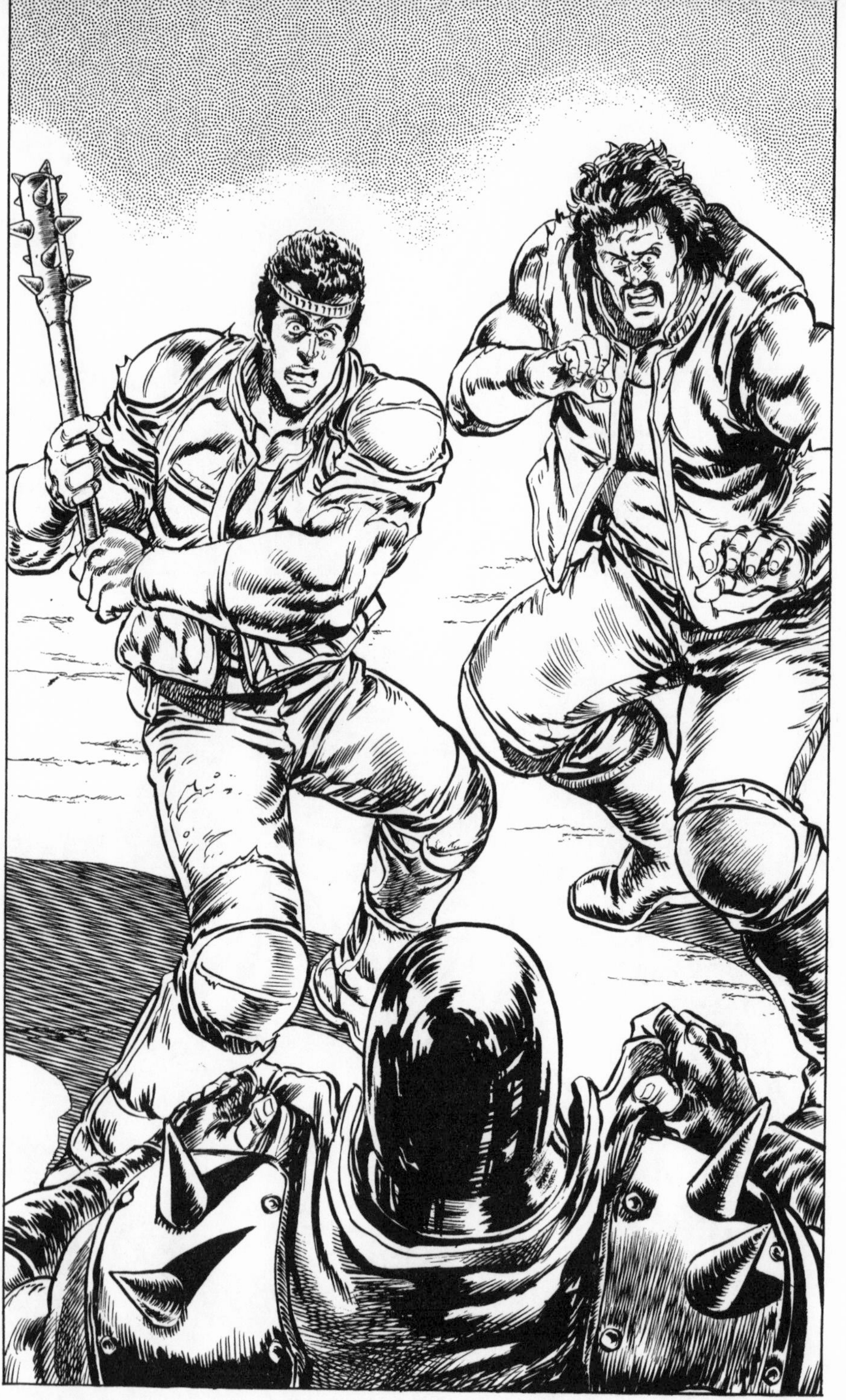

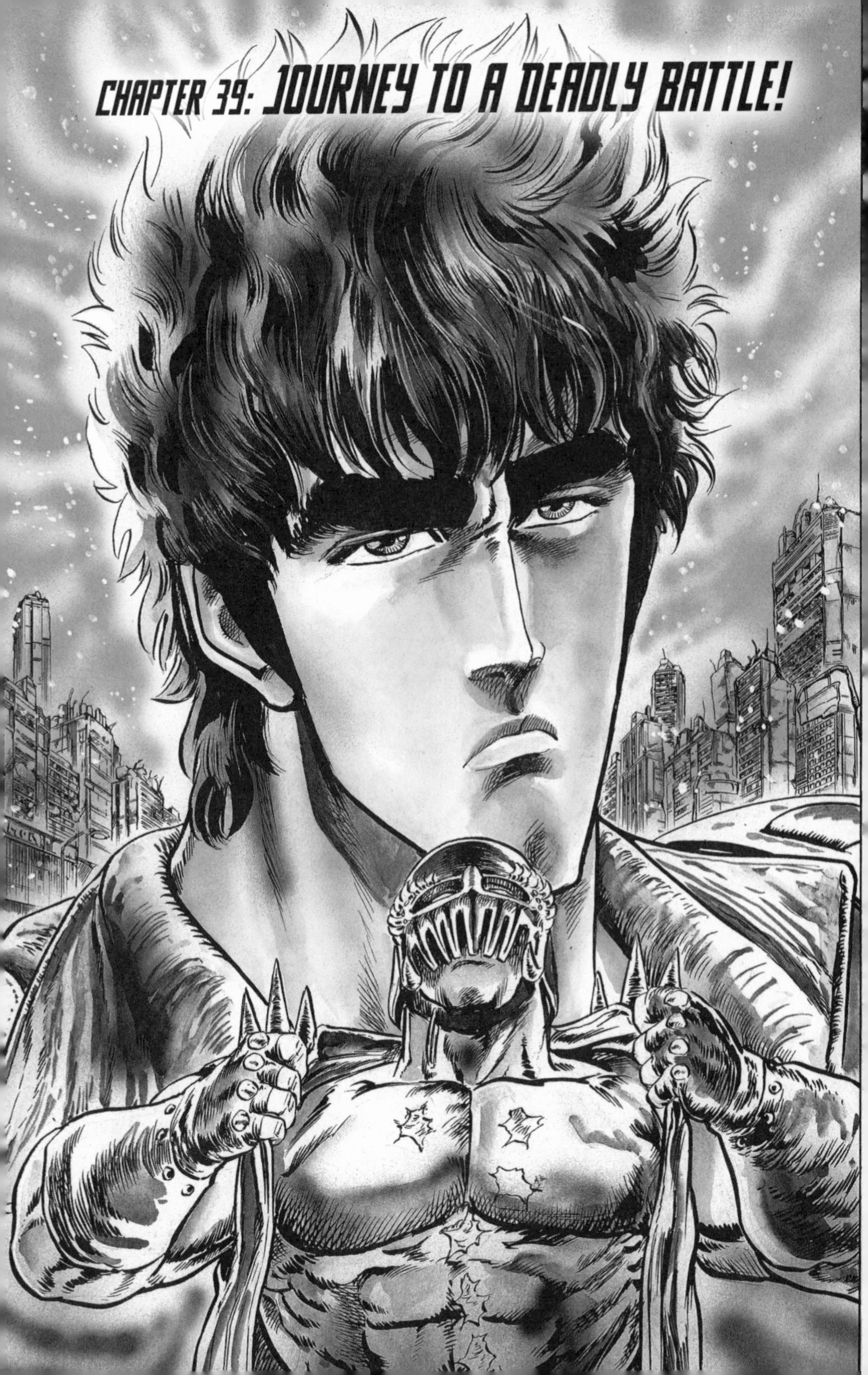
CHAPTER 39: JOURNEY TO A DEADLY BATTLE!

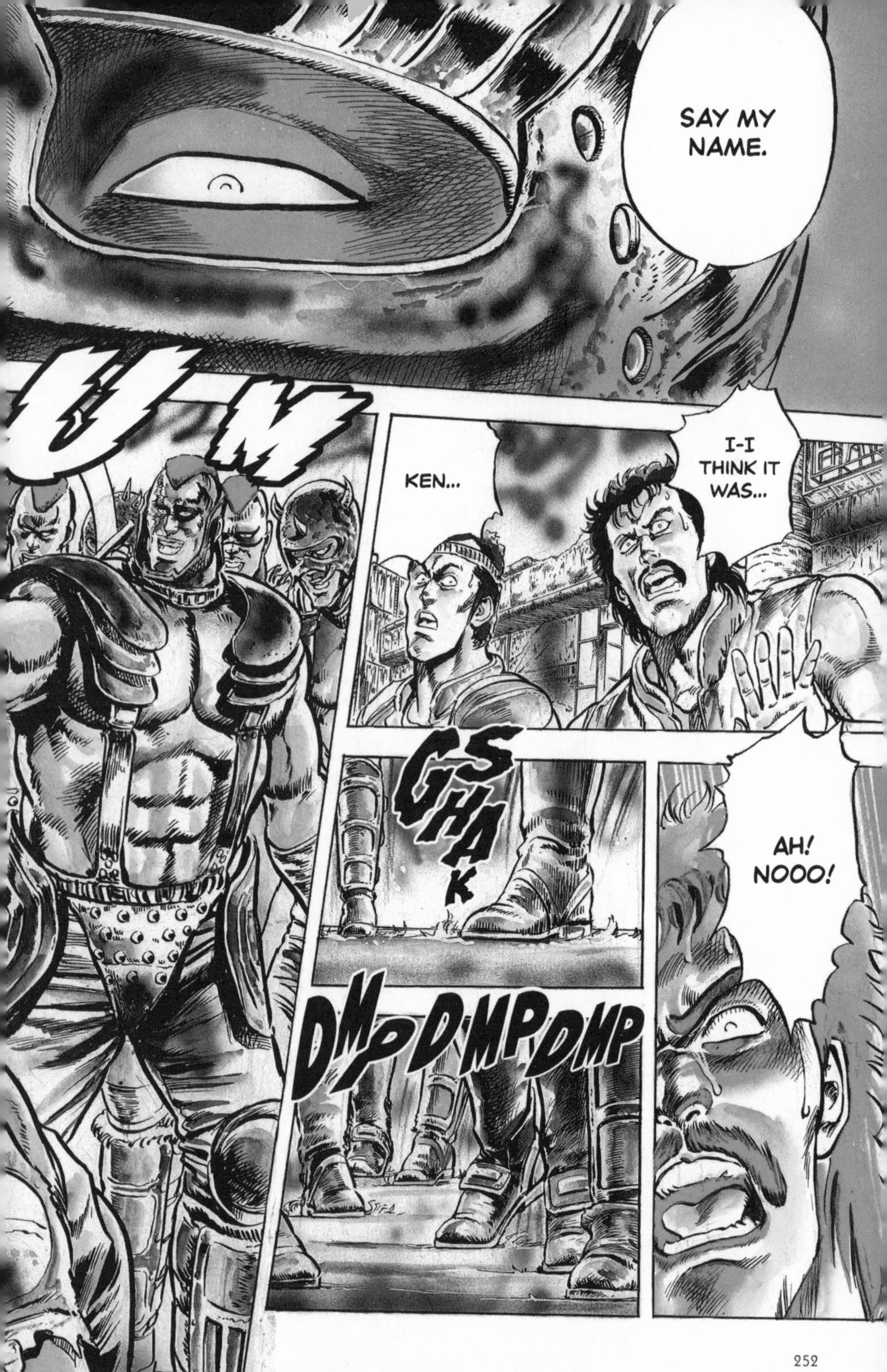
SAY MY NAME.
UM
I-I THINK IT WAS...
KEN...
AH! NOOO!
GSHAK
DMP DMP DMP

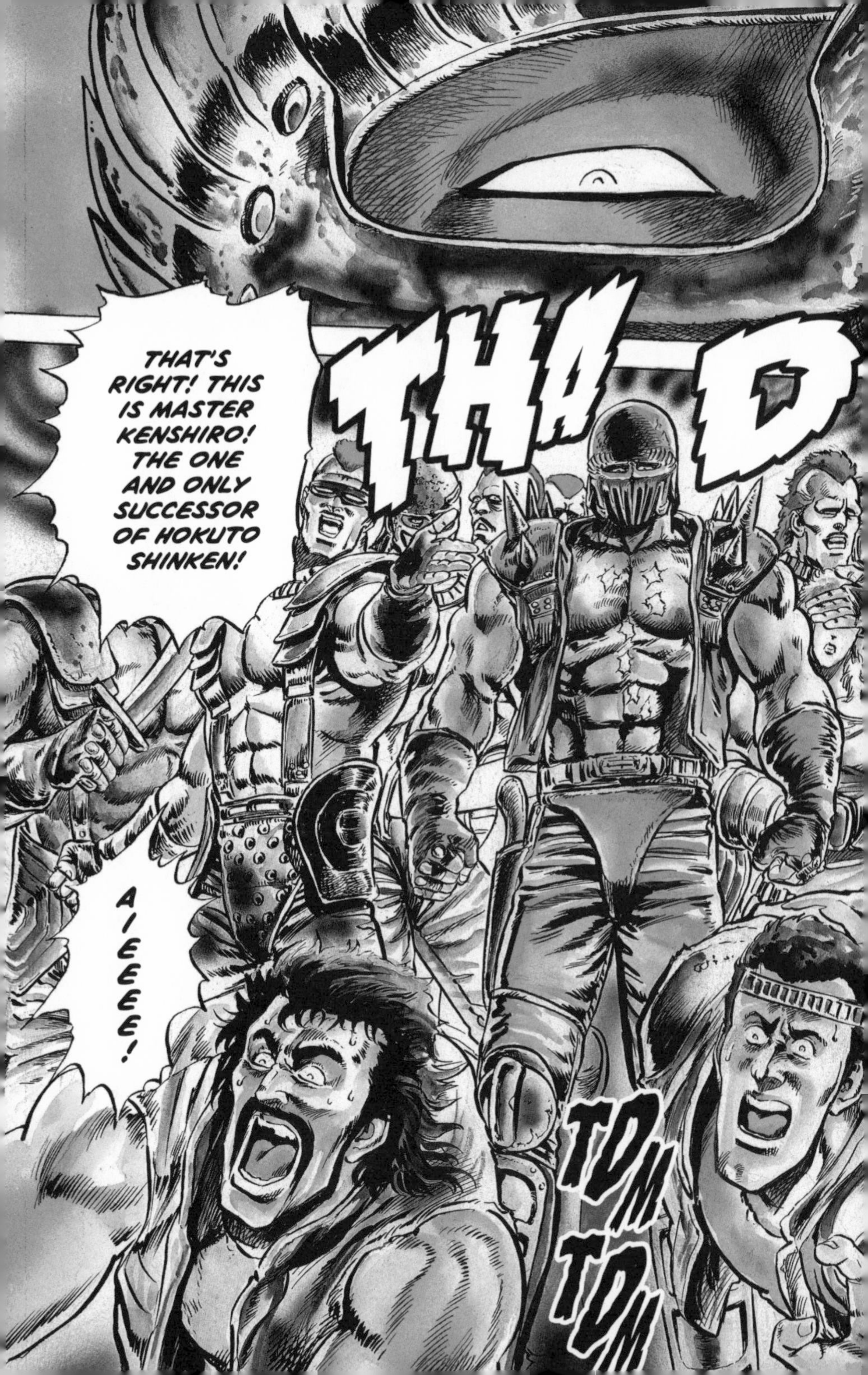
THAT'S RIGHT! THIS IS MASTER KENSHIRO! THE ONE AND ONLY SUCCESSOR OF HOKUTO SHINKEN!
THA D
AIEEEE!
TOM TOM

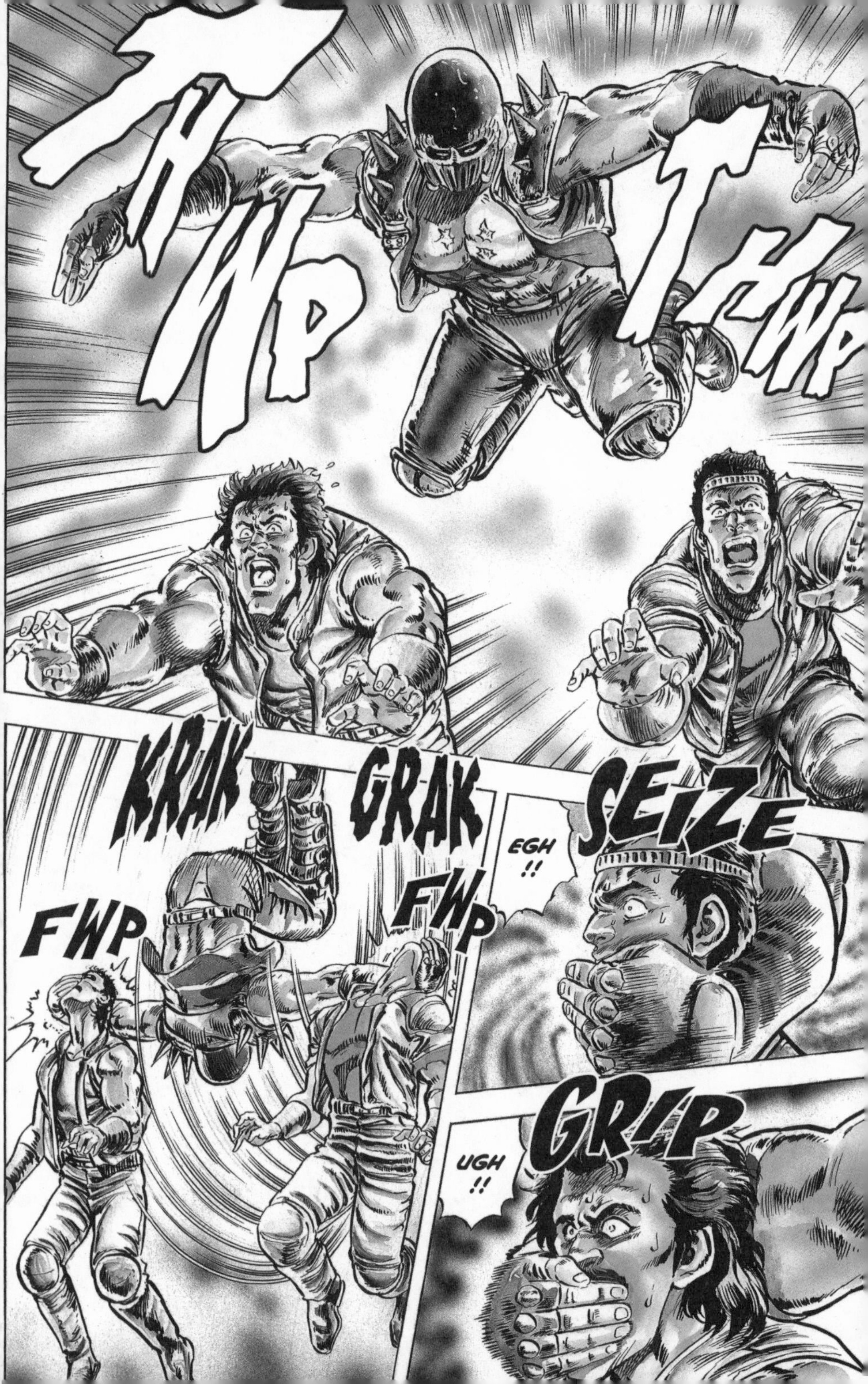
THWP
THWP
SEIZE
EGH !!
GRIP
UGH !!
GRAK
KRAK
FWP
FWP

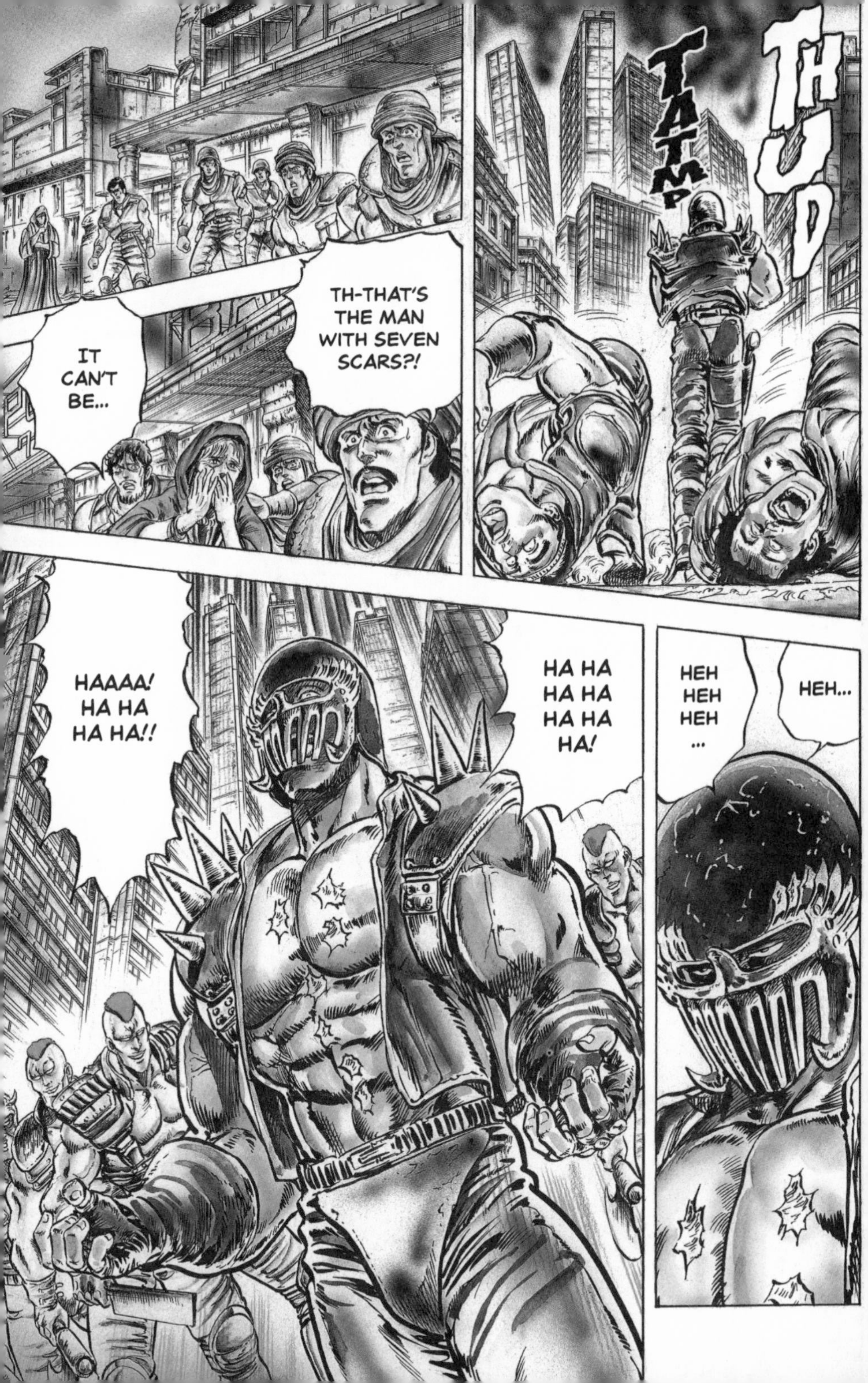
THUD
TATMP
TH-THAT'S THE MAN WITH SEVEN SCARS?!
IT CAN'T BE...
HEH...
HEH HEH HEH ...
HA HA HA HA HA HA HA!
HAAAA! HA HA HA HA!!

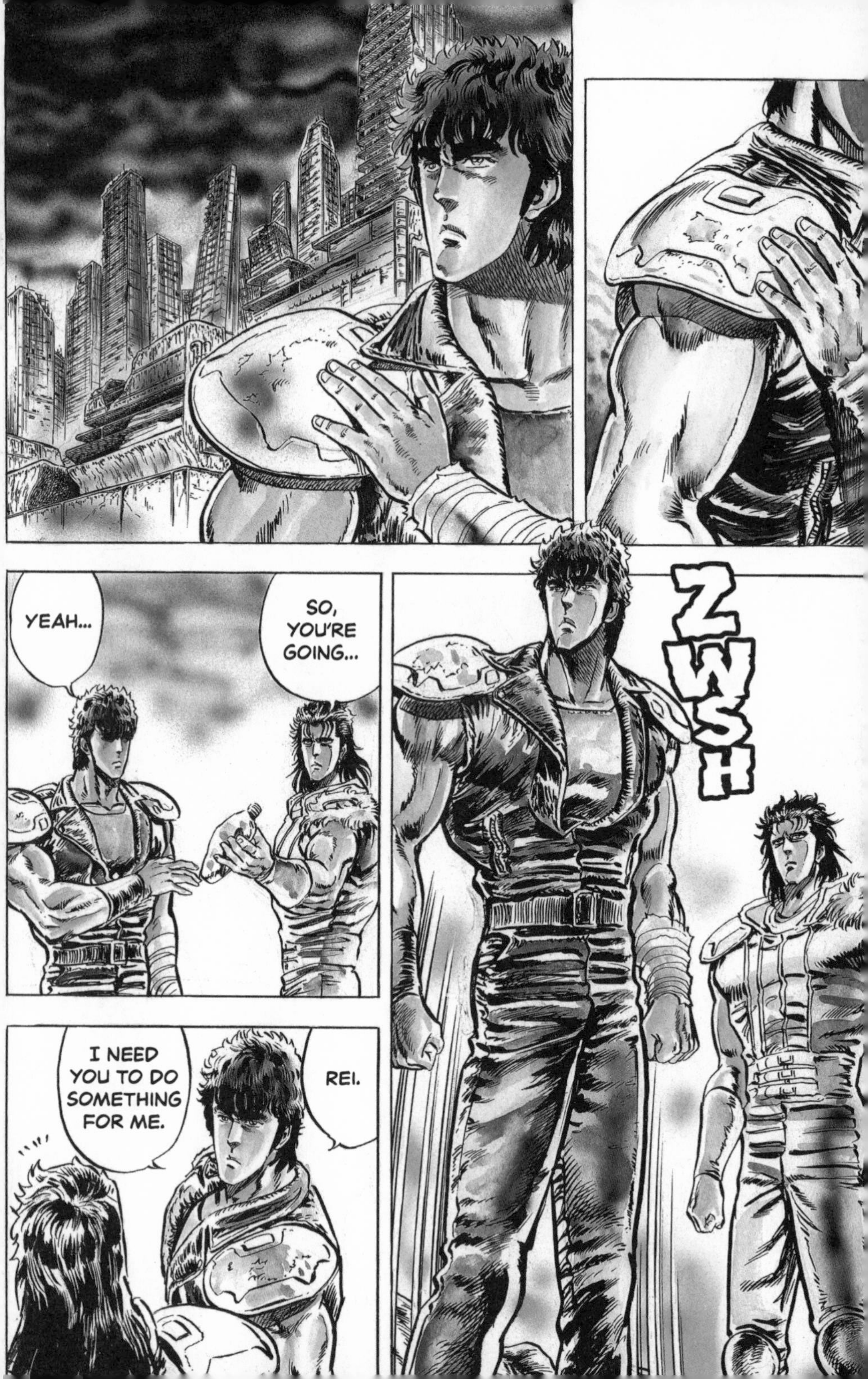
ZWSH
SO, YOU'RE GOING...
YEAH...
REI.
I NEED YOU TO DO SOMETHING FOR ME.

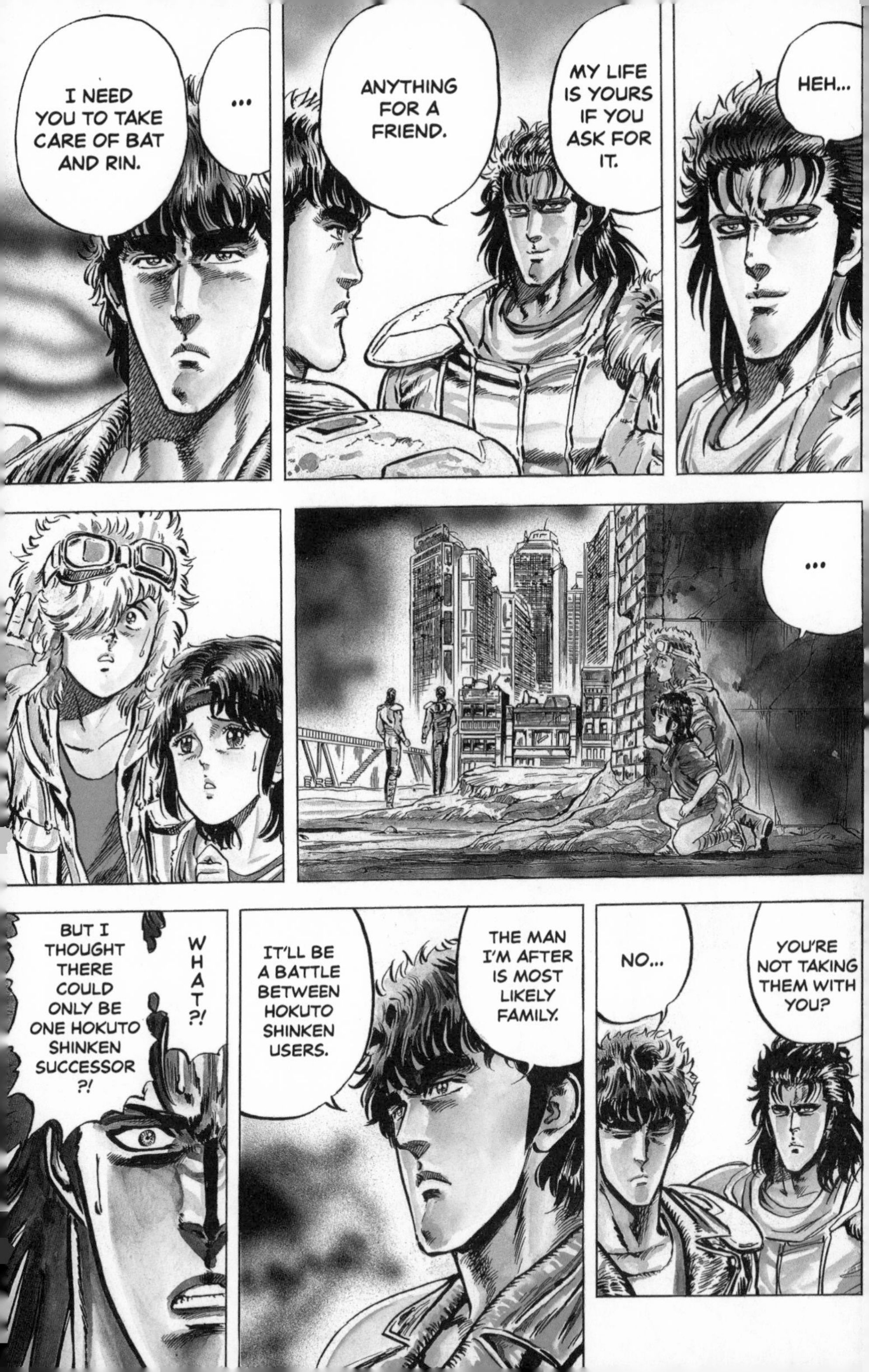
HEH...
MY LIFE IS YOURS IF YOU ASK FOR IT.
ANYTHING FOR A FRIEND.
...
I NEED YOU TO TAKE CARE OF BAT AND RIN.
...
YOU'RE NOT TAKING THEM WITH YOU?
NO...
THE MAN I'M AFTER IS MOST LIKELY FAMILY.
IT'LL BE A BATTLE BETWEEN HOKUTO SHINKEN USERS.
WHAT?!
BUT I THOUGHT THERE COULD ONLY BE ONE HOKUTO SHINKEN SUCCESSOR?!

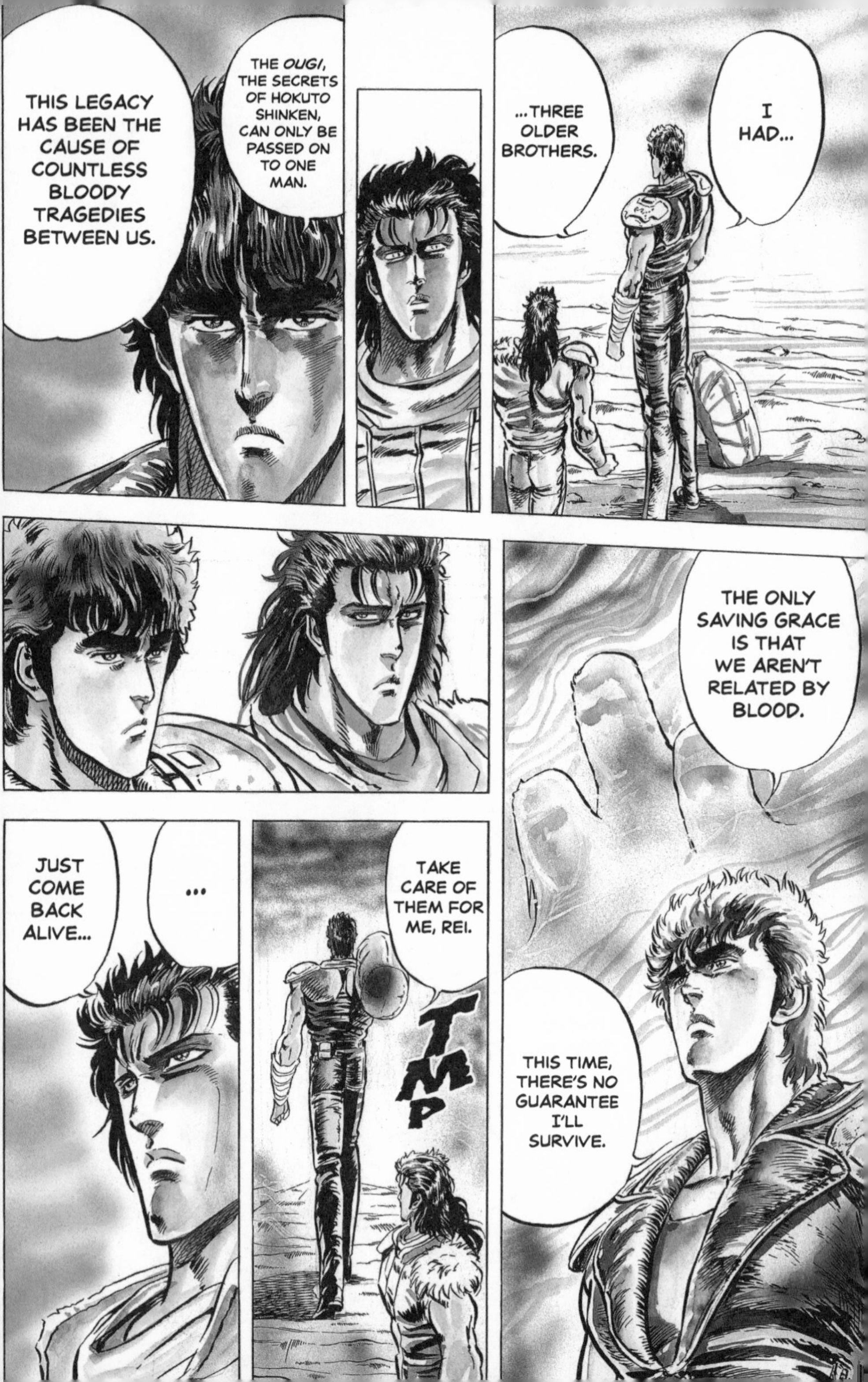
I HAD...
...THREE OLDER BROTHERS.
THE *OUGI*, THE SECRETS OF HOKUTO SHINKEN, CAN ONLY BE PASSED ON TO ONE MAN.
THIS LEGACY HAS BEEN THE CAUSE OF COUNTLESS BLOODY TRAGEDIES BETWEEN US.
THE ONLY SAVING GRACE IS THAT WE AREN'T RELATED BY BLOOD.
THIS TIME, THERE'S NO GUARANTEE I'LL SURVIVE.
TAKE CARE OF THEM FOR ME, REI.
TMP
...
JUST COME BACK ALIVE...

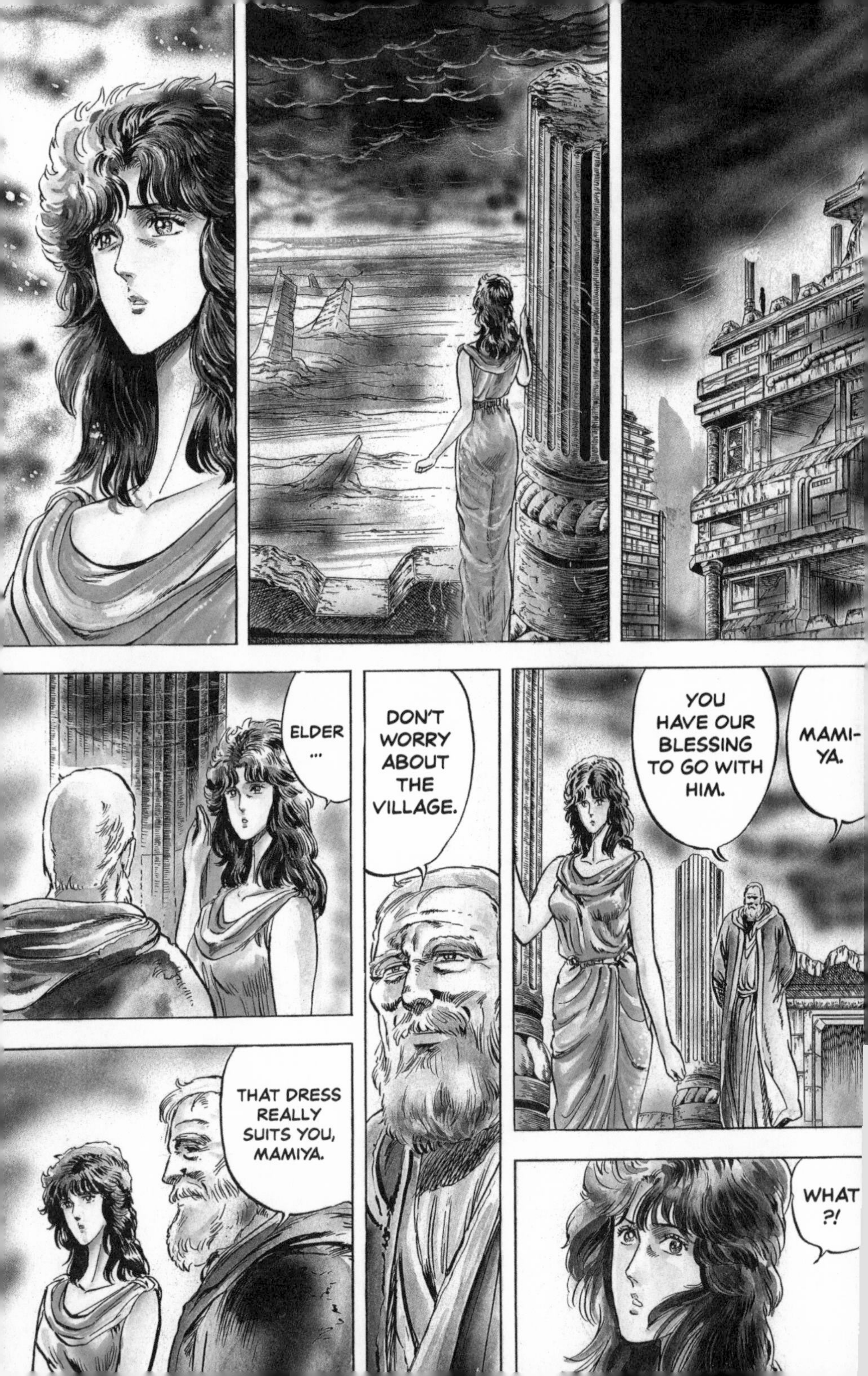
MAMI-YA.
YOU HAVE OUR BLESSING TO GO WITH HIM.
WHAT ?!
DON'T WORRY ABOUT THE VILLAGE.
ELDER ...
THAT DRESS REALLY SUITS YOU, MAMIYA.

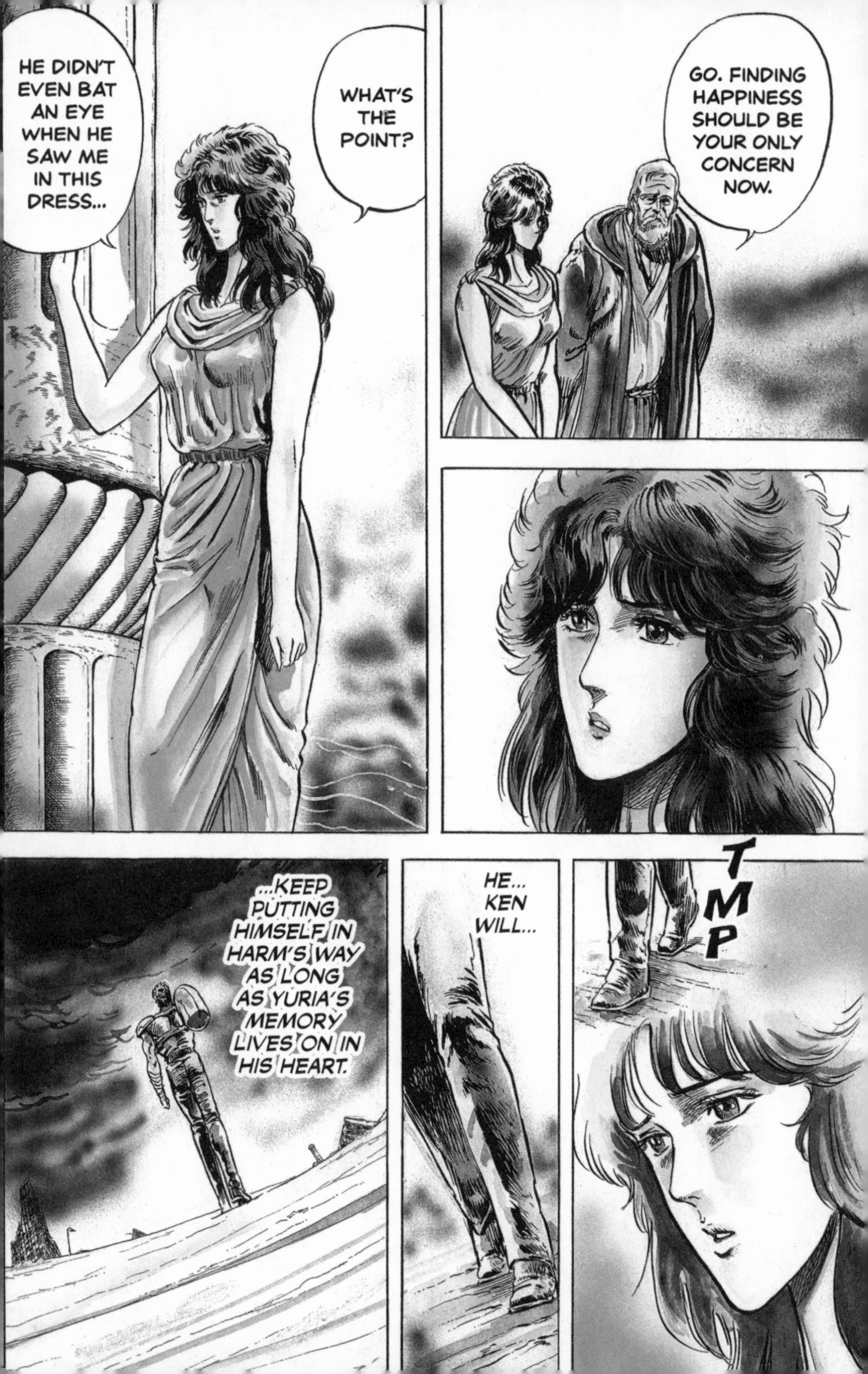
GO. FINDING HAPPINESS SHOULD BE YOUR ONLY CONCERN NOW.
WHAT'S THE POINT?
HE DIDN'T EVEN BAT AN EYE WHEN HE SAW ME IN THIS DRESS...
TMP
HE... KEN WILL...
...KEEP PUTTING HIMSELF IN HARM'S WAY AS LONG AS YURIA'S MEMORY LIVES ON IN HIS HEART.

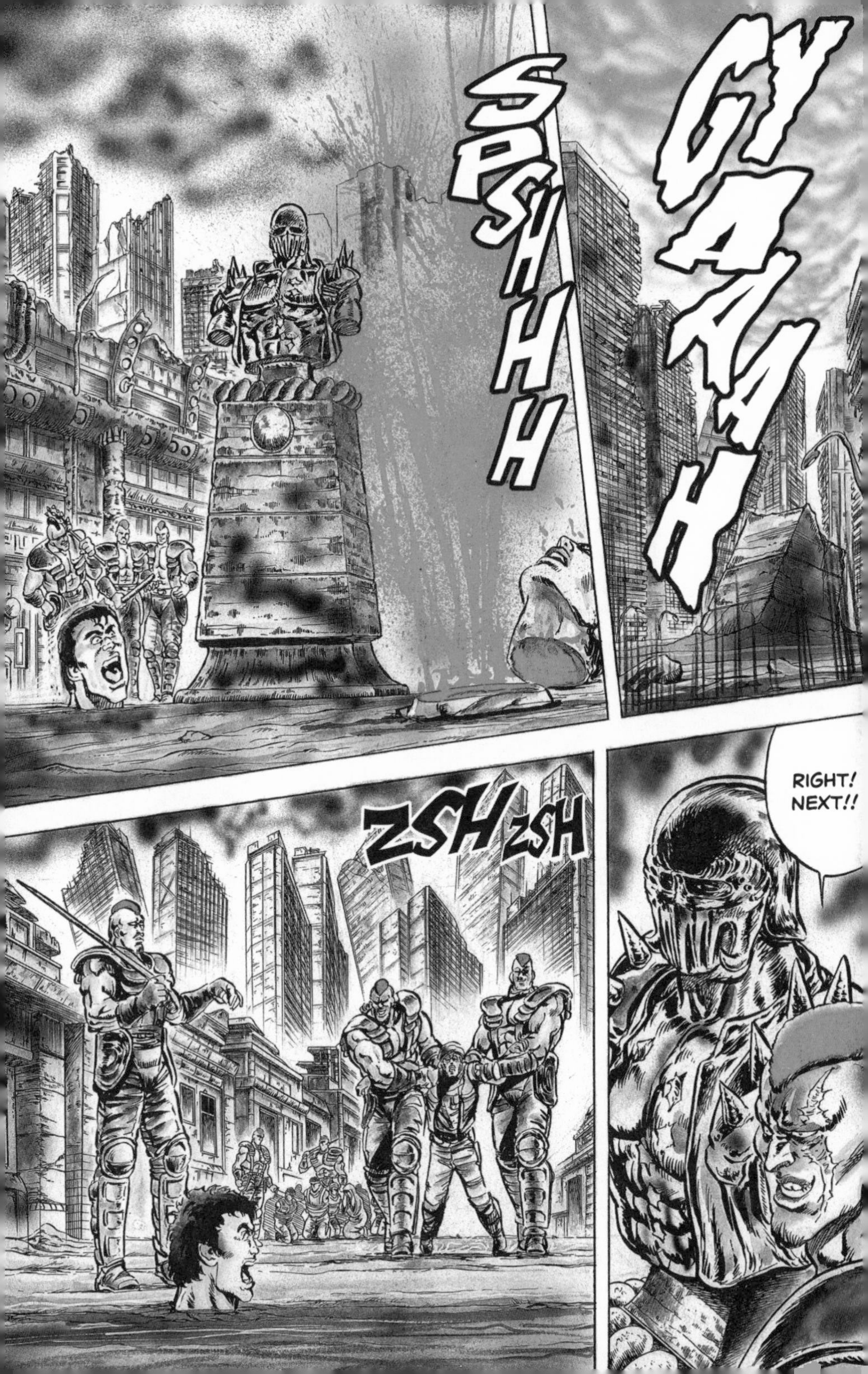
GYAAAAH
SPSHHH
RIGHT! NEXT!!
ZSH ZSH

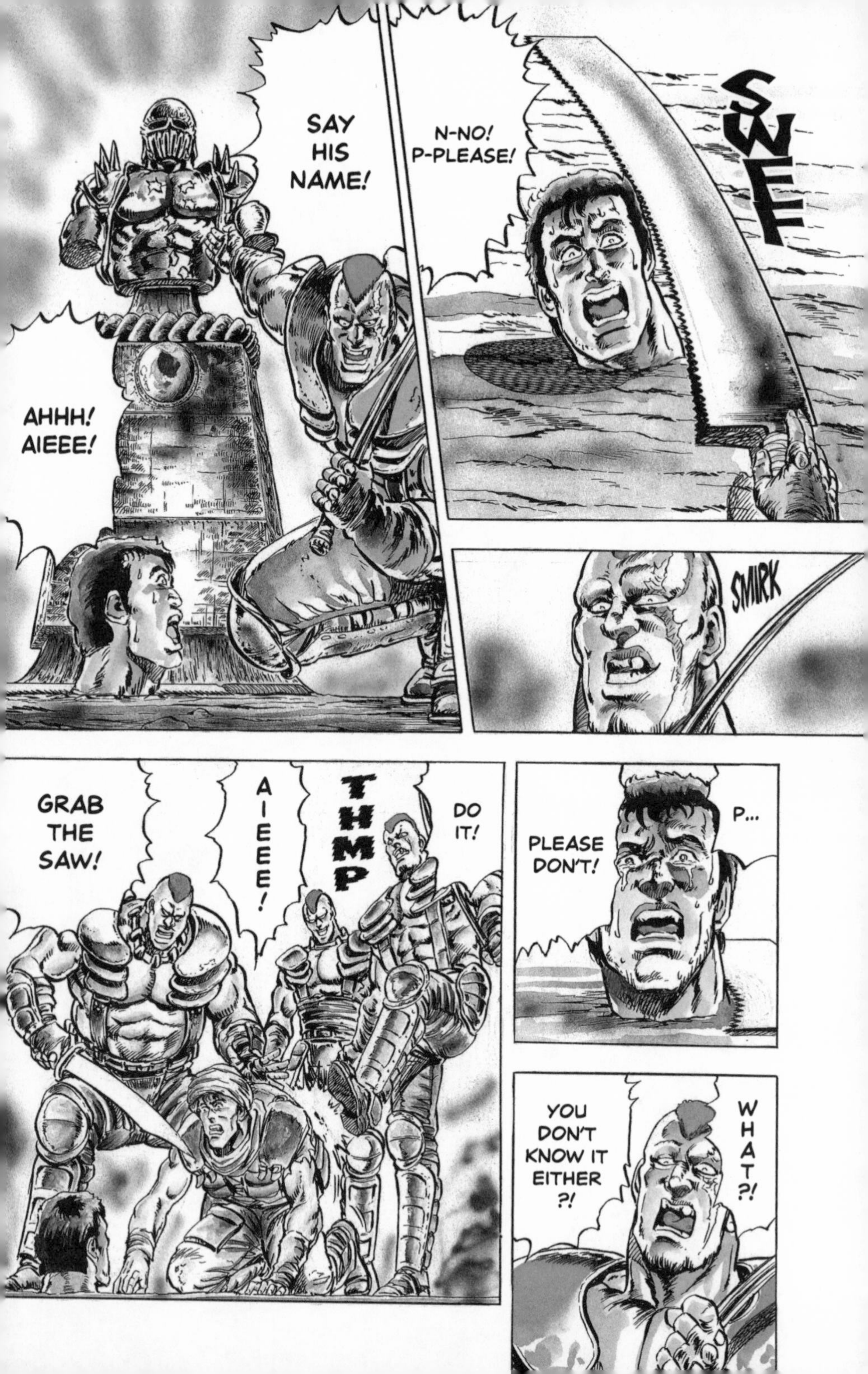
N-NO! P-PLEASE!
SWEE
SMIRK
SAY HIS NAME!
AHHH! AIEEE!
P...
PLEASE DON'T!
WHAT?!
YOU DON'T KNOW IT EITHER?!
DO IT!
THMP
AIEEE!
GRAB THE SAW!

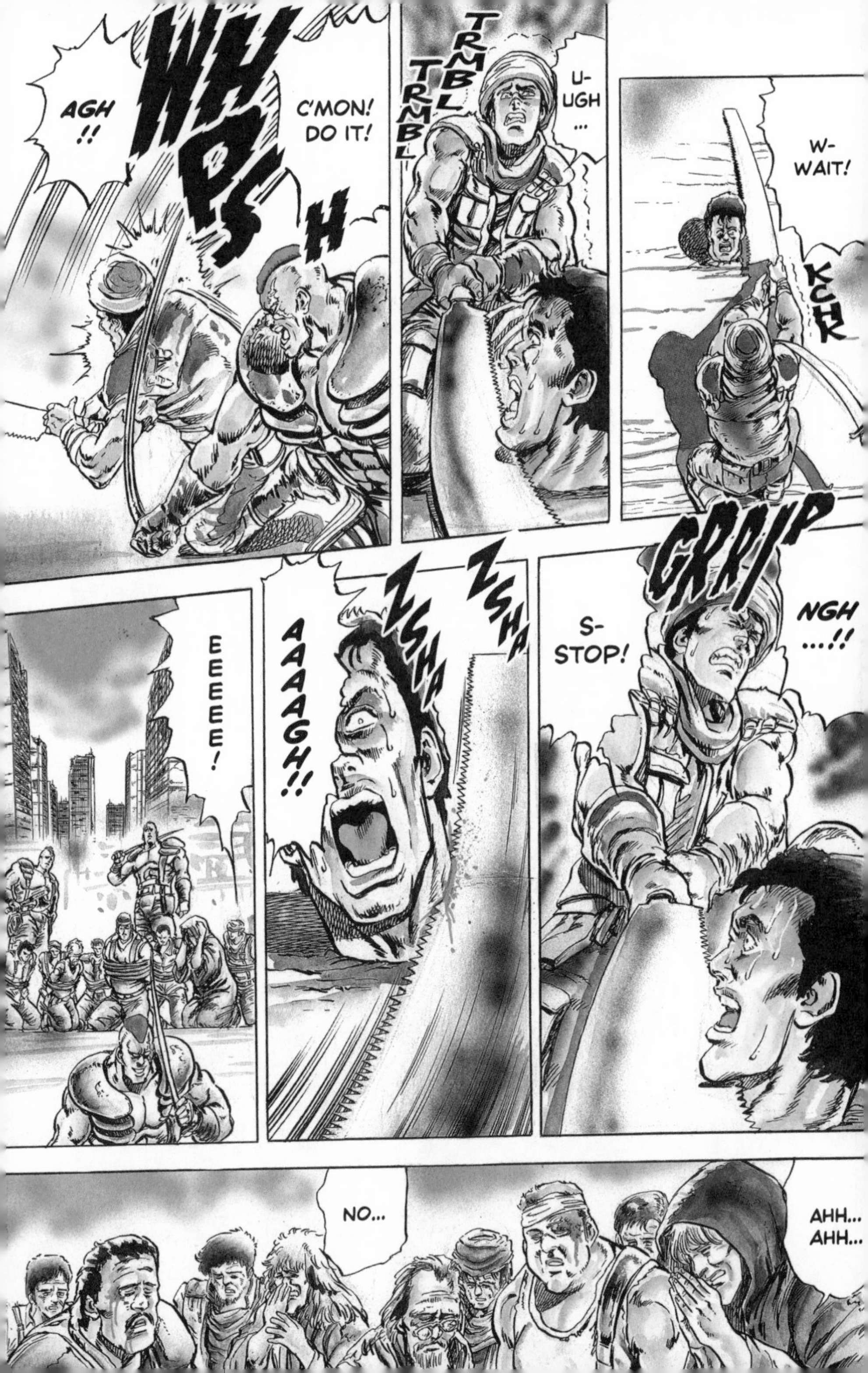
W-WAIT!
KCHK
U-UGH...
TRMBL TRMBL
C'MON! DO IT!
WHOSH
AGH!!
GRRIP
NGH...!!
S-STOP!
ZSHA ZSHA
AAAAGH!!
EEEEEE!
AHH... AHH...
NO...

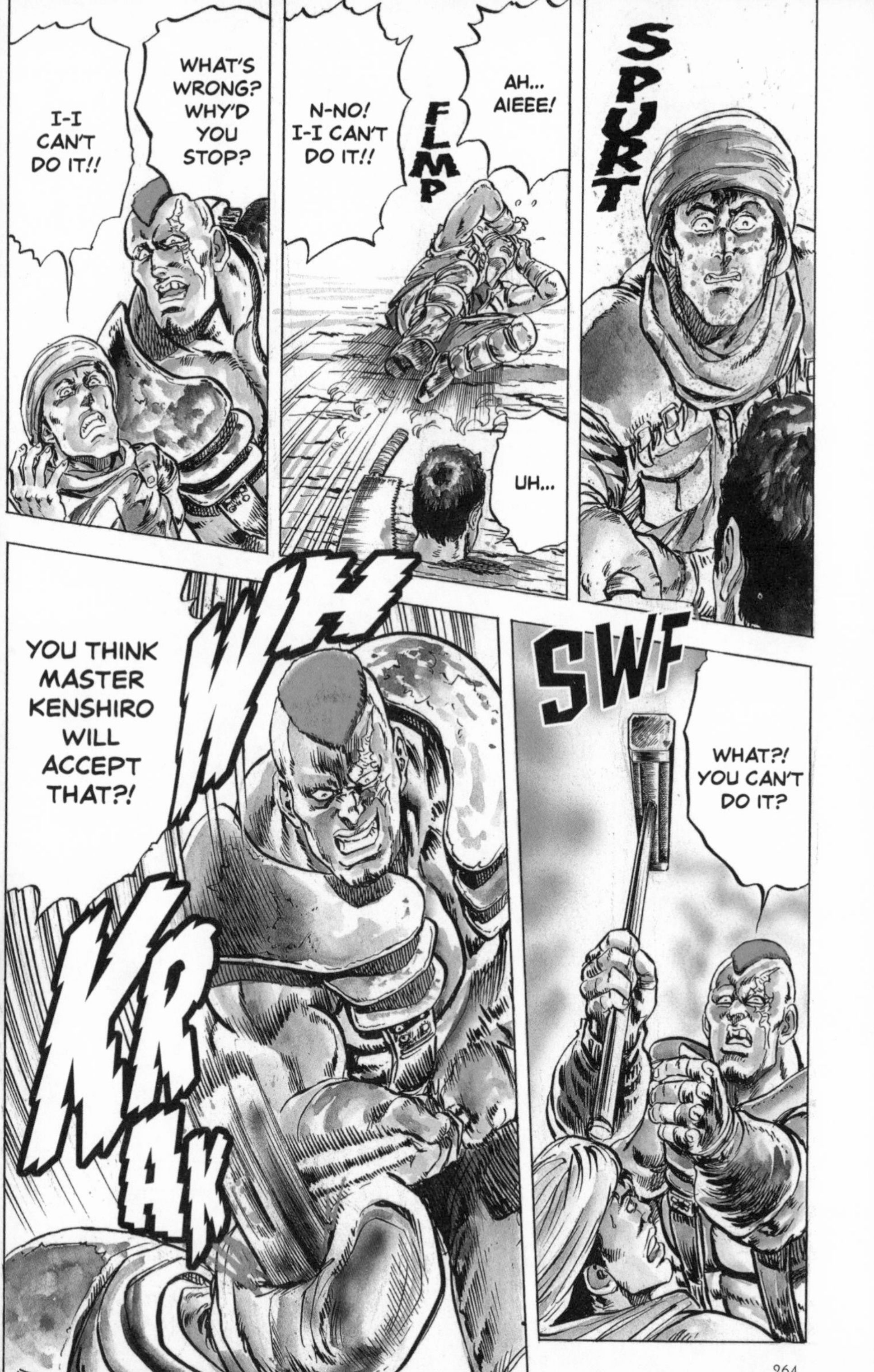
SPURT
UH...
AH... AIEEE!
FLMP
N-NO! I-I CAN'T DO IT!!
WHAT'S WRONG? WHY'D YOU STOP?
I-I CAN'T DO IT!!
SWF
WHAT?! YOU CAN'T DO IT?
WH
YOU THINK MASTER KENSHIRO WILL ACCEPT THAT?!
KRAK

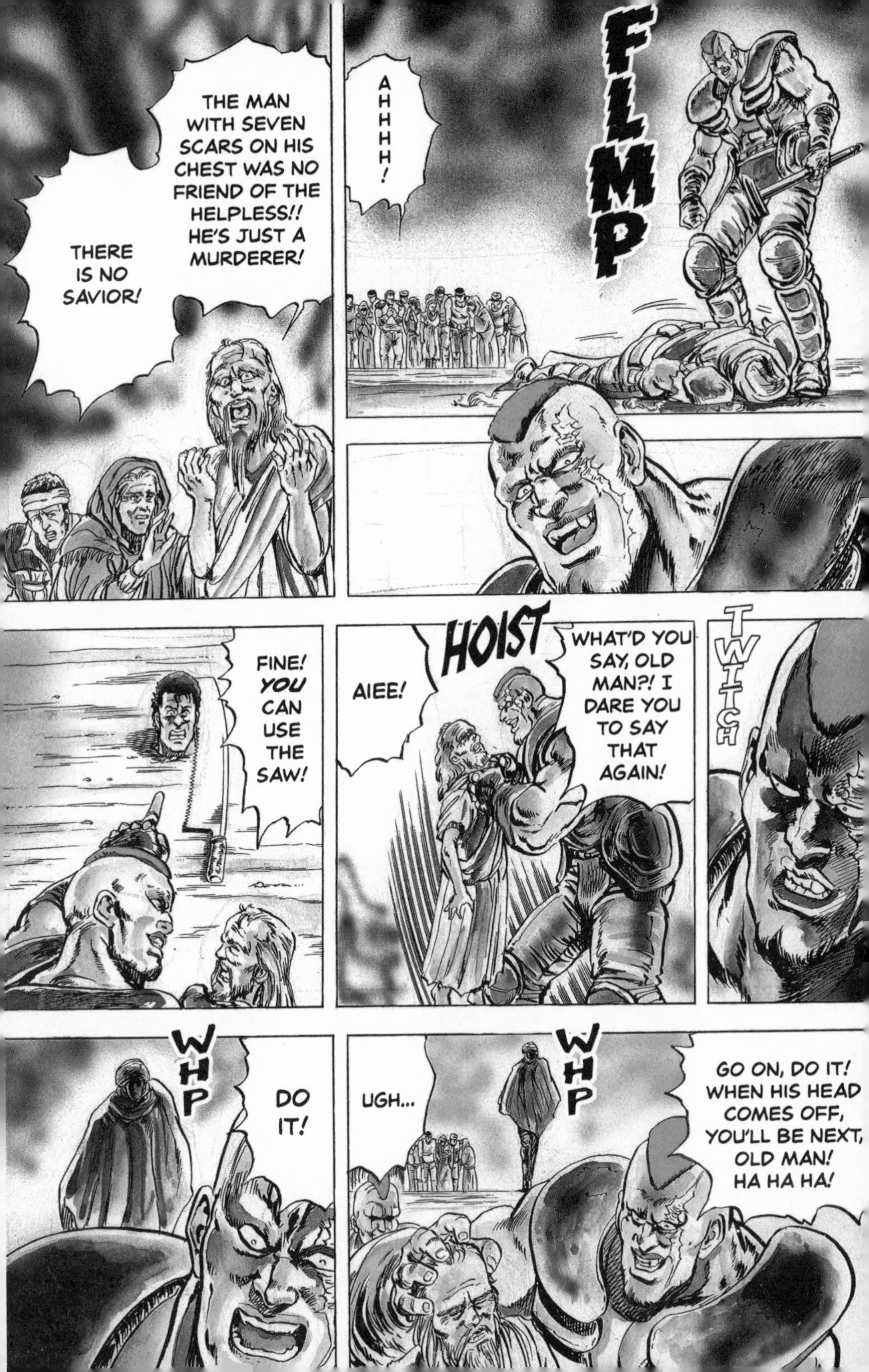
FLMP
AHHHH!
THE MAN WITH SEVEN SCARS ON HIS CHEST WAS NO FRIEND OF THE HELPLESS!! HE'S JUST A MURDERER!
THERE IS NO SAVIOR!
TWITCH
HOIST
WHAT'D YOU SAY, OLD MAN?! I DARE YOU TO SAY THAT AGAIN!
AIEE!
FINE! *YOU* CAN USE THE SAW!
WHP
GO ON, DO IT! WHEN HIS HEAD COMES OFF, YOU'LL BE NEXT, OLD MAN! HA HA HA!
UGH...
WHP
DO IT!

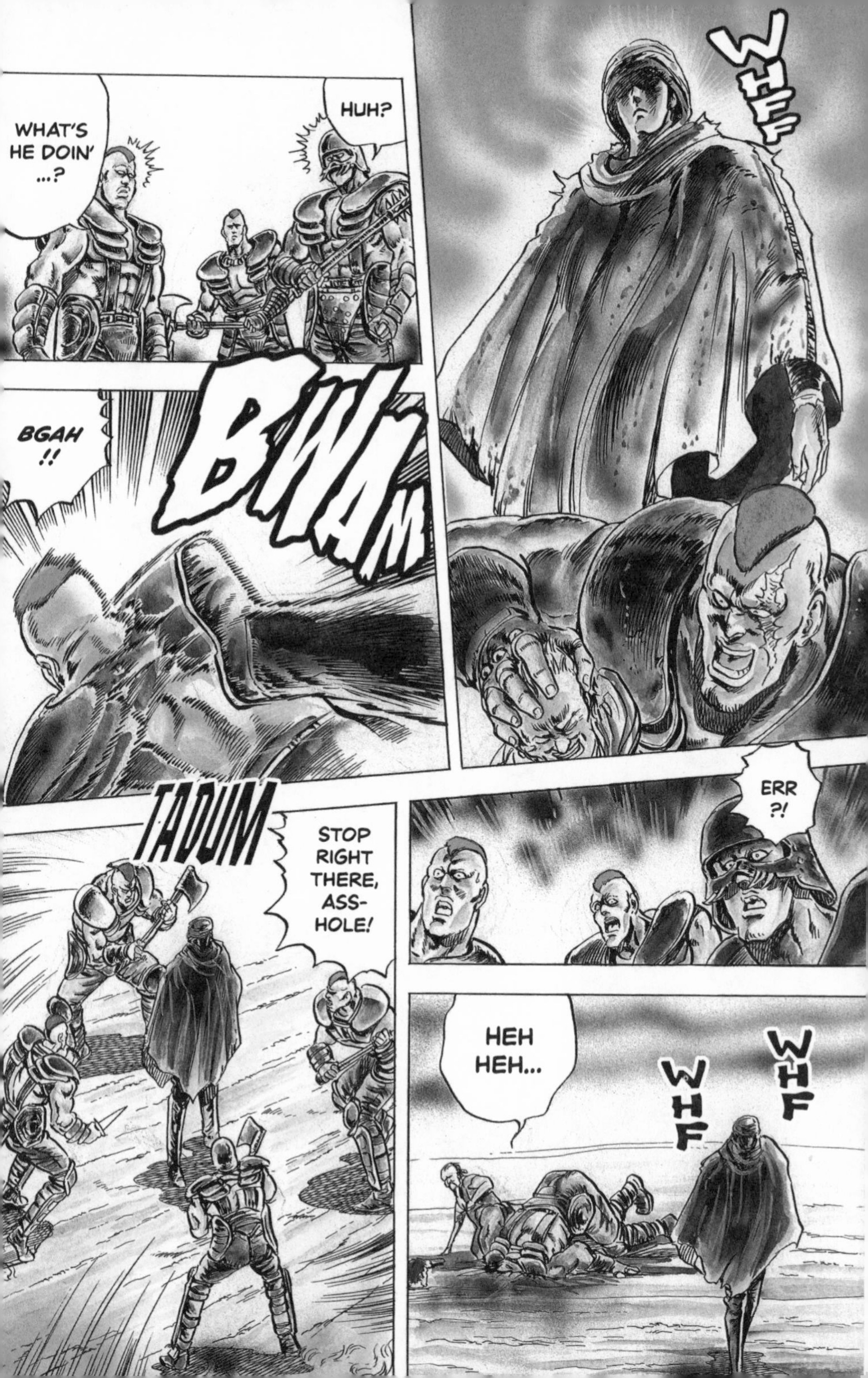
WHFF
HUH?
WHAT'S HE DOIN' ...?
BWAM
BGAH !!
ERR ?!
HEH HEH...
WHF
WHF
TADUM
STOP RIGHT THERE, ASS-HOLE!

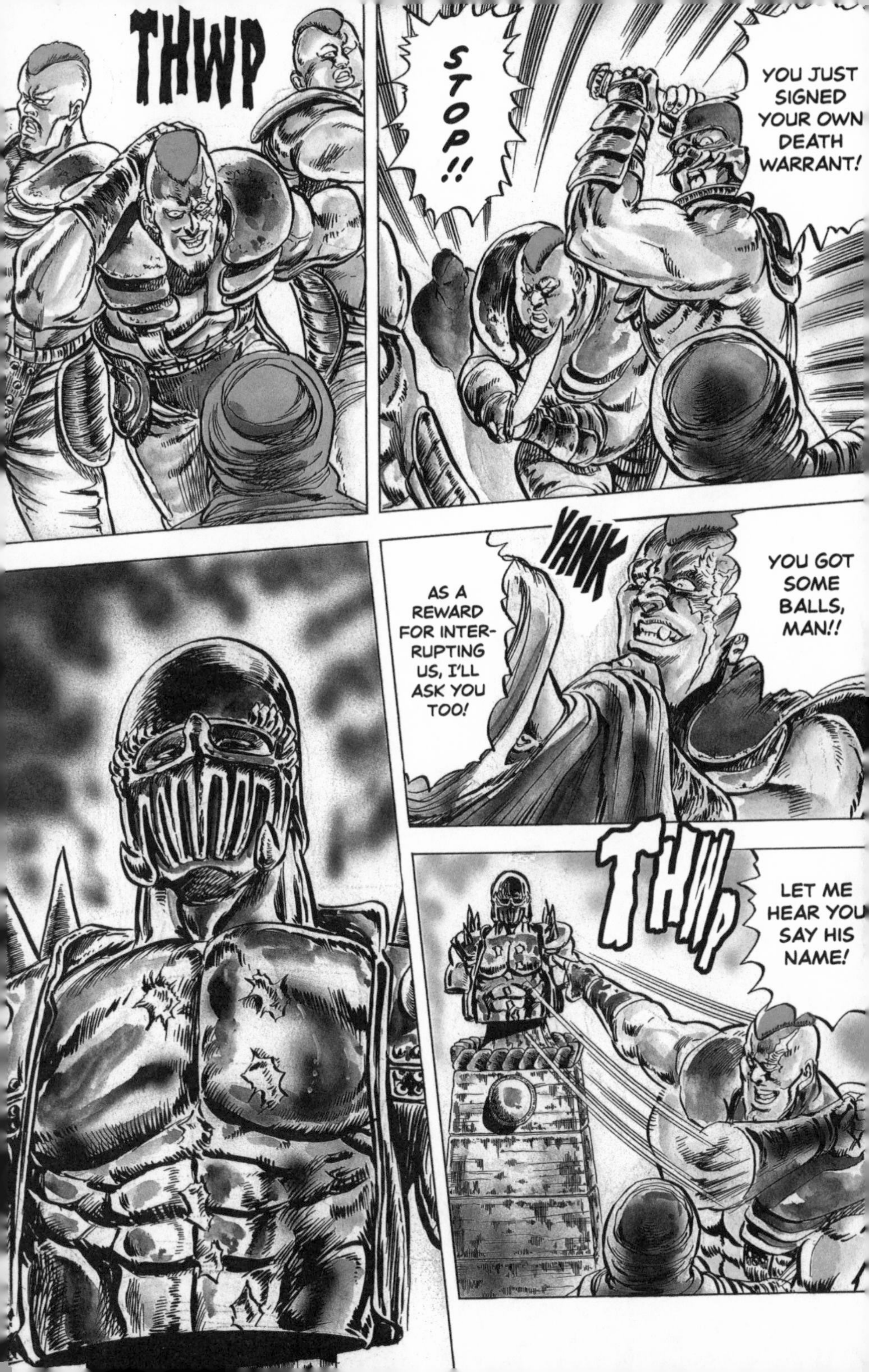
YOU JUST SIGNED YOUR OWN DEATH WARRANT!
STOP!!
THWP
YOU GOT SOME BALLS, MAN!!
YANK
AS A REWARD FOR INTER-RUPTING US, I'LL ASK YOU TOO!
THWP
LET ME HEAR YOU SAY HIS NAME!

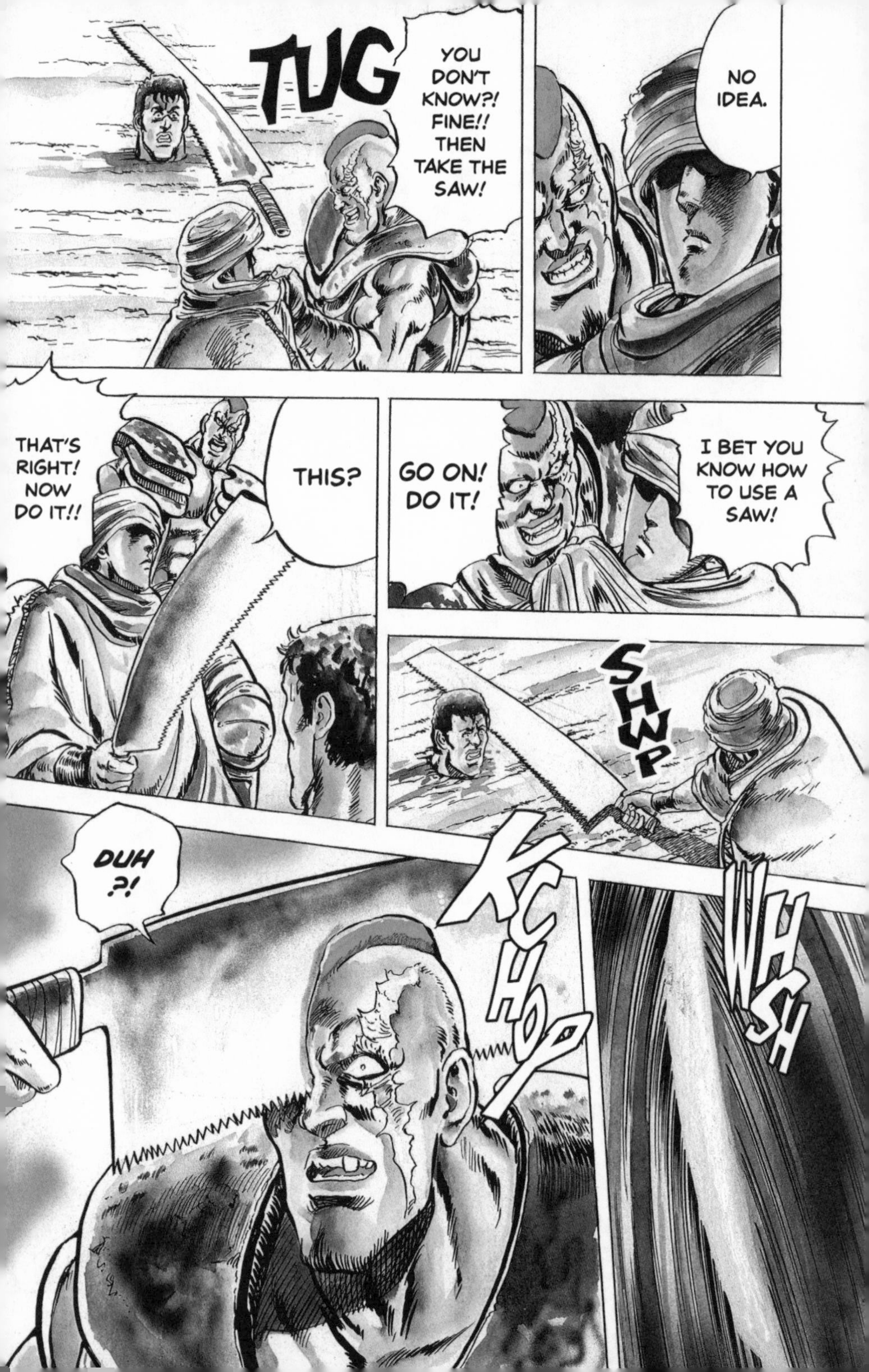
NO IDEA.
TUG
YOU DON'T KNOW?! FINE!! THEN TAKE THE SAW!
I BET YOU KNOW HOW TO USE A SAW!
GO ON! DO IT!
SHWP
THIS?
THAT'S RIGHT! NOW DO IT!!
WHSH
KCHOP
DUH ?!

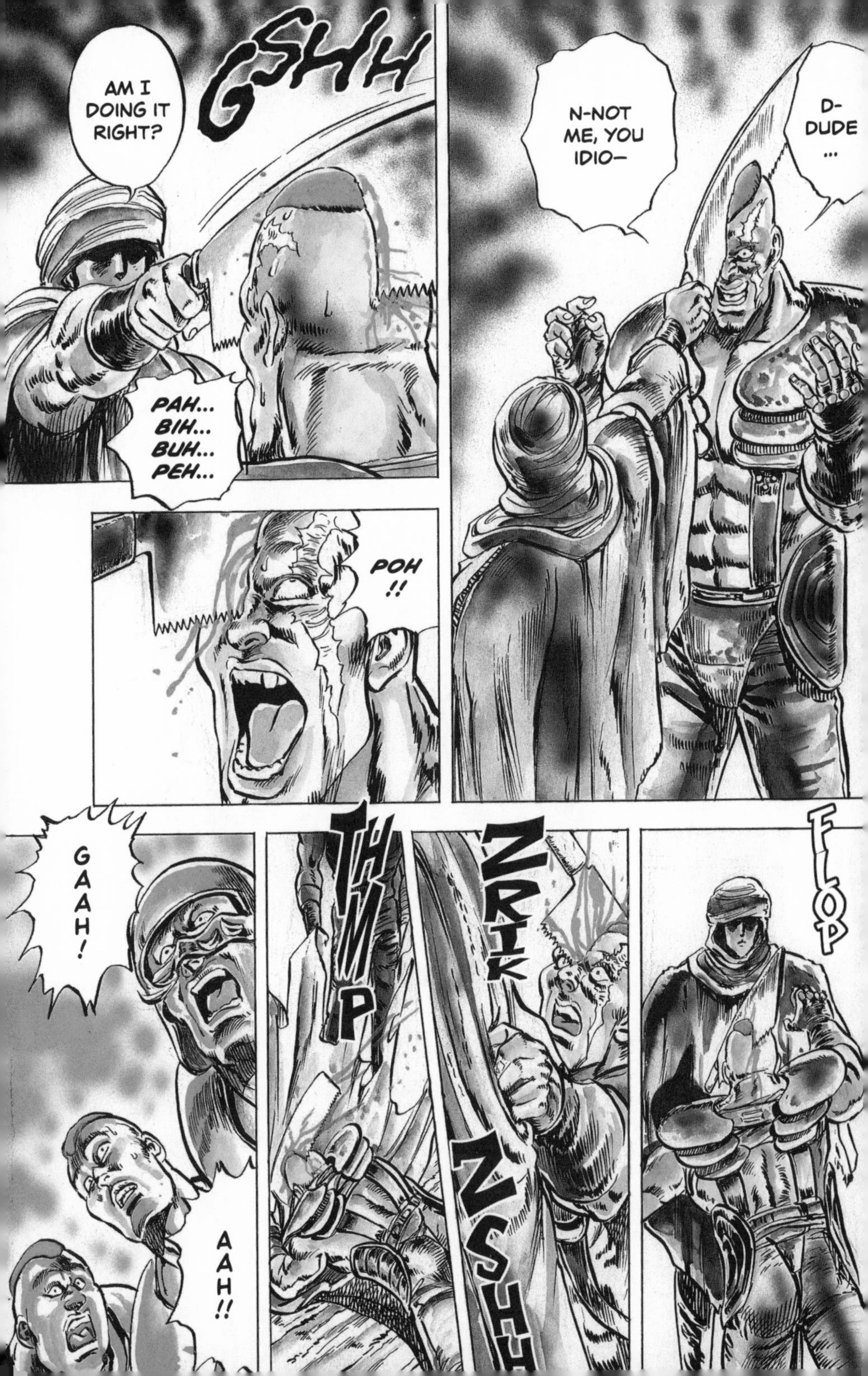
D-DUDE ...
N-NOT ME, YOU IDIO—
GSHH
AM I DOING IT RIGHT?
PAH... BIH... BUH... PEH...
POH !!
FLOP
ZRIK
ZNSHH
THMP
GAAH!
AAH!!

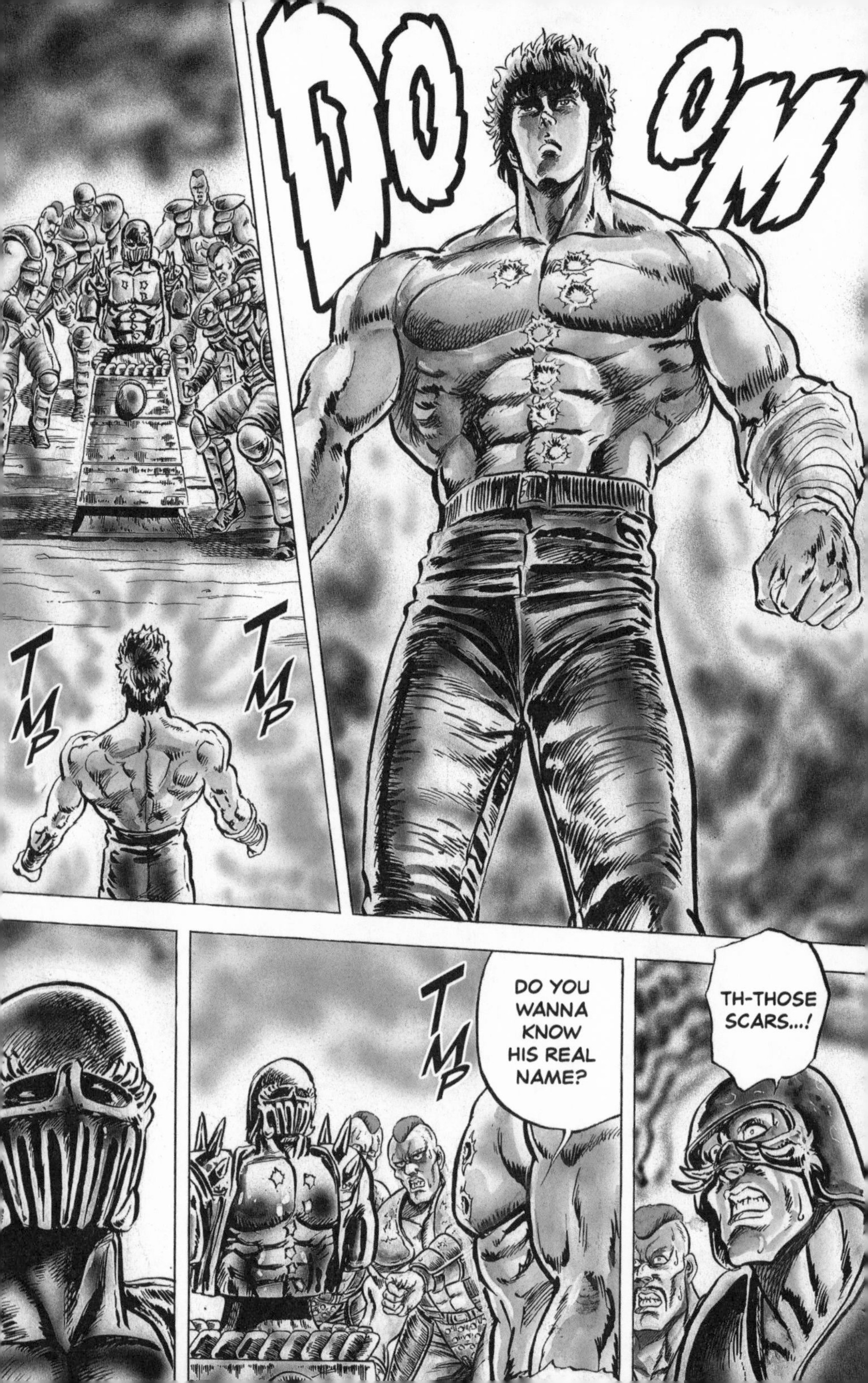
DOOM
TMP
TMP
TH-THOSE SCARS...!
TMP
DO YOU WANNA KNOW HIS REAL NAME?

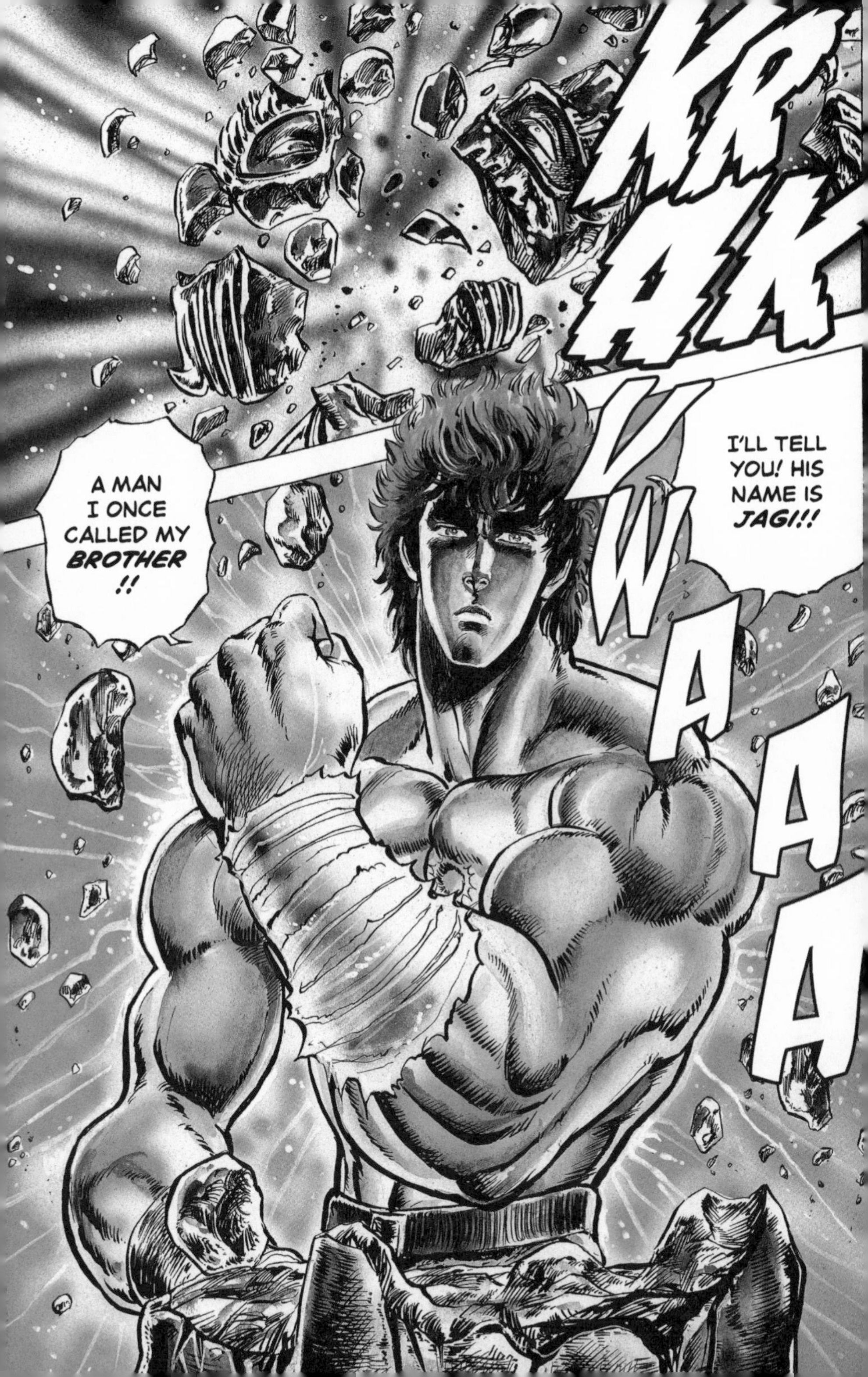
KRAK
VWAAA
I'LL TELL YOU! HIS NAME IS *JAGI!!*
A MAN I ONCE CALLED MY ***BROTHER*** !!

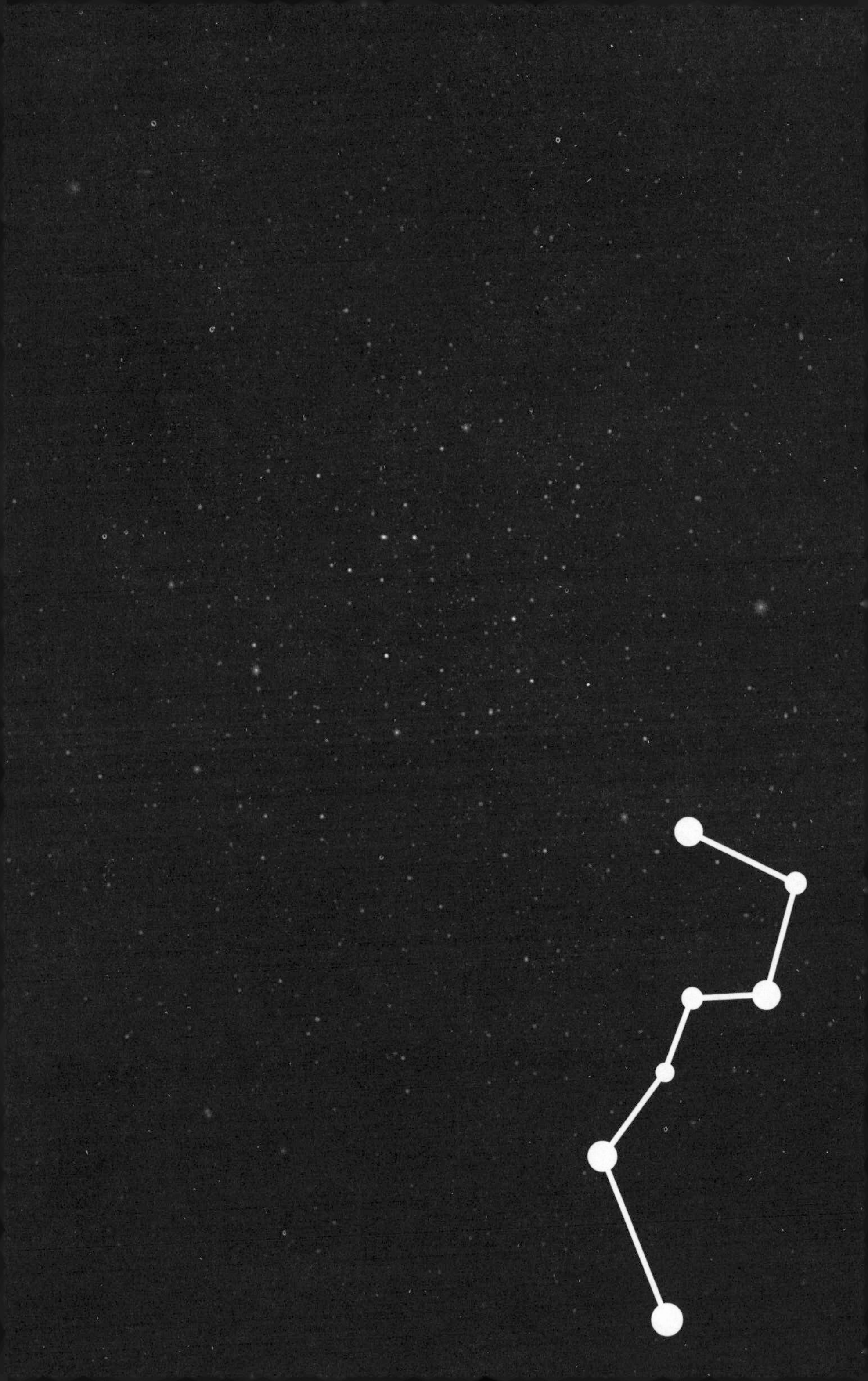

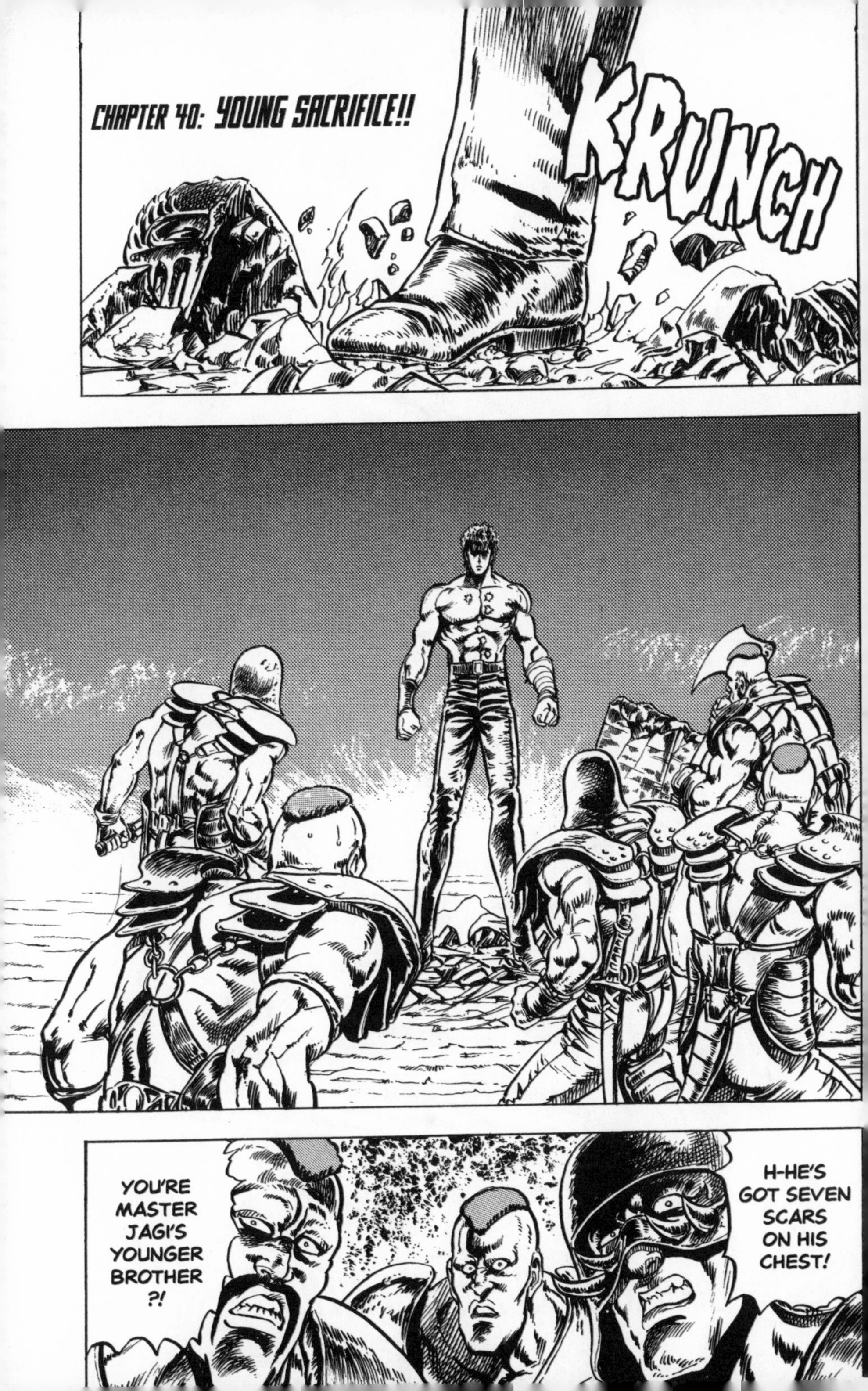
CHAPTER 40: YOUNG SACRIFICE!!
KRUNCH
H-HE'S GOT SEVEN SCARS ON HIS CHEST!
YOU'RE MASTER JAGI'S YOUNGER BROTHER ?!

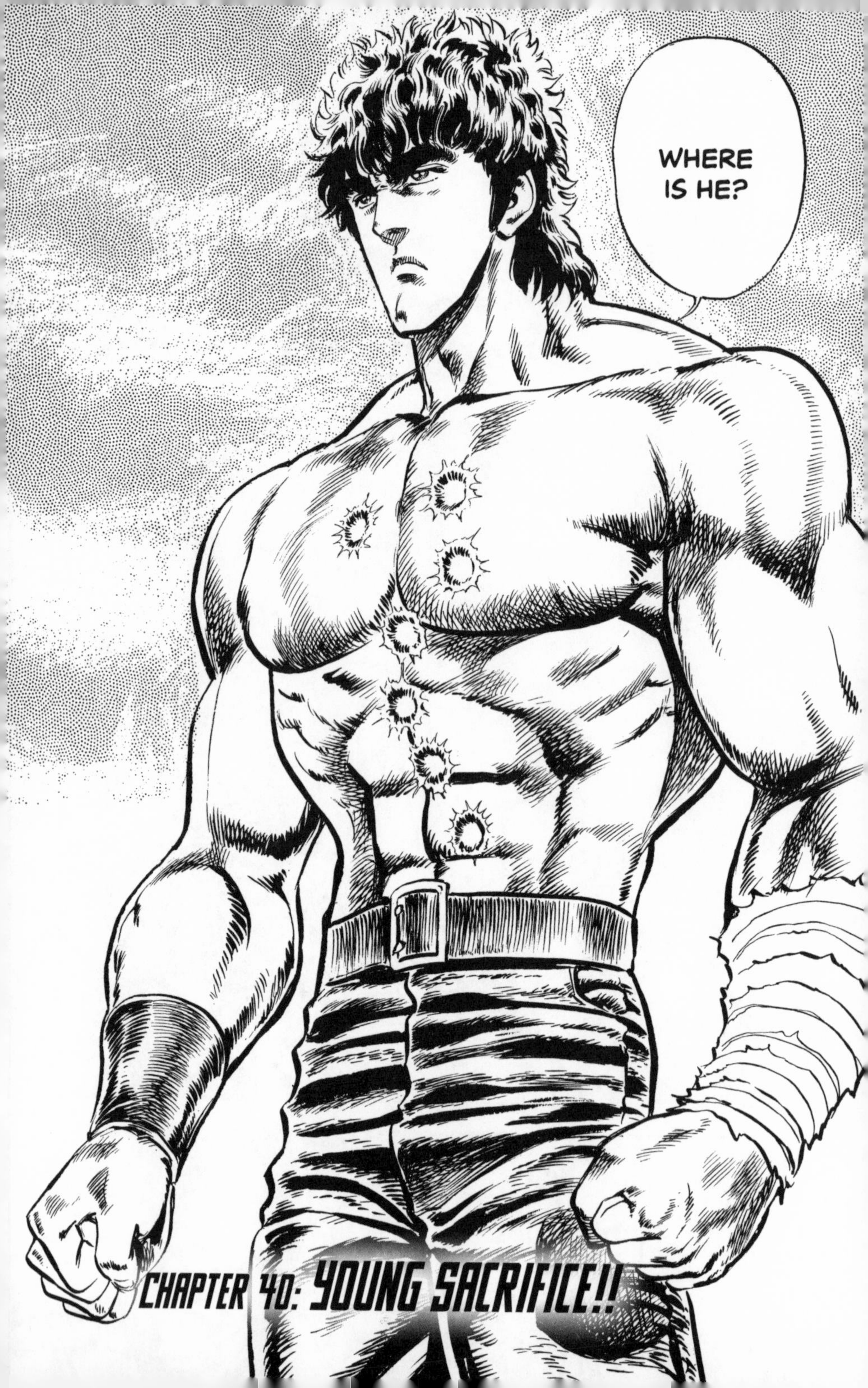
WHERE
IS HE?
CHAPTER 40: YOUNG SACRIFICE!!

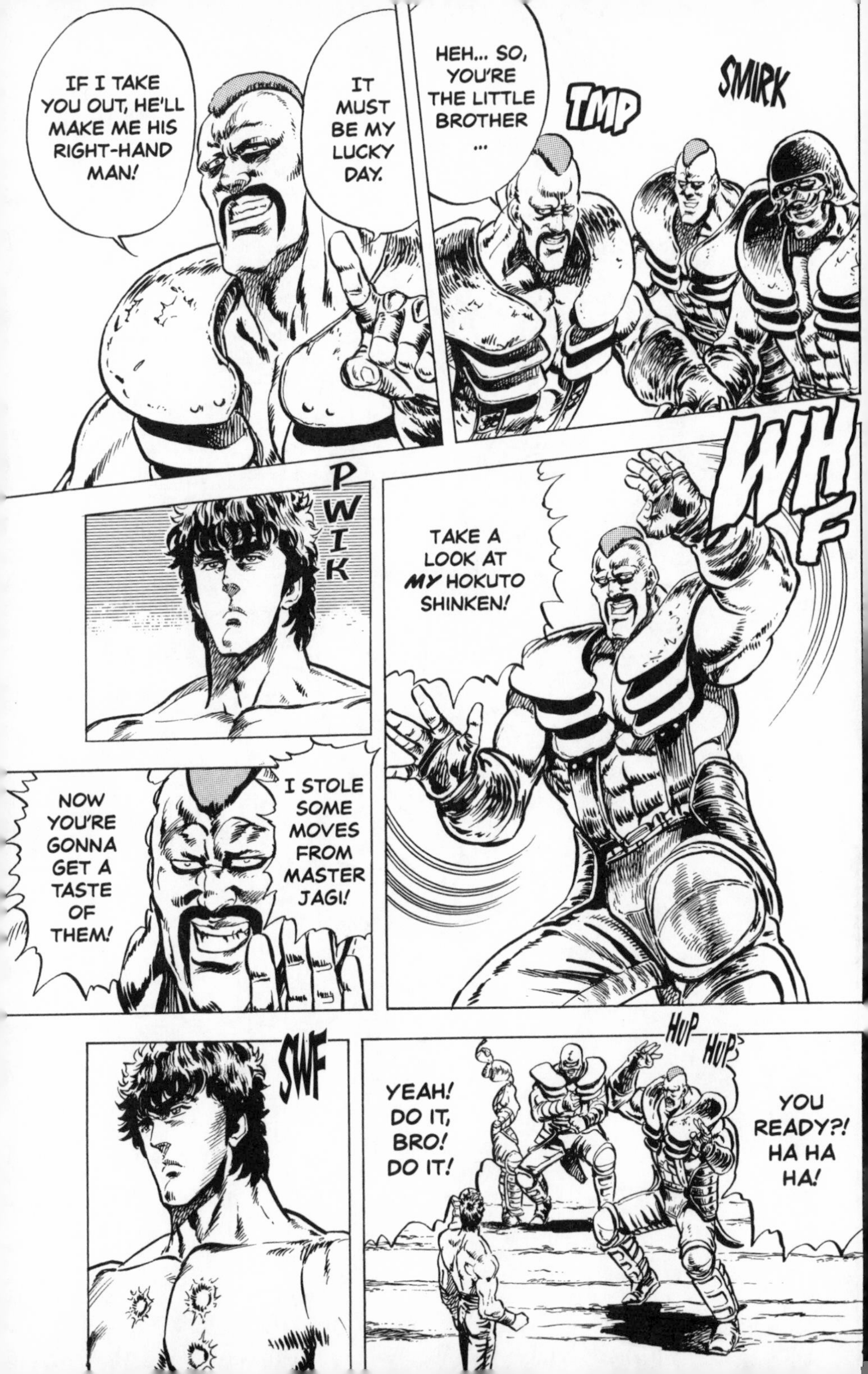
SMIRK
TMP
HEH... SO, YOU'RE THE LITTLE BROTHER ...
IT MUST BE MY LUCKY DAY.
IF I TAKE YOU OUT, HE'LL MAKE ME HIS RIGHT-HAND MAN!
WHF
TAKE A LOOK AT *MY* HOKUTO SHINKEN!
PWIK
I STOLE SOME MOVES FROM MASTER JAGI!
NOW YOU'RE GONNA GET A TASTE OF THEM!
HUP HUP
YOU READY?! HA HA HA!
YEAH! DO IT, BRO! DO IT!
SWF

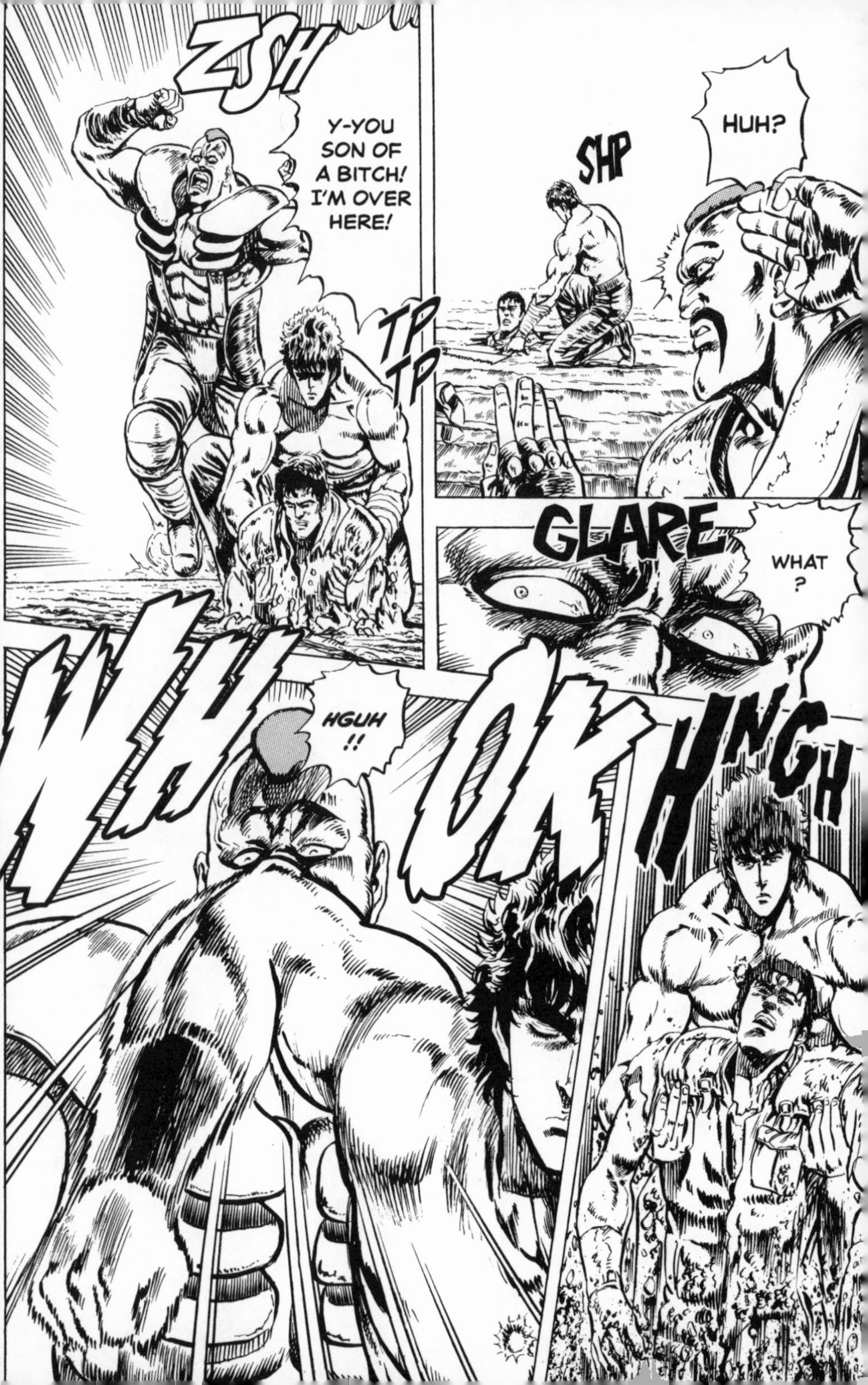
HUH?
SHP
GLARE
WHAT?
ZSH
Y-YOU SON OF A BITCH! I'M OVER HERE!
TP TP
HNGH
WHOK
HGUH !!

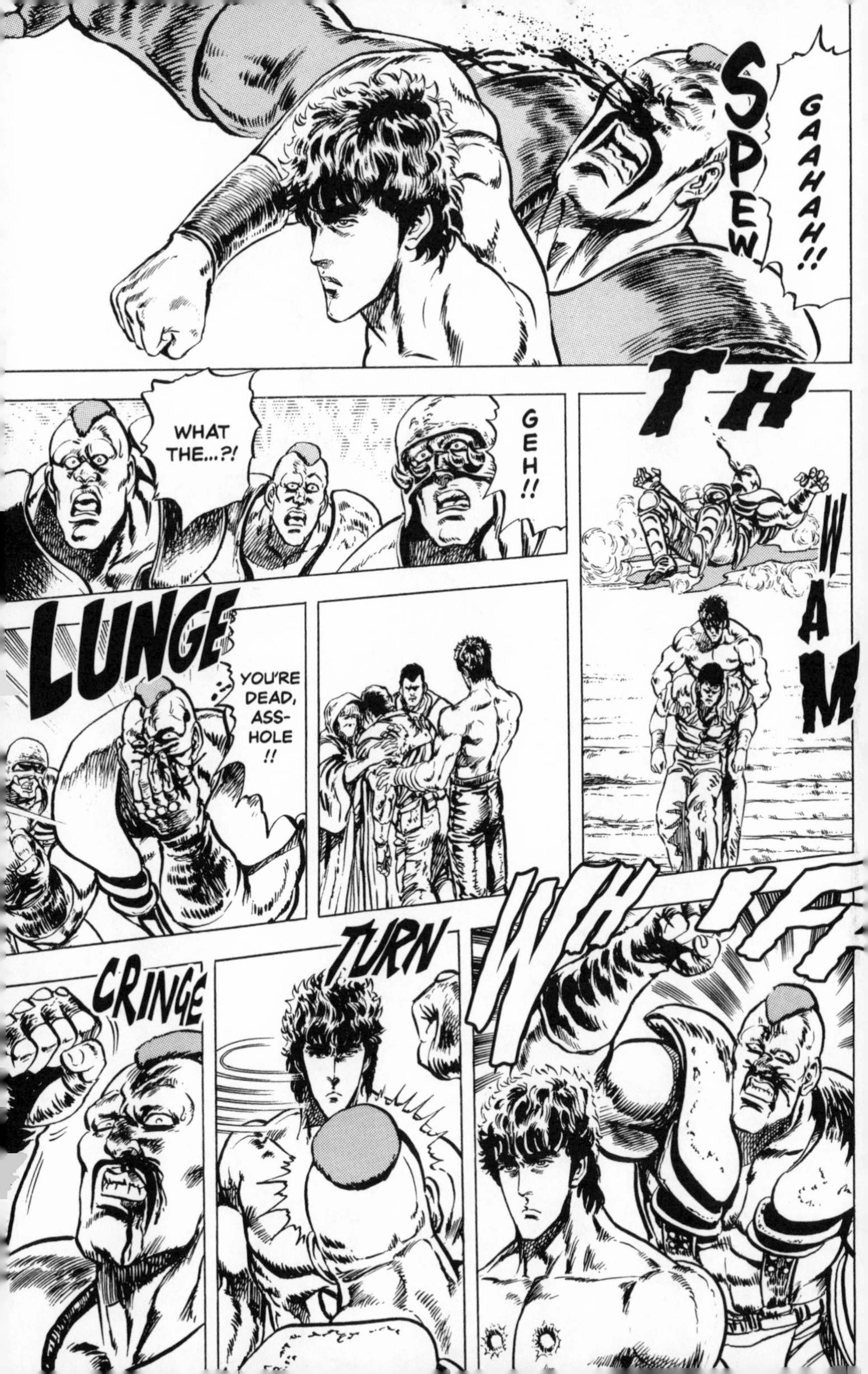
SPEW
GAAHAH!!
THWAM
GEH!!
WHAT THE...?!
LUNGE
YOU'RE DEAD, ASS-HOLE!!
TURN
CRINGE

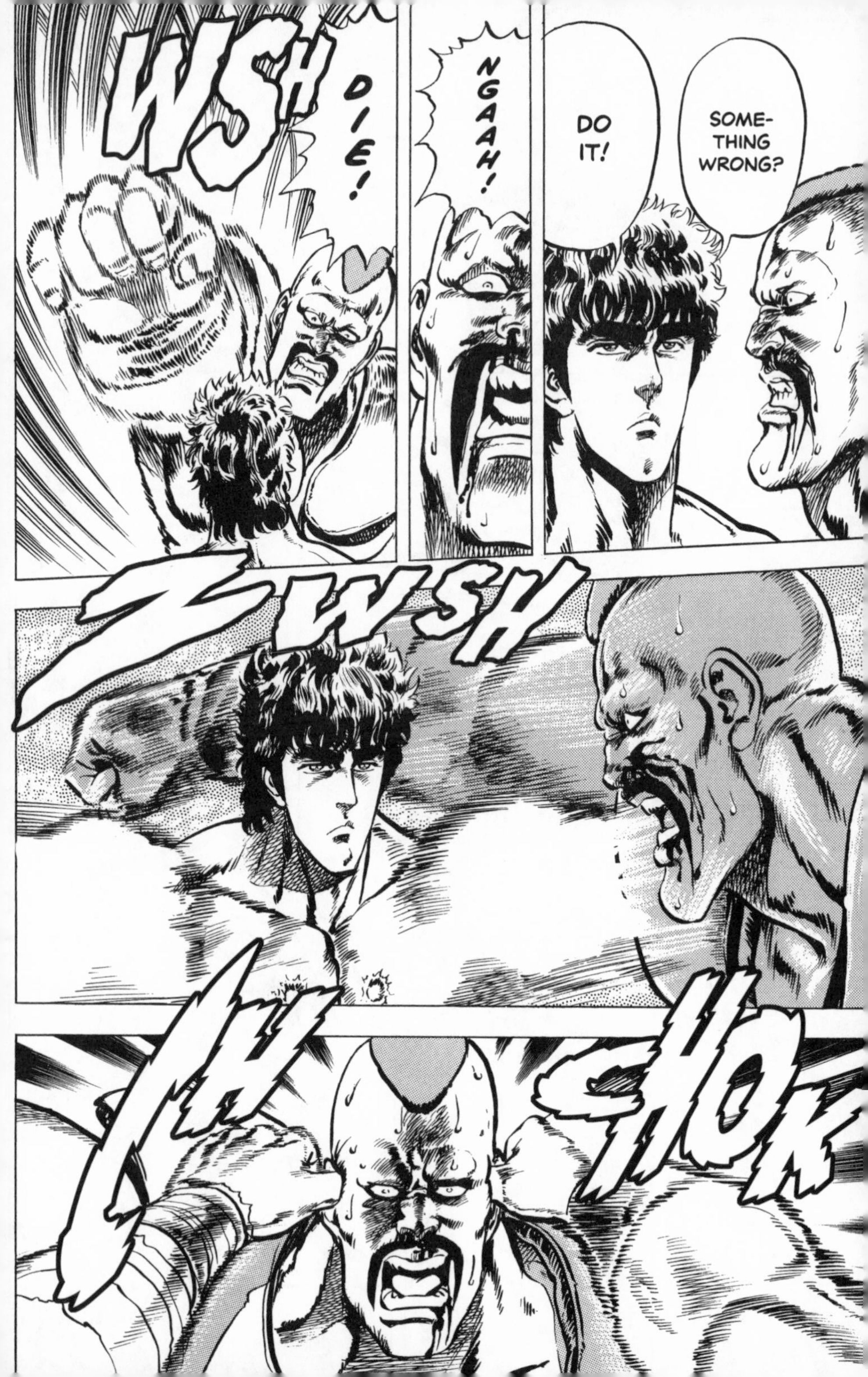
SOME-
THING
WRONG?
DO
IT!
NGAAAH!
DIE!
WSH
ZWSH
CHOK

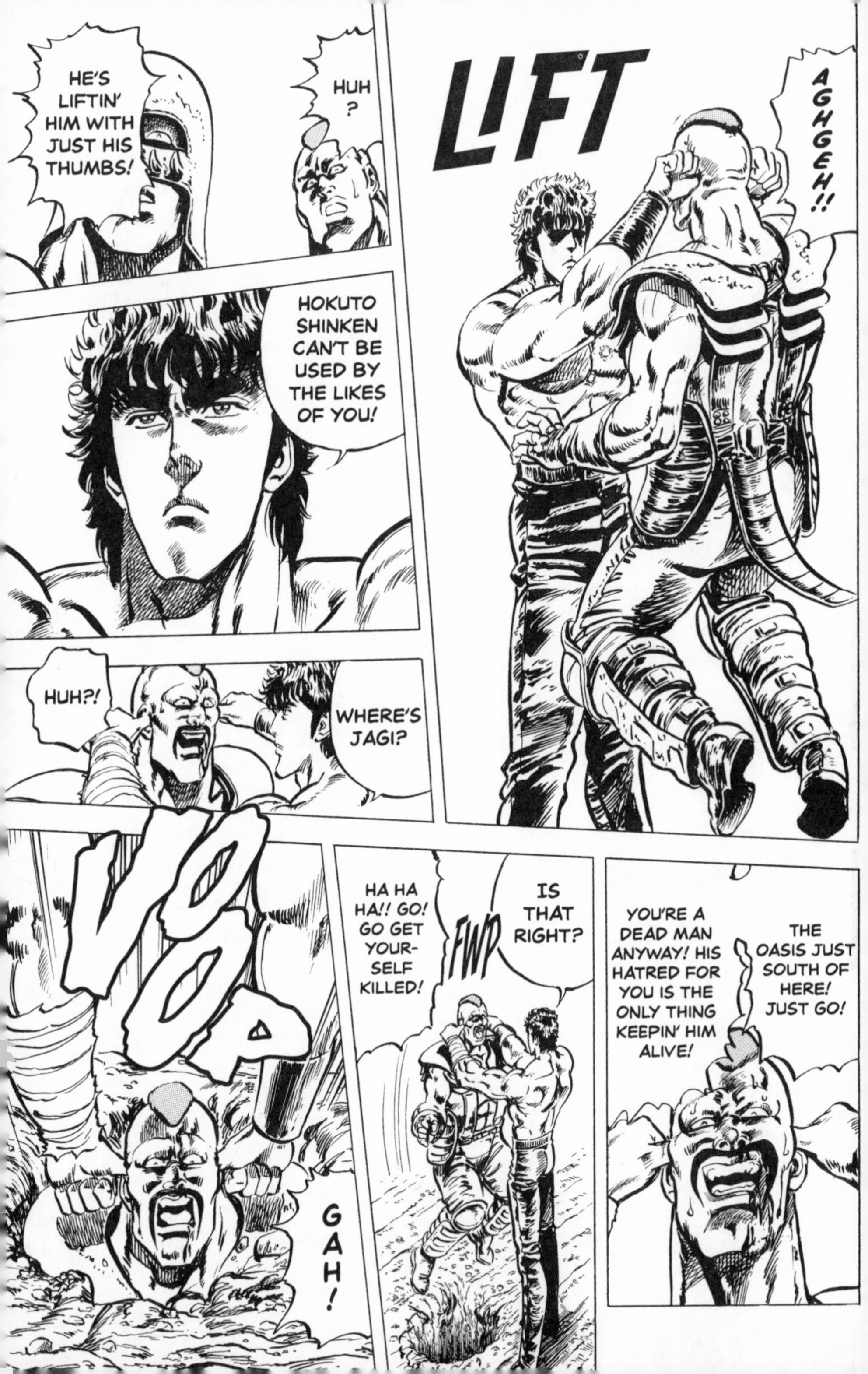
LIFT
AGHGEH!!
HUH ?
HE'S LIFTIN' HIM WITH JUST HIS THUMBS!
HOKUTO SHINKEN CAN'T BE USED BY THE LIKES OF YOU!
WHERE'S JAGI?
HUH?!
THE OASIS JUST SOUTH OF HERE! JUST GO!
YOU'RE A DEAD MAN ANYWAY! HIS HATRED FOR YOU IS THE ONLY THING KEEPIN' HIM ALIVE!
IS THAT RIGHT?
FWP
HA HA HA!! GO! GO GET YOURSELF KILLED!
VOP
GAH!

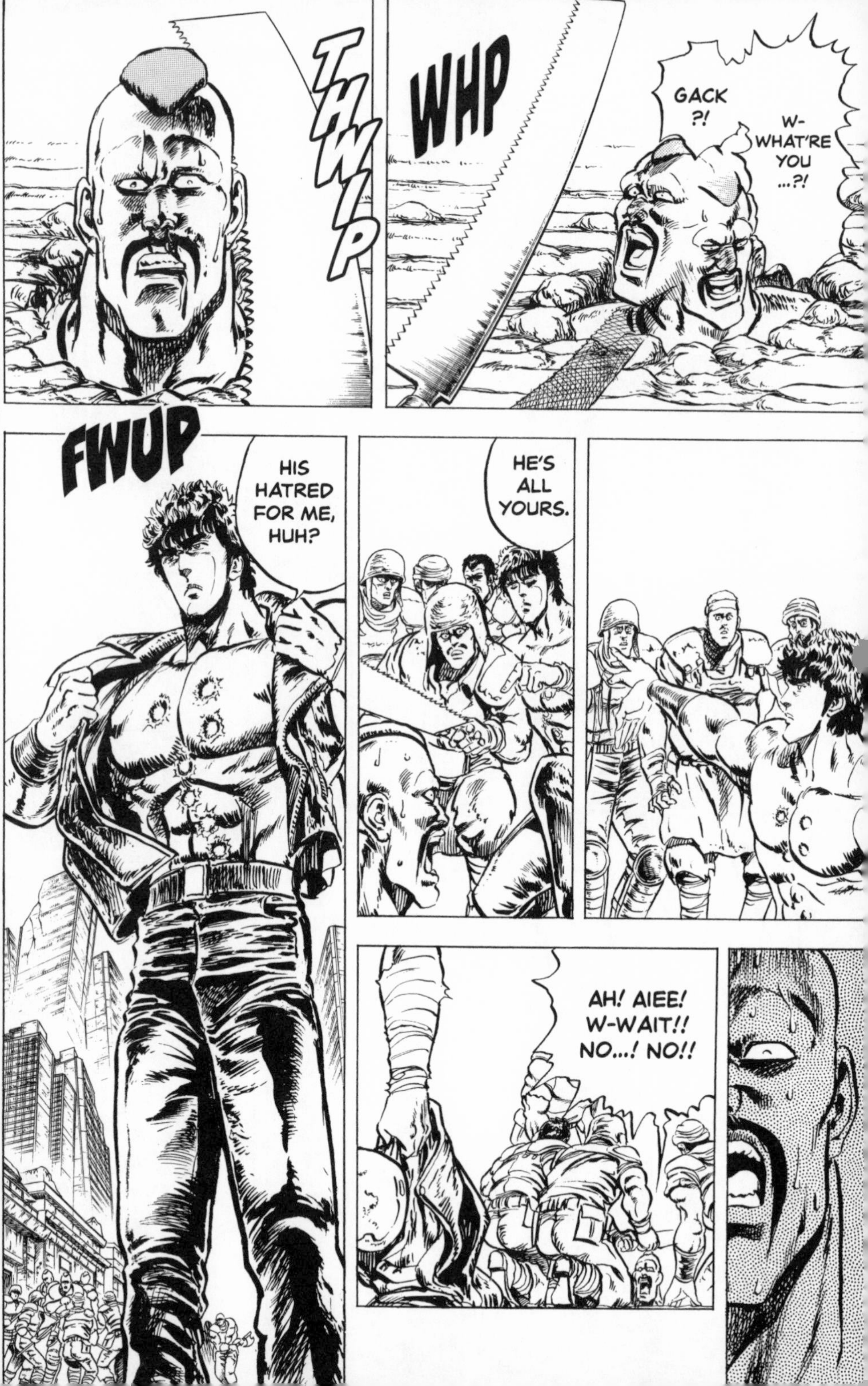
WHP
GACK ?!
W-WHAT'RE YOU ...?!
THWIP
HE'S ALL YOURS.
AH! AIEE! W-WAIT!! NO...! NO!!
FWUP
HIS HATRED FOR ME, HUH?

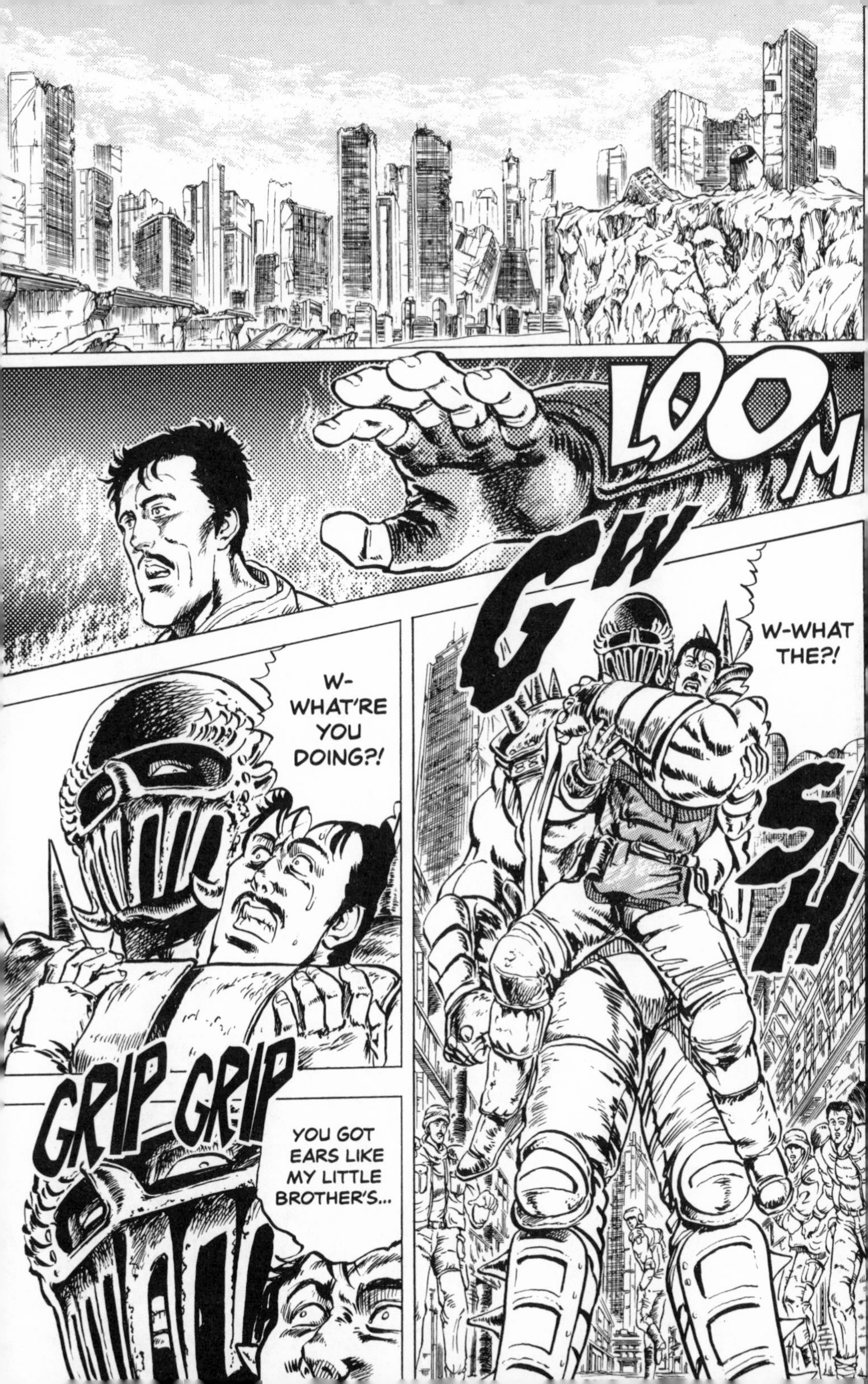
LOOM
GW
W-WHAT THE?!
SH
W-WHAT'RE YOU DOING?!
GRIP GRIP
YOU GOT EARS LIKE MY LITTLE BROTHER'S...

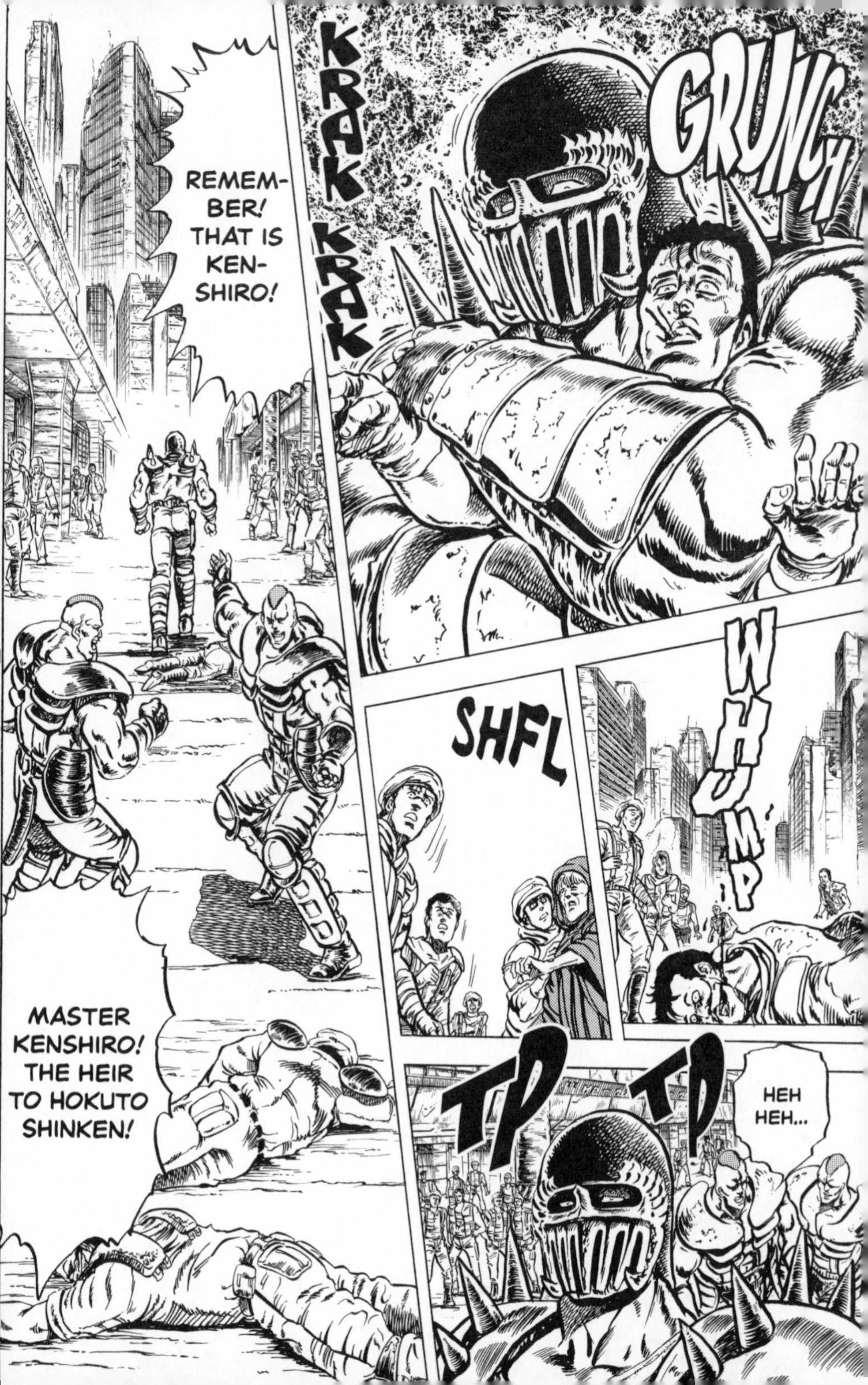
GRUNCH
KRAK KRAK
WHUMP
SHFL
TP TP
HEH HEH...
REMEMBER! THAT IS KENSHIRO!
MASTER KENSHIRO! THE HEIR TO HOKUTO SHINKEN!

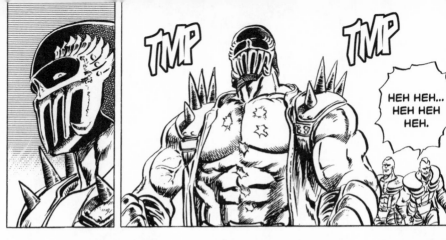

TMP TMP

HEH HEH...
HEH HEH
HEH.

AH!

THEY'RE
LIKE KEN-
SHIRO'S
...

THOSE
EYES...

TMP

C'MON, MAKO. LET'S GO!

TMP

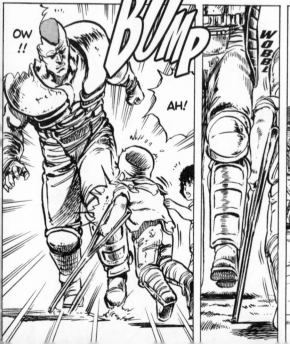

OW!!

BUMP

AH!

WOBBL

THAT'S RIGHT, MAKE WAY, FOOLS!

HYAH HA HA!

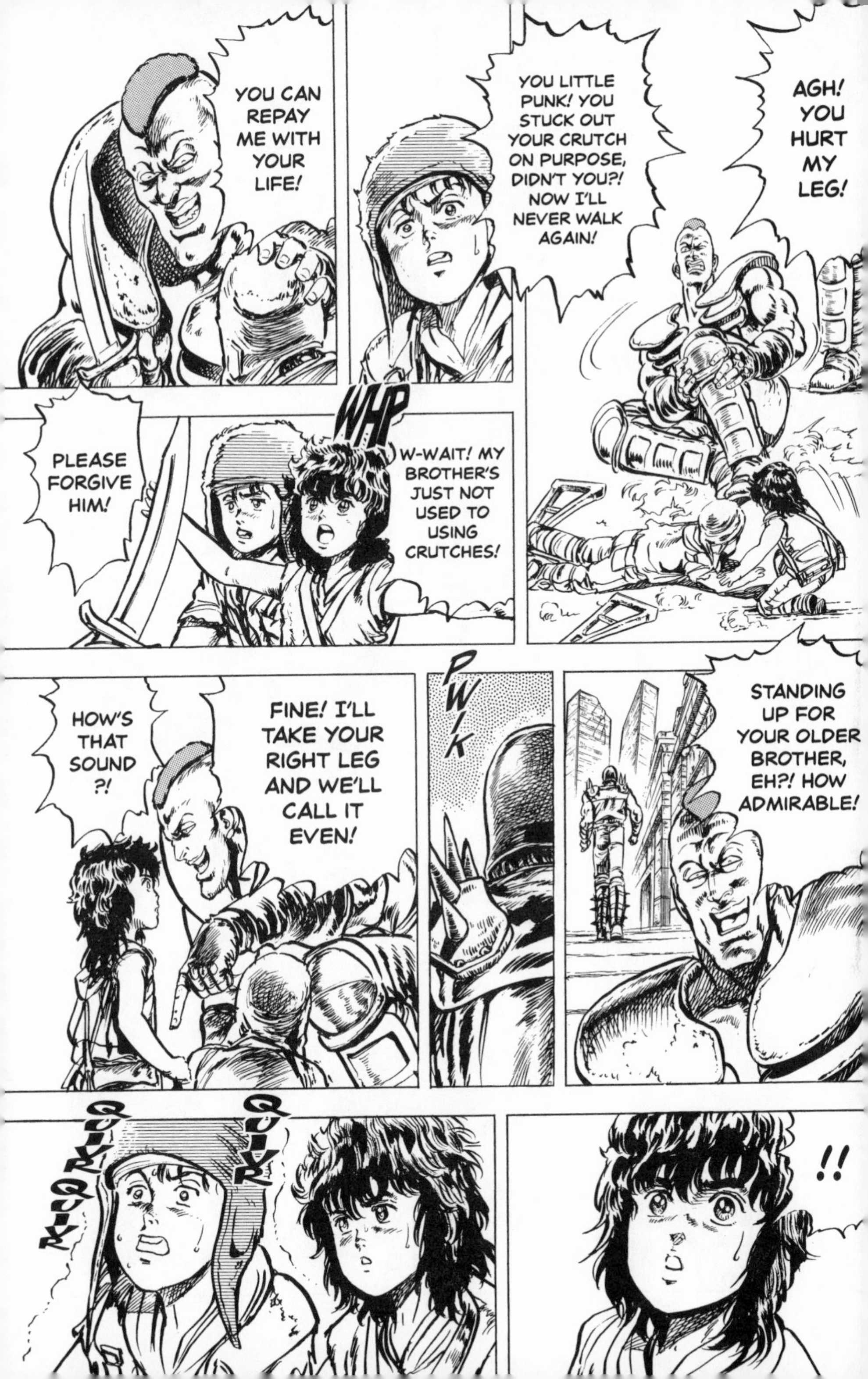
AGH! YOU HURT MY LEG!
YOU LITTLE PUNK! YOU STUCK OUT YOUR CRUTCH ON PURPOSE, DIDN'T YOU?! NOW I'LL NEVER WALK AGAIN!
YOU CAN REPAY ME WITH YOUR LIFE!
WHP
W-WAIT! MY BROTHER'S JUST NOT USED TO USING CRUTCHES!
PLEASE FORGIVE HIM!
STANDING UP FOR YOUR OLDER BROTHER, EH?! HOW ADMIRABLE!
PWIK
FINE! I'LL TAKE YOUR RIGHT LEG AND WE'LL CALL IT EVEN!
HOW'S THAT SOUND ?!
!!
QUIVR
QUIVR QUIVR

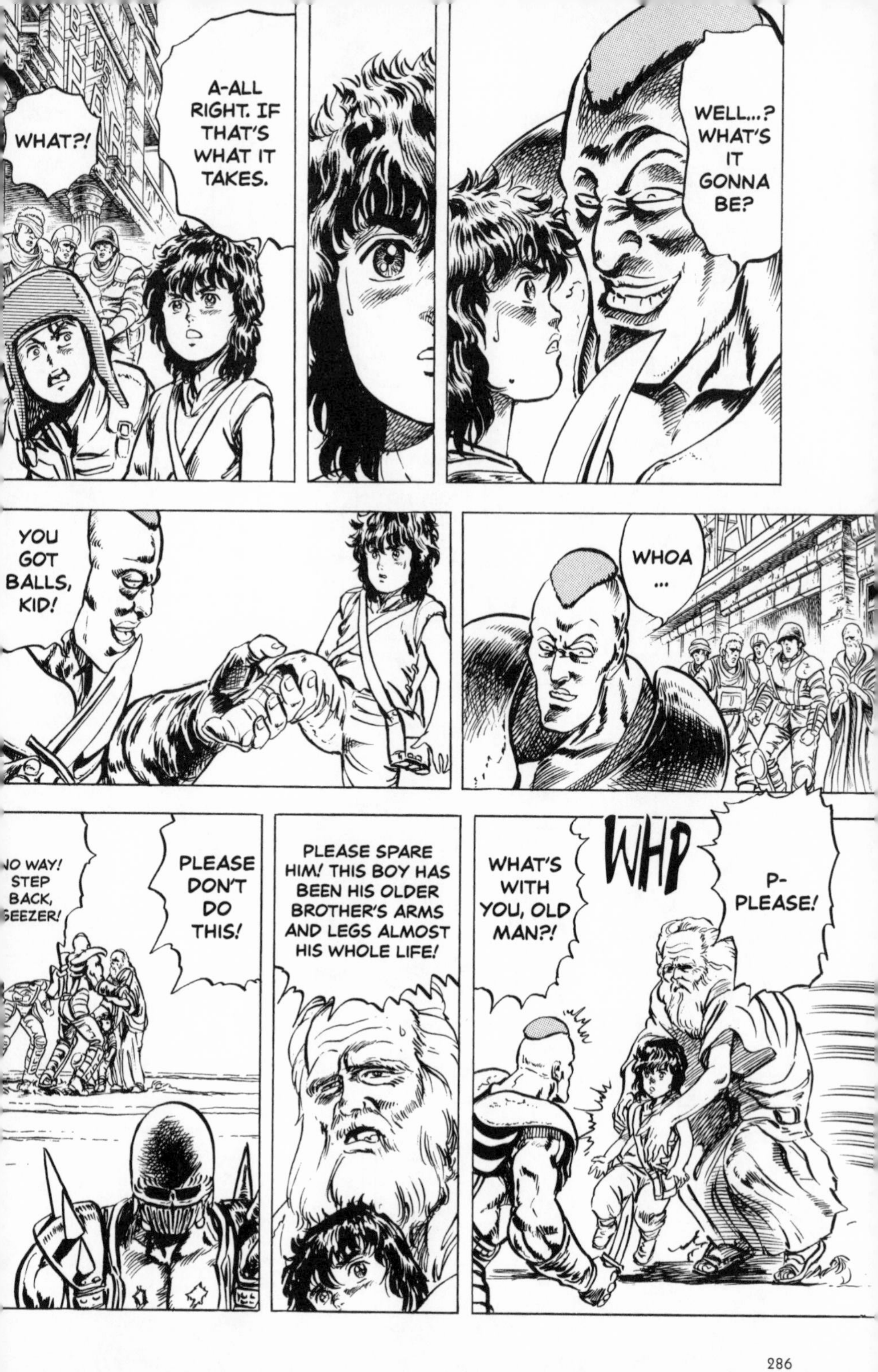
WELL...? WHAT'S IT GONNA BE?
A-ALL RIGHT. IF THAT'S WHAT IT TAKES.
WHAT?!
WHOA ...
YOU GOT BALLS, KID!
P-PLEASE!
WHP
WHAT'S WITH YOU, OLD MAN?!
PLEASE SPARE HIM! THIS BOY HAS BEEN HIS OLDER BROTHER'S ARMS AND LEGS ALMOST HIS WHOLE LIFE!
PLEASE DON'T DO THIS!
NO WAY! STEP BACK, GEEZER!

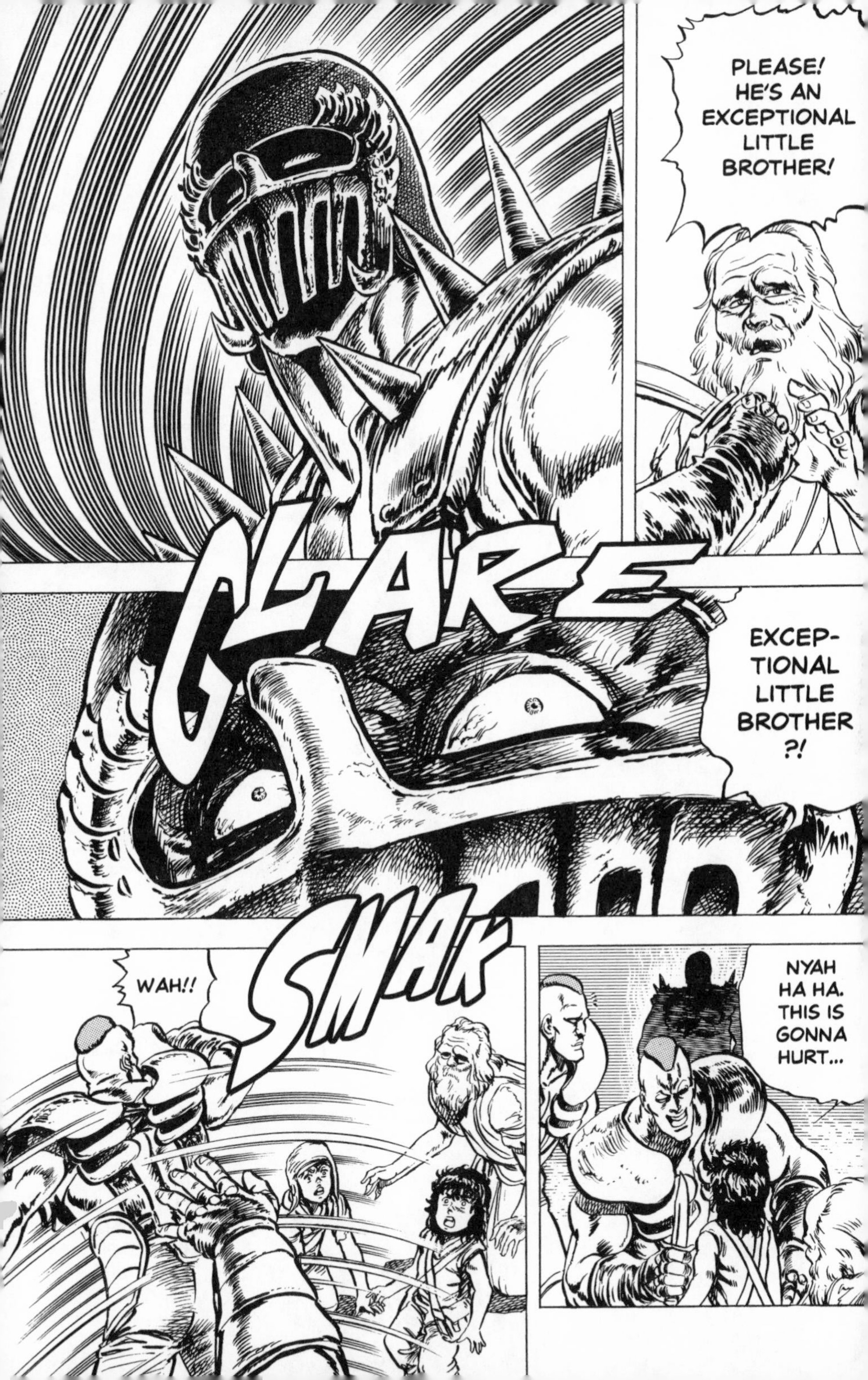
PLEASE! HE'S AN EXCEPTIONAL LITTLE BROTHER!
GLARE
EXCEPTIONAL LITTLE BROTHER ?!
NYAH HA HA. THIS IS GONNA HURT...
SMAK
WAH!!

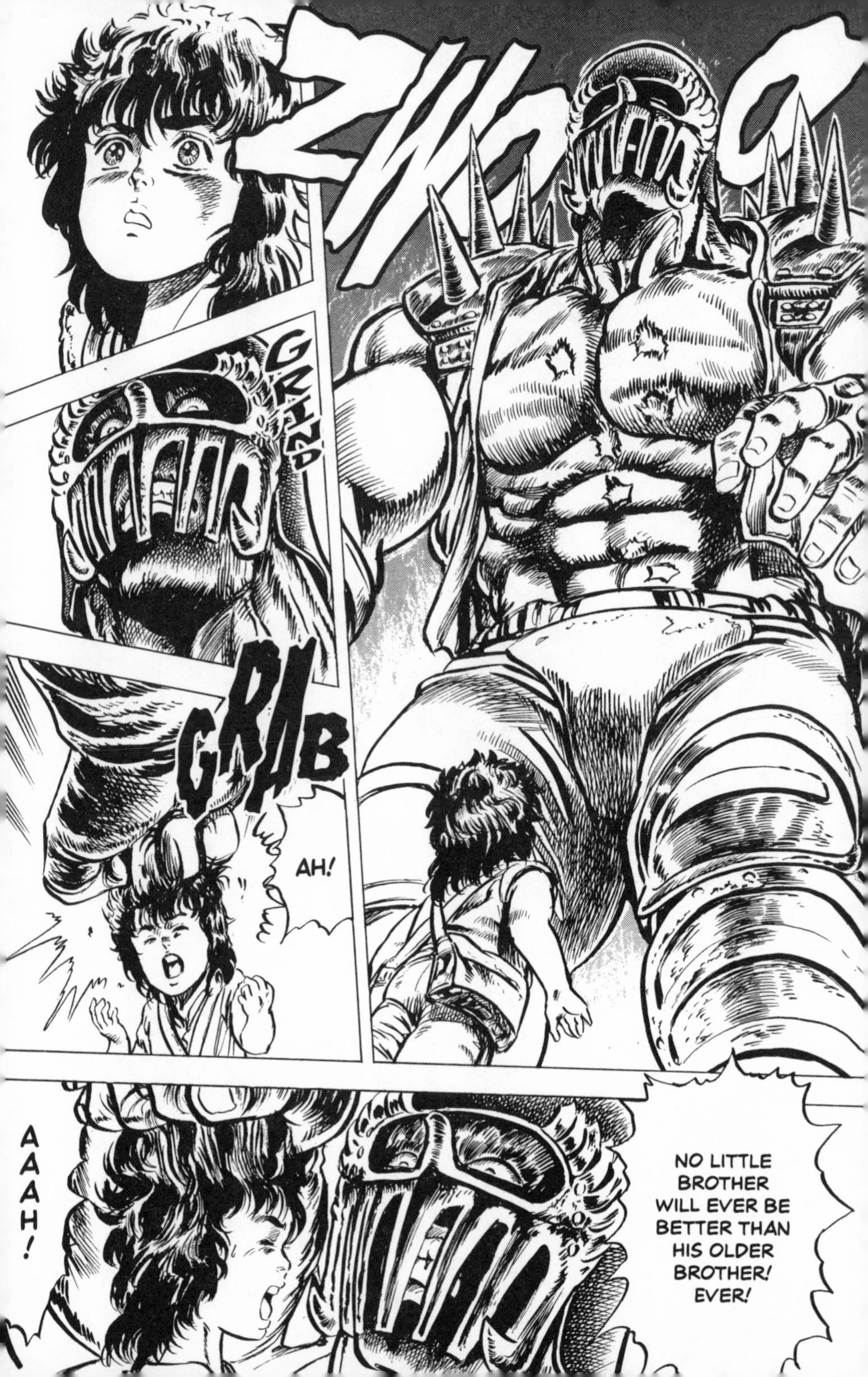
GRIND
GRAB
AH!
NO LITTLE BROTHER WILL EVER BE BETTER THAN HIS OLDER BROTHER! EVER!
AAAAH!

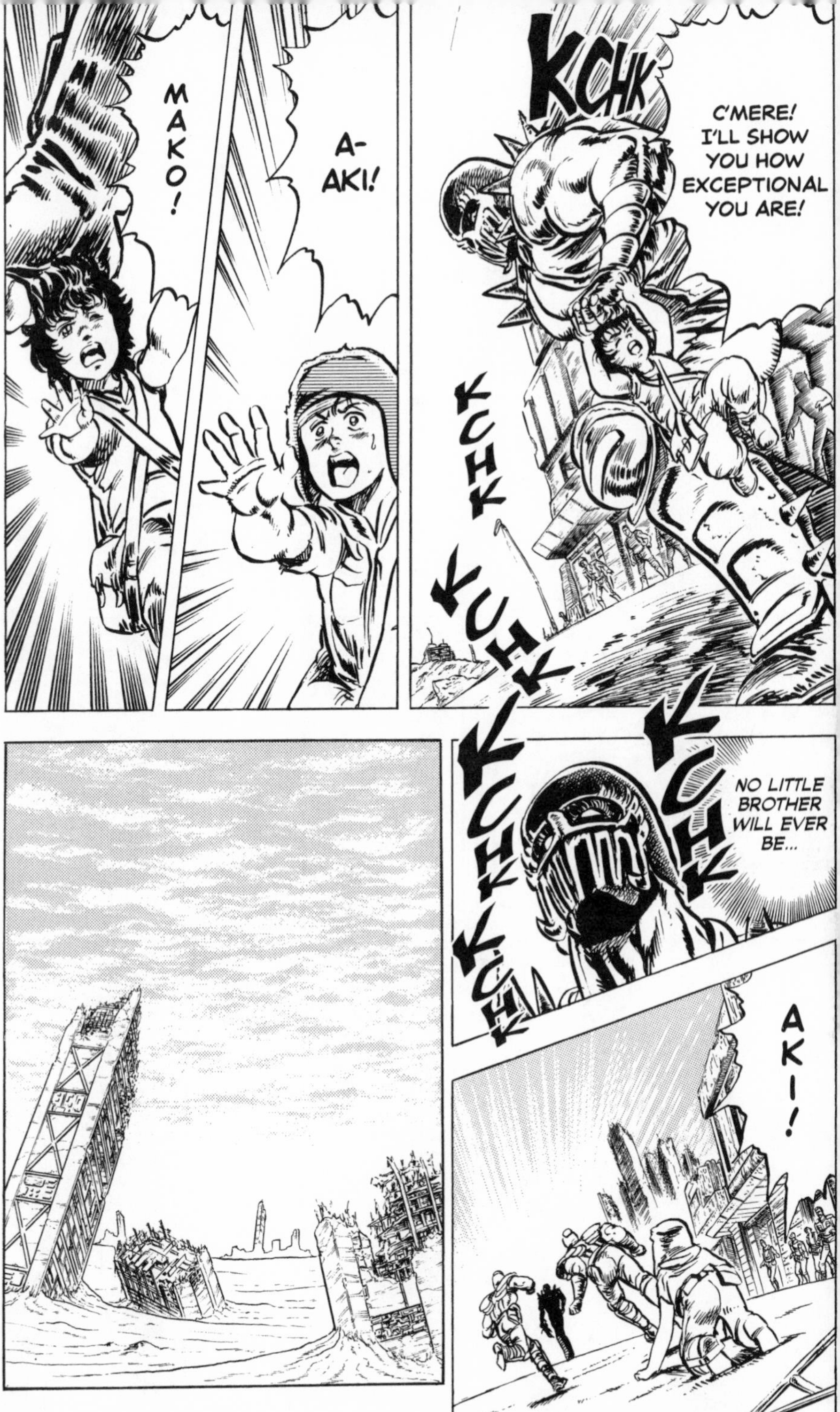
KCHK
C'MERE! I'LL SHOW YOU HOW EXCEPTIONAL YOU ARE!
KCHK
KCHK
KCHK
A-AKI!
MAKO!
KCHK
NO LITTLE BROTHER WILL EVER BE...
KCHK
KCHK
AKI-!

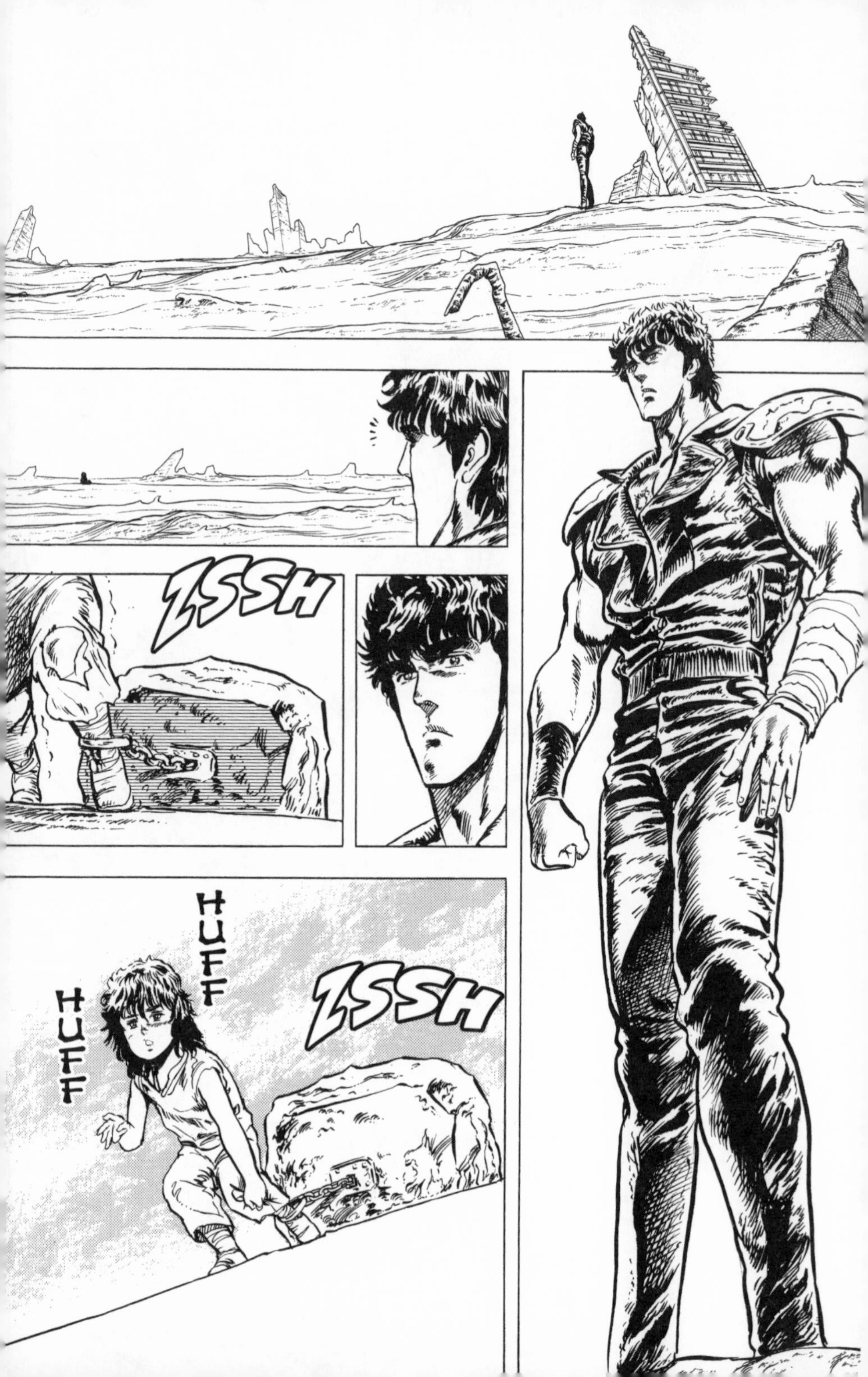
ZSSH
HUFF
ZSSH
HUFF

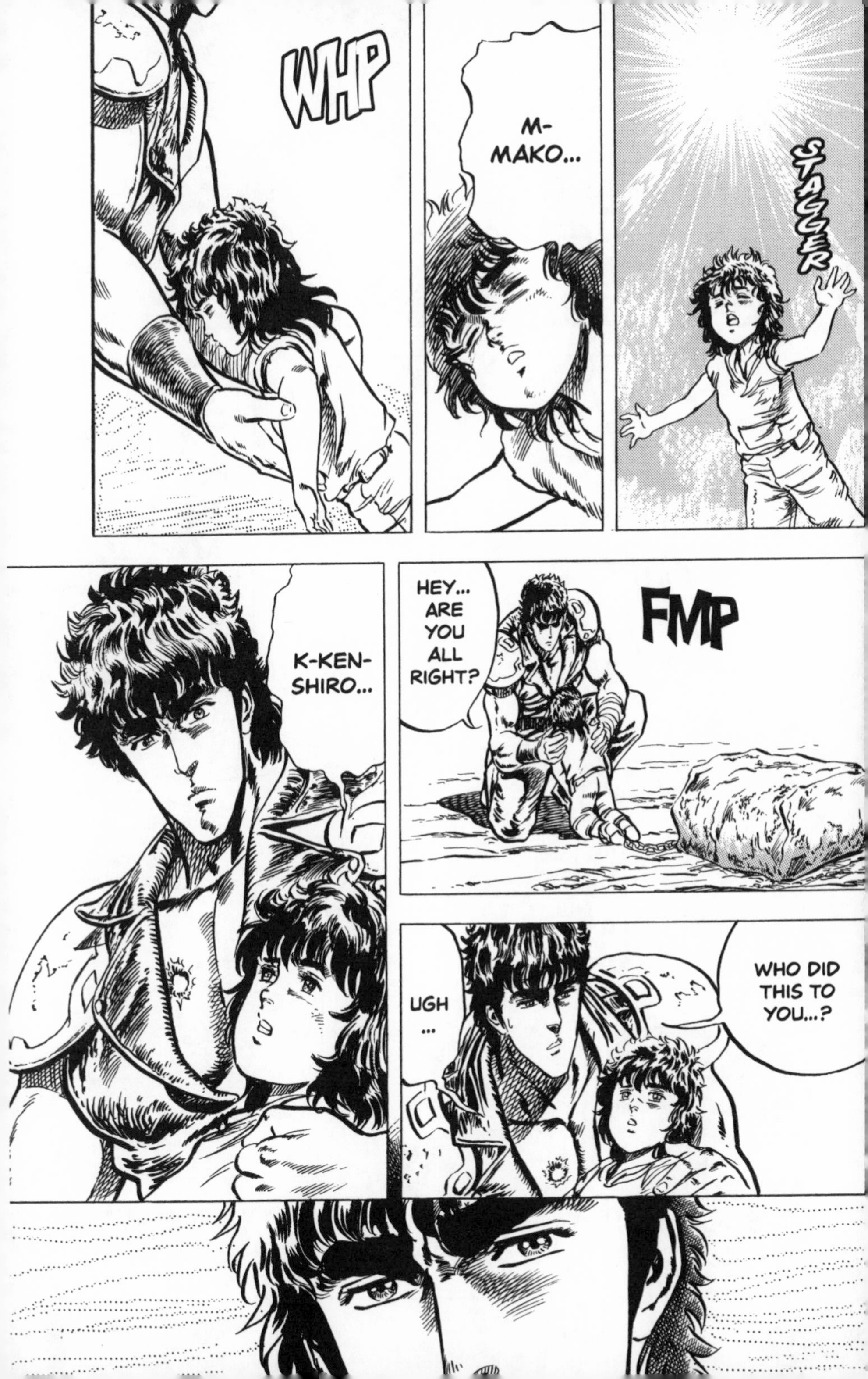
STAGGER
M- MAKO...
WHP
FMP
HEY... ARE YOU ALL RIGHT?
WHO DID THIS TO YOU...?
UGH ...
K-KEN- SHIRO...

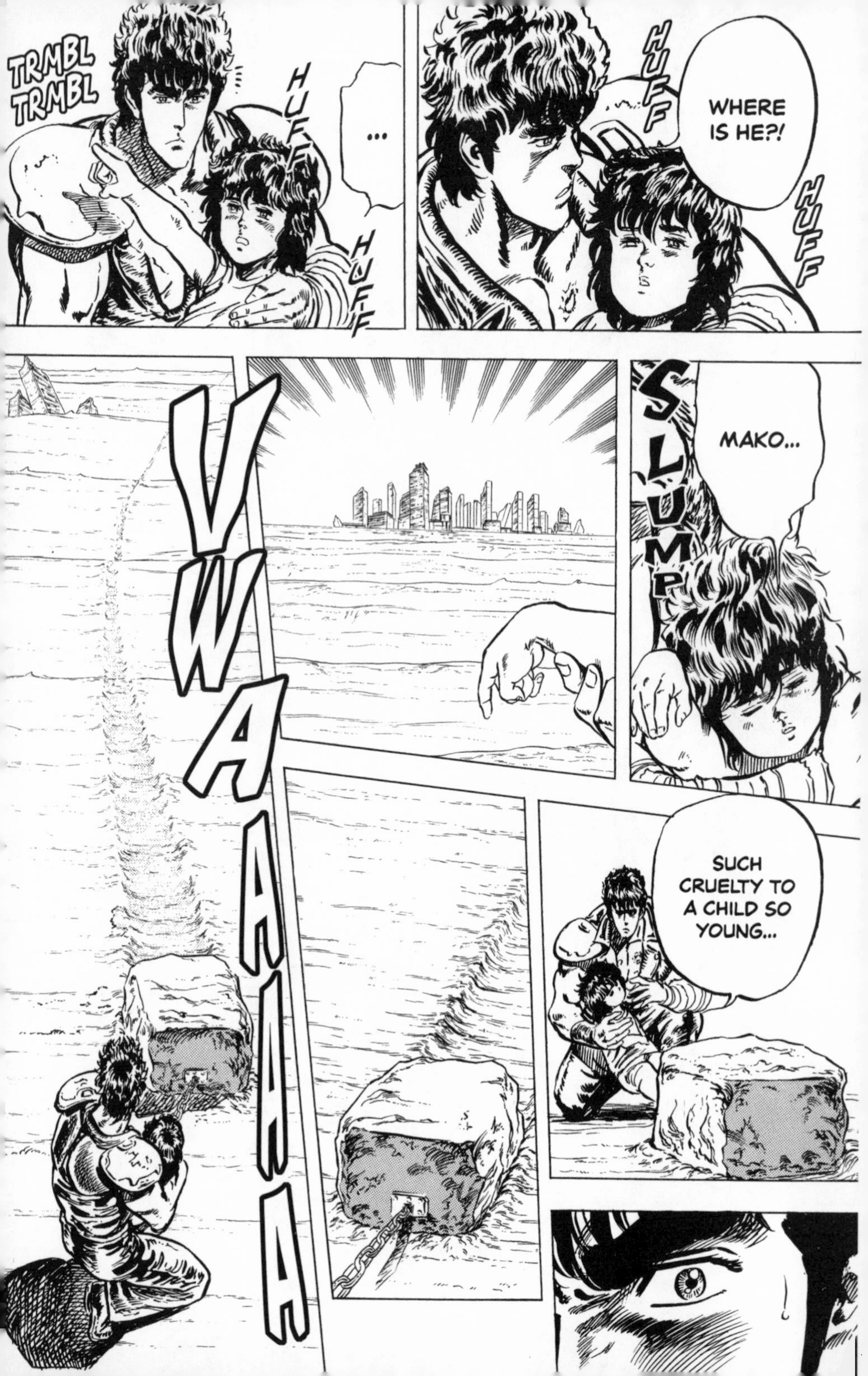
HUFF
WHERE IS HE?!
HUFF
TRMBL TRMBL
HUFF
...
HUFF
SLUMP
MAKO...
VWAAAAA
SUCH CRUELTY TO A CHILD SO YOUNG...

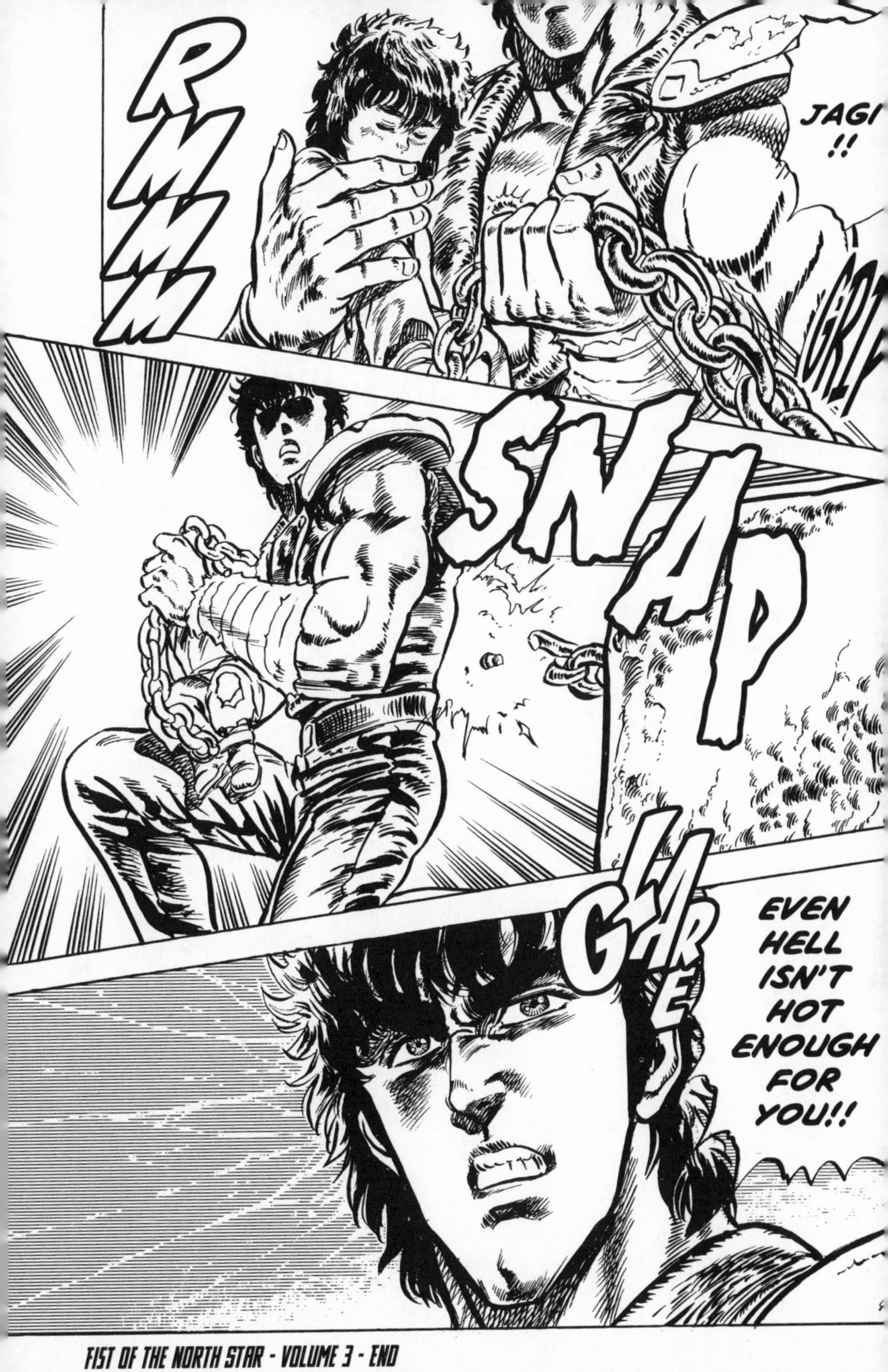
JAGI !!
RMMMM
GRIP
SNAP
GLARE
EVEN HELL ISN'T HOT ENOUGH FOR YOU!!

ABOUT THE AUTHORS

BURONSON started his career as a manga writer for *Weekly Shonen Jump* in 1972. He gained popularity with the hard-boiled action series *Doberman Cop* (with art by Shinji Hiramatsu). In 1983, he coauthored the massively successful *Fist of the North Star*. He has also written numerous hits under the pen name Sho Fumimura, including *Phantom Burai* and *Sanctuary*.

TETSUO HARA began his career with *The Iron Don Quixote* for *Weekly Shonen Jump* in 1982. *Fist of the North Star*, which began serialization in 1983, drew wide acclaim. In the 1990s, he released the historical period pieces *Hana no Keiji* and *Tokugawa Ieyasu's Shadow Warrior*. *Fist of the Blue Sky*, published in 2001, ran for nine years in *Weekly Comic Bunch*. His most recent series, *Ikusa no Ko: Oda Saburou Nobunaga-den*, began in *Monthly Comic Zenon* in 2010.

FIST OF THE NORTH STAR

VOLUME 3
VIZ Signature Edition

Story by BURONSON
Art by TETSUO HARA

Translation: JOE YAMAZAKI
Touch-up Art & Lettering: JOHN HUNT
Design: ADAM GRANO
Editor: MIKE MONTESA

HOKUTO NO KEN Ultimate Edition
©1983 by BURONSON AND TETSUO HARA/COAMIX
Approved No. ZDW-08E
All Rights Reserved.
English Translation Rights arranged with COAMIX, Inc.,
Tokyo, through Tuttle-Mori Agency, Inc., Tokyo.

Printed in the U.S.A.

Published by VIZ Media, LLC
P.O. Box 77010
San Francisco, CA 94107

10 9 8 7 6 5 4 3 2 1
First printing, December 2021

VIZ MEDIA
viz.com

VIZ SIGNATURE
vizsignature.com

THIS IS THE LAST PAGE.

FIST OF THE NORTH STAR

has been printed in the original Japanese right-to-left format
in order to preserve the orientation of the original artwork.